Logistical
Management

LOGISTICAL

MANAGEMENT

A Systems Integration of
Physical Distribution Management,
Material Management,
and Logistical Coordination

Donald J. Bowersox

Graduate School of Business Administration, Michigan State University

Macmillan Publishing Co., Inc.
New York
Collier Macmillan Publishers
London

Copyright © 1974, Macmillan Publishing Co., Inc.

Printed in the United States of America

All rights reserved. No part of this book may be reproduced or transmitted in any form or by any means, electronic or mechanical, including photocopying, recording, or any information storage and retrieval system, without permission in writing from the Publisher.

A portion of this material has been reprinted from *Physical Distribution Management*, First Edition, by Edward W. Smykay, Donald J. Bowersox, and Frank H. Mossman, © 1961 by Macmillan Publishing Co., Inc.; Second Edition, by Donald J. Bowersox, Edward W. Smykay, and Bernard J. La Londe, copyright © 1968 by Macmillan Publishing Co., Inc.

Macmillan Publishing Co., Inc.
866 Third Avenue, New York, New York 10022

Collier-Macmillan Canada, Ltd.

Library of Congress Cataloging in Publication Data

Bowersox, Donald J
  Logistical management.

  Bibliography: p.
  1. Physical distribution of goods—Management.
2. Materials management. I. Title.
HF5415.7.B66   658.7'8   73–8586
ISBN 0–02–313050–4

Printing: 1 2 3 4 5 6 7 8   Year: 4 5 6 7 8 9 0

Preface

For the past seventeen years, I have had the good fortune to participate actively in the formative years of business logistics. During this time, I have come to have a deep respect for the complexity of logistical performance and for its importance to the maintenance and growth of the free-enterprise system. To have the opportunity to attempt to describe the current content and future direction of this dynamic aspect of professional management is both a deeply felt privilege and a responsibility.

The history of the preparation of *Logistical Management* goes back to 1958. As many readers are aware, this book represents a third effort by the author to describe the direction and dimension of an emerging field. The first, presented in 1961, was a collaboration with two other authors and was the initial attempt to integrate corporate physical distribution activities in a single book. In 1968 *Physical Distribution Management*, again a collaboration, was substantially re-written as a new book because of the vast change that had occurred in the field during the intervening seven years. Although *Logistical Management* contains a great deal of the material I contributed to the earlier two works, the horizons of subject content have once again expanded so as to make a new approach desirable. Whereas the intent of both earlier books was to present a broad approach to physical distribution analysis, the events of subsequent years have far surpassed the range and depth originally envisaged for the field.

Logistical Management is presented as a systems integration of physical distribution, material management, and logistical coordination. With the exception of manufacturing processing, business logistics is viewed as involving over-all management of all aspects of physical movement to, from, and between facility locations that constitute the operating structure of the enterprise. I hope that the text, as an introduction to logistics, has achieved two fundamental objectives. First, the materials have been selected to present a comprehensive description of existing logistical practice within the business community. Second, a conceptual approach is provided as to how the discipline is likely to mature during the student's business career.

It would be impossible to mention all of the individuals who have made significant contributions to the contents of this book. Special mention is made of Professors Donald A. Taylor of Michigan State University, Thomas A. Staudt of Chevrolet Motor Division of General Motors Corporation, and Arthur E. Warner of the University of Tennessee. In addition, particular appreciation is due Professors Frank Mossman of Michigan State University, Bernard J. La Londe of The Ohio State University, Brian O'Neil of University of Miami, and James Johnson of the University of Tulsa for their specific aid with the manuscript. I am also pleased to acknowledge the guidance over the years of three close friends who counseled freely: Walter L. Jeffrey, Vice Chairman of the E. F. MacDonald Company; Robert J. Franco, President of Spector Freight System, Inc.; and Mark Egan, former Executive Director of The National Council of Physical Distribution Management; and two former mentors who are deceased: Edward A. Brand and George A. Ramlose.

I have been an active member of The National Council of Physical Distribution Management since its inception, and it would be impossible to elaborate the contributions of the many NCPDM members who have been of assistance in the preparation of this manuscript. In addition, over the past six years, those managers who have attended the annual Michigan State University Physical Distribution Executive Development Seminar have been exposed to the basic concepts developed in the text and have given freely of their time and experience.

The roll of those who actively teach various aspects of logistics around the world has expanded so as to make acknowledgment of key individuals impossible. To this group in general, and in particular to Professors E. Grosvenor Plowman of the University of Maine, Robert Pashek of Pennsylvania State University, Ernest Williams of Columbia University, and Lester Waters of Indiana University, I express sincere appreciation and dedication to the objective we all serve. In addition, I am grateful for the support of my colleagues at Michigan State University and Systems Research Incorporated, whose advice and assistance made it possible to complete this manuscript.

It is difficult to pinpoint the continuous contribution that a teacher receives from his students over the years. In many ways, the final day of judgment of a professional career comes in the seminar room. I have been fortunate to have the counsel of a great many outstanding young scholars who are currently making their marks upon the academic and business worlds. In particular, Dr. Omar Keith Helferich and other members of the research team that participated in a three-year simulation project, as well as the sponsor, Johnson & Johnson Domestic Operating Company, contributed in numerous ways to the manuscript.

I wish to single out the contribution of Felicia Kramer, who has served as the coordinator of manuscript preparation. Felicia and others who typed, edited, and prepared the manuscript art carried a burden over and above their normal assignments that is deeply appreciated. David Closs also made a substantial contribution to the manuscript by the preparation of mathematical and statistical examples.

Finally, every author has an understanding family, or the preparation of a manuscript would be impossible during the demanding years of life. In my particular case, this book is dedicated to Carol for reasons she full well understands.

With so much able assistance, it is difficult to offer any excuse for the shortcomings that might follow. However, the faults are solely my responsibility.

D. J. B.

The Logistician

Logisticians are a sad and embittered race of men who are very much in demand in war, and who sink resentfully into obscurity in peace. They deal only in facts, but must work for men who merchant in theories. They emerge during war because war is very much a fact. They disappear in peace because peace is mostly theory. The people who merchant in theories, and who employ logisticians in war and ignore them in peace, are generals.

Generals are a happily blessed race who radiate confidence and power. They feed only on ambrosia and drink only nectar. In peace, they stride confidently and can invade a world simply by sweeping their hands grandly over a map, pointing their fingers decisively up terrain corridors, and blocking defiles and obstacles with the sides of their hands. In war, they must stride more slowly because each general has a logistician riding on his back and he knows that, at any moment, the logistician may lean forward and whisper: "No, you can't do that." Generals fear logisticians in war and, in peace, generals try to forget logisticians.

Romping along beside generals are strategists and tacticians. Logisticians despise strategists and tacticians. Strategists and tacticians do not know about logisticians until they grow up to be generals—which they usually do.

Sometimes a logistician becomes a general. If he does, he must associate with generals whom he hates: he has a retinue of strategists and tacticians whom he despises; and, on his back, is a logistician whom he fears. This is why logisticians who become generals always have ulcers and cannot eat their ambrosia.

—Author unknown
Made available by Major William K. Bawden, RCAF.

Contents

Part
Three
Logistical System Design

Part
Four
Logistical System Administration

Introduction

The subject matter of this book—business logistics—is unique because it is one of the oldest and also one of the newest activities within a commercial enterprise. Logistical functions have been performed since the advent of specialization. These functions are transportation, inventory, warehousing, communication, and material movement. It is difficult to visualize any selling or trading that would not necessitate performance of such logistical functions.

The newness of logistics stems from a totally different approach to the management of these age-old functions that began to develop during the 1950s. Business logistics is defined as

The process of managing all activities required to strategically move raw materials, parts, and finished inventory from vendors, between enterprise facilities, and to customers.[1]

[1] In 1962 the National Council of Physical Distribution Management broadly defined physical distribution as follows: "A term employed in manufacturing and commerce to describe the broad range of activities concerned with efficient movement of finished products from the end of the production line to the consumer, and in some cases includes the movement of raw materials from the source of supply to the beginning of the production line. These activities include freight transportation, warehousing, material handling,

In the broadest sense, business logistics involves the over-all management of all aspects of everything that moves to, from, and between locations that constitute the facility structure of the enterprise. The responsibility of logistical management is

To design and administer a system to control the flow of material, parts, and finished inventory to the maximum benefit of the enterprise.

The subject matter of this book is a statement of concept and detail involved in the integrated approach to logistical management.

Prior to 1950, the typical commercial enterprise treated the over-all process of logistics on a fragmentary and most often secondary basis. Although a great many authors acknowledged the fundamental importance of logistics to marketing and manufacturing, no formalized or integrated concept prevailed.[2]

The following quote from a 1954 speech of the late Paul D. Converse provides a general appraisal of the physical distribution portion of logistics during the early 1950s.

... in the study of marketing and the operation of marketing departments and businesses a great deal more attention is paid to buying and selling than to physical handling. In fact, the physical handling of goods seems to be pretty much overlooked by sales executives, advertising men, and market researchers. ... problems of physical distribution are too often brushed aside as matters of little importance. I have for many years been reading business and economics magazines. Such publications over the years have devoted relatively little space to physical distribution.[3]

---

protective packaging, inventory control, plant and warehouse site selection, order processing, market forecasting, and customer service."

The main objection to this earlier definition is the limitation of the field to finished product distribution. The definition here presented includes material management and logistical coordination in addition to physical distribution as integral aspects of over-all business logistics.

[2] Numerous early references to logistics can be located in the literature. Arch W. Shaw, *An Approach to Business Problems* (Cambridge, Mass.: Harvard University Press, 1916), pp. 101–10, discussed the strategic aspects of physical distribution. Other early references are found in Fred E. Clark, *Principles of Marketing* (New York: Macmillan Publishing Co. Inc., 1922); Theodore N. Beckman, *Wholesaling* (New York: The Ronald Press Company, 1926); Ralph Borsodi, *The Distribution Age* (New York: Appleton-Century-Crofts, 1929); and Richard Webster, "Careless Physical Distribution: A Monkey-Wrench in Sales Management Machinery," *Sales Management*, Vol. XIX (July 6, 1929), p. 21. For a comprehensive review of early literature see Bernard J. La Londe and Leslie M. Dawson, "Early Development of Physical Distribution Thought," in *Readings in Physical Distribution Management* (New York: Macmillan Publishing Co., Inc., 1969), pp. 9–18. The historical review presented in this introduction is updated from an article by the author originally published in 1969; see Donald J. Bowersox, "Physical Distribution Development, Current Status, and Potential," *Journal of Marketing*, Vol. 33 (January 1969), pp. 63–70.

[3] Paul D. Converse, "The Other Half of Marketing," *Twenty-Sixth Boston Conference on Distribution*, Boston, 1954, p. 22.

The neglect and subsequent late development of logistics can logically be attributed to at least two major factors.

First, prior to the time that computers emerged and before applied analytical tools were generally at the disposal of business, there was no reason to believe that an over-all attack on logistical activities would accomplish improved performance. The 1950s were destined to witness a major change in traditional orientation since neither computers nor quantitative techniques were to be denied the fertility of logistical applications. Although neither the computer nor quantitative techniques are the private servants of business logistics, there is little doubt that they have been put to work on an operating basis as well in logistics as in any other area of the corporation.

A second major factor contributing to a reexamination of traditional viewpoints was the prevailing economic climate. The prolonged profit squeeze of the early 1950s, highlighted by the recession of 1958, created an environment conducive to the development of new cost control systems. Integrated logistics provided a productive arena for new methods of cost reduction.

Thus technology, as well as industrial need, abruptly changed during the 1950s. After a great many years of relative obscurity, the period from 1956 to 1965 was to become the decade during which the integrated logistical concept would crystallize. An interpretation of the literature reveals that logistical concept congealed as the product of several significant developments. Each is briefly discussed.

In 1956 a specialized study of air freight economics provided a major new orientation to logistics.[4] The study, which explained the economic justification for high-cost air transport, also introduced the concept of total cost analysis. Total cost was developed as a measure of all expenditures required to accomplish a firm's logistical mission. The authors illustrated that the high freight rates required for air transport could be more than justified by trade-offs, that would result in reduced inventory and warehouse operation costs.

The concept of total cost, although basic in logic, had not previously been applied to logistical economics.[5] Probably because of the economic climate of the times, the immediate reaction was a flurry of attention to logistical problems. Subsequent refinements provided a comprehensive treatment of cost characteristics and related functional analysis of available trade-offs.[6]

---

[4] Howard T. Lewis, James W. Culliton, and Jack D. Steel, *The Role of Air Freight in Physical Distribution* (Boston: Division of Research, Graduate School of Business Administration, Harvard University, 1956).

[5] The total cost concept, developed in greater detail in Chapter 10, is a specialized form of break-even analysis. For some early applications see J. Brooks Heckert and Robert B. Miner, *Distribution Costs* (New York: The Ronald Press Company, 1940), Chapter 15; and Donald R. Longman and Michael Schiff, *Practical Distribution Cost Analysis* (Homewood, Ill.: Richard D. Irwin, Inc., 1955), pp. 35–37.

[6] In particular, see Marvin Flaks, "Total Cost Approach to Physical Distribution," *Business Management*, Vol. 24 (August 1963), pp. 55–61, and Raymond LeKashman and John F. Stolle, "The Total Cost Approach to Distribution," *Business Horizons*, Vol. 8 (Winter 1965), pp. 33–46.

It is difficult to trace the exact origins of the systems approach to problem solving.[7] However, the notion of total integrated effort toward the accomplishment of predetermined goals rapidly found a home in logistical analysis. The systems concept provided a research posture, and total cost analysis offered a method of evaluating among alternative system configurations.

The first general articles directed to the subject of logistics relied heavily on systems technology.[8] In particular, it became apparent that the great deficiency of the traditional viewpoint was the prevailing practice of treating the many logistical activity centers as isolated performance areas. The result was a failure to capture the benefits obtainable only from integrated control.

When studied from a system viewpoint, integrated logistics create a new requirement for compromise between traditional business activities. For example, manufacturing traditionally desires long production runs and low procurement cost, whereas logistics raises questions concerning the total cost commitment of these practices. Finance, traditionally favorable to low inventories, may force a logistical system to adjust components in a less than satisfactory total cost arrangement. With respect to marketing, traditional preferences for finished-goods inventory staging, and broad assortments in forward markets, often stand in conflict to economies offered through total system evaluation. The basic belief that integrated system performance can and most often will produce an end result greater than is possible from non-coordinated performance rapidly became a primary focal point in the development of the integrated logistical concept.

By the early 1960s, the horizons of the emerging field of integrated logistics began to expand. During this period, emphasis began to shift toward a penetrating appraisal of the improved customer service capabilities possible from a highly integrated logistics system.[9] Increased attention was directed to issues of demand cultivation and to the over-all importance of logistics to

[7] For an expanded discussion, see Geoffrey Gordon, *System Simulation* (Englewood Cliffs, N.J.: Prentice-Hall, Inc., 1969), Chapters 1 and 2; Jay W. Forrester, *Principles of Systems* (Cambridge, Mass.: Wright-Allen Press, 1969); Stanford L. Optner, *Systems Analysis* (Englewood Cliffs, N.J.: Prentice-Hall, Inc., 1960); Stanley F. Stasch, *Systems Analysis for Marketing Planning and Control* (Glenview, Ill.: Scott, Foresman and Company, 1972); Van Court Hare, Jr., *Systems Analysis: A Diagnostic Approach* (New York: Harcourt Brace Jovanovich, 1967); and/or Robert H. Kupperman and Harvey A. Smith, *Mathematical Foundations of Systems Analysis* (Reading, Mass.: Addison-Wesley Publishing Company, Inc., 1969).

[8] For example, see Harvey N. Shycon and Richard B. Maffei, "Simulation—Tool for Better Distribution," *Harvard Business Review*, Vol. 38 (November–December 1960), pp. 65–75; Donald D. Parker, "Improve Efficiency and Reduced Cost in Marketing," *Journal of Marketing*, Vol. 26 (April 1962), pp. 15–21; J. L. Heskett, "Ferment in Marketing's Oldest Area," *Journal of Marketing*, Vol. 26 (October 1962), pp. 40–45; and, John F. Magee, "The Logistics of Distribution," *Harvard Business Review*, Vol. 40 (July–August 1962), pp. 89–101.

[9] For examples, see Peter Drucker, "The Economy's Dark Continent," *Fortune*, Vol. 72 (April 1962), pp. 103–104; William Lazer, "Distribution and the Marketing Mix," *Transportation and Distribution Management*, Vol. 2 (December 1962), pp. 12–17; and Wendell M. Stewart, "Key to Improved Volume and Profits," *Journal of Marketing*, Vol. 29 (January 1965), pp. 65–70.

corporate marketing vitality. Physical distribution management came into focus as representing a balance between product delivery capabilities and related cost. Material management, or physical supply, offered similar refinement in the manufacturing complex of the enterprise.[10] In both situations, several alternative operating system configurations exist. The management task is to select an operating system capable of accomplishing stated performance goals at the lowest associated total cost expenditure.

An additional development in logistical thinking relates to the dynamic aspect of channel management. The majority of logistical systems have been studied from the vantage point of vertically integrated organizations. A more useful viewpoint is that logistical activities and related responsibilities seldom terminate when product ownership transfer occurs.[11]

Emphasis on integrated logistics illustrates that many significant costs are experienced between separate firms, linked together in a channel arrangement. The interface of two or more different logistical systems may lead to excessive cost generation and customer service impairment for the over-all channel. Even under conditions of system compatibility, the total cost of logistics for the channel may rapidly accumulate as a result of efforts duplicated by member firms.

A different approach to channelwide logistical evaluation results from an evaluation of information lags and product assortment commitments inherent in channel organizations. In 1958 Forrester introduced a new view of channel relationships.[12] In terms of physical flow, Forrester dramatically illustrated the impact of information dynamics upon fluctuation in inventory accumulation. Until Forrester's work the impact of time delay had been generally neglected in logistics in deference to a primary emphasis upon spatial relationships. From this point forward, a more balanced approach to logistics developed which took integration of spatial and temporal forces into consideration.

With respect to product assortment commitments, it is now generally accepted that the options available to a single firm are directly related to the logistical systems inventory stocking locations. A great deal of the impetus toward understanding the relationship of commitment and location resulted from the classical work of the late Wroe Alderson.[13] The functional approach

[10] For examples, see Robert E. McGarrah, *Production and Logistics Management* (New York: John Wiley & Sons, Inc., 1963), and James L. Heskett, Robert M. Ivie, and Nicholas A. Glaskowsky, *Business Logistics* (New York: The Ronald Press Company, 1973). Dean S. Ammer, *Materials Management*, rev. ed. (Homewood, Ill.: Richard D. Irwin., 1968). To this author's knowledge, the term *physical supply* was first used by Heskett et al.

[11] The issue of legal ownership is critical to transaction analysis. Logistical responsibility may extend long after the time of actual ownership transfer. For an expanded treatment, see Chapter 2.

[12] Jay W. Forrester, "Industrial Dynamics," *Harvard Business Review*, Vol. 36 (July–August 1958), pp. 37–66; or Jay W. Forrester, *Industrial Dynamics* (Cambridge, Mass.: The MIT Press, 1961).

[13] Wroe Alderson, *Marketing Behavior and Executive Action* (Homewood, Ill.: Richard D. Irwin, Inc., 1957).

he provided served to revive, expand, and update the contributions of early marketing scholars concerning the relationships of risk and degree of commitment in logistical operations.[14]

In summary, the study of integrated logistics is relatively new. As a result of improved tools of analysis and the development of high-speed computers, new opportunities to improve logistical operations emerged during the 1950s. In addition, the 1950s provided an economic climate that encouraged the development of new methods of cost reduction. The result was a decade during which the concept of integrated logistics crystallized.

Although many factors contributed to logistical development, four appear to be of particular significance. First was the development of total cost analysis. Second was the application of systems technology. The systems approach provided a way to study complex relations. Total cost provided a measuring device. Beyond a purely cost orientation, a third factor of development was the realization that logistical performance could in fact stimulate revenue generation. Finally, development was further encouraged by increased awareness of the importance of timing, risk, and commitment of logistical resources in a channel context.

By 1965 management was afforded a rather segmented—but theoretically sound—approach to the formulation of logistical planning. The flurry of attention that Converse saw as a critical need in 1954 had by the mid-1960s become a reality. However, within the single enterprise, management began to place emphasis on one or the other of the two main parts of the total logistics system.

From the marketing orientation, physical distribution management emerged as the integrated approach to finished inventory movement. Among those concerned with physical distribution, emphasis centered on the logistical support of customer orders.[15]

In contrast, material management emerged as the applicational area for a similar approach to procurement and production scheduling.[16] Emphasis in material management centered around the orderly flow of raw material and parts to support manufacturing operations.

Although a great many differences exist between physical distribution and material management applications, the basic principles of system design, cost measurement, and tools of analysis are identical. The initial separation of physical distribution and material management was justified on the basis of the immediate improvements that could be readily realized in each operating area. The application of total cost and systems technology in each limited area provided a more workable arena for initial applications.

---

[14] In addition to references in footnote 2, see Percival White, *Scientific Marketing Management* (New York: Harper & Row, Publishers, 1927).

[15] The aspects of business logistics dealing with physical distribution are developed in greater detail in Chapters 1 and 2.

[16] The aspects of business logistics dealing with material management are developed in greater detail in Chapters 1 and 3.

Over the longer haul, a more integrated approach, which treats both physical distribution and material management as parts of an over-all logistical system, has begun to be adopted widely for at least two reasons. First, there is a great deal of interdependence between physical distribution and material management which often can be used to the advantage of the enterprise. For example, backhaul situations exist wherein transportation equipment used for customer delivery can also be dispatched to pick up material purchases. Even if such direct benefits as backhaul do not exist, separation of physical distribution and material management operations requires duplication within the enterprise. Prior to logistical emergence, it was not unusual for the corporate transportation department to service the requirements of both physical distribution and material management. However, rarely did such total enterprise cooperation exist with respect to the other components of integrated logistics.

A second reason for combining physical distribution and material management is the fact that a great deal of coordination is desirable between the two types of movement within the enterprise. This linkage is identified as *logistical coordination*.[17] The function of logistical coordination is to reconcile the differentials between physical distribution and material management to the maximum benefit of the firm. Separation of the two operational aspects of logistics at the neglect of effective coordination falls short of the true objective and benefits of integration.

The vantage point of the present treatment is to develop the concept of integrated logistics in the broadest possible context.[18] The total logistical system is viewed as consisting of three distinct but highly integrated operating systems. The physical distribution operating system is dedicated to the processing of customer orders. The material management operating system is dedicated to the support of manufacturing and assembly operations of the enterprise. The logistical coordination system is dedicated to planning and controlling all logistical activities that are captive within the enterprise.

The field of business logistics has evolved to the point wherein physical distribution and material management are increasingly being managed on an integrated basis. However, they remain largely separate focal points of specialized management attention within the enterprise. The area developed within the text as logistical coordination remains today highly fragmented and, to a significant degree, neglected in the typical enterprise. The potential and desirability of generally achieving full integration of all logistically related operating systems into one highly coordinated corporate structure remains to

---

[17] The term "logistical coordination" is introduced in this text to describe specific managerial responsibilities involved in reconciling physical distribution and material management operations. The specific aspects of logistical coordination are developed in greater detail in Chapters 1 and 4.

[18] For one interpretation of the types of changes expected in logistics in the decades ahead, see James L. Heskett, "Sweeping Changes in Distribution," *Harvard Business Review*, March–April 1973 pp. 123–32; or see Donald J. Bowersox, "Showdown in the Magic Pipeline: Call for New Priorities," Presidential Issue, *Handling & Shipping*, fall 1973, pp. 23–27.

be evaluated. If judged desirable, such integration will be accomplished during the forthcoming decades. This text is written on the assumption that such over-all integration will, in fact, materialize.

The over-all treatment of business logistics is divided into four parts. The objective of Part One is to introduce the subject detail of integrated logistics. Following an overview chapter, the orientation of the remaining chapters of Part One is to describe each of the three integral operating systems that combine to formulate the total logistical structure. Chapter 2 provides a detailed treatment of physical distribution management. In Chapter 3, material management is developed. The final chapter of Part One, Chapter 4, develops logistical coordination. In particular, forecasting is covered, coordination areas are developed, and the chapter directs attention to inventory replenishment objectives in integrated logistics.

The subject matter of Part Two develops the elements of logistical systems. Chapter 5 is concerned with transportation. In Chapter 6 the elements of inventory are treated. In Chapter 7, warehousing is presented. In Chapter 8, the subject of material movement is developed. Finally, communication and order processing are developed in Chapter 9.

Part Three is concerned with the managerial task of system design. The foundations of logistical policy are developed in Chapter 10. Chapter 11 treats system design procedure. In Chapter 12, attention is directed to techniques available to assist management in the design of a logistical system.

In Part Four, emphasis shifts from the design of logistical systems to administration. Chapter 13 is devoted to organization and administration. Chapter 14 deals with controlling logistical operations.

Thus the subject matter development starts with a comprehensive discussion of business logistics (Part One), followed by a detailed treatment of the fundamental elements that combine to form the logistical network of the firm (Part Two). At the conclusion of the first two parts, the stage will have been set for in-depth treatment of the two fundamental responsibilities of the logistical manager: system design (Part Three) and system administration (Part Four).

The decision to focus this text at the individual enterprise level made it necessary to select subjects of concern to over-all logistical management and omit others from explicit coverage. Three such omissions are noteworthy.

First, all logistical managers have a specific stake in the maintenance of a viable national transportation system. The determination of national policy and the encouragement of sound public investment in the transportation infrastructure require the active involvement of logistical professionals in all levels of government. Issues of macrotransportation are not specifically discussed at any point in the text material. Chapter 5 presents a background discussion of the transport infrastructure and regulatory framework within which logistical systems must be designed. This material also introduces the reader to major issues of national concern.

Second, many logistical managers have an active responsibility in multinational material management and physical distribution. All indications suggest that greater involvement in the international logistical arena can be expected during the years ahead. At the present time it is difficult to make generalized statements concerning multinational logistical patterns. Selected materials are presented in Chapter 8 in the sections dealing with containerization. However, with the exception of transportation and in particular containerization, most import–export arrangements are highly specialized relationships. Therefore, at the possible sacrifice of total subject coverage, it was decided to concentrate attention on domestic logistical operations.

Third, the text does not discuss the important subject of logistical ecology. Various aspects of logistical systems, particularly transportation and packaging, are significant causes of environmental pollution. On the positive side, the logistical delivery system is one of the nation's most available resources to be applied toward solving ecological problems. For example, solid waste disposal and package material recycling depend upon effective logistical movement for successful transfer of society waste to processing points. Once again, the prime reason for not including logistical ecology is the limited ability to generalize developments and responsibilities at this point in time.

A final note concerning subject matter development is the format used to integrate locational analysis and theory. The spatial network of fixed facilities deployed in the logistical system structure is the primary determination of potential effectiveness and efficiency of operations. Therefore, facility location to a large degree influences all components of the logistical system. To stress these interrelationships at the appropriate point in subject matter development, locational considerations are discussed at several points throughout the text. In Chapter 1 the network concept of fixed facilities is introduced in discussion of the logistical system concept. Treatment is also included as an integral part of Chapter 5 (concerning transportation) and Chapter 7 (on warehousing). The integration of spatial and temporal considerations in the formulation of logistical policy is developed in depth in Chapter 10. Techniques to assist managers in the selection of specific locations are covered in Chapter 12. The basic issues involved in industrial plant location and associated check lists are treated in appendixes. This format has the disadvantage of spreading the treatment of location across the text. In turn, it has the advantage of developing the salient aspects of location as an integral part of over-all logistical system design.

Part One

Integrated Business Logistics

1

Business Logistics

During the past three decades, logistics has emerged as a major concern of business managers and educators.[1] The objective of logistical operations is to deliver finished inventory and material assortments, in correct quantities, when required, at the location desired, and in usable condition at the lowest total dollar cost. It is through the logistical process that raw materials flow into the vast manufacturing complex of an industrial nation and finished products are distributed for consumption.

Logistical performance provides time and place utility in the business system. Thus value is added to either raw materials or finished products as the result of the logistical process. The value associated with time and place utility is costly to achieve. Although difficult to measure precisely, the annual expenditure required logistically to support the U.S. consumer–manufacturing complex consumes approximately 20 per cent of the total gross national

---

[1] Over the years, common titles used to describe all or parts of the material discussed in this text have been business logistics, physical distribution, material management, physical supply, logistics of distribution, marketing logistics, rhochrematics, and total distribution. See page 1 for the definition of business logistics followed in this text.

product. In a $1 trillion economy, the national logistical bill exceeds $200 billion annually.[2]

This book is concerned with various managerial activities involved in logistical operations of an individual enterprise. To achieve an orderly flow of products to the marketplace, managerial attention must be directed to the design and administration of a logistical system. The purpose of the logistical system is to control the flow of raw material and finished products. The goal of logistics is to achieve efficiently a predetermined level of manufacturing–marketing support at the lowest possible total cost expenditure. The logistical manager has the fundamental responsibility to design an operating system capable of realizing this goal. Once designed, his responsibility extends to the administration of the system.

Within the broad responsibilities of system design and administration, a multitude of detail and complex interrelationships exist. The hallmark of the new discipline of integrated logistics is a logical managerial approach capable of forging together the many dimensions and demands faced by a modern firm.

The objective of this chapter is to introduce and define the basic dimensions of business logistics. Attention is initially directed to an over-all perspective of the logistical task. Next, the systems approach to integrated logistics is examined and the component parts of a logistical system are introduced. The next section provides a synthesis of contemporary logistics within private enterprise and in a competitive environmental setting. In total, the chapter provides the foundation for all chapters that follow.

Logistics of the Firm

From the perspective of the individual firm, the over-all field of logistics is subdivided into three main areas of managerial concern: (1) physical distribution management, (2) material management, and (3) logistical coordination.

The process of *physical distribution management* is concerned with the movement of finished inventory to customers. The availability of inventory is a vital part of the marketing efforts of a firm. Unless the product is delivered at the appropriate time and in an economical manner, a great deal of the promotional efforts of a firm may be diluted. It is through the physical distribution process that time and space are introduced into marketing. Thus physical distribution links a firm with its customers. To support the wide variety of marketing systems that exist in a highly commercialized nation, many physical distribution systems are utilized. In total, such systems link

[2] Author's estimate based upon figures provided by U.S. government publications and industry reports.

together manufacturers, wholesalers, and retailers into a channel network for providing inventory availability in support of marketing.[3]

The process of *material management*, sometimes referred to as physical supply, is concerned with the procurement and movement of raw materials and parts from geographical points of purchase to manufacturing and assembly plants. Similar to physical distribution, material management is concerned with making available the correct assortment of materials, at the desired location, when needed, and in an economical manner. Whereas physical distribution is concerned with satisfying customer requirements, material management is concerned with the support of manufacturing and assembly operations.

Logistical coordination is concerned with the identification of internal requirements and the establishment of specifications that tie together a particular firm's physical distribution and material management. Coordination is required to establish operational continuity. Between physical distribution and material management substantially different operational requirements exist. The function of logistical coordination is to reconcile these differentials to the maximum benefit of the enterprise.

Logistical coordination constitutes a combination of planning and operational matters. The establishment of objectives to guide operations requires that estimates be compiled concerning future expectations and requirements. Forecasting is therefore an integral part of logistical coordination. Finally, to operationalize what a firm plans to accomplish during a specific time period, forecasts must be synthesized into specific plans. Such plans encompass material planning, production scheduling, and internal product replenishment. Forecasting, material planning, and production scheduling constitute the planning aspects of logistical coordination. Product replenishment represents the operational aspect of logistical coordination.

Product replenishment operations maintain control over semifinished goods between stages of manufacturing and finished inventory to and between warehouses utilized by the enterprise. Product replenishment has one major difference in contrast to either physical distribution or material management operations. Product replenishment operations are limited to movements within and under the complete control of the enterprise. Therefore, the uncertainties introduced by random order entry and erratic performance are removed from operational planning, thereby permitting more optional allocation.

From a vantage point of the total enterprise, the three subdivisions of logistics have substantial overlap. They combine to provide management of all material and finished inventory moving among locations, supply sources, and customers in the total enterprise. In this sense logistics is concerned with the integrated management for maximum benefit and economy of all material and finished inventory movement. The total logistical process is illustrated in Figure 1-1.

[3] Chapter 2 develops in detail the relationship of marketing channels and physical distribution.

FIGURE 1-1
The Total Concept of Business Logistics

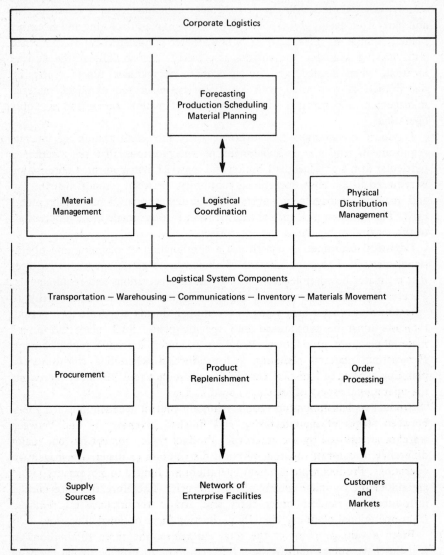

A Systems Approach to Integrated Logistics

Introductory comments stressed that one major deficiency of traditional logistical management was a failure to develop an integrated treatment. More often than not, management of individual parts of logistics has been under the direction and control of various departments within the corporation. Such diffusion of responsibility often resulted in duplication and waste, and sometimes in hindrance of mission accomplishment. Likewise, information flow concerning logistical matters was often sufficiently fragmented to prohibit both planning and administration of the total system. The basic belief that integrated system performance can and most often will produce an end result greater than is possible from noncoordinated performance rapidly became a focal point in development of the business logistics concept. The logic of systems technology offers a regimented way to penetrate the traditional viewpoint.

Some basic ideas of systems analysis are developed forthwith. First, a few comments regarding organization of logistics within the corporation will be helpful with respect to the material that follows. Implicit in the statements regarding duplication and waste is the assumption that if all management responsibility for logistics were centralized in a single organizational group, integrated control would automatically improve. This assumption has the basic fallacy of placing emphasis on structure rather than on results. Support for the fact that centralized organization alone is not sufficient to guarantee results can readily be illustrated. Many of the most effective logistical operations function without formal organizational grouping under a single management unit. Others with centralized grouping also achieve superior results.

Individual organization structures vary depending upon the specific mission, the given personnel, and the resource capabilities. Some basic patterns of organization are available to guide management; however, discussion and development are deferred until Chapter 13. At this stage the significant point is the development of a philosophy of operation that stimulates all levels of management within a firm to think and act in terms of integrated logistical capabilities and economies. Such a philosophy is found in the systems concept.

The Systems Concept

It is difficult to trace the exact origins of the systems approach to problem solving.[4] The first significant applications of system analysis can be traced to research during World War II. In fact, the concept of a system is closely related to all forms of organized activity. However, given the challenges of global war, scientists developed an organized methodology to guide the research and development of complex physical and organizational problems. This approach is referred to as *system analysis*. Technical aspects of logistical design are treated in Part Three. However, a basic knowledge of the systems concept is essential for a proper understanding of integrated logistics.

The systems concept is one of total integrated effort toward the accomplishment of a predetermined objective. Such an objective for a logistical system might be either the lowest possible cost or the fastest method of product delivery. Given the objective, a system capable of obtaining the desired results can be designed.

Under the systems approach, basic acknowledgment is given to the importance of all elements included in the system. These are normally considered

[4] See page 4 for a brief historical review of the systems concept.

components of the system. Each has a specific function to accomplish toward attainment of the basic objective of the total system. To illustrate, consider a precision high-fidelity stereotape player. Many different components are combined into an integrated system for the single purpose of reproducing sound. The speakers, the transistors, the amplifier, and other components only exist to the end that their combined performance results in the desired quality of sound.

From this basic illustration some principles can be stated concerning systems in general. First, it is the performance of the total system that is singularly of importance. Components only exist and find justification to the extent that they enhance total system performance. Second, components need not have optimum design on an individual basis, because emphasis is based upon their integrated relationship in the system. Third, there exists between components a functional relationship, which may stimulate or hinder combined performance. This relationship is commonly called a *trade-off*. Finally, it is explicit that components linked together as a system can, on a combined basis, produce an end result greater than that possible by individual performance. In fact, the desired result may not be attainable without such synergistic performance.

These principles are basic and logically consistent. There can be little doubt that a logistical system having balanced integration of all component parts should be able to attain greater results than one lacking coordinated performance. However, although logical and noncontroversial in concept, the effective implementation of the systems approach to logistics remains rare.

Until recently, various activities involved in logistics were more often than not performed within corporations as individual activities. For example, transportation and purchasing were managed by separate units in the corporation without any real effort at integrating the activities. To the degree that such isolated performance exists, a serious void may also exist in total integrated capability. In final analysis it makes very little difference whether a firm spends more or less dollars for an individual component—warehousing for example—as long as the over-all logistical objectives are achieved at the lowest total cost expenditure.

One useful way to view the implication of logistics as a corporate-wide system is to disregard organizational arrangements. Placing primary emphasis upon the arrangement of system components on a corporate-wide basis allows substantial freedom in system design without involvement in matters of traditional organizational control.

Logistical System Components

The major components of a firm's logistical system are grouped into five broad areas: (1) facility location, (2) transportation, (3) inventory, (4) communication, and (5) material movement. These five components combine to form a network that constitutes the logistical system of the firm. Two factors relating to development of a firm's logistical system are important to keep in mind while reviewing the material that follows.

First, whereas a firm desires to maintain a high degree of congruency with all other firms engaged in the distribution exchange channel, such alliances extend only to an agreement regarding common interfirm policies and programs. To a significant degree, firms will accept risk for performance of exchange functions only to the extent that it corresponds with potential return on investment or counterbalance of power. The decisions of who will perform what exchange functions are therefore matters of negotiation. Once these negotiations have stabilized, they, in effect, become operating parameters. Each firm involved in the exchange channel must legally make its own arrangements concerning implementation of their respective responsibility. The result of such negotiation becomes the basis for each firm's logistical system. It therefore follows that an individual firm may be more or less engaged in the various functions of distribution channel exchange and as a result will require more or less involvement in each of the five activity areas outlined.[5]

Second, those service firms included in a logistical system are considered capable of managerial control. Such control includes all the aspects of the system under direct ownership of the firm as well as the intermediary specialists performing specified activities for a price. Thus design of the logistical system includes for hire specialists such as transportation or public warehouse firms that perform a stated activity for a specified payment.

FACILITY LOCATIONS.   One deficiency in classical economic analysis is insufficient attention to the role of facility location. In an effort to study supply and demand relationships under a wide variety of market structures, economists in general often assumed location advantages and transportation cost differentials to be either nonexistent or equal among competitive firms. Businessmen, in contrast, are not able to neglect the impact of location decisions upon the subsequent success or failure of their firm to realize an adequate return on investment. In many ways, the network of facilities selected by a firm's management is basic with respect to ultimate logistical results. In particular, the number, the size, and the geographical arrangement of facilities operated or used in the system have a direct relationship to the customer service capabilities and corresponding logistical cost outlay of the firm.

It is a fact of business life that a great deal of disparity exists between geographical market areas. The top 10 trading markets in the United States account for over 42 per cent of the potential sale of any quality product or service.[6] It follows fairly well that any firm attempting to market on a national basis should give serious attention to the location of fixed facilities near these prime markets.

---

[5] The degree of involvement in each logistical activity area depends to a large degree upon the firm's vertical integration. For greater development, see Chapter 2.

[6] Derived from U.S. Department of Commerce census statistics.

When one realistically views competition, it is clear that all marketing transactions must be developed within and between a given framework of location points. From the viewpoint of physical flows, the facility network represents a series of nodal points through which materials and finished inventories physically move. In a planning sense, such facilities include production plants, distribution warehouses, and retail stores operated by a firm. If the specialized services of transportation firms or public warehouses are utilized, the facilities of these specialists represent part of the network.

The primary importance of selecting the best possible network of facilities cannot be overemphasized. Although it is unlikely that any firm can relocate all facilities at a given time, considerable latitude remains in location selection and facility design over a period of time. From the viewpoint of marketing impact, the selection of a superior set of locations can result in a substantial competitive advantage. Concerning the logistical support system, a superior network of locations can result in speedy delivery at a minimum dollar expenditure. The degree of logistical efficiency attainable is directly related to and limited by the network of facilities.

TRANSPORTATION.   Given a network of facilities, the first connecting link in the system is transport. Transportation and traffic management have received considerable attention over the years. Almost every firm of any size has a traffic manager who is responsible for administration of the firm's transportation program.

In a general sense, a firm has three alternatives in the establishment of a transport capability. First, a private fleet of equipment may be purchased or leased. Second, specific contracts may be arranged with firms and individuals who are transport specialists to provide an exclusive or contract movement service. Third, a firm may purchase the services of any legally authorized transport company that offers point-to-point transfer at specified charges. These three forms of transport are commonly called *private, contract*, and *common carriage*.

From the logistical system viewpoint, the firm must establish the ability to move materials and finished inventories between facilities from supply sources and to customers. Three factors are of primary importance in establishment of the transport capability: (1) cost of service, (2) speed of service, and (3) consistency of service.

The cost of transport results from the actual payment for a movement between two points plus the expense related to having inventory locked in transit. Logistical systems should be designed to minimize the transport cost in relation to the total system cost. As will be illustrated later, this does not necessarily mean that the lowest or cheapest method of movement between two facility points is desirable.

Speed of service relates to the actual time required to complete a transfer between two facilities. Speed of service and cost of service are related in two ways. First, those transport specialists capable of providing fast service normally charge higher rates. Second, the faster the service, the shorter is the time interval that materials and inventories are in transit.

Consistency of service refers to measured performance over a range of movements between two locations. In essence, how dependable is a given method of transfer with respect to time? In many ways consistency of service is the most important characteristic of the transport component. If a given movement takes two days one time and six the next, serious bottlenecks can develop in the flow of goods and cause impairment of inventory control. To the degree that transport capability lacks consistency, safeguards in terms of extra inventory in the form of safety stocks must be built into the system to prevent service breakdowns. Lack of consistency influences both sellers' and buyers' inventory commitments.

In the design of a logistical system, a delicate balance must be established between transfer cost and speed of service. The ultimate objective is to regulate and integrate speed of transfer into the total system. Under some circumstances, low-cost slow transfers are preferred, whereas under other conditions faster methods are desirable. Finding the proper balance in transport capability is one of the primary objectives of logistical system analysis.

Three aspects of transport capability should be kept in mind as they relate to the logistical system. First, the selection of facilities forms a network that in fact limits the range of transport alternatives available and establishes the nature of the transfer job to be accomplished. Second, the cost of physical transfer involves more than the freight bill received from a carrier for movement between two locations. Third, the entire effort to integrate transport capability into a logistical system may be defeated if the service received is sporadic and inconsistent.

INVENTORY.   The requirements for physical transfer between fixed facilities are based on the inventory policy followed by a firm. In a broad sense a firm could stock every item carried in inventory at every facility. Few firms, however, follow such a luxurious inventory program, because the total cost would be prohibitive. The objective of inventory integration into the logistical system is to employ the minimum quantities consistent with desired delivery capability and total cost expenditure. Excessive inventories can compensate for errors in the design of the basic system and may even help overcome poor administration of logistical activities. However, inventory used as a crutch normally will result in increased total cost.

Inventory programs should be initiated with the idea of the minimum asset commitment. The answer to a sound inventory program is found in selective deployment. Such selective deployment centers around four factors: (1) customer qualities, (2) product qualities, (3) transport integration, and (4) competitor performance. Each is briefly discussed.

Every firm selling to a variety of customers is confronted with a range of relative profitability. Some customers are very profitable to do business with and others are not. Such profitability stems, for example, from range of product line purchases, volume of purchases, price, marketing services required, and the necessary supporting activities needed to maintain a repetitious relationship. Customers who are highly profitable to do business with constitute the core market of a firm. Inventory policies should be designed to protect these customers by rapid and consistent logistical service.

Given a product line, most firms find that a substantial variance exists concerning the volume and profitability of individual products. It is often stated that most firms with a wide assortment find that 20 per cent of the products marketed account for 80 per cent of a firm's profit. Given this variance, a realistic appraisal should be made of the reasons low-profit items are carried in the assortment. On the surface it would seem obvious that a firm would want to provide a high degree of consistent delivery service on highly profitable products. The fallacy may be that many of the less profitable items are carried to provide full-line service to a core customer. Therefore, it is necessary to consider all factors when selectively deploying inventory holdings among facilities. Many firms find it desirable to centralize inventories on slow-moving or low-profit items and then utilize a fast method of transportation when such items are needed by a customer.

To a significant degree the selection of inventory assortments for given facilities is related to transportation cost. Most rates charged by transportation specialists are directly based on size of shipment. Therefore, it may be sound policy to stock more items at a specific facility in order to generate larger-volume shipments. The corresponding savings in unit transportation cost may more than offset the increase in unit inventory holding cost.

Finally, inventory stocking programs are not created in a competitive vacuum. The ability to provide rapid delivery of a complete assortment of products may well render a firm cheaper and more desirable to do business with. Therefore, inventory may be placed in a specific facility in order to improve over-all logistical impact even when such commitments increase cost. Such inventory policies may result from an effort to gain a differential advantage over a competitor or to neutralize one that a competitor currently enjoys. The strategy of competitively stimulated inventory stocking increases in tempo in direct relationship to the extent to which customers can substitute various manufacturers' products.

Three managerial tasks are related to inventory policy. The first is prediction and unit forecasting, which constitutes an evaluation of all pertinent and known facts to arrive at an estimate of anticipated future events. Inventory policy formation would require very little effort and involve little, if any, risk if future uncertainty could be eliminated. The second task is production scheduling. In essence this is the unit market forecast refined to a manufacturing work program. The third management task is material planning for procurement. Scheduling of the inbound flow of materials is harmonized with the outbound flow of finished goods via the logistical coordination task.

It is apparent that an integral relationship exists between facilities, transportation, and inventory. With respect to inventory, it is desirable to be as selective as possible in policy development.

COMMUNICATION. Communication represents an often neglected activity area in the logistical system. In part, such neglect has resulted from the lack of data processing and data transmission equipment capable of handling the necessary flow of information. Equally, the cause of neglect has been the lack of realistic understanding of the importance of rapid and accurate communication upon logistical performance.

A deficiency in the quality of information can result in countless problems. Such deficiencies fall into two broad categories. First, information received may be incorrect with respect to appraisal of trends and events. Because a great deal of logistical flow takes place in anticipation of future transactions, an inaccurate appraisal can result in a deficiency or abundance of inventory commitment with all associated logistical cost. Second, information may be incorrect with respect to a specific customer's needs. A firm that processes a wrong order confronts all the costs of logistics without the resultant sale. In fact, the costs are often compounded by the need to absorb the cost of returning the inventory and, if the sales opportunity still exists, once more attempting to provide the proper assortment.

The speed of information flow is directly related to the integration of fixed facilities, transportation capability, and inventory. It makes little sense for a firm to accumulate orders at a local sales office for a week, mail them to a regional office, send them to the data-processing department, assign them to a distribution warehouse, and then ship them via air express for fast delivery. Perhaps a direct phone call would have been justified from the customer's office, if such speedy order transmittal would have resulted in faster delivery at a lower total cost. Once again it is a question of balance among all components of the logistical system.

Two managerial tasks are directly related to logistic communication. The first is customer order processing. An order represents a critical information flow, which is the prime input to the logistical system. The second managerial task relates to customer adjustment. The adjustment function constitutes administration of an order until it is fully received by a customer in damage-free condition. Shipment of a customer order on time is not sufficient logistical performance. The order must also be received as promised with respect to quality and quantity. Performance concerning customer orders and adjustment has a direct impact on coordination of material management and physical distribution in the over-all logistical structure of the firm.

In general, the more efficient the design of a firm's logistical system, the more sensitive it is to disturbances in information flow. Finely balanced systems have no extra inventory holdings. Safety stocks are maintained at the minimum possible level consistent with transportation capability. Incorrect information can cause a serious disturbance in system performance. Delays in communication flow can amplify the error, which results in a series of oscillations in over- and undercorrection. It is communication that renders a logistical system dynamic. The quality and timeliness of information are the prime determinants of system stability.

MATERIAL MOVEMENT. The design of a basic logistical system is primarily concerned with four components: facility location, transportation capacity, inventory allocation, and communication network. These areas are subject to a wide variety of alternative design arrangements, each of which has a degree of potential effectiveness and a limit in attainable efficiency. In essence, these four activity centers provide a system structure for integrated product flow. One final area of design—material movement—also represents an integral part of the logistical system.

Material movement does not fit into the neat structural scheme of the other areas; it occurs throughout the system and is directly related to physical flow. Thus material movement involves flow of inventory through and between physical facilities. Such flow is only initiated in response to a message expressing a need at some point in the system.

In a broad sense, material movement involves handling, packaging, and containerization. Handling consumes a great deal of the cost of logistics in terms of operations and capital expenditure. It stands to reason that the fewer times a product has to be handled in the total process, the less restricted and the more potentially efficient will be the total physical flow.

To facilitate handling efficiency, individual products are combined into larger cartons, which contain a grouping of cans, bottles, boxes, or whatever. This *master carton* performs two functions. First, it serves to protect the product while the logistical process is under way. Second, the master carton serves as a primary load, which allows the handling of one larger package as opposed to a multitude of individual units.

For purposes of efficient handling, master cartons are normally grouped together into larger lots. These larger lots may be banded with steel strapping, combined with tape, shrink-wrapped, stocked into a wire cage, or stacked on a wooden pallet, to name a few common techniques. Each of these grouping devices provides a load of sufficient size to justify economically some form of specialized material handling equipment to assist in movement.

A container in the technical sense includes all devices used for grouping from, for example, the original can to be used to protect pineapple, to a 40-foot sea–truck box loaded on a ship in Hawaii for ultimate delivery in Lansing, Michigan. However, for ease of understanding, the term *container* is commonly used to describe loadings containing more than one master carton.

Material movement effectively integrated into a firm's logistical process can substantially reduce problems related to time and ease of product flow throughout the total system. In fact, several firms have been able to design unit loads that move large assortments of products from the production line directly to a customer's shelf. Although such programs have a related expense, if properly developed they may more than pay for themselves by reduced handling, lower transportation costs, improved customer relations, and general over-all efficiency.

Summary—Logistical Systems

The main strength of logistics appears foremost to evolve from the development of techniques and concepts for treating the range of inherent functions on an integrated basis. Systems technology provides the framework for studying alternative logistical designs and evaluating such arrangements on a total cost basis.

This system orientation stands in direct contrast to the traditional approach of treating the many activities integral to logistical operations on a separate or diffused basis. High-speed digital computers provide the tool required to evaluate complex system designs and to keep track of the multitude of details engaged in geographically dispersed logistical operations.

In a strategic context, the central or focal point of logistics is the corporate commitment to inventory. Individual products and raw materials are properly viewed as a combination of form, time, place, and possession utilities. Inventory has little value until form is placed in a temporal and spatial context which will provide the opportunity to enjoy the physical and psychological attributes related to possession. If a firm does not consistently meet the requirements of time and place closure, it has nothing to sell. Unless such time and place closure is efficiently achieved profits and return on investment may be jeopardized.

The Logistical Network, The Firm, and a Competitive Environment

Figure 1-2 illustrates a firm's logistical network with respect to internal and external forces influential in system design. The main objective of system design is to integrate the five primary components into a unified and balanced effort. Regardless of the firm's internal organization with respect to management responsibilities, the five components must be harmonized. The total logistical system exists for the sole purpose of accomplishing spatial and temporal closure for the firm's inventory. Until the utilities of time and place are achieved, little if any value has been added by the logistical process.

In Figure 1-2 the five main components of the logistical system are shown linked together as part of a corporate system. External to logistics are the other primary systems of a typical corporation. In essence, the logistics system is but one of four basic systems comprising the corporation. As such, logistics, marketing, production, and finance are all parts of the master system—the firm. Just as the five primary components of logistics must be in balance, so must the four significant parts of the master system function as a totality.

FIGURE 1-2
The Firm—A Competitive Environment

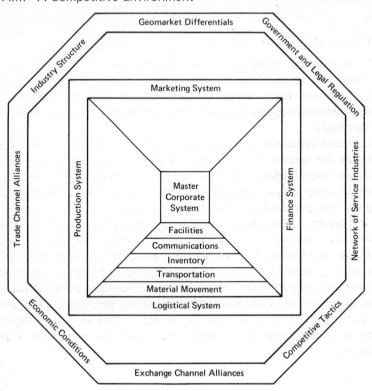

External to the four elements contained in a firm's master system are business environmental forces that limit flexibility of corporate design. In total, environmental forces form the ecology of the firm. These forces are (1) industry structure, (2) geomarket differentials, (3) network of service industries, (4) exchange channel alliances, (5) government and legal regulatory structure, (6) economic conditions, (7) trade channel alliances, and (8) competitive tactics.

In total strategy, the firm is viewed as a profit-generating enterprise within and adjusting to environmental constraints. Over a given planning period, environmental constraint remains relatively constant. The firm and competitors adjust corporate programs in an effort to obtain greater individual shares of the market for the particular product assortment offered. To the degree that any given firm gains favor in the eyes and behavior of buyers, that firm enjoys a differential advantage over competitors. Such advantage may be rapidly eliminated by competitors, or it may be retained over a substantial period of time. To the degree that a differential advantage prevails, the recipient firm gains lasting distinctiveness and long-run profitable growth.

The complexities of total corporate activity are important only to the degree that a firm is able to culminate all effort into profitable transactions. For any given firm to enjoy a continuous series of profitable transactians requires the efficient integration of all corporate resources. If a firm is to survive, all corporate systems—marketing, production, finance, and logistics—must function as a totality. Each system of the corporation or any of its activity centers viewed in isolation has no justification. Only to the degree that any given part contributes to the total corporate effort to realize profitable transactions does a given part, or the total corporate effort, gain economic justification.

Viewing business activity as a total system of goal-directed action has become commonplace. Equally common is the acceptance of an over-all corporate marketing orientation as an underlying philosophy of management. This market orientation viewpoint is not designed to place marketing on a pedestal but to underscore the importance of markets in corporate planning. Transactions are accomplished in the market place. Transactions are essential to survival. Therefore, all corporate action must be geared to the transaction.

Within the firm the logistical system is central to completion of the transaction. Those firms enjoying logistical efficiency gain an advantage in terms of cost and service that is difficult to duplicate. Firms that achieve a balanced network of facilities, transportation capacity, inventory deployment, communication, and material movement in harmony with the financial, marketing, and production systems of the corporation stand ahead of the competition with respect to long-range differential advantage.

This balance of components within the logistical system and of the logistical system to the balance of the firm must be subject to constant adjustment. In the long run, underlying quicksands of economic and institutional changes may render the existing system inadequate as well as uneconomical. This inadequacy may result in increased costs or a loss of competitive advantage to rival firms.

Defining the Logistical Mission

The logistical mission of the firm is to develop a system that meets the stated corporate customer service policy at the lowest possible dollar expenditure. Development of a satisfactory program requires two levels of adjustment: (1) integration of the logistical system with other corporate systems and (2) development of total cost balance between logistical system components. Both levels of adjustment constitute trade-offs.

Master System Integration

As stated earlier, the basic financial, production, marketing, and logistical systems of a firm must be integrated into a single effort. The logistical system is primarily concerned with support of the production and marketing systems. At the corporate level, the critical question centers around the expected level of support the logistical system will provide.

The question of corporate logistical support involves two factors: (1) delivery performance, and (2) total cost expenditure. In terms of total performance level, it is necessary to consider both required performance time and consistency of performance. With respect to cost expenditure, the problem centers around the dollar requirement related to alternative levels of total performance.

The problem at the corporate level is to establish a balance between performance and cost that will result in the desired return on investment for the firm. This balance reflects the corporate logistical policy and becomes the managerial parameter for guiding system design.

Logistical Performance

With respect to total performance, almost any level of logistical service is possible if a firm is willing to pay the price. For example, a full-line inventory can be situated in close geographical proximity to all major customers. A fleet of trucks can be held in a constant state of delivery readiness. To facilitate communications, a hot line can be installed between the customer's facility and the supplier firm's distribution warehouse. Under this hypothetical situation, it is conceivable that a customer's order could be delivered within a matter of minutes. Although such a service situation might constitute a sales manager's dream, such extreme performance is not practical or needed to support the marketing and production systems.

Logistical performance is, in final analysis, a question of priority and penalty. If a specific raw material is not available when required by the production system, it may necessitate a plant shutdown, with the resultant costs and the ultimate loss of sales. The penalty of such a failure is great, and therefore the priority placed upon performance will be high. In contrast, a 2-day delay in delivery of a product to a grocery chain store warehouse may cause little more than a delivery scheduling problem. Therefore, within limited ranges, the priority placed upon performance in this second situation will not be as severe, because the penalty for the failure is not as drastic.

As noted above, total performance is measured with respect to time and consistency. The time measure is concerned with the total elapsed time from the placement of the customer order or commitment to the delivery of the material or inventory in satisfactory condition. Naturally, a firm desires the fastest possible delivery program. However, a fast performance cycle is of little real value unless it is consistently met in actual practice. It does very little good for a firm to promise second-day delivery if in actual performance it can achieve such standards only a small percentage of the time.

Performance standards should be established on a selective basis. Some products are more critical than others because of their importance to the purchaser and consequent profitability. The stated level of delivery performance should be realistic and adjusted to the task at hand.

In general, firms tend to be overly optimistic when stating performance standards. Inferior or substandard performance to an unrealistic service policy often will cause greater operating and customer problems than the statement of less ambitious goals. The quality of consistency is of greater value than pure speed to a firm on the receiving end of a logistical pipeline.

Logistical Cost

It is currently in vogue to talk about profit centers within the modern corporation. The logistical system should be considered a cost center, and as with all other expenses of a firm, every effort must be made to hold expenditures to a minimum. Logistical costs have a direct relationship to a firm's selected service policy. The qualities of fast and consistent performance have related costs. The higher each of these aspects of total performance, the greater will be the cost to the logistical system.

A significant planning problem stems from the fact that logistical cost and increased performance have a nonproportional relationship. A firm that supports a service standard of overnight delivery at 95 per cent consistency may confront nearly double the logistical cost of one that develops a program of second-morning delivery at 90 per cent consistency. The same firm committed to a delivery policy of overnight service at greater than 95 per cent consistency could easily dissipate profits by attempting to provide performance not needed, expected, or even wanted by customers.

Logistical System Balance

The typical firm will find that the best over-all balance between logistical performance and cost is one that constitutes reasonable performance levels and realistic cost expenditures. Very seldom will either the lowest total cost or the highest service performance system constitute the best corporate logistical system. Most firms can be expected to select a reasonable balance between cost and performance.

Significant advances have been made in the development of tools to aid management in the measurement of cost–performance trade-offs. A sound decision concerning desired performance can be formulated only if it is possible to estimate expenditures for alternative levels of system performance. Likewise, alternative levels of logistical performance are meaningless unless properly integrated into marketing, production, and finance.

Typical Logistical Systems

The many aspects of logistical system development render the design of a program a very complex assignment. In addition to the development of a system having an acceptable balance of performance and cost, management must always keep in mind that change will require constant adjustment. Thus flexibility represents an important part of any system design. When one considers the wide variety of individual distribution systems operated by firms in the United States that service widely diverse markets, it might seem astonishing that any design similarity exists from one situation to the next. However, all systems have two items in common. First, they are designed to encourage maximum product flow. Second, the systems must be designed within the existing technological development of the five primary logistical components.

The limit of technology available in the performance of major logistical activities results in some common patterns among systems. Three basic patterns stand out as the most widely utilized designs for product flow: (1) echelon systems, (2) direct systems, and (3) dual or flexible systems.

Echelon Systems

The term *echelon* implies that the flow of products proceeds through a series of locational points or steps as it moves from production to point of ownership transfer or from raw materials sources to manufacturing locations. Such steps consist of the accumulation of inventory groupings in warehouses. Thus the essential characteristic of an echelon system is that inventory is maintained at one or more points in the product flow pipeline.

Two common echelon patterns are the establishment of break-bulk and consolidation points in the physical distribution system. The break-bulk distribution warehouse exists for the purpose of receiving large volume shipments from a variety of different suppliers for assortment into combinations required for individual customers or retailers. The food distribution centers operated by major grocery chains such as Kroger, A & P, and Colonial Stores constitute prime examples of break-bulk points. The consolidation distribution warehouse is normally operated by a firm that produces a product line at a variety of different production plants. By consolidation of all products at a central point, it is possible to ship large volumes consisting of the complete product. Major food-processing firms, such as Libby, Pillsbury, Del Monte, and General Foods, are prime examples of firms using consolidation points.

Echelon systems normally employ warehouses in order to combine a wide variety of products into a single large-volume shipment. However, intentories are also held in field locations in order to deliver customer orders rapidly. The general situation appears to favor warehousing in order to enjoy benefits of high volume and complete product assortment distribution. Rapid delivery can be realized without a warehouse network. When volume is sufficient, a network of strategically located field inventories offers the best balance of service performance and cost economies.

Direct Systems

In contrast to echelon pattern are those systems that operate direct to customer from one or a limited number of central inventory accumulations. Such firms find that their particular marketing efforts can best be supported by holding a central inventory from which customer orders are filled. Direct systems often utilize high-speed transport and electronic order processing to overcome the extensive geographical separation from customers. Examples of direct shipments are found in the mail order and electronic industries.

Dual Systems

The most common logistical patterns are those that combine the principles of the echelon and direct systems into a flexible operations pattern. As noted earlier, inventory selectivity is encouraged in the design of a logistical system. Some products may be held in warehouses, whereas others are distributed directly.

For example, one firm supplies after-market replacement automobile parts to support its new car distribution. Their system is designed to echelon inventories at various distances from prime markets. The slower the part turnover, the more centralized is the inventory. The slowest moving parts are held at a central location, which directly supplies the entire world.

In contrast, a second firm, which supplies industrial replacement parts, follows a completely opposite distribution policy. In order rapidly to meet unexpected demands, this firm inventories sufficient quantities of all slow movers at each distribution warehouse. In contrast to the first firm, fast- and medium-turnover products are supplied on a regular basis direct to customers from plants and central supply centers.

This different policy is easily explained when one examines the market each firm serves and the degree of product differential each enjoys. The automobile firm faces extensive competition on replacement parts on new models. However, as the original product ages, this competition decreases, making this firm the sole supplier. The industrial parts firm, on the other hand, sells a product that has very little style deterioration and a high degree of competitive substitutability. In this firm's market, a supplier is measured by purchasing agents with respect to how fast unexpected production breakdowns can be remedied.

Each firm faces a different marketing problem, and each utilizes a different flexible logistic policy with respect to warehousing finished product inventories. In general, each firm must study its own marketing situation to establish the logistical pattern that will best satisfy its customer service requirement at the lowest total cost.

Summary

The concept of integrated logistics is relatively new in business management. Substantial opportunities exist to improve logistical service and/or reduce total cost. The systems approach is essential to a comprehensive analysis of the logistical requirements of a firm. These requirements are satisfied by three logistical performance operations. Material management is concerned with the support of manufacturing operations, physical distribution is concerned with customer support, and logistical coordination is concerned with the planning and replenishment of inventories within the firm. The three operating systems form the over-all logistical sector of the enterprise.

To facilitate logistical performance, transportation, inventory, warehousing, material movement, and communication must be highly coordinated. Such coordination has three levels of concern: (1) within the over-all logistical system; (2) within the enterprise in consideration of marketing, manufacturing, and finance; and (3) within the competitive environment faced by the total enterprise. From within this maze of interacting forces, the job of the logistical manager is to design and administer an effective and efficient operating system.

Questions

1. Describe the differences among logistics, physical distribution, material management, logistical coordination, and transportation.
2. What is meant by the statement that the logistical management responsibility in a corporation involves both system design and administration?
3. What reasons can you give for the lack of attention to logistical coordination in the traditional organizational structure of the business enterprise?
4. Describe the similarities and differences of the order processing cycle in physical distribution, the material cycle in material management, and the product replenishment cycle in logistical coordination.
5. Would you agree that all organized behavior is to some degree systems oriented?
6. Describe the concept of trade-off and illustrate why it is an integral aspect of the systems concept.
7. Illustrate from your experience an example of failure to solve a problem on a total systems basis.
8. Why is location selection fundamental to the design of a logistical system?
9. Explain the difference between speed and consistency of service in transportation.
10. Why would a firm normally expect to find that 20 per cent of its products account for 80 per cent of its sales? Why do you think such relationships are significant to logistical planning?
11. In the illustration in Figure 1-2, why do corporate managers have various degrees of control over the environmental forces that form the ecology of the firm in comparison to the managerial factors?
12. Does the statement that the firm should seek to realize logistical performance at the lowest total cost mean that an over-all effort should be made to design and administer a logistical system of lowest total cost?

2

Physical
Distribution
Management

The aspect of over-all logistics concerned with the processing and delivery of customer orders is physical distribution management. Physical distribution is essential to marketing because timely and economical product delivery is necessary to accomplish profitable transactions. The over-all process of marketing can be broadly divided into transaction creating and physical fulfillment activities. Physical distribution is primarily concerned with the physical fulfillment activities.

The development of physical distribution systems to support modern marketing is a dynamic aspect of management because a firm is constantly changing parts of its marketing mix in an effort to gain and hold a competitive advantage in the market place.[1] The distribution or marketing channel is of fundamental importance to physical distribution because the channel is the arena within which marketing and logistics culminate into customer transactions.[2]

[1] For a detailed discussion of the marketing mix concept, see William Lazer, *Marketing Management* (New York: John Wiley & Sons, Inc., 1971), pp. 16–20. The concept is related to physical distribution on pages 37–39.

[2] For a historical review of the development of marketing channel logic and selected industry examples, see Richard M. Clewett, *Marketing Channels* (Homewood, Ill.: Richard D. Irwin, Inc., 1954).

Therefore, for a proper understanding of physical distribution, one should develop a sound insight into the over-all nature of distribution channels.

The initial section of this chapter is devoted to a description of modern marketing that includes a detailed discussion of the integral nature of physical distribution to the over-all marketing process. Next, attention is directed to descriptive contrast of traditional distribution channel treatment between those concerned with marketing and those with primarily a physical distribution orientation. The next section is concerned with channel structure. A general structural classification of channels is developed based upon separation of transaction and exchange activities. Given structure, the next section moves to a treatment of functions that must be performed by the total exchange channel to support the over-all marketing process. Essential to this functional development is a consideration of interfirm relations with respect to total channel considerations. All channel members need not play an equally aggressive part in functional activities nor engage in equal risk. Thus the next section of this chapter is devoted to a treatment of the tactics and strategy of total exchange channel management. The following section deals with cost and customer service measures of physical distribution performance. The final section of the chapter treats the dynamic nature of physical distribution performance over time. Although this chapter does not present a comprehensive treatment of over-all marketing, it does provide sufficient development for purposes of describing the interrelationship of physical distribution and marketing in a channel context.

Physical Distribution in the Marketing Affairs of the Enterprise

The introduction to this chapter stressed the fact that physical distribution is an integral part of the marketing affairs of the enterprise. The purpose of this section is to elaborate this relationship.

Marketing Concept Versus Marketing Management

As indicated in Chapter 1, modern business accepts an over-all corporate marketing orientation as the underlying philosophy of management planning.[3] This viewpoint is designed to underscore the importance of successful penetration of markets and the realization of profitable transactions to corporate survival. This corporate posture, commonly referred to as the *marketing concept*, emerged out of the shift following World War II from a seller's market to a prevailing buyer's market.[4]

The marketing concept is simply a market-based planning philosophy

---

[3] See page 27.

[4] A buyer's market condition is defined as one in which supply is abundant in relation to that demanded at a point in time.

orientated to identifying customer needs and mobilizing enterprise resources to serve selected needs at a profit.[5] The marketing concept starts with the goal of satisfying consumer needs at a profit. All systems of the firm must be integrated toward this fundamental goal. If a business enterprise is to survive, all corporate systems—marketing, production, finance, and logistics—must function as a totality aimed at generation of a stream of profitable transactions.[6] The marketing concept provides the integrative force in corporate planning.

Three basic pillars underlie the marketing concept: (1) customer needs are more basic than products, (2) products must be viewed in an end-use context, and (3) volume is secondary to profit. Each is briefly discussed.

The notion that customer needs are more basic than products places a priority upon studying market opportunities in an effort to determine what products are needed and will be purchased. Products that can be economically manufactured may or may not be profitably sold depending upon the perceived need of potential customers. Over time, all products will die as new and better methods of satisfying consumer needs are discovered from research and development. Thus the marketing concept starts with an orientation that markets must be studied in depth in order to discover potential product opportunities. Once a market opportunity is isolated, a product may or may not materialize depending upon a systematic integration of the joint feasibility of successful production, adequate financial resources, logistical capability, and marketing skill. It is important to realize that the opportunity to achieve profitable transactions initiates in the marketplace—customer needs are more basic than products.

In order to successfully market a product that is needed, products must be viewed in an end-use context. This second pillar of the marketing concept stresses the fact that products must be placed in a context wherein customers can readily make the transaction from concept to use. In this sense, once again the integration of total corporate resources is required. There are four economic utilities that can add value to a product in a use context. These are generally identified as form, possession, time, and place utility. The form utility of a product is generated in the manufacturing process. Marketing creates possession utility in the product through informing the potential customer of the availability of the product and facilitating the transaction phase of the over-all process. Physical distribution is concerned with creating time and place utility. Marketing can specify the color, shape, and style of the product as well as create a convenient and economical transaction between buyer and seller. Production can build a high-quality product at the lowest possible unit cost. It remains for physical distribution to ensure that the right product is at the right place at the right time. Profitable transactions will materialize only if all four utilities are integrated in a customer-use context.

---

[5] E. Jerome McCarthy, *Basic Marketing: A Managerial Approach*, 5th ed. (Homewood, Ill.: Richard D. Irwin, Inc., 1974), Chapter 2.

[6] For an early treatment of transaction analysis, see John R. Commons, *The Economics of Collective Action* (New York: Macmillan Publishing Co., Inc., 1950).

The final pillar of the marketing concept highlights the importance of stressing profitability as opposed to volume in selecting corporate priorities.[7] The important measure of success is not the number of units sold during the planning period. Rather, the appropriate measure is the degree of profitability resulting from accumulated transactions. Therefore, variations in all forms of utility offered—form, possession, time, and place—can be economically justified if a particular segment of the market is willing to pay for the adjustment in offering. Markets are appropriately viewed as consisting of many different segments, each of which has a particular preference for a combination of utilities. The refinement of market segmentation and product differentiation acknowledges that all aspects of an integrated offering are subject to modification when justified on the basis of profitability.

The integrated marketing concept provides the foundation for planning over-all operations for all aspects of the enterprise. The specifications to guide each separate system performance toward master system integration are realized from this corporate planning posture. Marketing management, in contrast, consists of the specific jobs that must be performed by the marketing organization as its part of the integrated enterprise activity.

Various attempts have been made to describe the activities of managerial marketing. For purposes of illustration, a functional approach developed by Staudt and Taylor is adopted.[8] Staudt and Taylor describe integrated managerial marketing in terms of seven functions that must be accomplished if profitable transactions are to materialize. They are (1) market delineation, (2) purchase motivation, (3) product development, (4) market communication, (5) physical distribution, (6) transaction, and (7) posttransaction.

Market delineation consists of a quantitative study of market potential to determine the economic justification of potential market segments. Purchase motivation consists of a determination of needs existent in the marketplace and a careful examination of what will motivate purchase. Product development consists of matching product offerings to market opportunities. Thus the first three functions of managerial marketing encompass the specific tasks that the marketing organization must perform in accordance with the pillars of the marketing concept.

Market communication consists of the planning of an integrated effort to stimulate purchase action. Although many different communication devices are available to the enterprise, the two main options are personal selling and advertising. The combined market communication effort is aimed at making potential customers aware of the product offering of the enterprise and stimulating purchase action through persuasion.

Physical distribution exists for the purpose of gaining time and place

---

[7] J. B. McKitterick, "Profitable Growth—The Challenge to Marketing Management," a speech before the 45th National Conference of the American Marketing Association, June 20, 1962.

[8] Thomas A. Staudt and Donald A. Taylor, *A Managerial Introduction to Marketing*, 2nd ed. (Englewood Cliffs, N.J.: Prentice-Hall, Inc., 1970), Chapter 3.

utility. The totality of this chapter is aimed at greater elaboration of the relationship of physical distribution to marketing; therefore, no further treatment is now developed. However, it is important to stress the integral nature of physical distribution to Staudt and Taylor's description of managerial marketing.

Finally, transaction and posttransaction consist of the many facets of marketing concerned with the successful completion of ownership transfer. In particular, posttransaction consists of the appropriate care of customers after initial purchase so as to assure repeat purchases. In essence, posttransaction blends with purchase motivation, product delineation, and product adjustment to render the managerial functions of marketing a circular or closed process that is continuous.

This brief review of managerial marketing from a functional viewpoint stresses the role of marketing as one part of the enterprise engaged in implementing the marketing concept. Two points are of particular importance. First, a clear distinction should be kept in mind between the corporate orientation to a market planning concept as contrasted to those functions associated with the performance of the marketing job. Second, it is important to realize the integral nature of physical distribution to marketing performance. Although logistics has been introduced as a major system of the corporation incorporating physical distribution, it is clear that considerable overlap exists between the logistical job and the marketing job. This integral relationship can be more fully understood by a discussion of a typical enterprise's marketing mix.

Marketing Mix

The term *marketing mix* is commonly used to describe the various aspects or elements of a firm's marketing plan.[9] Figure 2-1 illustrates the concept of the marketing mix. The use of "mix" results from the idea that all elements of the plan are blended together into an integrated effort. The mix results in a total customer offering of products and services that will stimulate transactions.

To further illustrate the notion of the marketing mix, a structure developed by Lazer and Kelley is adopted.[10] They have grouped the various marketing factors into three submixes: (1) the product and service mix, (2) the distribution mix, and (3) the communication mix.

The product and service mix represents all elements that are included as part of the physical product. It constitutes the bundle of utilities offered for sale at a specific price. The marketing factors included are brand, price, service, product line variety, warranty, style, color, and design. Consistent with the marketing concept, the specific nature and composition of the product and service mix at any point in time is based upon market needs.

[9] Lazer, *op cit.*, p. 16, with particular reference to footnote 10 of the cited work.
[10] William Lazer and Eugene J. Kelley, eds., *Managerial Marketing: Perspectives and Viewpoints*, 2nd ed. (Homewood, Ill.: Richard D. Irwin, Inc., 1962), p. 413.

FIGURE 2-1
The Marketing Mix—A Systems Concept

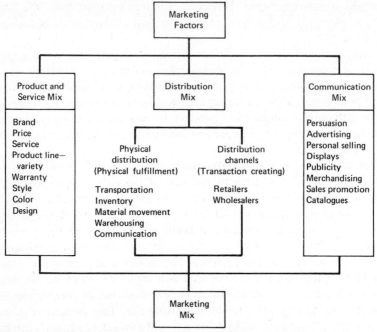

Source: Modified from William Lazer, *Marketing Management.* New York: John Wiley and Sons, Inc., 1971, p. 17.

The communication mix is concerned with information and persuasion. The prime objective in formulation of the communication mix is to influence the actions of customers and other firms who are members of a distribution system. The range of marketing factors involved in the communication mix is listed in Figure 2-1.

The distribution mix has two primary parts. The first is that portion of the logistics system concerned with physical distribution. Included is some mixture of all logistical components: location, transportation, inventory, communication, and material handling. The second part of the distribution mix concerns the selection of a *distribution* or *marketing channel*. The typical distribution channel involves a number of middlemen or intermediaries who assist the enterprise by performing some or all of the actions necessary to complete the final ownership transfer to an end user. The most widely known middlemen are wholesalers and retailers. However, many specialized types of middlemen exist. A complete review and classification of middlemen is provided in Appendix 2A.

The fundamental concern of logistics with respect to the marketing mix is the physical distribution portion of the distribution mix. The management task concerning the distribution mix is to organize a relationship between company facilities and middlemen that will result in completion of both the transaction creating and physical fulfillment activities of marketing. The end result is that both goods and their titles are moved to the market.

It is obvious that considerable overlap exists among the marketing concept, the marketing mix, and the functions of managerial marketing. The marketing concept is the over-all umbrella within which the total enterprise gains a goal-orientated planning perspective. The marketing mix and the functions of managerial marketing relate specifically to the responsibilities of the marketing organization. To a degree they represent alternative ways of conceptualizing the role of marketing management in a large-scale organization. Both approaches stress the integral nature of physical distribution within the firm's marketing effort. The marketing mix approach stresses the interrelationship of physical distribution and the distribution channel in formulation of an organizational approach to completing physical fulfillment. The next four sections develop a deeper understanding of the relationship of physical distribution and the distribution channel. A full understanding of this relationship is essential to planning physical distribution operations. The final sections of the chapter provide a more specific statement of the inter-relationship of physical distribution and marketing.

Traditional Development of Channel Structure

One of the least understood areas of business centers around institutions and activities normally grouped under the encompassing labels of distribution or marketing channels. A great deal of descriptive material has been written about the purpose and functions of institutions normally found in distribution channels. In contrast, the literature is less abundant in terms of comprehensive treatments of channel dynamics, structure, and strategy.[11]

Considerable difference exists between the way in which distribution channels are normally treated by those concerned with marketing management in contrast to those who have a major interest in physical distribution.

Typical Physical Distribution Approach to Distribution Channels

The physical distribution of any product requires the utilization of corporate facilities and/or intermediary specialists. By definition, a facility is considered a company-owned and -operated unit engaged in the performance of all or some part of the physical distribution process. Thus a distribution warehouse

---

[11] In the opinion of the author, several notable exceptions exist; these include Roland Vaile, E. T. Grether, and Reavis Cox, *Marketing In The American Economy* (New York: The Ronald Press Company, 1952); Wroe Alderson, *Marketing Behavior and Executive Action* (Homewood, Ill.: Richard D. Irwin, Inc., 1957); Bruce E. Mallen, ed., *The Marketing Channel* (New York: John Wiley & Sons, Inc., 1967); Edwin H. Lewis, *Marketing Channels: Structure and Strategy* (New York: McGraw-Hill Book Company, 1968); and Louis W. Stern, *Distribution Channels: Behavioral Dimensions* (Boston: Houghton Mifflin Company, 1969).

or a company-operated truck constitutes a logistical facility. However, either may also have the status of intermediary specialist. For example, the warehouse may be of a public variety, and the truck may be owned and operated by a common carrier. The intermediary specialist is an independent business operated for profit. In the design of a physical distribution system, the services of an intermediary specialist can be substituted for those of a company facility. The objective is to select the proper combination of facilities and specialists to meet objectives at the lowest total cost.

One serious deficiency of the traditional physical distribution approach to system development is that planning considerations are limited to the individual firm. A second deficiency results from a general subordination of physical distribution specialists to those intermediaries selected for reasons of marketing capabilities. Each of these deficiencies is discussed in turn.

DEFICIENCY OF LEGAL LIMITS. Traditional physical distribution planning seldom extends beyond the legal boundaries of the firm because normal control and profit measurement end when the product is transferred to a new owner. Depending upon conditions and terms of sale, legal ownership exchange is normally accomplished immediately before or after the final physical transfer of the product. However, in some special cases, such as consignment selling, a product's physical exchange may be completed long before the legal ownership exchange.

The problem is expanded by the fact that physical distribution of a product does not end once ownership transfer occurs. It does not end when the product is turned over to the next level or firm in the distribution channel or even when it is delivered to a buyer, unless all conditions of the transaction are satisfied. Ultimate responsibility for physical distribution does not end until the product in question is finally accepted by the person, family, or firm that will utilize it. All practitioners of physical distribution will agree that a product is not fully distributed until no additional physical transfer is possible. Some of the most difficult physical distribution problems are those of handling and moving return products. Such products may be returned for damage, improper performance, or even late delivery. Therefore, to properly direct physical distribution activities, planning horizons must transcend the total distribution channel.

Many significant costs of physical distribution occur between firms engaged in a distribution channel. To a large extent the control of such costs may rest with an intermediary specialist who has very little risk or vested interest in the over-all success of the marketing and physical distribution process. For example, an infrequently used common carrier who actually takes 20 days to transfer a shipment scheduled for 3-day delivery and who makes final delivery in split quantities of the original shipment may substantially increase total distribution costs.

In addition, a great many costs of physical distribution, such as inventory holding expense, may accumulate by duplicate effort at various levels within a channel. Such duplication increases the cost of total marketing, therefore adjustments in channel arrangement may be justified on the basis of a single firm's cost control program. However, such modification may increase the costs of all other firms in the channel and seriously hinder the ability of the total channel to survive. Physical distribution planning should be channel-wide in perspective.

As previously indicated, the main reason for a firm's limitation of physical distribution considerations to legal boundaries is the desire for control and profit. When a firm limits consideration to controllable limits within a channel, it, in effect, operates under artificial conditions of vertical integration. In short, the physical distribution system is often designed to include only vertically controlled operations.[12]

In system design, captive facilities are controlled, because they represent a geographical extension of general office authority. Specialized intermediaries are controlled to various degrees through service purchase contracts and obligations. The activities of both can normally be subordinated and co-ordinated to over-all performance of the firm's physical distribution system. Such control effort normally stops when ownership transfer occurs. This deficiency of legal limits on the part of each firm may have a detrimental result for the over-all distribution channel.

DEFICIENCY OF INTERMEDIARY SELECTION. The second main deficiency in physical distribution treatment of channels results from the over-all tendency to utilize a specialized intermediary selected for reasons of marketing competence. Traditionally, when a firm decided to locate a branch or district sales office, it was almost axiomatic that a field inventory would also be located at the facility. If a firm selected a market plan to utilize a specific wholesaler, it was normally assumed that the same wholesaler would inventory a full line of the firm's product assortment. The design of physical distribution systems to support marketing, in more cases than not, was identical with respect to intermediaries.

The deficiency of this single-structure system stems from the fact that a very effective marketing intermediary may not be either an effective or an efficient physical distribution intermediary. It is generally acknowledged that the successful marketing of a firm's product may require a wide range of channels to effectively reach different market segments.[13] Utilizing the same structure for logistical flows has the inherent weakness of forcing small uneconomical shipments upon the physical distribution system. Substantial economies of scale and related advantages might otherwise be realized in

[12] The term *vertically controlled* is adopted to describe a situation in which the next link of a channel is operationally controlled through purchase relationships to the extent that two independent firms function as a single entity—for example, the use of a public warehouse as an intermediary specialist.

[13] For a discussion of physical distribution complexity when markets become highly segmented see Staudt and Taylor, *op. cit.*, p. 179, or Philip Kotler, *Marketing Management*, 2nd ed. (Englewood Cliffs, N.J.: Prentice-Hall, Inc., 1972), Chap. 16.

physical flow. The most suitable structure for marketing channels may not, and often is not, highly satisfactory for physical distribution channels.

Typical Marketing Approach to Distribution Channels

Unlike those concerned with physical distribution, marketing men have traditionally acknowledged that distribution channels consist of a fantastically complex network of organizations grouped together in a variety of combinations.[14] The American Marketing Association defined the distribution channel as the structure of intracompany organization units and extracompany agents and dealers, wholesale and retail, through which a commodity, product, or service is marketed.[15] Others have defined the distribution channel as a grouping of intermediaries from first owner to last owner, who take title to a product during the marketing process.[16]

The main advantage of the over-all marketing approach is the basic acknowledgment of the complex process of marketing and the existence of a wide variety of organizational relationships. Each organization linked in a distribution channel exists for a reason and performs services in anticipation of a return on investment and effort. The marketing task is never considered complete until the final owner has been satisfied with respect to pretransaction anticipations. In fact, a considerable degree of marketing effort centers around measurement of pretransaction anticipations and posttransaction satisfactions. Thus marketing horizons are not limited by legal boundaries of the firm. It is the basic acknowledgment of a wider spectrum of planning and the realistic approach to interorganizational relationships that renders the marketing approach to channel structure superior to single-firm physical distribution planning. The marketing approach eliminates the limitation of dealing only with vertically controlled systems.

Four general approaches have been employed by marketing writers to study and describe channels: (1) descriptive institutional, (2) graphic, (3) commodity groupings, and (4) functional. A fifth and newer grouping, behavioral, will be treated later in the chapter. Although the first four groups are to various degrees concerned with structure as a primary focal point, the newer behavioral contributions expand structural considerations into a comprehensive treatment of interfirm strategies and relationships.

DESCRIPTIVE INSTITUTIONAL APPROACH. The descriptive institutional approach to distribution channels identifies the many participants who may be found within a channel structure. Such institutions are grouped with respect to the marketing services they perform. A complete listing of all intermediaries with

---

[14] This point is well developed in Schuyler F. Otteson, William G. Panschar, and James M. Patterson, *Marketing* (New York: Macmillan Publishing Co., Inc., 1964), pp. 302–22.

[15] Ralph S. Alexander, *Marketing Definitions: A Glossary of Marketing Terms* (Chicago: American Marketing Association, 1960), p. 10.

[16] Theodore N. Beckman and William R. Davidson, *Marketing* (New York: The Ronald Press Company, 1962), p. 44.

traditional classification is found in Appendix 2A. As one would expect, considerable differences exist in the type of institution employed in the marketing of consumer, industrial, and government products. Considerable differences in intermediary selection also exist between the marketing of products and services.

Those who have undertaken research into the various institutions of marketing generally acknowledge that the broad classifications of wholesaling and retailing are descriptive of the structure within which marketing is accomplished. Naturally, the wholesale structure is substantially different among industrial, agricultural, and consumer products. In addition, various categories of middlemen do not fall into a strict definition of either retailer or wholesaler. In an effort to prescribe when various institutions should be utilized, the basic descriptive institutional approach to channels has been expanded into the other treatments introduced later. Every student of marketing and physical distribution should have a detailed understanding of the institutional approach, because it serves as the basis for all other ways of studying channel structure.

GRAPHIC APPROACH. In an effort to identify the flow of ownership title of raw materials and finished products, a useful technique utilized in marketing has been the development of flow graphs. Such graphs illustrate the range of alternatives in institutional selection at all levels of the marketing process.

Figure 2-2 illustrates the many title levels that products or raw materials may pass through between original owner and final buyer. For example, retail stores may purchase from all levels of supply, from farm to wholesaler. Several of the neat classification lines illustrated in Figure 2-2 have been reduced by the expanding tendency toward *scrambled merchandising*.[17] An organization once considered only a wholesaler may now function within the channel as a retailer as well as a wholesaler. Retailers and manufacturers in turn have assumed many traditional duties of wholesalers. This extension of activities has been referred to as *integrated wholesaling*.[18] Under integrated wholesaling, the retail operation performs the functions traditionally performed by the wholesale intermediary.

The main advantage of graphs is that they illustrate the many links engaged in modern marketing. By the use of graphs the multiplicity of institutions is focused into logical sequence. However, the simplicity of flow diagrams tends to understate some complexities of designing the proper channel structure for an individual firm.

COMMODITY GROUPINGS. In an effort to limit the range of considerations in channel planning, several studies have been completed with the objective of

[17] *Scrambled merchandising* refers to the identical product being offered for sale in several different types of retail outlets: for example; garden rakes being sold at gasoline service stations as well as in hardware, garden, discount, and department stores. Also referred to as channel jumping, see pages 64–65.
[18] Beckman and Davidson, *op. cit.*, pp. 348–64.

FIGURE 2-2
Typical Channels of Distribution

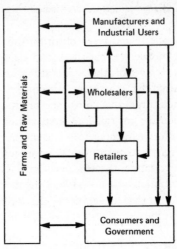

defining in detail channel structure for specific commodities.[19] Generally empirical in nature, commodities studies combine a description of institutions with a graphic illustration of primary ownership flows. Although they are very useful in specific situations, such commodity channel treatments are too specific for general physical distribution planning.

FUNCTIONAL TREATMENTS. The functional approach to channel structure has developed as a result of writers attempting to provide a logical explanation of the over-all marketing process. Figure 2-3 illustrates the most commonly agreed-upon listing of functions. In general, a function in a marketing sense represents a major economic activity that must be performed to some degree in the marketing of all products. In the marketing of many products, a given function may be performed by a number of institutions and intermediaries between the points of original sale and final sale. For example, storage may be performed by a producer, wholesaler, retailer, and even by a user. On the other hand, market financing might be performed by only one institution in the total process of marketing a given product. Beckman and Davidson[20] have summarized these functional relationships as follows:

Marketing has been defined as a process—one in which no person or institution is self-sufficient. It involves many participants and consists of various functional components. One must consider each of these functions and their interrelationships to understand the totality of the process.

[19] Clewett, *op. cit.*
[20] Beckman and Davidson, *op. cit.*

FIGURE 2-3
Marketing Functions[21]

The functional approach to marketing provides a framework for evaluation of alternative channel structures with respect to total channel capability.

Initial listing of marketing functions has been greatly expanded by subsequent developments of functional analysis. Functional analysis concentrates upon the interrelation of various functions in the total marketing process. Particularly noteworthy are the developments of Alderson with respect to the role of middlemen in the marketing process.[22] The essential role of marketing intermediary is, in the Alderson treatment, one of reconciling a narrow conglomeration of products from single sources into a wide inventory assortment at the point of final sales. This involves several steps, which can be best accomplished by a specialized middleman.

The entire process of changing conglomerations to assortments was labeled *sorting* in the Alderson treatment.[23] The marketing channel serves to perform the sorting activity, which consists of four steps. The initial step involves the *sorting out* of large conglomerations and results in one large supply being reclassified into small lots of various types of goods according to the requirements of the sorter. Next, a larger supply, perhaps from different locations, is *accumulated* over a period of time to provide a larger grouping of specialized but homogeneous goods. The third step in the sorting process consists of *allocation*. In allocation the total supply is apportioned either within corporate facilities or among market outlets. Finally, *assortment* takes place, which constitutes the building of individual supplies into a combination of different products or an assortment in accordance with an anticipated pattern of demand. Alderson's process or sorting is illustrated in Figure 2-4. In Figure 2-4 the four aspects of sorting are illustrated in the sequence most commonly found in the marketing process.

Staudt and Taylor[24] have built upon Alderson's concept of sorting and have generalized three principles that justify the existence of marketing

[21] Adopted from Beckman and Davidson, *op. cit.*, p. 390.
[22] Alderson, *op. cit.*, pp. 195–227.
[23] *Ibid.*
[24] Staudt and Taylor, *op. cit.*, pp. 266–68.

FIGURE 2-4
Alderson's Process of Sorting

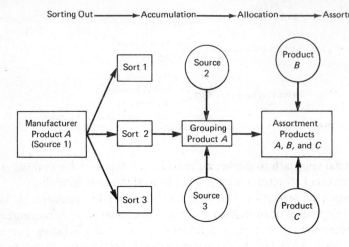

intermediaries: (1) the principle of minimum total transactions, (2) the principle of massed reserves, and (3) the principle of proximity.

The *principle of minimum total transactions* acknowledges that the total process of sorting is reduced by having a limited number of middlemen. This principle has wide application in finished goods and agricultural commodity distribution. In essence, the principle advocates specialization in the marketing process. Figure 2-5 illustrates the principle of minimum total transactions.

FIGURE 2-5
Principle of Minimum Total Transactions

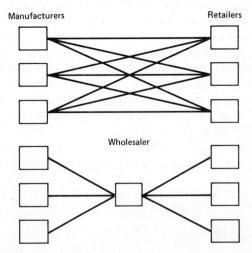

The *principle of massed reserves* is concerned with the storage of goods in the distribution channel. Staudt and Taylor acknowledge that goods in the form of inventories exist at each stop in the concentration and dispersion of goods. Such stops are defined as the producer level, accumulation level, assortment level, and the household. They conclude that the amount of goods in inventory when intermediaries are used is less than would otherwise be required.[25] This principle assumes exacting inventory control and consistent product delivery.

The *principle of proximity* states that the specialized intermediary should be located close to the marketplace. Close proximity provides better positioning to render final assortments in a manner most satisfactory and timely to market demand. In total, the three principles provide credence to the inclusion of a specialized intermediary in the channel of distribution.

DEFICIENCY OF MARKETING TREATMENTS.   It should be apparent from the brief review of marketing approaches to channel structure that they overcome the limitations of typical physical distribution treatments and move toward a systematic analysis of the complex situation that exists. However, marketing approaches have some limitations with respect to physical distribution planning.

Two primary kinds of transactions take place between intermediaries in a distribution channel. One is the physical exchange of products, and the other is the legal exchange of title. A product may never move physically, although legal ownership may change hands several times. This is particularly true of an agricultural commodity as demonstrated in the grain markets. On the other hand, a product may be handled many times within a single corporation, even moving across the entire nation, without changing legal ownership.

It appears that the specialized institutions most capable of performing marketing functions may differ from those desired for performance of physical distribution activities. The typical scheme of marketing institutions provides no allowance for the existence of a very important class of physical distribution intermediaries—common, contract, and exempt transportation carriers. For example, the functional role of a public warehouse as an accumulation and dispersion intermediary is most often subordinated to the role of the storage specialist in marketing treatments. Thus an integration of traditional marketing and physical distribution treatments is essential to the performance of business logistics.

Channel Structure

The term *structure* is widely used to describe a number of interrelationships which are part of but subordinate to the whole.[26] In distribution channels,

---

[25] *Ibid.*, p. 224.

[26] For a detailed discussion of marketing channel structure, see Kenneth R. Davis, *Marketing Management* (New York: The Ronald Press Company, 1961), pp. 131–33; and Lewis, *op. cit.*, pp. 136–47.

structure relates to the framework for classification of basic flows, which pass through the channel. A careful delineation of primary flows provides the basis for specialization of effort within the channel structure. In addition, it provides a logical framework to guide physical distribution planning.

The Concept of Separation

Several authors have developed the idea of flow separation within the over-all structure of the distribution channel.[27] The present approach singles out two flows. To accomplish a satisfactory marketing process, a flow of transaction-creating efforts and a flow of physical-fulfillment efforts must exist and be coordinated. There is no logical reason why these two flows must sequentially transpire through the same network of intermediaries. These two flows—physical fulfillment and transaction creating—are considered primary; all other flows in the total distribution channel are considered secondary.

Commons differentiated elements of bargaining transaction in contrast with the process of physical exchange.[28] He viewed the bargaining transaction as containing three essential steps: (1) negotiation (that is, reaching a satisfactory agreement); (2) contract (that is, establishment of obligations); and (3) administration (that is, performance of obligations). In the Commons scheme, exchange was viewed as the mechanical and labor process of physical delivery.[29]

The logic for separation of exchange fulfillment and transaction creation is based on the notion that no positive legal or economic laws require a simultaneous treatment or performance. Factors that tend to increase or decrease the total cost of physical flow have no real relationship to ownership boundaries, only an artificial one. Conversely, advertising, credit, personal selling, and other transaction-creating efforts of marketing have little influence upon the economics of physical flow. The responsiveness of each primary flow to specialization is unique to the circumstances surrounding that flow. In any given marketing situation, primary flows may best be accomplished by different middlemen. The most effective network for achieving profitable transactions may not be the most efficient arrangement of exchange intermediaries. Based upon specialization in primary flow, the total distribution channel is classified as containing transaction and exchange channels.

---

[27] A number of authors have developed the flow concept; contributions of noteworthy mention in this author's opinion were presented by Vaile, Grether, and Cox, *op. cit.*; Ralph F. Breyer, "Some Observations on Structural Formation and Growth of Marketing Channels," in Reavis Cox, Wroe Alderson, and Stanley J. Shapiro, eds., *Theory in Marketing* (Homewood, Ill.: Richard D. Irwin, Inc., 1964), pp. 163–75; George Fisk, *Marketing Systems* (New York: Harper & Row, Publishers, 1967), pp. 214–79; and Louis P. Bucklin, "Postponement, Speculation, and the Structure of Distribution Channels," *Journal of Marketing Research*, February 1965, pp. 26–31.

[28] Commons, *op. cit.*, p. 53.

[29] *Ibid.*, p. 45.

The transaction channel consists of a grouping of intermediaries engaged in the establishment of trading. The goal of the transaction channel is to negotiate, to contract, and to administer trading on a continuing basis. The full force of creative marketing action exists within the transaction channel. Participants in transaction channel activities are marketing specialists such as manufacturing agents, salesmen, jobbers, wholesalers, and retailers.

The exchange channel contains a network of intermediaries engaged in the functions of physical movement. Participants in the exchange channel are physical distribution specialists. Their concern is one of solving problems of time and space at a total expenditure consistent to trading specifications.

EXAMPLES OF SEPARATION.   Figure 2-6 illustrates the concept of separation for the distribution of color television sets. In this situation the transaction channel consists of five links: (1) general sales office, (2) district sales office, (3) distributor, (4) retailer, and (5) consumer. The exchange channel design consists of seven links: (1) factory warehouse, (2) company truck, (3) regional warehouse, (4) motor common carrier, (5) public warehouse, (6) local delivery, and (7) consumer. Only at the point of final transaction completion, the consumer's home, do the two primary channels merge.

Figure 2-6 also illustrates additional significant points. Concerning the exchange channel, three different specialized intermediaries are engaged in the physical distribution of the product. These three specialists are at level 4, a common carrier motor firm; level 5, a public warehouse; and level 6, a specialized local delivery firm. Three levels of physical distribution take place

FIGURE 2-6
Distribution Channel—Exchange and Transaction Separation

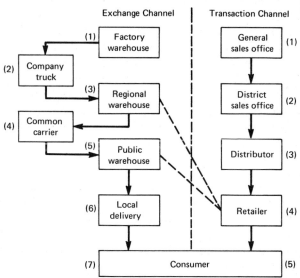

in the exchange channel utilizing organizational facilities of the producing firm. The television sets in question are warehoused at the factory, transported in company trucks, and stored in a regional warehouse before any specialized intermediary ever participates in the exchange channel.

The distributor, link 3 in the transaction channel, plays a unique role. He never physically handles the television sets; however, he has legal title from the time they depart the company warehouse (link 4, exchange channel) until they are delivered to the consumer. Of course, the distributor could elect to warehouse in his own facility, but his preference is to use a public warehouse specialist to service the needs of all his retailers.

The retailer illustrated is only one of many who sell the line of television sets. He displays limited sets offering next-day delivery to consumers who enter into a transaction. Delivery is then made from the distributor's stock, held in the public warehouse, using the services of a specialized local delivery intermediary. When sets are required for display in the retailer's store, they may be obtained by the distributor from either the factory's regional warehouse (link 3, exchange channel) or from his own stock in storage at the public warehouse (link 5, exchange channel). These two possibilities are illustrated as connections between the two channels utilizing common carrier transportation.

Retailers commonly limit stocks to display models. Sales are negotiated based on a commitment to deliver a specified model and color at a particular time and place. Although the transaction is initiated at a retail store, physical exchange may be completed by direct customer shipment from a warehouse strategically located many miles from the point of transaction.

An additional example of separation is the factory branch office that carries no inventory. The office exists for the sole purpose of transaction creation. The physical exchange between seller and buyer may move in a variety of combinations of transport and storage depending upon the value, the size, the bulk, the weight, and the perishability of the shipment. Generally, no economic justification exists for locating warehouses with each branch office. The network of branch offices is best selected to facilitate maximum transaction impact. The selection of exchange intermediaries is designed to achieve the desired physical distribution performance and economies.

A final example of separation comes from the rapidly growing mail order industry. An order placed at a local catalog desk may be drop-shipped from a distant factory direct to the buyer's home. Although the flow pattern described is only one of many observable arrangements in mail order, all such systems are designed to create separation and thereby the opportunity for specialization.

Interdependence of Transaction and Exchange Activities

The concept of separation of transaction flows and exchange flows should not be interpreted to mean that either can or should stand alone. Both must be completed as the basis for a satisfactory sale; both are essential to the marketing process. The main argument for separation of transaction and exchange is that it increases the structural opportunities for development of specialization.

Separation does not necessarily require separate legal enterprises to enjoy the benefits of specialization. The same intermediary may be very capable of performing both transaction and exchange. Many wholesalers successfully combine the performance of both flows. The degree of individual enterprise separation depends upon the necessity for specialization, economies of scale, available resources, and managerial capabilities.

Transactions are never complete until physical exchange is fully administered. Depending upon the category of goods—convenience, shopping, or speciality—the exchange process may start in anticipation of, be simultaneous with, or follow after negotiation is initiated.[30] The final exchange act occurs in accord with specifications established during the negotiation phase of the transaction. Such exchange specifications relate to time, location, or terms of transfer. Given any set of specifications, minimization of exchange expense is essential to achieve a mutually satisfactory transaction.

Contributions of efficient exchange are not limited to cost reduction. By achieving time and place utility, exchange can enhance transaction capabilities.[31] The ability to promise and provide dependable delivery of a proper assortment serves as a stimulant to purchase agreement. Actual performance according to specification creates a tendency toward repeated transactions and the benefits of routinization. Whereas present concern is with exchange mechanics, exchange capabilities may greatly enhance or dilute transaction potential.

Channel Functions of Exchange

Exchange channel goals are simply stated. The exchange channel consisting of a number of independent firms exists to deliver the specified product assortment to the right location at the right time. A number of functions must be performed jointly by all channel members in the exchange process. From the viewpoint of the total channel, these functions should be performed with a minimum of duplication between firms linked in a given channel structure. The reader will note that the discussion that follows incorporates

---

[30] This classification is widely used in marketing to describe conditions surrounding the availability of consumer goods in the marketplace. Different exchange channel considerations relate to each, which, in turn, may dictate different timing in actual physical distribution performance with respect to transaction.

[31] For a discussion of time and space utility, see James L. Heskett, "Spatial and Temporal Aspects of Physical Distribution," in Peter D. Bennett, ed., "*Marketing and Economic Development,*" *Proceedings of American Marketing Association,* 1965, pp. 679–87; and James L. Heskett, "A Missing Link in Physical Distribution System Design," *Journal of Marketing,* October 1966, pp. 37–41.

the basic components of the individual corporate logistical system expanded to include multiple firms in a channel context.

Exchange flow in a channel is analogous to the mechanical workings of a ratchet wrench. Physical movement is best designed for economies of one-way movement toward final customer location. Although it is a fact that products often have to be returned from retailer to manufacturer, such a reverse movement is an expensive exception rather than the rule.[32]

Adjustment

The *adjustment function* has received considerable treatment in marketing literature.[33] Some of the main contributions were reviewed earlier in this chapter.

Adjustment is the exchange channel function concerned with the creation of an assortment of goods. At some geographical point or points in the exchange process, goods must be concentrated, selected, and dispersed to the next level in the exchange channel.

Concentration refers to the collection of large lots of a single good or large groupings of several goods earmarked for final sale in an assortment. A manufacturer's distribution warehouse is a prime example of a concentration point in the exchange channel. Large shipments of products produced at each factory may be transferred to the distribution warehouse. The distribution warehouse, in turn, may hold such concentrations until an order is received for a particular assortment.

The process of grouping individual products into an assortment is referred to as *selection*. The selection process results in a custom offering, which meets one customer's specifications. It has become a common service for manufacturers to offer mixed carloads or truckloads of all marketed products based upon the functional capability of being able to sort in an economical manner. Such custom-selected shipments allow customers to carry the minimum necessary inventory of all items in the product line and to retain the benefits of lower per unit freight rates resulting from volume shipments.

Dispersement consists of placing custom assortments at the proper time in the right place. The dispersement aspect of adjustment refers to the establishment of the over-all specifications to guide the remainder of the exchange

[32] For examples, see C. G. Golucke and P. H. McGaukey, *Comprehensive Studies of Solid Waste Management*, Public Health Service Publication 2039 (Washington, D.C.: Government Printing Office, 1970); William G. Zikmund and William J. Stanton, "Recycling Solid Wastes: A Channels-of-Distribution Problem," *Journal of Marketing*, July 1971 pp. 34–39; and Omar Keith Helferich, Vernon Hoffner, and Douglas E. Gee, "Dynamic Simulation Model for Planning Solid Waste Management," *International Pollution Control Journal*, 1972 Pilot Issue, pp. 40–49.

[33] This concept has long standing in marketing literature. Two early treatments are found in Percival White, *Scientific Marketing Management* (New York: Harper & Row, Publishers, 1927), and Fred E. Clark, *Readings in Marketing* (New York: Macmillan Publishing Co., Inc., 1924).

functions. Dispersement is directive in nature and stimulates the performance of a given exchange process.

The particular facility performing the adjustment function may be either a company-operated facility or a specialized middleman. Wholesalers find economic justification by performing the adjustment function and thereby reducing some risk on the part of other channel members. A recent study indicates that merchant wholesalers have increased at the very time when vertical integration by large retailers and manufacturers was supposed to have eliminated their basis of economic justification.[34]

It would appear that the potential economies of integrated wholesaling by vertical expansion of the exchange channel may not offset the corresponding loss of innovative specialization and risk spreading. The strategically placed merchant wholesaler is able to perform the adjustment function for a number of different retailers and manufacturers, thereby reducing the number of transactions required in the total exchange channel.

Transfer

The *transfer function* consists of the mechanics of collection and dispersement. A single good or an assortment of goods must be physically transported to achieve temporal and spatial fulfillment of exchange contracts. In the collection phase of the adjustment function, the typical transfer consists of large limited commodity shipments. In the dispersement phase of the adjustment function, the typical transfer will be smaller shipments of a variety or assortment of products. As a general rule, transfers related to dispersement will be more costly than transfers related to concentration.

In total, transfer costs are the highest of all functions of exchange. Each transfer in the exchange process is a singularly conclusive act with associated costs. A shipment sent to the wrong destination or at the wrong time is double costly to one completed in the proper manner. As such, the margin for error in transfer is narrow, and the related costs or penalties cannot be recovered.

It is not surprising to find a grouping of transfer intermediaries who specialize in the mechanics of movement. Such specialists, in the form of motor, rail, water, and air carriers, number in the thousands in the United States. Transfer specialists exist because of the high cost of investment in equipment, which can be spread across many different shippers. In some cases, the performance of the transfer function is in part or total vertically integrated by the shipper through the purchase and operation of private transportation equipment. Normally the volume of movement must be heavy and balanced in both directions to justify the operation of private transfer facilities. In other cases, vertical control is achieved by establishment of contract commitments between the shipper and a specialized transfer intermediary.

---

[34] Reavis Cox, *Distribution in a High-Level Economy* (Englewood Cliffs, N.J.: Prentice-Hall, Inc., 1965), p. 56.

However, the majority of transfer specialists, the common carriers, provide their services to all shippers at a specified charge. A typical common carrier is regulated by either the federal or state government within the territory authorized for performance of the transfer function. For a specified charge the carrier assumes the risk for performance of the transfer mechanics. The risks of timing and directing the strategy of transfer remain with other intermediaries in the exchange channel.

Storage

The *storage function* occurs in the exchange channel because a great deal of concentration sorting and dispersement is performed in anticipation of future transactions. Given conditions of uncertainty in demand and supply, the exchange process must develop certain hedges to be able to satisfy future transaction requirements.

Accumulation of raw material or agricultural stockpiles in anticipation of future production requirements is a very common form of storage. Products produced year-round for sale during a very short period often require off-season storage: summer furniture and Christmas toys are examples of such products.

The risks of storage may be the greatest of all exchange functions, because damage and obsolescence can occur when inventories stand idle. Therefore, a continuous exchange flow from processing through adjustment and on to final consumption would contain less risk for all channel members. However, in a buyer's market, continuous movement seldom exists. At some point in the exchange channel, storage of at least a temporary nature must be performed.

Because of related risks, the function of storage is normally spread out among firms joined in a channel. Each firm is willing to assume the minimum amount of storage necessary to support its transaction activities. Because the total concentration of any one product tends to be reduced as the product moves through consecutive adjustments, it is not surprising to find that manufacturers are frequently forced to assume the largest share of product storage in a given exchange channel. In a given channel containing a manufacturer, a wholesaler, and a retailer, it appears logical that the retailer would perform the least amount and the manufacturer the greatest amount of storage.

Faced with the need to perform the lion's share of the storage, the manufacturer may elect to operate his own distribution warehouses. A common alternative is to purchase the use of storage space from an independent specialist called a *public warehouseman*. Historically, public warehouses were most commonly used for storage of off-season production. In more recent times, the public warehouse specialist has expanded his services to perform some additional exchange functions. The most common example is the performance of the adjustment function for manufacturers in a given market area or city.

As one would expect, the public warehouse specialist does not normally assume full risk for a product in storage. He does assume the risk for performance of the actual storage and related activities. The product in storage remains the property of the firm purchasing the specialized services of the public warehouse.

Handling

Handling is the least risky of exchange functions. However, expenses associated with handling are significant. Once a concentrated lot or an assortment of goods reaches a stopping point, shuffling begins. Cartons are moved in, placed, moved about, moved about some more, and finally moved out. The objective is to reduce handling in the exchange channel to an absolute minimum. Each handling has a separate and unique cost. Consequently, the fewer the total handlings in the exchange channel, the lower is the total cost.

Few specialized intermediaries exist for the sole purpose of performing the handling function. Handling is normally performed as part of adjustment, transfer, and storage functions. Therefore, handling must occur at all points in an exchange system through which the actual product passes. No function is more prone to duplication throughout the exchange channels than handling.

During the past decade substantial interest has developed around the use of containers and unitized loads. The basic idea of both is that products can be grouped together and handled as a single unit rather than multiple pieces. To the extent that products can be containerized from the manufacturer to the retailer, substantial handlings can be eliminated in the total exchange channel.

Communication

Communication is a two-way function in the exchange channel. In one direction, messages relay the need for exchange action. In the other direction, communication serves to monitor progress toward desired end results. Channel communication is continuous as products are transferred, adjusted, and stored in anticipation of future transaction requirements. Communications also exist between the transaction channel and the exchange channel with respect to assortment, quantity, location, and time of exchange.

At the outset it was noted that the total exchange channel was similar to a ratchet wrench in design concept with primary emphasis on forward movement to terminal user locations. A forward movement that subsequently requires reversal can be very costly to the total channel of exchange. From initial stimulant to feedback, the direct costs of communication are overshadowed by the resultant cost of a faulty message.

Because a great deal of exchange action is initiated in anticipation of future transaction requirements, communication containing an overly optimistic appraisal of potential may stimulate an exchange channel into a fever of ultimately useless work. Recent analysis of communication between channel members suggests that such anticipation has a tendency to increase in amplification as it proceeds between consecutive intermediaries in an exchange network.[35] Each such error in appraisal of transaction requirements has a tendency to introduce a disturbance for the total exchange channel. Faced with such a disturbance, the total channel may enter into an oscillatory corrective pattern resulting in a series of over- and underadjustments to real requirements.

By the nature of its basic mission, an exchange channel must be sensitive to transaction requirements. Therefore, the system stands ready to initiate the exchange process upon receipt of a stimulating message. Extreme care must be taken to structure communication in a manner that will result in a high degree of reliability.

The Exchange Network

Because a sequence of functions must be performed in the exchange process, it is not surprising that a number of individual enterprise units combine to create a channel or network. Only through coordination of all exchange functions can transaction requirements be fully satisfied. To the extent that duplication of functions exists in the channel, the total efficiency of the combined network will be impaired. To various degrees each channel member enjoys rewards or suffers losses based upon the over-all success of the total exchange channel.

Enterprises that make up the exchange channel are specialists in performing one or more exchange functions. Specialization by function has the end result of increasing efficiency and spreading risk. However, it is clear that risk in an exchange network is never equally spread among all participants. The greater the degree of specialization the intermediary has in the performance of exchange functions, the less risk he will assume in the over-all performance of any given exchange channel.

A motor carrier performing a single transfer function in a channel has relatively little risk with respect to the ultimate transaction. To the extent possible, such carriers will attempt to hedge risk involvement in any one exchange channel by performing similar functions for a wide variety of different channels. A retailer or a merchant wholesaler has risk involvement related to the sale of a single manufacturer's product assortment. Each attempts to hedge this risk by offering a total assortment far broader than any single manufacturer's product mix.

In contrast, a processor or manufacturer of a single product line may risk his total survival on the capabilities of a single exchange network. This disproportionate spread of risk among channel members is of central importance in the exchange process. Some channel members have a deeper

---

[35] See Jay W. Forrester, *Industrial Dynamics* (Cambridge, Mass.: The MIT Press, 1961), p. 62.

vested interest in the ultimate accomplishment of successful exchange than other members. Therefore, members with a vested interest are forced to play a more active role and assume greater responsibility for channel performance.

Without guidance, a great many exchange costs may be rapidly accumulated by functional duplication. In addition, costs may be unfavorably influenced by firms who have very little at stake in the channel. Such costs must be controlled if the channel is to realize maximum exchange capabilities. Control in an exchange channel is difficult to realize, because the only alternatives to ownership are persuasion or coercion.

Ownership control consists of vertical integration of two or more consecutive links in the exchange channel by a single enterprise. The ultimate of vertical integration in an exchange channel would be a manufacturer shipping via private transportation through his own storage points to his own retail outlets. Such complete vertical integration is rare. The exact extent to which vertical integration has materialized during the past two decades is difficult to appraise. As noted earlier, merchant wholesalers have tended to increase in number rather than decrease. There is increasing justification to conclude that the transaction channel has undergone more dramatic vertical integration than the exchange channel. The most radical shift in intermediaries has been within the transfer channel between agents and factory sales branches.[36]

Even when a firm is vertically extended with respect to integrated wholesaling, rarely can the services of a specialized transfer intermediary be fully eliminated. Sears Roebuck and Montgomery Ward utilize a high degree of common carrier transportation in addition to the vast fleet of private transportation vehicles they own and operate. It is doubtful that a firm could ever be fully integrated with respect to complete performance of every function required in the total exchange channel.

Tactics of persuasion and coercion are the most practical methods of directing and controlling exchange activities. Within the exchange channel, this basic need for common action under leadership guidance has been referred to as superorganization management.[37] The benefit of spearheading coordinated activity often resides with the channel member who has the greatest economic power. Such economic power most often rests with the channel member who directs activities at the point of transaction creation. Earlier in the chapter, domination by virtue of economic leverage was termed *vertically controlled*, in contrast to *vertically owned* operations. In a variety of situations, a firm is able to coordinate the activities of specialized intermediaries by virtue of market strength. The name of *channel captain* has been suggested for the firm that is economically able to stimulate interfirm coordination.[38]

Although all firms in a given exchange channel have a desire to cooperate,

[36] Cox, *op. cit.*, p. 55.

[37] J. L. Heskett, "Costing and Coordinating External and Internal Logistics Activities," unpublished paper before joint seminar, The Railway Systems and Management Association and the Transportation Research Forum, Chicago, October 6, 1964.

[38] McCarthy, *op. cit.*, pp. 389–90.

individual profit orientation and legal boundaries tend to create elements of conflict. In addition, there exists a degree of conflict over which member of a channel is willing to assume responsibility for performance of the more risky exchange functions. The firm having the greatest economic power may very well be the one least directly involved in the welfare of a specific exchange channel. The burden of economic power could very well be employed to shift risk rather than stimulate coordination.

The analysis of motivation for conflict and cooperation in both trading and exchange channels is currently receiving substantial attention in the literature.[39] Detailed treatment of the techniques of leadership are beyond the scope of immediate interest. The essential point is that the ultimate survival of a channel may depend upon constructive leadership. In addition, a great deal of future improvement in marketing efficiency could depend upon a substantial increase in managerial concern with channel group objectives as opposed to the preoccupation of the firm as an individual channel member.

Measures of Physical Distribution Performance

Physical distribution performance can be viewed from two perspectives with respect to integrated marketing. In part, physical distribution performs the exchange functions, thereby supporting the marketing mix offering of the enterprise. In a second sense, the quality of physical distribution performance can in fact encourage transactions by providing delivery service superior to that offered by competitors marketing near identical products. In the first sense, the primary measure of physical distribution performance is cost. In the second sense, degree of customer service is the primary measure.

Total Cost

As noted in the introductory chapter, the total cost of logistics within an enterprise can represent one of the highest costs of business operations.

[39] For a selection of examples, see J. C. Palamountain, Jr., *The Politics of Distribution* (Cambridge, Mass.: Harvard University Press, 1955); Valentine Ridgeway, "Administration of Manufacturer-Dealer Systems," *Administrative Science Quarterly*, March 1957, pp. 464–83; Bruce Mallen, "Conflict and Cooperation in Marketing Channels," in L. George Smith, ed., *Reflections on Progress in Marketing*, Proceedings American Marketing Association (Chicago: American Marketing Association, 1964), pp. 65–85; Bert C. McCammon, Jr., "Alternative Explanations of Institutional Change and Channel Evolution," in Stephen A. Greyser, ed., *Toward Scientific Marketing Proceedings* (Chicago: American Marketing Association, 1963), pp. 477–90; Bert C. McCammon, Jr., "Perspectives for Distribution Programming"; Donald J. Bowersox and E. Jerome McCarthy, "Strategic Development of Planned Vertical Marketing Systems"; and James L. Heskett, Louis W. Stern, and Frederick J. Beier, "Bases and Uses of Power in Interorganization Relations"; all published in Louis P. Bucklin, ed., *Vertical Marketing Systems* (Glenview, Ill.: Scott, Foresman and Company, 1970); Bert Rosenbloom, "Conflict and Channel Efficiency: Some Conceptual Models for the Decision Maker," *Journal of Marketing*, July 1973, pp. 26–30; and Louis P. Bucklin, "A Theory of Channel Control," *Journal of Marketing*, January 1973, pp. 39–47.

Within the marketing area of concern the total cost of physical distribution often ranges from 10 to 35 per cent of final sales price.[40] In the long run, the price of a product must cover all costs. Therefore, physical distribution efficiency is of vital concern.

The fragmented approach to physical distribution management that prevailed until recently created substantial room for cost reduction. In many cases, cost could be reduced while simultaneously maintaining or even improving the quality of customer service.

Whenever a new area for cost reduction is identified, it is natural that a great deal of attention will be attracted since the result of such savings is an immediate profit improvement. For example, if a firm is realizing a net profit of 2 per cent on the sales dollar, a cost reduction of $20,000 in physical distribution expense has a profit leverage equivalent to a sales increase of $1,000,000.[41]

The proper orientation toward allocation of physical distribution cost is that it represents a substantial marketing expense that must be subjected to careful control. The services provided by physical distribution represent an integral part of the over-all marketing mix. Therefore, physical distribution cost represents an investment toward the realization of profitable transactions.

The goal of physical distribution operations is simply stated. The degree of customer service desired as an integral part of the marketing mix should be provided at the lowest possible total cost. In this manner, physical distribution performance is blended with other marketing factors into an integrated offering.

Customer Service

The specific measures of customer service performance consist of level and response of delivery provided. Level relates to expected inventory availability. Response is concerned with the speed and consistency of delivery.

The level of customer service is a measure of the expected availability of a given product whenever ordered, or desired to be purchased by a customer. For example, what is the probability that you will find a specific brand and package size of soap each time you visit a particular supermarket? Similar measures can be developed for each inventory stocking location in a total exchange channel.

Response, as a measure of customer service performance, deals with situations whenever the typical practice is to place an order for subsequent

[40] Total cost includes all fixed and variable expenses related to physical distribution operations. The concept was introduced in the introduction and will be developed in greater detail in Chapters 10 and 14.

[41] This type of immediate profit impact will result from any form of cost reduction where sales and profit ratio remain constant. The main point is that there are many opportunities for cost reduction in physical distribution operations in the typical firm.

delivery. In Chapter 6 the specific terminology employed to structure inventory planning with respect to response is the inventory performance cycle. In physical distribution systems the typical practice is to provide rapid response and a high degree of consistency with respect to timely performance over a number of consecutive reorders. The cost and associated risk of holding inventory has become widely recognized among wholesalers and retailers. As a result, the pressures upon manufacturers to provide rapid and consistent delivery have also increased. Although the pressure for rapid response today is most acute among manufacturers servicing retailers, it appears clear that similar pressures are increasing across a broad spectrum of industry.

Physical Distribution Performance Over Time

From the foregoing discussion it should be clear that physical distribution performance is far more than a passive support for marketing. In attention to economical delivery, the level and response characteristics of customer service represent one of the elements of potential competitive superiority within the integrated marketing mix.

The nature of the marketing mix is that it must be dynamic with respect to changes in the marketplace and competition. Thus the level and response aspects of customer service will differ depending upon the specific situation confronted. In this final section physical distribution performance is viewed with respect to dynamics, flexibility, and aspects of complexity.

Tactical Adjustment Across Product Life Cycle

Perhaps the best illustration of the need for dynamic physical distribution performance is the product life cycle. The concept of product life cycle has been developed by marketing planners to illustrate the different competitive conditions that can be expected to exist during the market life of a product.[42]

Figure 2-7 illustrates a four-stage product life cycle. The stages illustrated are (1) introductory, (2) growth, (3) saturation, and (4) obsolescence or decline. It is beyond the purpose of this treatment to discuss all marketing ramifications associated with each stage of the life cycle. The purpose of illustrations is to highlight the fact that the marketing mix of a firm will be different in each stage and that the expectations concerning physical distribution performance will also vary.

During the introductory stage of a new product, a high level and response of physical distribution performance will normally be desired. Since initial distribution of the product is to be developed, a high premium will normally be placed on having an available stock for customers to draw upon and

---

[42] For an outstanding discussion of over-all competitive conditions surrounding each stage of the product life cycle, see Staudt and Taylor, *op. cit.*, Chap. 10.

FIGURE 2-7
Product Life Cycle Concept

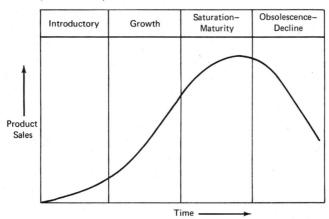

providing rapid and consistent service on replacement orders.[43] For example, a retail chain may add a new product but invest in a slim stock only. If the product gains customer acceptance, rapid and positive reorder will be required. In addition, marketing communication cost is normally high during the introductory stage as potential customers are being informed of product availability and being persuaded to purchase. Not having product availability during this critical time could have the net effect of diluting total impact of the marketing effort. Thus during the introductory stage physical distribution can be expected to play a prominent role in the integrated marketing offering. Since market position is not secure, it can be expected that shipment sizes will tend to be small and the frequency of orders erratic. Therefore, the physical distribution costs associated with providing the necessary level of service will be high.

During the growth stage of the product life cycle, the product in question has gained market acceptance and the potential of ultimate sales is now in better perspective. Emphasis in physical distribution performance during the growth stage can be expected to shift from a high level of customer service to one that can be realized at a more economical expenditure. Thus standards related to both level and response will be reduced provided a substantial per unit reduction in physical distribution cost can be realized. A characteristic of the growth stage is expanded distribution and a high level of profitability in transactions. Terms and conditions of sale will be adjusted to reflect economics associated with physical flow with efforts being made to encourage maximum efficiency. During the growth stage, particularly near the end of the stage and prior to intensive competition, the firm will enjoy maximum

---

[43] Because of the high cost of developing new markets, the cost of physical distribution is not as important as the impact of performance.

latitude in controlling physical distribution performance to reflect low total cost.

The saturation stage is characterized by competitive maturity. The product in question normally faces extensive competition with a variety of substitutes being marketed. Consequently, price competition is characteristic of competitive tactics. The desired physical distribution performance during the saturation stage can be expected to become highly selective. Competitors will adjust their service performance to provide high levels of availability and response to those customers who are major customers. To provide selectivity, higher expenditures will be allocated to physical distribution performance for those customers who represent the core of the enterprise's market.

During the obsolescence or decline stage of the product life cycle, the product's volume is declining. During this period, management is faced with a decision concerning whether to close the product out or to attempt to continue distribution on a restricted basis. During this stage, the physical distribution system must continue to support the degree of product distribution the firm is attempting to maintain while it continues to avoid excessive risk in the event that the product is discontinued. Minimum risk becomes a much more important attribute than realizing the lowest cost per unit of physical distribution performance.

The product life cycle illustrates a variety of different physical distribution strategies that a firm may select to implement during different points in time. No hard or firm rules exist because physical distribution performance, like all other elements of the marketing mix, must be altered to meet the market and competitive situation confronted. The level and response of performance will change over time. Likewise, the firm's willingness and ability to absorb physical distribution cost will also vary across time.

Performance Flexibility and Complexity

From the discussion of product life cycle, it is clear that the degree of customer service and associated total cost of physical distribution must be adapted to the marketing situation confronted. In addition to change across time with respect to a specific product, the physical distribution system must maintain flexibility and adjust to complexity at any specific point in time. Rather than the clear conditions of supporting a single product throughout one life cycle, the more prevailing condition is to be involved in the physical distribution support of multiple products, being serviced to many heterogeneous markets, through multiple exchange channels. In such a complex situation a firm's physical distribution system must be flexible and capable of coping with complexity. Some examples are provided in the remainder of this section.

NEW PRODUCT SUPPORT: A SPECIAL CASE OF INCREASING IMPORTANCE. The physical distribution support of new product introduction was briefly discussed under the introductory stage of the product life cycle. It was pointed out that the system would be expected to provide a high level of availability and rapid response during this critical period. In addition, some aspects of coordinating physical distribution support with introductory communications were noted.

The extent of new product activity anticipated for the future is worthy of note. Where in the past growth was more easily generated from existing products or the acquiring of other firms, the pattern for growth in the future appears to be more orientated to new product development. This change in emphasis is important to physical distribution for at least three reasons.

First, greater emphasis on new product development means that the physical distribution system will need to accommodate a far wider variation in product line. It is also likely that special handling, transportation, and packaging requirements will increase as the product line expands, forcing greater flexibility upon the system. To the extent that the expanded product line requires special equipment, such as refrigerated trucks or tank railcars, the task of physical distribution planning and coordination will become more complex.

A second consideration of expanded product line concerns the requirement to service many different markets through multiple channels. Given an expanding market offering, it is likely that products will become more specialized, being sold to smaller and highly service-orientated market segments. To reach these markets, a firm may need to utilize several different exchange and transaction channels.[44] The end result is small product volume flowing through any specific channel and less opportunity to aggregate volume for cost reductions.

A final implication of increased attempts at new product introductions results from the fact that marketing is far from a science when it comes to the development of new products. As noted earlier in this chapter, the development of new products requires a basic interpretation of customer needs to guide product developments. In addition, the potential new product must be projected into a use context in order to develop an effective communication program to inform and persuade potential buyers. In more than half the cases of new product development, the product offered does not enjoy sufficient longevity in the marketplace to repay its development cost.[45] From a viewpoint of physical distribution operations, it is difficult to project which products will win and lose. Extreme care must be taken not to cause product failure by not being able to support the product during critical points of introduction. On the other hand, the inventory stockpiling and advanced physical distribution of products to support sales that never materialize can be highly expensive for a firm. Physical distribution operations must walk a fine line with respect to new product planning. The requirement to

[44] If this is not clear, the reader should restudy pages 48–51.
[45] For further materials on this point, see Booz, Allen, and Hamilton, *Management of New Products* (New York: Company publication, 1960); Edgar A. Pessemier, New Product Ventures," *Business Horizons*, August 1968; and "Why Many New Products Fail," *Printers Ink*, October 23, 1964.

plan new product distribution can be expected to increase during the years ahead.

CUSTOMER SERVICE MYOPIA.   An area of complexity in physical distribution operations is the determination of just how much customer service should be provided to support the over-all integrated marketing mix. The provision of both high levels of availability and of rapid and consistent response to customer orders is a costly situation. As will be illustrated in detail in Chapter 10, which deals with the formulation of logistical policy, the added cost of improving the level of customer service performance increases at a far faster rate than the corresponding service increases. Therefore, firms that offer extremely high degrees of customer service will confront high total costs of physical distribution.

A failure on the part of managers fully to appreciate the relationship of incremental customer service and associated cost can result in commitments to high degrees of performance. The critical problem is to select a service level and response that will support sales without setting the standards so high that performance is prone to failure and costs are excessive. This proper degree of service can be determined only by experimentation and a willingness to take a firm stand concerning the degree of service to be offered.

Under modern technology of physical distribution, almost any degree of service can be provided if a firm is willing to pay the cost. In fact, it appears safe to generalize that most firms attempt to provide service in excess of that necessary to market products successfully. One of the major problems in physical distribution planning is to replace the tendency to overservice with a logical approach to the determination of customer service performance. The tendency to want to place a warehouse in every customer's backyard or to place consignment inventories in anticipation of sales must be replaced with a systematic approach to the design of a physical distribution system based upon cost–service benefit analysis. Facing the customer service myopia is one of the most complex aspects of physical distribution planning.

CHANNEL JUMPING.   In today's economy, retailers sell wholesale, wholesalers sell retail, hardware stores sell soft goods, department stores sell food, food stores sell appliances—they all sell toys and discount stores sell everything. This new structure of retailing is often referred to as *scrambled merchandising*.

Channel jumping is not limited to retailing. Finished goods often move to the same retailer from wholesalers, distributors, jobbers, assemblers, and direct from producers. In some cases, goods bypass retailers altogether and move directly to consumers. These changing patterns of exchange have forced a substantial alteration in the physical distribution complexity of individual firms.

In order to accommodate multiple channel physical distribution, a great many manufacturers and retailers have been forced into the operation of distribution warehouses in order efficiently to service many different types of customers. To a significant degree, manufacturer warehouses have replaced many of the specialized wholesalers, such as drug and hardware, that at one time were the dominant channel member. Such specialized intermediaries were unable adequately to service the distribution patterns associated with multiple channels.

Thus, in today's complex business arrangements, a firm must provide physical distribution service within many different channels. The simplicity of delivering almost all manufacturing output to a few wholesalers has been replaced by a variety of different physical fulfillment systems which deliver to numerous customer warehouses and, in many cases, direct to retail stores. The volume delivered to any one location is less under multichannel physical distribution, which often results in higher per unit costs. On the other hand, customer demands for high degrees of service are more direct since in many channels no middleman exists between manufacturer and retailers. The practice of channel jumping has increased the complexity of physical distribution while simultaneously proving a greater need for flexibility in operations.

Summary

The aspects of logistics dealing with physical distribution are an integral part of over-all marketing. The marketing concept sets a framework for over-all corporate planning. Within this framework, physical distribution performance is part of the marketing mix of the firm and represents one of the major costs of integrated marketing.

The distribution or marketing channel is of fundamental importance to physical distribution because the channel is the arena within which marketing and physical distribution culminate into customer transactions. The entire notion of loosely aligned middlemen linked together in pursuit of joint opportunity is not consistent with the logic of efficient physical distribution systems. One promising way to increase marketing efficiency is to improve physical movement within the distribution channel. Advantages in operation result when physical flow is separated from other flows in the total distribution process. The development of a specialized network of exchange intermediaries allows maximum control and economies of specialization in physical flow.

Many corporate costs of replenishment are hidden between departments of an enterprise, are not necessarily under the control of any given department, and are extremely difficult to identify. In addition, little consideration has been given to problems of coordinating and controlling physical distribution beyond the limits of legal control of an individual firm. Most physical distribution flow proceeds from production to consumption through specialized enterprises linked as an exchange channel. Each of these independent units or links may perform an excellent individual job of physical distribution, even though, as a totality, the over-all channel suffers from expensive duplication.

Therefore, the proper planning of a firm's physical distribution effort must transcend the total exchange channel.

As a total grouping of enterprises, an exchange channel must perform a specific sequence of functions in order to support transaction-creating efforts. Thus the total channel is, in effect, an integrated network with well-defined objectives. The most effective total channel is one capable of meeting objectives and controlling the flow of materials and finished goods in accordance with time and space demands.

The actual performance of physical distribution can be measured from the perspective of total cost and degree of customer service performance. The degree of customer service desired as an integral part of the marketing mix should be provided at the lowest possible total cost. Customer service can be measured in terms of level of product availability and response to order placement both in terms of speed and consistency of delivery.

The marketing mix must be dynamic with respect to changes in the market place and competition. The need to adjust the ratio of customer service capability and total cost expenditure to meet different conditions is illustrated by the product life cycle. Several aspects of complexity and the critical importance of maintaining flexibility were noted in the final part of the chapter. In particular, the importance of new products, the service myopia, and the increased complexity of physical distribution operations in a multiple channel environment were singled out for comment.

In total, the chapter provided an introduction to the role of physical distribution in over-all marketing. To provide a development base for the chapters that follow, physical distribution operations in a channel structure and function context were fully examined.

Appendix 2A
Definition and Characteristics
of Middlemen

The conventional approach to channel structure focuses on the path taken by the title of a product from producer or manufacturer to ultimate user. Included in this path are all middlemen, whether they take title directly or merely facilitate the title's passage. The purpose of this appendix is to provide a brief overview of the conventional approach to channel description.[1] Specifically, emphasis is placed on the wholesaling or middleman structure of

---

[1] *Note on Marketing Channels* (Boston: Harvard Business School, 1965), ICH 10M65, EA–M 480. This note provides additional coverage of distributional channels.

distribution. It should be noted that the terms *wholesalers* or *middlemen* are used in this section to describe specialists in the channel of distribution in addition to the term *intermediary* used in Chapter 2.

The conventional approach to channel description also focuses on the identification, description, and classification of middlemen. Figure 2A-1 typifies the analytical framework. At the first level, the distinction is made between merchant and functional middlemen. Merchant middlemen take title to the goods with all the ownership risks. Functional middlemen escape the risks of ownership but provide some necessary service to both client and customer.

At the second level, the distinction between range and type of wholesale services is made. Full-function middlemen typically buy in large quantities, break-bulk, assemble, assort, sell, and deliver. In performing these activities, the full-function middleman maintains a warehouse, employs a sales force that calls on the trade regularly, provides for physical distribution, extends trade credit, manages the collection of accounts, and serves in an advisory capacity or as an informational link to both suppliers and customers. The limited-function wholesaler is so designated because his range of services falls short of that provided by his full-function counterpart. On the other hand, the split-function middleman usually operates as both a retailer and wholesaler.

The third level of Figure 2A-1 represents descriptive criteria commonly applied to the various categories of wholesalers specified by the first two levels. The following section contains a more detailed description of the characteristics of specific classes of middlemen.

Merchant Middlemen

Included in this section are those wholesalers who buy and sell of their own initiative, thereby dealing with the risks of ownership.

FIGURE 2A-1
An Analytical Framework of Middlemen in the Structure of Distribution

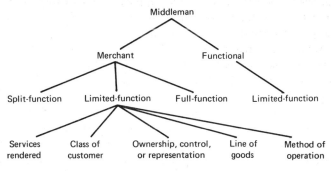

Regular Wholesalers

The service or regular wholesaler operates a full-function enterprise. Most commonly, the firm is independently owned and handles consumer goods. The regular wholesale firm purchases in large volume from producers and manufacturers, accepts delivery at one or more of its warehouses, breaks down and stores its purchases, sends out its sales force to canvass the trade, assembles orders in relatively small quantities, delivers orders to its customers, extends credit, assumes the risks of inventory and receivables, offers advisory service to its customers, and supplies marketing information to both customers and suppliers. The regular wholesale firm predominates as a retail source of supply in many mass-distributed consumer goods lines.

Industrial Distributor

The industrial distributor is also classified as a regular or full-function wholesaler. As such, he provides essentially the same services enumerated previously. The industrial distributor is differentiated from other full-function wholesalers by his customers and by the nature of his inventory. Customers purchase goods for consumption, use within their enterprise, or as an unfinished item subject to further processing. Although retailers are not technically excluded as a class of customer, in practice they provide a minimal source of patronage to the distributor. Most of the distributor's trade comes from such concerns as manufacturing firms, public utilities, railroads, mines, and service establishments (for example, doctors, barbers, beauticians, hotels, and restaurants). The industrial distributor often specializes in servicing one industry segment, such as automotive or mining.

Drop Shippers

Drop shippers are limited-function wholesalers in that they seldom take physical possession of the goods. Commodities such as coal, lumber, construction materials, agricultural products, and heavy machinery are bulky and require the economies of shipment by carload lots. The drop shipper typically purchases the carload from the supplier in anticipation of a future order. Once a buyer is found, the drop shipper assumes the responsibility and ownership of shipment until it is accepted by the customer. Because no warehouse facilities are maintained, the drop shipper's risk of title bearing varies with the time lag between purchase and sale of the carload. Apart from this risk, he also incurs the risks and costs of credit extension and receivables collection. This distinction between the practice of drop shipping and the drop shipper is important. Drop shipping is the practice of shipping an order direct from the supplier to the customer, although a middleman might be involved in the transactions. For example, headquarters purchasing might centrally purchase a large quantity of bulk merchandise. Instead of requiring shipment to the firm's distribution warehouse, the company might allocate portions of the shipment directly to its retail store. This practice is termed *drop shipping*. The drop shipper, on the other hand, is a distinct middleman who arranges for shipment, takes title, assumes responsibility for shipment, and functions as a merchant middleman in the over-all distribution channel.

Cash-and-Carry Wholesalers

Cash-and-carry wholesalers are limited-function middlemen who operate on a cash basis with no merchandise delivery. Chiefly found in the grocery trade, they were established to serve small retailers whose order size was typically not large enough to justify delivery. By stocking staple merchandise, employing no salesman, and eliminating delivery services and credit, such middlemen can economically serve the small retailer. To take advantage of such services, the retailer must travel to the warehouse, find and assemble his order, carry it to a central checkout location, pay cash, load on his truck, and carry the order to his place of business.

Wagon Distributors (Jobbers)

Principally utilized by the grocery trade, the wagon distributor is a limited-function wholesaler who specializes in high-margin specialty items or quick-turnover perishables. This middleman purchases from producers, may or may not maintain a warehouse, and employs one or more driver–salesmen to call regularly on the trade. Characteristically, sales and delivery are performed simultaneously. The customer fills his order from the truck's limited assortment and closes the transaction with a cash payment.

Rack Jobbers

Rack jobbers or service merchandisers are classified as full-function intermediaries in that they perform all the regular wholesaling functions plus some retailing functions. Dealing in extensive lines of nonfood merchandise, driver–salesmen regularly service grocer accounts. Typically, a salesman on call performs a stock control function in that he ensures that his display racks are adequately stocked, properly price-marked, and arranged in an attractive manner. Generally, a rack jobber will replace upon request of the retailer or at his own initiative unsold or slow-moving items. The retailer is usually billed on a consignment basis, paying only for merchandise sold since the jobber's last visit.

Assembling Wholesalers

Principally dealing in agricultural products, the assembling wholesaler reverses the common procedure in terms of order size. He buys the output of many small farmers, assembles and grades the product, ships in economical quantities to central markets, and sells in larger quantities than those purchased.

Semijobbers

Semijobbers are designated split-function middlemen, because they operate at both the wholesale and retail level of the channel of distribution. Usually semijobbers are limited- or full-function wholesalers who indulge in some retail sales; conversely, they are retailers who find it advantageous to be classified as wholesalers for at least a small portion of their operation. An illustration of the former is automotive suppliers. The second case is not typical of any particular retailing segment but is illustrative of a strategy aimed at gaining lower prices or developing business in two separate market segments.

Functional Middlemen

Wholesalers in the functional category do not take title; nevertheless they perform many wholesale functions. All middlemen included in this classification are, by definition, limited-function wholesalers, because they are precluded from assuming the risks of ownership.

Selling Agents

Selling agents serve their clients in lieu of a sales organization. They are contracted to sell output of one or more manufacturers as long as the lines handled are supplementary and do not compete directly. Because their principals are generally small firms, as illustrated by the textile industry, they are often called upon for financial assistance in terms of loans, carrying credit for the client, or collecting receivables. Furthermore, agents serve as collectors, analysts, and dispensers of marketing data. For these services, selling agents are remunerated on a commission basis.

Manufacturers' Agents

Manufacturers' agents are similar to selling agents in that they act as substitutes for a direct sales organization, are hired on a continuing contractual basis, represent relatively small enterprises, provide market intelligence, and are reimbursed by commissions. They differ from selling agents inasmuch as they do not sell the entire output of their clients, are limited to a specific geographic territory, and have little control over prices, discounts, and and credit terms. A manufacturer's agent or representative usually represents a number of manufacturers who produce noncompetitive but related lines.

Commission Merchants

Unlike agents, commission merchants rarely are used on a regular contractual basis. Instead, they are engaged for a single transaction, or, more commonly, to facilitate the disposal of a particular lot of goods. Once contracted, the commission merchant takes possession but not title of the goods, provides warehousing facilities, and displays either a sample or the entire lot to prospective purchasers. Once negotiations begin, the commission merchant is usually empowered to accept what in his judgment will be the best offer, as long as it exceeds a previously stipulated minimum price. To facilitate good offerings and speed the closing of transactions, the commission merchant may choose to extend credit at his own risk. In practice, he commonly extends credit, bills the customer, collects the account, provides a final accounting, and remits the proceeds less commission to his principal. Such a wholesaling operation is of vital importance to the marketing of livestock, grain, and other agricultural products.

Brokers

Brokers serve as catalytic agents to classes of buyers and sellers that would normally have considerable difficulty in meeting for purposes of negotiation. A broker's entire function is to stimulate and arrange contacts between the two groups. It is commonly understood that brokers do not permanently represent either buyer or seller. Furthermore, they do not handle the goods, rarely take physical possession, nor do they provide financial assistance to clients. The brokerage fee is paid by the principal, whether it is the buyer or the seller. In no case can a broker legally receive a fee from both parties to a transaction. Brokers are widely used in foreign trade by small manufacturers of convenience goods and by wholesale grocers.

Auction Companies

Auction companies are widely used in the marketing of fruit, tobacco, and livestock. They provide a physical setting conducive to the marketing of specific lots of commodities. Facilities are usually available to all those offering commodities and to all those bidding for them. The auction company is paid usually by the seller at a flat fee per transaction or a percentage of the sale.

Petroleum Bulk Stations

Stations provide the storage and wholesale distribution for the petroleum industry. Such establishments may be owned by refining companies and operated on a basis similar to that of manufacturers' sales branches; or they may be owned and operated independently.

Structural Alternatives in a Logistics System

In the first section of this appendix a description of the function and specific types of middlemen was presented. In this section a brief description of structural alternatives in product distribution is presented. Both sections treat structure in a graphic sense rather than in a strategic, dynamic context as presented in Chapter 2.

The graphic approach to describing a structure of distribution is described in Figures 2A-2 and 2A-3. In Figure 2A-2 the most common variations in consumer goods channels are illustrated. Of the four channels shown, the most typical for the consumer is the wholesale–retail–consumer channel. Most mass-produced consumer goods reach the market through a wholesaler and retailer. The channel selected by the manufacturer depends upon the characteristics of the product, the buying habits of the consumer, and the over-all marketing strategy of the firm. For example, a large personal sales force is required to market successfully a product nationwide directly to the consumer. Such companies as Avon Products and Fuller have selected this method of distribution. On the other hand, a manufacturer with limited capital resources and a limited product line might elect to hire a broker or an agent to sell his products in consumer channels.

In Figure 2A-3 a description of alternative channels for industrial goods distribution is presented. Most high-volume items in industrial markets move directly from producer to consumer. Supplies, replacement parts, and small orders of bulk items often use industrial distributors. In this sense the industrial middleman performs much the same function as the wholesaler in consumer channels. One major difference between consumer and industrial

FIGURE 2A-2
Typical Channel Structure Alternatives in Consumer Goods Distribution

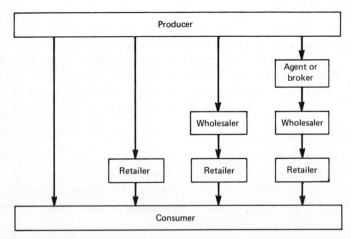

FIGURE 2A-3
Typical Channel Structure Alternatives in Industrial Goods Distribution

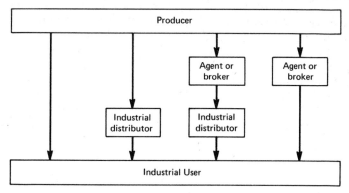

channels is that incidence of functional middlemen such as selling agents, brokers, and manufacturers' agents is much greater in industrial than in commercial channels.

The structures described in Figures 2A-2 and 2A-3 should be regarded as typical patterns. There are a great number of possible variations in channel structure in addition to those shown in these charts depending on the product, the customer, and the entrepreneurial vision of the channel members.

Questions

1. Describe the difference between the marketing concept and the job of management in marketing.
2. Why is it critical to think in terms of customer needs when designing a total marketing program?
3. How does physical distribution become an integral part of a firm's marketing mix? Is this consistent with the concept of over-all logistics developed in Chapter 1?
4. Describe the fundamental differences between the traditional ways in which distribution channels are viewed by marketing and by physical distribution managers.
5. What is the concept of separation and how does it lead to potential increases in over-all operating efficiency?
6. Why are exchange activities dependent upon the transaction channel for formulation of operational specifications?
7. Discuss risk with respect to the performance of the channel functions of exchange. Why is risk disproportionate among channel members?
8. Contrast vertically owned and vertically controlled distribution systems.

9. Discuss the different priorities placed on physical distribution performance during the product life cycle.
10. What is the impact of scrambled merchandising and channel jumping upon the design of a physical distribution system?
11. Discuss the impact of physical distribution performance upon new product introduction.
12. What is the concept of channel leadership, and how does it influence the design of physical distribution systems?

3

Material Management

The aspect of over-all logistics concerned with the procurement of raw materials and parts is material management. Material management is essential to manufacturing because timely and economical delivery is necessary to maintain efficient and continuous production. The cost of raw materials and parts constitutes the highest single expenditure of firms engaged in basic manufacturing. Therefore, extreme care is required to assure that the materials and parts purchased meet quality specifications at the lowest possible total cost of procurement.

The perspective of material management presented in this chapter is narrow in that the treatment centers on the logistical support of manufacturing. The primary reason for this orientation is that the manufacturing support situation is the most complex application of integrated material management. In addition to raw materials and parts, a typical enterprise must procure a variety of other items, such as supplies and equipment. This specialized form of logistical support is not treated in the present context. Finally, there exists a variety of retail and merchandising firms that do not engage in any form of manufacturing but do, in fact, have a great stake in economical purchasing. The basic principles of material management developed in the chapter directly apply to the purchasing requirements of nonmanufacturing firms. Sufficient similarity exists in the basic application of material management so as not to justify special treatment.

The initial section of this chapter is devoted to a description of material management as it interrelates with manufacturing. Next, attention is directed to the concept of the material cycle. The third section reviews basic procurement activities in greater detail, highlighting the fundamental areas of material management responsibility. The final section of this chapter treats some of the different approaches to decision making available to the material manager, who must cope with uncertainty concerning future price and supply availability.

Material Management in the Manufacturing Affairs of the Enterprise

The focal point of material management is procurement. The fundamental objective is to provide the correct assortment of materials and parts at the desired location, when needed, and in an economical manner. The efficient support of manufacturing engages all logistical components. Thus the material management subsystem, similar to physical distribution and product replenishment, involves transportation, inventory, warehousing, communications, and material movement.

Material management activities initiate from the material plan. The material plan is a statement of the quantity of raw materials and parts that will be required to support manufacturing. The plan contains specifications concerning when and where the materials and parts will be required. The task of material management is to economically satisfy the requirements outlined in the material plan.

The actual formulation of the material plan is not recommended as a material management responsibility. The plan is ideally formulated as part of logistical coordination. The sequence of events that culminates in the material plan is discussed in Chapter 4. At this point it is sufficient to note that the material plan is formulated on the basis of sales forecasts and the production schedule.[1]

Given the plan, material management is concerned with achieving six interrelated objectives.[2] Each is discussed in the following subsections.

[1] The sales forecast formulates the basic manufacturing assignment. The production schedule determines when, where, how much, and at what point in time they will be produced. See p. 102.

[2] The exact functions will vary depending upon author's coverage; for example, see Lamar Lee, Jr., and Donald W. Dobler, *Purchasing and Materials Management*, rev. ed. (New York: McGraw-Hill Book Company, 1971); Wilbur B. England, *The Purchasing System* (Homewood, Ill.: Richard D. Irwin, Inc., 1967); E. S. Buffa, *Production Inventory Systems: Planning and Control* (Homewood, Ill.: Richard D. Irwin, Inc., 1968), Dean S. Ammer, *Materials Management*, rev. ed. (Homewood, Ill.: Richard D. Irwin, Inc., 1968); Wilbur B. England, *Modern Procurement Management: Principles and Cases*, 5th ed. (Homewood, Ill.: Richard D. Irwin, Inc., 1970); and Stuart F. Heinritz and Paul V. Farrell, *Purchasing*, 5th ed. (Englewood Cliffs, N.J.: Prentice-Hall, Inc., 1971).

Best Price Procurement

Foremost, material management is concerned with purchasing the required raw materials and parts at the best possible price. The best possible price may not always be the lowest price available in the market place. Naturally, price must be viewed in terms of consistent quality and continuity of supply.

A great deal of the efforts of material managers is concentrated on price negotiation and programs to reduce cost. Since most prices are negotiated, it may be necessary to study supplier operations to the point of developing a detailed understanding of their costs in order to determine a fair negotiated price. A detailed understanding of cost is an important part of deciding if a firm should continue to purchase externally or if it is economically justified to internally manufacture the part.[3]

With respect to raw materials, the best price may well change as a function of supply and demand.[4] The actual timing of purchases must be based on an appraisal of most likely future prices in combination with the cost associated with maintaining stockpiles. A substantial element of risk is involved in procurement, which at times can make hedging economically justified.

Supply Continuity

The maintenance of a continuous supply of both materials and parts is an essential aspect of material management. Erratic availability of selected materials and parts may well require standing commitments with vendors so as to assure continuous supply. Such commitments are made in advance of the formulation of a specific material plan. Thus material management is involved in projecting availability and taking appropriate steps to protect the interests of the enterprise.

The serious nature of maintaining continuity is easily understood when one considers the high cost of manufacturing disruption in today's environment. If the shortage of materials or parts causes a work stoppage, in most cases the basic burden of manufacturing cost continues because of labor contract commitments and the high degree of capital investment in plant facilities. In addition, an unplanned work stoppage will in most cases have a direct impact upon marketing performance and consequently cash flow. At the very least, the orderly processes of product replenishment and physical distribution will be disrupted as emergency measures are taken to maintain continuity in customer order processing.

[3] For a comprehensive discussion of the factors involving the make versus buy decision, see England, *op. cit.*, pp. 71–81; J. W. Culliton, *Make or Buy*, Division of Research Study 27 (Boston: Harvard Business School, 1956); and Alfred G. Oxenfeldt, *Make or Buy: Factors Affecting Decisions* (New York: McGraw-Hill Book Company, 1956).

[4] Raw material speculation so as to realize an "appreciation" value on material stockpiles is less frequently practiced today than it was in the past. Nevertheless, the supply–demand relationship in the market has a major impact on evaluation of "best price." See Lee and Dobler, *op. cit.*, pp. 106–11.

Quality Maintenance

While materials and parts are normally procured to standard specifications, a considerable degree of latitude may exist in quality between alternative supply sources. It is a fundamental responsibility of material management to select the sources that most consistently meet quality specifications. In addition, a quality-control program must be maintained to safeguard against any deterioration in quality of materials or parts once a source commitment has been made. A sudden and unexpected quality variation in a major material or part can cause a prolonged work stoppage.

The emphasis on overall quality control has increased substantially in recent years as a direct result of broader interest in consumer protection. Manufacturers are increasingly involved in assuring consumers as well as production agencies that their products meet performance and safety standards. Maintaining this commitment starts with quality control of materials and parts. This is clearly evident in the history of automotive recalls. The basic reason for most recalls is subassembly failure.

Low Logistical Acquisition Cost

A basic objective of material management is to design and operate a highly efficient system for acquiring possession of materials and parts. Similar to physical distribution management, material managers must integrate transportation, inventory stocking, ordering communication, warehousing, and materials movement into a balanced support system. In this respect the logistical cost required to gain possession of materials and parts must be carefully evaluated in source or vendor selection. Although a particular vendor may offer the lowest purchase price for a given quality part, the logistical cost may prohibit the firm from doing business with that vendor.[5]

In the next section the material cycle is discussed, so further elaboration on acquisition cost is not necessary at this point. However, it is important to keep in mind that the expansion of managerial concern to the performance of the total logistical support system is the primary difference between material management and traditional purchasing.

Research and Development Assistance

A prime responsibility of material management is to be on the lookout for new ideas for product design engineering. This phase of material management encompasses a continuous search for new and better ways of meeting specifications as well as the transfer of new technology into the enterprise. Because representatives of the material management organization have regular contact

[5] For an excellent example, see James L. Heskett, Robert M. Ivie, and Nicholas A. Glaskowsky, Jr., *Business Logistics* (New York: The Ronald Press Company, 1973), pp. 171–93.

with the sources, trade shows, and specialized purchasing publications, they are better positioned than any other management group to be apprised of new developments.

For example, a specific part, given a change in technology, could perhaps be produced from a cheaper material or by a less expensive process with the end result of lower total cost and/or higher reliability. Thus one aspect of material management is to recommend changes in specifications that appear to be justified economically for review by the manufacturing research and development department.

Maintaining Supplier Relations

A final objective of material management deals with the development and maintenance of a positive relationship with suppliers. In the case of many large enterprises, suppliers may also be important customers. Therefore, an element of reciprocity will most often be involved in material management decisions. Providing the basic five objectives already discussed can be satisfied, there is good business reason to encourage reciprocal arrangements.[6]

Another aspect of good will with vendors concerns the inevitable emergencies that will develop regardless of how well the material plan is established. The ability to compensate for sudden failure of a supply source or a desire rapidly to increase production may depend upon the willingness of one or more suppliers substantially to modify their operations. At times it may be necessary to cancel outstanding commitments or even return materials or parts when actual sales lag behind forecasts or when a product is discontinued. The ability to get full vendor cooperation in such situations is fundamentally a question of economic leverage. However, if a positive relationship exists between the material management group and the supplier, such situations can be arranged with a minimum of friction.

The Material Cycle

For purposes of planning and designing the material management system, a useful concept is that of the material cycle.[7] To accomplish an orderly flow of materials and parts into manufacturing operations, several distinct activities are required. These are (1) sourcing, (2) order placement and expediting, (3) transportation, and (4) receiving and inspection. These specific activities are required in order to complete the procurement process. Once material or parts procured are in the possession of the enterprise, warehousing, inventory control, and material movement are required to complete their flow into the manufacturing complex.

---

[6] See Lee and Dobler, *op. cit.*, pp. 91–97.
[7] For an expanded discussion, see J. H. Westing, I. V. Fine, and G. J. Zenz, *Purchasing Management: Materials in Motion*, 3rd ed. (New York: John Wiley & Sons, Inc., 1969).

In many ways, the material cycle is similar to the customer order processing cycle involved in physical distribution. However, three important differences exist.

First, substantial differences exist in the delivery time, size of shipment, method of transport, and value of the products involved. As a general rule, material management requirements result in very large shipments, which may be transported by barge, deep-water vessels, multiple-car trains, and truck-loads. While exceptions do exist, transport emphasis in the material cycle is normally placed on realizing movement at the lowest cost. The lower value of materials and parts as contrasted to finished products means that a greater potential tradeoff exists between cost of maintaining inventory in-transit and low-cost modes of transport. Since the cost of maintaining materials and most parts in the supply pipeline is relatively lower per day than of maintaining finished products, no benefit is gained by paying premium rates for faster transport. Therefore, as a general rule lead times involved in the material cycle will be longer in duration than those typically found in customer-order-processing cycles.

A second major difference is the degree of middlemen who are normally involved in the material cycle as contrasted to the finished-product marketing channel. In Chapter 2 the marketing channel was viewed from a number of different vantage points.[8] In fact, a channel structure consisting of many different middlemen is the normal way in which the transaction creating and physical fulfillment activities of marketing and physical distribution are accomplished. In physical distribution planning, it is desirable to acknowledge that any particular firm is only a participant in an over-all exchange channel, which, through the combined efforts of all members, must achieve several specified functions.[9] In contrast, the material cycle is normally far more direct than the typical marketing channel. Materials and parts are purchased directly from the source and the procuring firm has little if any interest in the steps necessary to realize purchase source availability. From the viewpoint of the design of the material management system, the utilization of more direct channels is an important factor.

Finally, the customer-order-processing cycle must be designed to handle orders at the convenience of customers. Thus random ordering must be accommodated in the design of the physical distribution system. In contrast, the material management system places orders. Therefore, the degree of control is far greater in the material cycle as a result of a substantial reduction in the uncertainty of operational requirements.

The three major differences in the material cycle all are conducive to more orderly programming of logistical activities in material management than is characteristic of physical distribution operations. The major degree of un-certainty that exists in the material cycle is the appraisal that must be made

[8] See page 42.
[9] See page 51.

concerning the probability of future significant price changes or disruption in supply.

The next section reviews in greater detail various procurement activities involved in the material management cycle. The following section considers various decision criteria available to assist the material manager in coping with future uncertainty.

Material Cycle Design Considerations

The basic design of the material management operating system is based upon fulfillment of the material plan. However, the operating system will over time be expected efficiently to satisfy numerous material procurement plans. The objective is to establish an operating system that is sufficiently flexible to accommodate the peculiarities of different material plans while maintaining as much routinization as possible for the benefit of maximum economies. With this objective in mind, each of the activities involved in the material cycle is now reviewed in greater detail.

Sourcing

The fundamental concerns in sourcing are twofold: (1) the basic decision of whether to make or buy; and (2) in buy situations, the selection of vendors. In a theoretical sense, sourcing does not commence until the material plan is formulated. That is, unless necessary to protect enterprise interests, no commitments are made to vendors until the requirements of a material plan are being satisfied. In a practical sense, the initial selection of sources, as well as the evaluation of whether the part should be fabricated internally or purchased from an outside source, is completed during the product design phase of manufacturing. Unless circumstances change, the initial sourcing selection will normally be retained over a number of consecutive material plans.

MAKE OR BUY.   As a general rule, a manufacturing enterprise desires to make as many parts of its finished product line as is economically practical. For the most part, raw materials must be purchased from outside sources since few firms are vertically integrated to the point where they operate extraction or commodity processing facilities.[10]

Ammer has presented a general set of conditions that are helpful in the initial appraisal of the decision to make or buy.[11] These are summarized in Table 3-1. Beyond the general conditions favoring making or buying, the

---

[10] England, *op. cit.*, pp. 72–81, provides an excellent summary of conditions encouraging or discouraging making versus purchasing.

[11] Ammer, *op. cit.*, p. 271.

final decision results from the most efficient allocation of available capital. To aid in evaluation, the material manager can apply expected value analysis to project the probable gain of investing in the necessary fabrication equipment as opposed to alternative uses of capital. In general, any investment is expected to provide a return on investment that meets corporate financial planning criteria.

TABLE 3-1
Factors Favoring Make or Buy Decisions

Factors Favoring Fabrication	*Factors Favoring Procurement*
1. If the part can be more cheaply fabricated than purchased.	1. If the necessary facilities are not available and there are more profitable opportunities for investing company capital.
2. If the cost is nearly equal (because fabrication reduces the number of vendors the firm must rely upon).	2. If existing facilities can be more economically employed to make other parts.
3. If the part is vital and requires extremely close quality control.	3. If the existing personnel skills cannot be readily adapted to making the parts.
4. If the part can be produced on existing equipment and is of the type in which the firm has considerable manufacturing experience.	4. If patents or other legal barriers prevent the company from making the parts.
5. If the fabrication process requires no extensive investment in facilities that are already available at supplier plants.	5. If the expected requirements for the part are either temporary or seasonal.
6. If the requirements for the part are projected to be both relatively large and stable.	

Although the expected value criterion is one of the most widely advocated methods of evaluating alternative courses of action, it requires considerable knowledge concerning the decision.[12] In the case of the make or buy decision, the technique is extremely useful since the costs of each basic option are normally well defined. Assuming that the costs and other pertinent factors are nearly equal, the final decision is one of evaluating alternative application of financial resources. Rather than try to explain the expected value criterion, the basic concept is illustrated by an applicational example.

Assume that the material manager has a choice of spending $50,000 in any area that will improve over-all costs of procurement. Three major options are available. The first is to invest in fabrication equipment that would result in making rather than buying a specific part. The second option is to improve warehouse receiving facilities so as to reduce the amount of overtime currently

[12] For an expanded discussion, see Harvey M. Wagner, *Principles of Management Science* (Englewood Cliffs, N.J.: Prentice-Hall, Inc., 1970), pp. 340–42.

required by dock personnel. The third is to improve the existing methods used to control over-all procurement inventories. The problem is to select one of these alternative areas for investing the $50,000.

The first step is to project the potential cost savings of each option over a future time period. Assume that a basic corporate return on investment policy is that all capital investment must be recovered by cost–benefit savings within a three-year period. The best judgment of management is that the payoffs involved in each option are adequate to satisfy the cost–benefit criterion. The estimates of payoff are presented in Table 3-2.

TABLE 3-2
Expected Cost Benefit

Option	Three-Year Cost Reduction
Fabrication equipment	$100,000
Warehouse receiving	95,000
Inventory control method	125,000

However, each projected cost saving involves a certain degree of risk that the expected results will not in fact materialize. The second step in applying expected value is to assign a relative probability to the expected realization of each potential cost benefit.

Establishment of the probability is a judgment based upon evaluation of relative risk. For example, perhaps a potential vendor of the part in question will develop a new technology that will result in a price reduction if the part is purchased rather than fabricated. Alternatively, the demand for the part may not materialize at the level anticipated, which will result in noneconomical deployment of the new fabrication equipment. Each of the options has a similar number of contingencies that could result in the anticipated savings not materializing. Based on a careful evaluation of all facts, management on a scale of 0.10 to 1.0 estimates the following probabilities of realizing the expected cost reduction: (1) fabrication equipment 0.6, (2) warehouse receiving 0.8, and (3) inventory control method 0.5. The expected comparative value among the three options is simply calculated by multiplying the probability of attainment and the anticipated cost benefit. The results are presented in Table 3-3.

Using the expected value criterion to guide the investment decision, the choice would be to complete the improvement of warehouse receiving facilities. Even though this option has the lowest estimated cost benefit, it has the highest expected value, owing to the high probability that the expected cost benefits will indeed be realized. Although the expected value criterion does not replace the managerial judgment required to estimate potential consequences of alternative courses of action, it does provide a systematic logic for evaluation.

TABLE 3-3
Expected Value of Capital Expenditure

Option	Cost Benefit	Probability	Expected Value
Fabrication equipment	$100,000	0.6	$60,000
Warehouse receiving	95,000	0.8	76,000
Inventory control method	125,000	0.5	62,500

VENDOR SELECTION. If the economics of the situation and other pertinent factors support external purchasing, the specific source of supply must be selected. In most cases, a firm will desire to split purchases across two or more vendors in order to hedge against potential quantity, quality, or pricing problems. Assuming that a choice exists among several vendors with nearly equal pricing, quality, and no apparent quantity problems, the selection should, for the most part, rest upon a comprehensive analysis of the total logistical cost associated with procurement from each.

Beyond cost, the issues of reciprocity and relative stability of various sources are important to the final decision. A number of sources of information are available about vendor firm capabilities.[13] However, the acid tests are their financial stability and past performance record. In situations wherein vendor performance is extremely critical to the manufacturing and assembly operation, it is not unusual for a comprehensive financial analysis to be completed prior to source selected. In selected situations, a performance bond may be justified if any reasonable doubt exists about the vendor's capability.

Order Placement and Expediting

The exact amount of a raw material or part required over a period of time is based upon the material plan. Therefore, unless circumstances change, little uncertainty exists concerning the total amount to procure. It is necessary to arrive at a determination of how frequently purchases should be made and the size of each purchase.

In determining the frequency and size of orders, two extremes exist. If the selected course of action is to purchase in small quantities, the net result will be a high frequency of order placement. Under such a purchasing policy, little if any warehouse storage space and inventory carrying cost will be required, which will thereby reduce these elements of logistical cost. On the other hand, increased costs of order placement, expediting, and transportation, as well as the possible loss of volume discounts, may more than offset the cost reductions gained from frequently purchasing small quantities. The opposite extreme is to place very few large orders. When this policy is followed, the cost results of frequent ordering are reversed.

[13] See Lee and Dobler, op. cit., pp. 75–78.

The determination of an ordering policy can be approximated by determination of the economic order quantity (EOQ). EOQ determination will identify the precise size of order quantity which will result in the lowest total cost of ordering and maintaining raw material or parts inventory. If the EOQ is divided into the estimated total quantity called for in the material plan, the recommended frequency of ordering is readily determined.

Because the EOQ formulation is so basic to over-all inventory policy throughout all aspects of the logistical system, detailed treatment is reserved for Chapter 6.[14] At this point, two facets of the potential use of EOQ should be kept in mind. First, it will provide the precise order size wherein the costs of storage and ordering will be minimized. Second, the solution derived from the EOQ formulation in most cases will require modification to accommodate vendor capability, most economical transportation mode, and in some cases discount structure.[15]

Once an order is placed with a vendor, no additional action is necessary if everything proceeds according to expectations. However, it is not unusual for delays to be experienced. The expediting function of material management is to anticipate potential delays and to take corrective action in advance of an actual shortage.

In terms of anticipation a well-designed inventory control system can signal a potential problem prior to reaching a critical point. Most inventory policies provide a safety stock to accommodate minor variations or delays in vendor shipment. However, any major disruption in the vendor's ability to ship should be isolated long before safety stock reserves are the only remaining inventories available or in sight.

For the most part, expediting is concerned with making sure that the vendor is making every possible effort to avoid a discontinuity in supply. For example, it may be possible to release a partially completed order if authorized by the expeditor. In order for expediting to be helpful, the source of the potential problem must be solvable by vendor or procurement management action. If not, a rapid switch of vendors may be the only way to maintain supply continuity. The job of the expeditor is broader than mere problem solving. His regular involvement on a day-to-day basis with key vendors should be systematically scheduled to permit a continuous appraisal of potential supply problems far in advance of a serious operational problem.

Transportation

The element of transportation has been discussed thus far in the introductory chapter when reviewing the component parts of logistics and in Chapter 2 with respect to the channel of distribution. In addition, it is the sole subject of Chapter 5. Therefore, in the sake of avoiding redundancy only a few

[14] See page 193.
[15] See page 195 for an expanded development.

salient points specifically related to material management are noted at this point.

Transportation is a vital cost of procurement since typically very large shipments of raw materials are required to support manufacturing operations. Because the typical value of the material is relatively low and the tonnage great, freight rates among common carriers are normally substantially lower in material management than in physical distribution operations. In many material management situations, the total weight shipped is so large that even a minor reduction in cost per hundredweight can result in major dollar savings. Therefore, most traffic departments provide a continuous review of the rate structure applicable to these large-volume movements.

A second point concerning transportation in the material management cycle is that the size and regular frequency of movement makes the option of private or contract vehicles a worthy consideration. If two-way utilization of equipment is possible by combining some aspects of material management, product replenishment, and physical distribution transport, the potential for cost savings will normally be significant. The important point is that the regular nature of material management transport most often provides the nucleus around which an investment in private transportation capacity can be justified.

Receipt and Inspection

The final activity in the material cycle is receipt and inspection of the raw materials or parts. Depending upon the particular process under consideration, materials and parts may be placed into temporary storage or received and processed directly into the assembly operation. For example, in automotive assembly, it is not uncommon for components and parts to be scheduled for arrival for assembly usage right off the truck or freight car. Under such tight operating conditions, little latitude is available for bottlenecks in receipt or loss of quality control. The following subsections discuss both types of problems and solution approaches available to the material manager.

RECEIVING PROCEDURES. Material and part receiving represents only one of the areas in a corporation where potential waiting lines or queues can develop. However, it is a critical area because of the direct linkage of the material cycle to the manufacturing process. Queueing analysis is applicable to any situation where (1) some material, person, vehicle, or other element arrives at a facility for servicing; (2) at times, it is necessary to wait in line; (3) the desired service is received; (4) the object in question leaves the system.[16] Thus queueing analysis could just as readily be applied to a doctor's office, barber shop, to the over-all manufacturing process, or any other similar situation.

[16] For an expanded discussion, see Wagner, *op. cit.*, Chap. 15.

As in most areas of applied mathematics, queueing theory has a specialized terminology that should be understood by the reader. The *arrival rate* refers to the average rate at which trucks arrive at the unloading dock. Normally it is expressed as the number of arrivals per unit of time. The *service rate* refers to the average rate at which trucks can be unloaded. It is normally expressed as the number of trucks serviced per unit of time. The *distribution rate* for arrival and unloading has a significant impact upon waiting-line analysis. Basically, two rates exist. If no logical or consistent pattern of arrival and unloading exists, then a *random* distribution rate is experienced. If a pattern is present, then the distribution rate is *predictable*.

The probabilities of arrival and servicing can be expressed in the form of statistical distributions. Arrivals are typically expressed in the form of a *Poisson* distribution, whereas servicing is an *exponential* distribution.[17]

The Poisson distribution or the distribution of arrival times is espressed as

$$P(x) = \frac{(\lambda t)^x e^{-\lambda t}}{x'},$$

where

$P(x)$ = probability of arrival.

t = unit of time.

λ = average number of arrivals per unit of time.

x = arrivals.

The equation yields the probability that there will be x arrivals in time t with the average arrival rate of λ units. Figure 3-1 illustrates the Poisson distribution.

The probability of service time is exponential and is expressed as follows:

$$S(t) = M^e - Mt,$$

where

$S(t)$ = density function for service times.

t = unit of time.

M = average servicing time.

The average service time over-all is $\hat{\imath}s = 1/M$. Figure 3-2 illustrates the exponential density function.

A final term used in queueing analysis is *channel*. Channel refers to the number of processing devices in the situation under analysis. For example,

[17] The student not familiar with basic statistics should skip this section and resume reading at Inspection Procedures, page 92. For more detail, see pages 196–202.

FIGURE 3-1
Poisson Distribution

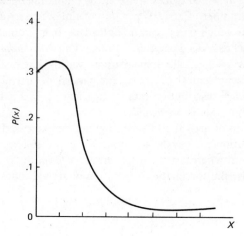

if one unloading dock is available, then the system is *single* channel. If more than one channel exists in the problem, then it is *multiple* channel.

The queueing analysis problem represents a quantification of the receiving situation so as to allow management to test different ideas or queue-reduction solutions. To illustrate, assume that an unbiased data bank has been collected about the arrival and unloading of trucks at a warehouse dock. The average time between arrivals of trucks at the dock is 30 minutes. Table 3-4 presents the measured unloading times for the trucks and the related frequency distribution.

Based on the data available, the unloading dock can be simulated. The first task is to simulate the arrival of a loaded truck. Based upon the average

FIGURE 3-2
Exponential Distribution

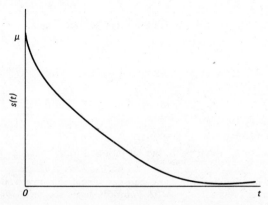

TABLE 3-4
Queue Analysis Data

Number of Trucks	Unloading Time (minutes)	Percentage Distribution Unloading Time	Weighted Average of Unloading Times
10	35	10	3.50
30	40	30	12.00
40	45	40	18.00
20	50	20	10.00

arrival-time analysis, there is a high probability that at least one truck will arrive every 30 minutes. Using a random number table, the number of arrivals each 30-minute period can be approximated. In a similar manner, random number tables can be used to approximate the expected unloading time for each arrival. A sample of the type of simulated operational data that can be generated using random numbers and the probabilities of arrival and unloading time is presented in Table 3-5.

TABLE 3-5
Simulated Arrival and Service Data

30-Minute Time Periods	Simulated Arrivals	Simulated Service Time (minutes)
1	0	
2	2	45–50
3	1	40
4	1	40
5	0	
6	0	
7	0	
8	1	50
9	0	
10	2	40–50
11	0	
12	1	45
13	0	
14	1	40
15	1	45
16	2	45–40
17	2	50–35
18	1	45
19	0	
20	0	
21	0	

Once the arrival and service pattern is determined, the queueing solution is to seek the lowest-cost way to complete the unloading. The cost of unloading consists of warehouse labor plus the idle time of truck drivers and equipment while in the queue. Assuming the necessary number of unloading docks or channels are available, the basic problem is to decide the size of the labor crew that will most economically service the arriving vehicles. The standard work rule is that trucks are unloaded on a first come–first service basis. For purposes of queue analysis, it is assumed if there is one arrival it will occur at the start of the 30-minute period, and if two trucks arrive, the second will be ready for servicing at the start of the sixteenth minute of the basic 30-minute period.

Figure 3-3 represents the simulated arrival and servicing patterns for the data displayed in Table 3-5. The numbers on the left side of Figure 3-3 represent 30-minute time periods. The dashed line represents waiting time once the truck has arrived. The solid line represents servicing time once the unloading starts. The total time in the queue is the combination of the waiting and servicing time.

Based on Figure 3-3, the total idle time of drivers and equipment is 1,285 minutes, an average time per driver in the queue of 85.69 minutes. Table 3-6 presents the basic cost of warehouse labor and idle drivers and equipment. The assumption is that idle transport equipment could be utilized if not in the queue.

TABLE 3-6
Queue Cost Factors

Warehouse regular rate/hr	$3.50
Warehouse overtime rate/hr	5.25
Driver and equipment rate/hr	20.00

Based on the data in Figure 3-3, it will be necessary for the warehouse dock crew to work 12.25 hours to complete the servicing of trucks scheduled to arrive on the simulated day. All hours over eight are paid at overtime rates.

The total cost of using a single seven-man unloading crew is presented in Table 3-7.

TABLE 3-7
One Warehouse Shift

Warehouse regular rate	$196.00
Warehouse overtime rate	156.19
Driver and equipment rate	409.32
Total cost	$761.51

FIGURE 3-3
Simulated Queue Time Pattern

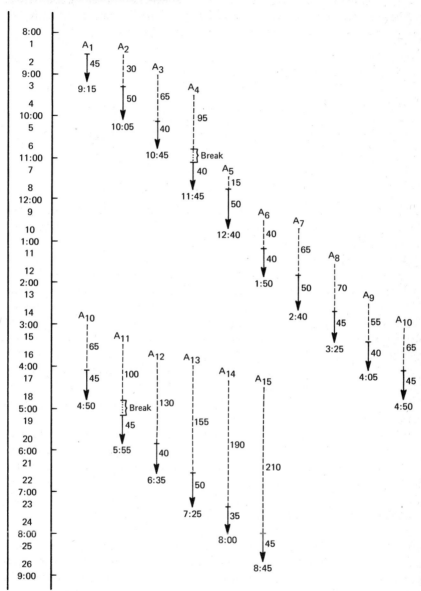

An alternative unloading procedure would be the addition of more warehouse personnel so as to unload or service the arriving trucks faster. To illustrate, a second crew of seven men is added under a work schedule that starts at 10 A.M. and ends when the last truck is unloaded. The regular crew is limited to an 8-hour shift.

While the simulated queue pattern is not presented, the result would be a reduction in average waiting time from 85.69 minutes to 25 minutes per truck. Table 3-8 provides the related cost data for the two-crew unloading alternative. A queue pattern for the two-crew unloading alternative similar to Figure 3-3 can be developed by the student from the data presented.

TABLE 3-8
Two Warehouse Shifts

Warehouse regular rate shift A	$196.00
Warehouse regular rate shift B	196.00
Warehouse overtime rate shift B	15.44
Driver and equipment rate	123.75
Total cost	$531.19

In the illustration, the queue has been substantially reduced by adding the second crew with a daily saving of $230.32. Based on a 250-day work year the annualized cost–benefit would be $57,580.

This simple illustration points out the type of analysis required by the material management organization in order to realize smooth operations at the lowest possible total cost. One frequent belief is that when common carriers are used, the in-queue time is not important. Therefore, the proper solution to the queue situation is to use the lowest amount of warehouse labor that will get the trucks unloaded in time for the materials or parts to be ready for manufacturing use. This logic is faulty for two reasons. First, over an extended time, driver and equipment idle time of common carriers will be reflected in the rate per hundredweight charged for their service. Second, most tariffs provide for a specific delay charge unless trucks are serviced within a specified time period.[18]

A number of variations can be applied to a waiting-line simulation to seek better servicing rate or lower costs. For example, when private trucks are used, an attempt can be made to eliminate random arrival by scheduling. Scheduled arrival will reduce the waiting queue. A second potential modification is to relax the first come–first service rule so as to move trucks with critical materials or higher than average delay charges rapidly through the queue.

In essence, the main point of emphasis in the receiving portion of the material cycle is the establishment of an unloading procedure that will meet manufacturing requirements at the lowest total cost. As in most areas of logistics, care must be exercised to assure that all relevant costs are considered in the decision process.

INSPECTION PROCEDURES.   One of the basic objectives of material management is quality maintenance. On the other hand, inferior quality is the single

---

[18] For an expanded discussion, see page 168.

greatest cause for the failure of supplies to be delivered on time. The material management inspection responsibility is aimed at checking a representative sample of materials and parts to assure they meet specification. Such inspection may be done at the vendor's manufacturing plant or after the material is received at the end of the material cycle. The location of inspection will depend upon the critical nature of the item in question and its over-all vulnerability to damage while in transit. As a general rule, the more susceptible a given material or part to inspection rejection, the greater the need to stockpile acceptable items in order to maintain continuity of supply.

The cost of 100 per cent inspection will, in most cases, be prohibitive.[19] Therefore, some form of inspection or quality control by statistical sampling is required. In most fabrication situations, a degree of random fluctuations in specific parts is expected to occur. The main purpose of the inspection sample is to measure the degree of fluctuation or damage to determine if the fabrication or transportation process was out of control.

Sampling consists of selecting a predetermined number of items from a large lot or shipment for careful inspection. The sample size and method of selection is structured in such a way to assure that it will be representative of the total group being inspected.[20] Based upon a careful inspection of the sample, the inspector follows a predetermined statistical inference procedure with respect to acceptance or rejection of the entire shipment. For each material or part, a predetermined required reliability sets the basic standard for acceptance or rejection.

For example, assume that a shipment of a specific part consists of 400 units. For purposes of inspection, it has been determined that a 10 per cent, or 40-unit sample is adequate to project the over-all condition of the shipment with a 95 per cent confidence of correct appraisal.[21] The sampling procedure under this situation could well be a complete inspection of every tenth part. If all 40 parts meet specifications, the entire shipment would be accepted. If one defect was discovered in the sample of 40, then several options might be followed.

First, the total lot could be rejected. However, this could result in unnecessary expense of return shipment and possible shortage of a critical part. Second, the total lot could be inspected, with a resulting separation of those parts which do and do not meet specifications. A final choice, if only one or a limited number of defects was discovered in the initial sample, is to take a second random sample to cross-verify results. The degree of tolerance in acceptance or rejection, as well as the amount of additional inspection caused by a defect, will depend upon the specific tolerance range established for the part.

---

[19] Robert E. McGarrah, *Production and Logistics Management* (New York: John Wiley & Sons, Inc., 1963), pp. 7–20.

[20] *Ibid.*

[21] Ninety-five per cent confidence means that the sample size will be adequate to make a valid inspection 95 of 100 times. It does not mean that deficiencies will exist 5 per cent of the time.

Design for Decision

The major variable in planning material management operations is the uncertainty that exists with respect to the future probability of a significant price change or a disruption in supply. In both situations, the material manager, unlike his counterparts in logistical coordination and physical distribution, must arrive at a decision concerning the probability of either type of event and take early corrective measures in the best interest of the enterprise.

To a significant degree, the best foundation for arriving at an operating decision is the familiarity of the material manager with the basic economic conditions that prevail in the marketplace and the extent to which labor contracts are scheduled to expire during the material cycle. However, given this basic knowledge, statistical decision techniques can be applied to uncertain conditions to help formulate a logical course of action.

Decision Criteria

A number of different criteria have been developed to help managers select between different available courses of action. To make a good decision, the material manager should evaluate the relative risks and expected payoffs associated with each of the courses of action.

As a general rule, the greater the potential payoff, the greater the corresponding risk. For example, a decision not to stockpile steel because of the probability of a strike is judged to be minimal will have a high payoff because normal material management operations can be maintained, excessive storage costs prevented, and cash flow regulated. However, the corresponding penalty associated with complete disruption of manufacturing operations in the event a strike does occur could make the decision in favor of a high payoff very risky.

MAXIMUM–MINIMUM RELATED CRITERIA. A number of different logic rules have been worked out to help a decision maker select a course of action that will either maximize payout or minimize risk. These basic criteria are useful in establishing the extremes of a pessimistic or optimistic outlook.

A maximum criterion is based on the assumption that all possible future events will go contrary to the best interest of the enterprise. Therefore, the pessimistic decision maker attempts to minimize future risk at the sacrifice of potential gains in payoff. Using the maximum criterion, the decision maker isolates the minimum risk–payoff relationship for each course of action and then selects the alternative that offers the maximum of the minimum risks.

The minimax criterion is also pessimistic in that the minimum alternative is selected from among a series of maximum seeking alternatives. In this situation, the maximum risk–payoff relationship for each course of action is identified. The alternative offering the minimum risk is then selected as the decision solution.

The most optimistic criterion under this grouping is to select the maximax course of events. Under the maximax outlook, alternatives are ranked similar to the minimax criteria. However, the alternative offering the highest payoff is selected with complete disregard to the associated risk.

The maximum–minimum associated criteria reflect the extremes of the decision-making perspective. In most material management appraisals, the appropriate decision criterion is found between the extremes of pessimistic or optimistic outlook.

HURWICZ CRITERION. The Hurwicz criterion makes use of an optimism-pessimism coefficient to incorporate the decision maker's feeling or appraisal of the likelihood of future events. To use this criterion, the decision maker must arrive at a measure of his degree of optimism and the potential payoff associated with alternative courses of action.

To guide the decision solution, a weighted average is calculated using the coefficient of optimism and the maximum and minimum payoffs associated with each alternative. The decision solution is based on the highest of the weighted averages.

To illustrate, assume on a scale of .01 to 1.0 that the decision maker feels his knowledge of the situation leads him to be slightly optimistic with a coefficient of optimism of 0.6. Table 3-9 illustrates the maximum and minimum payoff associated with three different courses of action.

Using the Hurwicz criterion, the decision maker uses the following mathematical procedure to evaluate each alternative:

1. Multiply the maximum payoff by the coefficient of optimism.
2. Multiply the minimum payoff by 1 minus the coefficient of optimism.
3. Add the two products together to rank the alternatives.

The result of ranking is illuatrated in Table 3-9. Using this criterion, the decision solution selected would be the second course of action.

TABLE 3-9
Example Hurwicz Criteria

| | Product | | Ranking |
Alternative	Maximum	Minimum	Product
1	$10,000	$6,000	$8,400
2	20,000	4,000	13,600
3	8,000	7,000	7,600

EXPECTED VALUE CRITERION. The expected value criterion was introduced earlier in the discussion of the make or buy decision. Using this criterion, a probability or measure of the likelihood of events is directly assigned to each possible outcome. This probability is then multiplied by the expected payoff to rank alternatives on the basis of the weighted value of each option. The fundamental difference of expected value and the Hurwicz criterion is that the best estimate of attainment is applied directly to the best estimate of accomplishment.

The main strength of using a criterion is that it provides a systematic method for reviewing alternatives that can be consistently applied. Judgment is integral to the use of all criteria in terms of the determination of payoffs and the likelihood of attainment. The benefit gained by use of a decision criteria scheme is consistency.

Decision Trees

Another approach to assisting the selection process is the use of decision trees. In most complex situations, a number of different options are confronted as a result of any initial decision. Formulation of an over-all plan requires evaluation of a total course of action. Initial probabilities and payoffs must be appraised followed by the conditional additional probabilities associated with each subsequent course of action. The decision tree enables the manager to assess a relatively complex situation systematically.

Decision trees consist of three parts: (1) the initial decision point, (2) the paths, and (3) the branches. The whole tree represents the decision problem. The paths, which may consist of several branches, represent the various probabilities and events of a particular outcome. The branches represent various outcomes. Each set of decisions has one outcome and an associated probability.

To illustrate, assume that a material manager is concerned with the likelihood of a strike and the associated possibility of a price increase. To assist in formulation of a strategy, it is necessary to estimate the initial probability of a strike occurring. Next, an estimated cost must be determined for fulfillment of the material plan with and without a strike as well as with or without a subsequent price increase.

The probability of a strike is estimated to be 0.6. The conditional probability of a price increase is judged to be 0.7 if a strike occurs and 0.8 if it does not. However, a price increase following the strike would be greater than if it is granted without a strike. Under each set of conditional probabilities, the cost of material management operations has to be calculated in terms of net profit impact. In other words, any loss of product sale caused by failure to maintain supply continuity has been taken into consideration in arriving at the estimated net profit of each event. The decision structure is presented in Figure 3-4.

FIGURE 3-4
Decision Tree Structure

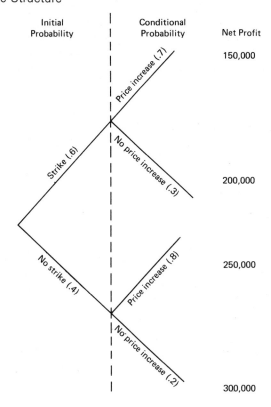

| Initial Probability | | Conditional Probability | Net Profit |

Price increase (.7) — 150,000

Strike (.6)

No price increase (.3) — 200,000

No strike (.4)

Price increase (.8) — 250,000

No price increase (.2) — 300,000

Table 3-10 provides the end product of the various events and the expected profit impact. Under the best estimate of probable future events and the impact of each upon expected profit, the most desirable course of action is for the material manager to take a chance that the strike will not occur but that a price increase will. Taking into consideration all associated costs and potential loss of revenue, the odds favor taking the risk that a strike will be postponed.

TABLE 3-10
Decision Tree Results

Event	Joint Probability	Expected Profit Value
Strike–increase	0.42	63,000
Strike–no increase	0.18	36,000
No strike–increase	0.32	80,000
No strike–no increase	0.08	24,000

The decision tree structure and problem illustrated are relatively simple in comparison to those which might result in an actual planning situation. Similar to all decision aids, the value of the decision tree is directly related to the correct assignment of probabilities, which is sometimes very difficult. For example, if the probability of a strike had been judged to be 0.7, the recommended course of action would have been to take the appropriate action necessary to continue to produce during the strike followed by a price increase. Under this set of circumstances, the cost of protection in comparison to the revenue gained from continued operation would have justified stockpiling the material. It is apparent that various procedures available to assist the decision process do not substitute for managerial judgment. Their main benefit is that they force a logical and consistent review of the facts.

Summary

The objective of Chapter 3 was to introduce the range of responsibilities included in material management. The primary purpose of the material management logistical subsystem is to provide an orderly and economical flow of materials and parts into the manufacturing complex.

The focal point of material management operations is the procurement of the materials and parts as specified in the material plan. The plan specifies when and where materials and parts will be required. The material management task is to satisfy economically the requirements of the plan. This involves the simultaneous attainment of the following six interrelated objectives: (1) best price procurement, (2) supply continuity, (3) quality maintenance, (4) low logistical acquisition cost, (5) research and development assistance, and (6) maintaining supplier relations.

The material cycle provides a useful way to view the distinct activities performed by material management. While several differences exist between the marketing channel structure of physical distribution and material management, the fulfillment of procurement requirements necessitates full use of the components of the logistical system. The activities identified as integral parts of the material cycle were (1) sourcing, (2) order placement and expediting, (3) transportation, and (4) receiving and inspection. Once the materials or parts procured are in the possession of the enterprise, warehousing, inventory control, and material movement are required to balance their flow into the manufacturing complex.

A major variable confronted in material management that is unique within the logistical system is the need to take a positive stand with respect to future probabilities of price changes or supply disruptions. In the final section of the chapter, attention was directed to the use of decision criteria and techniques to assist in logical and consistent evaluation of alternative courses of action.

In total, the chapter introduced the special circumstances surrounding the material management logistical subsystem. The next chapter is directed to logistical coordination and the elaboration of the product replenishment logistical subsystem.

Questions

1. In what major way does the design of a material management system confront uncertainty?
2. Define the role of the material plan in the formulation of a material management system.
3. What is meant by best price procurement?
4. Discuss the role of logistical cost in the acquisition of raw material and component parts.
5. Describe the similarities and differences between the material cycle and the customer-order-processing cycle.
6. Why would a firm under certain circumstances elect to purchase a component part even though it could manufacture it more economically?
7. What are the limitations of using expected value to help formulate make or buy decisions?
8. Discuss the role of expediting in the material cycle.
9. In utilization of queuing analysis, why are arrivals typically expressed in the form of Poisson distribution, whereas servicing is an exponential distribution?
10. Discuss the impact of single versus multiple receiving channels upon the queuing solution.
11. Why is it beneficial and safe to use sampling in the inspection procedure related to quality control?
12. What are the major limitations in using either the Hurwicz criterion or any other maximum/minimum criteria? To what extent is this overcome by the use of decision trees?

4

Logistical Coordination

Logistical coordination is concerned with the establishment of requirements and specifications that integrate a firm's physical distribution and material management operations. Material management has the primary objective of maintaining an orderly and economical flow of raw materials and externally purchased component parts into the manufacturing complex. Physical distribution operations are concerned with customer order processing and delivery. Between physical distribution and material management, substantially different operational requirements exist. The function of logistical coordination is to reconcile these differentials to the maximum benefit of the enterprise.

Unlike either physical distribution or material management, logistical coordination constitutes a combination of corporate planning and operational matters. The planning functions consist of *forecasting, production scheduling,* and *material planning.* The operational aspect of logistical coordination, called *product replenishment,* involves the movement of semifinished goods between stages of manufacturing and finished inventory to and between warehouses utilized by the enterprise. Thus the operational aspects of logistical coordination involve internal inventory replenishment.

In situations wherein a firm performs substantial operations in both physical

100

distribution and material management, there is little doubt that a high degree of coordination is desirable. The managerial functions that can be orientated to realize effective coordination are most often currently performed within a typical enterprise. Therefore, improved logistical coordination does not require the creation or formation of new managerial functions. Rather, a number of existing functions must be performed with their impact upon logistical cost and performance foremost in mind. The development of a clear perspective of the importance of coordination is the primary purpose of this chapter.

The initial section of the chapter develops the reasons why logistical coordination is singled out for special consideration. The next three sections cover the planning aspects of logistical coordination. The final section discusses product replenishment. Product replenishment is discussed and analytical techniques available to assist management in allocation are illustrated.

The Logistical Coordination Function

As noted in the historical review of business logistics, initial development in the over-all field was characterized by independent emphasis on physical distribution and material management.[1] This specialization was in part justified on the basis of immediate improvements that could be realized in each separate operating area. The application of total cost and systems technology in each limited area provided a more workable arena for initial improvements.

Specialization of physical distribution and material management within a single enterprise creates a gray area in control between the flow of material to manufacturing plants and the flow of finished production to customers. The purpose of logistical coordination is to reconcile this gray area.

The most significant coordination problem deals with over-all logistical performance of the enterprise. From the viewpoint of marketing, products must be consistently available from manufacturing sources in order to provide high levels of customer service. The level of product availability in turn depends upon decisions made with respect to production scheduling and the capability to procure the required materials. A second aspect of performance results from initial allocation of products from manufacturing plants to field warehouses. If allocation is not properly performed, adequate inventory may exist within the ownership of the firm; however, it may be located a substantial distance from where it is required by a customer. The key to coordinating logistical performance is to base all interrelated activities on the same forecast.

Significant coordination requirements also exist between the level of expenditure required to perform the logistical activities of physical distribution and material management. First, if these two aspects of logistics are totally independent, a duplication of facilities that otherwise might well be combined

[1] Page 7.

can result. Second, if the two areas are independent, the potential to aggregate transportation movements to realize lower rates as well as the benefit of potential backhauls may be overlooked. Finally, independence from the viewpoint of facility location can result in a network of manufacturing plants or warehouses that is efficient for one or the other parts of the logistical structure but highly inefficient for the two combined. In final analysis, the proper locational network of fixed facilities is the one that results in the lowest total enterprise logistical cost. It is important to keep in mind that the only valid perspective for logistical integration is the total enterprise.

Logistical coordination is realized by the performance of four functions. As noted earlier, three of the coordination functions have a planning orientation. The fourth is operational.

The first planning function of logistical coordination is forecasting. Since all business plans must be formulated within an uncertain environment, it is necessary to arrive at a common set of expectations concerning the level of future business activity and the anticipated sales performance of individual products. All activities that the enterprise performs in advance of actual transactions, including physical distribution and material management, should properly be guided by common expectation.

Based upon the forecast, the short-term production capability of the firm is committed to a specific level and combination of performance in the form of production schedule. Depending upon the nature of the particular business, the production schedule, once formulated, may have various degrees of flexibility. Regardless of the speed with which a production schedule may be modified, its initial influence is felt by both physical distribution and material management operations.

The impact of the production schedule upon material management is coordinated by the formulation of the material plan. The material plan is a time-sequenced specification of the raw materials and components that will be required to support the production schedule. The responsibility of material management is to procure and make available the required manufacturing input so as not to cause disruption in the planned production.

From the viewpoint of physical distribution management, the production schedule determines which products will be manufactured and when they will be available. The direct relationship between logistical coordination and physical distribution is the method employed in initial product allocation. Unless products are properly allocated when they are initially produced, substantial disruptions in physical distribution performance may result and thus create a subsequent need for reallocation.

The coordination tasks of forecasting, production scheduling, and material planning do not in themselves constitute operational matters. Rather, they establish operational expectations and specifications that are characteristic of planning. In contrast, replenishment is directly operational. As noted earlier, replenishment is concerned with the movement of semifinished goods between stages of manufacturing and finished inventory to and between warehouses operated by the enterprise. In this sense the firm is viewed as having three distinct performance areas, which combine to form the over-all logistical operation.

This viewpoint concerning the identification of replenishment as a distinct operating area is a relatively new concept in logistical management. The justification is that physical distribution and material management, as well as replenishment logistical subsystems, should be designed within a particular set of objectives and constraints. Therefore, to realize maximum benefits the deployment of logistical system components within each performance area should vary within a single enterprise. Although it is desirable to standardize as much as practical, each performance area requires specialized treatment because each faces a different assignment. The logistical coordination functions concerned with planning integrate the three performance areas into an over-all logistical system.

In logistical organizations in which prime emphasis is placed on physical distribution and material management, considerable risk exists that selected aspects of replenishment will be neglected. If not neglected, this aspect of logistical performance may be handled in part by physical distribution and material management, with the net result that an opportunity for specialization is overlooked in logistical system design.

The area of replenishment has one major difference in comparison with either physical distribution or material management. The replenishment performance area is captive to the enterprise, whereas the other two performance areas must deal with the uncertainty of external sources and customers. Therefore, in comparison, a differential of greater over-all control is enjoyed in the replenishment area. The maximum exploration of this control is the prime justification for a separation of replenishment from the other logistical performance areas. When forecasting, product scheduling, and material planning are combined with replenishment to form an over-all logistical coordination area, maximum opportunity exists to integrate over-all logistical performance.

Forecasting

The fundamental input to planning and coordinating logistical operations is a forecast of customer demand. The demand forecast provides the linkage between the enterprise and its environment. The desired result of forecasting is a common set of expectations concerning level of future business activity and the anticipated sales performance of individual products. To be useful in logistical coordination, the over-all demand forecast must be detailed to the individual product level.

Two basic procedures are available to arrive at product level demand. First, an over-all forecast of demand can be completed and geographically distributed to market areas. Once aggregate demand is segmented on a geographic basis, it can be broken down to product detail using historical records, salesmen's estimates, and other available information about specific markets. The end result is a formal statement of individual product sales expectations by market areas. When all product market estimates are aggregated, they reconcile to the initial over-all demand forecast.

A second approach is to apply forecasting techniques directly to the market area in an effort to generate product level demand. From this procedure, the over-all forecast of the corporation is realized by aggregation of individual product market estimates.

Logistical coordination requires as accurate an estimate of individual product–market demand as possible. Although forecasting is far from an exact science, it is becoming more and more common for firms to utilize mathematical and statistical forecasting techniques. Forecasts will vary, depending upon the planned use, time period covered, and level of detail.

The purpose of the forecast techniques discussed in this section is to generate expectations concerning future demand to be placed upon the combined physical distribution, replenishment, and material management operations. Therefore, only techniques capable of individual product demand estimates are discussed. Such techniques are mathematical and statistical. The term *forecast* is used exclusively to refer to these formal procedures for estimating future demand. All other methods of arriving at estimates concerning future demand are referred to as *predictions*.

The time horizon projected in logistical operational forecasts is normally 1 year or less. Depending upon the plan's intended use, forecasts may be required on a daily, weekly, monthly, quarterly, semiannual, or annual basis. A recent survey of 161 companies revealed that the most popular forecast period is 1 month.[2] While the forecast time period will vary from firm to firm, the important requirement is that the basic planning horizon should be selected to accommodate production scheduling and material procurement.

Finally, concerning level of detail, the purpose of the forecast is to develop an estimate of product requirements in individual markets. In the formulation of the production schedule and material procurement plan, the detail of components and raw materials required can be determined based on product demand estimates. Thus no level of detail below product-market forecast is required.

For purposes of presenting two commonly used mathematical–statistical forecast techniques, the simplifying assumption is made that a single product is being forecasted in a single market. In actual practice, several thousand different forecasts may be required to get a fix on over-all demand. The two techniques reviewed are (1) regression analysis and (2) mathematical smoothing.[3]

---

[2] *Sales Forecasting Practices: An Appraisal*, Experiences in Marketing Management 25 (New York: National Industrial Conference Board, 1970), p. 23.

[3] Emphasis in the following discussion is placed upon per unit sales forecasting. For illustration purposes, emphasis is limited to two techniques. For a comprehensive review of forecasting alternatives, see Fred Morgan, *A Simulated Sales Forecasting Model: A Build-up Approach* (unpublished doctoral dissertation, Michigan State University, 1972), Chaps. 2 and 3.

Regression Analysis

The technique of forecasting by regression analysis consists of estimating the sales of an individual product based upon information on one or more other factors. If the product forecast is based upon a single factor, it is referred to as simple regression analysis. The use of more than one forecast factor is referred to as multiple regression.

The use of regression simply means that the forecast of future sales is based upon a correlation of one event to another. In fact, no cause–effect relationship need exist between the product's sale and the independent event if a high degree of correlation is consistently present. However, the most reliable use of regression forecasting of sales is based on a cause–effect relationship.

Because multiple regression constitutes a major section of all business statistic textbooks, the present treatment is limited to the logic of regression forecasting. The reader not familiar with the technique should work through an example from a basic source.

The initial step in a regression-based forecast is to accumulate past sales history for the product to be forecasted. Given a reasonable sales history, the average monthly sales and standard deviation of sales around the average should be calculated to determine the general distribution of historical sales. A typical pattern of monthly sales is illustrated in Figure 4-1.

The mean or average monthly sale is determined by the formula

$$\bar{x} = \frac{\sum\limits_{i=1}^{n} s_i}{N},$$

FIGURE 4-1
Example of Monthly Unit Sales

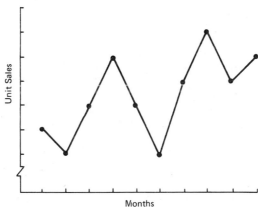

where

    $\bar{x}$ = average sales.

    s = monthly sales.

    i = sales of individual months for $1 \cdots n$.

    n = total number of months of data available.

The standard deviation formula is

$$\sigma = \frac{i\sqrt{\sum fd^2}}{n}$$

where

    σ = standard deviation.

    i = size of class interval (which is constantly 1 month in this example).

    f = frequency of event.

    d = deviation of events from mean [which is equal to $(S_i - \bar{S})^2$].

    n = total number of months of data available.

Once the average monthly sales and standard deviation are determined, it is possible to evaluate the degree of dispersion or likelihood that future months' sales will be nearly equal to previous months' sales. If the standard deviation is small, then it may be possible to make a forecast based upon average sales. If the deviation is large, some other method of forecasting must be determined.

The assumption in regression forecasting is that monthly sales can be correlated to another factor, which will result in a forecast with a smaller standard deviation than the prediction obtained using standard distribution probability.

The second step is to collect data concerning the independent factor that there is reason to believe will provide a better forecast. Assume for purposes of illustration that the objective is to forecast aviation propeller replacement sales. There is reason to believe that a positive correlation exists between total hours flown by private aviation in previous months and future months' propeller replacement sales. To test this assumption, historical data should be collected on private aviation hours flown and an attempt made to establish a correlation relationship. The independent data must be lagged to accommodate the time interval between the cause-and-effect relationship. Assume that the appropriate time lag is 3 months.

The third step, once the data on private aviation are collected, is to plot the results in the form of a scatter diagram. Although it is not necessary to develop a scatter diagram, it is easier to observe the likelihood of a positive correlation from such a display. Figure 4-2 provides an example wherein monthly total hours flown by private aviation lagged 3 months is the independent variable and monthly propeller sales is the dependent variable.

The fourth step is to fit the solid line displayed on Figure 4-2 to the data plotted in the scatter diagram. The assumption is made that a linear relationship exists; therefore, the regression line is established by the formula

$$S = a + bx,$$

where

s = predicted value of propeller sales associated with total monthly hours flown.

x = monthly hours flown.

a, b = coefficients of the regression equation.

Fitting the regression line resolves to finding the values for a and b that will minimize the sum of the squared deviations. Once the relationship of monthly sales and flying hours is determined, the regression line can be fitted, and a 3-month forecast of the expected sales is obtained.

FIGURE 4-2
Scatter Diagram for Regression Forecasting

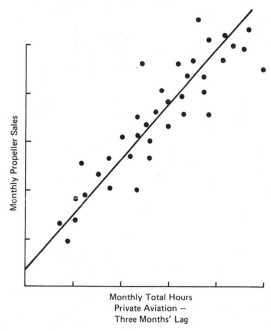

Monthly Total Hours
Private Aviation —
Three Months' Lag

A final step in regression forecasting is to determine if a reduction in standard deviation has resulted from the use of regression analysis as opposed to the use of a moving average based on probability distribution. This will help appraise the net gain realized from the attempt to correlate sales to an independent event.

The strength of the relationship between the dependent variable (sales) and the independent variable (flying hours) can be estimated by measuring the coefficient of correlation. The coefficient of correlation between two variables is determined by the formula

$$r = \frac{n \sum_i x_i y_i - \sum_i x_i \sum_i y_i}{\sqrt{\left\{n \sum_i x_i^2 - (\sum_i x_i)^2\right\}\left\{n \sum_i y_i^2 - (\sum_i y_i)^2\right\}}}$$

where

$r =$ coefficient of correlation.

$x_i =$ independent variable

$y_i =$ dependent variable (formerly noted as s; changed to y to conform to standard notation).

Correlation is measured by the regressive-line fit between the independent variable and the dependent variable. The closer the value of the coefficient of correlation to $+1$, the higher the correlation.

It is generally recognized that several assumptions underlie the use of regressive analysis for forecasting.[4] The most significant are

1. The basic relationships of x and y are strictly linear.
2. The regression error is randomly distributed.
3. The values of y are independent and express no autocorrelation.

In numerous situations, the use of regression analysis provides an adequate method for forecasting product sales. However, it is subject to seasonal effects that could dilute the direct value of the forecast. Finally, the most serious limitation is that it may not be possible to isolate a cause–effect relationship that has an acceptable coefficient of correlation. At best, using multiple regression for a broad number of product forecasts in numerous markets could be a cumbersome task.

Mathematical Smoothing

A method of short-term product forecasting that is highly adaptable to computerized processing is mathematical smoothing. The most commonly known technique in this class is exponential smoothing. However, second- and

[4] For an expanded discussion, see M. Hamburg, *Statistical Analysis for Decision Making* (New York: Harcourt Brace Jovanovich, 1970), p. 540.

third-order smoothing as well as adaptive smoothing techniques are available as modifications to the basic procedure.

MOVING AVERAGES.   The basic concept of exponential smoothing was derived as an improvement over forecasting on the basis of a moving average. In the previous section the notion of average sales and standard deviation around the average was introduced. If the standard deviation is large, the average cannot be relied upon to make useful forecasts. The use of a moving average bases the forecast upon an average of sales for a recent number of time periods. Each time a new set of data becomes available, it is used to replace the oldest set of data, keeping the number of time periods constant.

Thus the concept of a moving average can be expressed as

$$\bar{X}_M = \frac{\sum\limits_{n=1}^{n} st_i}{n},$$

where

$\bar{X}_M$ = moving average.

st = sales per time period; time periods are identified by the appropriate subscript.

n = total number of time periods.

Although a moving average is easy to determine, it has several obvious limitations. The most significant are that it relies upon an average of change to forecast, it is unresponsive or sluggish to change, and finally a great many historical data must be maintained and updated to calculate forecasts.

To partially overcome these deficiencies, weighted moving averages have been introduced as refinements. Basic exponential smoothing represents a form of weighted moving average.

EXPONENTIAL SMOOTHING.[5]   Exponential smoothing bases the estimate of future sales on the basis of the accuracy of the previous sales estimate. The new forecast is a function of the old forecast incremented by some fraction of the differential between the old forecast and actual sales realized. The increment of adjustment is called the alpha factor (α). The basic format of the model is

$$F(t) = F(t-1) + \alpha[D(t-1) - F(t-1)],$$

[5] This section draws heavily upon Robert G. Brown, *Statistical Forecasting for Inventory Control* (New York: McGraw-Hill Book Company, 1959), and W. A. Spurr and C. P. Bonini, *Statistical Analysis for Business* (Homewood, Ill.: Richard D. Irwin, Inc., 1967).

where

F = forecasted sales for a time period.

t = forecast time period of constant duration.

D = Most recent demand.

α = alpha factor.

To illustrate, assume that the forecasted sales for the most recent time period were 100 units and actual sales experienced were 110 units. Further assume that the alpha factor being employed is 0.7. Then, substituting,

$$F(t) = F(t - 1) + \alpha[D(t - 1) - F(t - 1)]$$
$$= 100 + 0.7(110 - 100)$$
$$= 107.$$

Thus the new forecast is for a product sales volume of 107 units.

The prime benefit of exponential smoothing is that it permits a rapid calculation of a new forecast without substantial historical records and updating. Thus exponential smoothing is highly adaptable to computerized forecasting.

The essential ingredient in using exponential smoothing is to determine the value assigned to the alpha factor. If a factor of 1 is employed, the net effect is to assume the most recent demand as the forecast of expected demand. A very low value, for example, 0.1, would have the net effect of reducing the forecast to almost a simple moving average. Thus high-alpha factors make the forecast very sensitive to change and therefore highly reactive. Low-alpha factors tend to react slowly to change and therefore provide sluggish or delayed reaction.

SMOOTHING ADAPTATIONS.   The determination of the proper alpha factor is critical; thus several variations on the basic exponential technique have been developed to assist management. Three such adaptations are briefly discussed.

Second-order smoothing includes an estimate of trend into the determination of the new forecast. The third-order modification further increases the sensitivity of the basic technique by including a measure of trend acceleration. Both of these modifications assist in increasing the usefulness of the technique in seasonal sales periods.[6]

Adaptive smoothing is a basic modification that encompasses a regular review of the validity of the alpha factor. The value of the smoothing constant is frequently reviewed after the fact to determine the exact alpha value that would have resulted in a perfect forecast. Once determined, the alpha factor currently in use is replaced by the one that would have produced an accurate forecast. Thus the managerial judgment element of determining an alpha factor is replaced by a systematic and consistent method of updating.

[6] Morgan, *op. cit.*, pp. 66–68.

Production Scheduling

The demand forecast has a number of uses within an enterprise. However, from the viewpoint of logistical coordination, the forecast is important for production scheduling and product replenishment. This section discusses production scheduling.

The sales forecast of individual products formulates the basic manufacturing assignment. The scheduling problem is to determine the products to be produced, how much of each to produce, and in what time interval or sequence to assure availability at the lowest possible unit production cost.

Logistical coordination and manufacturing organizations both have a major interest in production scheduling. The appropriate demarcation of responsibility is between what and how much will be produced, not how or where it will be manufactured. Logistical coordination is concerned with what and how much will be produced within a given time period and the time sequence of its availability. Manufacturing is concerned with where and the actual way in which a product is produced. The degree of logistical coordination involved in production scheduling is to select among the manufacturing options that combination of activities that will satisfy forecast requirements.

Master Production Plan

The master production plan is a long-term statement of the manufacturing capabilities of an enterprise. The plan is based upon an audit of manufacturing capabilities of each production plant. Two basic types of manufacturing process are widely employed.

The first is the job shop, in which the manufacturing function is spread across a number of work stations. Each work station performs a specific task in the production operation, such as stamping or machining, and each passes the product or component to the next work station. Under job shop processing, the flow of work does not uniformly proceed through successive stages, because of the variable time required to complete each process. Therefore, specific work stations may perform similar processes on a number of different products or components while others may be limited to processing a single item.

The second type of manufacturing process is a product line orientation. Under this arrangement all functions required to manufacture a product are performed in sequence. Although the assembly line is primarily a product line manufacturing process, this type of production is characteristic of all processes in which several manufacturing stages are continuous.

From the viewpoint of the master production plan, the job shop provides the greatest flexibility since it is not linked to a specific product. Therefore, with a reasonable lead time a variety of different products can be produced by a job shop. The degree of flexibility will vary between different job shops. Some have the capability of adapting on a per job basis. Others must complete at least sufficient processing once a station is activated to realize the economy of scale to which the machinery was designed and to spread the tooling cost.

The product line manufacturing process has limited flexibility since it is orientated around producing a specific product at a continuous, high-volume rate. Many product line facilities produce on a 24-hour, 7-day per week basis and possess no flexibility with respect to the product produced. Large paper-processing plants are prime examples of this category of manufacturing.

Thus, whereas the job shop can be regulated on the basis of anticipated product order, the product line process is committed to a volume orientation. Naturally, many variations exist wherein the features of these two basic processes are combined to achieve a balance between flexibility and economy. One way of combining the two basic methods of production is to use the maximum number of similar components in a variety of different end products. In this manner, maximum economy of scale can be retained with flexibility and be retained in highly adaptive assembly operations. Another technique is to postpone painting, accessory addition, and other more or less superficial aspects of production to the final stage of the manufacturing process.

No matter what type of manufacturing complex a firm has, it is considered fixed in terms of the master production plan. The plan provides a statement of manufacturing capabilities that can be adapted to the short-run requirements of sales forecasts. In particular, the master production plan should include but is not limited to

1. Identification of which products can be produced at specific plants.
2. A statement of the lead time required to provide production of a specific product.
3. A statement of the quantity of production that constitutes the economic lot size of production once a given product is placed into production.
4. A statement of the relative cost and desirability of producing a specific product at alternative manufacturing plants (when it is capable of being produced at more than one).

The complexity of the master plan will vary greatly, depending upon the complexity of the enterprise. In general, the more complex the manufacturing process, the more rigid the plan will be. In situations where a number of different job shops are linked together with product line assembly plants in a multi-echeloned network production sequence, it may not be possible, because of lead-time requirements, to switch over product assignments in a shorter time period than several months.

Development of the production plan, as well as the execution of a given production schedule, is the responsibility of manufacturing. Developing a schedule constitutes the involvement of logistical coordination.

Short-Term Scheduling

The master production plan provides the framework within which logistical coordination develops the production schedule. To the degree that flexibility exists in when and where a product can be produced, it is the function of scheduling to make specific manufacturing assignments.

Short-term schedules are adapted from the sales forecast in a manner that makes maximum utilization of the available manufacturing flexibility. The analysis of what particular product mix should be produced during a scheduling period depends upon available inventory or back orders, raw material procurement lead times, seasonality, and relative profitability among manufacturing alternatives.

A number of manual and mathematical techniques are available to assist in the formulation of a production schedule. The most widely used technique is linear programming. This technique is discussed and illustrated in a later section of this chapter which deals with product replenishment.

Even under extremely flexible scheduling conditions, it may require as much as 90 days lead time before a product will commence to flow from the manufacturing plants. Thus the scheduling process is continuously under revision as requirement appraisals are completed.

The primary purpose of including production scheduling as a logistical coordination function is that it is the logical outgrowth of forecasting and the prime determinant of procurement requirements. A concept of integrated logistical coordination provides the best corporate vantage point in terms of information and interrelated planning and operational activities to develop meaningful production schedules.

Material Planning

The third logistical coordination planning function is concerned with the establishment of raw material and parts requirements. The actual procurement activity is a part of the material management aspect of logistical operations. The coordination function is concerned with projecting material requirements in terms of quantity and timing. Material management is responsible for procuring the specified requirements when needed at the lowest possible total cost. Since purchasing was discussed in detail in Chapter 3, only a brief introduction into the material plan is necessary at this point.

Once the forecast is converted into a production schedule, a determination of raw material and component requirements is necessary. One method available to arrive at a statement of material requirements is to forecast directly. However, a technique that is growing in popularity is the use of a computer to explode in detail the specification of products contained in production schedule. Explosion consists of an identification of the aggregate quantity of materials and parts that will be required to produce the products scheduled to be manufactured. Since one of the ingredients that goes into the formulation of the production schedule is the procurement lead time, the results of the explosion analysis can be ranked on the basis of recommended purchasing sequence.

The combined planning functions of logistical coordination provide an orderly unification of logistics with the other major operational areas of an enterprise. Forecasting relates to marketing and provides the input for the production schedule. The production schedule coordinates the manufacturing operation and provides the input for development of a material requirement plan. The material plan in turn establishes specifications for the procurement aspects of material management.

As indicated earlier, in addition to the three planning functions of logistical coordination, one operational area is also necessary to realize integrated logistical performance. The operational area is product replenishment, which is discussed in the next section.

Product Replenishment

The aspects of coordination concerned with product replenishment engage all operational components of the logistical system. Thus transportation, warehousing, communication, inventory, and material handling constitute components of the product replenishment system. Similar to physical distribution and material management areas of logistics, product replenishment systems are expected to provide a level of service at the associated lowest total cost.

The product replenishment system initiates operational control over components, semifinished products, and finished products when they are released from manufacturing. The purpose of this phase of logistical coordination is to control the movements and storage of components and semifinished goods between stages of manufacturing and finished inventory to and between warehouses utilized by the enterprise. As such, product replenishment serves as a safety valve between all manufacturing plants and field inventories. In Chapter 6, the decoupling function of inventory will be introduced and discussed. At this point it should be noted that the decoupling benefit is achieved by the product replenishment system.

In sequence, material management feeds manufacturing raw materials and semifinished components when and where needed. Once the manufacturing operation is initiated and subsequent interplant movement of materials or semifinished products is required, such handling is performed by product replenishment. Product replenishment does not engage in manufacturing materials handling. Rather, replenishment operations are restricted to dock-to-dock movement and any intermediate storage required. When production is completed, product replenishment arranges for initial allocation of inventory to the warehouses that service customer orders. Unless inventory is subsequently shuffled between warehouses, the product replenishment task is completed when inventory is turned over to physical distribution operations.

In a multiplant manufacturing firm, the product replenishment system will constitute a vast network. To the extent that a number of different manufacturing plants participate in various stages of production and fabrication leading to final production, numerous handlings and transfers will be required prior to final product availability. In terms of finished inventory allocation, products may flow directly from manufacturing plants to field warehouses or they may be funneled through a series of intermediate warehouses for purposes of accumulating product assortments. Thus the complexity of the product replenishment system may far exceed that of either the physical distribution or material management subsystems.

As noted earlier, the product replenishment system has one major difference in contrast to either physical distribution or material management. Product replenishment operations are limited to movements within and under the control of the enterprise structure. Therefore, in conducting replenishment activities, the uncertainties introduced by random order entry and erratic vendor performance are removed from operational planning, which permits more optimal allocation.

The remaining portions of this section discuss three aspects of product replenishment operations. The first deals with allocation of products to warehouses under conditions of multiple manufacturing plants and when adequate supply is available. The others are concerned with the allocation of short supply and cross supply.

Product Allocation: Adequate Supply

The general nature of allocation problems is that the decision maker is certain about the conditions under which he must derive an operational assignment. Although a number of limitations and restrictions may exist, the objective of allocation is to determine the optimal course of action when taking all important factors into consideration.

One method for solving the allocation problem frequently confronted in product replenishment is *linear programming*. In a technical sense, linear programming is a method of allocation to optimize a given task. The method subjects the desired end result to whatever constraints exist and provides a process for selecting the most desirable course of action from among a number of available options.

In order for a problem to be solved using linear programming, several conditions are necessary. First, choice must exist in that two or more activities must be competing for limited resources. Second, all pertinent relationships in the problem must be precisely linear or capable of linear approximation.[7] Unless these conditions are satisfied, a solution derived from linear programming will not be valid.

Many procedures have been developed to solve allocation problems. Some

[7] For more detailed discussion of linear programming, see Ross A. Beaumont, *Linear Algebra* (New York: Harcourt Brace Jovanovich, 1965); George B. Dantzig, *Linear Programming and Extensions* (Princeton, N.J.: Princeton University Press, 1963); G. Hadley, *Linear Programming* (Reading, Mass.: Addison-Wesley Publishing Company, Inc., 1962); Nyles V. Reinfield and William R. Vogel, *Mathematical Programming* (Englewood Cliffs, N.J.: Prentice-Hall, Inc., 1958); or Robert Dortman, Paul A. Samuelson, and Robert M. Solow, *Linear Programming and Economic Analysis* (New York: The Ronald Press Company 1957).

are more useful or are easier to apply to specific problems than others. The general types of linear procedures will be briefly reviewed and then one will be illustrated to arrive at a product allocation solution.

The *algebraic technique* is similar to any method used to solve for a number of equalities with a number of unknowns. However, in allocation, since there are fewer equalities than unknowns, there are many possible solutions. The problem is to identify the optimum solution. The answer can be determined algebraically; however, it becomes difficult when a large number of variables are involved.

The next method is probably the easiest to understand, yet undoubtedly is the most restrictive. The *graphic method*, as its name implies, involves graphing the objective function and all constraints in order to determine the optimal point on the graph. The values are merely read from the graph and the optimal answer is obtained. With two variables, this method works well. With three variables, the problem is more difficult unless one is skilled at drawing in three dimensions. When the problem involves four or more variables, the graphic method does not present a possible means of solution.

The method presented to illustrate solving an allocation problem is the *transportation method*. This method is designed to optimize or maximize a single function that is referred to as the objective function. Even though it derives its name from its early use in transportation scheduling, the basic method is applicable to other situations. The transportation method is easier than the *simplex method*, which follows, because it does not involve the development and manipulation of equations.

The final linear programming procedure is the *simplex algorithm*. It is an iterative method of solving problems by finding successive feasible solutions and testing them for optimality. The simplex method is the most general of the algorithms in that it can either maximize or minimize an objective function that contains any finite number of variables. An additional point regarding the simplex method is the relative ease with which it can be programmed for computer processing.[8]

PROBLEM STRUCTURE.   The general structure of the allocation problem is that a given number of manufacturing plants and warehouses exist in a network and the cost of shipping a product from each plant to each warehouse is known. The problem is to select those assignments that will minimize shipping cost and satisfy the demand requirements of each warehouse.

To solve the problem using the transportation procedure, the following data are required:

1. The capacities of each manufacturing plant.
2. The requirements of each warehouse.
3. The product transport cost per unit from each manufacturing plant to each warehouse.

[8] Hadley, *ibid.*

The only general restriction beyond certainty and linear relationships is that a one-for-one substitution must be possible when using the transportation method. For example, if it is decided not to ship 100 units of a product from a specific plant to a specific warehouse, it must be possible to substitute a similar number of units from a different plant.

The structure of the example is that three plants located in New York, Chicago, and Los Angeles each produce the product in question. Shipments are made from the three plants to 10 warehouses located across the country.

PERTINENT DATA. Three types of data are required to operationalize the procedure. Tables 4-1, 4-2, and 4-3 present the data.

PROBLEM INITIALIZATION. The first step in the transportation method is to develop a matrix that arranges the supply, demand, and transportation cost data. However, this matrix must maintain a balance between supply and demand; so if supply does not equal demand, a dummy source or destination must be added to account for the difference. In the initial matrix, an "other" or dummy destination is added since the manufacturing capacity exceeds demand.

TABLE 4-1
Weekly Availability of Manufacturing at Each Plant

Plant Location	Manufacturing Schedule
New York	6,000
Chicago	3,500
Los Angeles	4,000
Total manufacturing (units per week)	13,500

Table 4-2
Requirements at Weekly Individual Warehouses

Warehouse	Unit Requirement
Boston	1,250
Pittsburgh	1,000
Washington, D.C.	1,500
Atlanta	1,000
Detroit	1,500
Dallas	1,250
Denver	750
Seattle	1,750
St. Louis	1,000
Miami	1,500
	12,500

TABLE 4-3
Transportation Cost from Each Plant to Each Warehouse in Ten Cities
(dollars per unit)

Plant Location	Boston	Pittsburgh	Washington	Atlanta	Detroit	Dallas	Denver	Seattle	St. Louis	Miami
New York	2	4	2	9	7	16	19	29	10	13
Chicago	10	5	7	7	3	9	10	21	3	14
Los Angeles	31	25	26	22	23	14	11	11	18	27

The transportation cost in the dummy column is zero since no product is actually shipped.

An initial solution is necessary to start the procedure. The initial solution can be determined in a number of manners, among which are (1) existing assignments, (2) present lowest cost solution found by inspection, (3) managerially preferred method, and (4) the northwest corner rule (NCR).[9] The NCR method is used in this example because it offers a systematic and logical method to arrive at an initial solution. The following procedures are used when implementing the NCR.

1. Begin in the upper left corner of the matrix and compare the demand of the column with the demand in the row. Place the smaller of these two values in that matrix location. If this fills the demand, move to the next location to the right and fill this demand, if possible. Continue this until the supply is exhausted for the row.
2. Moving to the next lower row, again compare the demand with the supply. Select the smaller of the two quantities and place in that location. Move to the next column or row and follow the same procedure.
3. After completing the second row, move to the third and fourth row, and so on, following steps 1 and 2.

Matrix I (see Table 4-4) is the cost matrix with the dummy column inserted. Since the transportation method is a maximizing procedure, transportation costs are expressed as negatives. If a negative value is used to express cost, a direct readout of the profit impact is possible. Matrix II shows the implementation of the NCR method.

Matrix II (see Table 4-5) represents a possible allocation but not necessarily the least-cost alternative. This matrix must now be evaluated for more economical alternatives. By analyzing each vacant square in the matrix, it can be determined if the least-cost solution has been found. If not, a better solution is possible by varying the shipping assignments within the established constraints.

SOLUTION PROCEDURE. To evaluate the matrix, the following steps are required.

1. Place a 0 in the margin of the first row. This is a row value. Now, for each *nonempty* location in that row, determine the column value by using the following equation:

$$\text{row value} + \text{column value} = \text{transportation cost}$$

or

$$\text{column value} = \text{transportation cost} - \text{row value.}$$

---

[9] Another approach to an initial solution is the Vogel approximation; see Reinfield and Vogel, *op. cit.*

TABLE 4-4
Matrix I: Cost Matrix with Dummy Column

| | | | | | *Warehouses* | | | | | | | |
Plants	Boston	Pittsburgh	Washington	Atlanta	Detroit	Dallas	Denver	Seattle	St. Louis	Miami	Other	Total Supply
New York	-2	-4	-2	-9	-7	-16	-19	-29	-10	-13	0	6,000
Chicago	-10	-5	-7	-7	-3	-9	-10	-21	-3	-14	0	3,500
Los Angeles	-31	-25	-26	-22	-23	-14	-11	-11	-18	-27	0	4,000
Weekly demand	1,250	1,000	1,500	1,000	1,500	1,250	750	1,750	1,000	1,500	1,000	13,500

TABLE 4-5
Matrix II: Initial Solution NCR Procedure

| | | | | | *Warehouses* | | | | | | | |
Plants	Boston	Pittsburgh	Washington	Atlanta	Detroit	Dallas	Denver	Seattle	St. Louis	Miami	Other	Total
New York	1,250 / -2	1,000 / -4	1,500 / -2	1,000 / -9	1,250 / -7	-16	-19	-29	-10	-13	0	6,000
Chicago	-10	-4	-5	-7	250 / -3	1,250 / -9	750 / -10	1,250 / -21	-3	-14	0	3,500
Los Angeles	-31	-25	-26	-22	-23	-14	-11	500 / -11	1,000 / -18	1,500 / -27	1,000	4,000
Total demand	1,250	1,000	1,500	1,000	1,500	1,250	750	1,750	1,000	1,500	100	

Place the column value in the margin of the column. The appropriate column should then be used to find the row value for another row and the process should be repeated until each row and column have a value. Only *nonempty* locations are used to find these values.

2. Now every vacant location is evaluated by means of the following equation:

$$\text{vacant value} = \text{row value} + \text{column value} - \text{transportation cost.}$$

This is done for all vacant locations and the value is put, in parentheses, in that location.

3. If all the values in parentheses are nonnegative, then the solution is optimal. However, if there are negative values, then a better solution exists. A better solution can be obtained by transferring units to the warehouse with the negative value, or the warehouse with the most negative value if there is more than one.

4. If units must be transferred, trace a path starting at the location that has the most negative value and put a plus $(+)$ in that location. Find another nonempty location in that column and place a minus $(-)$ in that location. Continue tracing a path until returning to the original row, alternatingly placing plus and minus in the *nonempty* locations. This process, in effect, is balancing the rows and columns so that units can be shifted to the desired location. Remember, all locations except the first one on this path must be *nonempty*, and all angles on the path must be right angles.

5. Review the path and find the warehouse with the smallest number of units and a minus in it. This is the number of units to transfer to the new warehouse. Transfer this number of units and balance the remainder of the matrix by adding or subtracting this value from the locations along the path as denoted by the sign. The number of nonvacant locations should at all times equal the number of rows plus the number of columns minus 1.

6. Return to step 1 and evaluate the new matrix.

SOLUTION EVALUATION.   Using the rules already given, the solution presented in matrix II can be evaluated for optimality. First, obtain row and column values using the nonempty locations. If a value of zero is arbitrarily assigned to R_1, then C_1 can be computed as follows:

$$C_1 = -z - 0 = -z,$$

where R_1 is row value for row one and C_1 is column value for column one.
    Additional column values can be identified in this method until column five is reached:

$$C_5 = -7 - R_1$$
$$= -7 - 0$$
$$= -7.$$

C_5 is now used to find R_2:

$$R_2 = \text{transportation cost} - C_5$$
$$= -3 - (-7)$$
$$= 4.$$

The value of R_2 is now placed in the margin and the process continues as before until all row and column values have been determined. Then each vacant location is evaluated with the formula

$$VV_{ij} = R_i + C_j - TC_{ij},$$

where

VV_{ij} = value to be put in the vacant location at the intersection of the ith row and jth column.

R_i = row value for row i.

C_j = column value for column j.

TC_{ij} = cost (negative) of sending one unit from warehouse i to wholesaler j.

To illustrate for the location designating New York to Miami, the calculation is as follows.

$$VV_{1,10} = R_1 + C_{10} - TC_{1,10}$$
$$= 0 + -41 - (-13)$$
$$= -28.$$

The -28 is placed in that location in parentheses. Matrix III is the matrix after all row and column values have been found and all vacant locations have been evaluated.

It is clear from matrix III (see Table 4-6) that units should be transferred into the New York to Miami route since it is the most negative; however, tracing the path would highlight that the lowest unit number with a minus sign appears twice on the path. Thus, when balancing the locations for supply and demand, two locations would be eliminated, and if only one is added, a degenerate matrix would be created. To avoid this problem, the second most negative value is selected. That is the value in Chicago–St. Louis. The resultant path is illustrated in matrix IV (see Table 4-7).

Next, the smallest value with a minus associated with it is transferred to the new location. In this case it is the value of 1,000 units in location Los Angeles–Seattle. To do this, 1,000 units are placed in the Chicago–St. Louis location by subtracting 1,000 units each from the Los Angeles–St. Louis and Chicago–Seattle locations and adding 1,000 units to the Los Angeles–Seattle location. This is accomplished in matrix V (see Table 4-8).

TABLE 4-6
Matrix III : Solution 1

	Row Value	Warehouses											
Plants		Boston	Pittsburgh	Washington	Atlanta	Detroit	Dallas	Denver	Seattle	St. Louis	Miami	Other	Total
Column Value:		−2	−4	−2	−9	−7	−13	−14	−25	−32	−41	−14	
New York	0	1,250	1,000	1,500	1,000	1,250	(3)	(5)	(4)	(−22)	(−28)	(−14)	6,000
		−2	−4	−2	−9	−7	−16	−19	−29	−10	−13	0	
Chicago	4	(12)	(5)	(9)	(2)	250	1,250	750	1,250	(−25)	(−23)	(−10)	3,500
		−10	−5	−7	−7	−3	−9	−10	−21	−3	−14	0	
Los Angeles	14	(43)	(35)	(38)	(28)	(30)	(15)	(11)	500	1,000	1,500	1,000	4,000
		−31	−25	−26	−22	−23	−14	−11	−11	−18	−27	0	
Total Demand		1,250	1,000	1,500	1,000	1,500	1,250	750	1,750	1,000	1,500	1,000	

Total cost = $137,000

123

TABLE 4-7
Matrix IV: Path to Balance Supply and Demand After Transfer

Plants	Warehouses											
	Boston	Pittsburgh	Washington	Atlanta	Detroit	Dallas	Denver	Seattle	St. Louis	Miami	Other	Total
New York	1,250	1,000	1,500	1,000	1,250			1,250 ⊖				6,000
Chicago					250	1,250	750		1,000 ⊖			3,500
Los Angeles								500 ⊕	1,000	1,500	1,000	4,000
Total	1,250	1,000	1,500	1,000	1,500	1,250	750	1,750	1,000	1,500	1,000	

TABLE 4-8
Matrix V: Reallocation

Plants	Warehouses											
	Boston	Pittsburgh	Washington	Atlanta	Detroit	Dallas	Denver	Seattle	St. Louis	Miami	Other	Total
New York	1,250	1,000	1,500	1,000	1,250							6,000
Chicago					250	1,250	750	250	1,000			3,500
Los Angeles								1,500		1,500	1,000	4,000
Total	1,250	1,000	1,500	1,000	1,500	1,250	750	1,750	1,000	1,500	1,000	

TABLE 4-9
Matrix VI: Solution 2

Plants	Row Value	Warehouses											
		Boston	Pittsburgh	Washington	Atlanta	Detroit	Dallas	Denver	Seattle	St. Louis	Miami	Other	Total
	Column Value	−2	−4	−2	−9	−7	−13	−14	−25	−7	−41	−14	
New York	0	1,250	1,000	1,500	1,000	⊖ 1,250	(3)	(5)	(4)	(3)	⊕ (−28)	(−14)	6,000
		−2	−4	−2	−9	−7	−16	−19	−29	−10	−13	0	
Chicago	4	(12)	(5)	(9)	(2)	⊕ 250	1,250	750	⊖ 250	1,000	(−23)	(−10)	3,500
			−5	−7	−7	−3	−9	−10	−21	−3	−14	0	
Los Angeles	14	(43)	(35)	(38)	(27)	(30)	(15)	(11)	⊕ 1,500	(25)	⊖ 1,500	1,000	4,000
		−31	−25	−26	−22	−23	−14	−11	−11	−18	−27	0	
Total		1,250	1,000	1,500	1,000	1,500	1,250	750	1,750	1,000	1,500	1,000	

Total cost = $112,000

TABLE 4-10
Matrix VII : Solution 3

Plants	Row Value	Warehouses											
		Boston	Pittsburgh	Washington	Atlanta	Detroit	Dallas	Denver	Seattle	St. Louis	Miami	Other	Total
		−2	−4	−2	−9	−7	−13	−14	3	−7	−13	14	
								Column Value					
New York	0	1,250 / −2	1,000 / −4	1,500 / −2	1,000 / −9	1,000 / −7	(3) / −16	(5) / −19	(32) / −29	(3) / −10	⊕ 250 / −13	(14) / 0	6,000
Chicago	4	(12) / −10	(5) / −5	(9) / −7	(2) / −7	⊕ 500 / −3	1,250 / −9	⊖ 750 / −10	(28) / −21	1,000 / −3	(5) / −14	(18) / 0	3,500
Los Angeles	−14	(15) / −31	(7) / −25	(10) / −26	(−1) / −22	(2) / −23	(−13) / −14	⊕ (−17) / −11	1,750 / −11	⊖ (−3) / −18	⊖ 1,250 / −27	1,000 / 0	4,000
Total		1,250	1,000	1,500	1,000	1,500	1,250	750	1,750	1,000	1,500	1,000	

Total cost = $105,000

TABLE 4-11
Matrix VIII : Solution 4

Plants	Row Value		Boston −2	Pittsburgh −4	Washington −2	Atlanta −9	Detroit −7	Dallas −13	Denver 3	Seattle 3	St. Louis −7	Miami −13	Other 14	Total
								Column Value						
New York	0		1,250 / −2	1,000 / −4	1,500 / −2	1,000 / −9	⊝250 / −7	(3) / −16	(22) / −19	(32) / −29	(3) / −10	⊕1,000 / −13	(14) / 0	6,000
Chicago	4		(12) / −10	(5) / −5	(9) / −7	(2) / −7	⊕1,250 / −3	⊝1,250 / −9	(17) / −10	(28) / −21	1,000 / −3	(5) / −14	(18) / 0	3,500
Los Angeles	−14		(15) / −31	(7) / −25	(10) / −26	(−1) / −22	(2) / −23	(−13) ⊕ / −14	750 / −11	1,750 / −11	(−3) / −18	500 / −27	1,000 / 0	4,000
Total			1,250	1,000	1,500	1,000	1,500	1,250	750	1,750	1,000	1,500	1,000	

Total cost = $92,250

TABLE 4-12
Matrix IX: Solution 5

	Row Value	Boston	Pittsburgh	Washington	Atlanta	Detroit	Dallas	Denver	Seattle	St. Louis	Miami	Other	Total
Warehouses													
Column Value		−2	−4	−2	−9	6	0	3	3	6	−13	14	
Plants													
New York	0	1,250	1,000	1,500	① 1,000	(13)	(16)	(22)	(32)	(16)	⊕ 1,250	(14)	6,000
		−2	−4	−2	−9	−7	−16	−19	−29	−10	−13	0	
Chicago	−9	(−1)	(−8)	(−4)	⊕ (−11)	1,500	1,000	(4)	(15)	1,000	(−8)	(5)	3,500
		−10	−5	−7	−7	−3	−9	−10	−21	−3	−14	0	
Los Angeles	−14	(15)	(7)	(10)	(−1)	(31)	250	750	1,750	(26)	① 250	1,000	4,000
		−31	−25	−26	−22	−23	−14	−11	−11	−18	−27	0	
Total		1,250	1,000	1,500	1,000	1,500	1,250	750	1,750	1,000	1,500	1,000	

Total cost = $89,000

TABLE 4-13
Matrix X: Optimal Solution

Plants	Row Value	Warehouses											
		Boston	Pittsburgh	Washington	Atlanta	Detroit	Dallas	Denver	Seattle	St. Louis	Miami	Other	Total
		Column Value											
		−2	−4	−2	−9	−5	−11	−8	−8	−5	−13	3	
New York	0	1,250	1,000	1,500	750	(2)	(5)	(11)	(21)	(5)	1,500	(3)	6,000
		−2	−4	−2	−9	−7	−16	−19	−29	−10	−13	0	
Chicago		(10)	(3)	(7)	250	1,500	750	(4)	(15)	1,000	(3)	(5)	3,500
		−10	−5	−7	−7	−3	−9	−10	−21	−3	−14	0	
Los Angeles		(26)	(18)	(21)	(10)	(15)	500	750	1,750	(10)	(11)	1,000	4,000
		−31	−25	−26	−22	−23	−14	−11	−11	−18	−27	0	
Total		1,250	1,000	1,500	1,000	1,500	1,250	750	1,750	1,000	1,500	1,000	

Total cost = $86,250

TABLE 4-14
Matrix XI: Optimal Shipping Assignments

Plants	Warehouses											
	Boston	Pittsburgh	Washington	Atlanta	Detroit	Dallas	Denver	Seattle	St. Louis	Miami	Other	Total
New York	1,250	1,000	1,500	750						1,500		6,000
Chicago				250	1,500	750			1,000			3,500
Los Angeles						500	750	1,750			1,000	4,000
Total	1,250	1,000	1,500	1,000	1,500	1,250	750	1,750	1,000	1,500	1,000	13,500

Total cost = $86,250

Notice that the totals in supply and demand must remain the same after the transfer.

Matrix VI (see Table 4-9) now brings together the new routes from matrix V and the cost data from matrix III.

The solution procedure is repeated until a solution is isolated which yields all nonnegative values for vacant locations.

In matrix VI the New York–Miami route is still the most negative. However, this time it can be transferred without making the new matrix degenerate. The transfer path is traced and matrix VII is generated (see Table 4-10). In total, it is necessary to generate 10 matrices before all negative values are eliminated.

No negative values exist in matrix X (see Table 4-13). Therefore, this matrix is the optimum method of allocation.

Matrix XI (see Table 4-14) provides a simplified form of matrix X showing only the loads to be shipped from each warehouse to each wholesaler. The savings between the initial matrix and the final one are $50,750. Although this problem could probably have been done just about as well using trial-and-error techniques, larger problems would require a more systematic approach. The transportation method provides a good technique for manual implementation of linear programming techniques; however, for larger problems manual calculations become tedious. An alternative algorithm for linear programming, the simplex method, provides an excellent method to program for a computer because it is mathematically structured.

Product Allocation: Short Supply

The short-supply problem occurs when the inventory available to ship falls short of that required at the destinations. The problem is to select a product allocation plan that will minimize the loss associated with the shortage.

The transportation method can be used to solve the short-supply problem by structuring a dummy plant (origin) rather than a dummy warehouse to handle the differential between supply and demand. In the example, two costs are treated. The first is the normal transportation cost per unit. The second is a per unit penalty cost associated with loss of sales if the warehouse is not supplied. Table 4-15 provides the estimate of per unit shortage cost to each warehouse. In the example, three actual plants, one dummy plant, and five warehouses are illustrated. All costs, including the shortage penalty, are shown as negative values. Using the NCR initialization procedure, the first solution is illustrated in matrix XII (see Table 4-16).

In the initial solution, there is a shortage of four units when the plant supply is depleted. Thus the dummy plant supplies four units at zero cost. The total cost of the initial solution is $145.

To achieve a final solution, the procedures presented for the transportation method are utilized. Omitting intermediate matrices, the final solution is shown by matrix XIII (see Table 4-17).

The total cost of the final matrix is $99.

TABLE 4-15
Penalty Cost per Unit
Short Supply

Warehouse Locations	Cost per Unit
U	$6
V	4
W	8
X	7
Y	6

TABLE 4-16
Matrix XII : Initial Condition—Short Supply

Plants	Warehouses					Total
	U	V	W	X	Y	
A	5	7	3			15
	−2	−5	−9	−3	−4	
B			5			5
	−8	−2	−1	−6	−9	
C			2	4	4	10
	−5	−2	−4	−2	−7	
"Dummy"					4	4
	−6	−4	−8	−7	−6	
Total	5	7	10	4	8	34

TABLE 4-17
Matrix XIII : Final Solution—Short Supply

Plants	Warehouses					Total
	U	V	W	X	Y	
A	5			2	8	15
	−2	−5	−9	−3	−4	
B			5			5
	−8	−2	−1	−6	−9	
C		3	5	2		10
	−5	−2	−4	−2	−7	
"Dummy"		4				4
	−6	−4	−8	−7	−6	
Total	5	7	10	4	8	34

Product Allocation: Transshipment

Reductions in transportation cost are often possible by shipping a product to final destination through an intermediate destination point. For purposes of this illustration of allocation, this procedure of shipping through an intermediate point is called transshipment.

Normal linear programming methods do not take transshipment potential into consideration when reaching a solution. However, with a small change in the solution procedure, transshipment potential can be evaluated using the transportation method. The primary modification in the technique structure to permit transshipment is that all locations, plants, and warehouses are treated as potential supply and destination points.

For contrast, matrix XIV (see Table 4-18) gives an initial solution and matrix XV (see Table 4-19) a final solution not including transshipment. The total cost of this solution is $97.

TABLE 4-18
Matrix XIV : Initial Solution—
No Transshipment

	Warehouses		
Plants	X	Y	Total
A	5	1	6
	−2	−4	
B		9	9
	−5	−8	
Total	5	10	15

TABLE 4-19
Matrix XV: Final Solution—
No Transshipment

	Warehouses		
Plants	X	Y	Total
A		6	6
	−2	−4	
B	5	4	9
	−5	−8	
Total	5	10	15

The transshipment modification requires that a positive quantity be available at all plants and that all warehouses have demand. This is accomplished by adding an artificial supply available from each plant. The quantity added should exceed the total that is otherwise required or available. Since the total required in the problem is 15, a suitable addition is 20. Thus warehouses X and Y require 20 more than the actual that is exactly available from the plants. Using the NCR method, matrix XVI (see Table 4-20) illustrates the initial transshipment solution. This problem is now solved exactly like a normal transportation problem. The final solution is shown in matrix XVII (see Table 4-21).

This solution shows that 9 units should be shipped from B to X, 15 units should be shipped from X to a, and 10 units should be shipped from a to x. If there had been no transshipment, all the locations on the diagonal would have value of 20. This solution has a total cost of $59, which is a reduction of $38 from the solution without cross supply.

TABLE 4-20
Matrix XVI: Initial Solution—Transshipment

Plants	Warehouses				
	X	Y	x	y	Total
A	20	6			26
	0	−2	−2	−4	
B		14	15		29
	−1	0	−5	−8	
a			10	10	20
	−2	−3	0	−2	
b				20	20
	−4	−3	−2	0	
Total	20	20	25	30	115

TABLE 4-21
Matrix XVII: Final Solution—Transshipment

Plants	Warehouses				
	X	Y	x	y	Total
A	11		15		26
	0	−2	−2	−4	
B	9	20			29
	−1	0	−5	−8	
a			10	10	20
	−2	−3	0	−2	
b				20	20
	−4	−3	−2	0	
Total	20	20	25	30	115

Summary

The main purpose of Chapter 4 was to establish the concept of coordination as the logistical area concerned with operational planning and intra-firm replenishment. Although physical distribution and material management are established concepts, logistical coordination offers a new approach to further integrating functions concerned with over-all inventory and raw material movement.

A logical operational planning sequence flows from forecasting to production scheduling to material planning. Because of their major impact upon over-all corporate operations, these three planning functions require a high degree of coordination. Together, the three planning functions more or less integrate over-all manufacturing, marketing, and logistical operations.

Product replenishment was established as a separate operating subsystem of logistics concerned with all material and inventory movements between enterprise facilities. In many large manufacturing organizations, the product replenishment system could very well be the most complex aspect of logistical operations. A unique feature of product replenishment is that its operating scope is totally internal to the enterprise. Because product replenishment is a captive system, maximum control is possible over the design and administration of operations. Linear programming was used to illustrate three different ways in which product allocations can be planned within the captive replenishment structure.

With the conclusion of Chapter 4, the basic field of integrated logistics has been introduced. Each of the three logistical operating areas has been discussed in sufficient detail to provide an insight into the types of functions each performs in the over-all logistical, as well as the corporate, structure. In Part Two attention is directed to a detailed discussion of the components of logistical systems.

Questions

1. Discuss the difference between the operational and planning functions of logistical coordination.
2. What is the similarity between the recent concern with the activities of logistical coordination and the concern in the early 1950s with physical distribution and material management?
3. What is the justification for placing unit forecasting in the logistical coordination group?
4. Describe the relationships among forecasting, production scheduling, and material planning.
5. What is the fundamental difference between the use of regression analysis and exponential smoothing in forecasting?
6. Why is it often stated that exponential smoothing is a refined form of moving average?
7. Discuss the range of sensitivity of alpha factors in an exponentially smoothed forecast. How does adaptive smoothing assist in the selection of alpha factors?
8. Discuss the difference between the formulation of a production schedule in an assembly plant and a job shop.
9. What is the short-term production schedule and how does it relate to the master production plan?
10. Discuss the formulation of the material plan. What is meant by exploding the production schedule?
11. In general terms, why is linear programming a useful tool for consideration when allocating product from plants to warehouses?
12. Describe the basic purpose of the northwest corner rule.

Part Two

Components of Logistical Systems

5

Elements of Transportation

Transportation provides logistical system spatial closure by linking geographically separated facilities and markets together. In most firms more dollars are spent on transportation than on any other single element of logistical operations. Total expenditures on intercity freight in the United States in 1970 were $62 billion and are projected to reach $100 billion by 1980.[1] Naturally the ratio of transportation to total logistical cost varies between industries. Industries that produce high-value products such as cameras, jewelry, and electronics have low transport cost as a percentage of sales. In contrast, coal, iron ore, basic chemicals, and fertilizers have high relative transport cost.

The requirement for transportation services varies greatly from industry to industry. In the case of basic commodities one way to view transportation requirements is in terms of total trains. In automobile logistics, the most common current method of transporting autos is the trilevel rail car. Several hundred trilevel rail cars are required to transport a single week's production

[1] 1972 National Transportation Report, Department of Transportation, and Summary of National Transportation Statistics, Department of Transportation, November 1972.

from an assembly plant. In iron ore transport, ships and barges flowing on the Great Lakes and inland waterways may most economically satisfy requirements. To the meat packer, transportation means refrigerated railcars or truck trailers. To the crude oil producer, the emphasis in transportation centers around pipelines. To the retailer, United Parcel Service, REA Express, or parcel post may constitute primary methods of customer delivery. In complete contrast, a producer of electronic components may use either air express or air freight as the primary method of product delivery.

There are many transportation options available to complete product or raw material movements in a logistical system. In addition to for-hire transportation, an enterprise may decide to operate its own or private transportation. The objective of this chapter is to provide an overview of transportation services available for utilization in logistical operations. The chapter development places emphasis on the range and cost of services. Special aspects of traffic management and administration are treated in Appendix 5A.

The first section of this chapter provides an overview of the role and functional purpose of transportation in the logistical system. Next, the transport infra-structure is discussed in terms of modal characteristics. Various transport modes are classified in terms of operating characteristics and legal alternatives. The final section develops the common carrier rate structure and describes special or accessorial services that are important to logistical operations.

Transportation Capacity and Location

Prior to the availability of cheap overland transportation, most of the world's commerce was transported by water. During this period commercial activity centered around port cities, and overland transport of goods was both costly and slow. For example, if a young lady in one of the Far Western states wanted to be married in an Eastern store-purchased dress, the lead time for ordering could easily exceed 9 months in duration. Although the need for fast and efficient transportation existed, it was not until the application of steam power to water and then the invention of the steam locomotive in 1829 that the transportation technological revolution began in the United States.

Today, the transportation system of the United States consists of a highly developed network of rail, water, air, highway, and pipeline services. Each transport alternative provides a somewhat different type of service which can be utilized within a logistic system depending upon the product line, raw material required, and the geographical area of operational concern.

The importance of transportation services to economic development has been recognized at least since the middle of the nineteenth century, when the German economist von Thünen developed "The Isolated State."[2] To von

---

[2] Joachim von Thünen, *The Isolated State* (Rostock, 1842–1863; reprinted Jena, 1921).

Thünen, the primary determinant of economic development was the price of land and the cost of transport to market. The price of land resulted from the relative cost of transport and the ability of a product to command a price capable of absorbing transport cost. His basic thesis was that the value of specific produce at the growing location decreases with distance from the primary selling market.

Following von Thünen, Weber generalized location theory from an agrarian to an industrial society.[3] Weber's theoretical system consisted of numerous consuming locations spread over an area and linked together by linear weight–distance transportation costs. With respect to materials, Weber developed the two major categories of localized and ubiquities. Ubiquities were those raw materials found in all locations which could not in themselves serve to command location. Localized raw materials consisted of mineral deposits found only in selected locations. Based upon an analysis of the relative weight of localized raw materials and finished products, Weber developed a "material index." The material index was a measure of the proportion of the weight of localized raw materials to the weight of the finished product. Each type of industry, based on the material index, could be assigned a "locational weight." Utilizing these two measures Weber generalized that specific industries would generally locate at the point of consumption if the manufacturing process was weight-gaining, near the point of raw material deposits if the manufacturing process was weight-losing, and at an intermediate point or location of convenience if the manufacturing process was neither weight-gaining or -losing.

Several location theorists followed von Thünen and Weber. The most notable contributions toward a general theory of location have been presented by Lösch, Hoover, Greenhut, and Isard.[4] All these authors have highlighted the importance of geographical specialization in industrial location, including a thorough development of the fundamental importance of transportation to industrial development.

In the most basic sense, transport capacity makes goods and commodities available that must be mined or produced elsewhere. Without economical transportation a community would have to be self-sufficient. The consequence would be limited variety of products, high prices, and inefficient utilization of resources.

From the vantage point of logistical planning, transportation links a geographically dispersed number of manufacturing, warehousing, and market locations into an integrated network. As such, transportation provides spatial closure, which in turn permits specialization. Transportation should be viewed

---

[3] Weber, Alfred, *Theory of the Location of Industries*, Carl J. Friedrich (trans.), (Chicago: University of Chicago Press, 1928).

[4] August Lösch, *Die Räumliche Ordnung der Wirtschaft* (Jena: Gustav Fischer Verlag, 1940); Egdar M. Hoover, *The Location of Economic Activity* (New York: McGraw-Hill Book Company, 1938); Melvin L. Greenhut, *Plant Location in Theory and Practice* (Chapel Hill, N.C.: University of North Carolina Press, 1956); and W. Isard *et al.*, *Methods of Regional Analysis: An Introduction to Regional Science* (New York: John Wiley & Sons, Inc., 1960).

as cost-reducing in the sense that expenditures for transport services allow greater economies in the processes of manufacturing and marketing.

In Chapter 6 the fundamental importance of transportation to the inventory performance cycle is developed. In Chapter 10 the integral nature of transportation to logistical policy is developed. In this chapter specifics related to transportation facilities, rates, and services are discussed.

Transportation Infra-structure

Infra-structure is viewed in terms of variety and characteristics of transportation modes. In addition, infra-structure is examined in terms of legal forms of transportation and the available range of multimodal systems.

Modal Variety and Relative Characteristics

The term *mode* is commonly used to differentiate between basic ways that goods or commodities may be physically transported. The five basic transportation modes are rail, highway, water, pipeline, and air. The relative importance of each mode can be measured in terms of mileage, traffic volume, traffic revenue, and the nature of traffic composition. The nature of each mode with respect to these relative measures is discussed below.[5]

RAIL.   Railroads have historically handled the largest number of ton-miles within the continental United States. As a result of the early establishment of a comprehensive network of railroads connecting almost all cities and towns, railroads dominated intercity freight tonnage through World War II. This early superiority resulted from the capability to transport large shipments economically, and from frequent service and a more or less monopolistic position. However, since World War II, with the advent of serious competition, the railroads' share of both ton-miles and revenues has been declining.

In 1970 railroads transported 35.9 per cent of total intercity ton-miles. In terms of relative decline, railroads transported 54.0 per cent of total ton-miles in 1947, 39.2 per cent in 1958, and 38.8 per cent in 1965. The decline in share of revenue has been even more significant, dropping from near 40 per cent in 1950 to less than 20 percent in 1970.

Naturally, the miles of railroads in service once ranked number one among all modes. In 1970 the total miles of railroads was 209,000 miles and ranked fourth among modes, only exceeding that of inland water. Although this change in relative mileage between modes is not surprising, it is important

---

[5] For a more detailed analysis, see D. Philip Locklin, *Economics of Transportation*, 6th ed. (Homewood, Ill.: Richard D. Irwin, Inc., 1966). The source of statistics that follow is the 1972 National Transportation Report, *op. cit.*, and George E. Harmon, *Transportation: The Nation's Lifelines* (Washington, D.C.: Industrial College of the Armed Forces, 1966).

to realize that since World War II the absolute miles of railroads have continued to decline. For example, 220,000 miles were reported in operation in 1960, contrasted with 209,000 miles in 1970.

The capability of railroads to transport very large tonnages efficiently over long distances is the main reason they continue to command a significant share of intercity tonnage and revenue. Railroad operations are characterized by high fixed costs as a result of extensive equipment, rights-of-way, switching yards, and terminals. This fixed capacity, coupled with the nature of rail power, results in a relatively small variable operational cost. The replacement of steam by diesel power reduced the railroad's variable cost per ton-mile, and the future potential of electrification offers even greater reductions. A minimal amount of power in combination with limited labor allows a large volume of traffic to be transported considerable distances at low variable cost per ton-mile.

In recent times the character of traffic transported by rails has shifted from a wide range of commodities to an emphasis on extracting industries, heavy manufacturing, and agricultural commodities. However, even in these categories a significant share of tonnage has been lost to competitive carriers. In 1970 the greatest sources of railroad tonnage are the raw-material-extracting industries located a considerable distance from improved waterways. Switching problems and car-tracing problems have created serious operational problems for railroads; the average speed between terminals has decreased to approximately 20 miles per hour.[6]

Despite operational problems, the inherent fixed-variable cost structure of the railroads still renders economic superiority for numerous long-haul movements. This distance advantage is one significant reason Western railroads have been better able to maintain revenues and tonnage than their Eastern counterparts. Since the 1950s, railroads have been tending toward a policy of market segmentation by the elimination of small shipment (LCL) traffic, the spinoff of REA Express, and the elimination of several accessorial services traditionally offered.[7] To provide improved services to major rail users, progressive railroads have concentrated on the development of specialized equipment such as the trilevel rail car, which is capable of transporting 16 automobiles; unit trains; and new pricing techniques.

These examples are by no means a comprehensive review of recent railroad innovations, but they are characteristic of the attempts being made to retain and improve railroad's share of the market. However, the plight of the railroads continues and is causing grave national concern. In 1971 rail passenger service was for all effective purposes nationalized with the creation of the National Railroad Passenger Corporation (Amtrack), a government-backed corporation. Although the loss of intercity passenger revenue was not

[6] For a comprehensive discussion of railroad operating characteristics and problems, see Harmon, *op. cit.*, pp. 6–13.

[7] See Charles A. Taff, *Management of Traffic and Physical Distribution*, 5th ed. (Homewood, Ill.: Richard D. Irwin, Inc., 1972), Chap. 18.

a serious concern to the railroads, which had less than 3 per cent of the total market, the creation of Amtrack, represented in the opinion of many transportation experts, a first step toward over-all nationalization. Following the financial demise of the Penn Central in 1970 and the Erie in 1972, at least the Eastern railroads appear to be prime candidates for nationalization. It is safe to conclude that radical changes can be expected during the 1970s in traditional railroad concepts of operation. The issues of survival and the resultant form of a viable rail network are of prime concern to logistical planning.

HIGHWAY. Highway transportation has rapidly expanded since the end of World War II. To a significant degree the rapid growth of the motor carrier industry has resulted from greater flexibility of door-to-door operation and greater speed of operation in comparison to railroads.

In 1970 expenditures on intercity freight moved by truck totaled $20.4 billion, which was greater than the combined total for rail, air, water, and pipeline. In terms of relative increase, motor carriers transported 5.2 per cent of total ton-miles in 1947, 12.5 per cent in 1958, 14.6 per cent in 1965, and 15.9 per cent in 1970. The increase in share of total revenue has been even more significant; it jumped from near 55 per cent in 1950 to near 75 per cent in 1970.

Motor carriers have the capability of operating on all types of rural highways, which means that over 3 million miles of roads are available. From the viewpoint of improved highways, the 1970 mileage available to motor carriers exceeds 3,170,000 miles, which is greater than the combined total of all other modes of transport.

In comparison to railroads, motor carriers have relatively small investment in terminal facilities and owned right-of-way. Although the cost of license fees and tolls experienced in operation is considerable, these expenses are regulated to the number of over-the-road vehicles in operation. The variable cost per mile of motor carrier is high because of the requirement that a separate power unit be operated for each trailer.[8] Also, the amount of labor is high because of restrictions by the drivers and substantial dock labor at shipper's locations and at carrier terminals. The net result is a structure of low fixed cost coupled with high variable cost. In comparison to railroads, motor carriers are more economically adapted to handling smaller shipments moving shorter distances.

The character of motor carrier traffic leans heavily toward the manufacturing and distributive trades. In particular, the motor carriers have made significant inroads into rail traffic associated with medium and light manufacturing. Because of the flexibility of store–door delivery, motor carriers have captured almost all freight moving in the distributive industries from wholesalers or warehouses to retail stores. In fact, the greatest source of competition to motor

---

[8] Some variations exist wherein more than one trailer may be pulled in a "double-bottom" or "truck-train" arrangement which exceeds 40 feet of combined trailers.

common carriers in this aspect of freight is the private or contract-operated truck.

The prospects for continued growth in highway transport remain bright. By the early 1970s almost all less-than-10,000-pound shipments (LTL), with the exception of small package goods, moving in intercity freight were captive to the motor carrier industry. This phase of traffic alone was capable of generating over 60 per cent of the revenue and more than 45 per cent of the tonnage of motor common carriers.

The motor carrier industry, however, is not without substantial problems. The primary difficulties relate to the increasing cost of labor as reflected in equipment replacement, driver wages, maintenance, and, in particular, platform and dock wages. The labor settlement of 1970, after a prolonged strike, had a substantial impact on labor rates with a subsequent increase in motor carrier rates. The 1973 labor settlement, which could not immediately be offset by a rate increase owing to Phase III inflation controls, created a major problem for many carriers. Although accelerating labor rates influence all modes of transport, the labor-intense nature of motor carrier operations causes the impact to be felt severely. To counteract this trend, carriers have placed a great deal of attention on improved line-haul scheduling that bypasses terminals, overhead billing systems, mechanized terminals; double-bottom line-haul operations that allow two trailers to be pulled by a single power unit; and utilization of coordinated transport systems, such as trailer on flat car (TOFC) to perform a portion of line-haul movement.

Perhaps the greatest threat to the common motor carrier industry is the performance of over-the-road transportation by trucks owned by shippers or by specialized carriers that perform transport services for shippers under contract. The low-fixed-cost structure of motor carrier operations encourages easy entry. Entry is blocked in terms of other common carriers because each must gain explicit operating authority from the Interstate Commerce Commission in the form of a Certificate of Public Convenience and Necessity.[9] However, private transportation need only comply with the federal, state, and local safety and licensing laws.

It is apparent that highway transportation will continue to function as the backbone of logistical operations for the foreseeable future. The area of greatest immediate concern to logistical planning is that of the increasing rates and special charges associated with shipments under 10,000 pounds.

WATER. The oldest form of transport is water. The original application of sailing vessels was replaced by steamboats in the early 1800s and later in the 1920s by diesel power. A division is generally made between deep-water and navigable inland water transport. In terms of domestic commerce the primary areas of concern are the Great Lakes, canals, and navigable rivers.

In 1970 water transport accounted for 28.4 per cent of total intercity tonnage.

---

[9] Issued by the federal government and most state government units.

In terms of relative share of intercity tonnage, water transport was 31.3 per cent in 1947 and 31.7 per cent in 1958; it declined to 27.9 per cent in 1965 but had increased by 1970. In terms of revenue, the water transport share has been approximately 3 per cent of intercity freight revenue since 1950.

The exact miles of improved waterways in operation depend in part on whether or not coastwise and intercoastal shipping are included. In terms of improved inland waterways, 25,000 miles were operational in 1960 and 26,000 miles in 1970. Fewer miles of improved inland waterways exist than of any other transportation mode.

The main feature of water transport is the capacity to move extremely large shipments. Deep-water vessels are restricted in operation, but diesel-towed barges have a fair degree of flexibility. In comparison to rail and high-way, water transport ranks in the middle with respect to fixed cost. The fixed cost of operation is greater than that of motor carriers but less than that of railroads. The main disadvantage of water is the limited degree of flexibility and the low speeds of transport. Unless the source and destination of the movement are adjacent to a waterway, prior or subsequent haul by rail or truck is required. The capability of water to transport large tonnage at low variable cost places this mode of transport in demand when low freight rates are desired and speed of transit is a secondary consideration.

The character of freight transported by inland water is heavily orientated to mining and basic bulk commodities, such as chemicals, cement, and selected agricultural products. In addition to being restricted by navigable waterways, terminal facilities in the form of bulk and dry cargo storage and load–unload devices limit the flexibility of water transport. Labor restrictions at dock level with respect to loading and unloading have created operational problems and have tended to reduce the potential range of available traffic. Finally a highly competitive situation has developed between railroads and inland water carriers in areas where parallel routings exist.

Inland and Great Lakes water transport will continue to be a viable part of future logistical system design. The full benefit of the St. Lawrence Seaway has not yet been realized with respect to domestic freight potential.[10] With respect to inland river transport, the slow nature of transport can in essence provide a form of warehousing in transit if fully integrated into over-all system design. Improvements in ice-breaking equipment appear on the threshold of eliminating the seasonal aspects of water transport.

PIPELINE.   The initial pipelines were placed into operation in domestic commerce in 1865. Although growth was not dramatic, by 1947, 9.5 per cent of intercity tonnage moved by pipeline. A major jump in utilization occurred between 1947 and 1958, when the percentage of total intercity freight ton-miles jumped to 16.5 per cent. In 1965 pipeline transport constituted 18.7 per cent of total intercity tonnage, and in 1970, 19.6 per cent.

[10] For more detail concerning research on this subject, see John Hazard, "The Second Decade of the Seaway," *Transportation Journal*, Summer 1970, pp. 33–40.

The main commodity transported by pipelines is petroleum. In 1960 there were 191,000 miles of pipeline operational in the United States. By 1970 the operational figure had jumped to 219,000 miles. Pipelines have the distinction of having the highest fixed cost and the lowest variable cost among all the transport modes. The high fixed cost results from the right-of-way for the pipeline, construction, and requirement for control stations and pumping capacity. Because pipelines are not labor intense once constructed, the variable cost of operation is extremely low.

The basic nature of a pipeline makes it unique in comparison to all other modes of transport. The pipeline operates around the clock 7 days per week and is limited only by the need to conduct emergency or preventative maintenance. The natural disadvantage is that the capacity of a pipeline is extremely limited with respect to commodities. Although tests to move solid products in the form of surrey or in hydraulic suspension have been and continue to be conducted, the main utilization of pipelines in the immediate future will be in the logistical operation of petroleum products.

AIR.   The newest, most glamorous, and by far the least utilized mode of transport is air freight. The glamor of air freight is linked to the speed with which a shipment can be transported. A coast-to-coast shipment by air between two major cities takes only a matter of hours, as opposed to days via other modes of transport. Likewise, the tradeoff of the speed of air as a substitute for other elements of the logistical system, such as field warehousing, has attracted considerable attention to the potential of air freight.

However, air transport remains in 1970 more a potential than a reality. Although the mileage related to airways is almost unlimited, in 1970 air freight accounted for less than 0.2 per cent of all intercity ton-miles and about 1 per cent of revenue. The capability of air transport is limited by the lift capacity and availability of aircraft. To date, most intercity air freight has been transported in the belly of scheduled passenger flights, with the subsequent reduction in freight operations of both capacity and flexibility. The high cost of jet aircraft, coupled with the erratic nature of freight, has limited the assignment of existing aircraft to all-freight operations. Likewise, research and development of special-purpose cargo aircraft, such as the C-5, special STOL-capable aircraft, and cargo helicopters, has lagged as a result of the slow maturity of high-volume air freight.

The fixed cost of air transport is not high in comparison to rail, water, and pipeline. Airways and airports are generally developed and maintained with public funds. Likewise, terminals are normally maintained by local communities. The fixed costs of air freight are associated with aircraft purchase and the requirement for specialized handling systems and cargo containers. Air transport ranks second only to highway with respect to low fixed cost. On the other hand, variable cost is extremely high for air operations, as a result of fuel, maintenance, and the labor intensity of both inflight and ground crews.

No particular commodity dominates the traffic carrier by air freight operations. Perhaps the best distinction is to classify the freight handled on the basis of emergency as opposed to regular movements. Most firms will utilize either scheduled or nonscheduled air cargo movements when the situation justifies such high-cost movement. In terms of regular air movement, the products having the greatest potential are those with high value or extreme perishability. When the marketing period for a product is extremely limited, such as in Christmas or selected high-fashion items, air transport may represent the most economical method for logistically supporting operations.

The future prospects for increased utilization of air cargo in logistical operations are still promising. Although movement by air requires prior and subsequent land movement, the speed of service possible between two distant points has the potential of reducing over-all logistical costs by sufficient margins to offset the added cost of air transport.

Modal Comparative Analysis

Figure 5-1 provides a distribution of intercity freight movement by each of five modes from 1947 through 1970. Trends in revenue per ton-mile from 1950 through 1970 are presented in Figure 5-2.

On the basis of revenue per ton-mile, air leads the five modes, with a revenue figure of 21.88 cents per ton-mile. Table 5-1 ranks the modes on the basis of revenue per ton-miles. The differential between rail and truck is over 6 cents per ton-mile, whereas the differential between water and rail is only slightly greater than 1 cent per ton-mile.

In terms of composition of traffic between modes, the value and bulk of the product and length of haul are the prime determinants of modal choice. Considering air and pipeline in a special category, the composition of freight tendered among truck, rail, and water would be expected to prefer truck as the value increases and water as the bulk increases.

Figure 5-3 presents a breakdown of participation by modes in hauls under and over 400 miles. Trucks dominate when hauls are less than 400 miles in length.

TABLE 5-1
Comparative Average Revenue
in Cents per Ton-Mile: Five
Basic Transportation Modes

Air	21.88
Truck	7.70
Rail	1.43
Pipeline	0.27
Water	0.30

FIGURE 5-1
Distribution of Intercity Freight Movement by Modes, 1947–70

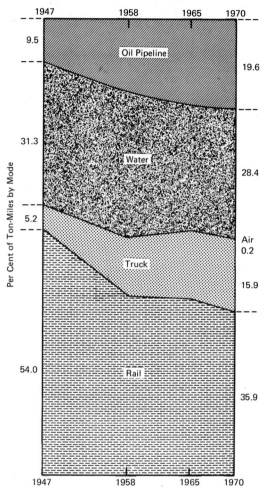

Source: Chart III–9, *1972 National Transportation Report,* U.S. Department of Transportation, pp. 2–55.

In terms of forecasted relative position among modes, Figure 5-4 provides a projection in annual freight growth rate by mode for the 1970s and 1980s. Although air transport leads in projected percentage growth, the most significant increases in absolute tonnage are projected for motor carriers.

Modal Classification

The five basic modes of transportation have been reviewed in terms of historical development and current share of intercity ton-miles and freight

FIGURE 5-2
Trends in Revenue per Ton-Mile Intercity Freight by Mode

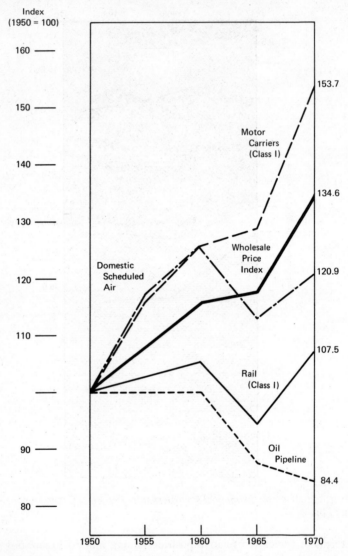

Source: Chart III–12,*1 972 National Transportation Report*, U.S. Department of Transportation, pp. 2–59.

revenue. The essential operating characteristics of each mode were noted, including the relationship of associated fixed and variable cost structures. Table 5-2 summarizes the operating characteristics of each mode with respect to speed, availability, dependability, capability, and frequency of service.

Speed refers to the elapsed time for intercity movement. Of course, air

FIGURE 5-3
Percentage Distribution of Ton-Mile of Nonurban Freight over and under
400 Miles by Mode in 1965

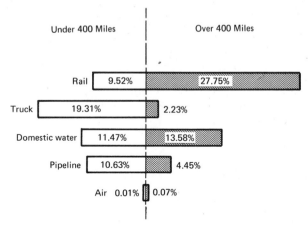

Source: Chart III–11, *1972 National Transportation Report,* U.S. Department of Transportation, pp. 2–57.

cargo is the fastest of all modes. Availability of service relates to the ability of a mode to service a given pair of locations. Highway carriers are the most capable among the five modes. Dependability of operations refers to potential variance from expected or published delivery schedules. Among the modes, pipelines, because of their continuous service, rank highest in dependability. Capability relates to the ability of a mode to handle any transport requirement. Water transport is the most capable among the modes. The final classification of service is frequency, which relates to the quantity of scheduled movements. Pipelines, because of their continuous service between two points, lead all modes in frequency.

From Table 5-2 the very rapid and significant growth of highway transport can be explained, at least in part, by the high ranking across all characteristics enjoyed by motor carriers. Operating on a highway system that comprises over

TABLE 5-2
Relative Operating Characteristics: Five Basic Transportation
Modes

Operating Characteristic	*Transportation Mode*				
	Rail	*Highway*	*Water*	*Pipeline*	*Air*
Speed	3	2	4	5	1
Availability	2	1	4	5	3
Dependability	3	2	4	1	5
Capability	2	3	1	5	4
Frequency	4	2	5	1	3

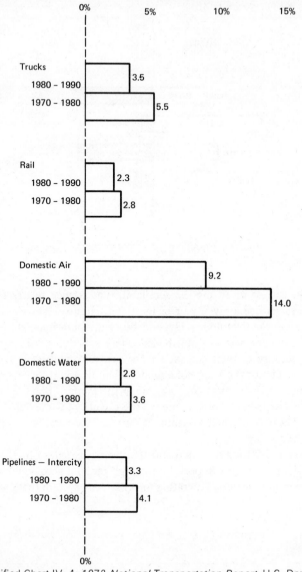

FIGURE 5-4
Projected Annual Growth Rates by Mode, 1970–80 and 1980–90

Source: Modified Chart IV–4, *1972 National Transportation Report*, U.S. Department of Transportation, pp. 2–182.

3 million miles, motor carriers rank first or second in all categories except capability. Although substantial improvements in motor capability result from relaxed weight limitations on interstate highways and approval of the practice of pulling tandem trailers, the prospects that motor transport will surpass rail or water in the immediate future are not promising.

Legal Forms of Transportation

In addition to classifying transportation alternatives on the basis of mode, another common grouping is based on the legality of carrier operating rights. Each carrier must comply with some form of legal authorization to transport goods and commodities. The four basic types of legal carriers are common, contract, private, and exempt. Each type of carrier may exist within any basic mode of transportation. As a general rule, for regulatory reasons, a single for-hire transportation firm will operate utilizing a single mode; however, more than one type of legal transport within the mode is commonly found.

The category of legal transportation represented most often consists of the common carriers. A common carrier is a company that offers to transport property for revenue any time and any place within its operating authority without discrimination. A common carrier is authorized to conduct for-hire transportation on the basis of receiving a certificate of public convenience and necessity from the appropriate regulatory agency. Common carriers are required to publish for the public all rates charged for transport services. These rates must be identical for similar movements of freight. The operating authority received by a motor common carrier may authorize transport of all commodities or may limit transport to specialized commodities such as steel, household goods, or computers. In addition, the operating authority specifies the geographical area the carrier may service and indicates if such service shall be on a scheduled or nonscheduled basis.

Contract carriers perform transport services on a selected basis. Although contract carriers must receive authorization in the form of a permit, such permits provide limited and for the most part less specific operating authority than do those for common carriers. The basis for contract cartage is an agreement between a carrier and a shipper calling for the carrier to provide a specified transportation service at an agreed-to cost for the shipper. The business agreement or contract becomes the basis for the contract carrier to receive his permit. The permit authorizes the contract carrier to transport specified commodities over specified routes. The contract carrier may transport for more than one shipper and is not required to charge the same rate for all shippers. Each agreement to transport requires regulatory approval.

Exempt carriers do not confront direct regulation with respect to operating rights or pricing policies. Exempt carriers must, however, comply with licensing and safety laws of the states in which they operate. If the exempt carrier is engaged in interstate movement, he is required to publish rates. The origins of exempt carriers for motor and water stem from the agricultural sector, wherein unprocessed farm products were authorized to be hauled to processing centers. Today, exempt carriers operate in a wider range of commercial activity. In addition to a broader list of exempt commodities, exemptions are also granted on the basis of area and to select associations. An example of area exemption is in local cartage within the commercial zones surrounding municipalities.

An association exemption refers to shipper alliances for the purpose of aggregating numerous small shipments at a buying center for transport to the shipper locations in one consolidated shipment. The two main modes engaged in exempt cartage are highway and water.

Private carriage consists of a firm providing its own transportation service. The general provision is that the firm must own or control through lease the transport equipment and be the bona fide owner of the goods or commodities being transported. In addition, the act of transporting goods must be incidental to the primary purpose of the business. Although private transport does not come under the regulatory laws of the federal or state governments, it is subject to license, safety, and weight restrictions.

Although the distinction between the legal forms of transport is slight, the related restrictions can have considerable impact upon the design of a logistical system. From the viewpoint of logistical planning the main differences between legal types are the degree of restriction, the extent of financial commitment, and the flexibility of operation.

The degree of restriction relates the law that surrounds the operation of each form of cartage. For example, private carriage of one subsidiary of a conglomerate cannot legally transport goods of another subsidiary in backhaul. The reader is advised to acquire a basic understanding of the differences and implications between the legal types.[11]

The extent of commitment refers to the degree of financial involvement or obligation the shipper has to the carrier. The least amount of commitment is experienced with common carriers wherein an agreement is reached for each shipment which specifies the obligation of all parties to the movement. Contract operations have a greater degree of commitment in the sense that the typical contract between the carrier and the shipper is of 6 months' to 1 year's duration. It is important to point out that the degree of involvement normally associated with both common and contract carriers is variable-cost in nature and is directly associated with the tonnage transported. In the case of private transport, the extent of commitment is of longer duration and normally involves both fixed cost of equipment and variable cost of operation. The duration of obligation can be reduced by equipment leasing; however, this form of financing only influences the cash flow related to equipment purchase and does not relieve the extent or magnitude of obligation. It is difficult to generalize the commitment associated with exempt cartage since it can range from very little to extensive. As a general rule, the degree of commitment would be greater than that of the common carrier and less than that of private carriage.

In terms of flexibility the greatest latitude of command is naturally associated with private transport. However, it should be pointed out that the failure to schedule private transport on an economical and routinized manner is one of the greatest pitfalls leading to costly operations. Exempt and contract cartage

[11] For expanded treatment, see Taff, *op. cit.*, or Locklin, *op. cit.*, and E. Grosvenor Plowman, *Elements of Business Logistics* (Stanford, Calif.: Stanford University Press, 1964).

rank next to private carriage in terms of operational flexibility. Since the contract operator is more or less captive to the shipper, a great deal of direction can be exercised in the operational scheduling. The number of common carriers, in excess of 14,500 motor carriers alone, means that the availability of service is great. However, the shipper does not legally enjoy a large degree of flexibility concerning the common carriers' operation. While the common carrier must service all shippers on an equal basis and at a common price, the prudence of good management dictates that the common carrier will design his service around the requirements of large and frequent shippers located within his operating territory.

The vitality of a sound national transportation system rests with common carriers, who provide the backbone of the transport network. Most enterprises that utilize private, exempt, and contract carriers also tender frequent shipments to common carriers. The tradition among professional traffic managers is that every effort should be made to utilize the capacity or the common carrier network. The utilization of contract carriers allows responsibility to be assigned to a management that has the sole task of operating transport capacity.

Finally, private cartage should be utilized when the nature of the transportation assignment requires specialized equipment or customized operations. Over the years, the bulk of intercity tonnage has been moved by for-hire carriers. However, in recent years there has been marked trend toward greater utilization of private transport. In part, this trend can be attributed to a decline in rail services and a substantial rate increase required to cover the cost of other common carrier operations. However, the greatest pressure encouraging greater utilization of private transport has been the trend toward broader product assortments and scrambled merchandising discussed in Chapter 2.

Multimodal Transportation Systems

In previous sections the transportation infra-structure has been viewed with respect to basic modes and legal classification. The student of logistics soon learns that every generalization has an exception. Two major areas of exception are the auxiliary users of for-hire transport and coordinated arrangements. An examination of each is necessary to have an over-all understanding of the transportation infra-structure. These two additional classifications of transportation supply are grouped under multimodal systems because they frequently utilize more than one mode of transport to perform their services.

AUXILIARY USERS.   Auxiliary users are transportation companies that, in effect, work in the exchange channels in a manner somewhat analogous to that of wholesalers in transaction channels.[12] They purchase a major share of their intercity or line-haul transport from the legal forms of transport. In some

[12] See page 67.

situations they operate their own over-the-road equipment by special authorization of regulatory agencies. It is common practice for auxiliary users to operate as exempt carriers within the commercial zone of municipalities for purposes of pickup and delivery.

The economic justification of auxiliary users is that they offer shippers lower rates for movement between two geographical points than would be possible by direct shipper utilization of common carriers. A more detailed explanation of the peculiarities in the common carrier rate structure that provide the opportunity for auxiliary transport will be discussed in a later section of this chapter; it is emphasized here that the enabling conditions are the existence of minimum charges, surcharges, and less-than-volume rates.[13] A quantity of small shipments from various shippers is aggregated by the auxiliary user, who then purchases intercity transportation on a volume-rate basis. The auxiliary users then offer the shipper a rate that is lower than the applicable common carrier rate for the shipment size. The profit margin of the auxiliary user is the per pound difference between the rate charged the shipper and the transport service purchased from the carrier. In some cases, auxiliary users charge even higher rates than shippers could obtain direct from primary carriers. The justification for higher charges is faster delivery and more complete service. The four main auxiliary users are freight forwarders, shipper associations, REA Express, and parcel post.

Freight forwarders are a quasi-legal form of transport in the sense that they are subjected to federal regulation and are treated as common carriers. They accept the full responsibility for performance on all shipments tendered to them by shippers. Freight forwarders are common in surface and air cargo. In both cases they consolidate small shipments and then tender a bulk shipment to common carriers for transport. At the destination the freight forwarder splits the bulk shipment back into the original shipments. Local delivery may or may not be included in the forwarder's service. The main advantage of the forwarder is a lower rate per hundredweight and, in most cases, speedier transport of small shipments than would be experienced by direct tender to a common carrier.

Shipper associations are similar in operation to the freight forwarder. However, as the name implies, shipper associations are voluntary nonprofit entities with membership centered around a specific industry in which small-shipment purchases are common. Department stores, for example, often participate in shipper associations since a large number of different products may be purchased at one location, such as the garment district in New York City. The basic idea is that a group of shippers establish an administrative office at a point of frequent merchandise purchase. The staff at the office arranges for all members' local purchases to be delivered to a central location. When sufficient volume is accumulated, the staff arranges for consolidated shipment to the association's membership base city. As indicated earlier, some

---

[13] See page 166.

associations operate their own intercity transportation with the legal status of an exempt carrier. Each member is billed on a proportionate basis to traffic moved plus a prorated share of the association's operating cost.

The U.S. Postal Service operates surface and air parcel service. The charges for parcel post are based on weight and distance. Generally, parcels must be delivered to the post office at a point of shipment origination. However, in the case of large users and when it is to the convenience of the government, post office service may be provided on the premises of the shipper. Intercity transport is accomplished using air, highway, rail, and even water. The legal forms utilized in parcel post include common and contract cartage. At destination delivery is provided by the post office. The importance of parcel service cannot be overemphasized. One of the fastest growing forms of marketing in the United States is nonstore retailing, in which orders are placed by telephone or mail from catalogues for subsequent home delivery. The bulk of nonstore retailing for home delivery which transcends a local municipal area is transported via parcel post and United Parcel Service.

REA Express was formerly known as the Railway Express Agency. One of the oldest forms of auxiliary transport, REA was originally formed on a cooperative basis by the railroads to provide express package service on small shipments using rail transport. With the advent of air transport, a division of the express company was created with the air carriers to provide a similar service utilizing intercity air movement. In the original concept, both surface and air express provided pickup at origin and delivery at destination. In terms of intercity transport express shipments were provided first priority on all vehicle space. In fact, the distinctive feature of express shipments was that they moved on passenger trains and planes as opposed to all freight vehicles, thereby enjoying more frequent shipment. With the decline of rail passenger service the nature of REA Express began to shift. In the 1960s REA became separated from railroad ownership and motor carrier transport began to dominate REA operations. The market orientation of REA also shifted from the small package area to concentration on shipments from 250 to 10,000 pounds. The fortunes of REA have varied over the years; however, today they remain a major auxiliary form of transport. Similar to freight forwarders, REA is regulated with respect to prices, operating authority, and authorized commodities on other than a package-goods basis.

The four auxiliary forms of transportation here reviewed all utilize to various degrees the capacity of one or more of the legal forms of transport and all major modes except pipelines. However, they do not represent coordinated transportation in the manner hereafter described.

COORDINATED TRANSPORTATION. Coordinated transportation arrangements refer to a combination of two common carriers representing different modes providing point-to-point service on a regularly scheduled basis. Numerous efforts have been made over the years to combine the inherent advantages of each transport mode into a single shipment. Initial attempts at modal coordination trace back to the early 1920s; however, the availability of such service did not become common until the 1950s.

In a technical sense coordinated transportation could be arranged between all basic modes. The common practice is to identify each type of arrangement by descriptive jargon. Consequently, piggyback, fishyback, trainship, and airtruck have become standard transportation terms. The important distinction related to coordinated arrangements is that the line-haul portion of the shipment is split between two different modes.

The best known and most widely used coordinated system is the trailer-on-flatcar (TOFC), which is commonly known as piggyback. As the name implies, TOFC consists of placement of a motor carrier trailer on a railroad flat car for some portion of the intercity line haul.

Five different basic plans of piggyback service are available. However, not all railroads offer all five. Two variations exist in the form of plans II$\frac{1}{2}$ and III$\frac{1}{2}$. The nature of the seven available plans is summarized in Table 5-3, which has been adapted from work of Taft.[14]

Containers also move via TOFC service. Containerization will be discussed in greater detail in Chapter 8. The basic concept is that goods are enclosed in a protective box (container) to facilitate handling during transit from origin to destination. The basic concept is similar to trailers on flat cars with the

TABLE 5-3
Summary TOFC Plans

Plan I. Railroad movement of trailers or containers of common motor carriers, with the shipment moving on one bill of lading and billing being done by the trucker. Traffic moves under rates in regular motor carrier tariffs. Currently, 23 per cent of TOFC moves under this plan.

Plan II. Railroad performs its own door-to-door service, moving its own trailers or containers on flat cars under tariffs usually similar to those of truckers. Thirty-eight per cent of TOFC moves under plan II.

Plan II$\frac{1}{2}$. A combination of plans II and III whereby the shipper furnishes the trailer but the railroad performs the terminal service.

Plan III. Ramp-to-ramp rates based on a flat charge, regardless of the contents of trailers or containers, usually owned or leased by freight forwarders or shippers. No pickup or delivery is performed by the railroad.

Plan III$\frac{1}{2}$. The same as plan III except one instead of two trailers per car at 60 per cent of the rate.

Plan IV. Shipper or forwarder furnishes a trailer or container-loaded flatcar, either owned or leased. The railroad makes a flat charge for loaded or empty-car movement, furnishing only power and rails.

Plan V. Traffic moves generally under joint railroad-truck or other combination of coordinated service rates. Either mode may solicit traffic for through movement.

---

[14] Taft, *op. cit.*, p. 106.

exception that containers are generally smaller than trailers and do not have under carriages. As would be expected, a special label (COFC) has been applied to container-on-flatcar service.

As noted earlier, TOFC is just one type of coordinated transport in current operation. One of the oldest is fishyback, wherein over-the-road trailers or containers are loaded on ships or barges for long-distance transport. Such services are provided in coastal waters between Atlantic and Gulf ports, Great Lakes to coastal points, and along inland navigable waterways.

Because of the economic potential of linking two modes together, in a coordinated effort, the basic concept has appeal to shippers and carriers alike. In fact, several authorities have suggested that the only way to maintain a strong common carrier network is to encourage and foster increased multi-modal combinations. Naturally, efforts toward increased multimodal coordination are of prime interest to logistical planners because such developments increase the options available to accomplish efficient spatial closure. The next decade should witness expanded development of coordinated arrangements because the greatest deterrent to growth in the past has been a tendency among modal representatives and regulator agencies to protect the status quo rather than participate in the added potential. The trend of shippers away from for-hire transport should challenge this protective attitude among common carriers concerning coordinated transport.

Package Services

One type of transportation service that represents an important part of the transport infra-structure does not neatly fall into any of the above classification schemes. Several different localized carriers offer package delivery services within the commercial zones of metropolitan areas under the category of exempt carriers. Some carriers offer package delivery services on an intrastate and interstate basis. The best known of these carriers is United Parcel Service (UPS).

The original service offered by UPS was contract delivery of local shipments for department stores. In this sense the service was limited to delivery of merchandise to consumers. During the last decade, UPS has made substantial inroads into over-all package movements, both in material management and physical distribution. Although UPS does not currently cover the entire United States, over-all operating authority has been constantly expanding. The basic concept is that individual packages conforming to specified size and weight restrictions may be shipped intercity via UPS. Shipments may include up to ten individual packages. By specializing in a specific size of package, UPS has been able to provide overnight service between most cities within 150 miles at rates for the most part equal to or less than parcel post or REA Express. Unlike parcel post, UPS provides both pickup and delivery service.

The growth of UPS has attracted considerable interest in transport circles since inroads are being made into the serious small-shipment problem confronting the distributive industries.[15] Of particular interest here is not UPS per se, but the modern advent of a specialized carrier who has developed an operating system customized to a specialized market segment. Similar developments have taken place within the limited certificate common carriers for shipments larger than package goods. Every indication is that specialization of carriers will continue during the 1970s.

Summary—Transport Infra-Structure

The transportation infra-structure available to the logistics planner in the United States is far superior to that of any other nation. Although problems do exist within and between the modes, the shipper has many different choices with respect to how a particular shipment will be transported between two locations. Within the five basic modes several legal forms exist. In addition, auxiliary users, coordinated arrangements, and specialized carriers exist to round out the array of alternatives. The task in design of a logistical system is to select from among available alternatives the combined transport capability or mix that best fits the needs of a particular enterprise.

Ultimately the selection of transportation mix must be fully integrated into the over-all logistical effort of the enterprise in order to design a balanced system. However, in evaluating the potential transportation mix, the value or service rendered by a specific combination of carriers must be measured in terms of corresponding cost. The next section discusses the common carrier rate structure.

Common Carrier Rate Structure

A comprehensive treatment of all aspects of common carrier rates is beyond the scope and intent of this brief overview. The primary purpose of the following is to introduce the nonprofessional to the basic logic and prevailing structure of common carrier rates.

The initial section provides a brief history and review of interstate regulatory authority associated with common carrier rates. Next, the most common types of rates are discussed. The final section reviews special services that carriers provide which are important to logistical planning.

---

[15] The small-shipment problem has caused serious concern for all modes of transportation in post-World War II commerce. For a more comprehensive discussion, see Merrill J. Roberts, *Intermodal Freight Transportation Coordination: Problems and Potential* (Pittsburgh: University of Pittsburgh, 1966), and James C. Johnson, "An Analysis of the Small Shipments Problem with Particular Attention to Its Ramifications on a Firm's Logistical System," *ICC Practitioner's Journal*, July–August 1972, pp. 646–66.

Regulatory Rate Making

To some degree all legal forms of transport are subject to regulation. Common and contract carriers are subject to direct authorization of operating rights, acceptable rates, and safety regulation by various agencies of the federal government if they operate in interstate commerce. If carriers' activities are limited to a single state, regulatory control is maintained by agencies of the various state governments. Of particular interest in this section is the influence of regulation with respect to rate making. Federal economic regulation affects 100 per cent of rail and air ton-miles, 80 per cent of pipeline, 43.1 per cent of trucking, and 6.7 per cent of domestic water carriers.[16]

BRIEF HISTORY OF INTERSTATE REGULATION.   The purpose of interstate regulation is to scrutinize the activities of common and contract carriers with respect to the over-all public interest. Since railroads dominated the early overland transportation network, they enjoyed the privileged position of a near monopolist. Individual states had attempted and gained the legal right to regulate discriminatory practices within their borders, and no federal regulation existed until the "Act to Regulate Commerce" was passed on February 4, 1887.[17] This initial act was the forerunner of the regulatory structure of today. It created the Interstate Commerce Commission (ICC), which remains today the chief transportation regulatory agency of the federal government.[18]

The gradual delineation of the federal government's regulatory power over carrier rate making resulted from a series of enactments and judicial decisions from 1900 through 1920.[19] At the turn of the century, rather serious competitive conditions had resulted from the practice of independent rate making among carriers. Although the ICC had the authority to review groups of rates with respect to the just and reasonable nature after the rates were placed into effect by individual carriers, no regulation existed over proposed rate making. Various attempts at joint rate making by railroads had been declared illegal, and in 1903 the railroads supported the passage of the Elkins Act. This act reduced the extent of under-the-table rebates, special concessions, and increased the penalty for departing from published rates. It did not, however, eliminate the cause of discriminatory practices, which was independent and nonregulated rate making.

[16] Derived from the 1972 National Transportation Report, *op. cit.*, pp. 2–44.

[17] For an early history of legislative attempts prior to 1887, see L. H. Hanley, *A Congressional History of Railways in the United States, 1850–1887*, Bulletin 342 (Madison, Wis.: University of Wisconsin, 1910).

[18] In recent years the ICC has been subjected to considerable review and evaluation by both Congress and critics of government regulation. Some have called for abolishment of the commission. However, the contents of the 1973 Surface Transportation Act, which Congress reviewed extensively and is likely to become law while this book is in press, continues to support the concept and scope of the ICC as the principal regulatory agency of the federal government.

[19] The discussion that follows is based upon that presented by Locklin, *op. cit.*, pp. 208–38.

The passage of the Hepburn Act in 1906 began to establish the federal regulatory powers over rate making. The just and reasonable review authorization of the 1887 act was expanded to include the examination of maximum rate levels. However, the regulatory posture remained *expost* until the passage in 1910 of the Mann–Elkins Act. Provisions of this act permitted the ICC to rule on the reasonableness of proposed rates and to suspend when the proposed rates appeared discriminatory.

The posture of modern rate regulation was completed with the passage of the Transportation Act of 1920. The review power of the ICC was expanded to prescribe minimum as well as maximum reasonableness of rates and the commission was instructed to assume a more aggressive nature concerning proposed rates. Rather than reacting, the original Act to Regulate Commerce was modified to instruct the commission to initiate, modify, and adjust rates as necessary in the public interest. The 1920 act also changed the name of the 1887 act to the Interstate Commerce Act.

Although several additional acts related to transportation have been enacted, with some exceptions their primary objective was to clarify issues related to the basic acts of 1887 and 1920. On 1935 the Emergency Transportation Act further instructed the ICC to set standards with respect to reasonable rate levels. Motor carrier competition was now a prime factor. In 1935 the Motor Carrier Act placed the regulation of common carrier highway transportation under the jurisdiction of the ICC. The Motor Carrier Act, which became Part II of the Interstate Commerce Act, defined the basic nature of the legal forms of common, contract, and exempt motor carriers.

In 1938 the Civil Aeronautics Act established the Civil Aeronautics Authority (CAA) as a counterpart of the ICC for regulating air transport. The powers and charges of the CAA were somewhat different than the ICC in the sense that the act specified that the CAA would be responsible to promote and actively develop the growth and safety of the airline industry. In 1940 the functions of the original CAA were reorganized into the Civil Aeronautics Board (CAB) and the Civil Aeronautics Administration, now known as the Federal Aeronautics Administration (FAA). In addition, the National Advisory Committee on Aeronautics was formed in the mid-1930s and in 1951 became known as the National Aeronautics and Space Administration (NASA). Through the 1960s NASA primarily concentrated attention on aerospace; however, NASA is specifically charged with the responsibility for increasing aviation safety, utility, and basic knowledge through the use of science and technology. From a combined viewpoint, the CAB regulates rate making, the FAA administers the airway system, and NASA is concerned with scientific development of aerospace, commercial, and civil (private) aviation.

The regulation of pipelines has not been as clear cut as that of railroads, motor carriers, and air. In 1906 the Hepburn Act declared that selected pipelines, primarily oil, were in fact common carriers. The need for regulation developed from the early position of market dominance that the original Standard Oil Company gained as a result of developing crude oil pipelines in competition with rail transport. In 1912 the ICC took action, which was upheld by the Supreme Court, to convert private pipelines into common carriers. While there are substantial differences between pipeline and other forms of regulation, today for all effective purposes, the ICC fully regulates pipeline traffic. As a point of interest, perhaps the greatest single difference in pipeline regulation is that common carriers are allowed to transport goods that are owned by the carrier.

Regulation of water transport prior to 1940 was extremely fragmented. Some regulation existed under both the ICC and the U.S. Maritime Commission. In addition, a series of specific acts had placed regulation of parts of the domestic water transport network under particular agencies. The Transportation Act of 1940 placed under the ICC the jurisdiction over domestic water transportation and gave the Federal Maritime Commission authority over water transport in foreign commerce and between Alaska and Hawaii and other U.S. ports.

It is important to understand that the ICC *does not* set or establish rates for carriers under its regulatory jurisdiction. Rather, the ICC reviews and either approves or disapproves rates. Carriers under federal regulation are exempt from the antitrust provisions of the Sherman, Clayton, and Robinson–Patman acts with respect to collaboration in rate making. Such exemption is provided by the Reed–Bulwinkle Act of 1948, which permits carriers to participate in rate-making bureaus. Cooperative rate making, according to a somewhat standardized procedure, is common among all modes with respect to their specific bureau's procedure. Motor carriers, for example, utilize eight rate-making bureaus to coordinate the establishment and publication of new or modified rates. The action of the bureaus is subject to ICC sanction.

Over the years a maze of different federal agencies has been created to assist in various phases of over-all transport regulation. In 1968 the Department of Transportation (DOT) was formed by Congress in an effort to draw the majority of transport-related agencies together under a single administrative head at the cabinet level. In 1971 President Nixon recommended a general reorganization of the Executive Branch of the federal government. Under the new structure, DOT would be abolished, with some functions going to the proposed Department of Community Development and most being assigned to the proposed Department of Economic Affairs.

Although the primary aspect of concern to this treatment is rate regulation, it is important to realize that national transportation policy has a direct impact on the vitality of the common carrier infra-structure and prevailing rates charged for services. Existing national transportation policy is primarily stated in the Amended Interstate Commerce Act, the Merchant Marine Acts, the FAA Act, the Department of Transportation Act, the actions of the ICC, court decisions, and economic messages of the various Presidents.

Table 5-4 provides a summary of the scope of federal economic regulation of interstate transport by mode. A review of the table illustrates that over-all regulation goes far beyond rate regulation.

TABLE 5-4
Scope of Federal Economic Regulation of Interstate Transport by Mode

Mode	Author- izing Statute	Agency	Functions Regulated		
			Rates	Carrier Agreements	Entry
Railroads	IC Act, Part I	ICC	Max-min-precise	Permitted	PCN[1]
Motor trucks	IC Act, Part II	ICC	Max-min-precise	Permitted	PCN,[1] permit
Buses	IC Act, Part III	ICC	Max-min-precise	Permitted	PCN[1]
Domestic water carriers	IC Act, Part III	ICC	Max-min-precise	Permitted	PCN,[1] permit
Surface freight forwarders	IC Act, Part IV	ICC	Max-min-precise	Permitted	Permit
Petroleum pipelines	IC Act, Part I	ICC	Max-min-precise	Permitted	Not controlled
Air carriers					
Domestic	FA Act	CAB	Max-min-precise	Not permitted	PCN[1]
International	FA Act	CAB	Not directly controlled	IATA agreement	PCN,[1] Presidential approval
Air freight forwarders	FA Act	CAB	Discrimination only	Not permitted	Operating authority
Noncontiguous maritime	Merchant Marine Act 1933	FMC	Max-min-precise	Permitted (limited)	Not controlled
International maritime	Merchant Marine Act 1916	FMC	Not directly controlled	Permitted	Not controlled
Maritime freight forwarders	Merchant Marine Act 1916	FMC	Not directly controlled	Permitted	Licensed

Source: Table III-1, *1972 National Transportation Report,* U.S. Department of Transportation, pp. 2–44.

[1] PCN indicates Certificate of Public Convenience and Necessity.

		Functions Regulated			
Service	Exit	Merger	Finance	Reporting	Exemptions
Car service only	PCN,[1] train discontinued	Controlled	Controlled	Specified	None
Not controlled	PCN[1]	Controlled	Controlled	Specified	Agricultural commodities, local transport
Not controlled	PCN[1]	Controlled	Controlled	Specified	None
Not controlled	PCN[1]	Controlled	Controlled	Specified	Bulk commodities
Not controlled	Not controlled	Controlled	Controlled	Specified	Shipper associations, minor carrier groups
Not controlled	Not controlled	Not controlled	Controlled	Specified	None
Little control	PCN[1]	Controlled	Controlled	Specified	Air taxi, agricultural commodities
Bilateral agreements	PCN[1]	Controlled	Controlled	Specified	None
Not controlled	Not controlled	Controlled	Controlled	Specified	None
Not controlled	Not controlled	Not controlled	Not controlled	Specified	Nonliner services
Not controlled	Not controlled	Not controlled	Not controlled	Specified	Nonliner services
Little controlled	Not controlled	Not controlled	Not controlled	None	None

A concentrated attempt is currently being made to review and modify existing national transportation policy in light of the demands and requirements of modern society. In 1972 the Department of Transportation published a report entitled *1972 National Transport Report* in an effort to frame an approach to developing new federal direction and legislation.[20] The report reviews the existing national transportation situation, projects future requirements, and clearly illustrates several alternative approaches to meeting future requirements.

Common Carrier Line-Haul Rates

Common carriers utilize three basic types of line-haul rates: (1) class, (2) exception, and (3) commodity. In this section each type of rate is reviewed.

CLASSIFICATION AND CLASS RATES.   The term *class rate* evolves from the fact that all products transported by common carriers have been classified for purposes of transportation pricing. The basic purpose of the classification scheme is to simplify the number of transportation rates charged by common carriers. The classification does not fix the monetary rate charged for movement of a particular commodity. The rate, once the products classification is determined, is obtained from the appropriate tariff. In standard transportation terminology a specific products classification is referred to as its rating. The charge in dollars and cents per hundredweight to move a specific product classification between two locations is referred to as the rate.

The purpose of the classification is to group products having similar transportation movement and handling characteristics. The classification ranks all products on a reference basis of 100. Therefore, those products with high transportation rates will normally be classified as greater than 100, while those having relatively lower rates will be less than 100.

In terms of classification, motor and rail carriers have independent systems. In addition, several regional classification schemes also exist. Thus a particular product may have different classifications depending upon how, where, or in what quantity it is being shipped. The how results from mode of transport. The where depends upon geographical locality. The quantity differential in classification results from the fact that the applicable classification of a product is normally lower for truckload and carload quantities than it is for smaller shipments.

Once the classification rating for a product is determined, the applicable rate per hundredweight between any two points can be determined from the tariff. All products that can legally be transported in Interstate Commerce can be shipped via class rates. The actual price charged for a specific shipment is normally subjected to a minimum charge and may also be subject to a surcharge or an arbitrary assessment.

---

[20] 1972 National Transportation Report, *op. cit.*

The minimum charge represents the least total charge a shipper must pay for a specific shipment. To illustrate, assume that the applicable class rate is $2.00/cwt and the shipper desired to ship 100 pounds to a specific location. If no minimum charge existed, the total cost of transport would be $2.00. However, if a minimum charge existed, assume it to be $5.00 per shipment, the cost for completing the shipment would be $5.00 rather than $2.00. Thus, under the assumed conditions, the minimum charge has the net effect of rendering all shipments from 1 to 250 pounds equal in transit cost.

An arbitrary refers to a special assessment added to a shipment charge. In some cases, such arbitraries exist to provide carriers special compensation for servicing selected destinations or areas. Such arbitraries are particularly common in the South, where added charges per shipment are placed upon all shipments in a particular weight category. In other cases, the applicable rates to specific destinations are published in terms of a hundredweight charge to a major city plus an arbitrary charge per cent for delivery beyond.

An additional charge, often added for small shipments, is a surcharge to help cover the cost of carrier handling. The surcharge may be a flat charge or a sliding scale based on the size of the shipment.

The combination of class rates, minimum charges, arbitrary charges, and surcharges form a pricing structure which, in various combinations, is applicable between all locations within the continental United States. The general classification provides a base rating for all products. Thus the classification and class rate structure combine to form a generalized pricing structure for rail and motor common carriers. Because of the general nature of class rates, they represent the highest transport prices.

EXCEPTION RATES.   Exception rates or exceptions to the classification are special rates published to provide shippers lower rates than the prevailing class rate. The original use of the exception technique was to provide a special rate for a specific area, origin-destination, or commodity when either competitive or high-volume movements justified a downward rate adjustment. Rather than publish a new tariff, an exception to the classification was published.

Just as the name implies, when an exception rate is published, the classification that normally applies to the product is changed. Such changes may be in the form of assignment of a new class or may be a percentage of the original class. Although, technically, exceptions may be higher or lower, most exception rates are reductions from class rates. Unless otherwise noted, all services associated with the movement remain the same as the class rate when a commodity moves under an exception rate.

COMMODITY RATES.   When a large quantity of a product moves on a regular basis between two locations, the common practice is to publish a commodity rate. Commodity rates are special or specific rates published without regard to classification. Commodity rates are normally published on a point-to-point basis and apply only on the specified products noted in the tariff.

Although at one time the majority of rail freight moved via exception rates, today the dominant tariffs are commodity orientated. Commodity rates are less common among motor carrier tariffs. Whenever a commodity rate exists, it supersedes the corresponding class or exception rate.

CONCLUSION LINE-HAUL RATES. The three main line-haul rates form the nucleus of the motor and rail common carrier rate structures. Each of the other modes has specific characteristics that are applicable to their tariffs. For example, in water, specific tariff provisions are normally made for cargo location within the ship or on the deck. In addition, provisions are made to charter total vessels. Similar specialized provisions are found in air cargo and pipeline tariffs. In addition, auxiliary users and package services publish tariffs that are specialized to their service.

Thus, while this section describes the most frequently used common carrier line-haul rates in a logistical system, it falls far short of providing a comprehensive treatment of all basic common carrier rates and tariffs.

Special Rates and Services

A number of special rates and services are provided by common carriers which are of particular importance to logistical operations. This final section provides a basic description of some of the more important examples.

FREIGHT-ALL-KINDS RATES. Rates for freight-all-kinds (FAK) are very important to physical distribution operations. Under FAK rates, a mixture of different commodities is delivered to a single or a limited number of destinations. Rather than charge each classification or freight within the shipment its appropriate rate, an average rate is applied for the total shipment. In essence, FAK rates are line-haul rates since they replace class, exception, or commodity rates. However, their main use is to simplify the paperwork associated with the movement of a mixture of different commodities. As such, they are of particular importance in distribution from warehouses to retail stores.

LOCAL, JOINT, PROPORTIONAL, AND COMBINATION RATES. Numerous special rates exist that may offer transportation savings on particular freight movements. When a commodity moves under the tariff of a single carrier, it is referred to as a local rate. If more than one carrier is involved in movement of the freight, a joint rate may be applicable wherein the freight moves on a through bill of lading even though multiple carriers are involved in the actual transport. Because many motor and rail carriers operate in restricted territory, it may be necessary to utilize the services of more than one to complete a shipment. Utilization of a joint rate can offer substantial savings over the use of two or more local rates to complete a shipment.

Proportional rates are in fact special price incentives to utilize a published tariff that applies only to part of the desired route. If a joint rate does not exist, and proportional provisions do, the cost of moving a shipment will be lower than combining local rates under the proportional arrangement. Proportional provisions of a tariff are most often applicable to origin or destination points beyond the normal geographical area of a local tariff. They provide a discount on the local tariff, thereby resulting in a lower over-all freight charge than the combination of two local rates.

Combination rates are somewhat similar to proportional rates in that two or more rates may be added together when no published local or joint rates exist between two locations. The rates may be any combination of class exception and commodity rates. The utilization of combination rates often involves several technicalities, such as intermediate rules and aggregation of intermediates, which are beyond the intent of this treatment. The use of combination rates substantially reduces the cost of an individual shipment. In most cases that involve regular logistical movements, the need to utilize combination rates is eliminated by the publication of a through rate.

TRANSIT PRIVILEGES. Transit privileges are, with some minor exceptions, limited to railroad operations. The basic nature of a transit privilege is that it permits a shipment to be stopped at an intermediate point for processing. When transit privileges exist, the shipment is charged a through rate from origin to destination plus a transit privilege charge. From the viewpoint of the shipper, the use of this specialized service is restricted to specific geographical areas once the product enters in transit service. Therefore, a degree of postponement is lost when the product is placed in transit because the area of final destination can be altered only at significant added expense, or at the least, loss of the through rate and assessment of the transit charge. Finally, the utilization of transit privileges increases the paperwork of shippers both in terms of meeting policing requirements of railroads and ultimate settlement of freight bills. The added cost of administration must be carefully weighted in evaluating the true benefits gained from utilizing a transit privilege.

DIVERSION AND RECONSIGNMENT. For a variety of reasons, a shipper, or for that matter the consignee (receiver of shipment), may desire to change routing, designation, or even consignee of a shipment once it is in transport. This flexibility can be extremely important to a logistical operation. It is a normal practice among certain types of marketing middlemen to purchase commodities with the full intention of selling while in transit with subsequent diversion or reconsignment.

Diversion consists of changing the destination of a shipment while it is enroute and prior to arrival at the originally planned destination. Reconsignment is a change in final destination once the shipment has arrived at the originally planned destination but prior to delivery acceptance by the consignee. Both services are provided by railroads and motor carriers for a specified charge.

DEMURRAGE AND DETENTION. Demurrage and detention are charges assessed by carriers when freight cars or truck trailers are held beyond a specified loading or unloading time. The term *demurrage* is used by the railroads for delay in excess of 48 hours in returning a car to service. Motor carriers use the term *detention* to cover similar delays. In the case of motor carriers, the permitted free time is specified in the appropriate tariff and will normally be limited to a few hours. The assessment of a penalty charge is mandatory on the part of carriers and is subject to ICC policing and fine if not properly administered.

From the viewpoint of logistical operations, the degree of demurrage and detention experienced must be carefully administered. Situations exist wherein it is desirable to pay the assessment in order to gain more operational time in the processing of a particular shipment. In effect, the boxcar or trailer can be used as temporary warehouse space by payment of demurrage or detention charges.

ANCILLARY OR ACCESSORIAL CHARGES. Motor and rail carriers offer a wide variety of services that can be of extreme importance in planning a logistical operation. In essence, diversion, reconsignment, transit, demurrage, and detention are examples of special services singled out earlier for more detailed treatment. The list of additional special services is almost unlimited. Of particular importance to logistics are environmental, special equipment, and special delivery services.

Environmental services refer to special control of freight while in transit. Icing, refrigeration, ventilation, and heating to prevent freezing are the prime examples of controlled environment transport. Special equipment charges refer to per trip assessment for the use of specific equipment which the carrier has purchased for the economy and convenience of the shipper.

Of particular importance to logistical operations are a range of special delivery services provided by carriers. This category of special service is most common among motor carriers, who, by the nature of their operation, provide door-to-door delivery. At destination, motor carriers will provide split delivery wherein a load is delivered to more than one destination. Under specified conditions, pickup and delivery will be extended to points beyond those normally considered as part of the point-to-point line-haul service.

Although this brief coverage of special services is not comprehensive, it does provide examples of the type of services carriers will provide for a specified fee. Thus the role of carriers in logistical operations can be far greater than simply transport between two locations.

Summary

The critical nature of transportation to logistical operations has to be developed from a number of viewpoints. Transportation provides spatial closure for the logistical system in the sense that geographically separated facilities and markets are linked together. Transportation is a total cost-reducing factor in the sense that expenditures for transport services allow greater specialization and economies in the process of manufacturing and marketing.

The transport infra-structure consists of five basic modes of transport. Rail, highway, water, pipeline, and air transport can be compared on the basis of speed, availability, dependability, capability and frequency of service as well as fixed and variable cost. Within the modes legal forms of transport identify specific carriers as common, contract, private, and exempt. In addition, multimodal transport exists in the form of auxiliary users and coordinated systems. Finally, the transport infra-structure includes a number of firms which provide package services. The task in the design of a logistical system is to select from among all alternatives the combined transport mix that best fits the needs of a particular enterprise.

The common carrier rate structure provides a basis for evaluating the benefits in over-all logistical operations in terms of corresponding cost. Common carrier rates are controlled by interstate regulatory authority, which dates to 1887. Specific common carrier line-haul rates can be grouped as class, exemption, and commodity rates. In addition, there exist a wide variety of special rates and services which are of particular importance to logistical operations.

Organization and administration of the over-all logistical system is reserved for Chapter 13. However, transportation management is sufficiently specialized so as to constitute an area of detailed professional administration that is essential to logistical operations. Appendix 5A outlines the duties and responsibilities of traffic management within the over-all logistical management organization.

Appendix 5A
Traffic Management and
Logistics

Historically, the largest single block of responsibilities in logistics has rested with the traffic department of the firm. With the advent of the logistical concept, responsibilities for exacting traffic management have increased substantially. In the past it was not at all unusual for the traffic manager to be strictly responsible for his major function—transportation purchasing. However, in the new context, his duties will frequently encompass packaging, material handling, inventory management, warehousing, and other areas of logistics.

Regardless of his exact scope of authority, under the logistical concept, the traffic manager will become more involved with other corporate activities, such as marketing, production, and finance. The recent awareness to total logistical systems has created confusion regarding the proper role of traffic management. In general, logistics is much broader in concept and function than transportation. Transportation management is but one aspect of over-all logistical management. However, it is one of the most important aspects of total control.

The advent of integrated logistics has increased the need for exacting transportation management. A system in total cannot function adequately unless the management of transport is effectively and efficiently performed and integrated to corporate efforts in all other areas. It appears safe to conclude that the demand for professional traffic management is at an all-time high. As long as logistics constitutes a major area of corporate effort, traffic management will be a vital ingredient of the total effort.

The purpose of this appendix is to develop the role of traffic management in a logistical organization. Because total books are devoted to this subject, the content of this appendix falls considerably short of a detailed professional development of the field of traffic management. The appendix aims to provide the nonprofessional reader with a basic familiarization of the specialized field of traffic management.

The major functional responsibilities of a traffic department can be grouped into two areas: (1) administration and (2) research. Each area of responsibility is reviewed below.

Traffic Administration

The administration responsibility of the traffic department consists of day-to-day control of freight movement. In cases where all movements are by for-hire carriers, this daily responsibility consists of purchasing services and movement control. If a firm operates private transport equipment, the traffic department is responsible for administration and scheduling of equipment. In both cases it is the objective of traffic management to provide a transport service that meets requirements of the physical distribution system. These system requirements relate to speed or service, size of order to be shipped, and assignment of the specific plant or warehouse to make the shipment. For any given period, the operating standards for transport are given and must be met if the firm is to achieve its desired logistical goals. However, the research responsibility of traffic management, discussed in the next section, outlines the way in which the transport sector of the firm can and should take an active role in setting logistical standards.

The administration of transportation consists of (1) freight classification, (2) obtaining lowest rate for a given movement consistent with service requirements, (3) equipment scheduling, (4) documenting, (5) tracing and expediting, (6) auditing, and (7) claims.

Freight Classification

All products normally transported are grouped together into uniform classifications. The purpose of the classification is to take into consideration characteristics of a product or a commodity that will influence cost of handling or transport. Products with a similarity are grouped into a given class, thereby reducing the wide range of possible ratings to a manageable size. The particular class that a given product or commodity receives is called its rating. A products rating is not the price that must be paid to have a product transported. The rating is a products classification placement. The actual price that must be paid is called the *freight rate*. As will be explained below, the rate is found from price lists called *tariffs*. Thus a products rating is used to determine the actual freight rate.

Motor carriers and rail carriers each have independent classification systems. The basic motor carrier system is the "National Motor Freight Classification," and rail classifications are published in the "Uniform Freight Classification." The motor classification has 23 classes of freight; the rail system has 31. In local or regional areas, individual groups of carriers may publish additional classification listings.

Classification of individual products is based on a relative percentage index of 100. Class 100 is considered the normal class with other classes running as high as 500 and as low as 35 in the national motor freight system. Each product is assigned an item number for listing purposes and then a class rating. As a general rule, the higher a class rating, the higher is the transport cost of a product. Thus a product classified as 400 would be four times more expensive to transport than a product rated as class 100. Products are also assigned classifications based upon the quantity shipped at an individual time. Less-than-carload (LCL) or less-than-truckload (LTL) shipments of identical products will have higher ratings than carload (CL) or truckload (TL) shipments.

To illustrate, take item 70660 from the National Motor Freight Classification A-7. Item 70660 is described as "carpet or rug cushions, cushioning or lining, sponge rubber, in wrapped rolls." Item 70660 falls into the general product grouping 70500 "floor coverings or related articles." For LTL shipments, item 70660 has a $77\frac{1}{2}$ rating, whereas in TL shipments it is assigned class 45, provided that a minimum shipment of 30.2 hundredweight is shipped. Many products will also be assigned different ratings based upon packaging. Sponge rubber cushions may have a different rating when shipped loose, in bails, or in boxes than when shipped in wrapped rolls. Thus a number of different classifications may apply to the same product depending upon where it is being shipped, the size of the shipment, the transport mode being used, and the packaging of the product.

One of the major responsibilities of the traffic department is to obtain the best possible rating for all products shipped by the firm. Although there are differences in rail and motor classifications, each is guided by classification rules. These rules are similar; however, the rail rules are more comprehensive and detailed than those for motor freight classification. It is essential that members of a traffic department have a comprehensive understanding of classification rules. These general rules handle all normal situations and specific rules are available as exceptions to the general rule.

It is possible to have a product reclassified by making written application to the appropriate classification board. These boards review proposals for change or additions with respect to minimum weights, commodity descriptions, packaging requirements, and general rules and regulations. All changes other than corrections in classification require public hearings prior to publication. Other interested parties are thereby provided an opportunity to be heard prior to acceptance or rejection of the proposal. After the proposal is accepted or rejected, methods of appeal are provided.

An alert traffic department must take an active role in classification. Many dollars can be saved by finding the correct classification for a product or by recommending a change in packaging or quantity shipped that will reduce the rating of a firm's product.

Freight Rates

The main body of Chapter 5 contained a description of basic transportation rates and rate regulation. For any given shipment it is the responsibility of the traffic department to obtain the lowest possible rate consistent with service requirements. Determination of transport cost by method of movement—rail, air, motor, pipeline, parcel post, United Parcel, REA Express, freight forwarders, and so on—is found by reference to tariffs. In this connection it is important that the traffic department have adequate access to current tariffs. The most important information resource available to the traffic department is its tariff library. Many tariffs exist and relevant ones must be kept up to date for all changes and modifications.

As indicated several times throughout this text, the lowest possible cost for transportation alone may not be the lowest total cost of distribution. The traffic department must seek the lowest rate consistent with service standards. For example, if 2-day delivery is required, the traffic department seeks to select the method of transport that will meet this standard at the lowest possible cost or freight bill.

Equipment Scheduling

In cases where private transportation equipment is used, one major responsibility of the traffic department is scheduling. This responsibility also exists when common carriers are utilized. One of the largest bottlenecks in physical distribution can occur by the building up of carrier equipment waiting to be loaded or unloaded at a shipper's dock.

Railroads and motor carriers each have special charges for equipment delay beyond normal times allowed in the tariffs. Motor carriers specify times based upon individual situations, and when these times are exceeded detention charges are made. Railroads normally allow 48 hours for unloading with time in excess charged as demurrage.

As a general rule, demurrage and detention should be held to a minimum, because they represent a penalty charge that increases the total cost of distribution. However, in special cases, it may be desirable to pay delay penalties in order to reduce other expenses. For example, demurrage charges may represent a favorable tradeoff if overtime can be reduced. Each situation must be evaluated on the merits of the alternatives. The objective is to eliminate special service charges unless they reduce other costs of physical distribution.

Documentation

Several basic documents are involved in transportation management. Two of the most important are the bill of lading and the freight bill.

BILL OF LADING.   The bill of lading is the basic document in the purchase of transport services. It serves as a receipt for goods shipped through the description of commodities and quantities as detailed on the document. For this reason, accurate description and count are essential. In case of loss, damage, or delay, the bill of lading provides necessary evidence for damage claims resulting from inferior carrier performance.

The bill of lading specifies the terms and conditions under which the carrier liability is extensive and includes all possible causes of loss or damage except those defined as acts of God. It is important that these terms and conditions be clearly understood so that appropriate actions may be taken in the event of nonperformance or inferior performance.

There are variations in bills of lading. In addition to the uniform bill of lading, others commonly used are order notify, export, livestock, and government. It is important to select the correct bill of lading for a specific shipment.

An order-notified or negotiable bill of lading is a credit instrument. It provides that delivery shall not be made unless the original bill of lading is surrendered to the carrier. The usual procedure is for the seller to send the order-notified bill of lading to a third party, usually a bank or credit institution. Upon payment of the invoice value of the goods, the credit institution releases the bill of lading to the buyer. The buyer then presents it to the common carrier, who in turn releases the goods.

An export bill of lading permits the use of export rates, which are sometimes lower than normal domestic rates. Thus, when a shipment is being moved domestically for export, savings in transport can sometimes be enjoyed. An export bill of lading also permits greater time at the port for transfer of freight from a rail car to ship. In many cases the export bill also eliminates the need for special broker services at the port facility.

Government bills of lading may be used when the product is owned by the U.S. government. A government bill of lading allows the use of *Section 22 rates*, which are normally lower than regular rates. Under Section 22 of the Interstate Commerce Act, when goods are shipped on government account, rates may be based on bids by carriers, which may result in more competitive rate structures.

The named individual or buyer on a bill of lading is the only bona fide recipient of goods. A carrier is responsible for proper delivery according to instructions contained in the document. In effect, title is transferred with accomplishment of delivery.

FREIGHT BILL. The freight bill represents a carrier's method of charging for transportation services performed. The freight bill is derived from information contained on the bill of lading. It may be either prepaid or collect. A prepaid bill means that transport cost must be paid for prior to the transportation performance, whereas a collect shipment shifts payment responsibility to the buyer.

Freight bill payment periods vary. Motor carriers must bill shippers within 7 days of delivery and the shipper must pay the carrier within an additional 7 days after receipt of the bill. In the case of rail, 96 hours are allowed for carloads and 120 hours for LCL shipments. Unless credit arrangements have been made with carriers, collect shipments are payable upon delivery.

A great deal of transportation administration is involved in preparation of bills of lading and freight bills. Several firms and carriers are jointly working to reduce this administrative burden. Some firms elect to pay at the time of creating the bill of lading, thereby combining the two documents into one. Such arrangements are based upon financial analysis of the relative benefits of advanced payment to reduce paperwork costs. Many attempts are also under way to produce all documents in the required number of copies simultaneously. This has become more practical with the advent of computer facilities to aid in document preparation.

Tracing and Expediting

One of the largest areas of transportation management is the responsibility of tracing and expediting. Shipments committed to the vast transportation network of the United States are bound from time to time to go astray or get delayed en route. Most large carriers maintain a tracing department to aid shippers in locating a shipment. The tracing action must be initiated by the shipper's traffic department. Once initiated, it is the carrier's responsibility to provide the desired information.

Under conditions of exacting product movement control, the shipper may desire to expedite a given shipment in order to overcome some unexpected change of events. Under these conditions the shipper is often provided a "pro" number, which corresponds to the carrier's waybill and vehicle number. Identification of the shipment's pro number allows rapid location at points of destination terminal and transfer terminals.

Auditing

Auditing of freight bills is another important function of the traffic department. Owing to the complexities involved in finding the correct rate, the probability of an error in rate determination is higher in purchasing transportation than in most other purchasing decisions. Given the fact that transportation costs in the United States exceed $60 billion, a 1 per cent error in calculating a rate will result in a $600 million potential loss to either carriers or shippers.

The freight audit is of two types: (1) preaudit and (2) postaudit. A preaudit determines the proper rate and charges prior to payment of a freight bill. A postaudit makes the same determination after payment. Either or both types of audits may be employed.

Auditing may be either (1) external or (2) internal. If external, specialized freight auditing companies are used whose personnel are usually assigned to specific commodity groupings, and this generally is more efficient than the use of internal personnel. Payment for an external audit is usually based upon the revenues reclaimed through inadvertent overcharges in the original payment. It is crucial that a highly ethical firm be employed for this purpose, because valuable marketing and customer information is contained in the freight bill, which, if not held confidential, may adversely affect corporate activities.

A combination of internal and external auditing is frequently employed. The division of this activity in such cases is based upon the freight bill. Thus, for a bill of $600, a 10 per cent error results in a $60 recovery, but for a $50 bill a 10 per cent error results in only a $5 recovery. Bills with the larger recovery potential may be handled by an external auditing firm.

External versus internal auditing may also be affected by the size of the firm and the degree of rate computerization. Large traffic departments are in a position to have specialized clerks for auditing purposes. Firms on computerized systems of freight payment can build in appropriate applicable rates on a large majority of points and weights. In that case, automatic checks on proper payment can be made by computer programs designed for that purpose.

Claim Administration

The transport carrier is a specialized middleman who agrees to perform a specified service for an agreed-upon fee. When these services or fees do not meet the predetermined standards, shippers can make claims for restoration. Naturally, carriers and shippers desire to prevent as many claims as possible.

The advent of a claim situation indicates that the planned physical distribution of a product has broken down and that corrective action is in order. Most claims can be settled between the carrier and shipper without resort to a higher authority. However, when necessary the framework for third-party settlement is detailed.

In general, claims break down into two categories: (1) loss and damage, and (2) overcharge–undercharge. Loss and damage claims represent a shipper's demand for carrier payment of partial or total financial loss resulting from improper fulfillment of the transport agreement. Charge claims result from variance in actual charges from those published in tariffs.

A specialized body of rules applies to the proper procedure for claim filing and the responsibility of the parties involved. A discussion of this detail is beyond the intent of this brief appendix. From the viewpoint of physical distribution management, two factors regarding claim administration are of primary importance. First, detailed attention should be given claim administration because such recoveries will be realized only by aggressive shipper programs. Second, the advent of a large volume of claims indicates that the carriers selected are not performing their specified service obligation with desired consistency. Regardless of the dollars recovered by claim administration, the breakdown in physical distribution performance from loss and damage claims constitutes a deficiency to the shipper firm in the eyes of customers.

Summary—Traffic Administration

The seven administrative responsibilities of traffic management herein developed could be expanded in substantial detail. In total, they break down to selection of carriers who can perform the desired service and follow-up required. Emphasis has been placed upon the purchasing of transport services rather than administration of private or contract fleets. Depending upon the transport mix used by a specific firm, the responsibilities of traffic management could very well encompass duties concerning common, contract, and private transport.

Traffic Research

Beyond traffic administration, the traffic department has a basic research responsibility with respect to the transport area and to the over-all logistical system. Almost all traffic managers are able to perform adequately the administrative responsibilities of transportation. To be sure, some are far superior to others in day-to-day administration. However, most all get the job accomplished. The true distinction of professionalism among traffic managers comes in their capabilities in the area here called traffic research.

Traffic research is divided into two areas of responsibility. The first represents activities to improve the cost of transportation services and/or the quality of service received. The second constitutes activities aimed at improving the total distribution effort of the firm. Each is discussed in turn.

Transport Services Research

Traffic managers should always be on the lookout for information to improve carrier service or obtain lower freight rates for a given quality of service. This means that an aggressive program of performance measurement and rate negotiation should represent a continuing function of transportation research.

Carrier performance measurement is perhaps one of the most void areas of traffic research. Information is normally accumulated regarding the number of claims required with individual carriers as well as tracing requirements. However, in addition, shippers should make an effort to measure how well carriers meet stated service obligations. Such obligations concern (1) equipment availability, (2) tracing efficiency, (3) expediting capability, and (4) transit consistency.

Among these four measures of performance, the one most difficult to obtain reliable information about is transit consistency. In Chapter 6 the subject of inventory control is developed. One vital aspect of control systems is the lead time required to obtain replenishment. Regardless of how fast a supplier is able to ship, if the transport carrier provides inconsistent delivery, problems in inventory control will result. Likewise, sales can be lost and production lines shut down if carriers fail to meet their service obligation. As a general statement, the smaller a given shipment, the greater the service variance between consecutive shipments. Thus, while a truckload or carload shipment may regularly meet published schedules, the same efficiency may not be enjoyed in LTL or LCL shipments. Some carriers are superior to others and the task is to determine which among the many available is most consistent.

One shipper that purchases from a number of suppliers for delivery to several different warehouses obtains this information as follows. When suppliers ship, they are required to record date and other critical information on a postcard. When the order arrives at the firm's warehouse, it is so noted on the daily data transmitter to the central purchasing headquarters. Both dates are retained in a computer file by individual carriers along with a statement of expected performance. The variation between actual and expected performance is determined by a simple computer routine and the average performance is calculated and updated on a regular basis. At specified intervals, the performance record of each carrier is printed in report form and forwarded for traffic management review.

This consistency report, coupled with statistics on equipment availability, tracing, and expediting performances, provides valuable information for evaluation of carriers. Unless this type of information is collected on a routine basis, it is difficult to be specific or take corrective action about erratic carrier performance.

Another vital area of transport research is the matter of negotiation. Such negotiations are of two types: (1) formal and (2) informal. In formal negotiations, shippers must actively participate in proceedings before regulatory boards. Such proceedings may be aimed at achieving improvements in rates, ratings, or service provisions of a specific tariff, or they may be aimed at preventing undue price increases or service detailments proposed by carriers. Informal negotiations consist of direct relationships between shippers and carriers. Despite the fact that transportation is a highly regulated industry, a great deal of latitude does exist between carriers and shippers. The effectiveness of both formal and informal negotiation will depend upon the shipper's ability to support proposals with accurate and complete information. Such information can only be collected by a well-administered research and analysis program. One very important area of transport research, therefore, is the constant review of carrier performance and continuous examination of beneficial changes in existing classifications and tariffs.

Logistical System Research

For any given operating period, traffic management is expected to meet the specified service requirements within the stated transportation budget. However, it is also a responsibility of traffic management to look for ways in which transportation can be effectively used to reduce total physical distribution costs. For example, a slight change in packaging may open the door for negotiation of a lower classification rating for a product. Although packaging costs may increase by a slight amount, this added expense may be offset by a substantial reduction in transportation cost. It seems safe to assume that unless such proposals evolve from the traffic department, they will go undetected in the average firm.

As indicated earlier, transportation is the highest single cost area in most logistical systems. Because of this cost and the dependence of the logistical system on an effective transport capability, the traffic department must play an active role in future planning.

Summary

In this brief appendix the responsibilities of traffic management in logistics have been developed. A basic differential was made between duties of an administrative nature and those related to research and development. Perhaps the greatest demands of professional traffic management relate to the areas of research and development. It is in the area of transport services and basic system research that the skills of the traffic management group are vitally needed. Many potential benefits of integrated logistical effort are first recognized and then accomplished by aggressive and innovative traffic management.

Questions

1. Why would early location theorists concentrate upon transportation as the prime determinant of industrial activity?
2. Describe the various modes of transportation and the concept of intermodal movement.
3. Describe the differences among common carriers, private carriers, and contract carriers in terms of fixed and variable costs of operation.
4. Why is a strong common carrier system considered essential to national growth and defense?
5. What has been the major shift in orientation in transportation regulation from the passage of the initial act in 1887 to the proposed surface transportation act of 1972?
6. Why is the Reed–Bulwinkle Act considered important to transportation pricing, and what current forces have subjected the provisions of this act to critical review?
7. Discuss the difference between class commodities and exception rates. What is the role of classification in determination of rates?
8. Why are transit privileges integral to the formulation of distribution systems?
9. Discuss the importance of demurrage and detention to the carriers and shippers.
10. Why would a freight-all-kinds rate be of extreme importance to a firm engaged in delivery of a broad product line from its warehouse to its retail stores?
11. Discuss the concept of alternating minimums in the selection of transportation rates.
12. What would be the major implications for the transportation industry and shippers if transportation were deregulated?

6

Elements of Inventory

Inventory management is one of the most risky decision areas in the modern business enterprise. Commitment to a particular inventory assortment and subsequent allocation to specific markets in anticipation of future sales represent the vortex of logistical operations. Without the proper assortment of inventories available, serious marketing problems can develop with respect to revenue generation and customer relations. Likewise, inventory planning is critical to manufacturing operations. Raw material shortages can force the production line to be shut down or the production schedule to be modified, which, in turn, introduces considerable added expense and a potential shortage of the finished product.

Just as shortages can disrupt planned marketing and manufacturing operations, excessive or overstocked inventories create serious problems. Overstocks increase cost and reduce profitability as a result of added warehousing, capital tieup, product deterioration, excessive insurance, added taxes, and even product obsolescence. The management of inventory is therefore properly viewed as the attainment of balance between a shortage of stock and an excess of stock within a planning environment characterized by risk and uncertainty.

In this chapter the basic principles of inventory management are developed.

The first section is concerned with an overview of the basic nature and function of inventory in the corporate structure. The risk related to inventory decisions is reviewed, and the section concludes with a statement of policy and control in a replenishment cycle context. Next, inventory cost is examined and the formulation of economic order quantity is related to the duration of optimal replenishment cycles. The following section considers sales uncertainty. Statistical probability is introduced as a technique for establishing safety stocks under a variety of situations. Special issues related to selectivity in inventory commitment are developed as they relate to safety stock policy. Next, uncertainty in both sales and duration of the inventory-replenishment cycle are treated as independent but compounded variables in the formulation of safety stock policy. The final section of the chapter switches emphasis from inventory planning and policy formulation to inventory unit control systems.

Nature and Functions of Inventory

Formulation of sound inventory policy requires a thorough understanding of the role of inventory in a manufacturing–marketing enterprise.[1] In this section the functions of inventory are examined first. Next, the degree of risk with respect to width, depth, and duration of inventory decisions for various types of enterprises is reviewed. Finally, the nature of managing inventory in a performance cycle context is examined with respect to policy formulation and unit control.

Functions of Inventory

The basic function of inventory is simply stated—to increase profitability through manufacturing and marketing support. The theoretically ideal concept of inventory commitment consists of manufacturing-to-customer specification for at-plant consumption. Such an ideal system would not require stockpiles of raw materials or finished goods in anticipation of future events. While obviously it is not practical to consider a zero-inventory manufacturing–distribution system, it is important to remember that each dollar invested in inventory should be committed to achieve a specific operational objective.

Inventory consists of a major area of asset deployment which should be required to provide an adequate return on investment. A measurement problem exists, however, since the typical corporate profit-and-loss statement does not adequately display the true cost or benefits gained by asset deployment in

---

[1] For a good background discussion, see John F. Magee, *Production Planning and Inventory Control* (New York: McGraw-Hill Book Company, 1958); M. K. Starr and D. W. Miller, *Inventory Control: Theory and Practice* (Englewood Cliffs, N.J.: Prentice-Hall, Inc., 1962), E. S. Buffa, *Production-Inventory Systems: Planning and Control* (Homewood, Ill.: Richard D. Irwin, Inc., 1968); and G. Hadley and T. M. Whitin, *Analysis of Inventory Systems* (Englewood Cliffs, N.J.: Prentice-Hall, Inc., 1963).

inventory. The lack of sophistication in the measurement of inventory investment means in part that it is difficult to identify the proper inventory level in
a complex organization. Substantial conflict exists within the organization
concerning the appropriate level of inventory commitment and allocation.
Financial management has a natural tendency to want inventories to be reduced
so as to improve cash flow. Marketing desires abundant finished goods inventories to protect against stockouts or back orders. The manufacturing department is inclined to desire large stockpiles of raw materials and components
to assure that there will be no disruption of plans designed to achieve
maximum economy of production.

As a generalization, most firms carry an average inventory that exceeds
their basic business requirement. This basic generalization can be better understood by a careful examination of the four prime functions that underline
inventory decisions.

GEOGRAPHICAL SPECIALIZATION.   One fundamental function of inventory is
to allow *geographical specialization* of individual operational units of the
enterprise. Owing to such factors of production as power, raw materials,
water, and labor, the most economical location for manufacturing could well
be a considerable distance from areas of prime consumption.[2] Geographical
separation also relates to the manufacturing of specific components of a
finished product. For example, tires, batteries, transmissions, springs, and
so forth become prime elements in the material management process of
automobile assembly. Geographical separation allows each component of the
automobile to be produced on an economical basis and later, as a result of
inventory coordination, to be fully integrated in assembly.

The function of geographical separation is also related to physical distribution. The collection of an assortment of goods from various manufacturing
plants within an enterprise so as to offer a mixed variety of all products
manufactured to a customer in a single mixed shipment is a prime example of
geographical separation and integrated distribution made possible by inventory.

Geographical separation therefore serves to permit economic specialization
between the manufacturing and distribution units of an enterprise. To the
degree that geographical separation exists, inventory in the form of raw
materials, semifinished goods or components, and finished goods must be
introduced to the logistical system. Each location requires basic stocks. In
addition, in-transit or pipeline inventories are necessitated to link the various
stages of manufacturing and distribution. Although difficult to measure, the
economies gained by geographical specialization are expected to more than
offset the additional cost of inventory and transportation.

DECOUPLING.   A second function of inventory is to provide maximum efficiency
of operations housed at a single geographical location. This function is referred

---

[2] See Appendix II.

to as the *decoupling* aspect of inventory.[3] Stockpiling work-in-process within the manufacturing complex permits maximum economies of production without work stoppage. Likewise, production to warehouse inventory allows economy of scale in manufacturing. In turn, warehouse inventory produced in advance of actual need permits distribution to customers in large-quantity shipments at minimum freight rates per unit distributed.

The decoupling function of inventory allows each product to be manufactured and distributed in economically sized lots. In terms of marketing, decoupling permits all products manufactured over a time period to be offered to customers as an assortment. Thus decoupling tends to buffer operations of the enterprise. The decoupling function of inventory is different from the geographical specialization function. Decoupling enables increased efficiency of operation at a single location. The function of geographical specialization provides the opportunity to introduce more than one location at which the advantages of decoupling may be enjoyed. Decoupling of operations requires investment in inventory in order to enjoy continuity of process.

BALANCING SUPPLY AND DEMAND.   A third function of inventory is *balancing*, which concerns elapsed time between consumption and manufacturing. Inventory in this capacity exists to reconcile supply availability with demand requirements. The most notable examples of balancing are manufacturing–marketing situations of seasonal production and year-round consumption: orange juice is one such product. Another example is year-round production and seasonal consumption: antifreeze represents this category. Inventories in a balancing capacity serve to link the economies of manufacturing with the demand variations of consumption.

The managerial reconciliation of differential time periods in manufacturing and demand encompass difficult planning problems. When seasonal demand is concentrated in a very short selling season, manufacturers, wholesalers, and retailers are forced to take an inventory position far in advance of the peak period of marketing. For example, in the manufacturing of lawn furniture, production must be in high gear by early fall for units that will not be sold to the public until the following spring or summer. In early January and February manufacturers' inventories peak and start to decline as orders for furniture begin to flow through the marketing channels on their way to wholesalers and large retailers. Retail sales begin in early spring and hit a peak between Memorial Day and Labor Day. However, after July 4 the nature of the retail market shifts from a seller's market to a buyer's market in the sense that price competition dominates as retailers attempt to reduce inventory and eliminate the possibility of seasonal carryover. Thus, from a retailer's viewpoint, an inventory position for the entire selling system must be planned six months prior to the peak selling season. Any attempt to supplement inventories after Memorial Day is extremely risky.

[3] Buffa, *op. cit.*

Although lawn furniture is an extreme example of seasonal selling, almost all products have seasonal variations. Inventory stockpiling serves to allow mass consumption or mass manufacturing of all products that are subject to seasonal patterns. The balancing function of inventory requires investment in seasonal stocks. Seasonal inventories represent a special case of asset deployment since such inventories are expected to be fully liquidated within the selling season. The critical planning problem with respect to seasonal inventories is how much to stockpile in order to enjoy maximum sales without running the risk of overstock and subsequent inventory carryover to the next selling season.

SAFETY STOCK. *Safety stock* is a function of inventory which concerns short-range variation in either demand or the operational capability to replenish inventories. This particular function of inventory is well appreciated by inventory managers since a great deal of their planning is devoted to determining the size of safety stocks. In fact, disregarding the special case of seasonal stocks, most overstocks are the result of improper planning of safety stocks.

The requirement for safety stock results from uncertainty concerning future sales and inventory replenishment. If uncertainty exists concerning how many of a given product will be sold during a future time period, it is necessary to plan an inventory position. In part, planning an inventory position consists of estimating sales, which, as indicated in Chapter 4, is a combination of statistical forecasting and prediction. The second part of planning an inventory position concerns the degree to which protection against forecast variations is desired. In a sense, this second part of inventory planning is similar to purchasing insurance. The inventory committed to protect against possible error in performance is commonly referred to as *safety* or *buffer stock*.

Safety stock is required to protect against two types of uncertainty or potential variations. The first type of uncertainty (type I) concerns sales that occur at random in excess of estimated sales during the planning period. The second type of uncertainty (type II) concerns time delays that occur at random in excess of the normal or standard time for replenishing inventory stocks between two locations in a manufacturing–marketing system. An example of type I uncertainty is the sale of more units per time period than was estimated. Type II uncertainty can be introduced to the planning situation by a delay in order receipt, order processing, or transportation.

Statistical and mathematical techniques for planning protection against both types of uncertainty are developed in detail later in the chapter. At this point it is important to realize that the probability and magnitude of each type of uncertainty can be estimated. The safety stock function of inventory is to provide a specified degree of protection against inventory shortages resulting from both types of uncertainty.

SUMMARY—INVENTORY FUNCTIONS. In summary, the four functions of inventory are identified as geographical specialization, decoupling, balancing supply, and demand and safety stock. All functions combine to prescribe a level of inventory investment necessary for a specific system to perform to management objectives. Given a specific manufacturing–marketing complex, inventories planned and committed to operations can be reduced only to a threshold level capable of performing the four inventory functions. All inventories that exceed the threshold level represent excessive commitments resulting from inaccurate appraisal.

At the threshold level, inventory investment to achieve geographical specialization and decoupling can be modified only by changes in the facility location and operational processes of the enterprise. Reductions in threshold inventory related to geographical specialization and decoupling are appropriately related to system design and manufacturing operations.

The threshold level of inventory required to balance supply and demand is the result of the difficult task of estimating seasonal requirements. With experience over a number of seasonal periods the related risks of attempting to achieve marginal sales during high periods of demand in comparison to costs associated with inventory stockpiling and carryover risk can be projected fairly well. A plan concerning threshold levels of seasonal inventory can be formulated based upon this experience. Although firms confronted with extreme seasonal supply-and-demand patterns may always experience a degree of error in estimating seasonal requirements, such error in threshold planning can be controlled within an acceptable range.

The inventories committed to safety stocks represent the greatest potential for improved inventory performance. Commitments to safety stocks are operational in nature and therefore subject to rapid adjustment in the event of error or a change in policy. A variety of techniques is available to assist management in the planning of safety stocks commitments. Therefore, a complete understanding of safety stock relationships and policy formulation constitutes the prime area of attention in this chapter.

Inventory Risk

During the discussion of inventory functions, risk related to inventory commitments was noted. It is important to fully appreciate that the depth, width, and duration of risk among business enteprises varies, depending upon the firm's position in the distribution channel.

RETAIL INVENTORY RISK. For a retailer the management of inventory is fundamentally a buying and selling process. The retailer purchases a wide variety of products from manufacturers and wholesalers, thereby assuming a substantial risk in the marketing process. The retailer's general inventory risk can be viewed as wide but not deep. The retailer, as a result of the high cost of store location, places prime emphasis on turnover or velocity of movement, which serves to minimize the duration of risk on any given product.

Although retailers will assume a risky position on a large variety of products, their position on any one product is not deep. For a typical supermarket inventory, risk is spread across over 10,000 stockkeeping units. A discount house with general merchandise and food could exceed 25,000 stockkeeping units. A full-line department store may need effectively to manage as many as 50,000 inventory stockkeeping units. Faced with this type of width in inventory risk, mass merchant retailers have made a concentrated effort to reduce risk by pressing manufacturers and wholesalers to assume greater and greater responsibility for safety stocks. Pushing safety stock functions "back up" the marketing channel has resulted in the demand by retailers for fast delivery of mixed product shipments from wholesalers and manufacturers. Specialty retailers, in contrast to mass merchandisers, normally have reduced width of inventory risk, owing to the fact that the lines they handle are narrower. Normally, however, specialty retailers are confronted with the need to assume greater risk than mass merchandisers with respect to depth and duration.

WHOLESALE INVENTORY RISK. The risk exposure of wholesalers is typically narrower but deeper and of longer duration than that of retailers. The traditional merchant wholesaler purchases in large quantities from manufacturers and sells in smaller quantities to retailers. The economic justification of the merchant wholesaler is that he can provide retail delivery of merchandise produced by many different manufacturers. Often, when such products are of a seasonal variety, the wholesaler is forced to take an inventory position far in advance of the selling season, thereby increasing risk of depth and duration by assuming seasonal stock responsibility.

One of the greatest hazards of wholesaling is to allow product lines to expand to the point where the width of inventory risk approaches the level assumed by the retailer while continuing to experience risk associated with the depth and duration that are characteristic of the wholesaling function. For example, traditional full-line hardware and food wholesalers have faced a difficult situation during the past decade. Extensive expansion of product lines has increased the width of inventory risk. In addition, their retail clientele has forced a substantial increase in depth and duration, which has caused a shift of safety stocks back up the marketing channel. The pressures of product-line proliferation, more than any other single factor, have caused a decline in the number of general wholesalers in favor of more specialized operations.

MANUFACTURER INVENTORY RISK. From the viewpoint of the manufacturer, risk takes on significant time dimensions. The manufacturer's commitment starts with a position with respect to raw materials and component parts, includes work-in-process, and ends with the finished goods. In addition, finished goods often must be distributed to warehouses in close proximity to wholesalers and retailers in order to provide rapid delivery. So, although a typical manufacturer may have a narrower line of products than his retail or wholesale counterparts, his operation will be relatively deep and long in duration of inventory commitment.

To the degree that an individual enterprise plans to operate at more than one level of the distribution process, it must be prepared to assume the related inventory risks at each level of the marketing channel. For example, the food chain that operates a regional warehouse assumes risk related to the typical wholesaler operation in addition to its normal retail operations. To the extent that a firm becomes fully integrated for a number of products from manufacturing to retailing, risks related to inventory must be managed at all levels of distribution. The management of echeloned inventories characteristic of vertically integrated firms is more complex because of the need for multilevel policy formulation and control. Regardless, if the inventory problem confronted is at the manufacturing, wholesaling, or retailing level and independent of whether or not it is single level or echeloned, the same basic techniques and principles of inventory management are applicable.

Inventory Policy and Control in a Performance Cycle Context

The task of managing inventory consists of policy formulation and unit control in a replenishment cycle context. Logistical replenishment cycles link together all inventory stocking locations in an enterprise with supplying locations that provide raw material or finished product. An over-all cycle from the viewpoint of inventory consists of order communications, processing, transportation, and updating. The performance times of the four elements combine to create the total elapsed time for inventory replenishment. The duration of the cycle represents the total time necessary to complete the replenishment of inventories. The determination of need (that is, when and how much to replenish) results from implementation of a specific inventory policy through an inventory control system.

Inventory policy consists of guidelines concerning what to purchase or manufacture, when to take the appropriate action, and in what quantity to purchase or manufacture. Unit control is concerned with maintaining accountability of inventory within the enterprise, tracking rates of usage, and, when appropriate, triggering appropriate action to implement inventory policy. The development of sound policy represents the difficult area of over-all inventory management. For purposes of policy formulation, inventories in an enterprise can be grouped as locational and transit.

Locational inventories consist of the combined level of finished products, raw materials, components, and work-in-process. From a policy viewpoint the appropriate level and combination of inventory must be determined for each location. The determination of level requires an appraisal of the basic quantity of each stockkeeping unit required to enjoy the maximum benefits of geographical specialization and decoupling. The determination of level of protection desired against uncertainty at each location must be specified in terms of safety stock units. When appropriate, policy formulation must also specify the level of inventories to be accumulated to satisfy seasonality of supply or demand.

From the viewpoint of *transit inventories*, policy formulation determines the quantity and time duration of all forms of inventory in the pipeline in order to provide an orderly replenishment of specified locational levels. Whereas over-all enterprise commitment on inventory exposure consists of all locational and transit inventories, only locational stocks are available for usage at any point in time. The task in formulating inventory policy is to plan locational and transit inventories for a specified level of availability while maintaining as low a risk of inventory exposure as possible.

The process of *inventory control* is a mechanical procedure required to implement a specified inventory policy. The accountability aspect of control consists of measuring how many units are on hand at a specific location and keeping track of additions and deletions to the basic quantity. In general, accountability and tracking of inventory can be performed by manual or computerized techniques, with the primary differential being speed, accuracy, and cost.

A second major aspect of inventory control is the determination of when action specified by a given policy should be performed. The implementation of policy requires comparison of combined inventory on hand and on order to the minimum level of inventory specified as a reorder point. When combined inventory on hand and on order is equal to or less than the reorder point specified to implement a given policy, the control system should signal the need for action. Inventory on hand can be compared with desired inventory on a periodic or a perpetual time basis.

One major problem in applied inventory management is the common failure clearly to separate the formulation of policy from the planning and implementation of a control system. The formulation of inventory policy is an executive-level responsibility. The determination of policy guidelines integrates inventory with all other aspects of logistics. In turn, all other functional areas of the enterprise are influenced by the implementation of inventory policy through logistical performance. The performance of inventory control is an operational management responsibility. While proper inventory control is essential to smooth corporate operations, problems in control do not normally create the same duration of disruption or failure to achieve goals as commonly experienced as a result of improper policy. Therefore, the major emphasis in the remainder of this chapter is centered on various aspects of the formation of inventory policy. The final section is devoted to a discussion of the fundamentals of periodic and perpetual control and the design of computerized control systems.

Inventory Cost, Economic Order Quantity, and Replenishment Cycle Duration: Conditions of Certainty

In the initial formulation of policy, it is necessary to determine a time for inventory replenishment. As a first approximation, the duration of the inventory replenishment cycle can be based on inventory cost. For purposes of illustration, assume the following conditions. First, the duration of the performance cycle has a high degree of time consistency. Second, the daily rate of sales during the replenishment cycle is constant: for example, the inventory replenishment cycle is always 20 days and the rate of sale is always 10 units per day. Third, as a matter of managerial preference, no more than one replenishment order per product is outstanding at any time. Although such assumptions concerning certainty remove the complex aspects involved in the formulation of inventory policy, they serve to illustrate basic principles.

Figure 6-1 illustrates these relationships. This type of chart is referred to as a *sawtooth diagram* because of the series of right triangles. Since complete certainty exists with respect to replenishment cycle duration and usage, orders would be scheduled to arrive just as the last unit in stock is used up. Thus no extra inventory is maintained in the system.

Since the rate of use in our example is 10 units per day and it takes 20 days to complete the inventory replenishment cycle, a sound reorder policy would be to order 200 units every 20 days. Given these assumed conditions, certain terminology related to policy formulation can be identified.

First, the reorder point is specified as 200 units on hand. Order size would never exceed 200 units an order. Every time an order was received, an additional order for 200 units would be placed.

Second, average inventory would be 100 units since stock on hand would exceed 100 units one half of the time (10 days) and would be less than 100 units one half of the time. In fact, average inventory would be equal to one half of the 200 order quantity. This is a useful rule to keep in mind.

Third, assuming a work year of 240 days, 12 purchases would be required during the year. Therefore, over a period of 1 year, 200 units would be purchased 12 times (2,400 total units). Sales would equal 10 units 240 times (2,400 total units). An average inventory of 100 units would be maintained. Thus the inventory would turn over 12 times.

FIGURE 6-1
Inventory Relationship Constant Sales and Performance Cycle

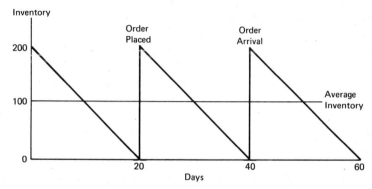

In time, the sheer boredom of such routine operations would in all probability lead management to ask some questions concerning the arrangement. What would happen if orders were placed more frequently than once every 20 days ? Why not order 100 units every 10 days ? Why order as frequently as every 20 days ? Why not reorder 600 units once every 60 days ? Assuming that the inventory replenishment cycle remains constant 20 days, what would be the net result of each of these alternative ordering policies on reorder point, average inventory, and inventory turnover ?

The policy of ordering a smaller volume of 100 units every 10 days would mean that two orders would always be outstanding. Thus the reorder point would still remain 200 committed units on order to service average daily sales of 10 units over the 20-day inventory replenishment cycle. However, average inventory on hand would drop to 50 units and inventory turnover would increase to 24 times per year. The policy of ordering 600 units every 60 days would result in an average inventory of 300 units and a turnover of approximately 4 times per year. These alternative ordering policies are illustrated in Figure 6-2. Despite this analysis, a dilemma would still exist concerning which ordering policy management should establish.

A first approximation to developing a policy can be achieved by calculation of the economic order quantity (EOQ). EOQ provides a deterministic answer by balancing the cost of ordering and the cost of maintaining inventory on an annual basis. By determining the economic order quantity and dividing it into annual demand, the frequency and size of orders that will minimize total cost related to inventory can be identified. Prior to introducing the formulation of EOQ, it is necessary to identify costs typically associated with ordering and maintaining inventory.

Identification of Inventory Costs

Because inventory is so fundamentally related to all aspects of logistical operations it is difficult to isolate costs related purely to inventory ordering and maintenance. In fact, there is a tendency to attempt to group all costs closely related to inventory into the formulation of economic order quantity with the net result that the pure cost of inventory cannot then be isolated for purposes of total logistical system costing.

MAINTENANCE COSTS. The accounts traditionally included in the cost of maintaining inventory are taxes, storage, capital, insurance, and obsolescence. With respect to taxes and insurance, the associated costs are relatively easy to determine. Insurance cost represents a direct payment based upon the degree of risk or exposure over time. Tax cost is a direct levy normally based on inventory holding on a specific day of the year or average holding over a period of time depending upon local tax laws.

The cost of storage must be allocated to specific products since it is not directly related to inventory value. Depending upon the type of warehouse facility

FIGURE 6-2
Illustration of Variable Order Quantity and Average Inventory

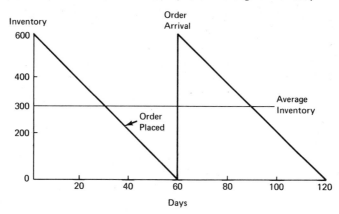

Example: Order 600

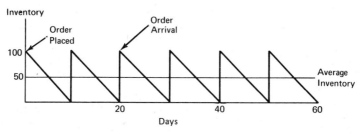

Example: Order 100

utilized, public or private, total storage charges may be direct or it may be necessary to impute costs.[4] In the case of privately owned facilities, the total annual depreciated expense of the warehouse must be reduced to a standard measure such as cost-per-day per square or cubic foot. The cost of total annual occupancy for a given product can then be assigned by multiplication of daily occupied space times the standard cost factor accumulated for the year. This figure can then be divided by the total number of units of merchandise processed through the facility to determine the average storage cost per merchandise unit. In assignment of such costs, care must be taken to make appropriate allowances for idle space.

Cost of obsolescence must be calculated on the basis of past experience. This particular type of obsolescence of concern in inventory planning is the

[4] Michael Schiff, *Accounting and Control in Physical Distribution Management* (Chicago: National Council of Physical Distribution Management, 1972), pp. 315–48.

deterioration not covered by insurance that takes place while a product is in storage. Obsolescence can also be expanded to include a form of marketing loss when a product becomes obsolete with respect to model or accepted customer usage. However, once again care must be exercised not to include costs that are not directly related to the inventory procurement decision. The assignment of obsolescence cost should be approached with care and be limited to direct loss that is related to the storage. Similar to storage cost, charges related to obsolescence should be expressed on a per unit basis.

The most controversial aspect of maintenance cost is the appropriate charge to place on capital invested in inventory. Experience with a variety of corporations indicates a range of figures from the prevailing prime interest rate of money to 25 per cent. The logic for using the prime interest rate is that cash to replace capital invested in inventory can be purchased in the money markets by payment of that rate. The logic of charges greater than the prime interest rate generally is based on a managerially expected return on investment expected from all dollars available to the enterprise. A dollar invested in inventory loses its earning power, restricts capital availability, and perhaps prohibits investment in a new opportunity.

General confusion results from the fact that many top managements have not formulated a clear-cut capital cost policy to be uniformly applied in decision making. With respect to logistical planning, the cost of capital must be clearly thought out since the final rate of assessment will have a profound impact on system design. Low cost of investment will tend to encourage multilocations and generally liberal inventory allocations. High costs will tend to have the opposite effect, almost to the point of restricting expansion.

The cost of maintaining inventory involves management judgment, estimation, assignment, and a degree of direct measurement. The finalized figure should be expressed on an annual basis as a percentage value of a single unit of merchandise. For example, maintenance cost for all categories of expense for a product could accumulate to 25 per cent. If the value of the unit of merchandise is $800, then the annual maintenance cost per unit would be $200.

Determination of maintenance cost across a broad group of products or raw materials requires substantial analysis. While cost of capital remains constant, expense associated with taxes, insurance, storage, and obsolescence will vary depending on value and physical attributes of each product. Once agreement has been reached on the appropriate total assessment for maintenance of all inventory units, the figures should be held constant, owing to their significant impact on over-all logistical planning.

ORDERING COSTS. The cost of placing an order consists of estimating the full expense of inventory control, order preparation, order communication, update activities, and managerial supervision. Similar to maintenance cost, ordering costs are built up for each element of expense until a total cost of order placement is obtained. The combined figure should include assignment of a share of fixed cost related to order preparation plus the direct variable cost associated with ordering. For example, if the total fixed cost associated with ordering activities is $550,000 per year and the historical pattern has been the placement of 220,000 orders per year, then the fixed cost factor per order would be $2.50. The variable cost of placing an order, namely direct communication cost and supplies, could represent $1.25 per order for a total cost of $3.75.

A great deal of variation exists between corporations concerning just what it costs to place an order. The main problem is to include all costs in assignment of fixed and variable expenses. Once the total cost of placing an order is estimated, the normal assumption is to hold it constant regardless of how many orders are placed during a planning period. This assumption of linearity is not fully accurate. However, as long as quantity of orders remains fairly constant from one planning period to the next, only a limited error is introduced.

Economic Order Quantity and Cycle Duration

The concept of EOQ balances the cost of maintaining inventory against the cost of ordering. The key to understanding the basic relationship is to remember that average inventory is equal to one-half order quantity. Therefore, the larger the order quantity the larger the average inventory, and consequently the greater the maintenance cost per year. Likewise, the larger the order quantity, the fewer orders required per planning period and consequently the lower total ordering cost.

The EOQ formulation finds the exact order quantity at which the annual combined total cost of ordering and maintenance is at the lowest point for a given sales volume. Figure 6-3 illustrates the basic relationship. The point at which ordering cost and maintenance cost intersect represents the lowest total cost. The exact quantity that should be ordered to enjoy economical relationships can be determined by dividing the number of orders into the annual volume.

To actually figure EOQ, the most efficient method is a mathematical one. The reader will recall that earlier in this section a policy dilemma was faced regarding whether to order 100, 200, or 600 units in the example situation. The answer to this question can be found by determining the applicable EOQ for the situation. The necessary information is contained in Table 6-1.

TABLE 6-1
Factor Input EOQ Sample Formulation

Annual sales volume	2400
Unit value at cost	$5.00
Maintenance cost	20% per year
Ordering cost per order	$20.00

FIGURE 6-3
Economic Order Quantity

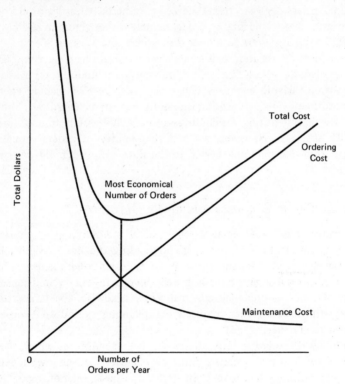

The facts of the situation are that to enjoy the most economical arrangement, orders should be placed in the amount of 300 units rather than 100, 200, or 600. Thus, over the year eight orders would be placed and average inventory would be 150 units.

The standard formulation for EOQ is

$$\text{EOQ} = \sqrt{\frac{2C_oS}{C_mU}}$$

where

C_o = cost per order.

C_m = cost of maintenance per year.

S = annual sales volume, units.

U = cost per unit.

Substituting from Table 6-1,

$$EOQ = \sqrt{\frac{2 \times 20 \times 2400}{0.20 \times 5.00}}$$

$$= \sqrt{96,000}$$

$$= 310 \text{ (rounded to 300)}.$$

Total ordering cost would amount to $160 and maintenance cost would be $150. Thus, subject to rounding for purposes of ordering in unit multiples of 10, annual ordering and maintenance costs have been equated.

With respect to replenishment cycle, ordering in quantities of 300 as opposed to 200 means that locational inventory has been introduced into the system. Since the over-all cycle is 20 days and usage rate is 10 units per day, each time an order arrives 100 units of stock or a 10-day supply will be on hand. In other words, it would not be necessary to place the next order for 10 additional days. Under these conditions of certainty with respect to sales and replenishment cycle duration, management can increase the inventory performance cycle by as much as 10 days without changing the basic order size or average inventory.

If the opportunity existed to enjoy lower costs of performance by substituting cheaper transportation, order communication, processing, or perhaps even purchasing from a more distant source, such changes would not influence performance as long as the modified replenishment cycle did not exceed 30 days. As a first approximation to the duration of the inventory replenishment cycle, under conditions of certainty, the length of ideal performance would be equal to or less than the economic order quantity divided by the average daily sales rate.

Based upon examination of the relationship of the inventory-replenishment cycle, inventory cost, and economic order formulations, several basic relationships useful for inventory planning have been introduced. Prior to dropping the assumption of certainty regarding sales and the replenishment cycle, the reader should fully understand these basic relationships.

First, the EOQ is found at the point where annualized ordering cost and maintenance cost are equal. Second, average inventory will equal one-half order quantity. Third, to retain no more than one order outstanding at a time, the duration of the replenishment cycle should be equal to or less than the EOQ divided by average daily sales. Fourth, the value of the inventory unit, all other things being equal will have a direct relationship on the duration of the replenishment cycle in that the higher the sales rate, the more frequently will orders be placed under EOQ relationships. Finally, the reader should carefully observe Figure 6-3 with respect to the shape of the total cost curve in the range of minimal value. Over a considerable range the total cost curve is relatively flat, which indicates that it would require a substantial change in either ordering cost or maintenance cost to result in a minor change in EOQ.

Therefore, the fact that inventory costs cannot be isolated with exact precision does not dilute the usefulness of EOQ. Likewise, the recalculation of EOQ need only be performed when a notable change occurs in cost or anticipated sales volume.

Setting Safety Stocks: Sales Uncertainty

Although it is useful to review basic inventory relationships under conditions of sales and performance cycle certainty, formulation of inventory policy must take into consideration the realistic situation of uncertainty. One of the main functions of inventory is to provide safety stock protection against the uncertainty of future events.

As noted earlier in this chapter, two types of uncertainty have a direct impact on inventory policy. Type I concerns the fluctuation in rate of sales during the inventory performance cycle; type II deals with variations in the duration or length of the inventory replenishment cycle. In this section sales uncertainty is treated with respect to setting safety stocks when the duration of the inventory replenishment cycle is assumed constant. Next, both types of uncertainty are handled on a simultaneous basis.

Nature of Sales Uncertainty: Type I

The purpose of unit sales forecasting is to project sales during the inventory performance cycle. Even with good forecasting, the typical situation confronted is that actual sales during the inventory performance cycle will either exceed or fall short of anticipated sales. To provide protection against a complete depletion of stock (a stockout) when sales exceed expectations, safety stock is added to basic inventory. Under conditions of sales uncertainty, average inventory is defined as one-half order quantity plus safety stock. Since safety stock exceeds the level of transit inventory associated with replenishment, it is identified as locational inventory.

Figure 6-4 illustrates an inventory-replenishment cycle under conditions of sales uncertainty. The dashed line reflects the forecast. The solid line illustrates inventory on hand from one cycle to the next. The task of planning safety stock consists of three steps. First, the likelihood of stockout must be gauged. Second, sales potential during periods of stockout must be estimated. Finally, a policy decision is required concerning the degree of stockout protection to introduce into the system.

Assume for purposes of illustration that the inventory replenishment cycle is 10 days. Historical experience indicates that daily sales range from zero to 10 with average daily sales of 5 units. The economic order is assumed to be 50, the reorder point is 50, the planned average inventory is 25, and sales during the replenishment cycle are expected to be 50 units.

FIGURE 6-4
Inventory Relationship Sales Uncertainty and Constant Performance Cycle

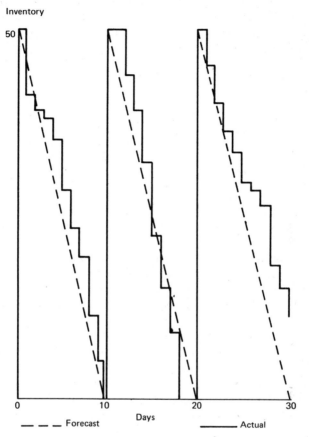

Table 6-2 provides a recap of actual sales history over three consecutive inventory performance cycles. During the first cycle, while sales experienced considerable variation from day to day, the average of 5 units per day was maintained and total sales during cycle 1 totaled 50 units, as expected. During cycle 2 sales reached 50 units in the first 8 days and inventories were fully depleted. As a consequence, no sales were possible on days 9 and 10 of the performance cycle. During cycle 3 sales reached a total of 39 units. The third replenishment cycle concluded with 12 units remaining in stock. Over the 30-day period total sales were 139 units, for an average daily sales of 4.6 units.

Based on the history recorded in Table 6-2, management can observe that stockouts occurred on 2 of 30 total days. Since sales never exceed 10 units per day, no possibility of stockout exists on the first 5 days of each replenishment cycle. Stockouts could occur on days 6 through 10, in case of the remote possibility that unit sales on the first 5 days of the cycle averaged 10 units

TABLE 6-2
Typical Sales Experience During Three Replenishment Cycles

	Forecast Cycle 1		Stockout Cycle 2		Overstock Cycle 3	
Day	Sales	Accumulated	Sales	Accumulated	Sales	Accumulated
1	9	9	0	0	5	5
2	2	11	6	6	5	10
3	1	12	5	11	4	14
4	3	15	7	18	3	17
5	7	22	10	28	4	21
6	5	27	7	35	1	22
7	4	31	6	41	2	24
8	8	39	9	50	8	32
9	6	45	stock-out	50	3	35
10	5	50	stock-out	50	4	39

per day and that no inventory is carried over from the previous period. Since over the three replenishment cycles 10 units were only sold once, it is apparent that the real risk of stockout occurs only during the last few days of the performance cycle and then only when sales have exceeded average by a substantial margin.

Some approximation is also possible concerning the amount of sales that could have been enjoyed had stock been available on days 9 and 10 of cycle 2. A maximum of 20 units could have been sold if inventory had been available. On the other hand, although remote, it is possible that even if stock had been available, no sales would have occurred on days 9 and 10. Based on average sales of 4 to 5 units per day, a reasonable appraisal of lost sales is from 8 to 10 units.

It should be apparent that the degree of risk related to stockouts created by variations in sales is limited to a short time duration and includes a small percentage of total sales. However, management will want to take some degree of protective action to realize available sales and to control the risk of possible deterioration in customer relations. Although the sales analysis presented in Table 6-2 helps to understand the problem, the appropriate course of corrective action is still not clear. Statistical probability can be used to develop a safety stock policy.

Application of Statistical Probability

The sales history over the 30-day period has been arranged in Table 6-3 in terms of a frequency distribution. The main purpose of developing a frequency distribution is to make an appraisal of variation around the average daily sales. Given an expected average of 5 units per day, sales exceeded

TABLE 6-3
Frequency of Sales

Sales/Day	Frequency (days)
Stockout	2
Zero	1
One unit	2
Two units	2
Three units	3
Four units	4
Five units	5
Six units	3
Seven units	3
Eight units	2
Nine units	2
Ten units	1

average on 11 days and were less than average on 12 days. An alternative way of illustrating a frequency distribution is by a bar chart. Figure 6-5, illustrating sales history, is a bar chart format.

Given the historical frequency of sales, it is possible to make an exact calculation of how much safety stock would be necessary to provide a specified degree of protection against lost sales. Probability theory is based on the random chance of a given occurrence appearing out of a large number of occurrences. In the situation illustrated the number of occurrences is 28 days of sales. Although in actual practice more than 28 events or observations would

FIGURE 6-5
Historical Analysis of Sales History

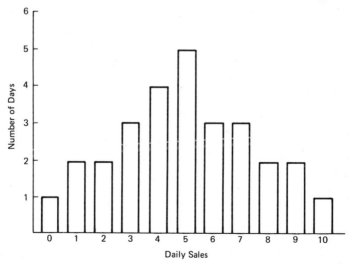

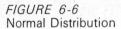

FIGURE 6-6
Normal Distribution

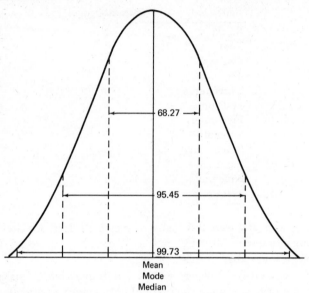

be desirable, a limited sample will serve to illustrate the application of probability theory to setting safety stocks.

The probability of occurrences can be expected to assume a standardized pattern around a measure of central tendency which is the average value of all occurrences. While a number of different types of frequency distributions are utilized in inventory control, the most common is the *normal distribution*.[5]

A normal distribution is characterized by a symmetrical bell-shaped curve, illustrated in Figure 6-6. The essential characteristic of a normal distribution is that the three measures of central tendency most commonly used in statistical analysis are identical. The mean, or average, value; the median, or middle, observation; and the mode, or most frequently observed value, all have the same numerical value. To the extent that these three measures of central tendency are the same or nearly identical, a frequency distribution is classified as normal.

The basis for prediction using a normal distribution is the standard deviation of observations around the measures of central tendency. The standard deviation is a measure of dispersion of events under the areas of the normal curve. With ± 1 standard deviation, 68.27 per cent of all events occur. Within ± 2 standard deviations, 95.45 per cent of all events occur. At ± 3 standard deviations, 99.73 per cent of all events are included. In terms of inventory

[5] For a more detailed application of statistical concepts, see Harry J. Bruce, *How to Apply Statistics to Physical Distribution* (Philadelphia: Chilton Company, 1967).

policy, the standard deviation provides a means of estimating the safety stock required to provide a specified degree of protection above the average sales.

The first step in setting safety stocks is to calculate standard deviation. The formula for standard deviation is

$$\sigma = i\sqrt{\frac{\sum fd^2}{N}},$$

where

σ = standard deviation.

i = size of the class interval (which is 1 day in this example).

f = frequency of event.

d = deviation of event from mean.

The necessary data to determine standard deviation are contained in Table 6-4. Substituting from Table 6-4,

$$\sigma = i\sqrt{\frac{144}{28}}$$

$$= \sqrt[i]{5.14}$$

$$= 2.26 \text{ units (rounded to 3)}.$$

Owing to the inability to add stock except in complete units, the standard deviation of the data in Table 6-4 is rounded to three units. In terms of setting

TABLE 6-4
Calculation of Standard Deviation of Daily Sales

Units	Frequency (f)	Deviation from Mean (d)	Deviation Squared (d^2)	fd^2
0	1	−4	16	16
1	2	−3	9	18
2	2	−3	9	18
3	3	−2	4	12
4	4	−1	1	4
5	5	0	0	0
6	4	+2	4	12
7	4	+2	4	12
8	3	+3	9	18
9	3	+3	9	18
10	1	+4	16	16
	$N = 28$ $\bar{x} = 5$		$\sum fd^2$	144

safety stocks, two standard deviations of protection, or 6 units, would protect against 95.45 per cent of all events included in the frequency distribution.

However, in cases of setting safety stocks, the only situations of concern are the probabilities concerning events that exceed the mean value. No problem exists concerning adequate inventory to satisfy sales that are equal to or below the average. Thus, on 50 per cent of the days, no safety stock is required. Safety stock protection at the 95 per cent level will, in fact, protect against 97.72 per cent of all possible events.

In order safely to use statistical probability to assist in setting safety stocks, it is important to test the compatibility of the historical data with the expected theoretical frequency distribution. Although the frequency distribution illustrated in Figure 6-5 or Table 6-3 is very similar to a normal distribution, such may not always be the case. In other situations wherein the actual data are expotential, binomial, Poisson; or even nearly normal, a test of goodness of fit should be completed.[6] One such test is the chi-square (χ^2) test of fit, the formula for which is

$$\chi^2 = \sum_{i=1}^{k} \frac{(o_i - e_i)^2}{e_i},$$

where

χ^2 = measure of fitness.

o_i = observed frequencies.

e_i = expected frequencies.

If the value of χ^2 is zero, the fit between the historical data and the theoretical expectation would be perfect. The larger the value of χ^2, the increasingly poorer the fit.

Statistical tables are available to assist in the acceptance or rejection of theoretical distribution as valid representations of actual history.[7] While the inventory planner does not need to understand the full process of evaluating the chi-square or other tests, he should be assured that the *fit* is a valid approximation prior to utilizing statistical probability to assist in establishing safety stock policy.

Establishing Selective Safety Stock Policies

In terms of the example situation, a safety stock of 6 units or an increase in average inventory from 25 units to 31 units would have the net result of meeting inventory needs, regardless of the possible variation in demand rate, on 97.72 per cent of stockout days. Six units represent a 25 per cent increase in average inventory. When one considers the broad number of stockkeeping

---

[6] For example, see Robert Schlaifer, *Probability and Statistics for Business Decisions* (New York: McGraw-Hill Book Company, 1959) or any standard statistical text used in business research courses.

[7] *Ibid.*

units in a typical inventory line an across-the-board 25 per cent safety stock could represent a rather substantial dollar investment.

To look at the situation from a different perspective, in the earlier example of sales uncertainty over three performance cycles (Figure 6-4), stockouts occurred on only 2 of 30 (or 6.6 per cent) of the days. To assure that stock will be available to satisfy demand on 97.72 per cent of the days that stockout might occur, a 25 per cent increase in average inventory is required.

It is important to realize that the size of safety stocks increases as higher and higher levels of stockout protection are desired. In Figure 6-7 the typical relationship between stockout protection and average inventory is illustrated. At lower levels of desired protection a substantial degree of protection is enjoyed with relatively low investment in safety stocks. As the desired level of protection increases, the size of investment necessary to gain each increment of added protection gets larger.

Table 6-5 illustrates the degree of incremental protection realized and typical inventory requirements for setting safety stocks at various levels within the range of from 1 to 3 standard deviations. To achieve protection at each of the selected levels of from 1 to 3 standard deviations, approximately a 4 per cent increase in inventory was required. In other words, it requires about a 12 per cent increase in inventory to obtain a standard deviation of protection. However, at the first standard deviation level, 34.13 per cent of protection is

FIGURE 6-7
Relationship of Average Inventory and Levels of Safety Stock Protection

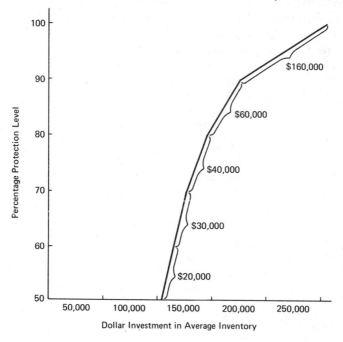

TABLE 6-5
Safety Stock Protection at Various Levels of Standard Deviation

Safety Stock Set at Standard Deviation	Degree of Protection	Incremental Protection	Incremental Inventory	Percentage* Increase over Average Inventory
1.0	84.13	34.13	12	12
1.3	90.32	6.19	4	16
1.6	94.52	4.20	4	20
2.0	97.72	3.20	5	25
2.3	98.93	1.21	3	28
2.6	99.53	0.60	4	32
3.0	99.86	0.33	4	36

* Inventory requirements based upon example of sales uncertainty used in this section. Although degrees of protection related to standard deviation are applicable to all normal distributions, related inventory requirements are special to each situation.

gained above the mean value for a 12 per cent increase in inventory. Moving from 1 to 2 standard deviations, the percentage of protection gained is 13.59. From the 2- to 3-deviations level the gain is down to 2.14. A rule to keep firmly in mind, then, is that the incremental protection realized by increasing safety stocks diminishes as safety stocks increase. As a general rule the ideal or optimal level of safety stock would be, assuming all other things equal, to protect each item in the line to the point wherein the marginal cost of protection equals the marginal revenue gained by the last unit sold.

From the viewpoint of practical planning, a high degree of selectivity must be exercised in establishing safety stock policy across a broad product line. Not all items are of the same degree of importance. The trick in establishing sound safety stock policy is to finely classify the inventory line on the basis of factors critical to meeting enterprise objectives.[8]

The fine-line classification of a product line can be based on a variety of different measures. The most commonly used are sales, profit, unit value, usage rate, and critical nature of the item. By classifying the over-all product line into categories, different safety stock policies can be established for each grouping. Those groups having extreme importance can be assigned high safety stock protection; those having limited importance can be given little or no protection.

Classification by sales volume is one of the oldest methods employed selectively to establish safety stock policy for an inventory line. In most marketing situations a small percentage of products account for a large percentage of sales. This generalization is often called the 20/80 rule, wherein 20 per cent of the products account for 80 per cent of the sales. The most common basis for sales classification is to rank-array and then group products into categories

[8] For a basic application, see W. Evert Welch, *Scientific Inventory Control* (Greenwich, Conn.: Management Publishing Company, 1962), pp. 19–22.

labeled ABC or similarly. Table 6-6 presents a rank array of 20 products with a grouping into three classifications. Given the fine-line classification, safety stock policies can be set for each group in order to be assured that the fast-moving products are afforded the lion's share of protection.

In special situations the classification system used to develop safety stock policy may best be established upon multiple factors. For example, sales, profitability, and critical nature could be weighted together in a combined index. The level of safety stock protection is then assigned according to the weighted rank array.

With respect to classification on the basis of unit usage it is important to realize that a differential will normally exist in a product line between total dollar sales and unit movement. Often items with a high frequency of unit sales during an inventory replenishment cycle account for only a small percentage of total dollar sales. Grouping of such items into broad categories can reduce the task of setting safety stocks.

With respect to unit value it is important to keep in mind that high-value items tend to be more expensive to protect by safety stock than items of lower value. The reader should recall from a previous discussion concerning the

TABLE 6-6
Fine-Line Classification on Basis of Sales

Product Identification	Annual Sales (in thousands)	Per cent Total Sales	Accumulated Sales (%)	Accumulated Products (%)	Classification Category
1	$45,000	30.0	30.0	5	A
2	35,000	23.3	53.3	10	A
3	25,000	16.7	70.0	15	A
4	15,000	10.0	80.0	20	A
5	8,000	5.3	85.3	25	B
6	5,000	3.3	88.6	30	B
7	4,000	2.7	91.3	35	B
8	3,000	2.0	93.3	40	B
9	2,000	1.3	94.6	45	B
10	1,000	0.7	95.3	50	B
11	1,000	0.7	96.0	55	C
12	1,000	0.7	96.7	60	C
13	1,000	0.7	97.4	65	C
14	750	0.5	97.9	70	C
15	750	0.5	98.4	75	C
16	750	0.5	98.9	80	C
17	500	0.3	99.2	85	C
18	500	0.3	99.5	90	C
19	500	0.2	99.8	95	C
20	250		100.0	100	C
	$150,000				

duration of the replenishment cycle that the higher the unit value and the greater the sales rate, the more frequently orders would be placed under the rules of economic order quantity. As a consequence, the desired duration of the inventory replenishment cycle would be short for items having high value and high usage. Therefore, the need to provide safety stocks for sales uncertainty during replenishment is thereby reduced.

The key to selective establishment of safety stocks is to realize from the outset that different products have various degrees of importance toward the accomplishment of enterprise objectives. Variations in the duration of the desired inventory replenishment cycle and in the degree of stockout protection during the cycle should be programmed to the best interest of meeting planned objectives. A final type of uncertainty that must be considered in formulating inventory policy deals with the expected and actual duration of the inventory replenishment cycle (type II).

Setting Safety Stocks: Combined Sales and Replenishment Cycle Uncertainty

The inventory replenishment cycle has been identified as the combination of order communication, processing, transportation, and update.[9] These elements combine to create an information and physical product flow between two geographical locations. The integrated replenishment cycle forms the central context for planning inventory policy. Up to this point, all discussions related to safety stock have assumed a constant time value for the duration of the replenishment cycle. For example, in the illustrations concerning the establishment of safety stocks to cover sales uncertainty, the duration of the cycle was assumed as a 10-day constant. The more typical situation confronting the inventory planner is illustrated in Figure 6-8, wherein both sales- (type I) and inventory-replenishment-cycle (type II) uncertainty are illustrated. In this section the nature of uncertainty concerning the replenishment cycle is reviewed, and methods for planning the joint probabilities of both types of uncertainty are introduced.

Nature of Performance Cycle Uncertainty: Type II

Uncertainty with respect to replenishment cycle duration simply means that inventory policy cannot be based on consistent delivery. As a general rule, the planner should expect that the time duration of the replenishment cycle will have a high frequency around the average and tend to be skewed in excess of the planned duration.

[9] To illustrate, see Richard R. Mead, "The Time Dimension and the Order Cycle" in D. McConaughy and C. J. Clawson, eds., *Business Logistics, Policies, and Decisions* (Los Angeles: University of California, 1968), pp. 117–27.

FIGURE 6-8
Combined Sales and Replenishment Cycle Uncertainty

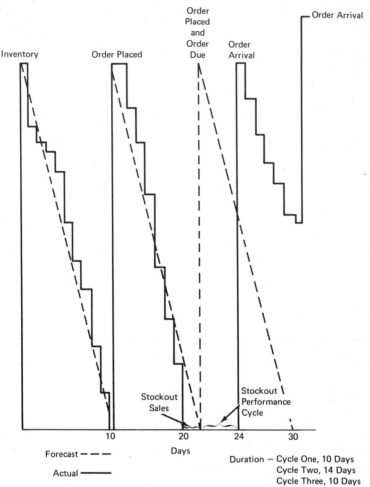

Forecast — — —

Actual ———

Duration — Cycle One, 10 Days
Cycle Two, 14 Days
Cycle Three, 10 Days

From a planning viewpoint, it would be possible to establish safety stock policy around the minimum possible days, the average expected days, or the maximum possible days of the inventory replenishment cycle. With respect to using the minimum or maximum limits, the resultant safety stock would be substantially different. Remember that safety stocks exist to protect against sales uncertainty during replenishment. Consequently, policies centered around minimum performance value would tend to provide inadequate protection, and those formulated around maximum value would result in excessive safety stocks.

If the impact of type II uncertainty is not statistically evaluated, the most common practice is to base safety stock policy on the planned or expected

TABLE 6-7
Calculation of Standard Deviation of Replenishment Cycle Duration

Performance Cycle Days	Frequency (f)	Deviation from Mean (d)	Deviation Squared (d)^2	fd^2
6	2	−4	16	32
7	4	−3	9	36
8	6	−2	4	24
9	8	−1	1	8
10	10	0	0	0
11	8	+1	1	8
12	6	+2	4	24
13	4	+3	9	36
14	2	+4	16	32
				$\sum 200$

$$N = 50 \qquad \bar{x} = 10$$

$$\sigma = \sqrt[t]{\frac{\sum fd^2}{N}} = \sqrt[t]{\frac{200}{50}} = \sqrt[t]{4} = 2 \text{ days}$$

days of cycle duration. However, if substantial variation in replenishment cycle duration is experienced, more formal consideration is necessary.

Table 6-7 presents a frequency distribution of replenishment cycle experience. Although 10 days is the most frequent experience, cycles range from 6 to 14 days. If one wishes to consider the full range of cycle possibilities, the standard deviation of the cycle is 2 days, if we assume that a goodness of fit exists between the data in Table 6-7 and the theoretical normal distribution. In other words, we would expect that total cycle time would fall within 8 to 12 days 68.27 per cent of the time.

From a practical viewpoint, when cycle days drop below 10, no immediate problem exists with respect to safety stock. If the actual replenishment cycle was consistently below the planned over a period of time, then adjustment of expected duration would be in order. The situation that is of most immediate concern is when the time duration of the replenishment cycle exceeds the expected value of 10 days.

From the viewpoint of the probability of exceeding 10 days, the frequency of such occurrences from the data in Table 6-7 can be restated in terms of performance cycles greater than 10 days and equal to or less than 10 days. In the example data, the standard deviation would not change because the distribution is normal. However, if the actual experience had been skewed in excess of the expected cycle duration, the theoretical distribution most appropriate may have been a Poisson distribution.[10] In Poisson frequency

[10] Schlaifer, *op. cit.*

distributions the standard deviation is equal to the square root of the mean. As a general rule, the smaller the mean, the greater the degree of skewness in the Poisson distribution.

Treating sales uncertainty (type I) and replenishment-cycle uncertainty (type II) consists of combining two uncorrelated variables. The duration of the cycle is independent of the daily demand. However, in setting safety stocks, the joint impact of the probability of individual variation in each must be related.

Table 6-8 presents a summary of sales and replenishment cycle performance. The key to understanding the potential relationships of the data in Table 6-8 is, if the replenishment cycle is 6 days in duration, total demand during the 6 days could range from 0 to 60 units of sales. On each day of the replenishment cycle the sales probability is independent of the previous day, and so forth for the 6-day duration. Assuming the full range of potential situations, total sales during replenishment could range from 0 to 140 units. With this basic relationship between the two types of uncertainty in mind, safety stock requirements can be determined by either numerical or simulated procedures.

Numerical Compounding: Types I and II Uncertainty

The exact numerical compounding of two variables involves the expansion of a multinomial of the type

$$p\{fm\} = \{p(S_1) + p(S_2) + \cdots + p(S_n)\}fm,$$

TABLE 6-8
Frequency Distribution: Types I and II Uncertainty

Sales Distribution		Replenishment Cycle Distribution	
Daily Sales	Frequency	Days	Frequency
0	1	6	2
1	2	7	4
2	2	8	5
3	3	9	8
4	4	10	10
5	5	11	8
6	3	12	6
7	3	13	4
8	2	14	2
9	2		
10	1		
	$N = 28$	$N = 50$	
	$\bar{x} = 5$	$\bar{x} = 10$	
	$\sigma = 2.3$	$\sigma = 2$	

where

f = replenishment cycle.

s = sales-replenishment-cycle duration.

m = number of replenishment cycles.

n = number of sales levels per day.

p = probability of an event.

Expanding this equation would determine the exact probabilities for all possible sales during all replenishment cycle durations. The resultant probabilities can then be used to set safety stocks by setting the desired level of protection corresponding to a probability of stockout.[11]

A more direct method is to relate the standard deviations of the two frequency distributions in order to approximate the combined standard deviation of the two sets of data:

$$\sigma c = \sqrt{\bar{t}\sigma t^2 + \bar{S}^2 \sigma s^2},$$

where

σc = standard deviation of combined probabilities.

$\bar{t}$ = average replenishment cycle.

σt = standard deviation of the replenishment cycle.

$\bar{S}$ = average daily sales.

σs = standard deviation of daily sales.

Substituting from Table 6-8,

$$\sigma c = \sqrt{10(2)^2 + (5)^2(2.3)^2}$$

$$= \sqrt{10(4) + (25)(5.28)}$$

$$= \sqrt{172}$$

$$= 13.115 \text{ (rounded to 13)}.$$

Thus, given a frequency distribution of daily sales of from 0 to 10 units per day and a range in replenishment cycle duration of from 6 to 14 days, 13 units of safety stock would be required to satisfy 68.27 per cent of all probable

[11] For an expanded treatment, see Robert B. Fetter and Winston C. Dalleck, *Decision Models for Inventory Management* (Homewood, Ill.: Richard D. Irwin, Inc., 1961), pp. 50–52.

TABLE 6-9
Summary of Alternative Assumptions Concerning Uncertainty and Impact on Average Inventory

	Order Quantity	Safety Stock	Average Inventory
Assume constant $\bar{x}$ sales and constant $\bar{x}$ replenishment cycle	50	0	25
Assume sales protection $\pm 2\sigma$ and constant $\bar{x}$ replenishment cycle	50	6	31
Assume constant $\bar{x}$ sales and $\pm 2\sigma$ replenishment cycle protection	50	10	35
Assume joint $\pm 2\sigma$ for sales and replenishment cycle	50	26	51

relationships. To protect at the 95 per cent level it would be necessary to plan a safety stock of 26 units.

In terms of average inventory, no safety stock would require 25 units, whereas protection for both types I and II uncertainty would require 51 units. An average inventory of 51 units would be sufficient to provide a combined 97.72 per cent protection against the independent possibility of daily sales or replenishment cycle variation. Table 6-9 summarizes the alternatives confronting the planner in terms of assumptions and corresponding impact on average inventory.

Simulating: Types I and II Uncertainty

As an alternative to numerically compounding types I and II uncertainty, the joint relationship of sales and replenishment cycle variation can be approximated by using Monte Carlo simulation.[12] The Monte Carlo technique consists of selecting values for representative replenishment cycles and corresponding sales levels of a random basis. Although the technique of Monte Carlo requires a large number of observations to establish safety stock policy, the procedure can be extremely useful when frequency distributions related to either sales or performance cycle history do not display a good fit to either a normal or a Poisson distribution.

To illustrate the Monte Carlo procedure, Table 6-10 recaps historical statistics similar to those of Table 6-8, with the addition of probabilities and random numbers. The probability related to each event indicates the frequency with which that value would be expected to occur over a large sampling of events. For example, with respect to daily sales, sales of five units would be expected to occur 17 of 100 times. The accumulated probability is also displayed and indicates the number of times the value of the occurrence would

[12] *Ibid.*, pp. 52–54.

TABLE 6-10
Summary of Demand and Replenishment Cycle Probabilities for Monte Carlo Simulation

Daily Unit Demand	Frequency Probability	Probability ≤ Demand	Random Number
0	0.04	0.04	001–040
1	0.07	0.11	041–110
2	0.07	0.18	111–180
3	0.11	0.29	181–290
4	0.14	0.43	291–430
5	0.17	0.60	431–600
6	0.11	0.71	601–710
7	0.11	0.82	711–820
8	0.07	0.89	821–890
9	0.07	0.96	891–960
10	0.04	1.00	961–1000

$N = 28$ $\bar{S} = 5$

Performance Cycle Duration	Frequency Probability	Probability ≤ Duration	Random Number
6	0.04	0.04	001–040
7	0.08	0.12	041–120
8	0.12	0.24	121–240
9	0.16	0.40	241–400
10	0.20	0.60	401–600
11	0.16	0.76	601–760
12		0.88	761–880
13		0.96	881–960
14	0.12	1.00	961–1000
	0.08		
	0.04		

$N = 50$ $\bar{S} = 10$

be equal to or less than a particular value. For example, 61 of 100 times the daily sales value would be expected to be equal to or less than 5 units. In addition, random numbers proportional to the frequency of each event have been displayed in Table 6-10.

The Monte Carlo process consists of selecting a random number for an inventory replenishment cycle. The actual selection of a random number can be made from a table of numbers or generated by a computer. To illustrate, assume that the random number 396 is selected for the inventory-replenishment cycle duration. The corresponding value is 9 days. Next, random numbers for each of 9 days of sales would be selected. Table 6-11 illustrates two rounds of Monte Carlo simulation wherein the random value of the replenishment cycle was selected as 9 and 11 days, respectively. In order to simulate a complete approximation of the joint relationships of types I and II uncertainty, a sample of several hundred replenishment cycles and related sales would be required to assure a reliable estimate.

If the purpose of the simulation is limited to the formulation of a safety stock policy, then all simulated results wherein average sales during replenishment cycle are equal to or less than average expected sales can be eliminated since no safety stock is required. For example, expected average sales are 5 units per day and assume that the replenishment cycle is 9 days. All situations wherein sales are 45 units or less could be dropped from the analysis. All situations in which simulated average sales exceeded the value of expected average sales during cycle would be tabulated for purposes of formulating a safety stock policy.

TABLE 6-11
Example Results of Monte Carlo Simulation: Two Observations

Replenishment Cycle Duration: R396 = 9 days		Replenishment Cycle Duration: R721 = 11 days	
Random Number	*Unit Sales*	*Random Number*	*Unit Sales*
097	1	796	7
542	5	520	5
422	4	805	7
019	0	452	5
807	7	685	6
065	1	594	5
060	1	481	5
269	3	124	2
573	5	350	4
		916	9
		085	1
$\sum s = 27$		$\sum s = 56$	
$\bar{S}p = 3$		$\bar{S}p = 5.09$	

Inventory Control Systems

The combination of economic order quantity, planned replenishment cycle duration, and establishment of safety stock policy sets the standards for inventory performance. The control of inventory is concerned with the mechanical process of carrying out the specified policy. A variety of different inventory control systems exists. However, most are based upon either the perpetual or periodic methods of maintaining inventory accountability. In this section each basic method of review is discussed and some comments concerning modified control systems are introduced.[13]

Perpetual Review

An inventory control approach based upon perpetual review is basically a reorder-point system. To utilize this type of control system, it is necessary to have an accurate accountability of all units of a particular stockkeeping line. If the line is broad, computer assistance is necessary effectively to implement the perpetual concept. The basic perpetual approach is described as follows:

$$ROP = S_s + \bar{S}dR,$$

where

ROP = reorder point.

S_s = safety stock.

$\bar{S}d$ = average expected daily sales.

R = duration of expected inventory replenishment cycle.

Thus, with an expected replenishment cycle of 10 days, expected average sales of 5 units per day, and a safety stock of 32 units to cover types I and II uncertainty, the ROP would be as follows:

$$ROP = S_s + \bar{S}dR,$$
$$= 32 + 5(10)$$
$$= 82 \text{ units}$$

and average inventory would be

$$\bar{I} = S_s + \frac{Q}{2},$$

where

$\bar{I}$ = average inventory.

S_s = safety stock.

Q = order quantity.

[13] The following section draws upon Starr and Miller, *op. cit.*

Implementing an economic order quantity of 50 units, average inventory would be as follows:

$$I = S_s + \frac{Q}{2},$$

$$= 32 + \frac{50}{2}$$

$$= 57 \text{ units}$$

Throughout this chapter most illustrations have been based on a perpetual review system with a fixed reorder point. The reorder formulation is based on the assumption that purchase orders for the item under control will be placed whenever the reorder point is reached and that the method of control provides a continuous monitoring of inventory status. When these two assumptions are not satisfied, the method of perpetual review must be modified.

Periodic Review

An inventory control system based upon periodic review is based upon the assumption that the status of items will be reviewed at a specified time. For example, the status of a particular item may be reviewed only every 20 days. Therefore, modifications in the basic reorder point must be implemented in order to take into consideration the fixed time interval of review.

The basic periodic concept is described as follows:

$$\text{ROP} = S_s + \bar{S}d\left(R + \frac{P}{2}\right),$$

where

$\text{ROP} =$ reorder point.

$S_s =$ safety stock.

$\bar{S}d =$ average expected daily sales.

$R =$ duration of expected inventory replenishment cycle.

$P =$ review period, days.

Since inventory status counts are completed only periodically, any particular item could fall below the desired reorder point during or within the review period. Therefore, the assumption is made that on the average the inventory will fall below ideal reorder status prior to the periodic count approximately one half of the time. Therefore, assuming a review period of 20 days, the

ROP, using conditions similar to those of the perpetual example, would be as follows:

$$\text{ROP} = S_s + \bar{S}d\left(R + \frac{P}{2}\right),$$

$$= 32 + 5\left(10 + \frac{20}{2}\right),$$

$$= 132 \text{ units.}$$

Implementing an economic order quantity of 50 units, average inventory could remain 57 units. However, because the review period is of greater duration than the replenishment cycle, the order quantity would have to be increased to accommodate the time duration between periodic review periods. Therefore, average inventory would become 98 units. Because of the time interval introduced by periodic review, the general rule is that periodic control systems require larger average inventories than perpetual systems.

Modified Control Systems

As one would expect, a number of variations and combinations of the basic periodic and perpetual control systems have been developed. Two of the most common are the replenishment level system and the optional replenishment system. Each is briefly noted to illustrate examples of the range of modified systems available for control purposes.

The replenishment system is a fixed order-interval system that provides for periodic review, however, in short intervals. For example, with complete status concerning inventory similar to the perpetual concept, an upper limit or replenishment level for reordering is established. The review period is added to the lead time and the replenishment level is defined as

$$L = S_s + \bar{S}d(R + P),$$

where

L = replenishment level.

S_s = safety stock.

$\bar{S}d$ = average daily sales.

R = duration of expected inventory replenishment cycle.

P = review period, days.

The general reordering rules become

$$O = \begin{cases} L - I & \text{if } R < P \\ L - I - q_o & \text{if } R > P, \end{cases}$$

where

O = order quantity.

L = replenishment level.

I = inventory status at review time.

q_o = quantity on order.

R = duration of expected inventory replenishment cycle.

P = review period, days.

Assuming a review period of 5 days, average expected sales of 5 units, safety stock of 32 units, and a replenishment cycle of 10 days:

$$L = S_s + \bar{S}d(R + P)$$
$$= 32 + 5(10 + 5)$$
$$= 107 \text{ units.}$$

Since the replenishment cycle is greater than the review period, it would be necessary to take into consideration outstanding orders. Assume that one order is outstanding for 25 units and the inventory status at time of review is 25 units. Then

$$O = L - I - q_o$$
$$= 107 - 25 - 25$$
$$= 57 \text{ units.}$$

If the review period had been greater than 10 days, assume 20. Then

$$L = S_s + \bar{S}d(R + P)$$
$$= 32 + 5(10 + 20)$$
$$= 182 \text{ units.}$$

and

$$O = L - I$$
$$= 107 - 25$$
$$= 82 \text{ units.}$$

Under the concept of the replenishment system, the size of order is determined without reference to the economic order quantity. Emphasis is placed upon maintaining inventory levels below a maximum, which is the replenishment or order-up-to level. The maximum is protected as an upper level since inventory will never exceed the replenishment level and can only reach the replenishment level if no unit sales are experienced between the order communication and update. Under conditions of the replenishment control system, the average inventory becomes

$$I = S_s + \tfrac{1}{2}\bar{S}dP.$$

The *optional replenishment system* is sometimes referred to as *Ss* or the *min-max system*. Similar to the replenishment system, the optional system substitutes a variable order quantity for the economic order quantity. However, a modification is introduced to limit the lower size of the variable order quantity. As a result, inventory is controlled on a perpetual basis between an upper and lower range. The upper range exists to limit maximum accumulation of inventory, and the lower limit serves to protect against small orders. The basic ordering rule becomes

$$O = L - I - q_o \text{ whenever } I + q_o \text{ is } < \text{ROP}$$

Do not order if $I + q_o$ is $> \text{ROP}$.

Summary

In summary, the basic functions of inventory have been identified as providing geographical separation, decoupling, balancing supply and demand, and providing safety stock protection against uncertainty. The risk related to inventory holding by level of the channel of distribution was discussed. In addition, a basic distinction was developed between inventory policy and control.

In terms of policy the inventory replenishment cycle, which consists of order communication, processing, transportation, and update, was introduced as the basic planning perspective. Duration of replenishment cycle was related to cost and the formulation of economic order quantity. Next, type I uncertainty, which concerns sales during replenishment, was introduced, and statistical probability was illustrated as a technique to cope with such uncertainty. The following section introduced type II uncertainty, which concerns the duration of the replenishment cycle. Methods for handling both types of uncertainty on a numerical and simulated basis were discussed.

The final section of the chapter treated basic concepts of inventory control. Systems based on periodic and perpetual review were illustrated and modified approaches that incorporate variable order size were reviewed.

In total, the chapter was designed to provide a working knowledge of the basic elements of inventory. Emphasis has been placed on the policy aspects of inventory, and even greater attention will be paid to the many implications of inventory in Chapter 10. Chapter 7 focuses attention on the basic nature of warehousing.

Questions

1. Where does the cost of carrying inventory show on the traditional profit-and-loss statement of the firm?
2. Describe the decoupling function provided by inventory.
3. Is it safe to say that safety stocks are the prime cause of overstocks?
4. Discuss the disproportionate risk in the holding of inventory by retailers, wholesalers, and manufacturers. Why has their been a trend to push inventory back up the channel of distribution?
5. Describe the difference between inventory management and inventory control.
6. Why is the performance cycle a critical concept in formulating inventory programs?
7. Describe the difference between type I and type II uncertainty as defined in the text.
8. Under conditions of uncertainty, describe the relationship between economic order quantity and order cycle duration.
9. How much protection would a firm be providing in percentage terms if safety stocks were set equal to 2 standard deviations?
10. Discuss the importance of selectivity in the formulation of inventory policy.
11. How does Monte Carlo simulation assist in the formulation of inventory policy?
12. Describe the difference between perpetual and periodic inventory control systems.

7

Warehousing

A warehouse is a specialized fixed facility included in the design of a logistical system to help accomplish the desired level of delivery service at the lowest total cost. Unless utilization of a warehouse meets this objective, there exists no justification for operation of such a facility.

In a logistical warehouse, primary emphasis is placed upon product flow in contrast to storage. Volume shipments are concentrated from supply points at the warehouse to realize maximum economies of transportation. Upon arrival, bulk shipments are sorted and grouped into specific assortments for either manufacturing or customer dispersement. The specific mission of a given warehouse determines the range of product assortment handled and the degree of storage performed.

In this chapter the concept of warehousing is first presented in detail with primary emphasis upon historical development. Next, attention is directed to the geographical positioning of warehouses in the over-all logistical system. Location strategy is directly related to the degree of differentiation in product-line assortment. The final sections of the chapter are concerned with an elaboration of warehouse functions, planning, and establishment of operations. The over-all objective of the chapter is to introduce the modern concept of warehousing as a vital link in logistics planning.

The Concept of Logistical Warehousing

Product storage has traditionally been an important part of economic activity. In the early stages of American development, the economy was essentially one of individual households serving somewhat as self-sufficient economic units. Consumers performed the function of storage and accepted the attendant risks. For example, meats were stored in smokehouses, and perishable products were protected in underground storage, such as food cellars.

As transportation facilities developed, specialized economic activity began to evolve. Product storage was shifted from the household to retailers, whole-salers, and manufacturers. Early literature indicates the warehouse was initially introduced as a storage unit designed to help satisfy basic marketing processes.[1] Product storage was viewed as an ancillary function required to match supply with erratic demand. The warehouse was the location for product storage until demand became sufficient to support distribution. The creation of the time utility principle was used to justify this type of economic activity.[2] This tendency to consider storage as merely a required facilitating function generally resulted in criticism of efficiency with little appreciation of the broader spectrum in which warehousing played a vital role. The warehouse served as a static unit in the material and product pipeline. The warehouse functions of order filling and reshipment were noted but given little emphasis. Internal management controls and maximum product turnover received little, if any, attention.

Literature of this early era correctly depicted the situation that existed. Firms attempting to effect closure among the points of procurement, manu-facturing, and final consumption gave little attention to internal warehouse economies. The formation of a rudimentary logistical network was essential for the initial survival of the firm, but little emphasis was placed on qualitative aspects. Engineering efforts were centered on the major problem of this early era, production.

The reported internal operation of early warehouses illustrates the general neglect of efficiency concepts. These warehouses received merchandise by car or truck, which was manually moved to the storage area. The merchandise was then hand-piled in stacks on the floor. When different products were stored in the same warehouse, merchandise was continually lost. Stock rotation was poorly handled, and products often deteriorated. When orders were received from retailers, selection was made by hand-picking merchandise for placement on carts. The carts were then manually pushed to the shipping area, where the merchandise was reassembled and hand-packed on outbound trucks for delivery.

[1] Hugh B. Killough, *The Economics of Marketing* (New York: Harper & Row, Publishers, 1933), p. 101.

[2] Theodore N. Beckman and William R. Davidson, *Marketing*, 8th ed. (New York: The Ronald Press Company, 1967).

Because of cheap labor rates, manpower was utilized freely, with little consideration of efficiency in space utilization, work methods, or material handling. To sum up, early warehouses, despite their shortcomings, were necessary to bridge the storage gap between marketing and production.

After World War II, managerial attention shifted toward increasing operating efficiency. Progressive firms became market-oriented and devoted extensive resources to the determination and satisfaction of customer wants. Increased competition soon forced firms to operate and obtain adequate profits on constantly diminishing margins. Although emphasis continued to be placed upon improved selling techniques, competitive pressures forced attention on cost reduction. Aggressive firms identified and began to critically appraise the logistical structure that had evolved, and gradually management devoted an increasing proportion of time to developing methods of physically serving manufacturing and markets.

General interest in the concept of developing warehouse capability is traced to (1) the logistic experience gained from wartime military operations, (2) the realization that strategic location of forward inventories has marketing implications far greater than those traditionally embodied in the warehouse storage concept, and (3) the postwar profit squeeze, which resulted in part from increasing logistical cost.

Management at the intermediate level of logistics was forced to justify the traditional warehouse in the product flow pipeline. Forecasting and production scheduling had improved, which had reduced the need for extensive inventories. Production processes had been perfected, eliminating long time delays during manufacturing. Seasonal production still demanded storage facilities, but the over-all need for storage had been reduced. However, the changing character of the retail order supported the need for warehouse facilities. The retail store, faced with the necessity of stocking a variety of different products, could not gain the advantages of consolidated shipments. Cost of procurement in less-than-quantity shipments made direct ordering largely prohibitive. The need for warehouses capable of providing rapid and economical inventory replenishment became increasingly important. At the wholesale level, the warehouse became a customizing unit for filling retail orders. Numerous alert firms developed integrated warehouse systems capable of providing increased retail service at reduced operating costs.

Improvements in warehousing at the wholesale level soon were adopted by material managers. For manufacturers producing multiple products at many locations, warehousing offered a method of reducing raw material and part storage, and handling costs, while maximizing production operations. A basic stock of all parts could be maintained at the warehouse, thereby reducing the need to stockpile at each plant. By use of volume shipments, products could be transported, when needed, to the warehouse and then to various plants at lower total expense.

Having a full line of products grouped at the same warehouse also opened the door for mixed carloads to customers. The mixed carload gained marketing importance because it increased the appeal of manufacturers who could provide this extra service. For the customer, mixed carloads had two distinct advantages. First, inventories could be reduced because the advantages of consolidation transportation were combined with full product assortments. Second, slow-turnover products could be economically ordered as part of the consolidated shipment. As competition increased, the manufacturer who could provide a mixed carload on 24-hour demand gained a competitive advantage.

The warehouse also offered economies to the manufacturer selling directly to retail outlets. For many firms, storage at the production point with direct shipments to retailers of relatively small lots had been the primary method of distribution. By decreasing logistical costs while increasing service, the warehouse offered more efficient physical distribution.

Physical Distribution: Warehouse Location Patterns

The prime emphasis on warehousing is in the physical distribution subsystem of the logistical network. The warehouse, viewed as a link in the dynamics of market logistics, renders service or cost advantages to a firm in a given market segment. The geographic location of a warehouse is controlled by production locations and markets to be penetrated.

Warehouses represent only a segment of a firm's total strategy for creating time and place utility. From a total corporate viewpoint, retail or customer locations represent the final point of product distribution. Nested in the center of demand, the final outlet for a firm's product stands at the apex of the total marketing effort. Thus the warehouse location is subordinated and perhaps only justified to the degree that it increases sales impact at the point of final product transfer.

Manufacturing or plant locations represent the originating point of the value creation process. Over the years a relatively refined body of knowledge concerning the location of manufacturing facilities has emerged. Today, firms are capable of drawing upon analytical sophistication tempered by sound theory to guide the selection of plant locations offering maximum economic and competitive benefits.[3]

Logically, three types of distribution structures evolve when warehouses are adopted. Under Hoover's plant location classification, these may be identified as being market-positioned, production-positioned, or intermediately positioned.[4]

Market-Positioned Physical Distribution Warehouses

A market-oriented warehouse serves the basic function of replenishing the inventory of retail stores and merchandise delivery to consumers. The ware-

[3] For a review of plant location theory and procedure, see Appendix II.

[4] Edgar M. Hoover, *Location of Economic Activity* (New York: McGraw-Hill Book Company, 1948), p. 35.

house, located near ultimate product consumption, affords maximum transport consolidation economies from distant shipping points with relatively short product movements in local delivery. The geographic market area served from a market-oriented warehouse is dependent upon the required speed of inventory replenishment to customers, size of average order, and cost per ton of local delivery.

Market-oriented warehouses may be owned by the retailer, the manufacturer, or independently. The mission of the warehouse will vary depending upon the ownership arrangement. Retailer-owned warehouses are designed to serve as break-bulk points for various products purchased from different sources. Because the product line processed through retailer-owned warehouses is extremely wide, the magnitude of demand for a given product need not be much of the warehouse's total volume.

The average retail store, large or small, does not have sufficient demand to order inventory in consolidated quantities directly from manufacturers. Retail product lines, manufactured or processed at widely scattered geographic points, are usually extensive. In order to obtain rapid inventory replenishment of this heterogeneous product line, the retailer normally requires the services of some form of warehouse.

The basic purpose of the warehouse is to consolidate purchases from distant procurement points and replenish inventory to retail outlets. A warehouse strategically located to provide a cost-and-service benefit to retail stores is best located near the outlets it serves. This allows maximum advantages of consolidated shipment with relatively short local delivery. Therefore, retail store location modifies warehouse location.

Good examples of market-oriented warehouses are found in the food industry. The modern food warehouse is typically located near the point of highest sales concentration. At this location, local deliveries are held to a minimum average length of haul. Delivery times determine the proximity of the warehouse to the most distant retail outlet. The Kroger Company, for example, operates two distribution warehouses to serve the Michigan market. If 2-day or overnight service were acceptable, one warehouse could satisfy demand requirements. In the food industry, generally, maximum local delivery of approximately 150 miles is desirable.

This description of market-positioned warehouses represents one location pattern. The basic point, their location close to the market served, rests upon the need to replenish customer inventory rapidly and the desire to achieve product distribution at lowest cost.

Production-Positioned Physical Distribution Warehouses

A production-oriented warehouse is located close to production plants in order to act as a collection point for many products manufactured at different plants. Shipments into these warehouses are normally the result of product allocation. The fundamental reason for production-oriented warehouses is the manufacturer's desire for maximum service to customers. Quantities of products from each plant are shipped to the collection center, from which customer orders are filled.

Upon order receipt, merchandise is shipped in the mixture necessary to satisfy customer requirements. Strategic location of warehouses with respect to manufacturing plants allows such mixed carloads to move to customer locations at consolidated transport rates. Under carload conditions, a customized order may be shipped to a customer faster than smaller quantities, thereby allowing rapid replenishment and lower basic inventories. This mixed carload service stimulates purchase of products that normally move under less-than-carload rates. Therefore, the advantage of a production-oriented warehouse is the ability to furnish superior service for a total product assortment. To the degree that a manufacturer can offer all products in custom assortments at consolidated transportation rates, a competitive differential advantage may be obtained in customer service.

Several major food-processing firms currently operate production-oriented distribution warehouses. Leading examples are Pillsbury, Johnson & Johnson, and Nabisco. At Nabisco, a shipping branch warehouse is located adjacent to each bakery. Quantities of all major products are shipped to each warehouse, thereby providing the ability to provide full-service shipments from each.

Intermediately Positioned Physical Distribution Warehouses

Warehouses located between customers and manufacturing plants are referred to as intermediately positioned. Such warehouses, similar to those that are production-oriented, find economic justification on the basis of increased customer service.

Industrial location theory points out that plants producing a particular type of product often must locate near required raw material.[5] For reasons of production economy, firms may be faced with geographically decentralized production plants.

Under conditions of joint product marketing, a warehouse may be located at an intermediate location and operated as a collection point for various products produced at decentralized locations. By grouping all products in the line, a firm can deliver mixed shipments with the advantages noted earlier.

Warehouse Location Strategy and Product Differentiation

From the preceding discussion it is clear that warehouses enter a physical distribution system only when a degree of differential advantage results from their inclusion between manufacturing site and final product destination. Differential advantage gained by adding warehouses culminated from achieving

---

[5] Melvin L. Greenhut, *Plant Location* (Chapel Hill, N.C.: University of North Carolina Press, 1956), p. 113.

a distribution cost or service advantage in a given market segment. The particular location strategy that a firm follows depends greatly upon the degree of product line differentiation that prevails in a particular industry.

Location Strategy with Nondifferentiated Products

In an industry characterized by nearly identical products, little consumer loyalty is commanded by individual firms. The industry demand curve is relatively elastic. Fundamentally, individual firms may attempt to differentiate their products by location dispersion. The major firms in the industry seek plant locations in prime markets and at low-cost production points. Smaller high-cost firms normally find economic justification by selecting locations in marginal markets. These locations are created by the inability of major producers to produce products within marginal markets at a competitive price. It is possible that major producers located in prime markets may utilize warehouses to service marginal markets. By locating warehouses in space islands, major producers can extend their effective market coverage. This type of market extension creates entry barriers to the location of high-cost producers in marginal markets.[6]

Consolidating shipments is a basic economic principle underlying the utilization of warehouses to extend market coverage to secondary areas. The major producer may initially sell FOB over his entire market area. Each customer is shipped products directly from the production point by some method of less-than-quantity shipment. The consolidation of product shipments to a warehouse substantially reduces transportation expenses. Thus the monopolist can move large quantities of his product into market areas previously beyond his reach at a total cost considerably below the consumer's price-acceptance level. The savings must be sufficient to cover the cost of facility operation and inventory. Products may then be distributed FOB warehouse in all directions to a point where total product price reaches the level of consumer indifference.

Figure 7-1 contains an example of market expansion through a warehouse.[7] The case of the spatial monopolist is illustrated in only one direction for the linear market. Under conditions of direct shipment, the monopolist can sell only as far into the market as point *D*. At the line *ED* the total cost of his product reaches the consumer-indifference price level. Beyond line *ED* the high-cost producer could exist in a marginal market. By placing a warehouse at some point in the market beyond *D*, the monopolist can consolidate shipments to the warehouse at a landed cost below the consumer-indifference price level. Shipments are then returned toward the production point and farther into the market area until total price once more becomes prohibitive to the consumer. The total market expansion achieved by utilizing a warehouse is expressed in the linear diagram by the line *DC*.

---

[6] For an expanded discussion, see Appendix II.

[7] Figure 7-1 is adopted from John H. Frederick, *Using Public Warehouses* (Philadelphia: Chilton Company, 1957), p. 81.

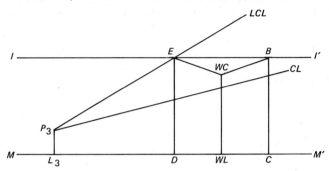

FIGURE 7-1
Market Extension by Use of a Distribution Warehouse

To generalize further, locating a number of such warehouses will produce full market coverage. However, marginal markets are now served by warehouses controlled by the major producer rather than by competitive high-cost producers. Thus one function of a warehouse is to extend prime markets under conditions of nondifferentiated products.

Location Strategy with Differentiated Products

Warehouses often are vital to the expansion of firms that sell differentiated products nationally. Because products offered by all firms are differentiated in the consumer's eyes, the theories of spatial monopoly break down. Each firm is forced to sell over a larger total market area in order to realize sales volumes sufficient for survival. These conditions probably will compel large producers to concentrate product plants where low production costs and much industry demand exist. This is necessary, because no individual submarket demands a firm's total production. Each producer can meet the service capabilities of competitors, and all confront similar transportation costs. Under these conditions, the industry initially settles down to conventional tactics of nonprice competition in order to achieve differential advantage.

The dynamics of spatial competition enter the industry when differentiated products begin to gain acceptance in distant markets. The firm finds it desirable to decentralize physical facilities when sales volumes become sufficient in submarkets to justify warehouses, and then branch plants. The transportation principle justifying the use of warehouses is the same as in geographically dispersed industries. When total demand in a given market segment becomes substantial enough to consolidate shipments, the resultant economies may justify a warehouse. Thus a second economic force leading to the use of warehouses is the normal expansion of firms selling differentiated products nationally.

Once a major producer obtains sufficient volumes to support a warehouse in a market segment, a location advantage is gained. In addition to transportation economies, firms that operate warehouses also gain a service advantage in these market segments. These select firms can replenish consumer inventories more quickly than can major competitors. For customers this means faster special order handling and an over-all reduction of basic inventories. Thus the firm with warehouses has one more method of gaining a differential advantage.

Warehouse Functions

The warehouse contains materials, parts, and finished goods on the move. Because the operation is essentially a break-bulk and regrouping procedure, the objective is efficiently to move large quantities into warehouses and customized assortments out of warehouses. A common and desirable practice is to have products arrive in and depart from the same warehouse during the working day.

The functions performed in the warehouse may be grouped into movement and storage categories. Movement is primarily emphasized, with storage receiving secondary concern. Within these two broad categories, movement is divided into four subfunctions and storage into two subfunctions.

Movement Function

In the movement function, quantity shipments are reduced to customized assortments. As previously noted movement consists of four basic subfunctions: (1) receiving, (2) transfer, (3) assembly, and (4) shipping. Each is discussed.

RECEIVING. Merchandise and materials normally arrive at the warehouse in carload and truckload quantities. The first movement function consists of unloading. In most warehouses, unloading is primarily manual except in the case of raw materials. No mechanized methods have been developed that are adaptable to varying product characteristics. Generally, one or two men unload the shipment. If the product is small enough to hand-stack, pallets are used to construct a unit load so as to maximize movement efficiency. In many cases, conveyors are employed to free vehicles rapidly. Larger merchandise may be unloaded directly from the car or truck for movement into the warehouse. The use of containerized shipment has greatly reduced the unloading time in many situations.[8]

TRANSFER. There are at least two and possibly three transfer movements within a typical warehouse. The merchandise is first moved into the warehouse and placed in a designated spot. The inbound movement is handled by fork-lift

[8] For a comprehensive analysis of the impact of containerization on handling, see Vernon Seguin, *An Investigation of the Factors Inhibiting Growth of Containerization in Domestic Surface Freight Shipments* (unpublished doctoral dissertation, Michigan State University, 1971).

trucks when pallets are used and fork-lift truck or other mechanical traction in the case of larger unit loads.

A second internal move may be required prior to order assembly, depending upon the operating procedures of the warehouse. If merchandise is stored primarily upon pallets, some units may be moved from the receiving dock to a remote storage area. When these products are subsequently required for selection, they will once more be moved by fork-lift trucks to a specialized selection area. When the merchandise is large or handled in full pallet loads, the second movement may be omitted.

In the final transfer, the specialized assortment is moved from the warehouse to the loading dock. The type of material handling equipment that is best suited for this operation depends upon the nature of the product and the order selection procedure utilized. As already noted, if the product is large or if it composes full pallet loads, this movement may be accomplished with fork-lift trucks. If the product is small and consists of a large number of different items, the final transfer may be handled by a small tractor and trailer or by a continuous-movement towline. In some special cases, conveyors have been employed.

ASSEMBLY.   Order assembly is the primary function of the warehouse. At this point, movements are primarily aimed at regrouping materials, parts, and products into assorted orders. For a large number of small products, one part of the warehouse may be established as a selection area. Automatic data processing may be utilized to facilitate accuracy in billing. Order pickers then place all items billed on selection carts for transfer to the shipping area.

SHIPPING.   The shipping function consists of checking and loading orders for outbound movement. As in the case of receiving, shipments in most systems are normally handled manually. It has become increasingly popular to ship full pallet loads, as considerable time can be saved in loading. Some firms have experienced considerable transportation savings; however, damage in transit normally increases. When delivery trucks are not company-owned, the additional problem of returning empty pallets may offset some of the savings. A checking operation is required when the merchandise is changing ownership as a result of shipment. Checking generally consists of item counts, but in some instances a piece-by-piece check for proper brand, size, and so on is necessary to assure proper receipt of all items.

Storage Function

In addition to processing custom or special orders, the warehouse performs all functions of the traditional storage warehouse. The basic subfunctions of storage are (1) temporary storage and (2) permanent storage.

TEMPORARY STORAGE.   As previously noted, primary emphasis is placed upon product flow in the warehouse. Regardless of inventory turnover, all goods received must be stored for some time period. Providing storage for basic inventory replenishment is referred to as temporary storage. Temporary storage duration will vary in different logistical systems, because elapsed time is based upon the inventory replenishment cycle. Temporary storage must provide a sufficient quantity of goods to satisfy demand and adequate safety reserves.

PERMANENT STORAGE.   Permanent storage, although a somewhat misleading, term, refers only to storage in excess of inventory required for normal replenishment. In some special situations, storage may be needed for several months. The logistical manager should understand the reasons why permanent storage may be required. A constant effort should be made to encourage warehouse managers to minimize permanent storage and concentrate upon maximum product flow. There are five basic reasons for a modern warehouse to store goods in excess of normal replenishment requirements. Each of these reasons is considered a special case rather than normal operating procedure.

Seasonal Production.   Regardless of advances in production scheduling, some products are seasonal because of growing periods. If the firm in question engages in this type of processing, extensive storage may be required during specific periods. Special storage warehouses or public warehouses may satisfy this requirement. Even if the firm does not engage in production but only in retail distribution, it may be necessary to purchase large quantities of seasonal products to assure a year-round supply. Canned tomato products are an example of merchandise often stored in a distribution warehouse.

Erratic Demand Requirements.   When a product with an extreme demand fluctuation is handled, it may become necessary to carry additional supplies in order to satisfy heavy demand requirements. An example is air conditioners. Because air conditioners are expensive items, retailers prefer to carry small inventories. When a period of high temperatures begins, the manufacturer has a very limited time to distribute additional units. With such products, surplus supplies may be held at warehouses in anticipation of excessive heat waves. Past experience has proved it not unusual for a carload of air conditioners to chase a heat wave across the entire country without ever arriving for distribution at a geographic point experiencing maximum temperatures.

Conditioning.   Conditioning is required for some products while at the warehouse. These products may be retained for a limited period of time in excess of temporary storage. The ripening of bananas is a case in point. Modern food distribution centers include ripening rooms to hold products until they reach peak quality.

Speculation.   The warehouse seldom stores goods for speculative purposes. The degree to which this activity takes place will depend upon the materials purchased. For example, it is not unusual to store grain for speculative reasons.

Realization of Special Discount.   The wholesale distribution warehouse often requires space for the storage of products offered at special discount.

The purchasing agent may be able to realize a substantial reduction during a specific period of the year. Under such conditions the warehouse contains inventories additional to those required for normal replenishment. Manufacturers of fertilizer often attempt to shift the warehousing burden on their product to customers by offering off-season discounts.

Warehouse Alternatives

In consideration of warehouse alternatives, four arrangements are available: (1) privately owned, (2) privately leased, (3) public, and (4) combinations of one through three, based upon seasonal variation in warehouse space requirements. As a broad grouping, warehouse facilities are normally classified as private or public.

A private logistical warehouse facility is one operated and managed by the firm which owns the merchandise handled through the facility. A public warehouse, in contrast, is operated by a professional warehouseman and provides a range of services to a number of different firms on a fee basis.

Public Warehouses

Public warehouses are widely used in modern logistical systems. About any combination of services desired can be arranged with the operator of a public warehouse. One classification of public warehouses has been developed based upon the range of specialized operations performed.[9] Public warehouses are classified as (1) general merchandise, (2) refrigerated, (3) special commodity, (4) bonded, (5) household goods and furniture, and (6) field warehouse. As would be expected, many public warehouses offer combinations of the above operations.

In physical distribution and product allocation, emphasis is placed upon the use of public facilities to assist in development of product assortments. In material management, emphasis is placed to a greater degree on storage. The current treatment is more concerned with the distribution capabilities of public warehouses. The distribution public warehouse performs four specialized services: (1) stock-spotting, (2) complete line assortment, (3) break-bulk, and (4) in-transit mixing. Each of these specialized services will be reviewed briefly.

STOCK SPOTTING.   The stock-spotting capabilities of public warehouses are most often used by manufacturers in their physical distribution systems. In addition, manufacturers with limited product lines are more prone to utilize this service. Rather than to place inventories in warehouse facilities near production plants, delivery time can be substantially reduced by pretransaction

---

[9] Frederick, *op. cit.*; for a complete review of each type, see Charles A. Taft, *Management of Physical Distribution and Transportation*, 5th ed. (Homewood, Ill.: Richard D. Irwin, Inc., 1972), pp. 174–76.

movement to strategic cities. Thus a consolidated carload of the firm's product line is "spot-stocked" in a public warehouse, from which customer orders are filled upon receipt. Utilizing public warehouse facilities for stock spotting allows inventories to be placed in a wide variety of markets adjacent to key customers.

COMPLETE LINE ASSORTMENT.   A public warehouse used for complete line assorting may be employed by either a manufacturer, wholesaler, or retailer. In this case the public warehouse performs the complete range of warehousing functions. Products are stocked in anticipation of customer orders, with customized assortments being grouped upon demand.

The differential between stock spotting and complete line assortment is one of degree. A firm following a stock-spotting policy will normally have a narrower product line and will place stocks in a wider range of different markets than one that uses public warehouses for complete line assortment.

BREAK-BULK.   Break-bulk public warehouse service represents a form of assistance in a logistical system that does not involve any storage. Public warehouse concerns often operate local delivery equipment, which can be hired by firms distributing in the general market area. A manufacturer can combine orders of different customers located in the market area into one pooled shipment and send the entire combined shipment to a public warehouseman. The public warehouse then separates the individual orders and performs a local delivery. Utilizing the services of a public warehouse in a break-bulk capacity allows the advantage of consolidated freight rates and reduces the difficulty of controlling a number of individual small shipments to a given market.

IN-TRANSIT MIXING.   In-transit mixing is similar to break-bulk services; however, when product plants are geographically separated, over-all transportation charges as well as over-all warehouse requirements can be reduced by this special service. In-transit mixing may involve shipments to one or more consignees. Solid carloads or truckloads are shipped from production plants to the public warehouseman, who provides the mixing service. Each large shipment enjoys the lowest possible transportation rate. The loadings of each product are designated to be mixed for specific customers at the public warehouse.

Upon arrival at the public warehouse, the solid cars are unloaded and the proper customer requirements of each product assorted. Shipment is then made to each individual customer. The total process of in-transit mixing is illustrated in Figure 7-2.

The economies of in-transit mixing have been increased by the development of special transportation tariffs.[10] These special tariffs are modifications of basic

[10] For an expanded discussion of public warehouse capabilities, see Kenneth B. Ackerman, R. W. Gardner, and Lee P. Thomas, *Understanding Today's Distribution Center* (Washington, D.C.: Traffic Service Corporation, 1972).

FIGURE 7-2
Public Warehouse In-Transit Mixing

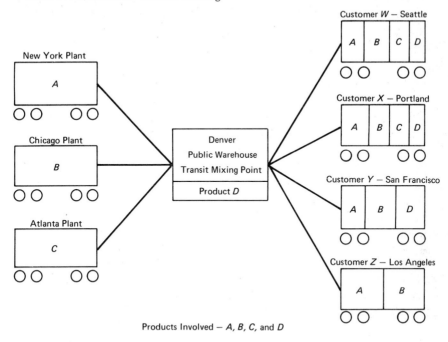

Products Involved — A, B, C, and D

storage in-transit privileges. Products are shipped from production plants, mixed as well as combined with products currently stored at the public warehouse, and then transported to customers under a special tariff provision. Although freight rates are applied on the basis of each commodity rather than on a mixed or freight-all-kinds rating. This special provision has the net effect of reducing total freight charges.

It will be apparent that the specialized public warehouse services of break-bulk and in-transit mixing have the net effect of reducing the amount of product storage required in product distribution. This objective is fully consistent with the total concept of logistics.

Private Warehouses

A private warehouse may be either owned or leased. The decision of which best fits an individual firm's requirement is essentially one of financial planning. It is often not possible to find a warehouse facility for lease that will fit the requirements of a given firm. In general, it is easier to locate facilities suitable for storage than for distribution warehousing. If a considerable amount of material handling is planned for the distribution warehouse, a readily available building may not be conducive to efficient product flow. As a general rule, an efficient warehouse should be designed around a material handling system in order to encourage maximum ease of product flow.

Increasingly, real estate developers will build distribution warehouses for specific firms to their specifications on a leased basis. Such custom construction is available in many markets on a lease arrangement as short as 5 years in duration.

Combination Systems

As would be expected, many firms utilize a combination of public and private distribution warehouses in product distribution. A private facility is used to cover basic requirements that are more or less constant the year around, whereas public facilities are used to handle peak requirements. Figure 7-3 illustrates the combined concept.

A public warehouseman normally charges on the basis of packages or hundredweight stored or handled by his facility. Such charges will normally exceed the cost of warehousing equivalent volumes in a distribution facility constructed to service basic demands. Public warehouse rates must be adjusted to different seasonal demands of a variety of customers. Full utilization of public warehouse space through the cycle of annual activities of all customers appears remote. For this reason the rate structure of a public warehouse used for only peak overflows will reflect lower efficiencies than can be experienced by construction of a private warehouse designed for stable demand.

As a planning rule, if a private warehouse is employed, it should be designed to be utilized to full capacity between 75 and 85 per cent of the time. Thus from 15 to 25 per cent of the time usable space is available to accommodate seasonal requirements. Public warehouses as a supplement should only be used temporarily to store requirements greater than the 15 to 25 per cent internal expansion capacity. When such public warehouse supplements are utilized, it can be expected that additional product handling and transfers will be required.

The preceding discussion is somewhat pessimistic regarding the resultant

FIGURE 7-3
Combined Private and Public Warehouse Facilities

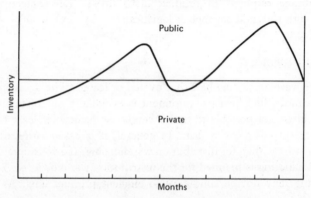

efficiencies from attempting to combine private and public warehouses to service a single market area or grouping of customers. However, this reluctance concerning joint utilization of private and public facilities in the same market should not be interpreted as a general rejection of combination systems. A firm may very well find that private distribution warehouses can be best used in specific markets, and public warehouses are used in other market situations. In logistical system design the objective is to locate whatever combination of the two types of warehouses most economically meets customer service objectives.

Comparative Benefits of Public Versus Private Warehouses

In recent years, the traditional role of public warehouses serving as supplemental storage facilities has dramatically changed in over-all logistics.[11] The nature of modern business places a great deal of emphasis on product turnover and rapid ability to satisfy orders. In order to achieve these two benefits, flexibility must be maintained within the logistical structure. Public warehousemen have been very progressive in designing warehouse systems that can be placed at the instant disposal of logistic managers with little, if any, fixed or long-term cost commitment.

Many individual public warehousemen have formed associations that allow a firm to purchase total order processing and local delivery systems in a number of different cities across the United States. The associations, in addition to basic warehousing, provide such additional services such as inventory control and billing.

In addition to association, some larger public warehouse firms are expanding their operations to encompass a network of warehouses located in key markets across the United States. In effect, this trend has the potential ultimately to offer manufacturers what amounts to a logistical utility. Under the utility concept, all functions required to service a firm's customers across the United States would be provided by a single public logistics specialist. For example, transportation, order processing, inventory control, warehousing, and selected administrative matters under the utility concept are provided by the public warehouseman. Although still in the formulation stages, indications are that these multifacility public warehouse networks under one management co-ordination will substantially increase in number and geographic coverage during the coming decade.

A final type of new logistical service being offered by public warehousemen is the multimanufacturer consolidated shipment. Under these arrangements, the public warehousemen consolidate merchandise orders from a number of different manufacturers destined to a specific customer as a single transportation shipment. The obvious benefit is the realization of the lowest possible

---

[11] For an expanded discussion, see Bernard J. La Londe *et al.*, "The Public Warehouse Decision: An Interim Report" (Columbus, Ohio: Division of Research Reprint Series, College of Administrative Science, 1973).

transportation rate and the reduction of congestion at the customer's receiving dock.

These innovative trends in public warehousing services are important in the appraisal of whether or not to use public or private warehouse facilities. Traditionally, the choice to use public warehouses was based on relative storage economics and flexibility. In the future, the choice will increasingly be based on the public warehousemen's ability to perform the necessary logistical task more effectively as well as more efficiently than if private facilities are utilized.

From an analytical viewpoint, the private versus public warehouse decision is very analogous to the material management decision concerning the making or buying of component parts.[12] The use of private warehouse facilities requires substantial investment or commitment. Such commitments should provide the same rate of return as other investments of corporate capital. If such prospects do not exist when viewed from a total cost perspective, then the use of public warehouse specialists could be carefully examined.

A final point concerning the use of public warehouse associations and single-ownership networks is the natural reluctancy of firms to turn over responsibility of an area as vital to operations as logistics. The risk considerations, which involve potential loss of control, problems in customer goodwill, and the inability of firms rapidly to replace or supplement a system that fails to perform, are the prime reasons given by logistical managers for not adopting single-management public warehouse networks. Although many firms exclusively employ public warehouses, each of such facilities is under individual management, with the logistical network control resting with the manufacturing, wholesaling, or retail enterprise. Whether future conditions will result in a significant change in the prevailing attitude and reluctance of public warehouse customers will remain to be seen.

Private Warehouse Establishment

The process of establishing a warehouse involves a series of decisions which, in total, mold the structure within which the logistical functions will be performed. The following discussion is management-oriented. Managers who have not previously experienced warehouse establishment often repeat the mistakes others have previously made. This brief review will provide a working background for such managers. In addition, it will indicate the type of information that will be expected from management by specialists called in to work on specific problems.

If a warehouse is economically justified, the problem of how it is established should be given primary attention. When planning a warehouse, management will find problems that cannot be separated; decisions made in one area will

---

[12] See pages 81–84. For example, Taft treats the subject in this context; see Taft, *op. cit.*, Chap. 8.

influence decisions concerning other areas. These interrelations must be recognized in order to develop an integrated warehouse system.

Planning the Distribution Warehouse

The first problems confronted are those directly related to planning the warehouse. The modern concept that a warehouse is an enclosure for a material handling operation requires detailed analysis before the size, type, and shape of the enclosure are determined. Too often the building is designed and construction is well under way before the material handling system is selected. A master plan of such related areas as material handling, layout, space requirement, and design should be developed. In addition, a specific site for the warehouse must be selected. Construction decisions are the most rigid decisions related to implementation. They establish the character of the warehouse, which, in turn, determines what degree of efficiency can be obtained in material handling.

SITE SELECTION.   Techniques of location analysis help in selection of a general area for warehouse location. Once this analysis is completed, a specific building site must be selected. Selection of a site for warehouse construction can normally be completed in all communities. Generally, three areas in a community may be considered for location: the transshipment zone, outlying areas served by motor truck only, and the central or downtown area. Selection of the site is based on the most economic satisfaction of the warehouse requirements.

In site selection, attention must be directed to cost analysis. Naturally, the direct cost of procurement is the primary governing factor. Normally, sites can be purchased at a cheaper price per square foot near the fringes of a metropolitan area than near the city center. A warehouse need not be located in a major industrial area. In city after city, one can observe warehouses among industrial plants, in industrial parks, and generally in areas zoned for light or heavy industry. This is unnecessary, because most warehouses can legally operate under the restrictions placed upon commercial property. The supply of desirable industrial sites may be limited in a given community, and one who desires such a site can expect to pay premium prices.

In addition to procurement costs, such setup and operating expenses as obtaining rail sidings, utility hookups, taxes, insurance rates, and highway access require evaluation. These expenses vary between sites and may render one site economically desirable over alternatives. For example, because of insurance rates, a food distribution firm recently rejected what otherwise appeared to be a totally satisfactory site. The parcel of land under consideration was located near the end of the water main. During most of the day, adequate water supplies were available to handle all operational requirements, in addition to any emergency demands. The only possible water problem occurred during two short periods each day. From 6:30 A.M. to 8:30 A.M. and from 5:00 P.M. to 7:00 P.M., the demand for water along the line was so great that sufficient supplies were not available to handle emergencies. Because of this deficiency, abnormally high insurance rates were required for necessary protection, and the site was consequently rejected.

In addition to low costs, several other requirements must be satisfied before the site is purchased. The site must offer adequate room for expansion. It is a good practice to purchase or option land totaling three to five times the total footage of the proposed structure for future expansion. The site should be serviced by a rail line capable of handling volumes considerably higher than those initially planned without excessive cost or delay. Highways to facilitate truck movements to and from the warehouse must be available. Utilities necessary for operation of the warehouse must be available. The site must offer a type of soil capable of supporting the structure, and it must be sufficiently high to afford proper drainage. Additional requirements will be situationally necessary depending upon the type of structure to be constructed. In summary, the final selection of the site must be preceded by extensive analysis.

PRODUCT MIX CONSIDERATIONS.   A second and independent area of quantitative analysis is a precise study of the products to be distributed through the proposed warehouse. This analysis provides information concerning the product mix that requires handling. The design and operation of a proposed warehouse is directly related to the character of the product mix. Each product should be analyzed in terms of annual sales, stability of demand, weight, bulk, and packaging. In addition, it is desirable to determine the total size, bulk, and weight of the average order processed through the warehouse. These data provide the necessary information for determination of the requirements of warehouse space, design and layout, material-handling equipment, operating procedures, and controls.

A firm that distributes a wide variety of unrelated products faces an entirely different distribution problem than does a firm that handles a few specialized products. For example, a food distribution warehouse may handle 10,000 or more products, each with different characteristics. In contrast, an appliance center may handle fewer than 100 products. The degree of complexity, therefore, depends upon the number and characteristics of the products distributed. Only by detailed analysis of the products can management specifically determine what factors are relevant in developing the warehouse. Analysis of these factors and the formulation of appropriate specifications provide the necessary guides for selecting among alternative handling systems. The character of the product line handled also helps establish which modes of intercity transportation can be utilized for product shipment.

EXPANSION.   Future expansion introduces a series of factors often neglected when a firm is considering an immediate extension of its warehouse facilities. Inclusion of a warehouse component into the logistical structure should be partially based upon estimated requirements for future operations. Well-managed firms often establish 5- to 10-year expansion plans. This results in a continual assessment of warehouse requirements as market conditions change in time.

Future plans calling for decentralization of newly constructed plants influence the location of a warehouse associated with existing plants. Likewise, a market-oriented physical distribution warehouse should be considered as one point in an expanding network of warehouses. Future plans will greatly influence the size of structure and location selection. For example, if a firm intends to expand the warehouse operation at some future time, construction must be guided by special requirements. A site that offers room for expansion must be selected. Transportation facilities must be adequate to handle increased volumes without delay or excessive cost. Although such planning may lead to increased short-run costs, it will yield long-run economic benefits.

To ease expansion without seriously affecting normal operations, special construction is often considered. Distribution warehouses can be designed and constructed to allow rapid expansion. Selected walls may be constructed of semipermanent materials to allow easy removal. Floor areas, designed to support heavy movements, are extended to these walls in a manner that facilitates expansion. Plans for future expansion also affect the selection of automated processing systems.

The projection of long-range logistical needs is unquestionably a difficult and delicate assignment. Careful analysis of such factors as past growth and population shifts, coupled with management expansion plans, may afford a reasonable estimate of future needs. These projections should be given consideration when determining final specifications.

BASIC POLICIES. Like expansion considerations, policies are seldom included in specifications. In actual operation, managerial preferences can become primary cost determinants. The newly proposed warehouses must be designed as part of an integrated system. To ease communications and control, operating procedures must be consistent with the remaining logistical structure.

The following example illustrates improper consideration of the total structure when planning a warehouse. Recently, a large firm developed a new physical distribution warehouse point. Product line analysis indicated that the most satisfactory method of internal material handling would be via a conveyor system. A material handling manufacturer designed an excellent system, which was subsequently installed in the warehouse. The system would have been sufficient if an earlier management decision to convert logistical operations to palletized unit loads had not been overlooked. Shortly after the warehouse was introduced into the system, all merchandise began arriving on pallets. The conveyor system, designed to handle easily the largest product case of the firm, was insufficient to handle full pallets. After a costly period of shipping in nonpallet loads to this warehouse, the conveyor system was discontinued.

Additional policy questions influence location preferences, inventory control, and ordering procedures. For example, the basic decision to buy or rent is, in part, the product of management preference. When a new warehouse is established, newly hired personnel may require training in company operating procedures; industrial or material handling systems may be analyzed by company staff or outside consultants; detailed consideration must be given in establishing operating specifications for the system.

SELECTION OF MATERIAL HANDLING SYSTEM. A material handling system is one of the initial considerations. Movement of various types is the main function within a warehouse. Consequently, the warehouse is viewed as a structure designed to facilitate maximum product flow. The subject of material handling is a major part of Chapter 8, which deals with over-all material movement. The following discussion relates some aspects of establishing warehouse operations with the detail developed in Chapter 8.

Several material handling systems are capable of satisfying required warehouse movements. Management should clearly understand the nature of the movement requirement in order to appreciate the reasons for selecting a specific system. The fact must always be kept in mind that handling, per se, adds no value to the product flow. Some examples of movement equipment currently utilized in warehouses are fork-lift trucks, various types of continuous movement towlines, tractors designed to pull one or more trailers, conveyors, and hand trucks. Each type of equipment is designed to do a specific job, normally more than one type of movement equipment is necessary in a total handling system.

The most common types of supporting equipment are pallets and skids. Pallets are recognized as one of the most efficient means of handling merchandise, which can be grouped into a unit load. The pallet provides a platform for the unit load. Unit loads permit movement of large quantities of small products at one time. A unit load also permits a single handling of merchandise before it is necessary to break bulk for customized order selection.

Complete pallet loads can be vertically stacked without the use of racks. Similar advantages cannot be achieved with partial pallets. Consequently, partial pallets of products awaiting order selection may be placed in storage racks. The rack also helps to increase the number of products that can be placed in a limited selection area. Partial pallets of two or more different products can be placed upon different shelves of the rack. The advantages of vertical stacking are not lost when racks are utilized to support partial pallets because full pallets may be placed on top of the rack.

Three factors, which can vary extensively among warehouses, determine what type of equipment is best suited for a particular system: (1) the product handled, (2) the volume of movements, and (3) distance and dimension of movement. If products with varying characteristics are to be handled, the type of movement and supporting equipment will be considerably different than for standardized products. For example, in the former case, a fork-lift truck palletized system might be most satisfactory, whereas in the latter a conveyor might best satisfy the movement function. In the selection of a handling system, the weight, bulk, size, and shape of the product are determinants of the most efficient type of equipment. Likewise, the volume of movements plays an important role. Normally a continuous movement system, for example, a towline, is economically justified only if the equipment can be kept in motion with a high degree of utilization during the total working period. The distance and dimension of movement are also important in selecting basic movement equipment. Some types of equipment are designed for long movements, whereas other types are designed primarily for shorter hauls. Although a single-level warehouse is ideal, for various reasons a multiple-story warehouse may have to suffice. Under such a condition, special equipment will be required for vertical movements between floors as well as horizontal movements on each floor.

WAREHOUSE AUTOMATION. Warehouses can be classified as manual, mechanized, or automated depending upon the degree to which labor applied to internal operations is supplemented by capital investment in handling equipment. Almost without exception, modern warehouses are mechanized to the extent that manual handling of labor is supplemented by equipment to facilitate material, parts, and merchandise transfer. The major area of the warehouse operation that remains highly labor intense is receiving, order accumulations, and shipping. These three areas of the warehouse remain the prime targets for increased mechanization, for semiautomatic or fully automated handling systems.

At this point, discussion is limited to where an investigation of highly mechanized or automated handling systems fit into over-all establishment of a private warehouse. As with all other types of capital investment decisions, in the final analysis the decision should be guided by projected cost benefits. Once again detailed treatment of this phase of material movement is deferred to Chapter 8.[13]

WAREHOUSE LAYOUT. The layout of a warehouse depends upon the proposed system of material handling. Normally a material handling system is designed with a specific layout in mind. Consequently, a layout and the material handling system must be planned together. Layout basically consists of developing a floor plan that will facilitate product flow.

It is difficult to generalize because of the vast difference between layouts designed to fit specific needs. If pallets are utilized, the first step is to determine the size of the pallets that may be stored. When specialized products are handled, a pallet of a nonstandard size may be desirable. Whenever possible, standardized pallets should be used because of their lower cost. The sizes

FIGURE 7-4
Alternative Methods of Pallet Placement

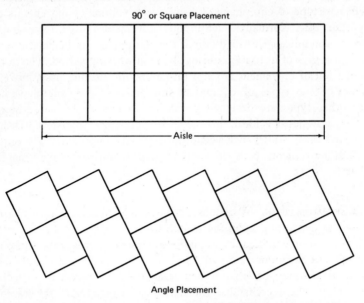

Angle Placement

most frequently utilized are 40 by 48 inches and 32 by 40 inches.[14] In general, the larger the pallet load, the lower is the cost of movement per pound or package over a given distance. One fork-lift truck operator can move a large load in the same time and with the same effort as is required to move a smaller load. The packages to be piled on the pallet and the related patterns that can be worked out will, to a certain extent, determine the size of pallet best suited to the operation. Regardless of the size finally selected, management should adopt one size for the total operation.

The second step in planning a layout involves the positioning of pallets. There are only two possible methods: (1) ninety degree, or square, and (2) angle. Ninety-degree, or square, placement means that the pallet is positioned perpendicular to the aisle, and angular placement means that the pallet is placed at an angle. The angles employed range from 10 degrees to 45 degrees, with $26\frac{1}{2}$ degrees most common. Figure 7-4 shows the two methods of positioning. The square method was widely utilized in early warehouses because of layout ease. The angle method is gaining in popularity because of greater operating efficiency. Aisle width can be reduced because the fork-lift truck can position a pallet in the angle placement system without making a full 90-degree turn. This offsets space losses due to angling. Operating efficiency is

---

[14] In reference to pallets, it is customary to name the dimension that is placed lengthwise of the forks in the lift truck first. Many pallets are designed with four-way entry; consequently, the two dimensions of the pallet may be used interchangeably.

FIGURE 7-5
Layout A

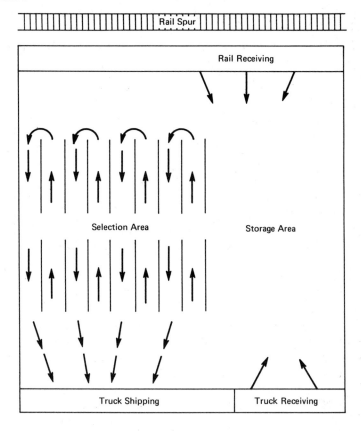

increased because of the ease of placement resulting from the shorter turn required. The method of pallet placement utilized in a particular layout will depend upon the specific problems experienced.[15] Often the two methods can be combined to arrive at the most efficient over-all layout.

Once all details have been isolated, the equipment selected must be integrated into a final layout. Normally the path of product flow will depend upon the material handling system. To indicate the relationship between material handling and layout, two systems and respective layouts are reviewed. The following illustrations represent only two of a multitude of potential layouts.

System A. Layout A, Figure 7-5, represents a material handling system

[15] For a detailed discussion, see Donald J. Bowersox, "Resolving the Pallet Layout Controversy," *Transportation and Distribution Management*, June 1962, pp. 43–46; and Ronald H. Ballou, *The Consideration of Angular Pallet Layout to Optimize Warehouse Space Utilization* (unpublished Master's thesis, The Ohio State University, Columbus, Ohio, 1963).

FIGURE 7-6
Layout B

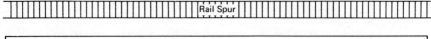

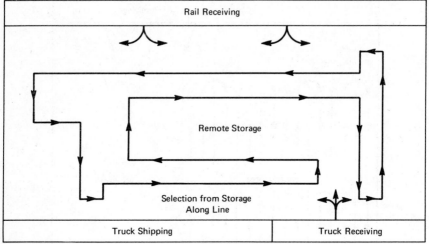

with related layout utilizing fork-lift trucks for inbound and transfer movements and tractor-trailers for order selection. The products are assumed
adaptable to a palletized operation. The layout is greatly simplified, because
offices, special areas, and details are omitted.

The proposed floor plan in layout A is approximately square. The advocates
of this particular system feel that a square structure provides the best plan for
operating efficiency. As indicated earlier, concerning utilization of some material
handling systems, products are clustered in a specific area of the warehouse
for order selection. Such is the case in layout A. This area is labeled the
selection area. The primary purpose of a small selection area is to minimize
the distance that order pickers must cover when selecting an order.

The selection area is normally supported by a storage area. When products
are received by rail or truck, they are palletized and placed in the storage
area. The selection area is then replenished from storage as required. When a
compact selection area is utilized, products are placed in this area according to
weight, bulk, and velocity characteristics in an attempt to minimize outbound-
movement problems.[16] Special orders are then accumulated by the order
selector moving a tractor and trailer through the selection area. The arrows in
layout A indicate the general flow of product movements.

[16] For a formulation to assist product space assignments see J. L. Heskett, "Cube-Pre-
Order Index—A Key to Warehouse Stock Location," *Transportation and Distribution
Management*, April 1963, pp. 27–31.

System B.   Layout B, Figure 7-6, represents a material-handling system with related layout utilizing fork-lift trucks for inbound and transfer movements and a continuous movement towline for order selection. Again, products are assumed adaptable to pallets, and once more the illustration is greatly simplified. The floor plan is a rectangular shape. In a system employing a continuous movement towline, the special selection area is omitted; selection is made directly from the storage.[17] Products are moved from rail and truck receiving areas into storage areas adjacent to the towline. The orders are then selected directly from storage and loaded onto four-wheel trucks, which are propelled by the towline. Merchandise is placed in the storage area to minimize inbound movement. Because the towline moves all products with the same degree of efficiency, the weight, bulk, and velocity concepts are not important for outbound movement. The arrows in layout B indicate major product movements. The line in the center of the layout illustrates the path of the towline.

Both layouts A and B have been greatly simplified, and, consequently, neither has been given detailed consideration. The main purpose of their inclusion is to indicate the relationship of material handling systems and proposed warehouse layouts.

PRECISE DETERMINATION OF WAREHOUSE SPACE.   Several methods are currently used to determine the exact amount of required warehouse space.[18] Each starts with a sales forecast or some other projection of the total tonnage that will move through the warehouse during a given period. This tonnage is then used to develop base and safety stocks. Some require consideration of firm and peak utilization rates; others do not. The neglect of utilization rates can result in overbuilding, with correspondingly increased costs. However, it is important to note that one of the major complaints of warehouse supervisors is the general underestimating of warehouse size requirements by management. A good practice is to allow 10 per cent additional space to account for increased volume, new products, and so on.

A product-line analysis, coupled with a sales forecast, provides the necessary information to determine specific space requirements. The first step is to convert the basic inventory requirements to pallet loads. The pallets can then be summed to arrive at the number of basic units to be placed in the warehouse. The second step is to arrive at the number of items to be placed along the selection line. This step is necessary whether a separate selection area or a selection line along a continuous movement system is to be employed. In the first case, the size of the area is relevant; in the second case, the length of the

---

[17] With the minor exception that some products have bulk storage in the center of the warehouse. Such bulk or remote storage occurs when extra heavy stocks of a given product are procured.

[18] For a comprehensive review of techniques, see Ronald H. Ballou, *Business Logistics Management* (Englewood Cliffs, N.J.: Prentice-Hall, Inc., 1973), pp. 380–96; also David A. Kind, "Measuring Warehouse Space Utilization," *Transportation and Distribution Management* (reprint), 1965.

line is relevant. The third step is to determine the size of the reserve area. The depth and the height of stacks depends upon the nature of the merchandise and the average inventory of the items temporarily stored. The final step is to determine the amount of space required for offices, grouping areas, maintenance areas, and so on. The summation of the area satisfying each requirement considered in the four steps is the total space necessary for the warehouse. Space is best considered in terms of cubic rather than square footage. The objective is to obtain maximum cubic utilization.

WAREHOUSE DESIGN.   Designing a warehouse is a special area of planning usually contracted to the architect. Design and construction characteristics must not hinder product flow. Consequently, management must communicate to the architect the need for primary emphasis upon unrestricted movement. In order to design a warehouse properly, the architect will require specifications for the size of the structure, layout, and predetermined path of material-handling equipment. The material handling specialist must work closely with the design specialist to develop an integrated system.

A number of small details directly related to efficiency are left to the architect. For example, doorway clearances must be carefully planned to ensure adequate widths and heights to accommodate material-handling equipment. If not correctly placed, a fire door can eliminate as many as 50 pallet positions. Assume that a firm has selected a layout using angle placement of pallets, five deep and five high, along the outer wall of the warehouse. Note in Figure 7-7 that if the door is placed in position *A*, 3 pallet positions, 5 high, are eliminated, a total of 15 positions. If the door is placed in position *B* or at any other point along the wall, 10 pallet positions, 5 high, are eliminated, a total of 50 positions.

Other items that require careful consideration are the placement of overhead obstructions such as lights, steampipes, sprinkler systems, and heating ducts.

FIGURE 7-7
Example of Correct and Incorrect Fire Door Placement

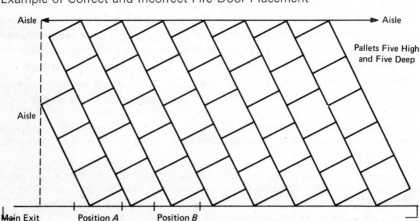

All these items must be kept above the tiering height if 20 feet of vertical clearance is planned for the material-handling operation. The placement of supporting columns is also an important design consideration. Generally, a latitude of positioning is available, depending upon which way the columns run with reference to the supporting walls of the structure. To ensure a minimum of restricted storage bays, it is of prime importance that the layout be planned in coordination with column placement.

The floor areas, which must be specially treated to ensure sufficient hardness, depend upon the predetermined path of the material-handling equipment. The choice of a square or rectangular design depends upon the characteristics of the selected material-handling system. The length and the width of receiving and shipping docks depend upon the volume of products handled, the systems of receiving and shipping employed, and the equipment used. The heights of the respective docks depend upon the height of trailer and railroad car bodies.

These items are but a few of the extensive reasons why the warehouse must be designed to facilitate product flow. The modern warehouse is founded on the efficient use of every cubic foot of space and available material-handling equipment. The structure is designed to stimulate this efficiency.

THE INTEGRATED PLAN.   Once management has selected a site and planned the size, layout, material-handling equipment, and design, construction may begin. It is generally a good idea to develop a small-scale physical model of the proposed structure. By utilizing a model and templates, a clear three-dimensional image of the proposed structure may be developed. A scale of $\frac{1}{4}$ inch equal to 1 foot provides a good model. Such a model will help point out minor shortcomings of the proposed structure so that modifications can be made prior to construction.

Initiating Warehouse Operations

To initiate operation, management must stock merchandise, hire personnel, develop work procedures, establish a method of billing and inventory control, and initiate a system of local delivery.

STOCKING THE WAREHOUSE.   The best procedure to follow when stocking a warehouse is to obtain the complete inventory prior to initiating operations. The individual products to be distributed through the warehouse and the quantities of each in the basic inventory were determined when the warehouse was planned. The problem in stocking is to schedule the arrival of this merchandise in order to obtain an even flow into the warehouse. Upon arrival, merchandise must be rapidly transferred to a predetermined position in order to avoid congestion and excessive delays on the receiving docks. The time required to initially stock a warehouse depends upon the number and quantity of products to be handled. For a warehouse containing 4,000 or more products, it may take from 30 to 60 days to complete initial stocking.

In the storage area, products are assigned in full pallet loads to a predetermined area. Specific products that fall into a designated area can be placed at any point within the area. In the selection area, a coding system is normally used to identify products and positions. The coding system consists of a numerical classification and a slot position. The numerical classification is assigned upon product arrival and is retained as long as the product is held in inventory. This number may be coded to an automatic data-processing installation to facilitate inventory control.

The assignment of slots refers to the floor position where merchandise is placed. A slot represents nothing more than a predetermined pallet position. Two methods of slot assignment are commonly used: (1) variable and (2) fixed. The variable slot system allows the product position to be changed each time a new shipment arrives in order to best utilize warehouse space. Under variable slot systems of placement, a given product may be in slot 1161 at one time and in slot 1831 the next.

Under the fixed slot placement system, a permanent position is assigned to each product placed in the selection area. The product retains this position as long as volume of movement maintains the same level. If volume increases or decreases, the product is reassigned. Fixed placement provides an advantage over variable slot placement because it provides a method of immediately locating a product. Regardless of what slot system is employed, each inbound product should initially be assigned a location. Upon arrival, the merchandise should be identified by position number and transferred immediately to the selection or storage area.

PERSONNEL TRAINING.   The hiring and training of personnel qualified to operate a warehouse presents a serious problem. Regardless of how good the proposed system is in theory, in practice it will be only as efficient as the operating personnel. Proper training is necessary to ensure optimum results from the system. The firm establishing a warehouse operation will undoubtedly have extensive experience in hiring desirable personnel; consequently, attention is directed to training.

Training personnel to operate a warehouse is not a difficult task if executed properly. Normally, the full work force should start work prior to the arrival of merchandise. People hired for specific jobs should be given extensive indoctrination in their jobs and the part their jobs play in the total system. Examination of the scale model and tours of the actual structure will rapidly familiarize the personnel with the system.

After a period of general indoctrination, each group of employees should be given extensive training in its specialized job. Personnel hired to operate a warehouse may be grouped in the following categories: administrators, supervisors, selectors, equipment operators, laborers, and miscellaneous workers, that is, maintenance, salvage, and so on. These categories may be large or small depending upon the degree of management activities to be housed at the warehouse. For example, it is not uncommon for the regional or district office personnel to be headquartered in the warehouse structure.

When initial stocking begins, the work force obtains actual training in merchandise handling. Normally, the manufacturer supplying the basic material-handling equipment sends an instructor to help train equipment operators. Once the basic inventory is in stock, it is a good practice to spend some time running sample orders through the warehouse. For example, simulated orders can be selected and loaded into delivery trucks. The merchandise may then be treated as new arrivals and transferred back into stock.

DEVELOPING WORK PROCEDURES. The development of work procedures goes hand in hand with the training of warehouse personnel. The specialist who develops the material-handling system generally establishes a work procedure that ensures maximum utilization of the system. It is the responsibility of management to see that all personnel understand and use these suggested procedures.

In the average distribution warehouse, approximately 65 per cent of the floor personnel are employed in some phase of order selection. Generally, modifications of two basic methods of order picking are employed in distribution warehouses: (1) individual selection and (2) area selection.

Under the individual system, one selector completes a total order. A number of trailers are placed behind the picker's tractor and, at a designated time, normally when the order is half completed, the trailers are hauled to the shipping dock. This system is not widely utilized, the primary application being when a large number of small orders are being selected for shipment on the same truck. Under the more commonly used area selection system, each selector is assigned a certain portion of the warehouse. Under this system, many selectors handle the same order. Because each man has a thorough knowledge of the selection area, no time is lost in hunting for items.

Specific procedures must also be established for receiving and shipping. Merchandise received must be checked to ensure inclusion into the inventory accounting system. If pallets are used, the merchandise must be stacked in patterns to ensure maximum load stability. For example, there are approximately 30 different patterns in which merchandise can be placed on a 40- by 48-inch pallet. Personnel working on receiving must be trained in which patterns to employ. Personnel working primarily in shipping must have a knowledge of loading procedures. In specific types of operations, primarily when merchandise changes ownership, items must be checked during loading.

Work procedures are not restricted to floor personnel. A definite procedure must be established for proper handling of inventory control records. Most firms employ some type of automatic data-processing equipment. The purchasing or reordering of merchandise for the warehouse can cause a serious operational problem if proper procedures are lacking. Normally there is little cooperation between buyers and the warehouse personnel if the warehouse is operating below capacity. The buyer tends to purchase in the quantity that will afford the best price, and little attention is given to the problem of space utilization. Under such conditions, it will not be long until the warehouse is overstocked and demurrage charges begin to occur. The problem can be eliminated before it develops if the proper procedures are employed.

Buyers should be required to check with the warehouse manager before any abnormally large orders or new products are purchased. Some firms feel so strongly about this point that buyers are required to obtain a space allotment for all merchandise ordered. An equally serious problem is the quantity of cases ordered at a given time. The buyer should be required to order in pallet-multiple quantities. For example, if a product is placed upon pallets in a pattern containing 50 cases, the buyer should order in multiples of 50. If an order is placed for 110 cases, upon arrival the cases will fill two pallets plus ten on a third pallet. The extra ten cases will require the same space as 50 and will require the same amount of movement effort.

These illustrations indicate a few of the operational bottlenecks that can result from a lack of work procedures. Only if the system is offered standard inputs can an efficient operation be realized. It is a basic responsibility of the warehouse manager to assure that such standard procedures are developed.

SECURITY SYSTEMS.   In a broad sense, maintaining security in a warehouse involves protection against merchandise pilferage and deterioration. Each form of security is worthy of management attention when initiating warehouse operations.

Pilferage Protection.   Protection against theft of merchandise has become a major factor in warehouse operations.[19] Such protection is required with respect to employees and as a result of the increased vulnerability of firms to riots and civil disturbances.

From a security viewpoint, all normal precautions employed throughout the enterprise should be strictly enforced at each warehouse operated. As standard procedure, only authorized personnel should be permitted into the facility and surrounding grounds. It is important to keep in mind that security begins at the fence. Entry to the warehouse yard should be controlled through a single gate. Without exception, no private automobile, regardless of the rank of management or importance of customer, should be allowed to penetrate the warehouse yard.

To illustrate the importance of the guidelines stated, the following actual experience reported to the author may be helpful. The firm illustrated generally enforced the rule that no private vehicles should be permitted in the warehouse yard. Two exceptions were made for handicapped office employees. One night following work, one of the employees, quite by accident, discovered a bundle taped under one fender of his car. Subsequent checking revealed that the car was literally a delivery truck. The matter was promptly reported to security, who informed the employee not to alter any packages taped to the

---

[19] Although no direct estimate of warehouse pilferage is available, the U.S. Department of Transportation estimates that annual losses due to cargo theft and pilferage range from $1.0 to $1.5 billion. See *1972 National Transportation Report* Washington, D.C.: (U.S. Department of Transportation, 1972), p. 15.

car and to continue the practice of parking inside the yard. Over the next several days, the situation was fully uncovered with the ultimate arrest and conviction of seven warehouse employees who confessed to stealing over $100,000 of company merchandise. The firm, in this example, would have been far better off to have originally purchased the small transport vehicle that was procured after the incident to provide rides from the regular parking lots to the office for the handicapped employees.

Shortages are always a major consideration in warehouse operations. Many are simply honest mistakes in order of selection and shipment. The purpose of security is to restrict the role of theft from all angles. As a general statement, the majority of thefts occur during normal working hours.

To a significant degree, computerized inventory-control and order-processing systems help in the protection of merchandise being carried out the doors. No merchandise should be released from the warehouse unless accompanied by a computer-release document. If salesmen's samples are authorized, a good procedure to follow is to separate this merchandise from other inventory used for customer order processing.

This discussion is not to imply that all pilferage is on a one-by-one package basis. Numerous examples have been discovered wherein organized efforts between warehouse personnel and truckers resulted in deliberate over-picking, or high-for-low-value product substitution in order to move un-authorized merchandise out of the warehouse "in system." Employee rotation, total counts, and, from time to time, complete line item checks can reduce vulnerability to such forms of collaboration.

Finally, a note is in order concerning the increased incident of total over-the-road trailer loads of merchandise being hijacked from yards or while in transit. The occurrence of hijacking has become a major concern during the past decade. For the most part, over-the-road hijack prevention is a matter of law enforcement. In-yard total unit theft can be eliminated by tight security provisions.

Product Deterioration.   Within the warehouse, a number of factors can reduce a product or material to a nonusable or nonmarketable state. The most obvious form of product deterioration is damage resulting from careless transfer or storage. Another major form of deterioration is noncompatibility between products stored in the same facility.

Some products are more susceptible to damage than others because they are more fragile or have poor packaging.[20] Of concern at this point is the deter-ioration that results from improper warehouse work procedures. For example, when pallets of merchandise are stacked in high cubes, the danger always exists that a marked change in humidity or temperature can cause packages supporting the stack to fall. From a planning viewpoint, the warehouse repre-sents an environment that must be carefully controlled or measured to provide proper product protection.

[20] For an expanded discussion, see page 262.

A constant concern of logistical managers is the degree of carelessness of warehouse employees. In this respect, the fork-lift truck may well be the manager's worst enemy. Regardless of how often a fork-lift truck operator is warned against carrying overloads, some still attempt such short cuts when not properly supervised. In one situation, a stack of four pallets was dropped off the fork-truck at the receiving dock of a food warehouse. Standard procedure was to move merchandise two pallets per load. From the viewpoint of the enterprise, the value of the damaged merchandise equaled the average daily profit of two supermarkets. Product deterioration from careless handling within the warehouse is a form of loss that cannot be insured against. Such losses constitute 100 per cent cost with no compensating revenue.

Noncapability refers to the fact that in special situations unanticipated chemical reactions can occur between products adjacently stored. Such reactions may cause odors or damage packaging or product exteriors. Product deterioration by exposure to foreign substances is more likely to occur in public warehouses than in private facilities. The reason is simply that a far greater variety of different manufacturers' products are stored simultaneously in a public warehouse.

BILLING AND INVENTORY CONTROL. Most firms handling a large number of products with various turnover characteristics find it economical to employ some type of automatic data-processing equipment to handle billing and inventory control. Under early systems, cards are normally punched for each case of merchandise received at the warehouse. When an order is received, the appropriate cards are pulled, and the order is printed, listing products in the order of warehouse placement. For example, if an area method of selection is employed, the order will be grouped by areas and printed in either numerical or slot order for the selector. Machine systems facilitate reordering, because warning cards may be placed in the inventory tubs to indicate reorder points. It is possible to make rapidly a card inventory of merchandise on hand at any given time. At selected times, the card inventory must be checked against a physical inventory in order to ensure continuous accuracy in receiving and shipping records.

The basic concepts of these early tab card systems have been computerized during recent years. While the same general functions are performed, product arrival data are placed directly into the computer from an on-the-line terminal. All functions related to order processing, inventory control, and procurement are then coordinated from a centralized data bank.

Management cannot be expected to understand the details of all available processing systems. Normally, a particular type of system is adaptable to an individual warehouse. The representatives of the various equipment companies will survey the problem and suggest a tailored system to meet the requirements of the particular warehouse.

INITIATING AND PROGRAMMING LOCAL DELIVERY. Most shipments from market-oriented warehouses are made to the retail outlet via motor truck. Three methods of local delivery are generally available: company fleet, common carrier, and leased carrier. Management must determine which is most economical for the specialized situation.

Common carrier is widely utilized when the shipments are varied in size, duration, and number. The common carrier offers the basic advantage of eliminating the problem of scheduling company-owned trucks in order to obtain maximum utilization. The leased carrier plan embodies the granting of a contract to a private carrier to handle all shipments. The main advantage of a leased carrier is the shifting of scheduling, maintenance, and load problems to a specialized operator. This plan is widely adopted because of these distinct advantages. For example, the A & P Company has a policy of utilizing leased carriers whenever possible. The company fleet has the main advantage of being adaptable to the requirements of the specific firm. When the operation requires extensive trucking facilities and trained personnel are available, the company fleet can offer a definite saving in distribution costs.

As noted before, when a company fleet is utilized, a problem is encountered in scheduling movements to ensure maximum utilization at minimum costs. Some aggressive firms have developed scheduling techniques to help solve this problem. In the case of programming local deliveries, the objective is to minimize the cost of distribution, which, for example, may be expressed as a function of vehicle mileage.

SAFETY AND MAINTENANCE.   Accident prevention is a paramount problem in each area of the warehouse. A well-balanced safety program should include constant examination of work procedures and equipment. The problem is to locate and correct unsafe conditions before they result in accidents. Accidents occur when workers become careless or when they are exposed to mechanical and/or physical hazards. The floors of a warehouse may become a major source of accidents if not properly cleaned. Through normal operation, rubber and glass deposits collect along movement aisles. From time to time, broken cases will cause all types of products to seep onto the floor. If proper cleaning procedures are followed, the risk of accidents resulting from these hazards may be minimized.

A preventative maintenance program for material handling equipment is necessary. Unlike production machines, movement equipment is not stationary. Consequently, it is easy to neglect proper maintenance. A preventative maintenance program requiring a periodic check of all handling equipment should be installed.

MEASURING WAREHOUSE EFFICIENCY.   Maintaining warehouse efficiency requires the development of measurement techniques and standards for evaluation. There are several measures of efficiency currently in use in warehouses. The two most popular measures are physical and dollar evaluations.

Physical Systems of Efficiency Measurement.   Physical systems of measurement consist of unit and weight evaluations. For example, a unit measure may be cases moved per man-hour or pallets per man-hour. Generally a tabulation is made of the number of units handled in each functional area of the warehouse: receiving, selection, and shipping. The physical unit system of measurement is also a convenient method for the evaluation of individual employees.

Weight systems normally employ a popular measure referred to as tons per man-hour (usually written TPMH). TPMH may be computed for the total warehouse or for individual functional areas. Normally the TMPH figure for the total warehouse is obtained by adding together the tons of merchandise received (TR) and shipped (TS) and then dividing the sum by the number of total direct handling hours. The formula is

$$TPMH = \frac{TR + TS}{hours}.$$

In some special cases where the shipment is via common carrier, it is not necessary to include handling hours spent in loading. Normally the merchandise is delivered to the dock, and the common carrier assumes the responsibility for loading. When such is the case, the TPMH figure should be figured excluding loading hours. Such measures are normally referred to as TPMH less loading.

Dollar System of Efficiency Measurement. The most widely used dollar measure is one expressing warehouse expense as a percentage of the cost of merchandise delivered to the warehouse during a given period. By weighting the relative dollar figures to a percentage figure, the problem of changing dollar values between time periods is partially omitted. The problem of different rates of change in prices and wages still exists, and the resultant figures should not be relied upon for period analysis. The dollar system is also inadequate for measuring efficiency between two warehouse systems during a given period because of regional cost differences.

MEASUREMENT STANDARDS. The selection of standards presents a delicate management problem. The standard is the primary reason for measuring various activities. The various measures result in figures that may be compared to standards, thereby determining whether specific functions or employees deviate substantially from the expected level of activity.

A performance standard can be set only after one has obtained a thorough knowledge of all particulars relating to the job. Extreme care should be taken in making warehouse comparisons on the basis of physical measures and related standards. Management should realize that there is no such thing as an absolute standard for measuring warehouse efficiency. Figures vary substantially between warehouses, depending upon methods of calculation and the various details of operation. Each warehouse should be considered as a special operation, and specific standards should be established on the basis of the potential of that operation. Physical standards do offer a convenient means of making internal employee comparisons. For example, order selectors may be evaluated to point out which workers are exceptionally fast or slow. The results of such an evaluation may be compared with accuracy figures to determine which selectors require additional training and supervision.

Regardless of what system of standards is employed, if applied to evaluate various workers, it should represent a reasonable goal rather than a measure of optimum effort. Setting of standards is a difficult problem worthy of management attention. Only if measuring techniques are consistently applied and performance standards realistically developed will management have a true picture of warehouse efficiency.

Summary

The concept of warehousing has made a dramatic change in the range of capabilities available for design of logistical systems. By utilizing the principles of warehousing, customers can often be rendered better service at lower cost. When product storage is required, it can often be accomplished at strategic locations in the product flow pipeline. Unfortunately, not all markets can support a warehouse operation. Therefore, the number of facilities, their location, and the product mix carried in each is of primary concern in logistical design. Chapter 8 concludes the discussion of logistical system elements by treating the movement of material.

Questions

1. How does logistical warehousing differ in concept from traditional storage?
2. Discuss the major principle in Frederick's economic justification of a warehouse.
3. What is the major difference between physical distribution warehouses which are market positioned and those which are either production or intermediately positioned?
4. What is meant by the statement that the warehouse should merely consist of a set of walls enclosing an efficient handling system?
5. Describe fixed and variable cost considerations of private versus public warehousing. Is this similar to the difference between private and common transportation carriers?
6. Discuss the importance of specialized services provided by public warehousemen in the formulation and design of a distribution system.
7. Under what conditions would one combine private and public warehousing in a single distribution system?
8. Why is there a tendency not to provide for adequate expansion when constructing a private distribution warehouse? What precautions can management take to prevent a future space problem?
9. What are the justifications used to support angle placement?
10. When designing a warehouse, what factors directly affect the capability to maintain a high degree of security?
11. Would damage in transit increase if the warehouse shipped full pallet loads? Why or why not?
12. Discuss the relationship between the number of warehouses in a distribution system and the aggregate level of safety stocks. Would safety stocks increase as a function of the number of warehouses? If so, why?

8 Material Movement

Material movement does not fit into the neat classification scheme of transportation, inventory, communication, and warehousing because it includes aspects of all these components. For example, material movement involves inventory as it flows through warehouses and as it is being transported. Material movement is initiated in response to an order within the physical distribution, material management, or product allocation system. Thus material movement is initiated by communication and is an integral part of all subsystems involved in total logistics.

In a broad sense, material movement is defined to include packaging, handling, and containerization. It stands to reason that the fewer times a product, raw material, or part has to be handled in the logistical system, the greater the potential efficiency in total system physical flow.

The chapter begins with a general discussion of material movement productivity. Improved productivity is the primary logic for grouping the traditional functions of handling, packaging, and containerization into a single area of managerial concern. In the second section packaging is treated. Emphasis is placed on protective packaging aspects as opposed to the marketing or motivational considerations. Next, attention is directed to material handling. In the fourth section, containerization is the focal point of attention. Containerization is defined so as to include all aspects and benefits derived from unitization. The final section of the chapter briefly reviews some important considerations in planning the material-movement capability of the total logistical system. In total, the chapter is developed from a managerial as opposed to a technical perspective. The main concern of the chapter is the development of a unified approach for the treatment of movement throughout the logistical system.

Productivity and Material Movement

In the simplest sense, productivity is a ratio of physical output to physical input. To increase productivity, it is necessary either to get greater output with the same effort applied or to maintain existing output with a reduction in the basic effort expended. Of particular concern to logistical system performance is labor productivity.[1] The basic nature of raw materials, parts, and finished goods flowing through and between a vast network of facilities makes logistics a labor-intense sector of business operation. The prime objective of improved material movement is to increase the labor efficiency of logistics.

In the period 1948–1971, over-all labor productivity in the private sector of the United States grew at an annual average rate of 2.8 per cent.[2] The most recent 10 years, in aggregate, experienced an annual average growth rate of 3.1 per cent. However, averages hide the real changes of the past decade. Labor productivity grew rapidly during the first half of the 1960s and stagnated during the last half. From 1967 through 1971, the annual average labor productivity growth rate dropped to 1.8 per cent. However, in 1972 and continuing into the first three quarters of 1973, the rate of growth increased to over 3 per cent. Figure 8-1 provides a summary of labor productivity from 1947 through 1971.

Naturally, labor productivity growth is influenced by the boom and recession pattern of business which has been characteristic of American industry since the early 1950s. When business is extremely good and the economy approaches full employment, output per man-hour characteristically falls as marginal workers are employed. The logistical sector of the enterprise gets more than its fair share of such new employees for the simple reason that few, if any, skills are required to perform many logistical tasks. When business activity turns downward, the nature of labor contracts and the requirement to continue to handle material and inventory backup prevent a rapid reduction in payrolls.

Productivity figures for logistical workers are not available separately. However, we can assume with a high degree of confidence that logistical labor productivity, if it differs from the remainder of privately employed labor, has lagged behind most other areas. Four factors contribute to this conclusion.

---

[1] Next to the service sector, the various combined aspects of logistical operations represent the highest employer of semiskilled labor in the over-all economy.

[2] U.S. Department of Commerce.

FIGURE 8-1
Annual Labor Productivity Growth Rate Private Sector 1967–71

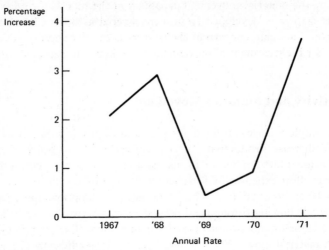

Source: U.S. Department of Commerce.

First, the sheer number of labor hours involved in logistical operations increases the vulnerability of this sector to any drop in output rate per labor hour. Second, the logistics area has not benefited from the substitution of capital for labor characteristic of manufacturing. Third, until recently logistical operations have not been managed on an integrated systems basis nor have they received a great deal of top management concern. Finally, the two major technological areas of logistical handling capable of reducing labor input—warehouse automation and domestic containerization—have not come to fruition as rapidly as expected.

Within the logistical system, material movement is the prime consumer of labor. The application of labor to movement transcends all other areas of the system accumulating into one of the highest total costs. Because of the relative levels of technological development in other areas of logistical operations, the prime prospect for improved productivity is in the technology of material movement.

A better perspective of the total material-movement task is facilitated by grouping packaging, material handling, and containerization as integral parts of a single managerial area. Each of these elements plays an important role in satisfying the over-all material-movement requirement.

Logistical Packaging

To facilitate handling efficiency, individual products or parts are normally grouped into cartons, bags, or barrels. These will all be referred to as *master cartons*. In the material-movement system, the master carton performs two basic functions. First, the master carton serves as the basic unit for material handling. Second, it protects the product or part from physical damage while moving through the logistical performance system. Each relationship is discussed in this section.

For purposes of handling efficiency, master cartons can be grouped into larger movement units. In a technical sense, all devices used for product grouping, including the master carton, are containers. However, within the present context, the term *containerization* is used to describe unit loads that contain more than one master carton. This section is concerned with the design of master cartons.

Standardized Packaging in the Logistical System

The master carton is the unit that is physically processed through a logistical system. The weight, cube, and fragility of the master cartons that combine to constitute a product line determine the basic configuration of transportation and warehousing utilized in the logistical system. Thus, if the package is not designed as efficiently as practical for logistical processing, the over-all system performance will fall short of what otherwise might have been accomplished.

Unfortunately, the final package is often based upon product design and marketing considerations at the general neglect of logistical requirements. For example, shipping certain products fully assembled, such as motorcycles, will result in a substantial reduction in density. In turn, a low-density package normally means higher transportation rates and greater cubic utilization of warehouse storage space. The proper perspective is to define what has been called "distribution or logistical packaging."[3] This, in essence, requires an evaluation of how the package influences all components of the logistical system.

From the viewpoint of package design, the traditional quantities in which products are sold at wholesale or retail should not be the prime determinant of the manner in which they are grouped into master cartons. There is no law of marketing or pricing that requires master carton packaging in even units or multiples of six units. The prime objective is to arrive at an assortment of master cartons that are as standardized as possible. Standardization of master carton size facilitates material movement and all other logistical system components.

The importance of standardization can be illustrated by a short example adapted from a shoe retailer. The initial physical distribution system employed by the retailer to ship shoes from the warehouse to retail shoe stores consisted of reusing cartons received from manufacturers for purpose of reshipment. Individual pairs of shoes were grouped into whatever repack cartons were available. The result was a variety of sizes of cartons going to each retail store.

The method of order picking used to assemble a store's pairage requirement

---

[3] Walter F. Friedman, "The Role of Packaging in Physical Distribution," *Transportation and Distribution Management*, February 1968, p. 38.

was to produce a warehouse-sequenced picking list by shoe style and quantity. The appropriate shoes were then selected in the warehouse and packed into cartons for shipment. In turn, the cartons were manually loaded onto a small four-wheel trailer for transfer to the shipping dock. Subsequently, the variety of carton sizes were loaded into over-the-road trailers for transport to the retail shoe store. While the order picking list provided a summary of all shoes in the total shipment, it was impossible for the retail stores to determine the contents of a given carton.

Viewing material movement as an integrated system resulted in a major change in the practice of reusing manufacturer cartons, the method of order picking, and material handling procedures within the warehouse. The revised system was structured around two basic concepts. First, standardized cartons were adopted, which facilitated continuous conveyorized movement from picking area direct to over-the-road trailers. Second, the integrated system utilized the computer to cube-out shoe pairs to assure that each standarized master carton was packed to maximum practical usage.

Under the new system, the cubed-out picking list was printed for each carton. After the individual pairs of shoes were placed into the carton, the pick list was attached to the carton, thereby providing a summary of contents for retail store personnel.

The advantages of using a standardized carton extended even to the retail store's back room. Because the contents of each master carton were easily determined, it was not necessary to search through many cartons for a particular style or size of shoe. Standardization allowed master cartons to be more efficiently tiered, thereby reducing back-room congestion. Finally, complete identification of master carton contents facilitated the completion of retail inventory and merchandise reordering.

As would be expected, the new integrated system required the regular purchase of master cartons since each could be reused only approximately three times. This added cost was more than recovered by less labor required in order picking, more continuous movement of cartons into over-the-road trailers, and the better utilization of the cubic content of the transportation vehicle. Since each master carton was cubed-out to near capacity, less dead space was experienced within packages placed on the truck. The standardized carton size was selected to achieve maximum conformity to a 40-foot-high-cube over-the-road trailer, thereby eliminating dead space in stacking. The final result of standardized master carton usage was a substantial reduction in total logistical cost combined with a far more effective material-movement system at both the warehouse and retail shoe store.

This example illustrates both the systems approach to logistical planning and the principle of total cost. However, the most important point to be derived from the example is that master carton standardization facilitated total system integration.

Naturally, few firms can reduce their master carton requirements to a single-size unit. When more than one size master carton is required, extreme care

FIGURE 8-2
Example and Benefits of the Modular System of Packaging

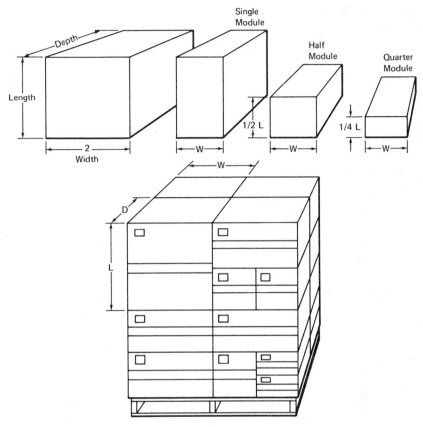

Source : Walter F. Friedman, "The Role of Packaging in Physical Distribution." *Transportation and Distribution Management,* February 1968.

should be taken to arrive at an assortment of units that are modularly compatible. Figure 8-2 illustrates one such concept utilizing four module sizes.[4] While the master carton sizes are not completely standardized, they are fully compatible.

Naturally, logistical considerations cannot fully dominate the design of packaging. The ideal package for logistical processing would be a perfect cube (equal length, depth, and width) to facilitate maximum density and minimum handling. Seldom, if ever, will such a package exist. The important point is that logistical considerations should be weighted along with marketing and product design to work out the best possible compromise, all factors taken into consideration.

[4] *Ibid.*

Protection

A major function of the master carton is to protect the product from damage while moving through the logistical system. In essence, achieving the desired degree of protection consists of tailoring the package to the product and selecting the material to be employed in package construction. The basic question that must be settled is the degree of product protection desired. To a degree, the master carton also provides product protection by serving as a deterrent to pilferage.

For most products, the cost of achieving absolute protection is prohibitive. The determination boils down to the value and fragility of the product. As a general rule, the higher the value of a product and the more fragile a product, the greater the economic justification for nearly absolute protection.

The susceptibility of a given package to damage is directly related to the environment within which it must be logistically processed. The over-all environment can be divided into two categories: (1) physical environment and (2) element environment.[5] Each aspect of the over-all environment is reviewed followed by a brief discussion of package material selection and damage prevention testing.

PHYSICAL ENVIRONMENT.   The first aspect of package environmental analysis is concerned with the physical nature of the logistical system arrangement that is employed to move a product to destination. This phase of the over-all environment both influences and is influenced by damage potential.

The potential package damage results from the transportation, storage, and handling systems that are employed to complete the logistical process. For example, if privately owned and operated transportation is used, the product will more or less move to destination in a controlled environment. On the other hand, if common carriers are utilized, the product is subjected to a noncontrolled logistical environment. Under the latter situation, the product is within the environment of the common carrier, wherein it may be handled by one or more terminals and loaded upon one or more different vehicles. The less control a firm has over its logistical operational environment, the greater the precautions required in packaging to prevent damage. Thus the logistical environment influences the packaging design decision.

During the logistical process, the product can experience a number of different shocks that could cause loss of usefulness or identity. The four most common causes of physical damage are vibration, impact, puncture, and compression. Within the logistical system, combinations of these four forms of shock can be experienced whenever a package is in transit or being handled. In addition, stacking failure can result in considerable physical damage while the product is in storage. The range of physical damage that can result from

---

[5] This distinction is used to separate sources of potential damage to the package while in transit.

shock is from surface scuffing and marring to complete product crushing, buckling, and cracking.

To a significant degree, shock damage can be limited while the product is in transit by securing the package. Typical methods of securing are strapping, tiedowns, and various dunnage materials that prevent product shifting or absorb vibration and impact shock. The best form of physical damage prevention is to load the over-the-road trailer or railcar in a tight pattern so as to prevent shifting. Securing and proper loading reduce the damage prevention burden that must be carried by the product package.

As noted earlier, the package requirement also influences logistical system design. The standard shipping practice in electronic data-processing equipment provides an excellent example. Because the basic product is of high value and extreme fragility, a substantial investment in packaging would be required to perform physical distribution using normal common carrier services. Consequently, electronic data processing equipment is normally distributed by specialized household movers. The type of equipment and the handling procedures employed by household moving specialists are highly orientated to damage prevention. Therefore, while the cost of transportation is higher, product packaging capable of providing absolute product protection is not required. Thus the product packaging requirement can substantially influence logistical system design.

ELEMENT ENVIRONMENT. The element environment of a package in the logistical system consists of potential damage created by temperature, humidity, and foreign matter. For the most part these environmental factors are beyond the control of logistical management. However, the protective nature of the package must be designed to cope with all reasonable possibilities of ambient conditions during transit.

To illustrate, it is not unusual for a package to be exposed to snow and below-freezing temperatures at time of loading, to be exposed to rain at a mid-destination transit transfer point, and to arrive at a hot and humid destination. The problem concerning evaluation of the element environment is to determine in advance how the content of the package will react with respect to instability and deterioration.

Temperature extremes will naturally influence package content. At very high levels of heat, specific products will melt, spoil, blister, peel, fuse together, and discolor. Exposed to cold, the contents may experience cracking, brittleness, or complete spoilage. With respect to extreme temperatures, the package can only offer minimal protection. For example, while in prolonged transit frozen foods cannot be maintained merely by package construction. However, the package design should accommodate natural environmental elements for a reasonable period of time during the logistical process.

The humidity impact upon product stability encompasses water and water vapor. The humidity problem is in many ways far more severe than the impact of temperature extremes upon package contents. The reasons are twofold. First, the typical product has extremely limited tolerances for water exposure without causing dissolution, separation, corrosion, or pitting. Second, since water exposure is for the most part limited to periods of time during which transfer between transport carriers or distribution organizations is taking place, the package may constitute the product's sole source of protection. Even if the product is protected, the package could very well lose identity if confronted with excessive moisture during movement.

The element of foreign matter influence upon the package consists of any damage or loss of content stability created by miscellaneous factors. For example, package contents can become contaminated or absorb tastes and odors if exposed for prolonged periods to chemicals or noxious or toxic elements. For certain kinds of products extreme care must be taken to protect against insects and rodents. Sometimes the package must protect against deterioration caused by prolonged air or light exposure.

Many products, such as film, chocolate, confectionery, livestock, and produce, are so perishable that design of logistical operating systems must be geared to provide controlled environmental movement. As surprising as it may seem, products clearly indentified as being perishable often do not create as severe an element environment deterioration problem as their more durable counterparts. It is the unexpected short-term excessive temperatures, high humidity, or foreign matter that cause product damage.

MATERIAL SELECTION AND PACKAGE TESTING.   The development of new packaging materials has been one of the most prolific areas of logistical research and development. A vast range of materials is employed in packaging, but the most commonly used are corrugated, solid fiber board, wood, and Styrofoam. The basic problem in selecting the optimum package is to determine just how much protection is required to cope with the anticipated physical and element environments. In essence, the optimal package design and material would combine to achieve absolute protection without incurring the expense of overprotection.

A typical situation is to have a package that is excessive in design or material but in practice does not provide the necessary protection of the contents. The process of arriving at a satisfactory packaging solution consists of defining allowable damage in terms of expected over-all environment and then isolating a combination of design and material capable of meeting the specifications. The important points are these: (1) in most cases the cost of absolute protection will be prohibitive and (2) package construction is properly a blend of design and material.

The determination of final package design requires a great deal of testing to assure that specifications are being satisfied at minimal cost. Such tests can be conducted in a laboratory or on an experimental shipment basis. During the past decade the process of package design and material selection has become far more scientific.

Today, computerized environmental simulations can be used to replicate the conditions a package will experience in the logistical system. Laboratory test equipment is available to evaluate the impact of shock upon the interaction of product fragility and packaging materials and design. New instrumented recording equipment is available that is capable of measuring severity and nature of shock while a package is in transit. By use of instrumented shipments on a scientifically selected sample of logistical movements, the bias of trial-and-error test shipments can be greatly reduced.[6]

Conclusion—Protective Packaging

The master carton provides the nucleus of the material-movement function of logistics. Extreme care must be taken to prevent product design and marketing purchase motivation to completely determine final package design. Logistical system factors must also be considered. From a logistical perspective the greater the degree of package standardization achieved, the more inherently efficient the material movement function. To this end, realization of a modular system of packaging is a noteworthy goal. The protective aspects of packaging consist of selecting a design and material capable of coping with physical and element environmental influences. Although absolute protection will in most cases not be necessary, the package should be scientifically designed to satisfy clear-cut protective specifications.

Material Handling

One extremely encouraging aspect of modern logistics is the concentration of capital investment toward keeping the freight moving. To realize logistical time and space closure, material handling cannot be avoided. It should, however, be minimized. The technical aspects of material handling are extensive and beyond the intentions of the present treatment. The following discussion places emphasis upon handling methods and efficiency measurement. A final discussion treats recent developments in automated handling.

Basic Handling Considerations

Material handling in the logistical system is concentrated in and around the warehouse facility. In particular, three warehouse handling activities must be performed: (1) receiving, (2) processing, and (3) shipping.[7] These three activities are common to the material management, product allocation, and physical distribution operations within a logistical system. The same three handling activities are common to in-plant material handling. However,

---

[6] For a discussion, see *5-Step Packaging Development*, publication of MTS-Monterey, Calif., 1971.

[7] For an expanded discussion, see page 228.

material handling within production and assembly plants is considered part of basic manufacturing and therefore not an element of logistical material movement.

A basic difference exists in the handling of bulk materials and master cartons. Bulk handling is a particular situation wherein no protective packaging is normally required and specialized handling equipment is employed to unload solids, fluids, or gaseous materials. The focal point in the following discussion is the handling of master cartons within the logistical system.

Modern handling systems can be classified as mechanized or automated. In mechanized systems, a combination of labor and handling equipment is utilized to facilitate receiving, processing, and/or shipping. As a general rule, labor constitutes a high percentage of the over-all input in mechanized systems. Automated systems, in contrast, attempt to minimize the labor element to the maximum extent practical by substituting capital investment in equipment. An automated handling system may be applied to all or any of the three basic handling activities, depending upon the situation. Mechanized handling systems are most common today, but automated systems are becoming more common and it is predicted that they will expand rapidly during the 1970s. As noted at the start of this chapter, one contributing factor to low productivity in logistics has been the failure of automated handling to achieve its full potential during the 1960s.

Mechanized Handling

Mechanized handling systems employ a wide range of equipment to facilitate efficient movement. The types of handling equipment used most commonly in logistical operations are powerized fork-lift trucks, towlines, tractor-trailer devices, and conveyors.

Powerized fork-lift trucks are able to move palletized loads of master cartons both horizontally and vertically. The pallet, which is discussed in greater detail in the containerization section of this chapter, provides a basic platform (see Figure 8-4) upon which master cartons are stacked. The normal operating procedure is for a fork-lift truck to transport a maximum of two pallets at a single time. Fork-lift trucks are not limited to handling pallets. Depending upon the nature of the product, skids or boxes may be transported.

Numerous types of fork-lift trucks are manufactured. For example, high-stacking trucks capable of up to 20 feet vertical movement, palletless side-clamp versions, and narrow aisle models are commonly found in logistical warehouses. The fork-lift truck is not economically adapted to long-distance horizontal movement because of the high ratio of labor per unit of transfer. Therefore, fork-lift trucks are most often employed in shipping and receiving, and to place merchandise in high cube storage. The two basic forms of power used to energize fork-lift trucks are propane gas and electricity. Because of ecological factors, electric-powered fork-lift trucks are becoming most popular.

Towlines consist of either in-floor or overhead-mounted drag devices. They are employed with four-wheel trailers on a continuous power basis.[8] The main advantage of a towline is the continuous power source. However, such handling devices do not have the flexibility of either fork-lift trucks or tractor-trailer devices. The normal application of towlines is in order selection within the warehouse. For example, order selectors or assemblers place merchandise on the trailer, which is then transported to the shipping dock. A number of automated decoupling devices have been perfected which route trailers from the basic line to selected shipping docks.

A rather continuous controversy has existed over the years between in-floor and overhead installation of towlines. The in-floor installation is costly to modify and is difficult to maintain from a housekeeping viewpoint. The overhead installation is more flexible, but unless the warehouse floor is absolutely level, the line may jerk the front wheels of trailers off the ground, causing potential product damage.

The tractor-trailer concept consists of a driver-manned powerized unit which tows a number of individual four-wheel trailers. The average size of the platform trailers is 4 by 8 feet. The most prevalent application of the tractor-trailer, as of the towline, is in order selection. This device for moving merchandise has a great deal of flexibility. However, it is not as economical as the towline because it requires greater labor participation and has a high potential of idleness. Experiments have been conducted with radio-controlled tractors and some special applications wherein the tractor follows a guide strip attached to the warehouse floor. Although remote control holds forth a potential for reduced labor involvement, the majority of tractor-trailer operations are of the conventional variety.

Conveyors are widely used in shipping and receiving operations and form the basic material-movement power for a number of order assembly systems. Conveyors can be classified on the basis of power or gravity and roller or belt movement. The conveyor is flexible, which allows the basic application to be modified with minimal difficulty. Gravity-style roller conveyors are often set up for a specific shipping or receiving task and in some cases are transported within over-the-road trailers to ease destination unloading. When power drive and belt configurations are employed, a great deal of the basic flexibility of conveyors is sacrificed.

The four basic types of material-handling equipment here discussed are far from exhaustive of the range available for the development of mechanized handling systems. Most systems employ a combination of handling devices, in an effort to develop specialized integration. For example, fork-lift trucks may be employed for primarily vertical movement while tractor trailers are utilized as the prime source of horizontal movement. As noted in Chapter 7 when discussing warehouse layout and design, the warehouse structure is properly viewed as a shell that surrounds an integrated material-handling system.

---

[8] Four-wheel trailers are similar to hand trucks or carts that are powered by attachment to the towline.

Over the years a variety of guidelines have been suggested to assist management in the design of mechanized material-handling systems.[9] The following six guidelines are representative.

1. Equipment for handling and storage should be as standardized as possible.
2. When in motion, the system should be designed to provide a maximum of continuous product flow.
3. In mechanized systems, maximum investment should be in movement as opposed to stationary equipment.
4. Movement equipment should be utilized to the maximum extent possible.
5. In equipment selection, effort should be made to minimize the ratio of dead weight to payload.
6. To the extent practical, gravity flow should be incorporated in system design.

As noted earlier, a distinct trend is developing to replace mechanized handling with more automated systems. Attention is now directed to warehouse automation.

Automated Handling

For a number of years automated handling has been long on potential and short on accomplishment. Initial efforts toward automated handling concentrated upon package good selection at the master carton level. Recently, emphasis has switched to the development of high-rise storage and automated handling of unit loads. Each is discussed in turn after a brief review of automated handling concepts.

POTENTIAL OF AUTOMATION.   The appeal of automation is that it substitutes capital investment in equipment for the high ratio of labor involved in mechanized handling systems. In addition to using less direct labor, the prospect of an automated system is that it will operate faster and more accurately than a mechanized system. The shortcomings are the high degree of capital investment and the complex nature of development and application.

To date, most automated systems have had to be custom designed and constructed for each application. Extreme care must be taken to plan existing and future applications so as to build in adequate flexibility and provisions for future handling requirements. The six guidelines previously noted concerning the selection of mechanized handling systems have little, if any, application to automated systems. For example, storage equipment in an automated system is an integral part of the handling capability and represents about 50 per cent of the total investment.[10] The ratio of dead weight to payload has little, if any, relevancy in an automated handling application.

---

[9] *An Introduction to Material Handling* (Pittsburgh: Materials Handling Institute, Inc., 1966), Chap. 4.
[10] *High-Rise Storage* (Boston: Modern Materials Handling, 1971), Chap. 2.

Although computers play an important part in all handling systems, they are essential to the performance of an automated system. The computer provides programming of the automated selection equipment and is used to link the warehouse to the remainder of the logistical operating system. Thus the logistical management control system will be vastly different if automated handling is utilized. One factor that prohibited rapid development of automated systems earlier was the high cost of minicomputers. Breakthroughs in electronic data processing associated with third-generation computers have eliminated this barrier.

AUTOMATED PACKAGE SYSTEMS. The initial application of automation was to the area of master carton selection or order assembly in the warehouse. Because of the high labor intensity involved in order selection, the basic objective was to integrate mechanized and automated handling into a total system.

The initial concept was as follows. An automated selection device was preloaded after merchandise was received from manufacturing or vendors. The device itself normally consisted of a series of merchandise racks vertically stacked. Merchandise was loaded from the rear and permitted to flow forward in the "live" rack on gravity conveyors until stopped by a rack door. Between or down the middle of the racks, power conveyors created a merchandise flow line, with several flow lines being positioned above each other, one at each level of rack doors.

Upon receipt of an order to be assembled, punch cards were created for each product to be selected and sorted in rack sequence. The cards were then processed through a reader which tripped the rack doors in sequence, allowing the desired merchandise to flow forward onto the powerized conveyors. The conveyor in turn transported merchandise to an order-packing area for shipment preparation.

In terms of modern applications, these initial attempts at automated package handling were highly inefficient. A great deal of labor was required at the merchandise input and output phases, and the expense of the automated equipment was high. Applications were limited to merchandise of extremely high value or to situations wherein working conditions justified such investment. For example, the order selection of frozen foods, wherein work temperatures are below freezing, was one area where these initial systems gained wide adoption.

More recently substantial advancements have been made in automated selection of case goods. The automated systems concept employed by the Johnson & Johnson Domestic Operating Company will be briefly described to reflect the current state of development.

At several Johnson & Johnson distribution warehouse facilities, the handling of fast-moving products in master cartons is fully automated from merchandise receipt to placement in over-the-road trailers for shipment. The system utilizes an integrated network of power and gravity conveyors linking together power-motivated live storage. The entire system is controlled by a computer that is coupled with the inventory and order-processing control systems for the warehouse facility.

Upon arrival, merchandise is automatically routed to the live storage position and inventory records updated. Upon order receipt, the merchandise desired is pre-cubed to vehicle size and scheduled for selection. At the appropriate time, all merchandise is selected in desired loading sequence and automatically transported by conveyor to the appropriate loading dock. In most situations, the first manual handling of the merchandise within the warehouse is when it is stacked into the transport vehicle.

The solution of the input–output interface problem and the development of sophisticated control systems resulted in a highly effective and efficient package-handling system. The Johnson & Johnson application is reflective of the nature of package-handling systems that are becoming more common today. However, the existing trend appears to favor what is called high-rise storage whenever the products handled can be adopted to utilized movement.

AUTOMATED UNIT-LOAD SYSTEMS. A recent review of developments in high-rise storage concluded that this concept represents the fastest-growing area of materials handling, with an annual growth rate of 25 to 35 per cent.[11] Perhaps the best way to describe the high-rise concept is to state that above all else it represents a highly integrated system. The high-rise method of handling is fully automated from receiving to shipping. Four main components constitute the basic high-rise system: (1) storage racks, (2) storage and retrieval equipment, (3) input–output systems, and (4) control systems.

The name *high-rise* comes from the physical appearance of the storage rack. The rack consists of a steel-structured vertical storage area commonly 50 to 75 feet high. Some buildings under construction are to be as high as 120 feet. When one considers that the stacking height of palletized cartons in a mechanized handling system is normally 20 feet, the high-rise concept potential comes through loud and clear.

The typical high-rise facility consists of a number of rows of storage racks. The rows are separated by aisles that typically run from 120 to over 800 feet. It is within these aisles between the high-rise rack rows that the storage and retrieval equipment functions. As described by *Modern Materials Handling*,

The storage and retrieval machine—this marvel of automated control—is basically a cross between the fork truck and the bridge-type stacker crane. It looks like a stacker crane but moves on wheels much like a truck. Locked within an aisle, it travels back and forth hoisting and lowering loads, moving them into and out of storage openings on either side of the aisle.[12]

A variety of different types of storage and retrieval equipment are available. Most require guidance at the top and bottom to provide the vertical stability needed to perform high-speed horizontal movement and vertical hoisting.

[11] *Ibid.*
[12] *Ibid.*, p. HR-6.

Today's horizontal speeds are in the range 300–400 feet per minute (fpm) with hoisting speeds of up to 100 fpm or more.[13]

The initial function of the storage and retrieval equipment is to reach the storage position rapidly; a second function is to deposit or retract a load of merchandise. For the most part, load deposit and retraction are achieved by shuttle tables, which can enter and exit from the rack at speeds up to 100 fpm. Since the shuttle table moves only a few feet, it must be able to accelerate and stop rapidly.

In some installations, the storage and retrieval machine can be moved between aisles by transfer cars. Numerous transfer arrangements and layouts have been worked out, but in concept they are simply dedicated or nondedicated. The *dedicated* transfer car is always stationed at the end of the aisle in which the storage and retrieval equipment is working. The *nondedicated* transfer car simply works a number of different aisles and retrieval machines on a scheduled basis to achieve maximum equipment utilization. The decision of whether or not to include aisle-to-aisle transfer in a high-rise storage system boils down to the economics of throughput rate and number of aisles included in the over-all system.

The input–output system in high-rise storage is concerned with moving loads to and from the rack area. Two types of movement are involved. First, loads must be transported from receiving docks or production lines to the storage area. Second, within the immediate peripheral area of the racks, loads must be positioned for entry or exit. The greatest potential handling problem is in the peripheral area. The common practice is to have pickup and discharge stations assigned to each aisle capable of staging an adequate supply of loads to fully deploy the storage and retrieval equipment. For maximum input–output performance, it is normal to have different stations for transfer of inbound and outbound loads assigned to the same aisle. The pickup and discharge stations are linked to the handling systems that transfer merchandise to and from the high-rise storage area.

The control system in high-rise storage is similar to that described earlier when discussing automated master carton handling. In the case of high-rise storage systems, a great deal of sophistication in programming and control measurement is required to achieve maximum equipment utilization and rapid command cycles. Recent advancements in the speed and cost of small computers that can be fully dedicated to the high-rise system have, for the most part, eliminated major control system problems.

Figure 8-3 illustrates the basic systems concept of a high-rise storage system. Merchandise flowing from the bakery is automatically stacked on 48- by 40-inch pallets and shrink-wrapped to create a unit load.[14] The unit

---

[13] *Ibid.*, p. HR-8.

[14] For a more detailed description of the system described in Figure 8-3, see James K. Allred, "New Developments in Computer Controlled Warehousing," presented at Materials Management Systems Seminar on Computers and Materials Handling, LaSalle Hotel, Chicago, Ill., October 24, 1972.

FIGURE 8-3
High-Rise Warehouse Facility.

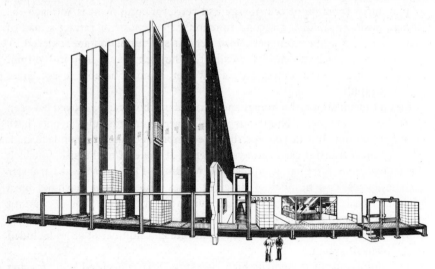

Reproduced by permission of Kenway Engineering.

load is then transported to the high-rise storage area by power conveyor. When the load arrives, it is assigned to a storage bin and transferred by power conveyor to the appropriate pickup station. At this point the storage and retrieval equipment takes over and delivers the unit load to its temporary home for storage.

In addition to scheduling arrivals and location assignments, the control system is concerned with inventory control and stock rotation. When orders are received, the command control system directs the retrieval of specified unit loads. From the outbound delivery stations, the unit load flows by power and gravity conveyor to the appropriate shipping dock. While retrieval and outbound delivery are being accomplished, all the paper work necessary to initiate product shipment is completed.

This example is just one of many high-rise storage systems currently in operation in a wide variety of industries. They are all designed to increase material movement productivity by providing maximum storage density per square foot of floor space and to minimize the direct labor required to perform handling. The highly controlled nature of the system provides extremely accurate control coupled with reliable pilferage-free and damage-free handling.

Evaluating Handling Efficiency

The basic managerial question is the determination of whether a handling system should be designed on a mechanized, automated, or combined basis. As a general rule, the initial cost of an automated system will be higher than that of a mechanized system. An automated system will require less building space, but the equipment investment will be greater. The return on investment from automation comes in the reduced cost of operation. In particular, an automated handling system, if properly designed and controlled, should outperform a mechanized system in terms of direct labor, reduced damage, increased accuracy, and quality of performance with respect to product protection and rotation. In the final analysis, the design to be used should be evaluated on the basis of return on investment, as should any other investment decision.[15]

To assist logistical managers in the design of a handling system, 20 basic principles have been delineated by the Materials Handling Institute, Inc., and the International Material Management Society. These principles are stated in Table 8-1. While any set of static principles offers at best guidelines for decision, those represented in Table 8-1 illustrate the comprehensive nature of planning integrated material handling within the material movement component as well as the over-all logistical operating system.

Conclusion—Material Handling

A major problem in handling is to increase productivity since a significant share of logistical labor is employed in moving materials and products. Today, a great deal of attention is being directed to keeping freight on the move. A wide choice of handling equipment and systems is available to process individual master cartons and unit loads. All have one objective—to eliminate unnecessary handling. The choice among mechanized, semiautomated, or fully automated handling systems depends upon the nature of the task confronted and the relative capital investment cost-benefits.

Containerization

A final aspect of the over-all materials movement component of logistics concerns containerization. The term *container* is employed to describe all grouping of master cartons for purposes of handling or transport. The concept of containerization includes all forms of unitization, from the strapping together of two master cartons to the use of specialized TOFC or other coordinated transport arrangements. All forms of containerization have one basic objective—to increase the material handling efficiency of the logistical operating system. For the present purposes, the over-all discussion is limited to methods of unitization that extend up to but not including total vehicle size. The first part of the section discusses unit loads that do not employ rigid enclosure. Next, the rigid-enclosure approach to unitization is discussed. Finally, the relative advantages and disadvantages of both types of containerization are reviewed. The reader is reminded that the failure of over-all

[15] For examples of this type of analysis, see *An Introduction to Material Handling, op. cit.*, Chap. 5.

TABLE 8-1*
The Twenty Principles of Material Handling[16]

1. *Planning Principle.* Plan all material handling and storage activities to obtain maximum over-all operating efficiency.
2. *Systems Principle.* Integrate as many handling activities as is practical into a coordinated system of operations, covering vendor, receiving, storage, production, inspection, packaging, warehousing, shipping, transportation, and customer.
3. *Material-Flow Principle.* Provide an operation sequence and equipment layout optimizing material flow.
4. *Simplification Principle.* Simplify handling by reducing, eliminating, or combining unnecessary movements and/or equipment.
5. *Gravity Principle.* Utilize gravity to move material wherever practical.
6. *Space-Utilization Principle.* Make optimum utilization of the building cube.
7. *Unit-Size Principle.* Increase the quantity, size, or weight of unit loads or flow rate.
8. *Mechanization Principle.* Mechanize handling operations.
9. *Automation Principle.* Provide automation to include production, handling, and storage functions.
10. *Equipment Selection Principle.* In selecting handling equipment, consider all aspects of the material handled—the movement and the method to be used.
11. *Standardization Principle.* Standardize handling methods as well as types and sizes of handling equipment.
12. *Adaptability Principle.* Use methods and equipment that can best perform a variety of tasks and application where special-purpose equipment is not justified.
13. *Dead-Weight Principle.* Reduce the ratio of dead weight of mobile handling equipment to load carried.
14. *Utilization Principle.* Plan for optimum utilization of handling equipment and manpower.
15. *Maintenance Principle.* Plan for preventive maintenance and scheduled repairs of all handling equipment.
16. *Obsolescence Principle.* Replace obsolete handling methods and equipment when more efficient methods or equipment will improve operations.
17. *Control Principle.* Use material handling activities to improve control of production, inventory, and order handling.
18. *Capacity Principle.* Use handling equipment to help achieve desired production capacity.
19. *Performance Principle.* Determine effectiveness of handling performance in terms of expense per unit handled.
20. *Safety Principle.* Provide suitable methods and equipment for safe handling.

* Adopted by the College–Industry Committee on Material Handling Education, sponsored by the Materials Handling Institute, Inc., and the International Material Management Society.

[16] *Ibid.,* p. 14.

domestic containerization to realize its expected potential was noted earlier in the chapter as a factor contributing to poor productivity.

Nonrigid Containerization

As the name implies, the nonrigid containerized load is not protected by complete enclosure. The most common of this variety of unitization is the stacking of master cartons on pallets for purposes of material handling. A basic hardwood pallet is illustrated in Figure 8-4. In order of development, pallet types and sizes are discussed first. Next, methods of sticking master cartons on pallets are briefly noted. Finally, alternative ways to secure the unit load on the pallet for transport outside the immediate handling environment are discussed.

PALLET TYPES AND SIZES.   Most industry associations have selected a standardized pallet size to be employed as extensively as possible by major firms within the industry. For example, the Grocery Manufacturers of America have adopted the 40- by 48-inch pallet with four-way entry as the recommended configuration for food distribution. Throughout industry, the sizes most frequently used are the 40 by 48, 32 by 40, and 32 by 36 (all dimensions in inches). It is common practice to identify the dimension of the pallet from which most frequent entry by handling equipment is first anticipated. If a pallet provides four-way entry, it can be moved by handling equipment from any side.

FIGURE 8-4
Example of Hardwood Pallet

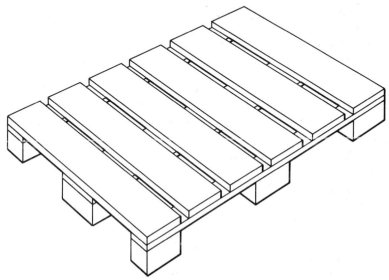

As a general practice, the larger a pallet, the more economical will be the resultant material handling. In comparison, the 40 by 48-inch pallet provides 768 more square inches per master carton tier than the 32- by 36-inch size. Assuming that master cartons can be stacked as high as 10 tiers, the total added unitization space of the 40- by 48-inch pallet is 7,680 square inches, which is 60 per cent larger than the 32- by 36-inch size. The final determination of pallet size should be based upon size of load to be handled, compatibility with the handling and transport equipment used throughout the logistical system, and standardized industry practice. In terms of modern handling equipment, few if any restrictions are encountered in weight limitations.

A wide range of material is used in pallet construction. The most dominant material used is hardwood, but pallets are also constructed from steel, corrugated, plastic, aluminum, and various synthetic materials. The material employed depends a great deal upon the use planned for the pallet. In many situations, the pallet is considered to be expendable after its initial use. Cheap construction is essential for such pallets. A corrugated disposable pallet can be purchased for less than $1, whereas a reinforced four-way-entry hardwood pallet is in the $7 to $10 range, depending upon the quality of the material used. Pallets constructed from other materials are correspondingly higher or lower priced, depending upon material and cost of fabrication.

MASTER CARTON STACKING. Four basic stacking methods are employed in tiering master cartons on pallets. The block method is used when cartons have equal width and length. When there are differential widths and lengths, the brick, row, or pinwheel pattern is employed. Figure 8-5 illustrates the four basic patterns. With the exception of the block method, cartons placed on the pallet are arranged in an interlocking pattern with adjoining tiers placed at 90 degrees to each other. The stability of the load is increased by interlocking. The block pattern does not provide this benefit.

Most firms find it advantageous to make a careful study of master cartons so as to develop a standardized pattern for each to be employed throughout the logistical system. For example, General Foods utilizes more than 90 pallet patterns to unitize over 400 master carton types.[17]

PALLET LOAD SECURING. Under a number of situations, the stability provided by the pallet pattern is not sufficient to secure the unit load while it is being handled or while it is in transit. The historical ways of providing stability include rope tie, corner posts, steel strapping, taping, and glue bonding. Recently, the use of shrink-wrap securing has gained in popularity.

Shrink wrapping consists of placing a prestretched plastic sheet or bag over the pallet and master cartons. The material is then heat-shrunk to lock the cartons to the pallet. Under shrink-wrap securing, the palletized unit load assumes many of the characteristics of a rigid container, with the exception

---

[17] L. G. Smiley, *General Foods Palletization Shipping Program* (New York: American Society of Mechanical Engineers, 1964), p. 4.

FIGURE 8-5
Basic Pallet Master Carton Stacking Patterns

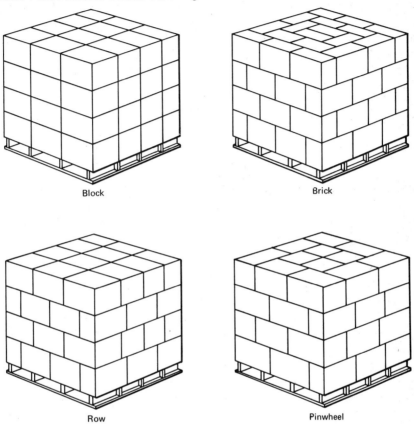

Adapted from palletization guides of the National Wooden Pallet Manufacturers Association.

that the same degree of physical protection is not provided during handling or transit. Other benefits gained by shrink wrapping are reduced exposure of master cartons to logistical environment, low cost, flexible adaptability to various shipment sizes, insignificant added weight, and easy disposal after usage.

Rigid Containers

The rigid container consists of a box within which master cartons or loose products are placed for handling and storage during warehousing and transit. The basic premise is that the placement of merchandise within a container will both protect it and make it easier to handle. The prospects for extensive domestic containerization have been the subject of a great deal of attention

TABLE 8-2
Potential Benefits of Rigid Containerization

Improves over-all material movement efficiency
Reduces damage in handling and transit
Reduces pilferage
Reduces protective packaging requirements
Provides greater protection of product from element environment
Provides a shipment unit that can be reused a substantial number of times, thereby
   reducing waste and the need to dispose of the container.

---

since the early 1950s. The potential for increased productivity by containerization is obvious. One expert estimated in the early 1960s that one-half the total
cost of transporting domestic goods was spent in shuffling between vehicles,
transporting across docks and platforms, in packaging, for claims of loss and
damage, for pilferage, and for insurance.[18] Table 8-2 summarizes the potential
benefits to be gained from increased containerization.

Despite the variety of potential benefits, domestic rigid containerized shipments have not become as common as was expected.[19] In contrast, the expansion of similar containerized movements in international commerce expanded
to the point where in 1970 at least one container ship departed from the North
Atlantic ports of the United States daily.[20] By the end of 1970, more than
one half of the nonbulk freight traveling on the North Atlantic and Pacific
oceans was containerized. Finally, the Port Authority of New York and New
Jersey projects that by 1975 nine million annual tons of cargo will be handled
by the Elizabeth port and that 90 per cent will be containerized.[21]

A comprehensive study of the reasons why domestic rigid containerization
has not materialized was completed in 1971.[22] The significant findings are
summarized in Table 8-3.

Conclusion—Containerization

While recent advancements in rapid expansion of automated handling are
encouraging, similar prospects are not materializing for rigid containerization.
The main advancements in domestic over-all containerizaton in domestic
traffic are centered upon nonrigid containers and coordinated transport
arrangements.

---

[18] Maritime Cargo Transportation Conference, *Inland and Maritime Transportation
of Unitized Cargo* (Washington, D.C.: National Academy of Science, 1963), pp. 33–36.
   [19] The discussion that follows draws upon Vernon C. Seguin, *An Investigation of the
Factors Inhibiting Growth of Containerization in Domestic Surface Freight Shipments*
(unpublished doctoral dissertation, Michigan State University, 1971).
   [20] *Ibid.*, p. 3.
   [21] *Ibid.*, p. 4.
   [22] *Ibid.*, p. 5.

TABLE 8-3*
Summary of Factors Inhibiting Growth of Domestic Containerization

---

Existing common carrier attitudes and practices
  Carriers do not feel that savings are adequate to offer rate reductions
  Empty containers are burdensome to handle
  Present volume is not adequate to earn a return on investment in specialized
    handling equipment
  TOFC is readily available as an alternative

Lack of domestic container standards
  No standardized domestic containers (in contrast to foreign) are universally
    accepted
  No single authority exists to establish such standards

Over-all leadership not evident
  Whereas major ocean carriers provided leadership in international containeriza-
    tion, no organized leadership is evident among domestic carriers or shippers
  Government and trade associations have not filled the leadership gap in a
    comprehensive manner

Existing domestic containerization lacks coordination, which discourages expansion
  Difficult to pinpoint source and responsibility for in-transit damage
  No intercity freight schedules are maintained by carriers
  The container itself is still in the development stage.
  Shippers are not coordinated among themselves in their individual efforts

---

* Adapted from Vernon Seguin, "An Investigation of the Factors Inhibiting Growth of
Containerization in Domestic Surface Freight Shipments" (unpublished doctoral
dissertation, Michigan State University, 1971).

Integrated Material Movement

Although treated separately in this chapter for purposes of clarity, packaging, material handling, and containerization all represent integral parts of the material movement component of the over-all logistical operating system. All three areas greatly influence each other with respect to integrated design. For example, unitized automated handling cannot be efficiently designed unless a high degree of master carton standardization is achieved, which in turn provides the opportunity to containerize individual products. This final section illustrates some aspects of the interaction of packaging, material handling, and containerization in the context of a total system of movement.

Integrated Customer Shipping Programs

A number of successful efforts have been made to develop integrated shipping programs between manufacturing firms and their customers. The idea behind such programs is to blend the material movement capability, transportation, warehousing, inventory policy, and communications into an integrated system that blends into the customer's logistical system. The end goal is to develop a system capability that will reduce to a minimum the exchange of merchandise between two separate corporations. To the degree that exchange interface friction can be reduced, cost savings are possible for both the manufacturer and the customer. This type of integrated exchange is most common in the physical distribution portion of the over-all logistical system.

The General Foods Corporation "Palletized Shipping Program" is an example.[23] This program consists of shipping unit loads of General Foods products to customers on 40- by 48-inch hardwood pallets. In addition to shipping in standardized palletized quantities, the program uses railcars and trucks that have been designed especially to facilitate unit load handling. Pallets are exchanged on a loan basis between GFC and customers.

From the viewpoint of the customer, the benefits of palletized shipment are numerous. First, the unloading time and congestion at the customer's warehouse are reduced to a minimum. Second, all material handling activities within the customer's warehouse are facilitated by receiving products in palletized quantities. Checking of inbound shipments is simplified, and the inventory can be rapidly positioned for order selection. The unloading of a palletized system requires approximately one fifth of the time needed to unload manually. Finally, damage in transit by use of pallet loads and specialized transportation equipment can be almost eliminated. All these factors mean reduced cost to the customer.

From the viewpoint of General Foods, the palletized shipment program permits products to be automatically placed on pallets at the end of the manufacturing line and maintained as a unit load during product allocation and physical distribution. No manual handling is required during the over-all logistical process. The pallet quantity creates a convenient focal point for standardizing order quantities. In turn, carload and truckload prices can be coordinated in terms of gross weight and palletized units. The shipper gains by lower costs and the ability to provide customers with improved service.

Although integrated shipping programs are not limited to food physical distribution, the Grocery Manufacturers of America have been very active in encouraging unitized shipment programs. In many industries, palletized shipments are common in the product allocation phase of logistics, wherein shipments are between company facilities. However, for such systems to function efficiently in physical distribution, a high degree of standardization and cooperation is required.

Special Considerations in Material Movement

As would be expected, the primary interest in material movement is the facilitation of merchandise flow in an orderly and efficient manner from manufacturing to point of sale. However, material movement systems must also be capable of handling reverse flow within the logistical network.

For a variety of reasons, merchandise may be recalled by a manufacturer or

[23] Smiley, *op. cit.*

returned to the manufacturer by customers. Normally such return flows do not have sufficient quantity nor regularity to afford the opportunity for any form of containerized movement. Therefore, the only convenient method of processing reverse flows is by manual handling. To the degree that is practical, material movement design should consider the cost and service impact of the probable level of return flows. Such flows often involve pallets, cartons, and packaging materials in addition to damaged, dated, or excessive merchandise.

Summary

Material movement facilitates flow throughout the logistical system. Within the over-all logistical network, the activities of material movement are prime consumers of labor. Because labor productivity has been dropping, considerable attention is focused on the improvement of efficiency of material movement.

The area of material movement consists of the highly interrelated functions of packaging, material handling, and containerization. Each function is concerned with specific elements of the total material movement activity. Recent years have witnessed substantial advancements in automated handling systems. To a significant degree, increased productivity has been obtained by use of nonrigid containers, such as shrink-wrapped pallets. To date, for a variety of reasons, the potential of rigid containers in domestic logistics has not been realized.

Questions

1. Why is the decline in labor productivity of critical concern to materials movement?
2. Discuss the role of master cartons in a material-movement system.
3. Why is standardized packaging essential to handling efficiency?
4. In the discussion in the text, what advantages would the shoe manufacturer realize by "cubed-out" packing?
5. What benefits can be gained by a modular system of packaging?
6. Discuss the difference between the physical and elemental environments of the package.
7. In basic handling, describe the role of a unit load.
8. What are the primary differences between a fork truck and a towline? Which application in the warehouse receiving, processing, and shipping activities best fits each type of equipment?
9. What is the justification for the guideline that once in motion a handling system should be designed to provide as continuous a flow of product as possible?
10. Why have automated handling systems failed to reach their potential?
11. What is the major justification for high-rise storage?
12. Discuss the differences between rigid and nonrigid containers. What is the role of shrink wrapping in the development of unit loads?

9 Communications

The communications message is the trigger mechanism for the entire logistical system. The quality and speed of information flow facilitates integration of the basic logistical system components. On the negative side, a poor communication network, which allows order bottlenecks or information errors to go undetected, can create havoc within the logistical system. Such errors amplify and distort stockout problems, production schedules, and inventory accumulation patterns.

Further, it is axiomatic that the more sophisticated the logistical system design, the more vulnerable it is to any internal or external communication malfunction. Take, for example, a zero-response inventory system, in which an order is placed following an item sale for replacement delivery. In such a system there is no safety stock at the retail level. The shoe retailer, for example, stocks one pair of man's black wingtips in size 11D. When this pair of shoes is sold, an order for another pair is placed. The retailer is out of stock of this particular size and style until his replacement order is filled from the warehouse. In such a system the lag between sale (impulse) and order fulfillment (response) must be dependable, or a prolonged out-of-stock situation will exist at the retail level. In this type of inventory system, the only way to ensure rapid response is through an efficient communications network. Companies that use the zero-response type of inventory system frequently rely on high-speed store-to-distribution center communication. The result of a communication delay, either through a mechanical failure or a transmission error, can be serious. Delay increases the probability of an out-of-stock condition at the retail store and possible amplification of these problems throughout the supplier channel.

Management has paid increasing attention to all forms of information flow in recent years. All too often in the past communication flows were a residual aspect of operations rather than a design element.

The purpose of this chapter is fourfold. First, the general nature and importance of logistical communication is discussed. Next, the specific role of communication in logistical operations is reviewed. The third part describes in detail an automated order-processing system. The final section presents a framework for developing and implementing a logistical communication system. Aspects of logistical communication are discussed at three points within the text. At this point, emphasis is placed upon the operational aspects of communication. In Chapters 13 and 14 the orientation is directed toward control and performance measurement.

Nature of Logistical Communication

The study of information within the business enterprise is a relatively new phenomenon. With the advent of the high-speed computer new opportunities for effective use of communication in logistical operations have emerged. Communications deals with the speed and accuracy of messages. Time in the logistical system is both limited and inelastic.[1] If time is not fully utilized, it cannot be retained for the future. Likewise, the faster a specific task can be performed in the logistical system, the more time is available for performance of other activities.

Two basic aspects of time are important in a logistical performance system. The first is the time expected to elapse while performing a specified activity, such as order transmittal. The second concerns message delay, experienced as a result of a variety of causes. These two aspects of time influence the performance of all logistical components. Since communication facilitates the activities of the other logistical components, the impact of elapsed time and delay in information flow is extremely critical to total logistical performance.

With today's level of information technology, a message can be transmitted with almost no elapsed time. Time saved in information transmission can be made available for the performance of other logistical activities. Since time is

[1] Richard R. Mead, "The Time Dimension and the Order Cycle," in D. McConaughy and C. J. Clawson, eds., *Business Logistics Policies and Decisions* (Los Angeles: University of California, 1968), p. 118.

expensive, the cost associated with rapidly receiving a customer order may be more than offset by savings realized in other logistical areas.

For example, assume that the total time elapsed in servicing a customer consists of 3 days for order transmittal, 2 days for warehouse processing, and 1 day for transport. Air freight is used to keep the total delivery time down to 6 days. An investment in data communications transmitting equipment integrated into warehouse operations could easily reduce transmittal and processing time to 1 day, which would allow 5 days for delivery. Given 5 days for possible outbound shipment, a number of options cheaper than air freight are capable of product delivery within a total elapsed time of 6 days. The resultant transportation rate savings could very well be more than adequate to offset the added cost of data communications.

This example illustrates the impact of speed or elapsed time upon logistical system design. The second impact of time upon communication concerns delay. Delay simply means that the message does not arrive when expected. Such delays can have a substantial impact upon logistical system performance. In particular, customer service can suffer as a result of stockouts, and production scheduling can be disrupted because of material or parts shortages. As noted in Chapter 6, one of the main functions of inventory is to provide protection in the form of safety stock to cover the probability of unexpected delays.[2]

The classical analysis of the impact of communication time and delay upon industrial performance was made by Forrester.[3] Figure 9-1, selected from his work, illustrates the importance of time lags in amplifying inventory and production requirements within an over-all distribution channel. The chart displays the interrelationships among sales, inventory stocks at various levels in the distribution channel, and production output. Some assumptions on time lags and functional relationships in the system are made, and the simulated impacts upon important variables in the system are presented. In Figure 9-1 the assumption is made that a sales increase of 10 per cent occurs in January. This in turn peaks out in March as a 16 per cent increase in distributors' orders from retailers. Manufacturing operations peak out at plus 40 in May.

The entire chart indicates the importance of time delays in amplifying inventory and production requirements of the firm. It should be noted that basically the same type of process, but reversed, would probably occur if sales dropped 10 per cent in early January.

For purposes of this discussion, Figure 9-1 illustrates the vital role of timely communications among production, distribution, and marketing. If the marketing department develops a program that will result in a 10 per cent increase in sales, it is important to assure physical distribution support of the program. Any anticipated shift in sales that is not carefully coordinated with production and distribution could result in lost sales due to stockouts or higher costs due to overtime and expedited shipments. Careful monitoring of the

[2] Page 184.

[3] Jay W. Forrester, *Industrial Dynamics* (Cambridge, Mass.: The MIT Press, 1961), and "Industrial Dynamics," *Harvard Business Review*, July–August 1958.

FIGURE 9-1

Response of a Simulated Production–Distribution System to a Sudden 10 per Cent Increase in Sales at the Retail Level

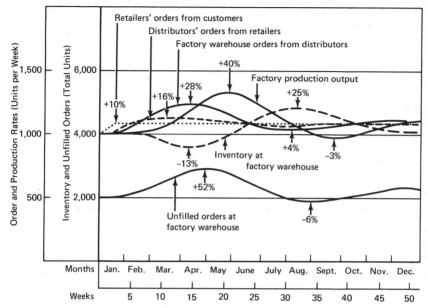

Source: Jay W. Forrester, "Industrial Dynamics," *Harvard Business Review*, July–August 1958, p. 43.

logistical system can reduce these amplifications through rapid relay of customer orders into adjusted production schedules.

Each communication network is designed and functions to serve the particular need of a particular firm. However, certain considerations influence to some degree the functioning of all communication systems. They are (1) system compatibility and balance, (2) systems complexity, (3) separation of physical flow and information flow, and (4) external versus internal information flow. Each is discussed briefly.

System Compatibility and Balance

The communication network of the firm must be balanced with the other components of the logistical system. This is true for all links in the communication network, as well as between communication and other system components, such as transportation and warehousing. A logistical communication system cannot realize its full potential as a management tool unless it is balanced and compatible with the system.

For example, there is marginal value in arranging for customer orders to be relayed from a sales office by direct communication if there is an average two-day backlog in key-punching a customer order for computer input.

Similarly, in the zero-response example noted earlier, the costs of store-to-distribution-center direct communication hookup are probably not justified unless coordinated with other components in the physical distribution system.

System Complexity

The communication network grows almost geometrically in complexity as new components are added to the system. Where one retailer is communicating with one customer and one manufacturer–supplier, the system is fairly simple. If the system includes different products, distinct classifications of customers, and multiple suppliers, the communication problem becomes more complicated.

An added dimension of complexity results from split control of the distribution channel. It is much easier to structure information flows in a channel where a firm owns or controls all channel elements. The opposite situation is illustrated in Figure 9-2. In the case of the appliance company the distributors are independent businessmen and cannot be forced to remit information regarding sales, inventories, or any other logistical related information. In the case where the channel is not integrated or controlled from one source, it is necessary to educate all channel members on the mutual value of efficient information flows.

Separation of Physical and Information Flow

There is usually a substantial difference between the physical channel for a product and the information channel. In Figure 9-2 the flow of products, parts, service, and communications is graphically presented. Note carefully that this exhibit is a simplified version of the actual physical distribution system. In addition to the segment presented, the firm has a substantial private-brand business with a split channel of distribution, which results in even more complex communication. Figure 9-2 also does not include the relationship to production or to over 300 major vendors of transportation, raw materials, subassemblies, and supplies that are part of the material management system. If the full range of information and physical flows here noted were graphically illustrated, it would require a separate systems manual.

However, for purposes of illustrating the divergence between communication and channels for product, parts, and service flow, the chart is descriptive. First, there is a clear split between the communication channel and the physical distribution channel of the product. Second, there is an equally apparent split in the control of the channel. That is, no segment of the channel controls all of the communication or all of the physical movement function. A third factor involves the variable time delays, which are controlled by different members in the channel. These factors are more or less typical of most businesses and dramatically illustrate the complexity of communications in logistical management.

FIGURE 9-2
Product, Parts, Service, and Communications Flow for a Large Manufacturer of Household Appliances

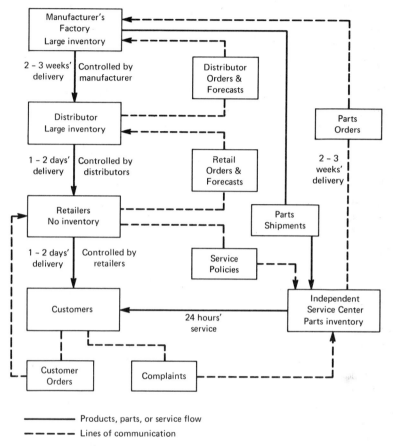

——————— Products, parts, or service flow
— — — — — Lines of communication

External Versus Internal Information Flows

A distinction is often made between internal and external flows in an information system. External flows are those that are either directed from an external source to the firm (customer order) or from the firm to an external
point (shipping instructions to a carrier). Internal flows are those that begin
and terminate within the company (requisition to purchase or warehouse
shipment notice). Although the internal–external division of information
flows provides a good perspective for understanding the role of communications, an analysis of information flows by principal linkage is more helpful
in systems analysis.[4]

[4] For more detailed discussion, see page 312.

The Communication Function in Logistical Management

The communication network, generally speaking, has the same role as the other components of the logistical system. All exist in integrated performance to balance customer service and total logistical cost. However, the method by which a communication network achieves these objectives is somewhat different from the other logistical components. The communication network has essentially four links. The first link consists of inbound communication in the form of a customer order, purchase order for raw materials or parts, or product replenishment requests. The second link in the system is coordination of information with other corporate activities affected by the order. The third link is the command function, which directs order fulfillment. The fourth link is the control phase, wherein management establishes and monitors feedback to ensure desired logistical system performance. Each aspect of the total communication network will be discussed in greater detail.

Order Transmittal

A wide variety of methods exist to accomplish the task of order transmittal. Some common methods utilized are personal delivery, mail, teletype, and various forms of telephone utilization. With respect to telephone usage, the methods of order transmittal can range from personal calls to automated data transmission. Each method or order communication can be classified according to speed, cost, dependability and accuracy of message delivery. Table 9-1 presents a comparative ranking of different methods of order transmittal.

As a general rule, the more speedy a form of order transmittal, the more costly per message unit. High-speed order communication may be desirable when quick replenishment of inventory is necessary or when rapid order transmittal can result in more economical accomplishment in other elements

TABLE 9-1
Relative Characteristics of Alternative Order Transmittal Methods

Type	Speed	Cost	Dependability	Accuracy
Personal delivery	Moderate	High	High	Moderate
Mail	Slow	Low	Low	High
Teletype	Fast	Moderate	Moderate	High
Telephone				
Personal	Fast	High	High	Moderate
Data	Fast	High	High	High

of the over-all logistical system. When evaluating the speed of order transmittal it is important to keep in mind the basic fact that no logistical activity can commence until the order is in hand at the processing point.

Any increase in order-processing speed should result in reduced inventories throughout the system. The effect of a decrease in the order-processing cycle results in a decrease in reaction time to a customer order and consequently a lowering of system safety stock. In general, if a supplier can reduce order processing time from 10 to 5 days, he can also reduce lead-time inventory. In this respect, there is a cost tradeoff between increased communication cost (for example, teleprocessing) and decreased inventory. However, as safety stocks are reduced and the system is brought into delicate balance, it becomes more vulnerable to any communication or information malfunction.

In terms of dependability, alternative methods of order transmittal are evaluated in terms of the consistency of message delivery with respect to expected or standard time. In a sense, dependability is a mechanical measure of performance. As a general rule, the longer the expected time of message delivery, the greater the inconsistency of average performance.

With respect to accuracy, the main element of potential error results from human involvement. Written methods of order transmission utilizing a standard format will be more accurate than verbal methods. In ordering systems in which data are encoded and verified for mechanical transmission, the degree of accuracy will be greater than in systems that utilize written or verbal transmission.

A number of methods can be used to detect errors in order transmission and ensure accuracy of data. Mechanical detection devices are available to perform consistency checks in the transmission of data. A computer can be programmed to provide review by exception of any orders that exceed certain established ranges in quantity or cost. The computer can also be programmed to check cost extension, product codes, and other order details. In general, it could be stated that the more times a piece of information is handled, the greater is the chance of error in transmission. This is particularly true where manual transmission of information occurs.

In summary, logistical performance is only initiated with the transmittal of a correct order. Available methods of order communication can be evaluated with respect to speed, cost, dependability, and accuracy. Regardless of the method selected to transmit orders, it is desirable to limit the options in an effort to derive the benefits of simplicity and routinization. Following are three principles of order transmittal. First, the time span for order transmittal should be as consistent as possible, considering the risks of systems malfunction and consequent stockout problems. Second, order transmission should be as direct as possible, with a minimum of change in order form and intermediate relay. Third, customer orders should be transmitted, wherever possible, by mechanical rather than by manual means to assure a minimum of human error.

Internal Coordination

The second function of the logistical communication system is to ensure a timely and accurate flow of information to corporate areas outside logistics. Useful information can be transmitted to most of the functional areas of the firm. For example, sales reports and market evaluation data can be generated in a more timely and accurate manner when orders first arrive than at any other time in communication flow. Finance and accounting are very much concerned, for purposes of cash-flow management, with anticipated accounts receivable, credit granted, and purchases.

In a sophisticated logistical communication system, a great deal of the coordination surrounding order processing is accomplished automatically. For example, production scheduling may be linked directly to order processing and warehouse inventory control in order to level out production and realize a more orderly over-all manufacturing process.

In summary, logistical communication has an impact on many functions within the business organization. A network must be designed that will ensure adequate two-way communication between logistics and other functional areas of the firm.

Logistical Command

After an order has been processed, the communication system must prepare logistical work directions. In terms of customer orders in the physical distribution, inventory must be assigned, credit cleared, assignment to a warehouse completed, and shipping instructions formulated. Similar logistical tasks must be specified in filling material management orders and product replenishment requests. The activity of creating logistical tasks is called the *command function.*

The command function is extremely important in logistical operations because it activates system components. Unless the command function is accurate and timely, a great deal of inefficiency can result in logistical operations. The command function can be performed automatically through an integrated data-processing system wherein inventories are automatically updated and shipping instructions prepared and released, or it can be done manually through verbal or written instructions. Modern logistical systems rely heavily upon automated communication command functions.

As a general rule command activities are limited to the logistical system. When common carriers and public warehouses are included as system components, logistical commands will extend outside the firm, to ensure proper performance.

In summary, communication command initiates logistical performance. The efficiency of the logistical performance system depends upon the timeliness and accuracy of command.

Monitor and Control

If the logistical communication system is used as a monitoring device, management must establish specific systems objectives that ensure feedback. Feedback is the return of information for management review of all logistical activities that require monitoring. These activities always relate to some aspect of customer service or to the cost of system performance. It is one thing to promise a customer service level of 2-day delivery for 95 per cent of the orders and another to make certain that this target level has been achieved. A multiplant or multiproduct supplier will typically not review each individual delivery to each customer but rather design a review on an exceptions basis. Standards might be established to allow plus or minus 1-day delivery deviation from programmed customer service levels. The only items reviewed are those that exceed the upper or lower limits of this range.

A similar type of review procedure can be designed to evaluate, on a continuous basis, vendors, transportation suppliers, back orders, and damaged merchandise. Exception reports from logistical monitoring can also be transmitted to other functional areas of the firm. For example, a listing of warehouse shipments expressed as turnover rates over time might be of interest to purchasing or marketing in evaluating suppliers or customers.

Another principal advantage of monitoring logistical system is the identification of developing trends. Shifts in color preferences and sizes, regional demand, and competitive actions can also be identified by closely observing movement within the physical distribution system. By properly reviewing and evaluating this information and relaying it to decision points within the firm, a more accurate reaction to unanticipated or uncontrollable factors in the marketplace can result. It provides the firm with a flexible management tool with which informed adjustments can be made to the total marketing program of the firm. The net effect of monitoring and control is to reduce amplification and distortion in the logistical system. Various additional aspects of performance measurement are discussed in Chapter 14.

Integrated Performance

The four basic links of the logistical communication system are essential to achieving over-all performance. The fundamental purpose of an automated order-processing system is to integrate the four linkages into a coordinated logistical information system. Figure 9-3 illustrates the basic concept of the logistical information system.

Automated Order Processing

Very few firms of any size depend upon manual methods of order processing in today's highly competitive environment. The trend toward automated processing has resulted from three benefits. First, the total time necessary

FIGURE 9-3
Logistical Information System

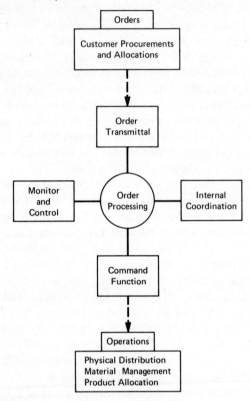

to process orders can be substantially reduced, thereby lowering total logistical cost and increasing customer service. Second, the accuracy of processing and over-all administration is much higher in automated than in manual processing systems. Third, the high cost of clerical help has resulted in greater productivity gains from the use of automated systems. This trend toward automating order processing has resulted in considerable research and development in terminal equipment, data transmission capability, and computerized processing programs.

No two automated order processing systems are identical. Because of the vast differences in operational requirements the automated order-processing system that constitutes the communication component of the logistical system should be highly customized. In this section we present a generalized concept of automated order processing rather than actual systems operated by businesses.[5]

---

[5] The generalized system illustrated is applicable to any situation characterized by a broad product line and a large quantity of orders.

Figure 9-4 presents a generalized concept of automated order processing. A total of 17 specific parts of the system are joined together and identified. In addition, four connector links are identified by alpha designators. The processing system is initiated by an order input and is completed when either a shipment or a purchase order is logistically processed (OUTPUT). Each aspect of the generalized system is briefly discussed.

Terminals (1)

The terminal aspect of order processing consists of the hardware utilized to originate the order into the system. The assumption is made in the generalized system that some form of data transmission is being employed. If not—for example, if orders are transmitted by government mail—then the system can be viewed as starting at point 3.

Development in data transmission terminals since the mid-1960s has been just short of phenomenal. Whereas just a few years ago the only device capable of transmitting orders was the teletype, today a wide variety of devices is available within a reasonable price range. The majority of terminals in use transmit over standard voice-grade telephone lines by first encoding messages on punch cards, paper tape, or magnetic tape. The orders using these terminal devices are encoded from hard copy and verified for accuracy. In a technical sense, the terminal merely transmits the message once it is encoded in data-processing format. The encoding and transmitting hardware is grouped here under what is called the *terminal*.

In some systems order transmittal is completed directly from computer to computer without the need to encode or to utilize an external terminal device. Internal computer communication capacity is commonly available in third-generation hardware. Such capacity provides the capability for the simultaneous handling of a number of transmission lines. When the computer is directly linked with a number of terminals, the communication capacity can automatically poll terminals in sequence by dialing each without manual intervention.

Most data-transmission systems operate by manual participation at the terminal location. Either the operator transmits an order directly to the receiving location, or a number of orders are prepared for transmission at a specified time. Either way, the system would not be classified as real time unless the entire order processing was completed during the on-line time. Real-time processing will be discussed later.

A recent development that is gaining widespread attention is the P-O-S (point-of-sale) terminal. Its use is primarily in retail establishments, wherein the traditional cash register is replaced by a device that encodes unit data while the customer transaction is being handled. Several types of P-O-S terminals are currently being marketed, and numerous retailers have tests under way.[6]

[6] "Chains Unlock Flood Gates for POS Systems," *Chain Store Age*, February 1972, pp. E-23–E-32.

FIGURE 9-4
Generalized Automated Order Processing System

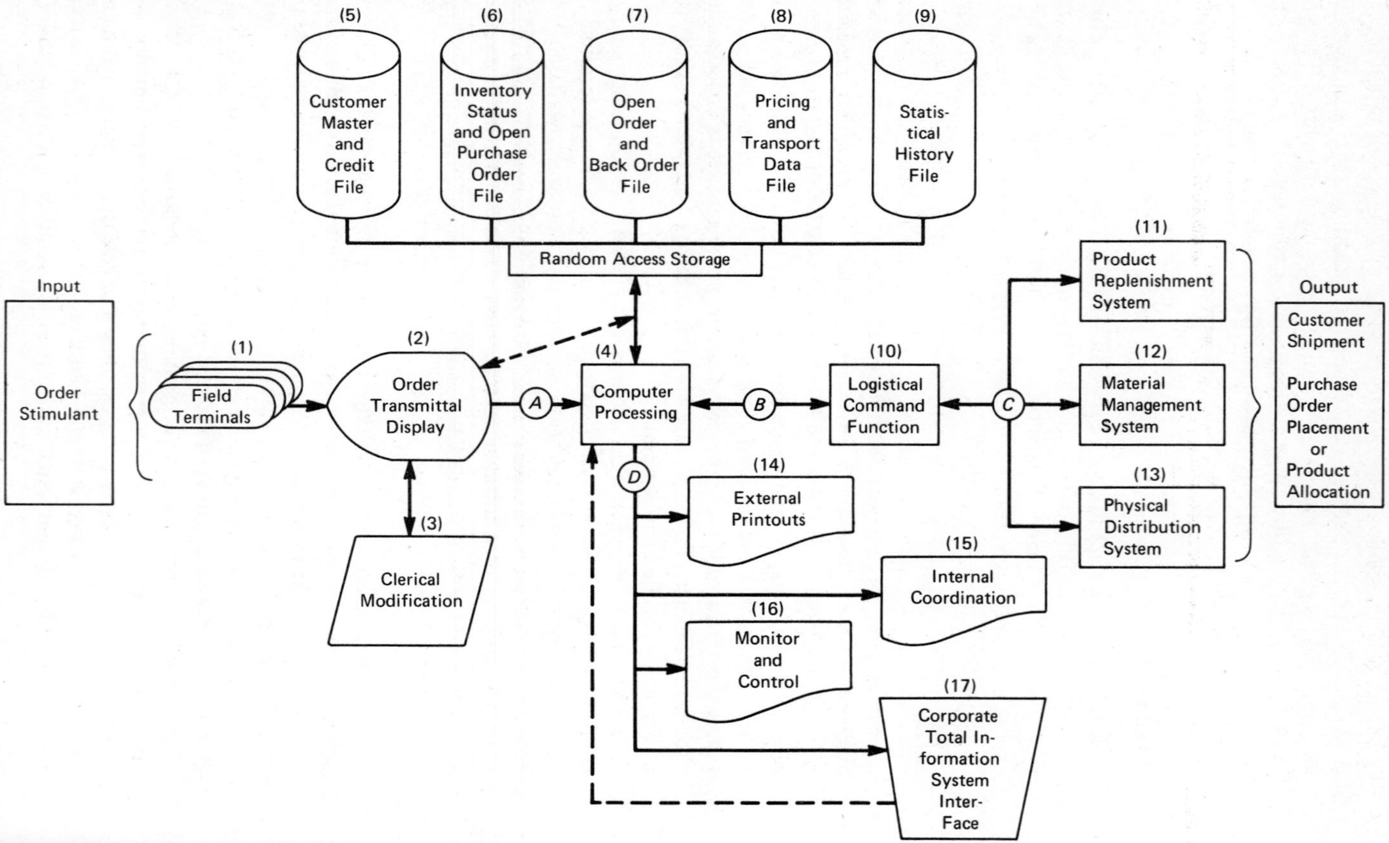

Input

Order Stimulant

(1) Field Terminals

(2) Order Transmittal Display

(3) Clerical Modification

(4) Computer Processing

Random Access Storage

(5) Customer Master and Credit File

(6) Inventory Status and Open Purchase Order File

(7) Open Order and Back Order File

(8) Pricing and Transport Data File

(9) Statistical History File

(10) Logistical Command Function

(11) Product Replenishment System

(12) Material Management System

(13) Physical Distribution System

(14) External Printouts

(15) Internal Coordination

(16) Monitor and Control

(17) Corporate Total Information System Inter-Face

Output

Customer Shipment

Purchase Order Placement or Product Allocation

Some experts predict that by the mid-1970s over half of the general retailing industry will be using P-O-S terminals and related information-processing systems.[7] The key to using P-O-S terminals is to automatically encode small ticket transactions so as to accumulate the data for effective inventory replenishment.

The specifics of the various terminals for order transmittal are not as important as the basic concept at work. Under all forms of terminal application, telecommunication is being employed to move order requirements rapidly into the processing system. In this sense, the use of a telephone for verbal order placement is classified as a terminal. In fact, many automated order-processing systems make a toll-free telephone number available to customers so that orders can be called directly to the processing location.

Order Transmittal Display and Clerical Modification (2 and 3)

As a general rule, orders do not flow directly from input terminals into the automated order-processing system. It may be desirable for a number of reasons to intercept the order for editing or to add information prior to processing. In order to intercept the order and carry out the necessary functions, it has become increasingly popular to install display units that provide a picture display of the order rather than to obtain hard-copy reproductions.

A number of display units are available. They are usually all referred to as CRT, which stands for cathode-ray tube. The CRT allows the total order to be displayed, with the available option of entering or extracting data. In Figure 9-3 a dashed line connects the order display unit (3) with the various random access files of the computer processor. This linkage is to illustrate the fact that it is possible to display selected information from computer files on the CRT for purposes of immediate identification of customer, credit, inventory, back- or open-order status, or statistical data. Thus, if a customer is on line, information concerning all aspects of order processing can be provided immediately.

For example, assume that a customer calls in an order to a CRT operator by telephone. Once the order is encoded, it is possible to read out inventory availability and to inform the customer when delivery can be expected. In fact, numerous systems make provision for reserving the inventory at this point for the specific customer.

The alert reader will note that the CRT is, in fact, a terminal unit located at a different geographical point from the field terminals. In fact, some field terminals utilize CRT equipment. Therefore, the combined function of parts 1 through 3 of the order-processing system is to capture the order and render it ready for processing. Thus the first link of the logistical communication network is complete at connector point A of the system.

[7] *Ibid.*, p. E-24.

Computer Processing and Random File Access (4–9)

The heart of the automated order-processing system is the computer and associated software. Most computer systems utilized in order processing have random access capabilities which permit random selections of data to be extracted from storage files, disks, or drums and merged together to formulate a completed order. Although a number of files may be incorporated in an order-processing system, five interrelated types of data are common to most.

The customer master and credit file contains complete information concerning all aspects of the customer being serviced. Of particular importance is credit-limit data, which can be automatically checked and updated during order processing. The exact data contained in this file will vary considerably. If multiple customer locations are serviced by the logistical system, then all should be identified in the file. In some applications, the extent of customer detail goes only so far as to require the entry of a code number to complete all necessary order detail. The extent of data contained in this file will depend upon the frequency and size of the customer's purchases.

The inventory status and open purchase order file (6) is perhaps the most critical file in order processing. This file contains the inventory on hand and in sight at all warehouse facilities within the logistical operating system. The inventory control system is implemented by use of data contained in this file.

The open-order and back-order file (7) provides the status of orders in process within the logistical system. An order is retained in this file while it is moving through the warehouse and transportation components of the logistical system. If the firm practices the policy of back-ordering merchandise it cannot provide at time of original order, a record must be maintained. In the generalized system, customer backorders are retained in this file.

The pricing and transportation data file (8) provides the information necessary to create the customer billing invoice. Depending upon the size, quantity, selection of products, or destination, the order may be shipped prepaid or collect. A great deal of sophistication has developed in the extension of pricing and transportation data at the time of order processing. For example, several firms currently route the shipment, apply appropriate rates, and extend the total freight bill at this point in the logistical process. In fact, some go so far as actually to pay carriers without the normal rendering of a freight bill.[8] If discounts of various types are offered by the firm, they are normally applied from data contained in this file.

The final file is concerned with the retention of statistical history. The purpose of the history file is self-explanatory. The standard practice is to retain short-term history in the integrated order-processing system for purposes of the generation later of operational reports. The amount and type of data generated by the logistical communication system is a vital aspect of the over-all corporate information data base.

---

[8] A payment system of this nature is used by Johnson & Johnson.

In total, the computer processor merges all data together in terms of response to an order and completes the necessary processing to initiate logistical performance. The actual assignment of operating tasks is achieved by the logistical command function.

Logistical Command Function (10)

The policies and operating rules of the logistical system are applied by the command linkage. In essence, the command function identifies the tasks that various logistical operating systems need to perform in order to carry out company policy. The communication system does not formulate policy. Rather, policy is formulated by management and is consistently implemented by the communication system. The logistical command function represents nothing more than the established operating policy expressed in usable decision rules.

For example, application of the command function provides the criteria for review of inventory status so as to initiate material management and product allocation operations. In terms of physical distribution operations, appropriate instructions are implemented to direct custom orders to specific warehouses and to arrange for necessary transportation to ensure delivery as specified.

Logistical Operating Systems (11–13)

The point of physical reaction to order processing is when any of the three operating systems is provided with a performance assignment. Although extensive elaboration is not in order at this point, we will stress the manner in which communications facilitate operational performance within the transportation, inventory, warehousing, and material movement components of each logistical operating system. It should be noted that the communication between the command function and the operating systems is two-way for purposes of file update and system monitor and control.

External Printouts (14)

A variety of documents that flow outside the corporation may be required to complete the logistical communication process. The most common are shipment notifications, invoices, and purchase orders. One benefit of automated systems is that invoices can be prepared and mailed simultaneously with order processing, thereby substantially reducing cash-flow lags.

Internal Coordination (15)

A third linkage of the logistical communication system is internal coordination. As noted earlier, a number of different areas of the corporation require information of a logistical nature adequately to perform their operational assignments. This information can be provided, as needed, by daily, weekly, or monthly reports generated from the statistical history file.

Monitor and Control (16)

The final link of the communication system is the operational manager engaged in running the over-all logistical system. This linkage is provided by the monitor and control aspect of the automated order-processing system.

Under the concept of automated order-processing systems, data are processed at speeds that allow discovery and interpretation of trends while they are forming. This information can be tapped at will by all levels of administrative control. At any given point in time all experience has been incorporated into the data statistical bank. The potential exists to examine any control or design problem from all dimensions. The most appropriate structure for utilizing total information flow is likened to a control nerve center.

The control nerve center of a logistical system is similar to an air-traffic-control system. Central management has direct up-to-date status information concerning all units of the logistical system. From a central vantage point, interrogation may be initiated of the status and performance of individual units of the system located at any geographical point. Performance can be evaluated with respect to the operating plan, allowing fast and efficient management response to any externally or internally generated change.

Daily sequence of logistical data provides a continuous two-way flow of information between all activity locations and the point of central data bank maintenance. All transactions and records are stored in central data files from original documents. Status reports can be developed as desired, and selected trend or special diagnostic reports can be generated as frequently as necessary. The essence of an information system is that all transaction documents are originated in a format that permits direct posting into data files. This posting results in a total information reservoir which contains relevant data in breadth as well as depth concerning logistical system status and performance. Reporting from an operational viewpoint is developed in greater detail in Chapter 13.

Time Connectors (A-B-C and D)

Within Figure 9-4, four connectors are illustrated to reflect the speed with which data flows into and out of the automated order-processing system. In effect, data flow can be instantaneous or subjected to a degree of predetermined delay. In the logistical sector of a firm, operations are carried on at widely separated locations. This geographical separation creates a need to rapidly collect and disseminate information.

Essentially three groupings of information flow can be identified, based upon speed: (1) batching, (2) short-interval sequencing, and (3) real time. Batching involves the grouping of data until sufficient volume is generated at a given location to justify entry into the tele-data processing system. Short-interval sequencing involves collection of information for a specific time period—for example, one day—with entry into the tele-data system at the end of the specified period regardless of volume. Real-time processing consists of a direct contact between all locations with immediate entry of information as generated. In a majority of logistical systems, a daily sequence of data entry is adequate. At the present time the cost of maintaining a broad real-time information network is, in most cases, prohibitive.

Corporate Total Information System Interface (17)

A final comment concerns the interface of logistical communication and the over-all corporate total information system. The logistical information system is part of a larger communication network. Provisions must be incorporated to pass data to and receive data from the corporate total information system.

Increasing information technology, on the one hand, and management's recognition of information potential, on the other, have given impetus to a corporate philosophy of total information systems. An information system may be defined as "An integrated corporate intelligence system designed to permit management by exception, based on timely information, randomly available, and guided by rigorously determined relationships and decision rules." [9]

When discussing a logistics information requirement, it should be recognized, therefore, that typically it is part of a total information system. One author identified three major elements of a typical management information system: (1) logistics or physical distribution information system, (2) financial information system, and (3) personnel information system.[10] He stated further that each of these major elements can be further broken down into subsystems. In the case of the logistics information system such subsystems might include procurement, raw material inventory control, production scheduling and control, finished goods inventory control, and order processing.[11]

Planning and Implementing a Logistical Communication System

When a firm initiates integrated logistical management, it is faced with the problem of designing a data communication system.[12] The data communication system is the actual physical method by which information is transmitted. The design of a data communication system is a never-ending management

---

[9] This defininition presented in 1961 represents a valid explanation of the objective of an information system. Roger Christian, "The Total System Concept," from a speech delivered before the 14th Annual International Systems Meeting, October 1961, p. 8.

[10] John Dearden, "How to Organize Information Systems," *Harvard Business Review*, March–April 1965, pp. 65–73.

[11] John Dearden, *Computers in Business Management* (Chicago: Dow Jones–Irwin, Inc., 1966), p. 122.

[12] This section is based on Edgar G. Gentle, Jr., ed., *Data Communications in Business: An Introduction*, published by American Telephone and Telegraph Co., 1965.

FIGURE 9-5
A Summary of the Steps Involved in Planning a Data Communications
System

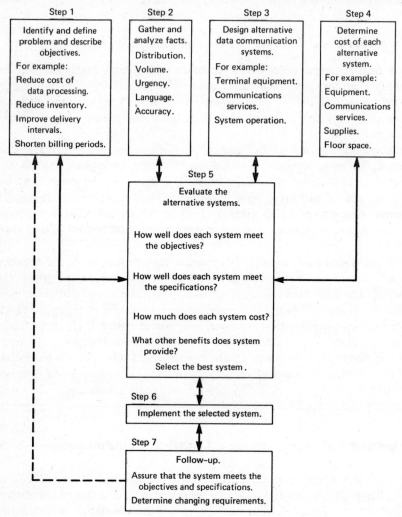

Step 1	Step 2	Step 3	Step 4
Identify and define problem and describe objectives. For example: Reduce cost of data processing. Reduce inventory. Improve delivery intervals. Shorten billing periods.	Gather and analyze facts. Distribution. Volume. Urgency. Language. Accuracy.	Design alternative data communication systems. For example: Terminal equipment. Communications services. System operation.	Determine cost of each alternative system. For example: Equipment. Communications services. Supplies. Floor space.

Step 5

Evaluate the alternative systems.

How well does each system meet the objectives?

How well does each system meet the specifications?

How much does each system cost?

What other benefits does system provide?

Select the best system.

Step 6

Implement the selected system.

Step 7

Follow–up.
Assure that the system meets the objectives and specifications.
Determine changing requirements.

task. Alterations in information inputs and communication technology must be constantly reviewed to maintain the most effective communication system for the individual firm.

Figure 9-5 shows a schematic diagram of the steps involved in building a data communication system. Each of these steps will be discussed briefly.

Identify and Define Problem and Describe Objectives

The establishment of a data communication system for logistical management may have a wide variety of objectives, which in many cases may overlap with other objectives of the firm. The primary objective of a logistical system is to provide the best service level at the lowest possible total cost. Both the over-all information system design and logistical data communication can facilitate objectives in the following ways.

First, the order-processing time may be shortened through the elimination of time delays in the system. This, in turn, leads to a reduction in inventory holding cost with no sacrifice in customer service level. Second, by improving customer service, management can immediately identify any deviation from standard and take corrective action. Third, logistical planning is improved by having timely, accurate, and reliable information for the purpose of short-run and long-range planning. Fourth, customer relations are improved through facilitating rapid and reliable communication flow on matters of mutual interest. Finally, the profit position of the company can be improved by reducing accounts receivable, by production leveling, and generally by providing rapid and reliable information required by other departments of the firm.

Generally speaking, the emergence of a managed information and communication system often results from a problem that has occurred in the business. Such problems as order errors, delayed shipments, noncompetitive service levels, and excessive back ordering can cause management to reevaluate its information handling procedures. When the analyst has determined the probable cause of the problem and has defined his objectives, he can then proceed to the next step in building a data communication system.

Gather and Analyze the Data

Information to be moved within a system has five basic characteristics: (1) structure of information flow, (2) volume, (3) urgency, (4) language, and (5) accuracy. Before a data communication system can be designed, each of these characteristics must be analyzed in depth.

STRUCTURE OF INFORMATION FLOW.   The source of input and the structure of information flow must be identified as they currently exist in the company. For example, sales orders can be generated directly from the customer, from manufacturer's salesmen, from distributors, and from other sources. Sales orders could be generated by salesmen within the district and accumulated at district level and again at regional level before transmission to the home office. It is often helpful to construct a chart that illustrates the two-way flow of communications.

FIGURE 9-6
Information Flow Format for a Small Company

From ＼ To	Headquarters	Factory	Factory Warehouse	Field Distribution Center	Sales Office A	Sales Office B
Headquarters		Order and Production Schedules	Shipment Releases	Shipment Directions	Administrative Messages	Administrative Messages
Factory	Production Reports		Shipment Notices	Shipment Notices		
Factory Warehouse	Stock Status	˙ Shipment Receipt		Order Status	Order Status	Order Status
Field Distribution Center	Orders		Shipment Receipt		Order and Shipment Status	Order and Shipment Status
Sales Office A	Orders			Inquiry on Orders		
Sales Office B	Orders			Inquiry on Orders		

In Figure 9-6 the information flow for a relatively small company is illustrated.[13] From the chart it can be noted that the company has a centralized information system with most of the information flowing out of the headquarters office. Regardless of the degree of complexity, almost all communication systems can be broken down into one or more of four basic patterns: (1) one point to one other point, (2) one point to many other points, (3) many points to one point, and (4) many points to many other points.

A "one-point-to-one-point" pattern is the most basic communications pattern. The flow of information is in one direction, in both directions alternately, or in both directions simultaneously. In communications technology the first alternative is termed *one-way*; the second, *half-duplex*; and the third, *duplex*.

The "one point to many other points" is a communications pattern in which a central location will transmit information to many other points. For example, a logistical system in which all data processing is centralized would likely have this pattern of communication. A situation in which the centralized source initiates the message to outlying points is also an example of this type of communication system.

[13] Figure 9-6 is designed to depict a two-way flow of communications between spatially separated points. There is communication of the nature described in this section within each of the areas. For example, communications patterns exist within the headquarters office. For additional background, see "Communications," *Modern Materials Handling*, January 1967, pp. 49–53, and Marshall McLuhan and John McLaughlin, *Information Technology and Survival of the Firm* (Chicago: Dow Jones–Irwin, Inc., 1966).

The third type of communication flow, "many points to one point," is probably best typified by an inquiry system to a centralized data source where calls are initiated outside the system.

The fourth and most complex communication pattern is the "many-point-to-many-point" system. In this system, every point in the system can communicate with every other point in the system. However, as a practical consideration, most of these systems have switching centers, which allow for temporary connections rather than permanent connections between points in the system. Many companies have more than one system in operation, to suit the particular needs of a division or department.

VOLUME.   The volume of information transmitted has a direct impact on the ultimate design of the system. The analyst must design a system that is able to handle adequate loads but without expensive excess capacity.

The volume of information within the current communications system must be analyzed if a more effective system is to be designed. This usually involves drawing a scientifically selected sample of actual messages at all points within the system. The sample should be drawn so as to eliminate any bias in message sending or receiving patterns. After the sample is selected, the following information should be collected from each sampled message: (1) origin and destination; (2) length, including all additional characters (for example, spaces) necessary to send the message; (3) filing time or time originator wanted to send the message; and (4) charges and other information relevant to the individual firm. On the basis of this survey, the average daily volume, message size, transmission time, and peak volume patterns can be calculated. A great deal of sampling and classification is required in such a survey.

URGENCY.   If it is critical that information be transmitted at a certain rate and at a certain time, the system must be built to accommodate this requirement. However, it is usually the volume of information rather than the urgency of information which is the prime determinant of communication system design. Priority messages are normally best accommodated on an exceptions basis.

LANGUAGE.   The term *language* is used in two different ways in communications. First, it is used to describe the physical form of the information. For example, the physical form could be handwritten, magnetic tape, microfilm, punched paper tape, and so on. The second use of the word "language" refers to the code used to record the information. Usually, if the message is carried in different media, such as punched cards and punched paper tape, the code language used will also be different.

When an analyst begins to design a communication system, he must pay careful attention to language compatibility within the system. Although it is possible to convert data (for example, punched paper tape to cards), this adds both time and cost to the system.

ACCURACY. In a communication system, errors can occur in the terminal equipment or in the transmission line. Such errors are usually rare and are easy to detect by verification procedures. Human errors are more difficult to detect, because they normally occur in a random manner.

In designing a communication system, every effort should be made to ensure the accuracy of information. However, there exists a tradeoff between the cost of error detection and the expense of an error. It is possible to increase accuracy by (1) moving as close to the source of information generation as possible, (2) decreasing the number of times information must be converted or handled, and (3) taking as much human input as possible out of the system.

Design Alternative Data Communication Systems

When the analysis has been completed, alternative data communication systems should be designed. This is generally done by drawing up a sketch of different communication configurations which meet the required specifications of the system. These charts should show the points of message origin and destination, the communication link between the points and the form of the information at various points in the system.

Using the statistics on volume and flow, it is possible to determine some of the specific equipment that will match the characteristics of information flow.

Determine Alternative Costs

Usually, five major cost elements must be measured in each data communications system. These expense centers are (1) personnel expense, (2) supplies, (3) space cost, (4) communication channel cost, and (5) equipment cost. The two largest cost items are generally the equipment and the channel.

The various costs should be reduced to a common denominator for purposes of comparison. A monthly estimated cost is commonly used, because most lease charges are quoted on a monthly basis.

Evaluate Alternative Systems

The alternative systems are evaluated in terms of relative costs and benefits. This analysis should be a thorough one, because factors other than direct cost must be analyzed. For example, the future anticipated needs of the company must be taken into account in selecting a system flexible enough to accommodate expansion.

Implement the Selected System

Prior to actual implementation, a careful plan of the sequence of implementation should be developed. Employees who operate the system should have adequate time for training and to become familiar with the equipment. Some time for "debugging" equipment, especially in a complex system, should be built into the implementation plan. If the system is large, it may be well to consider a gradual phasing in of the equipment over a period of time.

Depending on the complexity of the system and the critical nature of the data, it is often a good idea to arrange for temporary backup to the system. If any unusual "bugs" should develop in the new system, the backup system could be used until the problem can be identified and corrected.

Follow Up

After implementation of the system, it is a management responsibility to follow up and ensure that the proposed system satisfies the objectives and meets the specifications. Careful attention should be devoted to unanticipated bottlenecks that develop in the system.

As a company's needs change, its requirements for a data communication system will also change. It is a continuing management responsibility to review and evaluate the data communication system. In reevaluating an operating system, the type of analysis described in steps 1 and 2 should be performed. If this analysis indicates any significant change in pattern, the analysis should be completed.

Summary

The communication system is the component of the over-all logistical system that facilitates action. Technology has reached the point where combinations of data processing and data transmission equipment are available to handle most conceivable information system requirements. From among a wide choice, the logistical manager must select an information system capable of performing the necessary tasks while remaining compatible with the total corporate information system. The heart of any logistical communication network is the order-processing system.

Questions

1. Why is communication considered the trigger mechanism of the logistical system?
2. What is meant by the statement that time in a logistical system is both limited and inelastic?
3. What is meant by the total order cycle?
4. Discuss Forrester's analysis of time lags in the over-all distribution channel. What was his major finding?
5. Why must the capability of the logistical system be balanced with other activity centers in the logistical system?

6. What is meant by zero-response communication and when would you consider it to be effectively used in a logistical system?

7. Can information and physical flow be separated, and, if so, what is gained by such design considerations?

8. Discuss the relative capabilities of various techniques available for order transmittal.

9. In terms of order transmittal dependability, what factors are of critical importance?

10. What is the logistical command function and how does it relate to the order-processing system?

11. What is meant by automated order processing? At what points in an automated system must provisions be made for human intervention?

12. Discuss the potential of P-O-S terminals in relationship to order cycle and inventory control.

Part Three

Logistical
System
Design

10

Foundations
of Logistical Policy
and Planning

The essence of logistical management is to achieve balanced integration of all elements that form the logistical system. As indicated in Chapter 1, balanced integration of logistical operations must be achieved at three levels within the enterprise. First, within each of the operational areas of the over-all logistical system, the elements of facility location, communications, transportation, inventory, and material movement must be integrated. Next, to achieve over-all efficiency, physical distribution, material management, and logistical coordination must be integrated into a corporate logistical posture. Finally, the total logistical effort must be coordinated and integrated with the marketing, manufacturing, and financial efforts of the enterprise.

Chapter 10 has the objective of developing the framework for planning all three levels of integration. As such, the contents of the chapter serve to synthesize the material of the first nine chapters and as a prerequisite to the treatment of procedures and techniques of system design. The key to integration of the first two levels within the logistical system is total cost analysis. The spatial aspects of transportation are combined with the temporal aspects of inventory in a total network perspective that is measurable by total cost.

Integration at the corporate level requires that performance criteria with respect to both physical distribution and material management be planned within the constraints of available resources. The performance criteria consist of determining the desired elapsed time for delivery and a level of confidence that the desired time will be consistently realized. Once the level of performance for the over-all logistical system is specified, integration is achieved by developing the system capable of realizing the desired performance level at the lowest cost.

The initial section of the chapter integrates the material of the first nine chapters by introducing the logistical network concept. The components of facility location, communication, inventory, transportation, and material movement are synthesized on the basis of general network theory. Network theory provides the foundations for systems analysis and design. The next section of Chapter 10 treats the first two levels of logistical network integration. From a temporal and spatial viewpoint, integration is accomplished by identification of total cost relationships. The third section of the chapter concentrates on over-all enterprise integration by combining total cost and desired logistical performance. The final section develops the concept of the integrated cost–service planning curve.

The Logistical Network

Previous chapters developed the basic components related to each part of a logistical operating system. In total, facilities, transportation, communication, inventory, and material movement form the primary logistical system components. From a planning viewpoint all elements form a network that can be subjected to a wide variety of designs.

The logistical network is viewed as consisting of numerous performance cycles. At the most basic level each set or pair of locations that engages in any form of logistical activity must be related by a performance cycle that consists of order communication, processing, transportation, and update elements. Depending upon the purpose behind the particular performance cycle, all elements may or may not be under the complete control of the enterprise. For example, with respect to cycles utilized in replenishment within the enterprise, control would be the typical situation. However, the performance cycles related to physical distribution and material management normally include elements under separate management.

It is also important to realize that the frequency of activity will vary greatly among performance cycles. Some may exist logistically to support a one-time purchase or sales activity. In this case the cycle is designed, implemented, and abolished. In contrast, some performance cycles are operated almost continuously. An additional complicating fact is that any single location in a logistical system might well be involved in several hundred performance cycles. For example, a warehouse facility of a hardware wholesaler might well receive merchandise from many different manufacturers on a more or less regular basis.[1]

When one considers an enterprise of national or multinational scope, marketing a broad product line to a large number of different customers, engaged in basic manufacturing and assembly, and purchasing raw materials and components from a variety of sources, the basic notion of a performance cycle linking every pair of locations is difficult to comprehend. For example, it is almost impossible to attempt to guess how many individual performance cycles exist in the General Motors or Sears Roebuck logistical systems. Regardless of the number of performance cycles an enterprise utilizes to satisfy its logistical requirements, the important point is that each cycle needs to be designed and operated individually. For planning purposes the logistical network approach provides a basic framework for integration.

The logistical network consists of nodal points, linkages, levels, and flow rates. All aspects of the network are highly interdependant and, with the exception of flow rate, capable, to a significant degree, of partial substitution.

Nodal Points: Logistical Facilities

The nodal points of a logistical network consist of fixed facilities to and from which materials, components, and finished products flow. In a broad context, nodal points consist of all locations from which business operations are conducted. From the viewpoint of logistical operations, the nodal points of particular interest are the distribution and raw material warehouses. Market locations and manufacturing facilities represent fixed locations in that change is gradual and generally limited. The nodal points of the logistical structure, in contrast, are more flexible in the sense that they can be adjusted on relatively short notice.

Although it is unlikely that an enterprise could ever relocate all raw material or distribution warehouses at a single time, it is important to realize that some degree of change is almost constant in the geographical arrangement of such facilities. The fundamental question in the design of a logistical network is to determine how many raw material or distribution warehouses to utilize and where each should be located.

The aspect of the planning problem that concerns how many logistical facilities to include in a network is based upon efficient size, available resources, and potential operating economies. The planning aspects of where to locate individual facilities is based upon relative local economies and service potential.

From a conceptual viewpoint it is important to realize that the degree of service to be provided by the over-all logistical network is, with the exception of inventory availability, independent of the determination of how many facilities to employ. Rapid delivery can be accomplished in a specific market

---

[1] Prior to reading this chapter, the reader may wish to review the materials presented in Chapters 5 and 6 so that they will be fresh in his mind.

or to a specific customer from a distant location by use of telecommunication ordering and premium transportation. Therefore, geographical proximity cannot be directly equated to rapid or consistent delivery. As noted before, the fundamental determinant of how many facilities to include in a network is based on economic considerations.

Once the decision is made to utilize a given number of facilities, the actual locations selected will influence the threshold service potential of the system. *Threshold service potential* refers to the basic service that can be enjoyed in and around each facility utilizing the distribution method of lowest cost. Although it normally is possible to meet the same service level without the facility, once the economics of the over-all network justify including a facility, it should be located at the point of maximum threshold service potential among the locational alternatives that are economically justified.

To illustrate, it is within the capability of logistical technology to provide overnight service to Detroit, Cleveland, Chicago, and Columbus from a manufacturing plant located in St. Louis. However, if the economics of logistical performance justifies a distribution warehouse in the Great Lakes area, the location should be selected from among the alternatives on the basis of balance between logistical savings and threshold service potential.

The important point concerning nodal structure is that the number and location of facilities formulates the framework for the entire system. Each time a facility is added to the logistical network it becomes necessary to establish the appropriate number of performance cycles to integrate the new facility into the system.

Linkages: Transportation and Communication

From the viewpoint of the logistical network, transportation and communication linkages connect nodal points. As discussed earlier, a wide variety of options exists concerning each type of linkage. The particular linkage utilized between a pair of nodal points depends upon volume of activity and required time of performance. Alternatives within both transportation and communication linkages can be classified on the basis of cost, speed, and quality of performance. The network linkage requirements are directly related to the number of nodal points in the over-all system.

Levels: Inventory

The levels of a logistical network refer to the amount of inventory allocated to the system. Such inventory allocations consist of average inventory commitments for transit and locational requirements. Inventory levels can be viewed with respect to depth and selective exposure. If the level is deep, substantial safety stocks are incorporated to accommodate linkage uncertainty and expected duration.

With respect to selective exposure, two aspects influence level. First, individual stockkeeping items may be maintained at different locational inventory levels. Second, to the degree that some products are not located at a specific nodal point, it becomes necessary to arrange bypass performance channels. Thus locational selectivity has the net result of increasing the total quantity of inventory performance cycles required within the logistical network.

Flow Rate: Demand

The flow rate within the logistical network relates to the degree of activity or volume the system must handle over time. If the demand for performance is great, a substantial volume of throughput will be experienced. The net result will be a greater range of design alternatives. Likewise a high-volume throughput system will in all probability require a greater variety of inventory performance cycles to satisfy over-all requirements. If the flow rate is not large, the complexity of the network will be reduced. However, the design options will also be reduced, since little or no opportunity will exist to aggregate volume movements between any two nodal points.

Logistical Network Integration

From the perspective of a logistical network, the interrelation of nodal points, linkages, levels, and flow rates is of prime importance. Design decisions and options available concerning each part of the network are directly related to all other parts. The nodal points, for example, define the necessary linkages. Linkages, in turn, create the requirement for inventory levels. Selective inventory level policies can increase the necessary inventory performance cycles, hence the total number of linkages required to complete the network. Because of the high degree of interdependence among all parts of the network structure, no individual part of the over-all system should be designed in isolation.

Relationships among the network parts can be classified as spatial or temporal. The spatial structure relates to the combination of nodal points and linkages. The temporal structure of the logistical network relates to inventory levels and flow rates. It is important to realize that a logistical system could be designed on the basis of either spatial or temporal considerations. In fact, locational decisions have traditionally been solved without consideration of the temporal issues related to inventory level and flow rate.[2] The objective in such cases is to select the network of nodal points that will result in minimum linkage or transportation cost. Likewise, most attempts to plan inventory decisions over time assume as given the basic spatial or locational structure.[3]

---

[2] See page 138 for a more complete development.

[3] The material developed in the following sections is based on Donald J. Bowersox, "The Integration of Spatial and Temporal Factors in Physical Distribution System Design," *Der Markt*, 1972/1, pp. 4–8.

From the viewpoint of logistical network design the interrelation of spatial and temporal factors should be evaluated on a simultaneous basis. In the following sections the two relationships are first developed separately. First, the relationship of transportation and facility location is developed. Second, the relationship of inventory and facility location is developed. Finally, transportation and inventory are jointly integrated with respect to facility location.

Transportation Economies and Facility Location

The basic purpose of the transportation linkage in the logistical network is to achieve spatial closure between two or more nodal points. For purposes of illustration, assume that shipments are being made directly to a market area from a warehouse located adjacent to a distant manufacturing plant. If shipment quantities are large, volume rates to the market (for example, truckload or carload) will be possible. Therefore, in terms of logistical cost, no benefit would be gained by adding a distribution warehouse facility in the subject market.

However, if the size of shipment tends to be smaller than that necessary to enjoy volume rates, economic justification may exist for establishing a distribution warehouse. For example, assume that the average shipment size is 500 pounds and the rate between the manufacturing plant and the subject market for shipments of the product is $3.28 per hundredweight. Each shipment made direct from the manufacturing location to the market would have a transportation cost of $16.40. Assume that the volume rate for shipments of 20,000 pounds between the manufacturing plant and the market is 76 cents/hundredweight and that the cost of local delivery within the market area is 50 cents/hundredweight. Under these conditions, products shipped to the market via quantity rates and distributed locally would cost $1.26 per hundredweight or $6.30 per 500-pound shipment. Thus, if the warehouse facility and associated inventory level costs could be established for less than $10.10 per 500-pound shipment or $2.02 per hundredweight, the over-all cost of distributing to the market could be reduced. Under these conditions a distribution warehouse might be introduced into the logistical network in an effort to reduce total cost.

Figure 10-1 illustrates the basic principle of economic justification of adding a nodal point to a logistical network. *PL* is identified as the manufacturing location and *ML* is the center point of the market area. The vertical line at point *PL* labeled *PC* reflects the processing cost associated with the preparation of a 500-pound LTL shipment and a 20,000-pound truckload shipment. The slope of line *AB* reflects the freight rate from *PL* to and beyond *ML*, which are assumed to be linear with distance. The vertical line labeled *WC* at point *ML* represents the cost of warehousing and associated inventory maintenance. The line labeled *C* reflects the cost of local delivery from the warehouse located at *ML* to customers located within the area *Ma* to *Ma'*. The shaded area represents the locations to which shipment of 500-pound

FIGURE 10-1
Economic Justification of a Single Warehouse Facility Cost per CWT

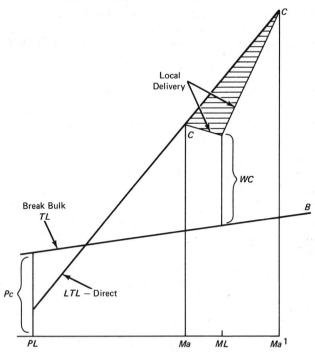

lots would be cheaper via the warehouse than direct from the plant to the customer. At points *Ma* and *Ma'* it would be indifferent from the viewpoint of total cost if customers located at those points were serviced from the manufacturing plant or the distribution warehouse, assuming equal total performance cycle duration and certainty. As a general rule warehouses would be added in situations where

$$\sum \frac{Pc_v + Fr_v}{N_{\bar{x}}} + Wc_{\bar{x}} + Ld_{\bar{x}} \leq \sum Pc_{\bar{x}} + Fr_{\bar{x}},$$

where

Pc_v = processing cost volume shipment.

Fr_v = freight cost volume shipment.

$Wc_{\bar{x}}$ = warehousing cost average shipment.

$Ld_{\bar{x}}$ = local delivery average shipment.

$N_{\bar{x}}$ = number of average shipments per volume shipment.

$Pc_{\bar{x}}$ = processing cost of average shipment.

$Fr_{\bar{x}}$ = direct freight cost average shipment.

The only limitation to this generalization is that sufficient annual volume of shipments would be required to justify the introduction of the warehouse facility. The impact of the annual volume would be reflected in the warehousing cost of the average shipment. As long as the total cost of all activities related to warehousing was equal to or less than the total cost of direct shipment to customers, the addition of warehouses would be economically justified.

In situations where the flow rate consists of orders too small to enjoy volume freight rates, the general relationship of transportation cost to location is as illustrated in Figure 10-2. The total transportation cost related to all performance cycles would reduce as warehouse locations were added to the logistical network. The reduction in transport cost results from consolidated volume shipments to warehouses coupled with short-haul small shipments direct from warehouse locations to customers. At the low point on the transportation cost curve the number of facilities to enjoy the lowest total cost of transportation is identified.

If facilities are added beyond the optimum number of warehouses, total cost will increase. The main reason for the cost increase is that the quantity of consolidated volume shipments to each warehouse would decrease, which would result in a higher rate per hundredweight. In other words, the frequency of small shipments to warehouses would increase. Finally, as more and more warehouses were added to the network, the benefit of consolidated shipments would diminish and total transportation cost would increase at an increasing rate.

FIGURE 10-2
Transportation Cost As a Function of the Number of Warehouse Locations

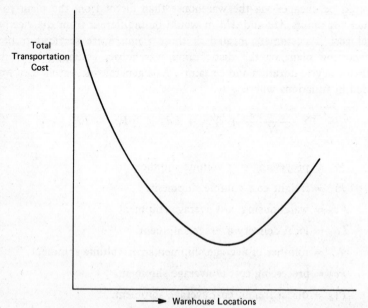

Inventory Economies and Facility Location

Inventory level and flow rate are concerned with achieving temporal closure throughout the logistical network. The basic framework for planning inventory level is the performance cycle. Although the cycle includes transportation, which provides spatial closure to the network, from the viewpoint of inventory the transit capability is measured in terms of time rather than cost.

The level of inventories required to provide temporal closure for each performance cycle consists of transit and safety stock. Transit stock level is based upon the planned or expected duration of the performance cycle. The order quantity is based upon a balance of maintenance and ordering cost. Under ideal conditions the duration of the performance cycle would be equal to EOQ divided by forecasted average daily sales.[4] In inventory control situations wherein EOQ is not utilized, such as in the replenishment or optional replenishment methods, the transit inventory would be equal to the expected days of duration of the performance cycle multiplied by the average daily sales forecasted. As a general rule, the shorter the duration of the performance cycle, the smaller the transit inventory.

The safety stock related to the inventory performance cycle provides protection against sales uncertainty (type I) and uncertainty in performance cycle duration (type II). Both aspects of uncertainty relate to time. Type I uncertainty is concerned with usage in excess of average daily sales during the performance cycle. Type II is concerned with the total elapsed days of a series of performance cycles over a planning horizon.

For the total logistical network, inventory commitment for a given structure of locations and a given configuration of performance cycles would be

$$\bar{X}Is = \sum_{i=1}^{n} \frac{Qi}{2} + SS_i,$$

where

$\bar{X}Is$ = average inventory total network.

n = number of performance cycles in the network.

Qi = order quantity for a given performance cycle identified by the appropriate subscript.

SS = safety stock for a given performance cycle identified by the appropriate subscript.

The net result of adding additional locations to a logistical structure increases the aggregate quantity of performance cycles required to perform logistical support. The question is this: What impact will the addition of locations have on average inventory? The impact on transit inventory and safety stock is different.

[4] See page 193.

TABLE 10-1
Transit Inventory Under Different Logistical Networks

Forecasted Average Daily Sales	Market Area	Warehouse X Only	Two-Warehouse Facilities		
			Warehouse X	Warehouse Y	Combined
6	A	36	36	—	36
7	B	70	—	40	40
	$\Sigma A + B$	106			76
	$\bar{X}Ia$	18			18
	$\bar{X}Ib$	35			20
	$\Sigma \bar{X}I$	53			38

LOCATIONAL IMPACT ON TRANSIT INVENTORY. From the viewpoint of transit inventories the expected result would be a reduction in average inventory as performance cycles are added to the logistical network. Assume that a single product is being sold in markets A and B and is currently being supplied from warehouse X, as illustrated in Figure 10-3. Assume also that the forecasted average sales per day is six for market A and seven for market B. The performance cycle duration is 6 days to market A and 10 days to market B.

FIGURE 10-3
Logistical Network—Two Markets, One Warehouse

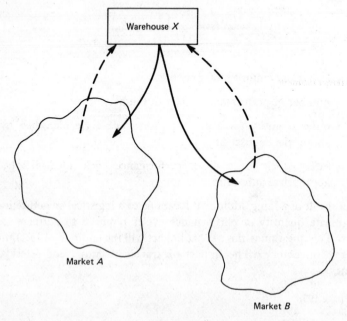

Warehouse X

Market A

Market B

FIGURE 10-4
Logistical Network—Two Markets, Two Warehouses

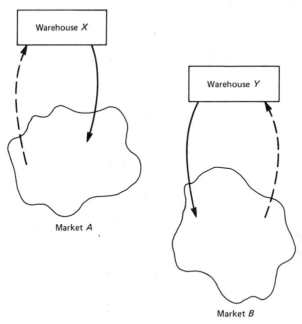

Without considering the impact of EOQ, the question is this: What will happen to transit inventories if a second warehouse is added, such as illustrated in Figure 10-4? Table10-1 provides a summary of the impact of adding a second warehouse, which reduced the performance cycle to market *B* from 10 to 4 days. The net result of adding a second warehouse is to reduce the average transit inventory of the network from 53 to 38 units. It should be noted that the addition of the second warehouse did not create additional performance cycles on the outbound or physical distribution portion of the logistical flow. However, on the inbound flow a new warehouse needs to be replenished. Assuming a full product line at each warehouse, the performance cycles related to replenishment will increase each time a new warehouse is added. However, the average in-transit inventory for the total network will normally drop each time a new warehouse is added to the network.

Assume that warehouse *X* is supplied by four manufacturing plants whose individual performance cycles and forecasted average usage are as illustrated in Table 10-2. For purposes of comparison, assume a unit value of $5 for all products handled at the warehouses. Utilizing only warehouse *X*, the average transit inventory would be 2,835 units at $5.00 each, or $14,175. Table 10-3 illustrates the addition of warehouse *Y*. Average transit inventory under the two-warehouse logistical structure dropped to 2,248 units or, at $5.00 each, $11,240. Thus, even though four new performance cycles were added to the logistical network, the average transit inventory was reduced.

TABLE 10-2
Logistical Structure: One Warehouse, Four Plants

	Warehouse X			
Manufacturing Plant	Performance Cycle Duration	Forecasted Average Sales	Transit Inventory	$\bar{X}I$
A	10	35	350	175
B	15	200	3,000	1,500
C	12	60	720	360
D	20	80	1,600	800
	57	375	5,670	2,835

TABLE 10-3
Logistical Structure: Two Warehouses, Four Plants

Manufacturing Plant	Performance Cycle Duration	Forecasted Average Sales	Transit Inventory	$\bar{X}I$
	Warehouse X			
A	10	20	200	100
B	15	100	1,500	750
C	12	35	420	210
D	20	30	600	300
	57	185	2,720	1,360
	Warehouse Y			
A	5	15	75	38
B	8	100	800	400
C	6	25	150	75
D	15	50	750	375
	34	190	1,775	888
	$\Sigma\, xy$ 91	$\Sigma\, xy$ 375	$\Sigma\, xy$ 11,695	$\Sigma\, \bar{x}xy$ 2,248

As a general rule, the addition of facilities will have the net effect of reducing the time duration of performance cycles and thus transit inventory levels. It is difficult to envision the planned addition of a facility that would increase the average duration of aggregated performance cycles throughout the logistical network.

From the viewpoint of performance cycle duration being set exactly equal to economic order quantity, the complete freedom illustrated in the examples given, wherein average transit inventory was assumed equal to one-half average sales multiplied by transit days, would not be possible. However, the general rule that additional performance cycles will reduce transit inventory is still valid. Recall that the formula for EOQ was presented as [5]

$$\text{EOQ} = \sqrt{\frac{2C_o S}{C_m U}},$$

where

$$C_o = \text{cost per order.}$$

$$C_m = \text{cost of maintenance per year.}$$

$$S = \text{annual sales volume, units.}$$

$$U = \text{cost per unit.}$$

The addition of a second warehouse facility would be expected to influence two factors in the formula: C_m, cost of maintenance per year, would shift its level in a two-warehouse network in contrast to a one-warehouse network; and S, annual sales volume in units, would drop by a substantial amount, approaching one half. No change would be experienced in the denominator of the formula. The net effect in the numerator would be a substantial reduction in the value as a result of the large drop in annual sales, the largest factor compounded. The result would be a reduction in the EOQ and therefore a reduction in average transit inventory since $\bar{X}I = \frac{1}{2}$ the order quantity.

In summary, the addition of nodal points to the logistical network can be expected to reduce the average transit inventory throughout the total network. This reduction can be expected to be independent of whether or not the number of performance cycles remains constant or increases as a result of the new locations added. Likewise, the addition of locations will have a net reduction in transit inventories independent of the use of economic order quantity formulations. The key to understanding the locational impact on transit inventory is that total performance cycle days are being reduced independent of the number of performance cycles included in the network.

LOCATIONAL IMPACT ON SAFETY STOCK.   From the viewpoint of safety stock the expected result is an increase in average inventory as locations are added to the logistical network. In Chapter 6 the uncertainty related to sales during performance cycle (type I) and performance cycle duration (type II) were evaluated for two frequency distributions.[6] In that example the standard deviation (σ) for type I uncertainty was determined to be 2.3, and for type II uncertainty, 2. Compounding the two independent variables resulted in a combined σ of 13 units; or it would require 26 units of safety stock to provide 97.72 per cent of stock availability during the performance cycle, taking types I and II uncertainty into consideration.

---

[5] See page 194.
[6] See page 209.

The addition of locations to the logistical network has two impacts upon the safety stock requirement to satisfy a given level of demand. First, since the planned duration of the performance cycle is reduced, the range of variability in sales during the performance cycle and the variability in the performance cycle are both reduced. Therefore, the first impact of reducing the duration of the performance cycle to some degree relieves the need for safety stocks.

The second impact of adding locations is, however, more serious. The addition of each new performance cycle creates the need for a new safety stock. In addition, the statistical data base for estimating the required safety stock is reduced in size with no corresponding reduction in the variability of sales. For example, when the needs of several different markets can be aggregated together to create a single usage requirement, the variability of demand across markets can be averaged out. In essence, the use of probability allows the safety stock of one market to be used to satisfy the requirements of other markets each time sales are less than the average forecasted for the first market.

To illustrate, Table 10-4 provides a summary of monthly sales in three markets on a combined and separate basis. Average sales for the three markets combined is 22 units per month, with the greatest variation above the average being in month 6, when sales reached 29 units, 7 more than average. Assuming that it is desirable to provide 100 per cent protection against stockout and

TABLE 10-4
Summary of Sales in One Combined and Three Separate Markets

Month	Combined Sales All Markets	Unit Sales per Market		
		A	B	C
1	18	9	0	9
2	22	6	3	13
3	24	7	5	12
4	20	8	4	8
5	17	2	4	11
6	29	10	5	14
7	21	7	6	8
8	26	7	7	12
9	18	5	6	7
10	24	9	5	10
11	23	8	4	11
12	23	12	2	9
Total Sales	265	90	51	124
Average Monthly Sales	22.0	7.5	4.2	10.3
Value Greater than Average	7	5	3	4

that total sales of 29 units had an equal probability of occurring in any month, a safety stock of 7 units would be required.

From the viewpoint of individual markets, the average monthly sales for markets A, B, and C are 7, 4, and 10 units (rounded). The maximum demand in excess of forecast is for market A, 5 units in month 12; for market B, 3 units in month 8; and for market C, 4 units in month 6. The combination of each of these three extreme months equals 12 units. Thus, if safety stocks were being planned for each market on a separate basis, 12 units of safety stock would be required as opposed to 7 units on a combined basis. Thus a total increase in safety stock of 5 units would be required to provide equal protection.

Although this example is not complex, it serves to illustrate the impact of additional locations on the aggregate level of safety stocks in the logistical network. The important point to understand is that the increase in aggregate safety stock in the network is the result of an inability to aggregate sales across a large market area. As a consequence, separate safety stocks must be established for each market which take into consideration the total impact of local variation in demand.

GENERALIZED LOCATIONAL IMPACT ON INVENTORY.   The impact of expanding locations in the logistical network upon average inventory is generalized in Figure 10-5. The reduction in average transit inventory is illustrated by the line labeled $\bar{X}t$. The assumption is that a general linear relationship exists between average transit inventory and the number of locations in the network. In actual situations, the line would decrease; however, it would never equal zero. At some point in the expansion process the quantity of average transit inventory would not be reduced by the additional reduction of aggregate performance cycles.

The curve labeled $\bar{X}ss$ (average safety stock) increases as the number of locations in the network are expanded. The actual increase is at a decreasing rate since the net increase per location is the added safety stock less the reduction in uncertainty as a result of short performance cycle duration. However, this relationship reduces as more and more performance cycles are added. The total inventory curve represents the summation of the two inventory functions. The significant point is that the safety stock factor related to aggregate average inventory dominates the total average inventory commitment throughout the logistical network. This impact results because the average inventory for each performance cycle is the full safety stock plus one half of the order quantity or transit inventory. Thus the total inventory increases as the number of locations in the network is raised.

Spatial–Temporal Integration

The total cost related to the logistical network is illustrated in Figure 10-6. The low point on the total transportation cost curve is at a configuration of

FIGURE 10-5
Average Inventory As a Function of Number of Warehouse Locations

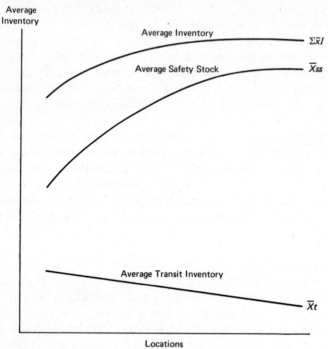

eight locations. Total cost related to average inventory commitment increases with each additional location. The lowest total cost for the over-all logistical structure is for a network consisting of five locations.

The identification of the least-total-cost combination illustrates the potential of trade-offs among cost generating activities. The minimal total cost point for the integrated system is not at the point of least cost for either activity displayed.

Over the past several years the total cost concept has received considerable attention in the literature related to logistics.[7] The original application of the concept in logistics was presented by Lewis and Culliton in an examination of how air freight can represent the lowest total cost of physical distribution when costed from the vantage point of all expense related to gaining spatial and temporal closure.[8] LeKashman and Stolle refined the basic concept by identification of 10 categories of tangible and intangible costs related to the

[7] For complete development of the total-cost concept, see Raymond LeKashman and John F. Stolle, "The Total Cost Approach to Distribution," *Business Horizons*, Vol. 44 (Winter 1965), pp. 33–46; or Marvin Flaks, "Total Cost Approach to Physical Distribution," *Business Management*, Vol. 24 (August 1963), pp. 55–61.

[8] Howard T. Lewis and James W. Culliton, *The Role of Air Freight in Physical Distribution* (Boston: Harvard University, 1956).

FIGURE 10-6
Total-Cost Logistical Network

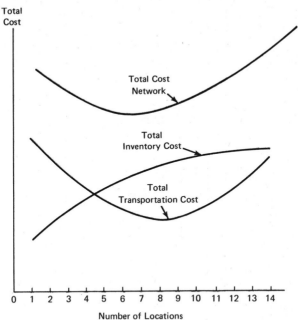

total-cost approach.[9] Figure 10-7 is reproduced from the LeKashman–Stolle article. Each of the 10 costs identified is illustrated in terms of its respective relationship to an increase in the number of locations added to the logistical network.

For purposes of present illustration, emphasis is placed on the two main cost categories: inventory and transportation. Each primary cost is defined sufficiently broadly to include more than the capital invested in inventory or the basic freight rate in transportation.

In terms of inventory, total cost includes all costs related to maintenance and ordering. Maintenance cost includes taxes, storage in terms of fixed facility cost, capital, insurance, and obsolescence. The cost of ordering includes the full expense of inventory control, order preparation, order communications, update activities, and managerial supervision. The total cost of transportation includes published rates and accessorial charges plus expenses related to the hazards incurred in utilizing the various modes and legal forms of transport and the associated administrative costs.

A summary of total costs of logistical activities is presented in Table 10-5. A number of groupings of logistical accounts have been developed to assist in total cost accounting and analysis. The most recent was a comprehensive

[9] LeKashman and Stolle, *op. cit.*, p. 38.

FIGURE 10-7
Ten Cost Categories As a Function of the Number of Warehouse Locations

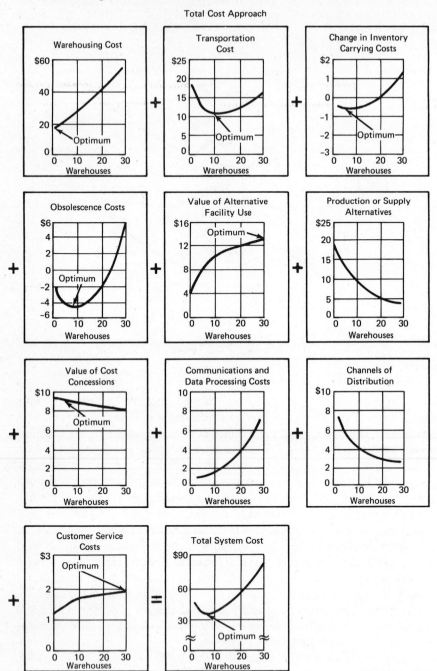

Reproduced with permission from Raymond LeKashman and John F. Stolle, "The Total Cost Approach to Distribution." *Business Horizons*, Winter 1965, pp. 33–46.

TABLE 10-5
Total Cost Grouping by Inventory and Transport Components

Inventory-Related Costs	*Transportation-Related Costs*
Maintenance	Direct
Tax	Rates
Storage	Accessorial charges
Capital	Indirect
Insurance	Liability not protected by carrier
Obsolescence	Managerial
Ordering	
Communication	
Processing, including material	
handling and packaging	
Update activities, including	
receiving and data processing	
Inventory Control	
Managerial	

study completed by the National Council of Physical Distribution Management.[10] In Table 10-5 emphasis is placed upon grouping of cost accounts for purpose of total cost analysis.

Thus, from the perspective of total cost managerial accounting, provision must be made to assign all tangible and intangible costs related to logistical system design. The technique of grouping costs in association with the major accounts of inventory and transportation highlights the basic interrelation of all related costs while retaining a clear perspective of the critical factors in logistical planning.

Total Cost and Desired Customer Service Performance

The basic total-cost approach to logistical network design identifies the most economical arrangement of facilities with respect to inventory and transportation. In Figure 10-6 the least-total-cost network consisted of six warehouses. Beyond pure logistical considerations it is necessary to integrate the degree of service performance required by marketing and manufacturing into the over-all design of the network. The integration to over-all enterprise operation is achieved by evaluation of the total cost–service relationships.[11]

[10] Michael Schiff, *Accounting and Control in Physical Distribution Management* (Chicago: National Council of Physical Distribution Management, 1972).

[11] For an example of the applied use of total cost analysis, see Donald J. Bowersox and Robert J. Franco, "Physical Distribution, a New Concept of Critical Importance to Government Procurement When Priorities Escalate," *Defense Management Journal*, Winter 1968–69, pp. 30–34.

As noted earlier, a logistical system designed around the least total cost of transportation and inventory will have an inherent threshold for service capability. Service in the present context refers to the capability of the network to provide a certain level of delivery performance on a consistent basis. The least-cost position illustrated in Figure 10-5 has an inherent or threshold level of service related to the six locations in the network. The aggregate amount of service provided at the point of least total cost would be a function of the extent of demand or manufacturing requirements located within the time duration of the various performance cycles and the level of safety stock related to each performance cycle. For example, if the level of safety stock is set at 97.75 per cent protection for the combined probability of type I and type II uncertainty, it would be expected that about 98 of 100 orders would receive the planned threshold service.

The level of threshold service related to total least cost can be expanded by adding facilities beyond those that represent total least cost. Assuming that the measure of logistical service is related to the percentage of demand that can be serviced within a time interval, the general nature of expanding the degree of service provided is illustrated in Table 10-6. Although the results displayed in Table 10-6 are hypothetical, they do serve to illustrate the basic need when designing networks of providing very high levels of demand service.

First, incremental service is a diminishing function. For example, the first five locations provided 24-hour performance to 48 per cent of all customers or plants at a 97.75 confidence level. This degree of customer or plant service is

TABLE 10-6
Service Capabilities at Time Intervals of
Performance Consistency 97.75

Network Locations	Percentage Demand by Performance-Cycle Duration (hours)			
	24	48	60	84
1	15	31	53	70
2	23	44	61	76
3	32	49	64	81
4	37	55	70	85
5	42	60	75	87
6	48	65	79	89
7	54	70	83	90
8	60	76	84	90
9	65	80	85	91
10	70	82	86	92
11	74	84	87	92
12	78	84	88	93
13	82	85	88	93
14	84	86	89	94

the threshold service related to total least cost. In order to nearly double the percentage of 24-hour service, from 48 to 84 per cent, eight additional locations needed to be added to the logistical network.

Second, high degrees of demand service are reached for customers or plants at the longer performance intervals much faster than at the shorter intervals. For example, only four locations can provide 85 per cent performance to demand within the 84-hour performance cycle. Increasing the total locations from 5 to 14 improved the 84-hour performance only to incrementally 9 per cent more demand locations.

Finally, with respect to total cost, reference to Figure 10-6 indicates that the total cost associated with each additional location added to the logistical network increases dramatically. Thus, while the incremental service resulting from additional locations is a diminishing function, the related incremental cost associated with each new location is an increasing function.

In summary, integration of the logistical system into over-all corporate planning consists of selecting the level of service that is desired for customers or manufacturing plants. This level of service is viewed from the time interval of delivery and the confidence level that the desired delivery service will in fact materialize given types I and II uncertainty. The total cost curve defines the point of least cost associated with each level of potential service. From a design viewpoint, the point of total least cost with its associated threshold service capability offers a structure that enjoys optimum cost trade-offs. From the viewpoint of over-all enterprise objectives, incremental service in excess of the threshold level may be justified from the perspective of marketing or manufacturing operations. Thus, from the level of total enterprise planning, service–cost trade-offs may be structured which will result in the logistical network being designed to operate at other than the point of least total cost. Given the desired level and confidence of service, the logistical network should be designed to provide the desired service at the related total least cost.

Alternative Logistical Policies

Establishment of service and cost objectives constitutes a critical managerial policy preceding logistical design. The system must be designed to meet service objectives and to stay within anticipated costs. Extreme care should be taken in the establishment of objectives. As a generalization, firms fall into the trap of being overly optimistic in the statement of service policies. The result is an excessively high commitment to customers, followed by erratic performance. This dichotomy results from failure to have a realistic appreciation of the cost of facilities and operations required to support high service commitments.

As indicated throughout this book, the objectives of individual departments responsible for logistic activities often stand in conflict. Therefore, formulation of system objectives cannot be left exclusively to department managers.

Service policies must remain the responsibility of top management. Four basic strategies are available to guide managerial planning: (1) minimum total cost, (2) maximum customer service, (3) short-range profit maximization, and (4) maximum competitive advantage. Each basic strategy normally requires a different system design.

Minimum Total Cost Policies

Just as a physical map of a geographical area shows the elevations, depressions, and contours of land surface, an economic cost map illustrates differences in the cost of logistic activities between different areas. Generally, peak costs for labor and government services occur in large metropolitan areas. However, because of geographical demand cluster, total logistic cost resulting from reduced expenditures on transportation and inventory often is at a minimum at these metropolitan points. Lower total cost results from the density of demand in these major markets.

At first approximation, a policy of least total cost will seek to select a combination of facilities that will require lowest fixed and variable costs. Such a system will be designed purely for economies, with resultant customer service capabilities being a function of cost relationships among distribution activity centers. In terms of basic relationships, the point of total least cost was illustrated in Figure 10-6.

Under the conditions of least total cost, each customer is serviced on the basis of cost equalization between warehouse and plant locations included in the system. In a multiproduct situation, selection of service territories of each facility will depend upon the products stocked at each location and the degree of product mixing on individual customer orders. Because costs have significant geographical differentials, the service area of any given facility will vary in size and configuration. Figure 10-8 provides an illustration of warehouse territory boundaries based upon an equalization line of total delivered cost. The irregularity of service territories results from distribution cost differentials in various directions out of the three warehouse points illustrated.

In Figure 10-8 the three warehouse facilities are identified by the letters X, Y, and Z. The cost illustrated at each facility location represents the average order cost for all logistic costs not related to transportation. The differential of average order cost between facilities is reflective of geographical and individual system differentials.

Around each facility three total cost lines are displayed at intervals of $1.50, $2.50, and $3.50. The value on the line represents the total cost of distribution to points located along the line. The area within a given line can be serviced at something less than the parameter cost displayed on the line. In actual practice, equal total cost lines ($1.20 costs) would be constructed at smaller dollar intervals than the $1 range illustrated in Figure 10-8. The irregularity of the cost interval lines is reflective of the nonlinear characteristics of transportation rates.

FIGURE 10-8
Determination of Distribution Territories—Three-Point, Least-Cost System

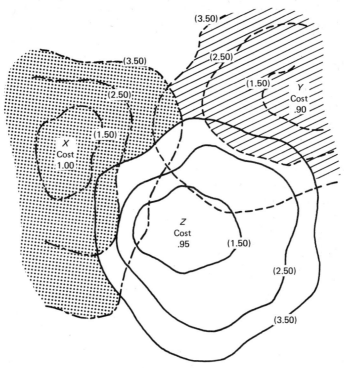

The actual area serviced by each facility is based on lowest total cost. This territory boundary line represents the point of equal total cost between two facilities. Along this line of equal costs, the firm is indifferent as to which facility services the specific customer involved.

The reader should be aware of two conditions contained in Figure 10-8. First, the illustration is based upon an average order, and thus distribution costs are equated on the average. To the degree that order size varies from the average, alternative territory boundaries will be required. Second, an element of time is included because transportation cost is calculated upon the basis of common carrier rates and costs occurred while inventories are in transit. Thus the conclusion cannot be made that delivery times will be constant within territories or to the point of equal total logistic cost between two service areas.

The fact that a least-cost physical distribution system is designed for maximum economy does not mean that customer service standards are omitted from managerial policy. The elapsed time from the customer's order placement to product delivery in a least-cost system will be longer on the average than for other types of systems. However, customers located in the heart of the market will enjoy very high threshold standard of service. Because the least-cost array will tend to favor areas of highest demand concentration, a substantial number of customers will enjoy fast delivery.

Regardless of the resultant delivery time, management will be in a position to make customer commitments concerning expected delivery. Such a statement might be expressed as follows: Order cycle for area A will be 10 days from receipt of orders at our warehouse facility. It is our policy to be able to fill 90 per cent of all orders within the 10-day period.

The operational capability of the firm's logistical system is measured by the degree to which service standards to established areas are constantly met in practice.

Maximum Customer Service Policies

In actual situations, a maximum service strategy is rarely found. In essence, a system designed to provide maximum service would not attempt to deliver products faster than on a 24-hour basis.

Emphasis in maximum service shifts from cost to delivery time. Thus a territory division is developed similar in appearance to the least-cost service areas illustrated in Figure 10-8. However, the cost lines are transformed into time or service lines. The limits of each facility service area are determined by the capability to provide overnight delivery. Similar to cost-oriented service areas, time-oriented areas will be irregular, because of transport route configurations.

The amount of total cost variation between least-cost and maximum-service models will be substantial. To service the total U.S. market on an overnight basis would require from 30 to 40 distribution facilities or the use of very high-speed, high-cost transportation.

Maximum Profit Policies

Objectives of maximum profit policies are those to which firms most commonly aspire in the design of logistical systems. At a theoretical level, the service area of each facility is determined by establishing a minimum allowable profit margin for customers located at varying distances from the facility. Because the warehouse facility will normally be located in high-volume markets, the greater the distance a customer is located from the service area center, the greater are the costs of logistics. This occurs, not only because of distance, but also as a result of lower customer density at the periphery of the service area. At the point where the costs of serving peripheral customers result in minimum allowable margins, further extensions of the service territory become unprofitable on a total-cost-delivered basis.

If the customer were offered better delivery service in terms of speed or frequency to complete an order, more of the product assortment might be purchased. Therefore, additional service is introduced to the point where marginal revenues equal marginal costs. At this point of equilibrium, no additional service is economically justified. The addition of service may or may not result from increasing the number of warehouses. The service may best be provided by a supplemental system of direct or dual distribution. The theoretical profit maximization position is easier to state than to accomplish in practice. However, the goal of equated marginal revenue and marginal cost represents a normative situation management should strive to approximate.

In the development of a highly profitable system, management is seeking a balance between service and cost. By referring to Figure 10-6, the balance will normally be found along the total cost curve to the right of the least-cost point but considerably short of the point where total costs rise rapidly. For the situation illustrated in Figure 10-8, the profit maximization system could, as a first approximation, be expected to fall between a network of 6 and 10 warehouses.

Table 10-6 presented a quantification of the service capabilities of the 14 best networks of distribution points in comparison with a hypothetical customer configuration. The assumption is made that all systems are geared to a 97.75 per cent probability of inventory availability upon receipt of a customer order. The actual service gains accruing will vary by each firm and every market situation. The amount of dollar variation between each of the systems under consideration shows the additional total costs of reaching higher service levels. These dollar estimates provide an assessment of the value of added service against added cost. Given a schedule of these cost–service relationships, management is afforded considerable information to help in the establishment of service delivery standards.

Maximum Competitive Advantage Policies

Under special situations, the most desirable policy to guide logistical system design may be the accomplishment of maximum competitive advantage. Although there are many cases where systems may be modified to gain competitive advantage, two are developed here to illustrate this range of policy considerations.

CORE MARKET CONSIDERATIONS. The first general case concerns modifications in system structure aimed at protecting major customers from competitive inroads. In the case of a firm that is able to provide 42 per cent of the customers with 24-hour delivery at 95 per cent inventory availability, management should be concerned with the welfare of major customers under this service policy.

To illustrate, assume that this firm is typical among those engaged in mass marketing and that 20 per cent of their customers purchase 80 per cent of their product output. Further, assume that 20 per cent of the customers represent 75 delivery or terminal points to be serviced. Is this 20 per cent of core customers included in the 42 per cent of total customers receiving 24-hour delivery? Under conditions of equal customer geographical dispersion, the probability is about 0.5 that the array of 42 per cent of total customers would include all the significant 20 per cent. In other words, one would expect that on the average approximately 40 to 45 of the core customers would get 24-hour service. However, because we know the system is biased toward location of distribution facilities at points of highest demand, it would be safe to assume that a higher number of our core customers would receive prime service.

By identification of core customers, it is an easy process to isolate the service received by each. Core customers are identified as critical terminal points, and the frequency by delivery service interval is obtained by an interrogation process. Table 10-7 presents the results of a hypothetical interrogative process.

The actual number of core customers receiving 24-hour delivery is 53. Thus, although 42 per cent of all customers receive 24-hour service, 76 per cent of the core customers receive prime consideration. In addition, the interrogative process points out that the remaining core customers receive varying degrees of service with two of these critical customers obtaining only 60-hour delivery.

Providing management is so disposed, this situation can be rectified by a restatement of objectives. The cost of a system providing 24-hour service to 90 per cent of all customers can be isolated. Thus management can equate the dollar-and-cents requirements of a core-customer policy.

Several additional systems modifications may be evaluated similarly to the core-customer illustration shown. Management may wish to examine service provided to the most profitable customer. Evaluations can be made regarding customers or noncustomers having the greatest potential. In addition, a firm may wish to evaluate the incremental cost of providing prime service to the core customers of major competitors. Although all such modifications may increase total cost and decrease short-range profits, the long-range gain may be a substantial improvement in competitive position.

ECONOMICALLY JUSTIFIED HIGH-COST FACILITY. An additional application of design modification to capitalize on competitive activities is the case of the economically justified high-cost facility. This situation is especially pertinent to a small business enterprise. Because of rigidities inherent in large firms, pricing policies are likely to be somewhat inflexible. Present antitrust legislation tends to reinforce these rigidities. The result is that large firms selling in broad geographical markets tend to disregard unique cost and demand

TABLE 10-7
Core-Customer Interrogative Results

Total Core Customers	Number of Core Customers Serviced by Hour Intervals			
	24	36	48	60
75	53	16	4	2

conditions in localized markets or find it legally impossible to adjust marketing and logistical systems to accommodate these localized situations. This inflexibility creates opportunities for smaller and localized operations. Such opportunities may encourage management of these smaller firms to make significant modification in least-cost distribution policies.

Location of a small-scale plant or warehouse facility in a minor market some distance from major competitors results in a localized space island that is more or less insulated from competition. The logic of this special situation was developed under the general discussion of factors influencing distribution facility location. At this time it is sufficient to point out that major firms follow one of two courses concerning these localized situations with respect to logistical design.

First, a major firm can elect to avoid these localized situations with respect to providing special service. This policy of concentrating on primary markets results in an opportunity for the higher-cost, smaller firm. Second, major producers may introduce smaller-scale facilities or institute direct logistical systems in an effort to create a differential advantage in these local demand situations. Following the first policy will result, more or less, in a system approaching a least-cost configuration. The second policy will require substantial system modification, with resultant higher costs and lower short-range profits. It is interesting to note that firms which adjusted to the localized West Coast situation in the late 1930s find their market position very desirable today.

The Integrated Cost-Service Planning Curve

In the previous sections the concept and foundation for isolating the total-least-cost logistical network were developed. As indicated in the last section, in many operational situations it may be necessary to seek greater service performance than offered by the least-cost network in order to achieve integration with manufacturing or marketing. Thus the concept of cost–service trade-off was introduced. In development of basic cost–service relationships a variety of simplifying assumptions were necessary. In order to develop a more realistic planning perspective, it is now necessary to relax several assumptions. In this section the complex nature of designing the logistical network is examined in the perspective of the integrated cost–service planning curve.

The two-dimensional display in Figure 10-6 represents a single level of sales volume across a single planning period. The assumption is made that all business activity consists of an average shipment of a single size. In actual operations neither of these conditions will hold true. First, the nature of logistical network design is not a short-term planning problem. Because of the basic nature of fixed facility decisions the planning horizon should encompass several years of operation each with a range of likely annual sales volumes. Second, actual shipment size or order size can be expected to have substantial variation around the average shipment size. In fact, the assumption that average shipment size must be less than that necessary to enjoy volume rates in order to introduce the transportation cost curve displayed in Figure 10-2 must be relaxed to encompass volume shipments direct to customers or manufacturing plants. A more realistic approach to planning must take into consideration the fact that the range of shipments across the planning horizon will be handled by a variety of different logistical methods depending on size and urgency of shipment.

The analysis of expanded network service capability presented in Table 10-6 embodied the assumption that the addition of nodal points was the sole method of upgrading performance. In practical operations all modes of transportation can be employed and delivery service can be upgraded by selection of a transit method independent of the locational structure. The level of service provided by a given logistical network will jointly depend upon locational structure and selection of transport mode.

The locational selection aspect of planning is far more complex than deciding how many facilities to utilize along a limited scale such as illustrated in Figure 10-6. For example, if a firm is engaged in nationwide logistics, a wide latitude of potential warehouse locations exists. There are 50 potential states within which one or more distribution warehouses can be located. Assuming that the total practical number of warehouses does not exceed 50, the range of possible locations consists of one in each state, for a total of 50, or only one warehouse in any one of the 50 states. Given this range of options, there are 1.1259×10^{15} different combinations of warehouses that could be selected in seeking the total-least-cost network.

In order to take into consideration the wide range of variables that exist in designing a logistical system, complex models have been developed. Several such models will be discussed in Chapter 12. At this point, the nature of the integrated cost–service planning curve for logistical system design is important from the viewpoint of policy formation. The integrated cost–service planning curve must take into consideration all relevant variables that influence logistical system design.

The initial perspective in developing the planning curve is to introduce a variation in shipment size and transportation alternatives to the two-dimensional display contained in Figure 10-6. This initial step involves a series of two-dimensional relationships linked together similar to the pages in a textbook. The three variables under consideration are shipment size, transportation mode, and number of locations. The constants or givens are level of inventory protection, the level of desired performance cycle duration, and the specific range of locations under consideration.

In constructing the first planning perspective, shipment sizes are grouped in terms of frequency and the transportation mode economically justified to handle each shipment size is identified within the constraint of desired performance cycle duration. For each shipment size a total cost curve is determined. This will result in a series of two-dimensional charts, one for each combination of shipment size and related transportation mode. Next, the individual charts are bound together somewhat as in the textbook analogy and the points of least total cost are joined together by the cost–service planning curve (CSPC), which cuts through the hypothetical book. In a technical sense the CSPC is an envelope curve that joins the low points on the total cost curve related to each individual shipment size–transport mode relationship. Figure 10-9 illustrates the basic concept.

The cost–service planning curve joins points of total least cost for the range of shipment sizes. It does not join locational points. For example, the desirable number of locations for one size of shipment may be more or less than for another. Therefore, a second perspective to the problem is necessary. However, before discussing the second perspective two points are important to recognize. First, because the desired level of inventory protection and the duration of the desired performance cycle are given as constants or parameters, the CSPC does integrate the logistical structure with other operational units of the enterprise. As a result, the CSPC is joining points of least cost related to a specified service performance and not the points of total least cost. Second, the entire analysis is conducted with respect to a projected volume of business. Therefore, the first perspective is limited in terms of planning horizon to a relatively short interval.

The second perspective of the CSPC is to fit the curve to the range of potential locations created by joining the least-cost point for each shipment size and transport combination. Assume that the locational range consisted of from 1 to 14 alternatives. Within this range the CSPC will select out a smaller range of applicable locations. In Figure 10-9 the points of least cost for six different combinations indicate that the range of four to eight locations will accommodate the least cost for each shipment size–transport arrangement.

FIGURE 10-9
Three-Dimensional Cost Service Planning Curve (First Perspective)

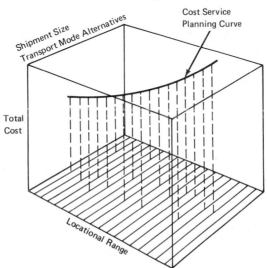

Although a compromise is in order in terms of the exact final number of locations to select for the logistical structure, the duration of the performance cycle cannot be violated. Therefore, the final selection or fit will tend toward the higher number of locations. The final fit of the CSPC will consist of measuring marginal cost changes for each shipment size–transportation mode combination for the logistical network functional at four, five, six, seven, and eight locations. Providing that within the range of four options the service duration constraint is not violated, the lowest-total-cost result after marginal adjustment among the four locational alternatives would be selected.

A third perspective on the planning problem concerns the locational array selected. In the case of Figure 10-9, the best-fit CSPC number of locations may not be superior with respect to least total cost to a different sequence of potential locations. For all sets of locations a least-cost CSPC will result. Among the different locational sets that are practical alternatives the best CSPC must be identified. While the third perspective requires only comparison of the total cost related to the CSPC for each locational set, the number of potential locational sets is almost unlimited. For each locational set, the first and second perspective of integration must be gained prior to the comparison of the third perspective. The third perspective is achieved by relaxing the locational constraint.

A fourth perspective on the planning problem can be gained by relaxing the performance cycle duration. The reader will recall that the duration factor dealt with the number of customers or manufacturing locations that would be serviced within specific time intervals. In terms of desired service this constraint can be set high or low with respect to percentage service within 24-, 48-, 72-, or 96-hour intervals. The net result for each service duration will be to shift the CSPC and consequently the best locational fit described as the second perspective. The third perspective will be based on the duration related to an analysis of different locational sets and will vary as each new level of performance duration is introduced.

A fifth perspective on the planning problem relates to the constraint of service confidence level. This particular constraint is related to the desired degree of protection against type I and type II uncertainty. As the confidence level is increased, the inventory cost curve illustrated in Figure 10-5 will tend to shift upward. It will shift downward as the confidence level is decreased. The reason for the shift is that different levels of safety stock will be required to satisfy each confidence level. The net result of varying confidence level will be to shift the CSPC for each analysis and consequently the best-fit CSPC. Once again, the third perspective conclusion will be based on the confidence level related to an analysis of different locational sets and will vary in solution as each new level of confidence is introduced.

The sixth and final perspective of planning relates to the planning horizon. The first five perspectives have been related to a period of business. For example, the related solutions were based on one year's business. For purposes of logistical system planning a longer-range horizon should be considered.

A planning perspective of 10 years is realistic for the design of a logistical network. Consequently, the best-fit CSPC should be determined in the third perspective over a planning horizon. As annual volume across the planning horizon expands, it is likely that the number of locations associated with the CSPC for any locational set will increase. Likewise, there is a high probability that the set of locations associated with the third perspective will shift with respect to the best set across time. As will be pointed out in Chapter 12, one of the main reasons for utilizing dynamic analysis in system design is to isolate the path of locational change across the planning horizon.

In summary, the theoretical foundations for formulating logistical network policy center around the variables of locational sequence, shipment size, transportation mode, performance cycle duration, confidence level with respect to service performance under uncertainty, and expected volume over the planning horizon. The interrelationships of these variables are measured on a total cost basis. The essence of integrated logistical planning is to achieve a balanced relationship among variables that results in the desired performance at the lowest total cost.

The process of achieving integration has been staged in six perspectives. The first takes into consideration shipment size and related transportation modes capable of meeting performance cycle durations. The result is a cost–service planning curve that links together the least-cost locational network associated with each shipment size. The second perspective represents a fit between the range of identified locations among a single set as the least-cost number of locations. The third perspective relaxes the constraint on locations and introduces additional location sets. The least-cost CSPC best fit will vary between locational sets, and one CSPC fit will be superior to all others. The fourth and fifth perspectives related to desired performance cycle duration and confidence levels with respect to sales and performance-cycle-duration uncertainty. In essence, perspectives four and five deal with total service provided by the network. To the degree that the levels of perspectives four and five are adjusted up or down, the CSPC fits of perspectives one, two, and three will be modified. The final perspective, six, relates to planning beyond a single time period and serves to illustrate that the vitality of any limited time CSPC will change with time.

Summary

Chapter 10 has developed the foundation of logistical policy. In perspective, the chapter presents a theoretical foundation to guide logistical system design. In the initial section of the chapter, the logistical network was described in the context of general systems theory by identifying nodal points, linkages, levels, and flow rates. The purpose of the initial section was to structure the logistical network in appropriate relationships and transformations to guide systems analysis and subsequent modeling in later chapters.

Next, spatial–temporal integration and synthesis was developed by examining the interrelation of transportation cost and inventory cost with respect to facility location. The basic purpose of transportation is to achieve spatial closure. Inventory serves to provide temporal closure. Each aspect of closure was first developed on an independent basis. Next, spatial and temporal integration was presented by development of the total-cost approach for measuring logistical system performance.

The next section related total-cost measurement to logistical system performance. Whereas total cost provides a balance within the logistical structure, performance level serves as the basis for integrating logistical operations with marketing and manufacturing operations. The over-all integration of logistical operations was identified as isolating the least-total-cost system capable of providing a level of service and a degree of confidence that the desired level will be accomplished. The next section reviewed the fundamental policy variations available to guide logistical system design. The final section of the chapter introduced the concept of the integrated cost–service planning curve.

Many assumptions were necessary to develop the basic notion of spatial–temporal integration within logistics and then logistical systems integration within the total enterprise. In development of the cost–service planning curve, assumptions regarding size of shipment, transportation mode, locational sequence, performance cycle duration, confidence level, and time period were relaxed by the introduction of six levels of planning perspective. The end result was a multivariant perspective of the range of factors that influence the formulation of logistical policy.

Questions

1. Describe the logistical network concept. Why would a logistical network have numerous different performance cycles ?
2. What are the relationships among nodal points, linkages, and inventory in a system network perspective ?
3. Why do transportation costs decrease as number of warehouses in a system increase ?
4. Why do inventory costs increase as the number of warehouses in a system increase ?
5. In your own words, what is the locational impact of inventory ? How does it differ on transit inventories and safety stocks ?
6. What is the significant characteristic of the total-cost system illustrated in Figure 10-6 ?
7. In Table 10-5, why are costs associated with all aspects of the logistical system grouped under inventory and transportation ?
8. What is meant by the level of threshold service of a least-cost system ?
9. Why does customer service not increase proportionately to increase in total cost when a logistical system is being designed ?

10. Discuss the differences between improving customer service through faster and more consistent transportation, higher inventory levels, and/or expanded numbers of warehouses.
11. What is the difference between minimum-total-cost and short-range profit maximization policies in system design?
12. Under what conditions would a firm design a maximum-customer-service system?

11

System Design Procedure

The establishment of a revamped logistical policy will normally involve a substantial modification in the existing system network. Logistical redesign studies involve a great deal of data collection and analysis to arrive at a final system design. The object of system redesign is to bring the logistical network to the desired performance level at the lowest possible associated total cost. The design procedure and related techniques of analysis should incorporate the capability to experiment with different network arrangements prior to selection of the system modifications to be recommended for implementation. The primary purpose of Chapter 11 is to provide a systematic approach to be followed when conducting a logistical study.

The initial section of the chapter presents a managerial guide to system design. The final section is concerned with project scheduling.

Managerial Guide to System Design

Just as there exists no ideal logistical system suitable to the needs of all firms, procedures followed in the conduct of a design study vary extensively. As one

FIGURE 11-1
Flow Diagram Managerial Guide to System Design

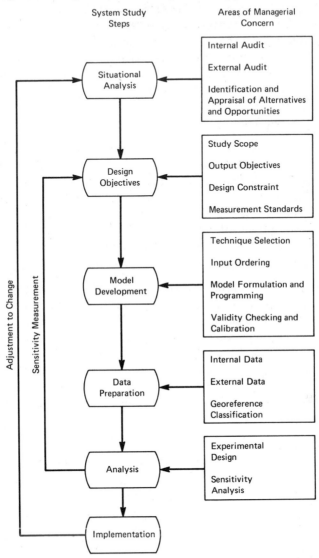

would expect, the format for a total logistical system redesign would be considerably different than for a study concerned with a limited aspect of either
the physical distribution, material management, or product replenishment
subsystem. However, in the design process several definable steps should be
completed in all studies. The purpose of this section is to present a managerial
guide to the research process.

Figure 11-1 illustrates a flow diagram of a generalized managerial guide for logistical system design. Each of the major steps recommended is noted with reference to areas of managerial concern. The left-hand side of the flow diagram illustrates the process of (1) sensitivity analysis and (2) continuous adjustment to change. From a managerial viewpoint, a final system design never really exists. The system should be under constant review to take advantage of change. Thus the total process of logistical system design is a never-ending responsibility subject to change with passing time. Each of the major areas illustrated in Figure 11-1 is discussed in the remainder of this section.

Situational Analysis

Appropriately, the over-all study process begins with a comprehensive analysis of the logistical planning situation confronted. The immediate concern of management is to determine what, if any, modifications are needed in the existing logistical system. Thus situational analysis involves an internal and external audit of existing practices to determine if a substantial area for improvement exists. Finally, the situational analysis should include a comprehensive review of logistical alternatives available to the enterprise. Each of these tasks is discussed.

INTERNAL AUDIT.   The purpose of the internal audit is to develop a clear perspective of the existing logistical network. In particular, the audit is directed at a comprehensive evaluation of the existing system's capabilities and deficiencies. Each subsystem of the over-all logistical network should be carefully examined with respect to how well its stated objectives are in fact being realized. For example, is the physical distribution support system consistently meeting the level and response of customer service performance desired by the marketing department? Likewise, is the material management system meeting its goals with respect to manufacturing requirements? Are the three primary functions of logistical coordination—forecasting, product scheduling, and material planning—being conducted in an orderly and integrated fashion? Finally, does an integrated concept of product replenishment which takes maximum advantage of the captive nature of internal product allocation exist in practice? These and many similar questions form the basis of the self-appraisal involved in the internal audit. It is from this comprehensive review that the opportunities that cost-justify potential system redesign are delineated.

The specific content of the audit is concerned with, but not limited to, such matters as these:

1. Developing a specific understanding of the existing geographical arrangement, capacity, and assignment of all fixed facilities utilized throughout the logistical network.
2. A careful review of the order-processing systems and procedures employed in the customer service cycle and the material procurement cycle.
3. Delineation of the internal communication network employed in the product replenishment process.

4. Examination of the current policies and control systems utilized to manage inventory.
5. A thorough review of the practices of traffic management employed within the over-all logistical network, including an evaluation of usage of the full range of common carrier services available and an audit of private fleet capabilities and condition.
6. Development of a clear understanding of existing material movement techniques and practices employed in various facilities, including an evaluation of the effectiveness of any existing automated or extensively mechanized handling.
7. Review of existing forecast techniques employed with an appraisal of their effectiveness.
8. Examination of the methods employed to develop product schedules.
9. Delineation of the techniques employed to formulate the material plan, including evaluation of the over-all accuracy of specifications concerning material and part requirements and timing.
10. Evaluation of receiving and inspection procedures employed throughout the logistical facilities.
11. A detailed review of finished products from the perspective of packaging, special handling, relative volume, relative profitability, and existing facility stocking policies.
12. An accounting of existing expenditures for performance of logistical activities by function, including an evaluation of the existing investment and turnover in inventory committed to physical distribution, material management, and product replenishment.

It would indeed be a rare firm which had all the data concerning the 12 basic areas involved in the internal audit. Unquestionably, considerable research would be required to assemble all data related to each area. The purpose of the audit is not data collection. Rather, it is a diagnostic review of what is currently taking place in logistical operations as well as a probe to determine the availability of data. Most significantly, the internal audit is aimed at the identification of areas wherein a substantial opportunity for improvement exists.

EXTERNAL AUDIT. The focal point of the external audit is the competitive environment within which the physical distribution and material-management subsystems function. Of the three logistical operating subsystems, these two have constant involvement in the material and finished product markets. In particular, the external audit is concerned with an evaluation of how well the existing logistical system is functioning in terms of customer requirements and competitive practices.

Although an internal audit will indicate if the physical distribution subsystem is meeting the marketing organization's specifications, the external audit is aimed at evaluation of the validity of the existing standards. For example, does the potential service myopia discussed in Chapter 2 in fact exist?

The specific content of the audit is concerned with, but not limited to, the following four areas:

1. Examination of the logistical systems being employed by major competitors in both the material and finished-goods markets.
2. Evaluation of existing marketing channel arrangements as well as major structural trends, including an evaluation of the extent of separation in transaction-creating and physical exchange processes.
3. Quantification of existing and potential customers and supply sources with respect to volume purchased, special logistical requirements, and structure of facilities that must be linked to the firm's logistical network.
4. Measurement of delivery service being consistently offered by major competitors.

As with the internal audit requirements, it would be rare to find all the data desired about the competitive and market environment readily available in a firm. Once again, the purpose of the audit is to appraise what is available and to develop as comprehensive an insight as possible into the effectiveness of the existing logistical system.

IDENTIFICATION AND APPRAISAL OF ALTERNATIVES AND OPPORTUNITIES. The fundamental combined purpose of the two audits is to provide management with the best possible appraisal of the strengths and weaknesses of the existing logistical system. From a comprehensive review of internal and external conditions, three specific end products are desired.

First, a determination must be made if sufficient areas for improved logistical performance exist to justify detailed research and analysis. In a sense, completion of the situational analysis provides a convenient go–no go point for further study. The desirability, as well as the feasibility, of conducting a detailed system design study can be evaluated in terms of expected cost and benefit. While conducting the remaining steps in the managerial design procedure does not commit a firm to implementation or even guarantee a viable new system design, the potential benefits of change should be fairly clear at the completion of the situational analysis.

Second, the typical end product of the combined audits will be a confirmation that a great many aspects of the existing logistical system are more right than wrong. This should not be a surprising conclusion. However, it is one that should be reached based upon comprehensive factual analysis and not opinion. The delineation of areas wherein improvement potential exists, as well as those wherein operations are satisfactory, provides the foundation for delineating the size of the system design study. For example, it may be apparent that a serious problem exists in inventory, which holds forth the potential for significant cost and service improvement. Correspondingly, if there is no justification found to question the existing structure of fixed facilities with respect to location or size, then all subsequent analysis can focus on improvement of the inventory component without serious risk of suboptimization.

The third end product of the audits and over-all situational analysis should by a clear statement of the logistical alternatives available as options of the existing system. At this point in the study process, it is normally well worth the effort to construct flow diagrams that illustrate the basic networks associated with different alternatives. These diagrams will illustrate the opportunities for engaging dual logistical patterns, clearly outline the transportation and communication linkages, and more or less serve to provide a comprehensive overview of the study situation. Some variables available in identifying logistical options will be difficult to illustrate in a flow diagram context. For example, regional variations, product mix variations, and differential shipment policies are difficult to illustrate, whereas they do form the basis for design alternatives. Nevertheless, an attempt should be made to delineate the options. The techniques involved in this form of presentation are discussed in Chapter 12.

Design Objectives

The second step in the logistical design procedure is the establishment of design objectives. Four specific tasks must be accomplished at this stage of the design effort: (1) the study scope must be delineated, (2) output objectives stated, (3) design constraints established, and (4) measurement standards specified. Each will be discussed briefly.

STUDY SCOPE.   Based upon the situational analysis, the exact aspects of the logistical system to be subjected to potential design modification must be specified. The alternatives and opportunities delineated during the situational analysis provide the basis for final determination of the study scope.

Specifically, it must be decided if the design study is to be concerned with all three logistical subsystems or only select parts. In situations wherein a comprehensive redesign is being conducted for the first time, it is not unusual for the study to be limited to either the physical distribution, material management, or product replenishment subsystem. At a later point, potential benefits of total logistical system integration can be examined.

In addition to identification of the extent of subsystem coverage, it is necessary to specify which logistical components will be included in the analysis. In this respect, the study scope should be as broad as possible in order to approach the design problem on a total system basis.

Whatever the managerially determined limits, they will have a significant impact upon the research results. Alternative strategies to guide the selection of study scope were presented at the conclusion of Chapter 10.

OUTPUT OBJECTIVES.   Output objectives deal with cost and service expectations of the revised system. It is essential that such objectives be stated specifically in terms of measurable factors. A typical procedure at this point in the study is to state specific service objectives setting cost considerations aside until later in the study. The following is a typical format of service objectives: (1) the system will be designed to provide 95 per cent inventory availability for category A products, 92 per cent for category B products, and 87 per cent for category C products; (2) desired delivery of all customer orders will be within 48 hours of order placement for 98 per cent of all orders; (3) customer service from secondary service points will be held to a minimum; (4) mixed commodity orders will be filled without back order on a minimum of 85 per cent of all orders; (5) back orders will be restricted to 5 days' aging; (6) the 50 most profitable customers will receive these minimum performance capabilities on 98 per cent of all orders.

Given these statements of customer service, a system can be designed that will provide the desired performance. The total cost of such a system will be derived. To the extent that such cost does not meet managerial expectations, various levels of alternative performance can be tested.

An alternative approach to the statement of output objectives is to fix a maximum allowable total cost expenditure and then design a system to achieve the highest possible degree of service. Such cost-oriented objectives have the feature of practicality, because results will be within acceptable budget ranges. However, they lack the selectivity of the service-oriented approach to system design.

DESIGN CONSTRAINTS.   A second category of managerial policy deals with design constraints. From the situational analysis, it is expected that management will place restrictions on the scope of permissible modifications. The nature of such restrictions will depend upon the specific circumstances of individual firms. However, two typical examples are here provided.

One restriction common to distribution system design concerns the network of manufacturing facilities and the product assortment produced at each. To simplify the study, management may elect to hold existing manufacturing facilities constant in the system design. Although such constraints reduce the optimization of a study, they are justified on the basis of financial considerations and capacity for immediate change.

A second category of constraints deals with marketing channels and physical distribution activities of separate divisions. In firms with a traditional pattern of decentralized profit responsibility, management may elect to omit certain divisions from study consideration. Thus some divisions may be managerially determined to be candidates for consolidated physical distribution operations, whereas others will be omitted from consideration.

All design constraints serve to limit the scope of the study. However, as one executive stated the problem: "Why study things we don't plan to do anything about?" Unless there exists a reasonable chance that management is favorably inclined to introduce change, the subject in question should be structured as a study constraint. Once the model is developed, all such constraints can be evaluated at will with a minimum of structural change.

MEASUREMENT STANDARDS. In most situations the situational analysis will illustrate the need for managerial determination of measurement standards. Such standards will concern (1) the structure of synthetic costs, (2) the cost of performance penalties, and (3) the study period. Each of these categories of standards has been discussed previously. The essential point is that management must provide guidelines for each category as a prerequisite to the formulation of the system model. Once formulated, such standards must be held constant throughout the design analysis. Although considerable managerial prerogative exists in the formulation of standards, care must be exercised not to dilute the validity of the model and thereby subsequent study results.

Model Development

Determination of the type of model and the associated technique of analysis in a logistical design study requires creative talent as well as analytical ability. This is normally the domain of the specialist. However, management still must play an active role in order to maintain control and to develop appropriate data into a usable format. A detailed treatment of modeling from a more technical view is the subject matter of Chapter 12. At this point, emphasis is placed on the nontechnical manager's role in the logistical modeling process. Several steps are involved in model development: (1) technique selection, (2) input ordering, (3) model formulation and programming, and (4) validity checking and model calibration. Each is discussed in terms of managerial involvement.

TECHNIQUE SELECTION. The major responsibility of management in technique selection is to evaluate the recommendations of the specialist in terms of time and cost. It is to be expected that the specialist will be more concerned with development of broad-gauged models requiring complex integrative techniques. Management must balance this desire for exacting answers and perfect information with related cost and time requirements. In addition, management must understand the capability and limitations of all proposed techniques. Although technical evaluation of problem requirements is an area of specialized talent, deciding if a firm can commit the necessary resources is a managerial responsibility. Neglect of this responsibility at an early stage of study development is perhaps the greatest cause for subsequent failure.

INPUT ORDERING. Given the study period, transactions must be developed for use as flow input and as set constants to the study model. The flow input represents historical records placed into a georeference code for study use. Set constants represent a restatement of managerial parameters in terms of the system model. The technical aspects of each of these input formulations is not a managerial responsibility. However, the validity of each must be checked prior to use.

MODEL FORMULATION AND PROGRAMMING. Model formulation involves development of equations to handle system-state operating relationships and, to the degree utilized, feedback mechanisms. Programming consists of writing computer instructions to handle the required computations. Managerial responsibility in model formulation and programming is limited to a control of expense and constant review of progress. It is not unusual to have weekly briefings on development progress. Although excessive managerial pressures can be a deterrent to creativity, a lack of progress control can result in a substantial waste of resources.

VALIDITY CHECKING AND CALIBRATION. A critical managerial responsibility is checking the validity of the system model. Because mathematical model building and computer simulation is a complex task, the risk is always present that the technical expert will not understand or have sufficient knowledge of the specific business under study. Thus, before a model is used for system design, its validity must be tested. If the model is not a reasonable approximation to the situation under study, little in terms of improvements can be anticipated.

In development of a validity test two conditions are desirable. First, the original model state should be structured to simulate a known situation. As a start, the first system state is often structured as a replica of the existing system operated by the firm. Second, extreme care must be exercised to use all input flow data associated with the study period. Given these two conditions it is possible to test validity by appraising the model's capability to simulate results of a known situation.

Regardless of the care taken in testing model validity, an element of error remains a constant possibility. First, it is impossible to calibrate for all possible situations. This danger increases as the model becomes more dynamic. Second, it is never possible to eliminate or identify all compensating errors in a specific validity test. Although such errors may wash out in a validity test, their interrelation may become significant under alternative test situations. Every effort should be made to develop the best possible model, keeping in mind inherent limitations of the modeling process when evaluation results.

Data Preparation

In actual system design practice, the process of data collection began with the situational analysis. In addition, a fairly detailed specification of data is required in the formulation or adaptation of the system model. However, at this point in the procedure, the detailed data must be accumulated and organized for use in analysis. One aspect of data collection is that the model can often be initially calibrated and validated using assumed or dummy data. Once operational, the model can be subjected to sensitivity analysis to determine the categories of data that are of particular interest to the design solution. Once identified, the data preparation area can be concentrated on the critical information categories.

For purposes of discussion, the types of data required in a logistical design study are grouped as internal and external. Each is briefly discussed, followed by a review of different georeference classification schemes that can be employed to order model input.

INTERNAL DATA.   The majority of data required in a logistical study can be obtained inside the firm. Although considerable digging may be required to come up with all the necessary pieces of information, normally most of the information is available from corporate records.

The first category of required data is that related to sales and customer orders. The annual sales forecast and percentage sales by month are necessary to structure the total volume to be modeled as well as seasonality patterns. An historical sample of customer order invoices is necessary to classify order characteristics. This sample, stratified by size and type of customer, is used to generate orders to be processed by the system model.

Specific customer data are required, and ideally the data should be classified on a georeference basis. In particular, location, type, size, order frequency, growth rate, and special logistical services required are the main information needs, perhaps the most significant grouping of data needed.

For the material management subsystem it is necessary to identify the sources of manufacturing and purchasing. In addition, a classification of raw materials and parts by demand and type is required.

While manufacturing plant locations are not normally considered variable in a logistical design study, it is necessary to specify the number and location of plants, the product mix produced, production schedules, and seasonality of production.

With respect to the product replenishment subsystem, reorder priorities, shipment policy, warehouse processing times, and cost must be identified. In particular, inventory control rules and product allocation procedures are required.

For each warehouse either currently in the system or a potential addition, it is necessary to establish operational costs, maximum-product-mix storage, and service capabilities. For the model structure it is necessary to identify the location and size of all existing warehouses as well as those locations that may potentially be added during system redesign.

In the area of transportation, the number and type of modes utilized, as well as the criteria for selecting each mode, must be established. In addition, rates and transit times by modes, as well as shipping rules and policies, must be quantified. If private transportation is to be included in the analysis, then all relevant data are required.

In the areas of inventory and communication, it is necessary to identify reorder policies, costs of inventory maintenance, order-processing time, and cost. Definition of the existing and potential reliability and capability of the order-communication system is required to provide the basis for alternative systems analysis.

Needless to elaborate, the collection of data for a detailed logistical system is a time-consuming and expensive task. The problem is complicated by the fact that synthetic costs and operating data are necessary to accommodate system modifications that require modeling of nonexistent logistical component arrangements.

While the various types of data here noted may be more or less than those required to evaluate a specific type of logistical system modification, the description provides an over-all perspective of the types of detail required. The prime justification of placing formal data preparation as the fourth step in the design process is to limit the chance of collecting information not necessary to a specified design problem.

A final note concerns the quality of the data used in analysis. Simply stated, the design solution will be no better than the data it is based upon.

EXTERNAL DATA.   In most logistical planning situations, a selected amount of basic environmental data is required to model the system into future time. Management can normally provide an estimate of expected or desired sales for a planning horizon up to 10 years. The difficulty comes in obtaining a market-by-market distribution of the total forecast.

One solution to the problem is to use demographic factor projections that correlate highly with sales. For example, assume that a multiple correlation exists among sales, school enrollment, family size, and total population.[1] Based on this correlation, future sales in any geographic area can be forecast by projection of these demographic factors.

The task of collecting demographic base data has become relatively simple. The U.S. Department of Commerce has made available the 1970 Census of Population and Housing Fifth-Count Tallies Classified by ZIP Code Areas.[2] These data are available on computer tapes, which provide all necessary information to develop a positive correlation. A variety of different projections concerning demographic factors are regularly published by various government agencies and universities.[3] Thus a reasonable data bank of environmental information is readily available.

Additional areas of external data required will be information concerning competitive logistical system designs and the marketing channel. For the

---

[1] A great deal of the section that follows is based upon Omar Keith Helferich, *Development of a Dynamic Simulation Model for Planning Physical Distribution Systems: Formulation of the Mathematical Model* (unpublished doctoral dissertation, Michigan State University, 1970).

[2] This is expected to represent standard procedure from 1970 forward.

[3] Helferich, *op. cit.*

most part, the area of interest will be competitive facility locations. In most cases this is readily available from published reports, annual reports, and the general knowledge possessed by company executives. The main purpose in collecting these data is that during the analysis phase of the study, it is normally desirable to compare the customer service capabilities of one or more major competitors to the system under design.

GEOREFERENCE CLASSIFICATION OF DATA. For modeling purposes, data concerning sales, customers, product raw materials, and demographics need to be classified on a geographical basis. Distribution of such data by individual markets provides the geographical structure of demand or material source that must be logistically serviced. The purpose of the model is to arrange the logistical system components in such a manner as to provide a level of service to individual markets at the lowest total cost. Thus selection of the georeference classification method is an extremely important aspect of the system design procedure.

A number of georeference classification structures have been developed. The six most useful to logistical modeling are (1) customer point locations, (2) county, (3) standard metropolitan statistical area (SMSA), (4) economic trading area, (5) zip code, and (6) grid structure.

For purposes of selection in any given modeling situation, the alternative georeference structures can be evaluated on the basis of two criteria: (1) demand unit attributes and (2) specific modeling requirements. Table 11-1 provides a summary of the major considerations in evaluating each criterion.

Customer Point Locations. The individual customer or material location is the most detailed georeference classification. One disadvantage of developing a model structured on individual customers is that the sheer number can greatly slow down processing. However, in some cases wherein a relatively

TABLE 11-1
Criteria in Georeference System Evaluation

Comparative georeference system attributes
    Size of unit
    Stability
    Homogeneity
    Flexibility
    Mutual exclusiveness
    Geographical continuity
    Availability of periodically updated data

Model-oriented georeference system attributes
    Availability of relevant data at the basic data unit
    Appropriateness of data unit coverage to the markets serviced by the firm
    Ability to determine distance from logistical facilities to data unit
    Compatibility of data unit to the firm's management information system

---

few customers or supply sources are critical to logistical system design, specific customer detail may be justified.

When it is desirable to classify on the basis of specific customers, their geographic location can be identified by latitude and longitude or by use of a point reference system. The most widely used point reference system is PICADAD,[4] which stands for PI, place identification; CA, characteristics of area; and DAD, procedure for computing distance and direction. Developed by the U.S. Department of Commerce, PICADAD provides a method to pinpoint almost every city of any consequence in the United States. A special feature is that the reference system includes the computation procedure for calculation of distance.

The primary determination of whether or not a point reference system is used rests with the level of detail desired. All other systems conglomerate geographical areas for purposes of data collection.

County. The county provides a reference system that for the most part is structured on historical political patterns. A great deal of data is available on a county basis. For example, it is the basis for grouping of census data and can be readily identified to larger data sources such as SMSAs and states. Thus the county structure is easily controlled from the viewpoint of data availability and processing.

In terms of model usage, it is sufficiently homogeneous for many products, is mutually exclusive, stable, and provides geographical continuity. Distance can be determined by use of key or central city in the county without introducing significant error.

The primary disadvantage of the county is that it does not represent a trading area. The number of counties, approximately 3,000, is also a disadvantage in terms of the practical problem of system model processing.

Standard Metropolitan Statistical Area. The SMSA is defined as a county or group of 300 continuous counties that contain at least one city or twin cities with a population of 50,000 or more.

The primary advantage of using the SMSA as a georeference base is that 300 data units can be used to represent over 70 per cent of the consumer sales or other demographic information needed to project future demand. Data are easy to collect and a great deal is readily available in computer processing format. As with the county, distance can be determined on a key-city basis.

The major limit is that the total set of SMSA units does not result in a geographically continuous control structure. In addition, the SMSA structure is designed to change as a function of growth patterns.

Economic Trading Area. The concept of an economic trading area (ETA) is to design a georeference system specifically to suit the requirements of a specific firm's demand and management information.

For example, an ETA classification system could be developed on the

---

[4] Donald E. Church, "Picadad: A Sytem for Machine Processing of Geographic and Distance Factors in Transportation and Marketing Data," Bureau of the Census, U.S. Department of Commerce, 1965.

following basis: (1) all SMSAs; (2) each county where sales exceed a specific minimum that is not included in an SMSA. However, a set of rules for grouping other georeference systems would be acceptable. The main advantage is custom design. Distance can be calculated on a key-city basis.

The primary disadvantage of ETAs is that they will be on the average geographically large. The number would fall between the 300 SMSAs and the 3,000 counties.

ZIP Code. A zip-based georeference system is formulated on the U.S. Postal Service ZIP Code Sectional Center System, which divides the country into 552 areas, including about 314 multicoded cities. The Postal Service describes an area as follows: [5]

1. It includes a hub city that is a national center for local transportation.
2. It includes between 40 and 75 post offices.
3. The most remote post office is no more than 3 hours' normal driving time from the hub city.

It is possible to further subdivide the ZIP areas into up to 20,000 specific areas if the full classification is employed. In fact, the census data, available on a ZIP basis for the first time in 1970, are detailed to the most detailed level.

The primary advantage of the ZIP georeference system is flexibility. The classification is geographically continuous and relatively stable. It is common for firms to maintain ZIP codes in their data files, which greatly assist in obtaining internal data. Finally, distance can be determined on a hub-city basis.

The only significant limitation of the ZIP Code reference system is that it is not so homogeneous as some other data classification units. The geographic size of an area can vary greatly.

Grid Structure. Under a grid structure classification base, the United States is divided into geographically standardized blocks. The primary example of this form of classification is the REA grid. [6] REA originally developed the grid for purposes of pricing their transportation service. The concept divides the United States into 1-degree-square blocks based on latitude and longitude. Each block is further divided into 256 smaller squares each containing approximately 41 square miles.

The grid system unit has the major attributes of being relatively the smallest, most homogeneous, completely stable, highly flexible, mutually exclusive, and geographically continuous among the georeference systems available. In addition, it has been modified to accommodate distance by the elimination of curvature distortion. [7]

[5] U.S. Postal Service ZIP Code Index.
[6] For a detailed study of geocoding systems, see Pamela A. Werner, *A Survey of National Geo-Coding Systems* (Washington, D.C.: U.S. Department of Transportation, 1972).
[7] Richard Lewis, *A Logistical Information System for Marketing Analysis* (Cincinnati, Ohio: Southwestern Publishing Co., 1970) pp. 33–34.

The primary limitation of a grid reference system is significant. In most cases it cannot be used without significant modification and adjustment of both internal and external data. The relevant data required in logistical design are not grouped in a manner compatible to grids.

Summary Georeference Groupings.   Depending upon the situation, one or more of the georeference systems may be combined to formulate the data classification structure for a system model. For example, it is not uncommon for the ZIP sectional areas to be used as the primary reference base supplemented by identification of a large number of customers on a point basis.

Among the six georeference systems reviewed, the ZIP Code appears to be most widely used for logistical system models.[8] The ZIP configuration meets all the desirable attributes specified in Table 10-1 about as well as any other georeference system. The only serious limitation is that the areas do not have uniformity of size, which somewhat prohibits analysis based on density. However, above all else, the increasing availability of data is the main attribute of a ZIP-based reference system.

Analysis

The fifth step in the over-all procedure is to apply the selected model and associated data to arrive at a logistical system design solution. The analysis phase consists of experimental design or modeling procedure and sensitivity analysis. The entire process of analysis is the subject matter of a considerable part of Chapter 12. At this point the two aspects of analysis are briefly commented upon as the next logical step in the system design procedure.

EXPERIMENTAL DESIGN.   The experimental design phase of study completion consists of establishing a set of runs for the model and analyzing the data that result. Assuming that the model is validated, it is neccessary to plan a series of model runs or replications to arrive at an acceptable solution.

In a technical sense, the formulation of an experimental design is concerned with measuring dependency. For example, given an independent event such as an increase in orders, what will be the impact on the dependent event, logistical cost? To date, there has been relatively limited development of techniques to assist the manager in analysis of experimental data generated by computer models.[9] If only one cause-and-effect relationship were of concern, a number of basic statistical measurements could assist in evaluation.[10] The problem is that a logistical design analysis is multivariate. Therefore, basic

---

[8] Helferich, *op. cit.*, p. 121.

[9] For a discussion, see Geoffrey Gordon, *System Simulation* (Englewood Cliffs, N.J.: Prentice-Hall, Inc., 1969), pp. 18–22.

[10] For example, see Thomas H. Naylor, Joseph L. Balentfy, Donald S. Burdick, and Kong Chu, *Computer Simulation Techniques* (New York: John Wiley & Sons, Inc., 1966), Chap. 4; and K. D. Tocher, *The Art of Simulation* (London: English University Press Ltd., 1963), Chap. 2.

techniques of solution variance measurement do not offer a great deal of practical help.[11]

In the use of a model, the researcher must arrive at several basic decisions aimed at zeroing in on a solution. The structure and sequence of carrying out these decisions serves as the experimental design for analysis. In logistical system design problems, four basic determinations are necessary to form an experimental design.[12]

1. State the initial conditions and objectives in the form of parameters and constraints to limit the range of analysis.
2. Decide to what degree or over what range of values particular parameters and/or constraints will be permitted to vary in order to establish the necessary measures of system response to arrive at a solution.
3. Define the number and sequence of model applications or runs necessary to arrive at a solution.
4. To the extent that is practical, measure significant differences in output values (total cost and customer service) as a function of parameter or constraint variance.

To a significant degree, the utilization of a logistical design model involves a great deal of trial-and-error analysis preceded by postulation concerning probable outcomes. Thus, in practical application the number of model runs (determination 3) to include in the experimental design will, to a significant degree, be a function of the range and variance of output values. This trial-and-error procedure is normally referred to as sensitivity analysis.

SENSITIVITY ANALYSIS. In sensitivity analysis, the objective is to see how design solutions vary as a result of systematically changing parameter and constraint values. The process of sensitivity analysis provides a way in which management can pretest alternative distribution policies. In many ways, the real payoff from an integrated logistical system study depends upon the range of sensitivity testing completed. Given a valid model, the design solution will represent the best possible logistical arrangement in terms of management parameters and constraints. However, this does not mean that the study is over. One of the greatest benefits of a system model is the ability to ask "what if" questions without taking a chance with the existing business.

In the modeling procedure, management parameters are introduced concerning output objectives, design constraints, and measurement standards. Each introduces an unknown degree of restraint on the problem solution.

[11] For a research-oriented discussion related to model validation, see Peter Gilmore, *Development of a Dynamic Simulation Model for Planning Physical Distribution Systems: Validation* (unpublished doctoral dissertation, Michigan State University, 1971), Chap. 2.

[12] Developed from P. J. Kiviat, *Digital Computer Simulation Modeling Concepts* (Santa Monica, Calif.: Rand Corporation, 1967), p. 18; and M. Asimow, *Introduction to Design* (Englewood Cliffs, N.J.: Prentice-Hall, Inc., 1962).

By holding all other factors constant, the influence on managerial parameters can be evaluated in terms of total cost and customer service impact.

To illustrate the importance of diagnostic procedures, consider a typical problem confronted by management in logistical system design. Namely, what level of customer service should we decide to provide to our customers? The reader will recall that measures of customer service level are concerned with inventory availability, which, in turn, is reflected by the size of safety stock incorporated into the system.

Figure 11-2 provides the results of using sensitivity analysis to isolate the cost effect of increasing service availability from the existing level of 92 per cent to as close as 100 per cent as possible. To complete the analysis, the parameter dealing with service was relaxed on a systematic basis and total least cost for achieving the specified performance level was determined. For

FIGURE 11-2
Illustration of Using Sensitivity Analysis in Logistical Design

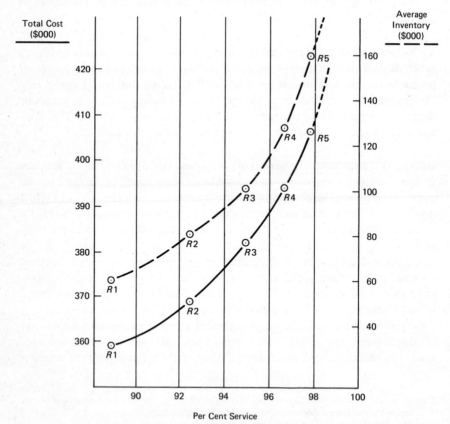

Per Cent Service

100 per cent minus per cent of orders stocked out
or per cent of orders filled

example, the parameter was first relaxed from 92 to 94 per cent and the associated design solution was then determined. This procedure was continued until the total cost curve associated with the service function could be constructed. In the example illustrated in Figure 11-2, five computer runs were required to construct the curve. The chart illustrates both total cost and inventory cost associated with increasing service.

A typical procedure in sensitivity analysis is to select what appear to be critical variables in a design problem for early diagnosis. By making large-scale value differentials in potentially critical variables and measuring how violently the design solution reacts, it is often possible quickly to limit analysis to those factors that really matter.

In reference to Figure 11-1, a feedback loop is incorporated in the recommended study steps between analysis and design objectives. This linkage reflects the recursive nature of sensitivity analysis.

Implementation

The most common question asked by business executives is "What can I expect to see as the end result of a logistical study?" Unfortunately, unless considerable evaluation is completed and a report prepared, the executive will see a voluminous stock of computer printouts. The mental barrier of approaching such a mass of data can greatly reduce the benefit gained from the study as a result of the need to "dig it out." Therefore, the best procedure is to develop a study summary report of significant findings. Such a report will contain the following information:

1. A statement of system customer service capabilities, including an estimate of performance probability.
2. An estimate of total fixed and variable cost expressed as a percentage cost of sales for a specified operating period.
3. A comparison of service and cost projections for the redesigned system in comparison to the current system for identical time periods.
4. Estimated results of several alternative service policies and related costs of performance.
5. A format of required transport, facility, communication, and inventory capabilities under the integrated system.

The results of a logistical system study will contain infinitely more detail than the information here listed. Once management has selected a final system redesign, such detail is used to develop an implementational program. Prior to final selection of a system, a series of additional tests may be instituted.

It would be a rare firm that could move into an across-the-board revision of all elements in a logistical system. Thus the planning model becomes a valuable tool to use to select the steps that will provide the greatest payoff if implemented at once. Thus a five-year (or any other time period) program can be developed with a measure of expected results. Priorities and check points can be established to guide over-all revamping of the existing system. The changing nature of business requires that constant checks be performed to test the continued validity of the system model.

From a managerial viewpoint, a final system design never really exists. The redesign implementation plan is constantly being adjusted to take advantage of change. The firm that develops a logistical planning model, formulates a redesign implementation plan, and then disregards the model dissolves a powerful planning tool. The continuous process of planning is illustrated in Figure 11-1 by a feedback linkage between implementation and situational analysis.

Project Scheduling

The major over-all management responsibility in logistical design studies is to assure that valid results are realized within time and budget expectations. Fortunately, several scheduling techniques are available which can be easily adopted to the logistical research project.

Scheduling is concerned with planning and the accomplishment of nonrepetitive projects. In addition, scheduling is concerned with the most efficient utilization of resources during the study. During the 1950s sophisticated project planning and progress evaluation techniques were developed. The techniques help managers maintain control over manpower, money, material, and machinery allocated to a project. Two scheduling techniques, the *program evaluation review technique* (PERT) and the *critical path method* (CPM), are reviewed in this section.[13] Both PERT and CPM are variations of more general critical path planning approaches. First, characteristics common to both techniques are reviewed and then the peculiarities of each discussed. For purposes of illustration, the techniques are discussed in terms of the development and implementation of an order-entry system.

Basic Critical Path Concepts

The heart of critical path planning is a graphic portrayal of the project work plan. This graph, or network as it is commonly called, displays the interdependencies between activities leading to project completion.

The critical path concept is designed to satisfy the following five project management requirements:

1. Evaluate progress toward attainment of project completion.
2. Focus attention on potential and actual problems during the project.
3. Provide frequent and accurate status reports at critical check points.

[13] For more detail, see Harvey M. Wagner, *Principles of Management Science* (Englewood Cliffs, N.J.: Prentice-Hall, Inc., 1970), pp. 150–55.

4. Provide a regular and updated prediction of when the project will be completed.

5. Provide at any time during the project determination of the shortest completion time if priorities and resources are shifted.

The Network

The network is a flow chart of project events joined by lines that represent activities. The activities illustrate project interrelationships and interdependencies. Events are usually represented by circles and activities are illustrated by arrows that connect events. A project event is a significant occurrence. Events signify the start or completion of at least one activity and represent the achievement of a project goal.

Activities in a project network may be real or dummy. Real activities represent tasks that must be completed to advance from one node to another. Real activities expend project resources. Dummy activities illustrate the dependency of one event to another for project-planning purposes. Although a dummy activity may involve waiting or lead time, it does not expend project resources. All events are numbered in the network chart. Although the activity arrow lengths have no relationship to the time required to accomplish an event, arrows always connect lower- and higher-numbered events.

PERT Project Illustration

To illustrate the planning and control of a project, the PERT technique is discussed as applied to the installation of a computerized order-entry system. Thus the system development illustration deals with a special aspect of over-all logistical system design. The system, when developed, will enable orders to be entered into computer terminals for direct processing by the computer. The computer programs, in turn, will provide inventory assignment and invoicing and will allocate the order to the appropriate warehouse for shipment to the customer.

The illustration that follows could be developed using either PERT or CPM. The primary difference is that PERT deals only with the time aspect of the project, whereas CPM illustrates both time and cost.

PROJECT DESIGN.   The initial step is to divide the over-all project into specific tasks. These tasks become events in the project network. Since events only represent a point in time, it is necessary that the start, completion, or an intermediate point in time be selected for representation. For purposes of illustration, both the start and completion time for each event are identified. It is also assumed that variable lead times exist between the completion of one event and the start of the next.

Since activities represent the time necessary to complete an event, the second step is to estimate the time necessary to complete each activity. A fundamental

FIGURE 11-3
Pert Network for Computerizing an Order Entry System

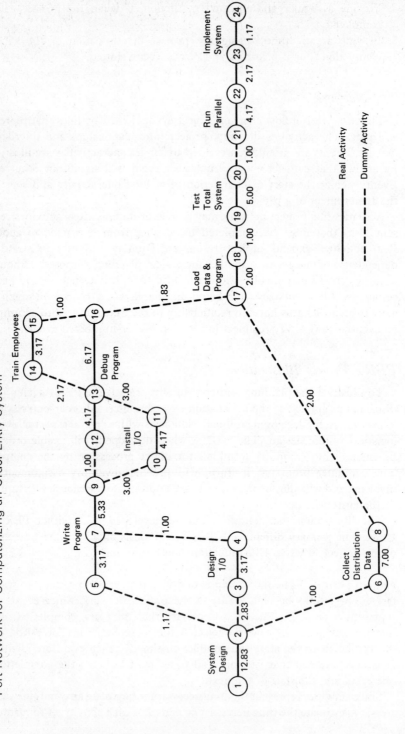

difference between PERT and CPM is the nature of time estimates. CPM uses exact or expected times while PERT uses variable time estimates. A PERT schedule requires three time estimates for each activity. They are

1. Optimistic time—the elapsed time if the activity proceeds perfectly, represented by a.
2. Pessimistic time—the elapsed time if extreme difficulty is experienced, represented by b.
3. Most likely completion time—the expected time, represented by m.

The basic activities and time estimates for the example project are contained in Table 11-2.

The third step is to structure the project in a PERT network, identify the necessary dummy activities, and calculate the mean elapsed time (T_e) for each activity. The network is illustrated by Figure 11-3. The following formula is used to develop mean elapsed time giving a weight of 4 to the most likely time and one each to the optimistic and pessimistic times:

$$T_e = \frac{a + 4m + b}{6}.$$

The resultant data are presented in Table 11-3.

The fourth and final step is to identify the critical path for the project. The path with the largest or highest total mean elapsed time (T_e) represents the critical path. All other paths are called slack paths because the final project completion date does not depend upon completing events along the slack path. Table 11-4 presents the determination of the critical path in the example project.

Table 11-2
Project Activities and Variable Time Estimates

Event No.	Activity	a	m	b
1–2	Design system	9	12	20
3–4	Design I/O for distribution offices	2	3	5
5–9	Write computer program	6	8	13
6–8	Collect distribution data	5	7	9
10–11	Install I/O system	3	4	6
12–16	Debug program	7	10	15
14–15	Train employees on system use	2	3	5
17–18	Load data program into system	1	2	3
19–20	Test total system	3	5	7
21–22	Run parallel with present system	3	4	6
23–24	Implement system	0	1	3

TABLE 11-3
Actual and Dummy Activities and
Weighted Elapsed Time

Activities		a	m	b	T_e
1–2		9	12	20	12.83
2–3	D*	1	3	4	2.83
2–5	D	0	1	3	1.17
2–6	D	0	1	2	1.00
3–4		2	3	5	3.17
4–7	D	0	1	2	1.00
5–7		2	3	5	3.17
6–8		5	7	9	7.00
7–9		4	5	8	5.33
8–17	D	1	2	3	2.00
9–10	D	2	3	4	3.00
9–12	D	0	1	2	1.00
10–11		3	4	6	4.17
11–13	D	2	3	4	3.00
12–13		3	4	6	4.17
13–14	D	1	2	4	2.17
13–16		4	6	9	6.17
14–15		2	3	5	3.17
15–16	D	0	1	2	1.00
16–17	D	0	2	3	1.83
17–18		1	2	3	2.00
18–19	D	0	1	2	1.00
19–20		3	5	7	5.00
20–21	D	0	1	2	1.00
21–22		3	4	6	4.17
22–23	D	1	2	4	2.17
23–24		0	1	3	1.17

* Designates "dummy" activity.

Once the schedule analysis is completed, a reevaluation of resource allocation to each activity is needed to determine if the project could possibly be completed in less time if resources from the slack paths could be diverted to the critical path. The final project schedule is based upon the network having the lowest total elapsed time. The highest T_e of this network is the project critical path.

CPM

The procedure for CPM is almost identical to that for PERT. The fundamental difference is that CPM uses two exact time estimates and incorporates cost or budget figures.

TABLE 11-4
Path Identification and Average Elapsed Time

Path	Activity Average Elapsed Time	Total Elapsed Time
1–2–6–8–17–18–19–20–21–22–23–24	12.83 + 1.00 + 7.00 + 2.00 + 2.00 + 1.00 + 5.00 + 1.00 + 4.17 + 2.17 + 1.17	= 39.35 weeks
1–2–5–7–9–10–11–13–14–15–16–17–18–19–20–21–22–23–24	12.83 + 1.17 + 3.17 + 5.33 + 3.00 + 4.17 + 3.00 + 2.17 + 3.17 + 1.00 + 1.83 + 2.00 + 1.00 + 5.00 + 1.00 + 1.00 + 4.17 + 2.17 + 1.17	= 57.35 weeks
1–2–3–4–7–9–10–11–13–16–17–18–19–20–21–22–23–24	12.83 + 2.83 + 3.17 + 1.00 + 5.33 + 1.00 + 4.16 + 3.00 + 6.17 + 1.83 + 2.00 + 1.00 + 5.00 + 1.00 + 4.17 + 2.17 + 1.17	= 59.84 weeks
*1–2–3–4–7–9–10–11–13–14–15–16–17–18–19–20–21–22–23–24	12.83 + 2.83 + 3.17 + 1.00 + 5.33 + 3.00 + 4.17 + 3.00 + 2.17 + 3.17 + 1.00 + 1.83 + 2.00 + 1.00 + 5.00 + 1.00 + 4.17 + 2.17 + 1.17	= 60.01 weeks
1–2–3–4–7–9–12–13–14–15–16–17–18–19–20–21–22–23–24	12.83 + 2.83 + 3.17 + 1.00 + 5.33 + 1.00 + 4.17 + 2.17 + 3.17 + 1.00 + 1.83 + 2.00 + 1.00 + 5.00 + 1.00 + 4.17 + 2.17 + 1.17	= 55.01 weeks

* Critical path.

The time estimates formulated for CPM are the best estimates of the project manager. The normal time estimate is the elapsed time expected to complete the activity. The second time estimate is a crash estimate of how rapidly the project could be completed if no costs or effort are spared.

Along with the time estimates, the project manager should develop costs for each of the two time estimates. At the outset, the project manager can project two total project costs. These cost differentials for normal and crash efforts provide the basis for measuring the added cost and time saved if the project is expedited. In addition, the necessary data are available for estimating time and cost at any point during the project in the event it becomes desirable to expedite the remainder of the project.

Summary

In this chapter a six-step procedure recommended as a managerial guide line for conducting logistical system design studies was presented. The second part of the chapter introduced PERT and CPM scheduling concepts. Emphasis throughout the chapter has been placed upon managerial responsibility rather than on excessive technical detail. Particular attention was directed to the critical nature of the manager in data collection, sensitivity analysis, and overall project administration. Attention is now directed to modeling techniques available for use in the over-all logistical system design procedure.

Questions

1. What is the basic objective in a system redesign study? Is it normally a one-time activity?
2. In performing a situational analysis, why is an internal audit extremely important?
3. Why must extreme care be given to measurement of competitors' service when undertaking redesign of a system?
4. Are design constraints specified at the early stage of a study capable of being modified at a later point in the system redesign? Why would this be done and to what extent is it practical?
5. Does the nontechnical manager have responsibility in model development?
6. What is meant by validity checking and calibration?
7. Why is geoclassification of data important to logistical studies?
8. Discuss the major differences between the six georeference classification systems presented in the chapter. Which method of classification does the author appear to favor, and why?
9. What is sensitivity analysis and what part does it play in experimental design?
10. Discuss the formulation of an implementation program as a result of a logistical redesign study. What would you consider to be the major ingredients of such a plan?
11. What can one hope to gain by the use of a project-scheduling technique?
12. Discuss the differences between PERT and CPM. What is the role of a dummy activity in the PERT analysis?

12

System
Design Techniques

This chapter presents system technology from the viewpoint of a logistical system designer. Throughout earlier chapters, the systems approach has been presented as a method whereby complex arrangements can be analyzed. The logistical system is measured by two performance standards: (1) level and consistency of customer service and (2) total cost expenditure. The objective in system design is to bring a firm's logistical structure to a specified performance level at the lowest possible associated cost. Chapter 11 presented procedures for conducting over-all logistical research and development. This chapter focuses on system modeling and associated techniques.

The initial section of the chapter introduces modeling concepts. An over-all approach to modeling is presented and various models are described according to approach and mathematical technique. Next, elements of model structure are reviewed in terms of variable classification and interrelations. The third section illustrates a generalized system model. Next, desirable system design characteristics are reviewed. The fifth section presents modeling procedure. In the sixth section an analytic model for selecting single locations is presented. Next, models available for comprehensive system analysis are reviewed and four simulation approaches discussed. The final section reviews a dynamic simulation planning model.

System Modeling

The fundamental purpose of systems analysis is to attempt to make a valid prediction of how potential logistical configurations will perform in advance of actual implementation. A model constitutes a body of information and restrictions about a unique situation accumulated for the purpose of systems analysis.[1] The model represents a substitute for testing actual logistical designs. By developing and testing a model, it is possible to evaluate the impact of alternative policies prior to resource commitment. Thus modeling permits experimentation with different potential system designs without resorting to trial and error or arbitrary modifications to existing operations.

Models are of two general types: (1) physical and (2) abstract.[2] Physical models are replicas of the object under study. Common examples are the scaled replications of aircraft within a wind-tunnel environment used to deduct performance of full-size aircraft. The process of physical modeling is frequently used in construction. Most logistical managers use physical models when planning a new warehouse layout. The main disadvantage of using physical models in total system design studies is the complexity, time, and cost requirements of constructing the replications.

The abstract model uses symbols rather than physical devices to represent a system. A variety of abstract models exist, but the two most commonly used in logistical system design are mathematical symbols and block-flow diagrams. In a mathematical model, the components and interrelations of a system are expressed in terms of equations. In a block-flow symbolic treatment, the system is illustrated by communication and product flow diagrams. The primary concern of this chapter is mathematical modeling. Mathematical modeling can be classified in terms of (1) static–dynamic structure and (2) analytic–numeric technique.

Static-Dynamic Structure

The fundamental difference between static and dynamic mathematical models rests around time interrelationships. A model is static if it deals with time periods on an exclusive basis wherein the system model is in equilibrium during analysis. For example, a static model may replicate system performance over a 13-period operating year. As such, the model would cover an extended time horizon. The modeling process is static if each of the time periods is treated independently. The design of the system is mathematically expressed as given and the model replicates operational performance.

[1] The classical classification of model types is found in Jay W. Forrester, *Industrial Dynamics* (Cambridge, Mass.: The MIT Press, 1961), Chap. 4.
[2] *Ibid.*, p. 49.

If the time periods are linked in a manner wherein one time period's performance can influence the next time period's design, then the model is dynamic.[3] The 13-period replication is dynamic if each of the time intervals is linked on a recursive basis. Such linkage is accomplished by mathematical representations of feedback mechanisms in the model construction.

Feedback mechanisms treat system outputs as inputs for the next activity period. Given any single time period, the prevailing system design must have excessive capacity, adequate capacity, or be deficient to the task at hand. The optimum situation would be a system design that remained adequate to the desired performance over the entire design horizon. However, adequate capacity is seldom the case in logistical system design under conditions of uncertainty. Thus the prevailing system capability will normally be either abundant or deficient. Both situations result in operational penalties. A condition of excess capacity results in higher than necessary total cost. Excess penalties can be handled properly in both static and dynamic models. A deficient condition is more critical.

Deficiencies influence both cost and service performance. For example, inventory shortage at a given warehouse may (1) result in shipment from a secondary location at greater cost and possible reductions in customer service; (2) result in a backorder with related cost and service penalties; or (3) result in an order cancellation with possible penalty of customer loss. In any event, the actual system under analysis must cope with the deficiency in terms of specific action or a significant element important in design is omitted. Likewise, the model used in analysis should be capable of handling deficiencies. Dynamic models include feedback elements to provide a more realistic approximation of actual logistical operating situations.

Of particular concern to logistical system planning is the implementation sequence of design modifications. From a purely operational viewpoint, no firm of any substantial size has the capability, nor could it justify the risk, of simultaneously changing all aspects of a logistical system. Thus the sequence of implementing a system modification across time is of critical importance. The nature of dynamic modeling is such that sequential planning can be more comprehensively treated than is possible under static design.

The determination of whether a static or dynamic approach should be used in logistical modeling depends, for the most part, on the type of planning situation confronted. As a general rule, the more complex and comprehensive the design task confronted, the more desirable is dynamic mathematical modeling. For example, a static model may be fully adequate for the purpose of locating a single warehouse. In contrast, total system designs can be more realistically modeled on a dynamic basis.

---

[3] For a clear understanding of dynamics, see Thomas H. Naylor, Joseph L. Balentfy, Donald S. Burdick, and Kong Chu, *Computer Simulation Techniques* (New York: John Wiley & Sons, Inc., 1966), pp. 16–20.

Analytic-Numeric Technique[4]

Mathematical models may be classified as analytic or numeric depending upon the specific analysis technique used to generate design solutions. Analytic techniques seek a precise answer to the design situation confronted. To utilize analytic techniques it is necessary that all relationships in a system design be capable of full description. When such system definition is attainable, analytically optimum design solutions can be determined.

In complex logistical system design situations, it may be next to impossible to identify all the relationships that exist within the potential combinations of warehouse locations, inventory allocations, transportation alternatives, order processing, and material movement. It is necessary to make a great number of assumptions to avoid overcomplication of the model. In such situations a useful alternative to an analytical technique is to employ numeric techniques in model construction.

A numerical model utilizes computation methods to replicate system design and performance. However, it contains no specific mathematical procedure that assures identification of the best possible solution. A numerical model does not attempt specifically to identify relationships within the model. Emphasis is placed upon the way that various components interact in terms of system performance.

The primary objective in logistical system design is to identify an arrangement of components that will meet specific cost–service performance specifications. Thus, consistent with the systems concept, emphasis is placed on performance of the total system and not on relationships among variables. Therefore, although it is theoretically desirable to isolate optimal design solutions, it is not necessary for purposes of improving logistical system design.

The tempo of business change coupled with the inability to consider all facilities and resource commitments variable at a given point in time permits considerable imperfection in the system design process. Even if an optimum system could be conceived and modeled, it is doubtful that construction and over-all implementation could be completed in sufficient time to enjoy the perfect arrangement. Thus the selection between analytic and numeric techniques depends upon the type of planning situation confronted.

In terms of over-all business logistics, both types of techniques have substantial applications. Analytic techniques can be employed in design situations wherein the nature of the problem is sufficiently limited to allow full description of relationships. Later in this chapter, models using analytic techniques for single-facility location are illustrated. The most abundant use of analytic techniques in logistical management is found in operational decision making.[5]

In planning situations that require simultaneous treatment of all components of the logistical system over a time horizon, numeric techniques have received

---

[4] The type of model discussed in this section is often referred to as deterministic.
[5] For example, see Peter P. Schoderbek, ed., *Management Systems* (New York: John Wiley & Sons, Inc., 1967).

widespread utilization. The two numeric techniques most utilized are static and dynamic simulation. Simulation is discussed and illustrated in the final section of this chapter.

In conclusion it is interesting to note that large-scale models in the logistics field have begun to combine both types of techniques within a single structure.[6] For example, a dynamic simulation model may include one or more analytical techniques to handle specialized design solutions at a given point during the planning horizon, that is, the determination of economic order quantities or the location of a specific warehouse.

Mathematical Model Structure

A well-defined body of knowledge exists concerning model design.[7] The purpose of this section is briefly to introduce model structure concepts. Mathematical models can be explained in terms of four elements: (1) components, (2) variables, (2) parameters and constraints, and (4) functional relationships. Each is described in terms of logistical system models.

Components

The components of a model consist of the entities that are being described by a set of equations. They are the objects of primary interest in the system design. In terms of logistical system models, the entities or components are facility type and size, transportation, inventory, communication, and material movement. These five factors constitute the resources of the firm that must be integrated to formulate a logistical system.

Variables

The variables in a model serve the purpose of relating components. A number of different types of variables exist within a complex model structure. The most common classification is as exogenous, status, and endogenous variables.

EXOGENOUS VARIABLES. Exogenous variables are independent of the system being modeled. They constitute inputs to the model. As such, an exogenous variable's impact upon the system causes it to react or perform in a specified manner. Exogenous variables can be classified as instrumental or environmental on the basis of control exercised by the model builder or user.

---

[6] Alfred A. Kuehn, "Complex Interactive Models" in *Quantitative Techniques in Marketing Analysis* (Homewood, Ill.: Richard D. Irwin, Inc., 1962), pp. 106–23.
[7] For a summary, see Omar Keith Helferich, *Development of a Dynamic Simulation Model for Planning Physical Distribution Systems: Formulation of the Mathematical Model* (unpublished doctoral dissertation, Michigan State University, 1970), Chaps. 2 and 3.

Instrumental variables can be controlled or manipulated by the model user for purposes of experimental design. They are taken as given by the model but are controlled by the user. Thus they can be changed at will for purposes of testing their impact upon system design. In terms of logistical models, order-size policies, inventory dispositions, and customer service standards all represent instrumental variables.

Environmental variables cannot be controlled by the model user since he has no direct influence upon their nature or value. Thus the impact of environmental variables must be taken as given. A prime example of an environmental variable influencing logistical system design is the geographical distribution of product demand. The logistical system must service the product orders that evolve from basic demand determinants; however, no control exists over the geographical distribution of demand for the purpose of improved logistical design.

Environmental variables may have constant impact upon logistical system performance or may impact only at specific points in time. For example, while we hope that demand impact will be continuous, we hope that the impact of a fire, flood, or other acts of nature will occur rarely, if ever. Both types of environmental factors impact the model's performance and must be accommodated in design.

While variables generated by the environment cannot be controlled with respect to real impact, they can be manipulated by model users to test their impact upon system design. In this form of sensitivity analysis, it is possible to determine how the logistical system would perform if environmental variables changed. As a result of such analysis, a logistical system design having a high degree of capability to handle the most probable environmental changes with the least system disruption can be determined.

A critical aspect of model design is to define the system's boundary or dividing line between instrumental and environmental variables. The boundary influences the system's design range and will have a major impact upon the accuracy and relevancy of the resultant model.

Exogenous variables can also be viewed in terms of their purpose to the model. In this sense they are classified as set and flow variables. With respect to input, set and flow variables constitute the data necessary to establish and use the model.

Set data establish the prevailing condition prior to the design process. To initiate the modeling procedure, it is necessary to define customers by location, size, and product demands. In addition, georeference coding is also required for raw material sources, suppliers, existing manufacturing plants, inventory accumulations, distribution warehouses, transport capacity, and all other factors involved in the existing logistical system. Set data also include values for various managerial-determined constraints on system design. The degree of desired customer service is of critical importance as well as a statement of available resources. If any given data are considered beyond the boundary of the model but influential to the system design, they are classified as environmental.

Flow data represent the stream of operational demands to be placed upon the system during the study or planning period. At an operational level, flow data will be constructed as a series of shipment requirements by customers or other terminal locations. Such activity may be listed sequentially or randomly generated in order of occurrence for each time period under study. In seeking the best system design, flow data are held constant during analysis. The end result is a system status that will most effectively meet managerial-determined service policies at the lowest total cost.

STATUS VARIABLES.   Status variables describe the system's state at any given point in time. In a logistical model, system state reflects the condition of all components with a particular design relationship or state. Each system state is based upon a set of relationships among components that will have a system service capacity and associated cost.

The starting system state is defined by the set data formulated under initial conditions. In logistical system modeling, initial state formulations must be sufficiently broad to allow all desirable system configurations to be tested. The fundamental purpose of the model is to modify state variables as a result of flow data processing, thereby providing an improved system design.

Here, perhaps, better than from any other vantage point, the difference between numeric and analytic models can be illustrated. Analytic models deal with a limited number and range of status variables and seek the best or optimal relationship between those considered. Numeric or simulation models are more comprehensive with respect to the range of variables treated. The more comprehensive range is obtained at a sacrifice in determining the optimal relationship or system state arrangement.

ENDOGENOUS VARIABLES.   Endogenous variables are dependent upon system performance and constitute output of the system. As a result of the interaction of exogenous and status variables, endogenous variables are generated according to the operating characteristics of the model.

The main managerial involvement with logistical design models is with the output printouts. Given an initial system state and both set and flow endogenous variables, the output expresses for management the degree of improvement obtainable from variations in system design. As will be elaborated later, depending upon the model under consideration, such output may take the form of operational status reports, profit-and-loss statements, or special analysis of problem situations.[8]

Parameters and Constraints

In the design and operation of a model, parameters represent variables that do not change as a function of model operation. In other words, they

[8] See page 402.

constitute restrictions upon the model. The literature contains considerable contradiction between the exact meaning and difference of a parameter and a constraint.

For purposes of this treatment, a parameter is defined as a design limitation concerning what is contained within a model's structure and the boundary of the model. Parameters define the components that will be formulated by system state variables and the set limits of the endogenous variables that define system boundary.

Constraints are limits that are placed upon the values of system state variables as well as both endogenous flow and set variables. These limits, both upper and lower, are enforced by the model builder in order to exclude specific aspects of the study situation from system design modification. For example, manufacturing plant locations may be held constant in the design of a logistical system.

Both parameters and constraints may be varied by modification of the model's set data. The general procedure is to hold both constant in initial design of a logistical system. Once a system design is isolated that meets a specific operating requirement, parameters and constraints may be varied for purposes of sensitivity impact upon the design solution.

Functional Relationships

Functional relationships describe the interaction of all types of variables as the model functions. In modeling terminology, functional relationship, transformation, and algorithm are used interchangeably.

It is necessary to formulate the relationships among all variables included within the system structure. In essence, functional relationships are behavioral because they reflect the impact of change in system state. For example, the addition of a warehouse will result in substantial changes in transport, inventory, and communication demands placed upon the system. The functional relationship formulas provide a means for determining resultant changes in system state occasioned by the modeling process. As such, functional relationships are flow formulations, whereas system states are level equations.[9]

An important part of the transformations of a model is the feedback mechanisms. As indicated earlier in the chapter, feedback is essential to rendering the model dynamic. Given an initial system state flow, exogenous variables are processed to determine if an improved system state is possible. The degree of improvement is measured by change in the endogenous variables or output of the model. Such an improved system state results from analysis of operational relationships over a period of time. Feedback transformations are the manner by which time-related performance penalties and delays are formulated in a model.

The impact of feedback transformations influences the derived system state.

[9] Helferich, *op. cit.*

Thus stability is introduced into the modeling structure.[10] A stable model will strive to maintain its original or initial state and make appropriate modification as disturbing events occur. An unstable model tends to amplify disturbances. Instability results because lags and unplanned interruptions are not dampened out by the ability of the system's functional relationships to take corrective system state action. The end result may be destruction of the system as it loses complete control.

Given a stable system, a disturbance, like a 2-week out-of-stock on a fast-moving product, would be expected to result in temporary adjustments in stock levels to protect the desired level of inventory availability. However, unless demand stabilized at a higher level, the model would seek to reinstate the original condition. In any event, a stable model would retain the desired performance level with a minimum of oscillation. In contrast, an unstable system would be more likely to experience prolonged oscillation between excessive and deficient inventories.

The typical manager may not view out-of-stock performance in terms of stability; however, the odds are high that he has experienced instability at work. An unstable situation seldom improves until some external force intervenes. In consecutive periods, such external force may well be the controller when inventories peak and the sales manager at times of inventory drought. The development of stability in the logistical system can greatly reduce this conflict.

Generalized System Model

The structure of a mathematical model has been presented in terms of its components, variables, parameters and constraints, and functional relationships. The treatment was abstract in the sense that no particular model was illustrated. The final sections of this chapter will provide specific illustrations of analytic and simulation models. At this point, a generalized model of a logistical system is introduced.

At a basic level all models can be generalized on the interrelationship of their structural elements. In a logistical design situation, the objective is to isolate the system that will satisfy customer service requirements at the lowest total cost given managerially determined constraints.

The initial condition of the model is derived from flow and set data. Flow data provide a stream of operational confrontations for the model. Set data establish the model's initial component state, functional relationships, parameters, and constraints. Each time the flow data are processed or generated, a study cycle is completed. The processing of flow data results in operational output. Such output is generated by the interaction of the flow data with components according to functional relationships and within the limitations imposed by parameters and constraints.

---

[10] *Ibid.*

If the model structure does not incorporate feedback, it is considered static. In static models no attempt is made to allow output to influence future set data values. Thus set data are held constant and the initial condition of state variables of the model will not change as an internal feature of the model based upon output. If the model is dynamic, it incorporates the internal capability of altering system state on the basis of output.

The total process is generalized as a dynamic model in Figure 12-1. The functional interrelationships of the model are displayed so as to illustrate the recursion relationships.

The initial study cycle results in a system state identified as $t + 1$. Operational relationships and feedback influence the system state in two ways. First, for the initial cycle, the study-period deficiencies in system capability are generated in terms of extra demand loads with related operational penalties. Second, given initial system status, deficiencies lead to modifications in system status, shown as $t + 1 \cdots n$. Such modifications are reflected as new values for system state set variables. This process is repeated until no improvement in system state is possible, and the system t_f (final system) has been structured. A model that isolates the optional system state is classified as analytic.

FIGURE 12-1
The Dynamic Modeling Process

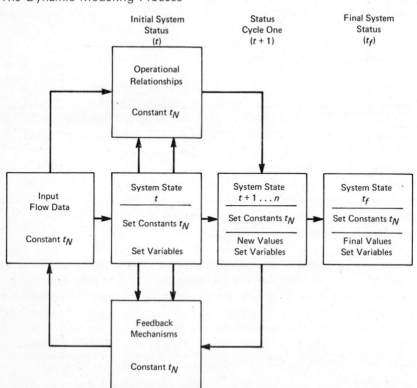

Desirable Model Characteristics

Regardless of the specific model structure, a well-designed model will more or less reflect a number of desirable characteristics. Four such characteristics are reviewed in this section.

Modular Construction

Although modular construction is not critical to all types of system models, the approach is recommended for the development of logistical models. The modular or building-block approach begins with a single module of the system being modeled and then adds modules until the total system is modeled.

The main advantage of modular construction is that it permits a complex system to be divided into a number of smaller subsystems. With identification of basic modules, a variety of different system designs can be combined from the modules, thereby introducing considerable design flexibility.

Each module represents a part of the total system that is influenced by limited input variables and produces limited outputs. Ideally, it can be initially represented by a block diagram and the system, in total, can be illustrated graphically by connecting the blocks.[11]

Accuracy

Naturally, unless a model is accurate with respect to the situation under study, its output will be of little, if any, value to management. Accuracy involves both data collection and the verification of model design.

One of the most costly aspects of modeling is the collection of data necessary to formulate all elements of the system model. One benefit of a modular approach is that it permits data to be collected and refined on a buildup basis. To an extent, the collection of unnecessary data and duplication are safeguarded against.

To a significant degree, the exactness of data required rests with the purpose of model construction. In analytical formulations, where precise answers are anticipated, extreme care must be taken to realize the best possible data. In numeric formulations, some latitude exists.

When using numeric formulations, a procedure gaining in interest is to operationalize the model on the basis of assumed flow data and to some degree assumed set data. Provided that the components and the functional relationships of the model can be defined, the model can be utilized on a diagnostic basis to determine the sensitivity of specific flow and set data to the design solution. Once priorities are established between the importance of different data, emphasis can be placed on collecting the critical data.

[11] See page 413.

Design verification is concerned with the operational validity of the model. A well-defined body of model verification theory exists which provides guidance to this critical area of modeling.[12] At least two aspects are important in logistical modeling: (1) surface relevancy and (2) internal consistency.

Surface relevancy relates to the believable nature of model outputs. In essense, does the model output reflect what the manager expects to see about the situation under study? Managerial confidence is critical to the ultimate implementation of a design solution. Therefore, a common procedure in system simulation is to start the analysis by replicating the existing logistical system. This provides outputs for managerial review that correlate with operating results of the existing system, thereby proving model capability.

Within the model, a number of relationships must be validated to assure that the model will not lose its surface validity once it is utilized in experimental design situations. The manner in which flow data are handled must be free of bias, the functional relationships must be consistent, and the feedback mechanisms must be stable. Mathematical and statistical tests are available to assist in the validation of a model's internal consistency.[13]

Simplicity

As a general rule, the models constructed should be as simple as the situation under design will permit, thereby reducing the complexity of data collection and model verification. One method of reducing complexity is to aggregate as many modules as possible, thereby eliminating the sheer number of functional relationships modeled.

Another interesting approach to simplifying a model is to concentrate design efforts upon the most important linkages of a planning situation.[14] This has the net effect of neglecting weak linkages. Procedures have been developed to identify the relative importance of linkages in a model's structure.[15]

The reader will recall from Chapters 4 and 10 that the logistical system can be viewed as a series of nodal points connected by transport and communication linkages. The notion of strong link concentration is to forget about the occasional shipment that may take place between a pair of nodes unless it represents a regular relationship. Thus the emergency shipment of a product from the manufacturing plant to a customer to supplement a critical warehouse out-of-stock situation could very well be a one-time linkage that should be eliminated from system redesign efforts. One-time and weak linkages can render a model very complex, while adding little to or even reducing the relevancy of the design solution.

[12] For a summary, see Peter Gilmore, *Development of a Dynamic Simulation Model for Planning Physical Distribution Systems: Validation* (unpublished doctoral dissertation, Michigan State University, 1971), Chaps. 2 and 3.

[13] *Ibid.*, Chap. 2.

[14] Important or strong links are defined as those between which important activity takes place.

[15] William K. Holstein and William L. Berry, "Work Flow Structure: An Analysis for Planning and Control," *Management Science*, February 1970, pp. 324–37.

Adaptability or Universality

Adaptability or universality of a model refers to the ease with which it can be adapted to different analysis situations. From a managerial viewpoint, a high degree of adaptability is desirable in order to reduce the cost of additional model construction as planning situations are confronted.

A model constructed along the basis of nodal locations, levels, and linkages has a high degree of adaptability to any planning situation involving temporal and spatial integration. In this respect a logistical system model has a great deal in common with any other network model.[16]

The more specialized the model becomes, the greater its relevancy to a specific planning situation and the less its over-all adaptability. However, special-purpose models can incorporate greater redundancy, which may be a desirable feature in model design.

Redundancy in a modeling context increases reliability by providing backup functional relationship structures. Although important to select types of system performance, such as aerospace guidance systems, system backup assumes greater importance in logistical operating systems such as order processing and inventory control. The important point from the present viewpoint is that more universal models have greater difficulty in incorporating redundancy features.

Summary—Desirable Model Characteristics

The four characteristics reviewed are considered as the more important aspects of logistical system design models. The characteristics covered are neither exhaustive nor necessarily the most important claracteristics in terms of models in general. The important point is that a considerable degree of judgment must be integrated into model design. No exact rules exist to guide the model builder in these critical design areas.

Modeling Procedure

Modeling, by nature, is an interactive process wherein the user attempts to solve a design situation by developing the best aid possible. To a significant degree modeling is more an art than a science.

The process of designing the model requires a continuous balancing of cost of development and data collection against the benefits of precision and comprehensiveness. Thus the final model is a compromise between what is desired and what is possible within a cost–benefit relationship.

From a managerial viewpoint, the development as well as the utilization of a system model involves a great deal of trial-and-error procedure preceded

[16] For example, see Omar Keith Helferich and Robert M. Monczka, "Development of a Dynamic Simulation Model for Planning Material Input Systems," *Journal of Purchasing*, August 1972, pp. 17–33.

TABLE 12-1
Model Development Process

Stage 1: Statement of a problem in general system terms. Definition of gross system boundaries. Statement of output(s) needed to solve the problem.

Stage 2: Statement of (initial) assumption. Definition of static and dynamic system structure. Construction of minimal system model assessment of assumptions in light of stage 1 goals.

Stage 3: Determination of input data requirements and availability. (If input data required are not available, modify assumptions and model structure by returning to stage 2.)

Stage 4: Determination of output possibilities. (If output is insufficient, modify assumptions and model structure by returning to stage 2.)

Stage 5: Prepare precise specifications for final model. Select a modeling and programming language. Reassess the implications of all assumptions for the future. Prepare a detailed plan for use of the model.

by postulation concerning probable outcomes. A number of different approaches have been recommended to guide model development and utilization, but most of them simply lead to a logistical procedure to reduce the range of options to a solution. It is becoming increasingly common to refer to the solution procedure as the heuristic approach.

A heuristic approach to problem solving closely parallels the thought process of the human mind. In essence, it is a steplike procedure that narrows in on the solution by systematic elimination of the alternatives. Such an approach does not necessarily result in selection of an optional solution. The step procedure requires review at each decision point with related explanation of logic postulations at each step of the procedure. Thus the solution once derived requires little interpretation on the part of the designer. Brief comments follow concerning the use of heuristic procedure in model development and utilization.

Heuristic Model Development

In model design the objective is to arrive as efficiently as possible at a final model. The final model structure will be influenced by such factors as (1) the model's design objective; (2) the precision required; (3) the complexity of structural design and data necessary to achieve the required precision; (4) the scope of the system with respect to components, functional relationships, boundaries, parameters, and constraints; and (5) data availability.

The compromise or cost–benefit analysis between these factors requires considerable evaluation. The process is necessarily iterative in that subsequent results of investigation should modify earlier assumptions. Table 12-1 provides an example of a five-stage iterative model-development process.[17]

[17] Kiviat, *op. cit.*, p. 18.

A procedure of the type illustrated in Table 12-1 is necessary regardless of whether the model under development is analytical or numerical. In application an analytical technique provides a precise answer, whereas in design considerable judgment and choice must be exercised.

Heuristic Model Application

In logistical system design, the application of models constitutes only one aspect of the over-all study. Regardless of the technical nature of the model employed, chances are it will be used a number of times under different design constraints to arrive at a design solution. The very nature of system design is experimental since management is seeking a more satisfactory level of cost and/or service performance. Thus, whereas the technique employed may be precise in its analytical capabilities, the managerial process of application discussed in Chapter 11 is not.

For example, assume that the desired end result of the analysis is to select the number, size, and location of distribution warehouses to include in the physical distribution subsystem of a firm's logistical network. Inventory policy is assumed constant and a logical assortment consisting of a maximum number of warehouses is assumed to start the analysis procedure. The total heuristic process attempts to keep reducing the range of alternatives to a minimum consistent with achievement of the cost–service objectives. Managerial intervention is planned at critical points in the search process in order to guarantee acceptable results.

Under heuristic procedures, a given network of facilities (system state) will be modeled and measured on the basis of cost and service capability. This information is given to management for evaluation. The assumption is made that management has sufficient appreciation of realistic requirements not to eliminate a vital aspect of the solution. As a result of this evaluation, additional distribution facilities are added to or deleted from the network by managerial discretion.

The modified system state is then evaluated. As new facilities are added or deleted, existing warehouses are reviewed in terms of continued desirability. Once again results are compiled for managerial review. This process continues until the most acceptable network of distribution warehouses is determined.[18]

Single-Location Determination

This section illustrates the use of an analytic technique to assist in the location of a single distribution warehouse or manufacturing plant.[19] A number

---

[18] The initial model using this procedure was reported by Harvey N. Shycon and Richard B. Maffei, "Simulation—Tool for Better Distribution," *Harvard Business Review*, November–December 1960, pp. 65–75.

[19] This technique illustration is adapted from Donald J. Bowersox, *Food Distribution Center Location: Technique and Procedure*, Marketing and Transportation Paper 12 (East Lansing, Mich.: Michigan State University, 1962).

of methods, both mathematical and nonmathematical, can be applied to the problem of a single location. The cost and complexity of the technique should be matched to the difficulty of the problem. Here an algebraic model for solving the location problem is presented. By use of this model it is possible to locate a facility at the ton-center, mile-center, ton-mile center, or time-ton-mile center of a physical distribution service territory—whichever results in lowest total cost. Where it is necessary to locate multiple distribution warehouses in a total system network, techniques similar to those discussed in following sections should be used.

For purposes of illustration, the location of a food distribution center is demonstrated. Although the retail food industry is somewhat unique, the principles demonstrated have application over a wide range of consumer and industrial logistical situations. The input variables will change, because basic market configurations vary by industry, but the analytic technique and model remain the same.

The Analytic Model

The mathematical technique employed evolves from analytic geometry. The model is based upon Cartesian coordinates. In a system of Cartesian coordinates, the horizontal, or east–west, axis is traditionally labeled the x axis. The vertical, or north–south, axis is labeled the y axis. Together these two axes differentiate four quadrants, which are customarily numbered as illustrated in Figure 12-2.

Any given point in a quadrant can be identified with reference to the x and y coordinates. The y coordinate of a point is called its *ordinate*. The ordinate is found by measuring its distance from the x axis, parallel to the y axis. The x coordinate of a point is referred to as its *abscissa*. This is the distance from

FIGURE 12-2
Cartesian Coordinates

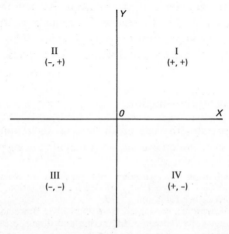

the vertical y axis, measured parallel to the x axis. Taken together, the abscissa and ordinate form the coordinates of a given point, the abscissa being given first. Figure 12-3 illustrates the abscissa and ordinate of point A in the positive or northeast quadrant. In Figure 12-3 the distance Ox_1 equals the abscissa of point A, and the distance Oy_1 equals the ordinate. Assuming the values of 40 miles for x_1 and 30 miles for y_1, the coordinates of point A would be read as $A(40, 30)$. The use of uniform mileage scales along the axes permits all points in the quadrant to be relatively located.

By use of this basic system of orientation, it is possible to replicate the geographic market area in which the warehouse facility is to be located. All retail stores are plotted in the Cartesian plane. Each store is identified by a subscript and placed in the replicated market with reference to its coordinates. In other words, retail stores are plotted with reference to their abscissa and ordinate, measured on a uniform mileage scale.

The algebraic method for solving the location problem identifies the coordinate position of the proposed distribution warehouse. The problem is essentially a weighted average of a given number of independent variables, with the dependent variable being the warehouse location. The algebraic process is solved for the abscissa and ordinate of the warehouse. For simplicity, it is convenient to solve independently for the x- and y-coordinate location of the warehouse. The formula for this calculation depends upon the independent variables, which are expressed in the location measure employed. Therefore, the exact formulations will be presented in the following section.

The Algebraic Solution

In the algebraic formulation the data utilized as basic measurement input represent independent variables. The resultant warehouse location is the dependent variable. The location problem is structured with identical service standards required from all potential distribution warehouse locations. Given this service standard, the location goal is to minimize physical distribution costs.

FIGURE 12-3
Location of a Point in the Positive Plane of Cartesian Coordinates

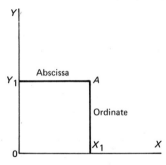

Generally, it is accepted that private carrier trucking costs are a function of time, weight, and distance. However, historically, when mathematical techniques were employed, not all of these cost factors were included as independent variables in the measurement device. Four measurement devices are available for analysis: (1) ton-center solution, (2) mile-center solution, (3) ton-mile-center solution, and (4) time-ton-mile-center solution. As the titles suggest, the first three contain combinations of only those variables related to weight and distance. The fourth measurement device includes both of these plus time as cost-influencing factors. By utilizing the Cartesian reference system and related algebraic formulations, the location problem is presented for each measurement device.

TON-CENTER SOLUTION. In the ton-center solution, the point located represents the center of gravity or center of movement in the market area. When obtaining a ton-center solution, the assumption is that the center of movements represents the least-cost location. However, accepting cost as a function of time, weight, and distance reveals the basic limitation of the measurement device—only weight is given consideration.

All outlets are plotted in the Cartesian plane and identified by subscripts. To express tonnage requirements to each supermarket, annual tonnage is reduced to standard trailer units. The standard trailer employed is a 40-foot semivan capable of handling 38,000 pounds of dry grocery merchandise. Once each supermarket location is determined and the total trailer loads to each are known, the warehouse location may be determined.

The location solution is found by adding the products of store location and trailer frequency for each supermarket from the x coordinate and dividing by the total number of trailers. The process is repeated from the y coordinate. The result is a location in terms of x and y for the distribution center. The final location solution indicates the point that provides the balance of weight between stores for the given period. This basic algebraic procedure is followed for all mathematically derived location solutions with appropriate modifications necessary to handle the inclusion of different variables.

The algebraic formula for the ton-center computation is

$$x = \frac{\sum\limits_{i=1}^{n} x_i F_i}{\sum\limits_{i=1}^{n} F_i} \qquad y = \frac{\sum\limits_{i=1}^{n} y_i F_i}{\sum\limits_{i=1}^{n} F_i},$$

where

x, y = unknown coordinate values of the distribution warehouse.

x_n, y_n = supermarket locations, designated by appropriate subscript.

F_n = annual tonnage to each supermarket, expressed as standard trailers, identified by appropriate subscript.

MILE-CENTER SOLUTION. The mile-center solution isolates that geographical point which results in the least distance to all delivery points. The assumption underlying the solution is that delivery costs are a function of mileage. Therefore, if mileage is minimized, a least-cost location is determined. The basic deficiency in the mile-center solution is the omission of tonnage and time considerations.

Unlike the ton-center solution, the mile-center solution cannot be determined simply by solving for the weighted average along each coordinate. To find the mile-center it is necessary to establish the distance of each store location from an original warehouse location, thereby obtaining a mileage value. This value is determined by utilizing the general formula for finding the length of a straight line connecting two points. The exact procedure for this measurement is developed below.

Because the solution requires an initial x and y value for the distribution center, the final solution is found by a trial-and-error procedure. Starting with initial values for x and y, each time a computation is completed, new values are generated for the distribution warehouse in terms of x and y. The location problem is solved when the new values are equated to zero or within an acceptable tolerance of the last previous values. For example, if the initial values of x and y are 30 and 40, respectively, the location solution is obtained by utilizing these values to determine the new distribution warehouse coordinates. Assuming that the new values obtained are $x = 36$ and $y = 43$, the procedure has failed to set the new values equal to the original values. Thus additional computation is required. For the second computation, the most recent values, $x = 36$ and $y = 43$, are employed. If the second computation results in the values $x = 36$ and $y = 43$, the location solution equates to zero, and the problem is optimized.

In trial-and-error solutions, an acceptable tolerance of ± 1 mile is usually established for the x and y distribution warehouse coordinates. This means that solutions are correct within a 4-mile-square area. If through trial and error values for x and y within this tolerance are reached, the location is accepted as the center of the 4-square-mile area. This results in a maximum location error of 1 mile.

The algebraic formula for determining the mile-center solution is

$$x = \frac{\sum_{i=1}^{n} \frac{x_i}{d_i}}{\sum_{i=1}^{n} \frac{1}{d_i}} \qquad y = \frac{\sum_{i=1}^{n} \frac{y_i}{d_i}}{\sum_{i=1}^{n} \frac{1}{d_i}},$$

where

x, y = unknown coordinate values of the distribution center.

x_n, y_n = supermarket locations, designated by appropriate subscript.

d_n = location until the trial-and-error procedure is completed.

The value for d expressing the distance from a distribution center location can be determined from direct measurement on the coordinate plane or by utilization of the following straight-line formula:

$$d_n = \sqrt{(x_n - x)^2 + (y_n - y)^2},$$

where

d_n = distance between store and distribution warehouse, designated by appropriate subscript.

x, y = given coordinates of distribution warehouse.

x_n, y_n = supermarket location, designated by appropriate subscript.

Because the value of d for all supermarkets changes each time a new set of distribution warehouse coordinates is determined, the distance formula is utilized in each step of the trial-and-error procedure.

TON-MILE-CENTER SOLUTION.   The ton-mile-center solution combines the variables of weight and distance in selecting the distribution warehouse locations. The assumption is that costs are a function of ton-miles. The ton-mile solution is superior to the mile-center solution, because it takes frequency of delivery to each store into consideration in selecting the location. It is superior to the simple ton-center solution since the impact of distance is taken into consideration. The solution once more calls for trial and error since d is included in the formulation.

The ton-mile formulation is

$$x = \frac{\sum\limits_{i=1}^{n} \dfrac{x_i F_i}{d_i}}{\sum\limits_{i=1}^{n} \dfrac{F_i}{d_i}} \qquad y = \frac{\sum\limits_{i=1}^{n} \dfrac{y_i F_i}{d_i}}{\sum\limits_{i=1}^{n} \dfrac{F_i}{d_i}},$$

where

x, y = unknown coordinate values of the distribution warehouse.

x_n, y_n = supermarket locations designated by appropriate subscript.

F_n = annual tonnage to each supermarket expressed as standard trailers identified by appropriate subscript.

d_n = supermarket location differentiated in miles from the initial distribution warehouse location and sequentially from each new location until the trial-and-error procedure is completed.

TIME-TON-MILE-CENTER SOLUTION.   The fourth location measurement device includes all cost-influencing variables. Because costs are a function of time, weight, and distance, the distribution warehouse location derived as a product of this device should represent a superior least-cost location. The procedure for selecting the time-ton-mile solution is trial and error, because both the time and distance factors are differentiated from a given distribution warehouse location.

The formulation is as follows:

$$x = \frac{\sum\limits_{i=1}^{n} \dfrac{x_i F_i}{M_i}}{\sum\limits_{i=1}^{n} \dfrac{F_i}{M_i}} \qquad y = \frac{\sum\limits_{i=1}^{n} \dfrac{y_i F_i}{M_i}}{\sum\limits_{i=1}^{n} \dfrac{F_i}{M_i}},$$

where

x, y = unknown coordinate values of the distribution warehouse.

x_n, y_n = supermarket locations, designated by appropriate subscript.

F_n = annual tonnage to each supermarket, expressed as standard trailers, identified by appropriate subscript.

Mn = supermarket location differentiated in terms of miles per minute from the initial distribution warehouse location and sequentially from each new location until the trial-and-error procedure is completed.

To arrive at a value for M_n it is necessary to ascertain both the distance and time to all supermarkets from the given distribution center location. The distance value is determined by use of the basic distance formula. The time in minutes to each supermarket is found by calculating a time value from the coordinate plane. An estimate of delivery time must include number of miles, type of highway, and traffic. A general rule is that time per mile decreases as the number of miles per stop increases. To account for the basic factors that influence driving time, zones representing attainable movement rates are constructed in the simulated market area. These zones consist of two basic types: rural and urban. Movement rates that account for the influence of these factors have been adopted for each zone from a U.S. Department of Agriculture publication.[20] This publication represents a study of the trucking operations of eight wholesale grocery firms. The purpose of the study was to develop methods for establishing time standards for dry grocery delivery in urban and rural areas. A time-estimation table was developed that can be utilized for estimating delivery times between two points.

For use in a distribution warehouse location problem, the development of such estimating tables represents a substantial saving in research cost. Utilizing these tables, the total time necessary to traverse the distance between a given distribution center location and a supermarket can be rapidly estimated. This eliminates expensive engineering time studies for each alternative distribution warehouse location. The time zones and respective movement rates are presented in Table 12-2.

[20] Charles Crossed and Martin Kriesberg, *Procedures for Evaluating Delivery Operations of Wholesale Food Distributors* (Washington, D.C.: U.S. Department of Agriculture, 1960), pp. 8–14.

TABLE 12-2
Time-Estimation Table*

Urban Area		Rural Area	
Distance (miles)	Minutes/ Mile	Distance (miles)	Minutes/ Mile
Under 1	8.8	All rural	2.2
1.0–1.5	7.0		
1.6–2.0	4.8		
2.1–3.0	4.0		
3.1–4.0	3.5		
Over 4.0	3.4		

Example: If a delivery trip consists of 16 urban miles and 38 rural miles, total time would be 138 minutes (16 × 3.4) + (38 × 2.2).

* Adapted from Charles Crossed and Martin Kriesberg, *Procedures for Evaluating Delivery Operations of Wholesale Food Distributors* (Washington, D.C.: U.S. Department of Agriculture, 1960).

In this illustration, urban zones are defined as the geographic area of all cities with a population greater than 25,000. All other areas are considered rural. Given the values of distance and time through rural and urban zones, M_n is calculated in the following manner:

$$M_n = \frac{d_n}{t_n},$$

where

M_n = attainable miles per minute to the appropriate supermarket.

$d_n = \sqrt{(x_n - x)^2 + (y_n - y)^2}.$

t_n = total time to the store, minutes.

Summary—Single Location Determination

The location of a single logistical facility is commonly confronted in logistical planning. The very fact that a total system revision is rarely conducted for immediate implementation makes a simple approach to the evaluation of a single-facility location a useful aid to management. In cases where inbound transportation is an important cost, the model can easily be modified to include both inbound and outbound transportation cost.

The model is limited in that it does not incorporate the total cost of logistics. In addition, the solution is formulated in a static context. However, with these limitations in mind, the model represents an economical and efficient method for finding the precise location of a facility as a function of minimum transportation cost. The next section introduces more comprehensive models.

Simulated Systems Analysis

Comprehensive analysis of a total logistical system requires the full integration of all five components in the evaluation of total cost and customer service capability. Until recently, few models existed that were capable of a comprehensive analysis of the total logistical system. The primary purpose of this section is to introduce simulation. The section first presents a comparative evaluation of the current state of the art in logistical modeling and the reasons simulation models are preferrable in logistical system analysis. Next, four types of simulation models are presented and compared.

Comprehensive Models[21]

Logistical planning is a prime candidate for quantitative analysis because the major variables involved are readily measured: product, time, distance, flow rate, inventory accumulation, and spatial demand. Although the variables are readily measured, existing logistical planning models have major deficiencies: (1) Most models are not comprehensive (e.g., they do not consider all elements inherent in a logistical system), (2) they are unable to integrate time and space as the unifying system dimensions, and/or (3) they fail to incorporate dynamic behavior.

Existing logistical planning models can be grouped as analytical or simulation.[22] Analytic models strive mathematically to optimize particular objectives such as service or cost. In contrast, simulation models numerically represent a system but do not guarantee reaching or even indicating the direction in which one might expect to find an optimal solution. As a general statement, both analytic and simulation models fail to provide a comprehensive logistical planning tool.

Analytic models sacrifice comprehensive treatment of system components and relationships in order to ensure that a mathematical solution for optimality is achieved. These models concentrate on a single or a limited number of components, such as location, transportation, or inventory.[23] The solutions,

---

[21] This section draws upon Helferich, *op. cit.*, and Donald J. Bowersox, "Planning Physical Distribution Operations with Dynamic Simulation," *Journal of Marketing*, January 1972, pp. 17–25.

[22] M. A. Geisler and W. A. Steger, "The Combination of Alternative Research Techniques in Logistics Systems Analysis," in *Operations Management: Selected Readings*, G. K. Groff and J. F. Muth, eds. (Homewood, Ill.: Richard D. Irwin, Inc., 1969), pp. 324–32.

[23] W. J. Baumol and P. Wolfe, "A Warehouse Location Problem," *Operations Research*, Vol. 6 (March–April 1958), pp. 252–63; Ronald H. Ballou, "Dynamic Warehouse Location Analysis," *Journal of Marketing Research*, Vol. V (August 1968), pp. 271–76; B. F. Rowan, "Linear Programming: A Straight Line to Distribution Efficiency," *Handling and Shipping*, Vol. 6 (November 1965), pp. 56–60.

while optimizing the few components considered, usually present results that are suboptimal for the system as a whole. Although the goal of achieving optimal solutions is desirable, the current state of analytic modeling limits its ability to represent the total system.

Simulation is frequently selected by model builders as a more comprehensive alternative to analytic techniques. Currently, there are many simulators which include most components of the logistical system.[24] The primary deficiency in the comprehensiveness of existing simulation models is their failure to incorporate multiechelon structure and variable channel product flow. Both features are desirable in logistical system planning.

Multiechelon structure refers to the model's ability to represent a number of consecutive levels in the physical distribution channel. For example, a multi-echeloned model would be able to simulate product flow from manufacturing plants through consecutive warehousing levels to final geographical destinations. Variable channel product flow refers to the ability of a model simultaneously to simulate more than one echelon structure. In Chapter 1 this was referred to as dual distribution.

Different echeloned arrangements may be utilized on a shipment-by-shipment basis. To be comprehensive a planning model should include all components of logistics and have multiechelon and variable channel features.

A second deficiency of existing analytic and simulation models is their failure to combine spatial and temporal unifying factors.[25] The unifying dimension of a model is classified as spatial if the cost and service measurement is based on transportation. If the model unifies on total order-cycle time, it is classified as temporal. To date, most location models are spatially unified, whereas inventory models unify on time. The actual measurement of both cost and customer service is based on the combined impact of time and space. Therefore, a desirable modeling advancement in total system planning is a more complete integration of these two elements.

A planning problem is classified as static if the desired solution relates to a specific point in time.[26] However, if a series of decisions must be made in which current time-period actions influence future decisions, the planning problem becomes dynamic. There is increasing support for the desirability of framing planning models in a dynamic context.[27] A dynamic structure

---

[24] Shycon and Maffei, *op. cit.*, and Alfred Kuehn and M. J. Hamburger, "A Heuristic Program for Locating Warehouses," *Management Science*, July 1963, pp. 543–666. For other reported simulation models incorporating dynamic features see Robert E. Markland, "Analyzing Geographically Discrete Warehousing Networks by Computer Simulation," *The Journal for the American Institute for Decision Sciences*, Vol. 4, No. 2, April 1973, and Michael M. Conners, *et al.*, "The Distributor System Simulator," *Management Science*, Vol. 18, No. 8, April 1972, also WHAMOL (Benton Harbor, Mich.: Whirlpool Corporation Physical Distribution Department), 1973.

[25] James L. Heskett, "A Missing Link in Physical Distribution System Design," *Journal of Marketing*, October 1966, pp. 37–41.

[26] W. Hausman, "Sequential Decision Problems: A Model to Exploit Existing Forecasters," *Management Science*, October 1969, p. B-93.

[27] Ballou, *op. cit.*, p. 271, and R. A. Howard, "Dynamic Programming," *Management Science*, January 1966, p. 317.

requires incorporation of information feedback to measure the dependency of current actions upon environment reaction and necessary future actions.[28]

To date, analytical models have advanced further with respect to dynamics than simulation models.[29] However, in selecting a modeling approach for total system analysis the comprehensive advantage of simulation, coupled with the relative ease of temporal and spatial unification, outweighs the dynamic superiority of analytic techniques. The remainder of this section concentrates on simulation models.

Simulation Models

A number of simulation models exist which are useful in logistical planning. The label *simulation* can be applied to almost any attempt to replicate a situation. Simulation is a process by which a model of a particular situation is developed and tested using facts from real-world conditions. As one would expect, the range of simulations in terms of complexity and subject studies is unlimited.

In logistical system design, concern is with models containing various combinations of activity centers. The simulation process attempts to measure anticipated performance given a specified set of business conditions. With the exception of some very simple simulations, the complexity of the distribution system design process requires the use of computers to handle numerical computations. This section reviews four types of simulation models frequently employed in logistical planning. The progression is from the least to the most comprehensive type of simulation.

SYMBOLIC SIMULATIONS.   Symbolic simulation refers to the use of block flow charts to replicate alternative logistical systems. The procedure consists of diagramming the physical product and communication flows as connecting linkages between facility nodes. Once the diagram is completed, cost accounts associated with each node and category of linkage are identified. These costs are then grouped together to formulate a total cost projection for the system configuration illustrated by the flow diagram at a specified volume level.

Flow diagrams represent the first step in the development of most simulation models. However, the emphasis in general simulation flow diagramming is on identification of components, variables, functional relationships, parameters, and constraints for purposes of model formulation and programming. In the case of symbolic simulations the flow diagram is used as the primary tool of

---

[28] Forrester, *op. cit.*, p. 14.

[29] C. Hadley, *Nonlinear and Dynamic Programming* (Reading, Mass.: Addison-Wesley Publishing Company, Inc., 1964), R. A. Howard, *op. cit.*, and R. E. Bellman and S. E. Dreyfus, *Applied Dynamic Programming* (Princeton, N.J.: Princeton University Press, 1962).

analysis. Thus a different flow diagram must be developed for each alternative system.

In terms of capability and comprehensive treatment, symbolic simulations have numerous limitations. First, the array of shipment sizes must be averaged. Second, the approach has limited capability to evaluate alternative volume levels. Third, symbolic simulations are completely static. Fourth, the range of designs tested is limited to those which the distribution analyst feels are acceptable alternatives. Fifth, facility locations must be assumed and held constant under any given design configuration. Thus the interrelationship of facility location is not treated in design configuration. Finally, symbolic simulation is not able to handle trade-offs between customer service and cost requirements with the same precision as other integrative techniques.

The limitations of symbolic simulation analysis render it deficient for large-scale integrative studies. The technique is useful for evaluation of proposed modification to limited parts of an existing system. For example, it can be employed to check if a given market area has reached a sufficient volume to support replacement of direct shipments with a warehouse. The technique is fast and inexpensive, and it requires a minimum amount of technical expertise or computation capacity. If used with care and on specific types of problems, symbolic simulation can represent a useful short-range planning tool.

A recommended set of symbols for use in logistical system blocking is presented in Appendix 12A, as well as an example of a symbolic simulation. A set of typical accounts used to summarize cost accounts was illustrated in Table 10-5.

BREAK-EVEN SIMULATION. A second level of sophistication in comprehensive logistical system design consists of total cost break-even analysis. In a technical sense, break-even analysis is not a form of simulation. However, depending upon how it is employed, it falls between a purely analytic and a simulation tool.

The purpose of introducing break-even analysis is to evaluate the changing nature of total cost as a function of volume. Two or more alternative system designs are identified as potential logistical systems. For example, direct air distribution, rail–single-warehouse–truck, and rail–dual-warehouse–truck represent three ways a particular market could be serviced.

The initial step is to complete all the activities here discussed as necessary in symbolic simulation. Once total costs have been identified, the major difference is that an attempt is made to divide the costs related to each alternative into fixed and variable groupings.

Each alternative will have different cost functions in each category. Some will have higher fixed costs than others. The variable cost of handling more or less average shipments will also be substantially different among alternative systems. For any given volume one system will have the lowest combination of fixed and variable costs and therefore will be the lowest-cost logistical alternative under consideration.

When using break-even simulation, an attempt is made to express variable cost relationships for each system in a formula. These formulas are linear in relationship and represent the variable cost of an additional average shipment to the market under study. Fixed costs are held constant. By testing alternative volumes of average shipments, it is possible to locate the level at which one system achieves lower cost than the next. The series of formulas represent the models of alternative systems under study.

Break-even simulation has many of the same limitations as symbolic simulation. Location is assumed, range of system alternatives is limited, and service–cost relationships are lacking. Because testing can consider performance at alternative volume levels, break-even analysis eliminates one of the main deficiencies of symbolic simulation.

Break-even simulation has limited usefulness as a planning tool. It is frequently utilized to aid operational decision making. For example, if alternative methods of direct distribution exist to service a given market, break-even simulation can be formulated on the basis of fixed and variable costs of each as a function of shipment size. Given a particular shipment, it is possible to select the direct distribution alternative that should be utilized. Even if a warehouse exists in the service area, the model can provide valuable cost information to help decide if the shipment should be sent directly from the factory. Under certain conditions it may be less expensive to bypass the warehouse and ship direct. A break-even simulator can be of great aid in daily management.

Thus, although symbolic and break-even simulation provide techniques useful for limited research, training, and operational guidance, more powerful and comprehensive analysis models are needed for tackling complex distribution system studies.

STATIC SIMULATION. Static simulation represents the first level of models capable of total system replication. All components of the total logistical system are replicated. The primary difference between dynamic and static simulation is the sacrifice of feedback in static models. In addition, most static simulators do not incorporate dual distribution capabilities. Such simplicities result in lower cost and faster solutions. In terms of the rapid rate of change in modern business, such "satisfactory solutions" may well be adequate for some system design situations.

In static simulation the model is formulated around a group of plausible distribution facility locations. In the majority of cases, the type of facility is limited to distribution and plant warehouses with production capacity are assumed constant. In addition, the model is often structured around finished-goods distribution. Because the range of potential distribution facilities is limited, operational cost relationships are formulated on a point-to-point basis. This ability to work on a point-to-point basis overcomes the major hurdle of developing the all-encompassing operational relationships required in dynamic simulation. In static simulation no attempt is made to structure the model to handle time-period interplay. The static simulation treats each operating period within the over-all study period as a finite interval. Final results represent a summation of operating performance for each period in the study.

The static-simulation procedure seeks the best network of facilities among those included in the study structure. The initial state of the system assumed that all plausible locations are included in the network. In subsequent cycles, distribution facilities are added and deleted on a trial-and-error basis until the best combination among the locations is ascertained. No assurance exists that the selection of facilities included in the study will represent the best possible range of alternatives.

The advantage of static simulation is that it is simpler, less expensive, and faster than dynamic simulation. Although the solution lacks unlimited design possibilities, it is sufficiently broad to include all apparent facility locations, transport alternatives, and communication subsystems. Inventory allocations are made based upon the network of distribution facilities included in each study cycle, and service territories for each facility are delineated.

DYNAMIC SIMULATION. Dynamic simulation is the most comprehensive technique within the group of existing simulation models. However, it is also the most complex and requires the highest degree of expert capability.

The dynamic simulation solution relies upon sequential tests of a system model. A study period, for example, 1 to 10 years, is held constant to test system capability. This business activity, called *flow input*, is used repeatedly to test design modifications. Each sequence in the simulation procedure results in an improvement in total system design. The final solution is determined when no additional worthwhile improvements can be made in the design then existing. As such, dynamic simulation models are structured on a recursive relationship and rely upon numerical analysis for design solutions.

The dynamic simulation process, if properly structured, should result in a configuration of facilities ideal to support logistical requirements. Specifications concerning inventory allocations will be delineated for each facility. Perhaps the most beneficial result of dynamic simulation is a priority assignment of customers to specific supply facilities. This permits a detailed analysis of the cost–benefit relationship of high levels of customer service. In addition, the most desirable order processing and communication subsystem will be determined by the simulation. A final output of primary importance is a transportation scheduling scheme which will achieve the desired performance at lowest total system cost.

The final section of this chapter provides a comprehensive description of a dynamic logistics simulator.

The LREPS Model[30]

This section reviews a dynamic simulation model, LREPS (long-range environmental planning simulator), which is capable of simulating comprehensive logistical systems. The model was developed through a joint industry–university research project, which had six specific development objectives.

1. A comprehensive model of logistical operations as an integrated system capable of total cost and customer service performance measurement.
2. A dynamic model that permits logistical planning over time with sufficient feedback to ensure that the future impact or consequence of any decision is adequately treated.
3. A model capable of simultaneously coping with inventory allocation and facility location, thereby integrating temporal and spatial attributes.
4. A model capable of representing one or more total order cycles on a probabilistic basis and in an echeloned structure, thereby introducing the capability of staging, variable channel product flow, and performance delays.
5. An environmental model that permits experimentation between the boundary of the operating model and critical environmental factors that influence performance.
6. A model structure with sufficient adaptability to be efficiently applied to a variety of enterprise situations.

Model Design

The multiecheloned structure of LREPS is illustrated in Figure 12-4. Each echelon may be used to replicate any sequence of nodal point in a logistical system structure from raw material sources to final product delivery destinations. Any number of echelons may be included in the model structure and no requirements exist to have the same number of nodes in each echelon.

Linkages between and within echelons are defined in terms of product and information flows. Product flow is treated in multiproduct fashion. Unlimited individual products may be tracked. Information flow, related specifically to the order communication function, occurs between and within echelons. Product flow is measured by standard units such as value, weight, cube, and density. Order cycle time, the primary measure of customer service, is measured

---

[30] For a complete report on the LREPS project, see Donald J. Bowersox *et al.*, *Dynamic Simulation of Physical Distribution Systems* (East Lansing, Mich.: Division of Research, Michigan State University, 1973); Donald J. Bowersox, *op. cit.*; Donald J. Bowersox, "Dynamic Simulation of Physical Distribution," *Distribution Worldwide*, December 1972, pp. 24–31; and Donald J. Bowersox, Omar Keith Helferich, and Edward J. Marien, "Physical Distribution Planning with Simulation," *International Journal of Physical Distribution*, October 1971, pp. 38–42. Portions of the following sections and figures are based upon these references by the author.

FIGURE 12-4
Structure of the Physical Distribution Network

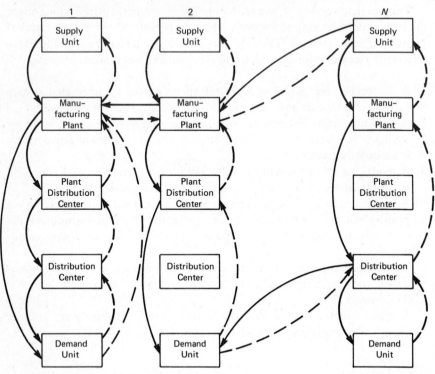

in terms of four elapsed time intervals: (1) order communication time, (2) order processing time, (3) transportation time, and (4) total penalty time accumulated under (1), (2), or (3) resulting from delay, deficiency, or queuing. Orders and products are treated on a multichanneled basis. Both information and product flows related to specific requirements can be specifically assigned to alternative channel paths between manufacturing and point of demand. The system structure of LREPS thus allows the simulation of multiproduct and information flow to occur in a multichanneled pattern through a multi-echeloned logistical system.

To illustrate a planning application, Figure 12-5 provides a simplified simulation structure. The structure illustrated on Figure 12-5 and during the remainder of this section is based on a simulation limited to physical distri-bution. The model has also been applied on a total logistical system basis, which includes material management and physical distribution operations in an integrated network structure. In this case the first echelon comprises three manufacturing plants with adjacent warehouses. Each plant may be designated as either a partial- or full-product-line producer. The second echelon in Figure 12-5 is comprised of six warehouses, which may stock any

FIGURE 12-5
Illustration of Echelons in a Physical Distribution Application

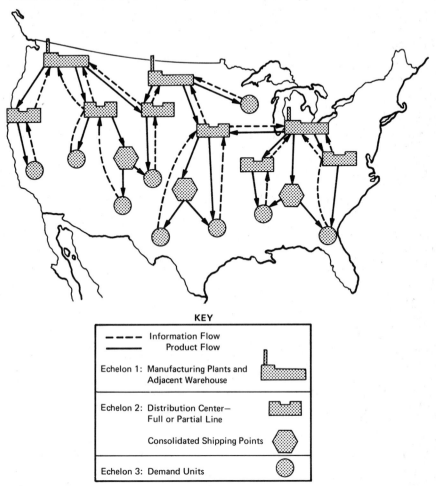

KEY

– – – –	Information Flow
———	Product Flow

Echelon 1: Manufacturing Plants and
Adjacent Warehouse

Echelon 2: Distribution Center—
Full or Partial Line

Consolidated Shipping Points

Echelon 3: Demand Units

inventory assortment. If desired, warehouses can be stocked in product flow sequence and thus become primary and remote facilities. An additional feature illustrated in the second echelon is the ability to simulate shipping consolidation points for the sole purpose of aggregating transportation tonnage. The final echelon provides demand units that represent individual and/or aggregations of customers. Although only nine are illustrated on Figure 12-5, several thousand can be identified in any particular simulation.

LREPS has three modes of operation. First, LREPS may operate on a probabilistic or deterministic mode with regard to the total order cycle–time relationship. Communication, order processing, and transportation times can

TABLE 12-3
LREPS Controllable System Variables

Variable Groupings	Design Options
Marketing-oriented variables	
Order characteristics	Actual or hypothetical
Product mix	Actual or hypothetical
New products	As desired
Customer mix	Actual or hypothetical
Distribution-oriented variables	
Facility structure	Actual or hypothetical by echelon
Facility connection	Actual or hypothetical between echelons
Inventory policy	Reorder point, replenishment, or hybrid by echelon
Transportation	Truck, rail, air, private and contract truck in any combination between echelons
Communication	Computer, teletype, mail, telephone between echelons
Material handling	Automated or mechanized by echelons

be present for any specified linkage, or discrete probability distributions may be specified. In the latter case the model operates in a probabilistic mode.

Second, LREPS is oriented to *variable time-planning horizons*. The model operates on a time-interval-dependent basis (that is, results achieved at the end of a time period are noted and influence operations during the next time period) and functions for a specified combination of days, quarters, or years. Ten years is the most common maximum period chosen.

Third, feedback loops are utilized to provide *dynamic behavior* when desired. For example, future sales of a product group can be altered if customer service varies from a target value. In addition, two locational algorithms may be utilized with LREPS. The heuristic algorithm is similar in nature to that reported by Kuehn and Hamburger.[31] The other algorithm is an on-the-fly linear programming routine that determines an analytic solution to the location structure for a single point in time during the planning horizon. If activated, the algorithms have the capability to alter the second echelon structure as necessary throughout the planning horizon. Alteration is achieved subject to stated management-specified parameters such as permissible facility size, cost, locational option, and construction startup delays.

Variables Considered

Three groupings of variables are defined in LREPS: (1) target variables, (2) environment variables, and (3) controllable variables. The major target variables are customer service and total cost. Environmental variables are

---

[31] Kuehn and Hamburger, *op. cit.*

grouped into major categories of demographics, technologies, and acts of nature. Each of these categories is broken down into variables that are inter-active with the model itself; that is, demographic variables defined in terms of cost-of-living indices, real-estate-value indices, and demand determinants.

The major controllable variables illustrated in Table 12-3 structure the major physical distribution and marketing overlap. Included to the right of each variable is a summary of design options for simulated experimentation.

Model Operation

For illustrative purposes, two versions of the LREPS are presented in Figures 12-6 and 12-7. Given the supporting data necessary to simulate a planning situation, the operation of the model embodies four steps.

First, daily orders by demand units are generated. This is achieved by randomly selecting blocks of actual orders in such a manner as to satisfy the daily sales requirements of each demand unit. An over-all sales forecast is allocated to demand units on the basis of independent market variables. This initial activity is performed by the model's demand and environmental sub-system (D&E).

FIGURE 12-6
Generalized LREPS System Concept—Physical Distribution Model

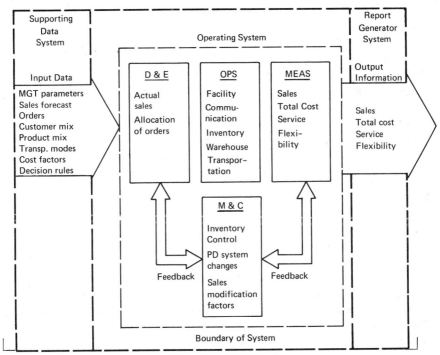

FIGURE 12-7
LREPS Computer System Flow Chart—Physical Distribution Model

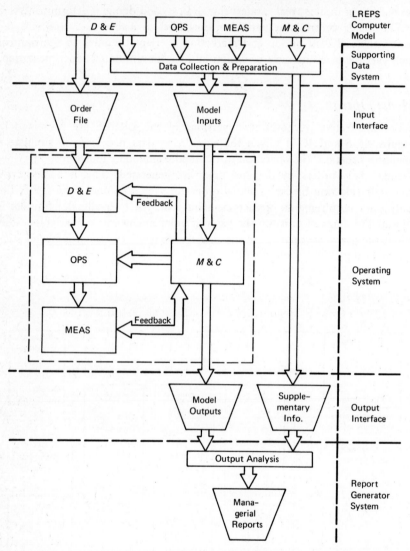

Second, the actual processing is simulated. All order cycles between demand units and other echelons are simulated, and appropriate elapsed times are computed. The operations subsystem (OPS) of LREPS performs this processing function and thereby constitutes the model's system structure.

As orders are processed at each distribution center, inventories are appropriately reduced; if unavailable, products are back-ordered. As reorder points or periods are reached at one echelon, replenishment orders are dispatched to the next echelon. There time delays are computed and inventory replenishment decisions are made.

Third, all this relevant information is used to compute target variable values. Total cost is measured on the basis of cost parameters and mathematical transformations related to each component of the system. Fixed facility investment cost by size and type of facility is based upon annual depreciated amount. Order processing costs for each distribution center are calculated using regression equations with different cost factors based upon size and location of the facility. Communication costs are calculated using regression equations where the independent variables are the number of orders and lines processed. Inventory carrying and reorder costs are calculated for all nodal and pipeline inventories. Inbound transportation costs to distribution centers are calculated on specific point-to-point rates. Outbound transport costs to demand units are calculated from sets of regression equations based on distance. The measurement subsystem (MEAS) provides necessary measurement for evaluation of system performance.

The interplay here described must be monitored and controlled (M&G subsystem). The introduction of new variable values at the proper time, the addition or deletion of distribution facilities according to management rules, and the impact of changes in the environment are handled internal to the model by this subsystem.

Design Assumptions

As a generalized simulation model, LREPS does not incorporate many assumptions common to other physical distribution simulators. Simplifying assumptions such as a single average product, one manufacturing location, or single-channel distribution are not made. The development of cost functions based upon historic corporate data and representation by regresssion equations also reduces the need to assume a variety of data relationships.

Two major operational assumptions are contained within the LREPS model structure. First, the procedure by which demand is generated from a single sales forecast requires statistical validation. The primary need for this assumption is to free the simulator's operation from the requirement to input thousands of individual orders into the computer. Second, the procedure wherein tracked products are selected to represent a total product line requires statistical validation.

Validation

Three major areas were considered in the over-all validation of LREPS: (1) stability of output data, (2) sensitivity to assumed relationships, and (3) comparison of simulated output to historical data.[32]

[32] Gilmore, *op. cit.*

Results using graphical correlation, Theil's inequality coefficient, and spectral analysis indicated that the model does generate persistent and stable output over time. Using the techniques described, plus analysis of variance, multiple comparison, F test, regression analysis, chi-square test, and factor analysis, the two major assumptions—demand generation and product selection—were proved valid. Although a series of tests was conducted concerning the quality of simulated output, the model's long-range predictive capability has not been scientifically established. Although the model has surface validity, final determination of design validity must await the availability of more extensive historic data.

Limitations

The following major areas of limitation appear to be most important:

1. The flow and set data required to initialize LREPS are large and not all firms possess the required data, thereby limiting applicability if pure data are desired.
2. The complexity makes LREPS unsuited for many minor studies, and a scaled-down version is often needed.
3. In all areas of forecasting and cost predicting, improvement over regression equations is desirable.

Output Capabilities and Selected Applications

This section illustrates the output capabilities of the LREPS report generator and provides three illustrations of LREPS applications to date. The examples were selected to illustrate areas of overlap between physical distribution and marketing planning. They also demonstrate how LREPS improves upon the deficiencies of existing planning models. All output data presented have been slightly altered to ensure confidentiality of results.

The output capabilities of LREPS are partially illustrated in Table 12-4. Section A presents a summary of information generated for the total system and the type of detail available concerning each nodal point evaluated. The most significant data in section A concern total cost accumulation by system component and various measures of service based upon total order cycle time. Section B demonstrates the capability of LREPS to track multiproduct flow in a multiechelon network. The comprehensive nature of the data generated by LREPS provides the basis for measuring total cost and customer service trade-offs.

In addition to the operational data given in Table 12-4, financially orientated data in the format of profit-and-loss statements or cash-flow schedules can be produced directly from the LREPS report generator.

ILLUSTRATION I.   Initial utilization of LREPS to analyze cost–service trade-offs demonstrates the model's capacity to integrate spatial and temporal aspects of

TABLE 12-4
Representative Information Output LREPS

Section A—Total System and Individual Distribution Center Data

Summary for Selected Period—On Facility in Solution

Sales $	Cost $	Profit. Contrib. $	Order Cycle Time	Inventory on Hand
7,079.8	607.3	6,472.5	6.2	227.0

Sales information:

Dollars	Weight	Cube	Cases	Lines	Orders
7,079.8	4,574	580	400	80,100	13,650

Component cost information:

Outbound	Inbound	Throughput	Commics.	Fac.	Invn.	Total
123.3	30.7	180.2	12.6	200.0	60.5	607.3

Order cycle time information:

Total Order Cycle	Back-Order Penalty (BP)	Order Cycle W/O-BP	Standard Deviation Cycle	Average Transit Time	Standard Deviation Transit Time	Desired to Actual Service Ratio
6.2	0.3	5.9	0.6	2.0	0.3	0.91

Proportion within order cycle time:

Days	3 days	5 days	7 days	9 days	11 days
Orders	0.10	0.70	0.85	0.95	1.0
Dollars	0.15	0.75	0.88	0.98	1.0

Section B—Product Track Information

Summary for Selected Period per product and Total All Products by Individual Warehouse and Demand Units

Manufacturing replenishment:

	Plant 1	Plant 2	Plant N
Reorder	55	60	45
Av. Days Lead Time	1.5	6.0	7.5

Distribution center period performance:

Inventory on Hand	Total Stockouts	Total Reorders	% Case Units Back-Ordered	Av. Stockout Delay	Standard Deviation of Av. Stockout Delay
200	135	899	1.0	6.3	3.2

Distribution activity period performance by demand unit:

Demand Unit	Dollars	Weight	Cube	Cases	Lines	Orders
Unit 1	283.2	180.3	23.2	16.0	3,204.0	546.0
Unit 2	709.1	480.5	60.3	42.0	8,120.0	1,465.0
Unit N	141.1	92.1	12.6	8.0	1,610.0	268.0

system redesign on a comprehensive basis. The planning situation called for a 10-year evaluation of required warehousing capacity. The existing system consisted of six regional distribution warehouses. A sales growth of 50 per cent was forecast over the 10-year planning horizon. Management specified that customer service be maintained at or above the current level of 80 per cent of all orders being serviced at lowest possible total cost and within a 5-day total order cycle.

Preliminary analysis using LREPS established three design alternatives that management desired to simulate in detail: (1) expand existing facilities, (2) expand existing facilities plus add two facilities, and (3) expand existing facilities plus add three facilities. The cost–service results of the detailed simulation runs are graphically illustrated in Figures 12-8 and 12-9.

A surprising result was that total logistical system cost over the planning horizon was similar for each alternative. Each alternative experienced increasing costs over time; however, trade-offs between the various physical distribution components in each situation were substantially different. Alternative 1 experienced highest transport costs coupled with lowest inventory costs. The situation was reversed in the case of alternative 3.

Despite similar total system costs, a significant differential existed between the customer service capabilities of the three alternatives. Although not expected, all three systems did realize the stated managerial service goals. Over the planning horizons, however, alternative 3 realized greater than 90 per cent of all orders being serviced within a 5-day order cycle. Thus alternative 3

FIGURE 12-8
Total Cost—Illustration I

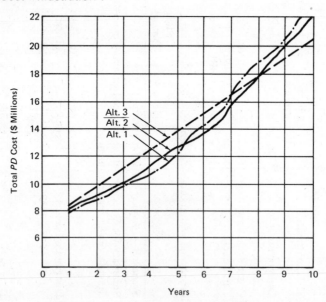

FIGURE 12-9
Order Cycle Time—Illustration II

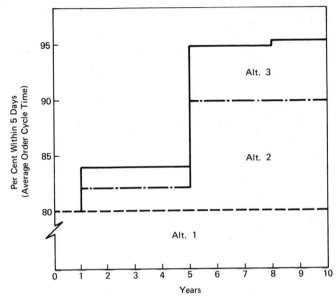

was about 10 per cent more effective than alternative 1 at approximately the same total cost.

The presimulation management expectation was that additional warehouses would be required to maintain desired service standards, and that the total system cost associated with adding facilities would increase substantially. The simulated results provided a flexible plan for expanding service capabilities if and when desired as part of the total marketing offering. In the interim, cost-service objectives could be realized by retaining the simplicity of a six-facility warehouse network each of expanded size.

ILLUSTRATION II.   The relationship of inventory and location has also been simulated for a single market area consisting of eight states. In this situation the marketing organization desired the addition of a second warehouse to improve service capability and average order cycle by reducing transit time. Expectations were that the total cost of servicing the over-all market would increase as a result of adding the second facility. A second alternative for improving customer service was to increase the safety stock at the existing warehouse. Increased safety stock was expected to improve average order cycle time via a reduction in back orders. The existing average order cycle time was 4.6 days; 75 per cent of all orders were filled within 5 days. Marketing desired a 10 per cent improvement at minimum total cost.

Addition of the warehouse (alternative 1) reduced the average order cycle time to 4.1 days, which was the equivalent of increasing the orders filled within 5 days from 75 to 92 per cent. Increasing safety stock at the existing warehouse (alternative 2) reduced the average order cycle by 0.3 days, to 4.3 days. This was equivalent to improving the percentage of orders filled within 5 days from 75 to 87 per cent. Over the 10-year planning horizon, the addition of a second warehouse provided the lowest-total-cost alternative.

The service–cost relationships of the two alternatives are illustrated in Figures 12-10 and 12-11. In this situation the warehouse addition resulted in the lowest cost and provided the highest average level of customer service. It is interesting to note that the addition of a warehouse was the more costly alternative for approximately the first three years of simulated operations but the least costly for the aggregated 10 years. Thus marketing could realize a 12 per cent increase in service capability for the initial three years at the lowest total cost by increasing safety stocks at the existing warehouse. Establishment of a second warehouse to be operational by the fourth year would realize an additional 5 per cent improvement in service and a continuation of the least-cost arrangement. This relationship of cost and service over the planning horizon is one of the many situations simulated to date which illustrates the importance of a dynamic planning structure.

ILLUSTRATION III.   A final illustration of LREPS shows the model's capacity to simulate total system service relationships on (1) the number and sequencing

FIGURE 12-10
Order Cycle Time—Illustration II

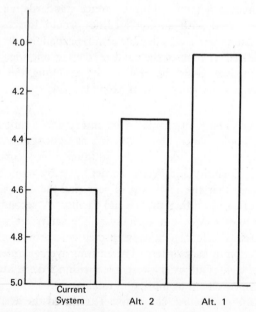

FIGURE 12-11
Total Cost—Illustration II

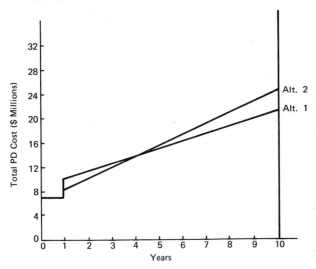

FIGURE 12-12
Relationship Distribution Centers to Total Order Time—Illustration III

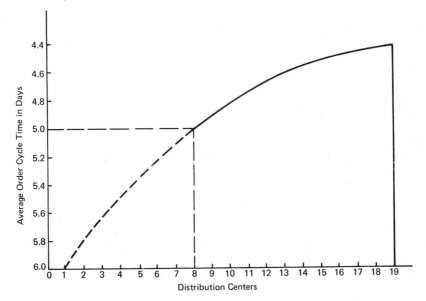

of warehouse locations, (2) inventory cost related to performance delays for an eight-location structure, and (3) market area adjustment to postpone timing of warehouse additions. Simulation runs of the type described in illustration III are regularly used to isolate design alternatives which are subjected to detailed simulation analysis.

The general relationship of service as a function of the number and sequencing of warehouse additions is illustrated in Figure 12-12. A specific marketing situation was simulated over a 10-year period in an effort to determine the shortest possible average order cycle duration. The facility location algorithm of LREPS was permitted to select the sequence and number of warehouse locations constrained only by the rate of permissible annual capital investment. Inventory performance was held constant at 85 per cent of all orders being filled within the average order cycle time. Given the initial six warehouse locations of the firm, an expansion plan was selected from a list of 35 potential warehouse additions. The facility location algorithm isolated the expansion

FIGURE 12-13
Percentage of Orders Filled in 5.0 Average Order Cycle Days—Eight Warehouse Configuration—One Year—Illustration III

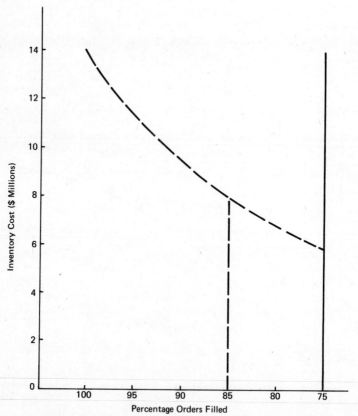

Percentage Orders Filled

sequence by selecting additional warehouses on the basis of the incremental relationship between minimum added cost and maximum added service.

In total, order cycle time was reduced from 6.0 to 4.4 days by expanding the locational structure from 1 to 19 warehouses. As anticipated, improvement in simulated average order time increased at a decreasing rate as additional warehouses were added. No improvement was realized beyond 19 warehouses.

Based upon the expansion sequence illustrated in Figure 12-12, management elected to evaluate the addition of two warehouses beyond the existing six. A specific simulation was conducted to determine the relationship of inventory investment cost to average performance delays for the eight-warehouse configuration. In effect, the original constraint of 85 per cent of all orders being satisfied within 5.0 average order cycle days (dashed lines, Figure 12-12) was simulated to obtain the service improvement possible from increased safety stock levels. For the particular number and location of warehouses it was determined that an increase from $7 to $14 million of annual inventory cost would be required to increase service from 85 to 100 per cent of all orders filled within 5.0 average order cycle days (Figure 12-13).

Next the initial plan of adding two warehouses was subjected to sensitivity analysis, wherein market area assignments to specific warehouses were allowed to shift a maximum of twice during the 10-year planning horizon. The objective was to determine if a trade-off could be realized between investment and operating cost at little or no sacrifice in customer service. The sensitivity testing resulted in a plan to postpone the first facility by one year and the second facility by two years.

The situations illustrated demonstrate the general planning capabilities of dynamic simulation. Each example was selected from an over-all planning problem to illustrate the overlap between decisions made at any given echelon and the importance of time horizon analysis in logistical system planning.

Summary

Chapter 12 presented basic concepts in modeling, introduced and classified techniques available for use in logistical design, and provided illustrations of both analytical and simulation applications. The chapter generally supported simulation as the most applicable technique to comprehensive logistical planning problems. Modeling represents only one aspect of over-all logistical planning; therefore, Chapters 10, 11, and 12 provide a comprehensive treatment of the design responsibility of logistical management. The next part of the text focuses on system administration.

Appendix 12A
System Terminology and Flowcharting

Flowcharting of any type of a system represents the alignment of the steps followed by the system in performance of a specified activity. Flowcharts are widely used in automated data processing (ADP) for the purpose of outlining sequential steps in both general systems and computer programs. In distribution system design, the use of flowcharts provides a means by which the physical and the information flows can be visualized. To date no standardized set of symbols has been developed for use in specialized physical distribution flowcharts. The purpose of this appendix is to outline some standard symbols for use in such flowcharting.

Standard Data-Processing Flowchart Symbols

In the field of automated data processing, standard symbols have been developed. In general, three basic symbols are used:

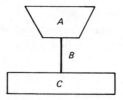

Symbol *A* is the basic notation for an input or output of a given system flow. Symbol *B* is used to describe the direction of flow within a system. The direction is normally read from top to bottom and from left to right. It is not standard practice to use arrowheads, if the flow is in either of these directions. In the event flow is to the opposite or reverse direction, an open arrowhead is used to indicate this condition. Bidirectional flow is charted by dashed lines or double lines. Symbol *C* represents the basic identification of a processing function. The processing symbol is used for the purpose of illustrating a major activity on the data flow. For example, the preparation of a payroll is indicated by a processing symbol.

These basic symbols are supplemented by a variety of special symbols that define in greater detail the type of input, output, or processing to be performed in a data-processing system. A great deal of effort has been centered on the development of these standard symbols. Both basic and special symbols are fairly interchangeable between major data-processing systems. When physical distribution systems are flowcharted for computer processing, these basic notations should be used. However, when flowcharts are developed for purposes of visualizing a physical distribution system, standard symbols used in ADP are too restrictive. Therefore, more descriptive symbols are desirable.

410

Recommended Physical Distribution Flowchart Symbols

Nine basic symbols are used to develop a physical distribution flowchart. Each is listed below with a brief description.

Fixed Location
Activity Center

Symbol *A* is used to denote those physical distribution activities that are performed at a fixed location such as a distribution warehouse.

Transit Activity
Center

The transit activity center is noted by symbol *B*. It is useful to distinguish between fixed-location and transit activity centers because of the wide range of alternatives in transit performance.

Input/Output

Symbol *C* is used to illustrate inputs and outputs of the physical distribution system.

Activity Centers
External to Physical
Distribution System

A great many activity centers or other areas of the corporation come into direct involvement with the physical distribution system. These external activity centers are indicated by symbol *D*.

Data Processing

Symbol E is used to indicate points of data-processing control. It is at these points that computer facilities are employed in the physical distribution system.

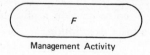

Management Activity

From time to time, special managerial action is generated as part of the over-all system. Although such action is a part of almost every system segment, when special attention is desired symbol F is recommended.

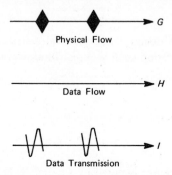

Physical Flow

Data Flow

Data Transmission

Three different symbols are used to illustrate flow in the physical distribution system. Symbol G is used to illustrate physical product flow. Symbol H is employed for information flow, and the special symbol I is used to denote the existence of data-transmission equipment.

In addition to these nine basic symbols, any number of special symbols may be used to illustrate additional or more detailed physical distribution activities.

Example of a Physical Distribution System Flowchart

Figure 12A-1 illustrates a two-production plant–three-distribution warehouse logistical system. This system has the following characteristics: (1) each of the production plants ships to all three distribution centers; (2) distribution warehouses have a communication capacity with each other and with central control; (3) distribution centers can interbranch-transfer when the situation is warranted; (4) when conditions justify, shipments can be made direct from production plants to customers; (5) customer orders are routed direct to distribution warehouses for shipment, if possible; and (6) inventory and production control is maintained at the central inventory control location, which is linked to distribution warehouses by data transmission.

The system detailed in Figure 12A-1 represents a major simplification, because no detail is developed for major activity centers. In flowcharting the complete structure of a physical distribution system, the normal procedure would be development of diagrams for each subsystem.

FIGURE 12A-1
Two-Plant–Three-Distribution Warehouse System Flowchart

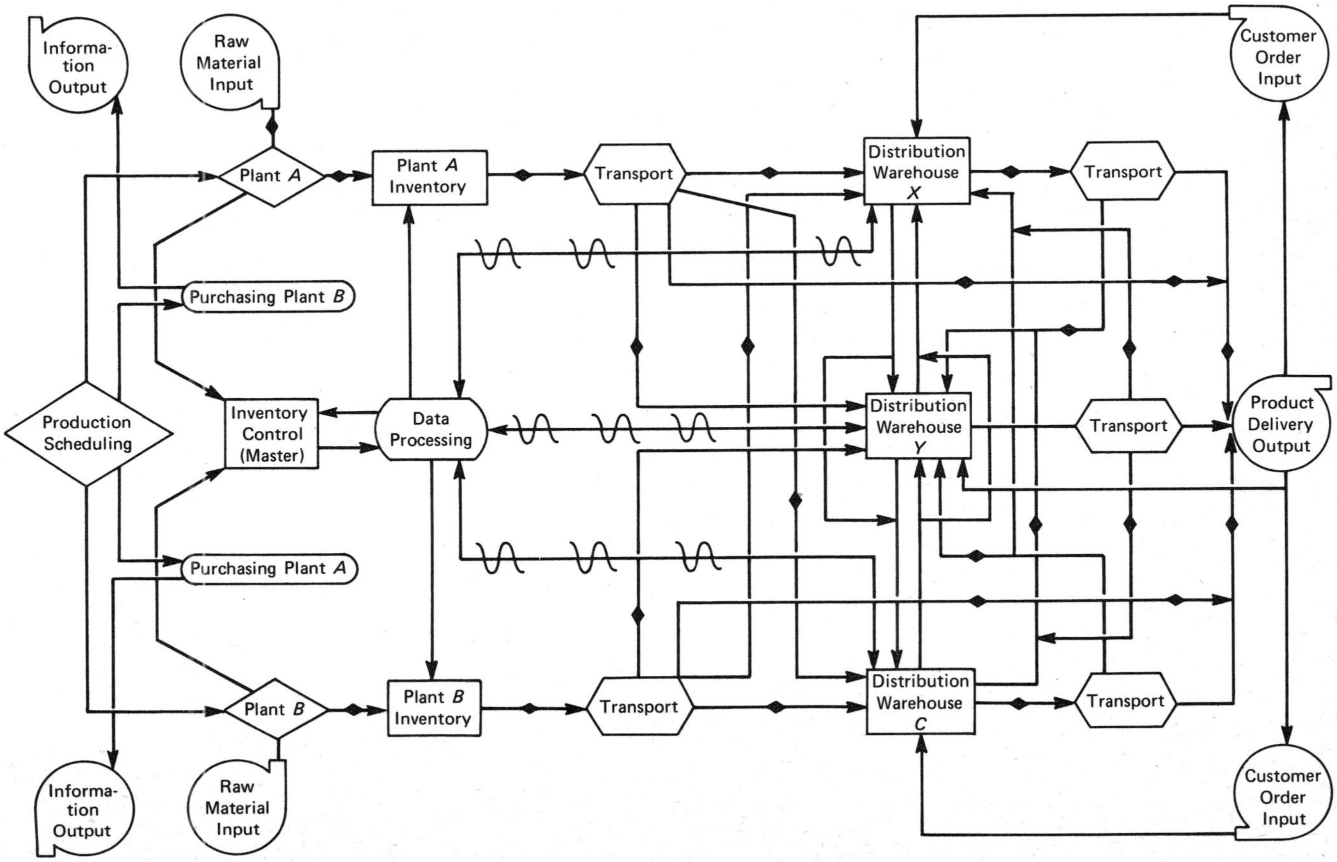

Questions

1. Describe the difference between a physical model and an abstract model. Are both useful to the logistical manager?
2. What is meant by a dynamic model?
3. Contrast analytical and numeric mathematical models.
4. What is the role of a functional relationship in the mathematical model structure?
5. Discuss the differences among exogenous, status, and endogenous variables.
6. Why is the generalized system model described in Figure 12-1 considered dynamic?
7. What benefit is gained by modular construction of a model?
8. Describe the concept of redundancy in model design.
9. What is meant by the phrase "heuristic approach"?
10. Can a heuristic procedure be utilized with the employment of an analytical model?
11. In the model illustrated for single-location determination, what is the major reason for attempting to include time as a variable in the problem solution?
12. In discussion of large-scale simulations, what is meant by the feature of multiechelon and multitrack? Why is dynamic representation essential to spatial and temporal unification?

Part Four

Logistical
System
Administration

13

Administration
and Organization

Given a logistical system design, the second broad area of managerial responsibility is administration. Logistical administration is concerned with the process of resource allocation and control of the five activity centers included in system design. Organization is the structure by which human resources are aligned in a particular logistical operation. Among the many subject matters of logistical management, the areas of integrated system administration and organization are the least understood. This lack of clearly defined principles is the result of the relative newness of integrated logistical systems and related performance measurement techniques.

This chapter is concerned with system administration and organization for logistical management. The basic format is one of integrated management by objectives. It is through the establishment of clearly defined goals and continuous review of progress that administration is most effective. The first section of this chapter develops the basic concept of management by objectives. Next, the operational planning process is developed. Following is a discussion of organization for logistical management.

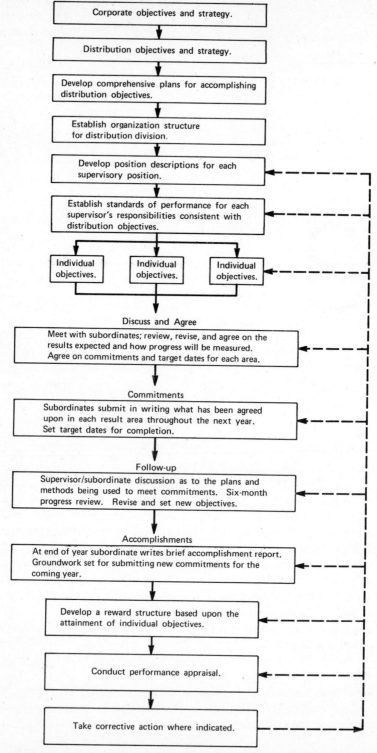

FIGURE 13-1
Process of Management by Objectives (MBO)

Corporate objectives and strategy.

Distribution objectives and strategy.

Develop comprehensive plans for accomplishing distribution objectives.

Establish organization structure for distribution division.

Develop position descriptions for each supervisory position.

Establish standards of performance for each supervisor's responsibilities consistent with distribution objectives.

Individual objectives.

Individual objectives.

Individual objectives.

Discuss and Agree

Meet with subordinates; review, revise, and agree on the results expected and how progress will be measured. Agree on commitments and target dates for each area.

Commitments

Subordinates submit in writing what has been agreed upon in each result area throughout the next year. Set target dates for completion.

Follow-up

Supervisor/subordinate discussion as to the plans and methods being used to meet commitments. Six-month progress review. Revise and set new objectives.

Accomplishments

At end of year subordinate writes brief accomplishment report. Groundwork set for submitting new commitments for the coming year.

Develop a reward structure based upon the attainment of individual objectives.

Conduct performance appraisal.

Take corrective action where indicated.

Source: Bernard J. LaLonde and James F. Robeson, "Organizing and Managing the Corporate Distribution Function," *Jounal of Business Policy.*

Management by Objectives

The essential concept of management by objectives (MBO) is the establishment of goals and controls. In MBO it is not the content of a job in terms of description which is important. The important facet is the objective for individual job accomplishment established for each administrative period. The job objective is the goal. Given a goal or a series of goals, logistical administration is concerned with control in order to measure progress toward goal accomplishment.

The concept of professional management is illustrated in Figure 13-1. It is based on an MBO approach, which is summarized as follows:

1. At the beginning of the planning period, top management establishes overall goals or objectives for the entire organization. These overall objectives are then translated into action plans for every manager in the organization so that each has clear, unambiguous objectives for his particular area of responsibility—objectives in keeping with the over-all organizational objectives.
2. Next, an organizational structure consistent with and capable of achieving these objectives must be established. Whereas objectives represent the "end," organization represents the "means" or the vehicle by which objectives will be achieved.
3. Position descriptions which clearly define the responsibilities of each individual in the organizational structure must then be developed.
4. The next phase involves establishing performance standards to guide and direct each individual's activities. These performance standards must be supportive and consistent with functional area and overall corporate objectives.
5. This step involves developing a reward structure that fairly and adequately compensates each individual when he achieves the performance standards established for his position.
6. Finally, and perhaps most importantly, each individual's success or failure in achieving his standards of performance *must* be appraised and corrective action taken where necessary. This represents the key to professional management.[1]

The over-all administrative task is concerned with planning to establish goals and controls to guarantee logistical performance. The next section is concerned with planning followed by a section on logistical control.

Logistical Planning

During the past few decades there has been increased interest in all forms of business planning. This interest in planning flows from two sources. First,

[1] Bernard J. LaLonde and James F. Robeson, "Corporate Strategy and Organization for Distribution," *Journal of Business Policy*, Spring 1972, p. 55.

the over-all business enterprise has become increasingly complex and the competitive environment extremely dynamic. Second, data-processing technology has developed a tool to assist management in fulfillment of the planning task. Further, the information base provided by data processing gives management the capability for continuously monitoring short- and long-range performance in relation to plans.

The logistical operating system is no exception when it comes to increased complexity over the past several decades. The multiplication of lines, brands, sizes, colors, and geographical scope of operations, coupled with increasing customer service demands characteristic of modern operations, has forced the logistical manager to shift from a posture of reaction to one of anticipation.

Along with this growth in complexity, the entire logistical function began to be treated in a more scientific way. It became necessary to develop a data base for implementing inventory-control systems. Other applications of the computer to logistical and transportation problems required more rigorous and analytical thinking on the part of management. This requirement created a need for more aggressive logistical planning.

A third impetus toward increased logistical planning grew out of the increasing cost of fixed facilities utilized to perform the logistical function. As construction and wage costs mounted, the impact of logistical costs became more obvious. These factors, combined with an over-all profit squeeze on U.S. business during the latter part of the 1960s, shifted the perspective of management toward anticipation and planning for logistical requirements.

Types of Logistical Planning

In Table 13-1 various levels of logistical planning are defined and outlined. As is the case in any classification scheme, it undoubtedly does not cover all contingencies or every planning requirement confronted by logistical managers. The classification scheme divides the planning function of logistics into three basic categories: (1) strategic, (2) tactical, and (3) operational. The basic criteria for delineation are the time duration and the likelihood that the anticipated event will occur.

In tactical and operational planning, the effect of any management decision is likely to be of short duration. Strategic planning typically requires a significant commitment of corporate resources. It is anticipated that strategic planning will alter significantly the method of conducting operations over the long run.

The second dimension of classifying plans is based upon the future likelihood of an event occurring. Strategic plans have a high element of probability that the event anticipated will not materialize. Operational and tactical plans, in contrast, have a much higher potential of materialization during the planning period. Relatively speaking, as the planning horizon is extended from the immediate future to 5 or 10 years hence, the degree of certainty concerning conclusions diminishes.

TABLE 13-1
Typology of Logistical Planning*

Classification	Subtypes	Example	Definition
Strategic planning	Long-range Project	Distribution system for 1980 Phasing in a corporate regional warehouse system	A process for dealing with allocation of distribution resources over an extended time frame which is consistent and supportive of over-all corporate policy and objectives.
Operational planning	Automatic Periodic	Add new item to inventory control system Yearly distribution budget	A process for developing distribution policy and objectives to handle routine or regularly anticipated management action in an ongoing distribution organization
Tactical planning	Special marketing support Nonstandard support requirements	Distribution support for new product introduction Maintaining distribution service levels during severe snowstorm	A process for developing short-range plans for optimum adjustment of distribution resources to irregular or unanticipated corporate, competitive, or environmental conditions

* *Source:* Bernard J. LaLonde, "Technique and Procedure for Developing the Strategic Plan," *Proceedings NCPDM Fall Meeting,* Chicago, 1970, p. 54.

The strategic planning aspect of logistical management is concerned with system design. This aspect of logistics was covered in detail in Part Three. Operational and tactical planning is part of the day-to-day management function in logistics, which deals with contingency preparation and short-term operational adjustment.[2] Thus operational and tactical planning considerations are treated throughout Part Four. The main subject of concern at this point is operational planning.

[2] *Ibid.*

Operational Planning

Operational planning is of critical importance, because managerial talent is always in short supply. This deficiency is expected to become more acute in the future. Therefore, top and middle management cannot afford the luxury of becoming fire fighters bogged down in operational detail. One important technique for directing the efforts of an organization is the operational plan.

The operational plan for logistical administration is short-range to the extent that it covers projected operations for months rather than years. The exact period of time covered will normally not exceed a single fiscal year. The operational plan covers a segment of over-all system implementation programs. The reader will recall that the system implementation strategy was the result of system design research outlined in Chapter 11.[3] Given a system implementation strategy (long-range), operational plans (short-range) must be developed to direct day-to-day work efforts. Long-range implementational strategies represent a set of guideposts for short-range operational planning. The operational plan details expected accomplishments during a specified time period. Such accomplishments concern (1) facility adjustments and (2) performance.

ACTIVITY CENTER ADJUSTMENT.   During any period, several adjustments in operating structure may be planned for implementation. For example, a firm may have a long-range system-implementational strategy calling for the consolidation of 25 warehouses into 10 regional distribution centers. The full implementational program may cover a number of years and will therefore embrace several operational plans. The initial operating plan may call for a commitment to build or lease two of the regional facilities and to close a selected number of existing warehouses as a result of new customer service policies. Future operational plans may provide for the initial occupancy and use of these first two regional distribution warehouses, the commitment to building additional facilities, and the closing of other outdated warehouses scheduled for elimination. Logistical system redesigns encompass a number of years, and consecutive operational plans will contain elements of the over-all implemental strategy.

In consideration of activity center adjustments included in operational plans, two factors must be clearly understood. First, budget allocations must isolate the expense of the initial setup as well as once-and-for-all savings separate from day-to-day operational expenditures. Second, special efforts required to maintain customer service commitments during the period of activity center readjustment must be adequately programmed. Each of these expenditures is a function of the long-range program for implementation of a new system rather than the operation of an existing system. As such, the

[3] Page 359.

expenditures are not expected to prevail between consecutive operational planning periods. Unless such one-time expenditures are isolated, the capability of comparative analysis of operational results from one period to the next is diluted.

The operational plan must provide for scheduled adjustments in activity centers. It contains an allocation of resources to accomplish the expected results and specifies a responsibility to achieve desired adjustments within the operational period.

PERFORMANCE. The bulk of the operational plan consists of a statement of management objectives for day-to-day operations and a commitment of resources to meet stated goals. Customer service objectives are outlined in detail. Thus the goals are clearly stated for the total system. Each segment of the system is assigned specific responsibilities in terms of customer support, product-line storage, and response time to meet marketing requirements. Such assignments are based upon a combination of forecasting and managerial judgment regarding future requirements. To meet these specified responsibilities, allocations of capital are made to each control unit in the total system.

Thus the total operational plan provides the structure for meeting the logistical objectives. It assigns specific responsibilities regarding activity center adjustments and performance and allocates authorized resources. As such, the total logistical effort is synchronized through the operational plan.

Development of the Operational Plan

The operational plan can be developed in many different ways. Following is one approach to development.

ESTABLISHMENT OF PLANNING PERIOD GOALS. The goals specified for any planning period must be formulated at a top management level. These goals should result from extensive system design studies. As before indicated, they relate to (1) system activity center adjustments and (2) day-to-day performance. Each category of goals for a specified operating period must be clearly stated.

ESTIMATES OF EXPENDITURE. Given a statement of goals, the next step in the planning process is to estimate required expenditures needed to accomplish desired objectives. A typical procedure is to request budgets from individual management units. Thus, line management, given a statement of objectives, is asked to formulate a request for operational funds. The budgets, once requested, constitute each manager's financial estimates to achieve goals.

The review of individual budget requests is the critical juncture of logistical administration. Top management should be concerned with the total performance of the system and not any one of the individual parts. Development of an integrated system provides top management with an estimate of the total dollars required to meet specified system objectives. The planning process at this point becomes one of reconciling individual budget requests with total system resources.[4]

Budget desires of individual managers will almost always exceed funds required to assure good performance. This can be expected because no single unit manager is in a position to view the total system. A tendency also exists to view performance in any activity center on a unit cost basis. This bias in unit cost budgeting often forces uneconomic performance in one area without full evaluation of interrelationships to other areas. A traffic manager, concerned with unit cost, will tend toward low-cost transport selection, which he may be able to achieve only by delay of shipments.

The reader may ask: Why are individual managers asked to formulate budget requests if we anticipate such deficiencies? The answer is twofold. First, it is essential that the individual manager participate in budget formation in order to gain a complete understanding of the integrated nature of total system programming. Budget formation is one of the most potent training tools available to top management. Second, individual unit managers are often aware of factors that must be considered in a specific operational plan and that have not come to the attention of top management. The greatest danger of total system planning is to develop a top-management complacency concerning the continued validity of the long-range implementation strategy. Cross participation between individual control-center managers and top management is essential to the development of a realistic but demanding operational plan.

THE FINAL PLAN.   The final operational plan provides a blueprint to guide short-range performance. The plan should be in written format and contain a statement of objectives plus detailed cost budgets for each operational unit. It will focus on total system performance and objectives. The total budget package should be designed to combine all relevant cost centers into a single unified plan. By this method each management specialist will be more likely to aim for his budget performance goal on an over-all cost basis, because cost increases or decreases in one function are no longer relevant. It is the over-all cost performance that counts. This concept of total accountability is one of the essential aspects of management by objectives. For the total system to accomplish the highest possible performance, all managers must assume correlative responsibility for everyone else's job.

PLAN MODIFICATION.   Once the final plan is developed, printed, and distributed, some aspect or element of the plan can be anticipated to be in need of modification. Thus tactical adjustments to the operational plan will be required throughout the total planning period. Such modification results from planning errors and from the need tactically to adjust to unanticipated events.

Because the individual manager has participated in development of the

[4] For more detail, see page 450.

integrated plan, he will be aware of the impact of his decisions upon other functional areas. In his day-to-day operations, he may also become aware of environmental changes that may adversely or favorably affect corporate distribution activities. Thus a change in freight rates, packaging, material handling, and so on may come to the attention of an individual manager. As these changes occur, the individual manager is in a position to engage in planning and to recommend adjustments in the current operational plan.

Significant modifications to operational plans are encouraged, because results are obtained by exploiting timely opportunities. However, two rules must be followed in all such modifications. First, tactical modifications must be formally requested prior to any deviation from planned operations. Second, it follows that all such modifications must be evaluated in terms of total system performance. Once proposed modifications are adopted, formal written amendments to the operational plan should be distributed to all managers engaged in logistical administration.

CONTROL.   The operational plan provides the measurement base for over-all control of logistical operations. The purpose of a control system is to assure that resources are devoted and monitored in application to achieve managerial objectives. Because of the fundamental importance of control to the administration of logistical operations, the totality of Chapter 14 is devoted to this subject.

Summary—Operational Planning

Management by objectives is dependent upon the development of a sound operational plan. The approved plan becomes the basis for performance measurement during the operating period. The process of developing an operational plan is time-consuming and tedious. The problem is complicated by the need to view the total system on an integrated basis. Such integration often requires information beyond that normally available from a firm's standard costing or accounting systems.

Special emphasis should be made between the relationship of operational planning and total system implementation programs. The process of logistical system design results in an implementational program. Reference to Figure 11-1 highlights that the system design responsibility is a continuous process.[5] A feedback loop exists between the development of an implementational program and the distribution audit. This feedback loop exists to allow for the advent of change upon system design. The need for such change is more often than not initially detected through the operational plan.

As noted earlier, consecutive operating plans represent short-range elements of longer-term system implementational strategy. Therefore, logistical system design and administration are unified through the relationship between operational plans and implemental strategies. Attention is now directed to logistical organization.

[5] Page 344.

Organization

Management is simply defined as the process of getting things done through others employed by the enterprise. Thus an integral part of all forms of management is the motivation of personnel. As one corporate president recently stated,

> There are three possible relationships between a superior and a subordinate. The first is "you do," wherein the subordinate is able to perform his operational assignment with little, if any, supervision according to the plan. The second is "we do," wherein the superior is called upon to assist a subordinate in execution of his responsibilities. The third is "I do," wherein the superior is forced to usurp the authority delegated to the subordinate in the best interest of corporate performance. *Simply stated, if I do, I don't need you.*[6]

The fundamental responsibility of top management is to create an environment wherein each operating manager is provided maximum opportunity to fully perform to the best interest of attaining corporate objectives. To this end organization structure is one vital part of management.

Responsibility for logistical management has traditionally been fragmented throughout the organizational structure. One basic premise underlying the integrated logistical concept is that organizational fragmentation of responsibility is highly vulnerable to duplication, waste, and, at times, outright hindrance of mission accomplishment. The fundamental weakness of fragmented organization is that communication flows become distorted and lines of authority and responsibility become blurred.

Organizational structuring of logistics as a separate integrated function is relatively new. The fact that logistical functions have always been performed within industry has created a great deal of controversy over whether or not a unified organizational group is necessary or even desirable. The objective of this section is to provide an overview of logistical organizational practices. Initially, an evolutionary approach to logistical unification is described which reflects patterns that are commonly observed and that appear to be merging in organizational revamping. Next, several perspicuous and persistent issues in organizational structure are discussed.

Two comments are in order concerning the manner in which organization structure is developed within this chapter. First, in recognition that organization of any function within an enterprise is a highly customized activity, no attempt is made to present a number of individual firms' organization charts as representative models.[7] No model fits all structures. Rather, emphasis is based upon the logic of unified grouping of logistical functions based upon

---

[6] Unpublished speech by Robert J. Franco, Michigan State University Physical Distribution Executive Development Seminar, June 1972.

[7] Numerous examples can be found in professional journals in the logistics field.

the maturity level of integrated logistics within an enterprise. Accordingly, three stages or types of organizations are discussed as development points along a unification continuum. The applicability of the general comments presented will vary greatly depending upon individual firms' requirements.

A second noteworthy point is that widely acknowledged principles of management are not discussed in this section. These principles apply to all forms of organization and represent a valuable guideline for managers concerned with designing a structure. Because they are widely published and discussed in detail in all basic management textbooks, no elaboration is justified in this specialized treatment.

Organizational Evolution

If one is willing to accept the premise that top management in general is not prone to revolutionary change, the notion follows that unified logistical organization must evolve over time. As noted repeatedly, all functions engaged in logistics have always been performed within successful enterprises. It is only natural that resistance is experienced when an attempt is made to relocate management authority and responsibility deeply seated in existing organizational units. As more than one logistical manager can testify, attempts at rapid or instantaneous reorganization are often met with rivalry and mistrust as well as charges of empire building. The nature of management organization is that budgets flow with operational functions. Likewise, power and visibility result from large budgets. Therefore, the process of logistical reorganization can be expected to be evolutionary in all but a few exceptional situations and will be preceded by substantial educational effort in all situations.

TYPE I ORGANIZATION.   Unified organization is not a prerequisite to improved logistical efficiency. Neither is it a guarantee that over-all performance will automatically become more efficient and/or effective. The first condition that must exist within an enterprise is recognition that over-all logistical performance can be improved by integrated coordination of all parts of the system. To flatly state that unified organization is essential to achieve widespread recognition and cooperation has the fallacy of placing emphasis on structure at the possible sacrifice of end results.

The first type of organization that reflects any degree of functional unification will normally emerge only after the basic concept and potential of logistics has gained management visibility. The typical pattern is for two or more traditional logistics functions to be grouped together without any significant change in positioning within the organizational hierarchy. Such grouping may initially occur at the staff or line level of organization. In most cases the first stage of unified organization will consist of grouping established units of the organization. Seldom will organizational units engaged in what has been defined as material management and physical distribution management be joined together at this initial level of unification. Finally, seldom will the initial groupings make organizational provisions for separate and distinct management of the product allocation system.

Figure 13-2 provides a typical traditional organizational structure with dispersed logistical related functions. Only those functions involved in logistical operations are highlighted by the hypothetical organization chart. It should be noted that several logistical functions that will be introduced at a later stage do not exist in the traditional organization structure displayed in Figure 13-2.

Figure 13-3 illustrates the first type of unified organization that is likely to emerge. Although totally separated, physical distribution and/or material management are identified as areas of functional control and selected activities are grouped under these new control centers. No definite studies are available concerning what specific functions are initially unified and whether or not

FIGURE 13-2
Traditional Organizational Structure of Logistical Related Functions

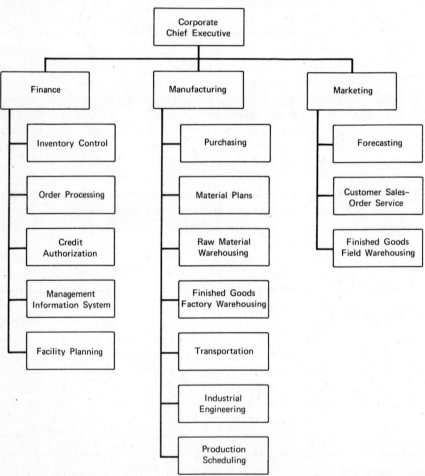

FIGURE 13-3
Type I Logistical Organization

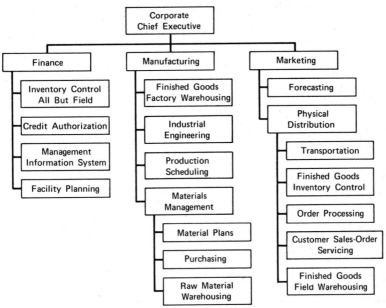

both physical distribution and material management emerge separately as control areas at stage I development.

The point is that as recognition of integrated logistics develops within an enterprise, two clusters of unified operations are likely to emerge. In the marketing area, the cluster will center around customer servicing. In the manufacturing area, the center of concentration will be material and parts procurement. However, with some minor exceptions, no traditional functional departments will normally be repositioned nor will the level of the newly created organizations be significantly altered. For the most part, organizational change of the type I variety consists of regrouping within the traditional areas of marketing and manufacturing.

TYPE II ORGANIZATION.   As the over-all enterprise gains operational experience with unified logistics and the cost benefit of the approach becomes apparent, a second stage of reorganization may be applicable. Figure 13-4 illustrates a type II organization posture.

The significant point in the second stage of development is that the logistical area is isolated and elevated to a position of authority and responsibility equal to that of other major areas of the enterprise. The most likely candidate to achieve independent status is physical distribution. The reason is simply one of visibility as a result of improved customer service performance. Material management will, in all probability, increase operational authority and responsibility. However, as a unified group the chances are it will remain nested under manufacturing.

In order to realize type II organization, it is necessary to reallocate functions and to provide the newly created organization with an independent position at some level within the over-all enterprise structure. It is interesting to note that the logistical coordinational functions—management information system, production scheduling, and forecasting—are the most likely holdouts at this stage of unification. In addition, because of a predominance of concern with material handling internal to manufacturing operations, the chances are that industrial engineering will not be reassigned to logistical operations. It is during the second stage of organizational evolution that system planning emerges as a new logistical function.

It is significant to point out that the notion of fully integrated logistics is still secondary to the separate fields of physical distribution and material management in the type II organization. This failure to synthesize all movement management into an integrated system approach results in part from a preoccupation with specific tasks, such as order processing and purchasing, which are essential to continued operations. A second limiting factor to total

FIGURE 13-4
Type II Logistical Organization

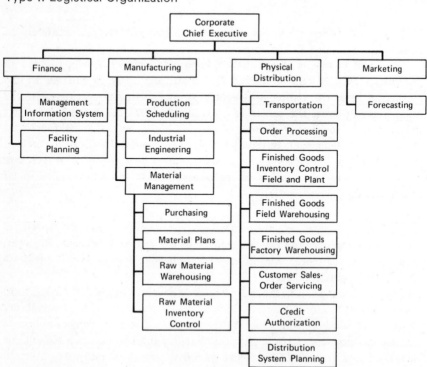

unification is the failure at this stage of development to have a fully operational logistical information system. Based on the findings of an in-depth survey of 14 companies in 1972, it would appear that most firms with a high degree of expertise in logistics currently have organizations roughly equivalent to what is here classified as type II organization,[8] the main exception being that independent status from the traditional functional organization has usually not been achieved.

TYPE III ORGANIZATION.   The third type of organization involves complete unification of all logistical functions and activities into a single management structure. At this point in reorganization, the concept of logistical management as developed throughout this book emerges as a fully integrated system. Type III organizations do not exist today in the comprehensive nature illustrated in Figure 13-5. However, the trend in organization grouping is clearly moving toward the unification of as many logistical planning and operational functions as practical under single authority and responsibility. The goal is to manage all material and finished product movement to the maximum benefit of the enterprise.

The rapid development of logistical information systems is one reason why the potential of the type III organization is emerging. The information technology is currently available to plan and operate systems that fully integrate logistical performance. Several features of the type III organization are noteworthy. The structure illustrated in Figure 13-5 will be discussed from bottom to top.

First, each performance system of over-all logistics is structured as a separate line operation. The lines of authority and responsibility are, therefore, clear concerning each major task to be performed within the over-all logistical effort. Because of the clear areas of operational concern, it is possible to establish product allocation as an operational unit similar to material management and physical distribution. Each of the three units is operationally self-sufficient. Therefore, each is able to maintain the flexibility necessary to accommodate differences in the peculiar nature of their respective operational areas. In addition, since all logistical activities are planned and coordinated on an integrated basis, the similarities among operational areas can be exploited.

Second, four component areas of over-all logistics are represented at the operational planning level. This facilitates total integration of the logistical system. Care is taken not to describe the operational planning level as a staff group. Rather, the operational planning group is involved in day-to-day management with direct liaison with their respective groups assigned to material management, physical distribution, or product allocation.

Third, at the processing and coordination level, the full impact of the logistical total information system can be deployed throughout planning operations

---

[8] Michael Schiff, *Accounting and Control in Physical Distribution Management* (Chicago: National Council of Physical Distribution Management, 1972), Chap. 2.

FIGURE 13-5
Type III Logistical Organization

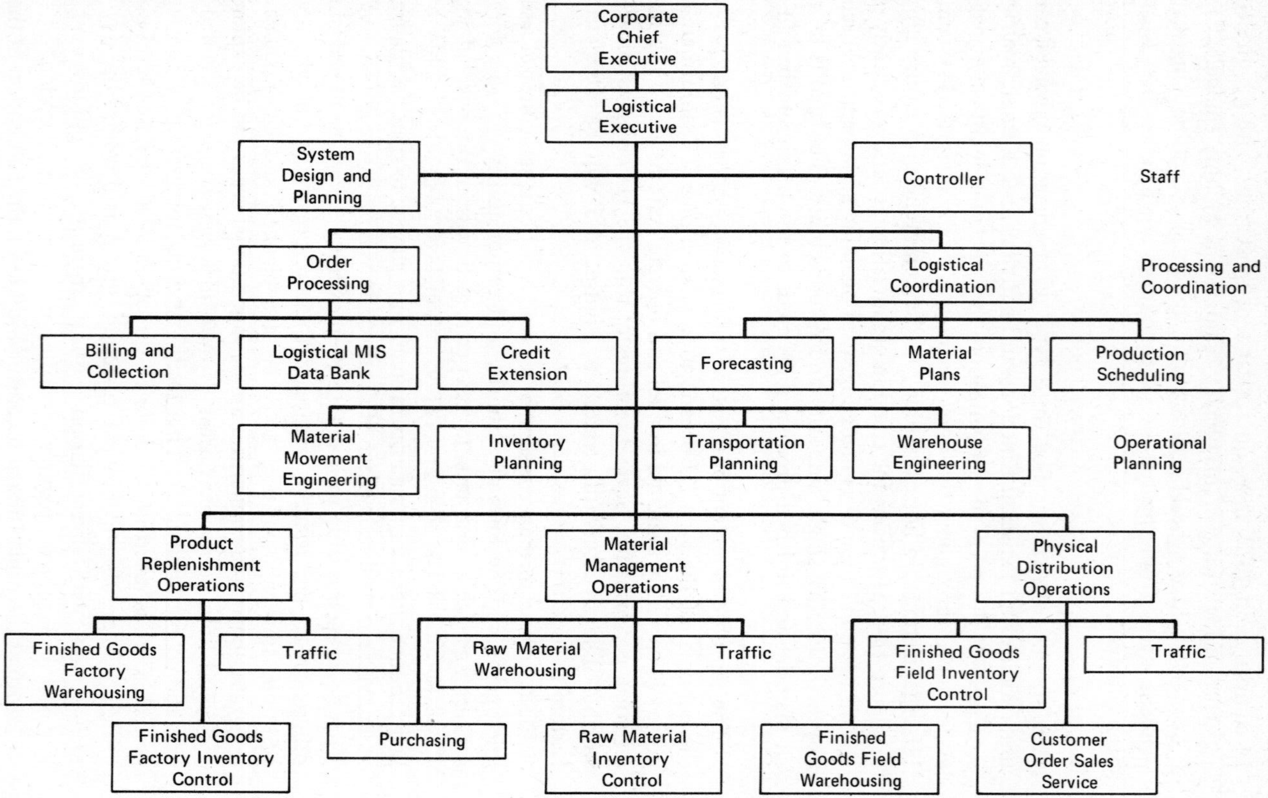

and line operations. Order processing triggers the logistical system into operation and generates the data bank for controlling all phases of the operation. The logistical coordination group integrates forecasting, production scheduling, and development of the material plan to guide logistical operations performed in anticipation of future sales.

Finally, total system planning and controllership exist at the last, or highest, level of the type III organization. These two groups represent staff services for the integrated organization. The logistical systems planning group is primarily concerned with longer-range planning of the strategic variety. Therefore, this group is primarily concerned with logistical system design.

The controller, as a logistical staff group, is becoming common in type II organizations.[9] The purpose of the controller is to measure performance of the logistical operation and to provide data for managerial decision making. For the most part, this function originated because of the inability of the standard corporate financial reporting group to provide functional logistical costs. Although he will continue to provide functional cost data in the future, the controller's role in logistical operations should properly extend to all forms of decision making throughout the unified organization. Controllership is the subject of Chapter 14.

CONCLUSION. There is every reason to predict that logistical organization will continue to move toward greater unification. The next logical step is to unify management control over all movement in the organization except movement within the plant. The process of unification is evolutionary. It will transpire as long as the payoffs are substantial. While the type III organization posture represents a look into the future, some progressive firms are actively studying the fully integrated organizational concept. Although organization is not a substitute for matured management, proper organization can increase the effectiveness of a sound managerial approach.

Perspicuous and Persistent Issues in Organization

The subject of organizational structure always raises a number of issues in the mind of the corporate manager. These issues are classified as perspicuous and persistent because they are both easy to identify and difficult to solve. In this section the following four organization issues are discussed: (1) centralization and decentralization, (2) line and staff, (3) conglomerate structures, and (4) organizational positioning.

CENTRALIZED VERSUS DECENTRALIZED STRUCTURE. The distinction between centralization and decentralization in organization structure is based upon the degree of authority and profit responsibility vested in specific operating units.

[9] *Ibid.*

Within a corporation, units or divisions would be considered highly decentralized if each were able to function on an almost autonomous basis. In a fully decentralized organizational structure, each division would be responsible for providing its own logistical requirements.

Current trends in logistical organization are highly supportive of centralized positioning. The development of logistical information systems no longer requires decentralization in order to provide high performance levels. Second, the high cost of logistical facilities and equipment is prohibitive to duplication between divisions. Therefore, while logistical centralization may run contrary to developments in other functional areas of the corporation, it appears in the best interest of efficient performance to make provisions to realize the inherent benefits of centralized operations.

LINE AND STAFF. Business managers have been attempting to reconcile the real difference between line and staff responsibilities since almost the advent of business organization. The traditional distinction is that line performs the operational tasks while staff is concerned with planning. As suggested earlier under the discussion of the emerging type III organizations, this traditional distinction may no longer be valid. Today, all managers are involved to a significant degree in both operations and planning. What could be defined as a line function one day may very well be a staff function the next, depending upon the nature and urgency of the task. It would appear that the impact of total information management upon logistics is beginning to remove the traditional staff–line classification. The two types of groups are being merged together into a managerial resource base dedicated to maximum integration of the logistical operating system.

CONGLOMERATE STRUCTURES. During the mid to late 1960s, a great many firms developed what amounts to a conglomerate structure as a result of acquiring control and ownership over other business enterprises. Unlike earlier mergers, the conglomerate approach preserved the organizational integrity of each firm and allowed it to operate on a decentralized basis. Whereas the earlier discussion dealt with centralization versus decentralization within a single corporate structure, the conglomerate issue involves several different corporations jointly owned.

A pressing question in corporate planning for the 1970s is whether or not selected operating areas of separate corporations in a conglomerate should be consolidated. For example, the idea of forming a separate service company to provide integrated logistics for all firms within the conglomerate as a profit-making distributive organization is one such consideration. The idea is that the potential cost saving from consolidation would be sufficient to reduce each individual corporation's existing logistical expense with additional savings to show a substantial return on investment for the service company.

When one considers that several major corporations have, on a combined basis, total annual logistical operating costs in excess of $100 million, the service corporation concept would appear to have potential. To date, a few initial steps have been taken along the lines of service company development. If a trend materializes, even the organizational approach outlined as type III (Figure 13-5) would not be sufficiently comprehensive to provide multi-corporation logistical service operations.

ORGANIZATIONAL POSITIONING. Organizational unification has had the net impact of improving the relative position of logistical management in over-all corporate structure. Whereas 20 years ago executives with any form of logistically related title were nearly impossible to locate, functional vice presidents are common today.

In general, the logistical function has not yet achieved the organizational status that would place it on an equal footing with marketing, manufacturing, and finance. In most organizations the stage of organizational evolution is between type I and type II structures. A recent study of the positioning of the physical distribution (P.D.) function concluded that

1. P.D. has received significant status in the corporate organization.
2. What has been disclosed in the field study probably reflects a stage of development that will lead to the identification of P.D. as equal to the traditional functional areas.
3. In the course of the process of development, a high level of effectiveness in the management of the P.D. function has been achieved whatever its positioning in the organization, principally as a result of the abilities and personal qualities of the P.D. manager. Perhaps in these cases his success stems from the fact that he functions in his role as if he were, indeed, on a par with other functional areas.[10]

Although the trend cannot be questioned, development of the concept of integrated logistical management to the point where it is generally independent and functionally positioned in top management can be realized only over an extended period of time.

Summary

Logistical administration consists of operational planning and control. Administration in the logistical organization should be guided from an approach of management by objectives. The operational planning approach should be designed to result in a clear statement of objectives. The control process provides a measure of accomplishment.

Logistical organization is an evolutionary process. Responsibility and authority for logistical performance has traditionally been fragmented. Definite

[10] *Ibid.*, pp. 1–7.

trends have developed over the past decade toward unification of logistical functions under a single management. This trend has not evolved to the point where logistics has gained equal stature with manufacturing, marketing, and finance, but the gap is closing. There is every reason to project that in the future logistical organizational structures will continue to gain independence from traditional functional areas of management and achieve top management positioning.

Questions

1. Describe the concept of management by objectives. Is this limited to logistics in its application?
2. Describe the differences among strategic, tactical, and operational planning.
3. What types of factors or activities would be included in a typical operational plan?
4. Describe the role of a system activity center adjustment in an operational plan.
5. Is it a good practice to modify operational plans once established?
6. Is the organization of all logistical activities into a single management unit essential to the achievement of efficient operations?
7. What is a type I organization?
8. Why is it common for physical distribution and material management to develop as separate entities in a firm? Is this bad?
9. Describe a type II organization and distinguish it from type I.
10. Why is it logical that forecasting will remain with marketing after physical distribution becomes a unified organization?
11. What is the major distinguishing difference of a type III compared with a type II organization? Describe the role performed by the logistical controller.
12. Among the perspicuous and persistent issues in an organization, why does centralization versus decentralization remain a constant issue? Why does logistical operation favor centralized operation?

14

Logistical
Controllership

This final chapter is concerned with logistical control. Control is the administrative process whereby logistical costs and services are maintained as planned. The operational plan provides the measurement base for logistical control. The purpose of a control system is to assure that resources devoted to logistics satisfy managerial objectives.

This chapter is developed in three sections. First, the nature of the control process is reviewed. The second section deals with specifics of cost control. The final section is devoted to the measurement of service performance.

Nature of the Control Process

Control of a logistical system should always be relative to the operational plan. Without an operational plan, it is difficult, if not impossible, to measure performance. For example, in the retail field it is not unusual to purchase Christmas toys in early spring in order to realize special discounts and allowances. From a control viewpoint, such practices, although justified on a total cost basis, may result in significant temporary increases in logistical costs

437

far in advance of the normal season. Such cost expenditures, when viewed in terms of the operational plan, cause little more than advanced planning for cash flow. When viewed without the benefit of an operational plan, early expenditure for advanced physical distribution of Christmas merchandise could appear as an uncontrolled cost trend.

The basic concept of logistical control should be one of management by exceptions. The comprehensive and detailed nature of logistics requires that management review be limited to deviations from anticipated results. However, few managers are willing to sit back and wait for an exception to appear. The exception, by its very nature, is proof that a problem exists. Although solving such problems is a vital aspect of management, something more is needed. The something extra is a mechanism for system monitoring. The monitoring network exists for the purpose of reassuring management that the total system is tracking along the course desired. A deficiency noted from system monitoring should call for a diagnostic evaluation of causal factors. The advent of a significant exception means that a trend leading to a major deviation was overlooked during its formation stages.

To illustrate the relationship between system monitoring and exceptions, the following is a typical example from inventory management. Dollars allocated to an open-to-buy program at a given point in a planning period may be near exhaustion. At the same time a critical item may be approaching a reorder point. Placement of the required order size as indicated by economic order quantity formulations could very well result in a commitment over and above authorized expenditures. One might assume that the individual merchandise controller would bring this situation to management's attention. If so, appropriate adjustments could be made.

However, if the original open-to-buy program was sufficient to cover needs, the current deficiency of funds resulted from a past purchase decision made by the same contoller in which he improperly allocated dollars. Therefore, resort to management means that the controller needs help to rectify his error. Unfortunately, too few individuals feel free to place themselves under open management scrutiny. This common fallacy of human nature is likely to cause the controller to gamble. In essence, he gambles that existing stock on the critical item will last until new funds are authorized, at which time he plans to place a rush order. In reality he gambles a major segment of a firm's customer service policy by running a risk that a critical item will go out of stock. Given their opportunity, management might well select the choice of adding dollars to the open-to-buy program, overrunning the risk of an out-of-stock situation. The problem is that unless the firm enjoys a comprehensive monitoring system, management may never get the chance to express their choice until the out-of-stock situation turns up as an exception to stated policy.

In the case of inventory control, the monitoring system could be expected to signal that a critical item had reached and passed the inventory level of normal reorder without the issue of a purchase order. The inventory control manager would be expected to take appropriate action and if necessary request aid from higher management. The combined process of management is to prevent the monitored trend from becoming a full-scale exception.

From this discussion it is clear that management would rather prevent than correct exceptions. The monitoring system exists for this purpose. The exception reporting system exists to signal a breakdown within a segment of the organization that requires corrective action to prevent recurrence.

Types of Control

The control of a logistical system relates to expected level of performance and related expenditures. The over-all operational plan calls for specified accomplishments in terms of performance and expenditure relating to two types of activity: (1) logistical component adjustments and (2) over-all logistical operating performance. The control system should be capable of providing status reports concerning each type of activity.

LOGISTICAL COMPONENT CONTROL. As noted in Chapter 13, an individual operational plan may call for adjustments in the components that constitute the logistical system.[1] Such adjustments are planned, funds are authorized, and the actual implementation is placed on a time table. One function of the control system is to provide status reports concerning conformity to the agreed-upon plan. Such status or progress reports are for the purpose of anticipating problems that might occur if the implementational schedule were not met. A lag in development which cannot be prevented is often more efficiently handled if rescheduled than if overcome by the commitment of additional resources.

Reports concerning planned component adjustments are most often developed by middle management on a customized basis rather than from automated records. Care should be taken to see that such reports are provided on a regular basis and that they are sufficiently comprehensive to include all critical information. In one case of branch plant relocation, progress reports indicated that all was well. In fact, the new building was ahead of schedule. Appropriate plans were made to hire new workers. Personnel were transferred, and the product was stockpiled as scheduled in field warehouses to accommodate customers during the switchover. The undetected problem was that a new series of automated finishing machines were not meeting specifications at the plant of a long-time, reliable equipment supplier. The final result was that a national-brand appliance was for all practical purposes out of stock in the market place for well over 3 months. By the time the full problem was detected, the old facility had been closed down and the equipment sold for salvage. A deficiency in reporting placed this firm in a situation beyond the control of management. The final impact of this deficiency will not be known for some time to come, because of the serious void in market supply and its influence upon long-range market position.

[1] Page 422.

Equally important to reports concerning planned component adjustments are those that indicate unplanned changes. Although it is difficult to visualize a situation in which a plant or warehouse is added or deleted without pre-planning, inventories are subject to substantial changes over a single planning period. In general, the more variable the cost associated with a specific component, the more vulnerable is the center's unscheduled accumulation or depletion. The operational plan should specify maximum and minimum inventory levels by individual stocking location. One important aspect of total system monitoring is a current report concerning trends that could lead to unplanned modifications. Such deviations materialize over time and have a tendency to reach rather large proportions once the trend is fully developed. The causal force may stem from significant changes in sales patterns or from internally generated factors. In either case, such trends must be detected early to prevent serious readjustment problems and lags.[2]

PERFORMANCE CONTROL. Assuming that all is well with basic components, a critical need still exists for measurement of over-all logistical performance. The control system of a firm must be capable of measuring efficiency and effectiveness of performance in comparison to the operational plan.

Efficiency is a dollar measure of expenditure to get a specific job done. A specified level of expenditure is authorized in the operational plan. Management is concerned with the relationship of authorized and actual expenditures. It should be noted that efficiency as developed here is concerned with the plan and subsequent performance. No attempt is made to state that the plan is the most efficient method for accomplishing the required logistical performance. That decision and related compromises were made earlier during system design. Given a design, a level of resource allocation is structured into an operational plan. Management, from an operations control viewpoint, is concerned with the efficiency of the authorized resource expenditure.

Effectiveness is a measure of accomplishment in terms of objectives. For example, if the objective is to never be out of stock of a specific item at any location, the system would not be fully effective if a single stockout occurred. Effectiveness, then, is a measure of how well the integrated logistical system performs in terms of goals. It would be a rare system that obtained 100 per cent operating effectivenesss over the total planning period.

Measures of effectiveness and efficiency combine to provide performance controls. Effectiveness provides an indication of whether or not the desired job is getting done. Efficiency is a measure of the actual in comparison to planned cost for whatever level of performance the system is generating. For example, considering transportation expenditures, 95 per cent of all orders may be arriving on time. However, the cost for the first three intervals of the planning period may be 103 per cent of the budget. In this example, effectiveness might well be within acceptable ranges; however, management may feel that steps are necessary to select more efficient transportation.

[2] See page 285 for further development of this idea.

Levels of Control and Information Flow

The nature of system control requires that several different levels of information be developed within the corporation. As a general rule, the higher the level of management review in the organization, the more selective are the control information and the reporting. The following four levels of information are appropriate to logistical control systems: (1) direction, (2) variation, (3) decision, and (4) policy revision. At each level the information may be related to trend monitoring or exception correction.

DIRECTION.   At the level of direction, information flow and control are concerned with execution of the operational plan. A stream of transaction documents signals a need, and the action document commands that appropriate steps be taken to satisfy the need. For example, an order is received, credit is checked, the order is assigned to a warehouse and picked, packed, and shipped. Upon shipment, the customer is billed in accord with the agreed-upon terms of sale. The order receipt is a transaction document; the remainder of the activities are generated as a result of action documents.

At specified time intervals, all transaction and action documents are combined in a series of status reports. Such status reports summarize individual activities in terms of existing capabilities to meet future transaction requirements. For example, total inventory usage may be summarized by each item in the product line, and a comparison is made to current inventories. As a result of status reports, additional action documents may be issued to replenish stock on specific items.

Two important features should be kept in mind concerning information flow and control at the direction level. First, information at the direction level is concerned with the day-to-day running of the business on an individual transaction basis. Selectivity of information at the direction level is limited to review of status in accord with predetermined decision rules. In total, information flow at the direction level is concerned with execution of predetermined programs.

The second feature of information flow at the direction level is that accumulation of records formulates a data bank for all other levels of control. It is from this data bank that all reports concerning effectiveness and efficiency are generated, all trends are monitored, and all exceptions are detected. Although managerial discretion at the direction level is limited, all that follows is based upon the accuracy of information processed and generated from transactions and action documents.

VARIATION.   The variation level of control is concerned with accumulation of information which indicates that all is not going according to plan. As indicated earlier, the variation level of control ideally results in interpretation of a trend that could lead to future trouble. However, the variation may very well first appear as an exception to the desired level of performance at the direction level.

Managerial discretion concerning the allocation of resources of capabilities first comes under consideration at the variation level. The manager concerned must ascertain if the situation discovered is an isolated event or if it is symptomatic of a more serious problem. Second, the manager must determine if a solution to the problem is within the scope of his delegated authority or if it will require additional resources. Depending upon the manager's interpretation of these two questions, he will either issue corrective instructions to the direction level of operations or request assistance from the decision level.

It is important to realize that the scope of information reviewed at the variation level has been considerably reduced in comparison to the direction level. Management at the variation level is concerned with the broader issues of effectiveness and efficiency related to a series of transactions.

DECISION. Control at the decision level of management is concerned with modifications in the operational plan. In essence, situations have materialized at the direction and variation levels that require a reappraisal of the original operational plan. As the reader would expect, the assortment of information presented at the decision level will be very selective. It is significant to note that the decision level is the first control level at which a change in the operational plan is considered.

Such modifications will normally require allocation of additional resources. In accord with the format of control outlined here, the range of decision will never involve a modification of system objectives. In other words, at this level customer service standards will not be changed if performance has been deficient. Rather, a greater expenditure will be authorized as required to meet system objectives. Managerial activities at the decision level must be evaluated in terms of total system consequences. As noted earlier, decisions that modify the plan must be relayed to all managers involved in total system performance.

POLICY. Control at the policy level relates to a basic change in logistical objectives. Once again, the areas of system design and administration merge when questions of policy are confronted. The level of concern becomes corporate-wide in scope and embodies all members of the corporation. The formulation of new policies will require an evaluation of planned system design as well as the required total cost of achievement. Requests for policy revisions may originate from any point within the total corporation. Thus far, this discussion of control has centered around information generated from the logistical data base and in general around deficiencies in either logistical performance or expenditure plans. However, policy situations may be occasioned from other areas of the corporation. For example, the marketing department may desire an over-all upgrading of customer service standards.

To illustrate, assume that the current system is geared to servicing at least 90 per cent of all customers at a 95 per cent inventory availability within 60 hours of order receipt. Further, assume that the current logistical network is meeting these objectives at lowest total cost utilizing seven warehouses. However, marketing is not happy. Marketing management is of the opinion that service capability should be increased to the point where 90 per cent of all customers at 97 per cent inventory availability would receive 24-hour delivery. Top management is faced with a critical policy consideration. In accord with the steps of distribution system design, sensitivity tests are in order.

Figure 14-1 highlights results that might be isolated from such sensitivity testing. Marketing is requesting a 2 per cent improvement in inventory availability coupled with a 36-hour improvement in delivery time. To achieve these goals, the existing network warehouses would have to be expanded by 13. The simulator, through sensitivity testing, determines that 20 facilities would be the lowest-cost method for achieving the new service standards. The total cost of this expanded service capability is measured on the vertical axis of Figure 14-1 as the distance between points *A* and *B*. The total cost of meeting the new managerial service standard will be $200,000 per year greater than current expenditures. If the firm in question had a before-tax profit margin equal to 10 per cent of sales, it would be necessary to generate additional sales of $2 million to justify the added service on a break-even basis.

FIGURE 14-1
Comparative Total Cost for Seven- and Twenty-Distribution-Point Systems

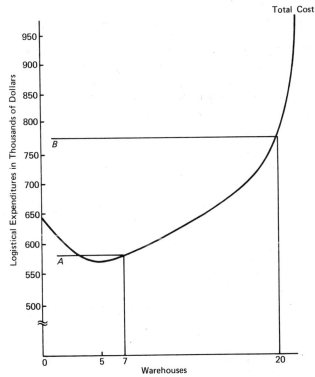

The policy decision of acceptance or rejection of the marketing proposal for increased service must rest with top management. Policy changes, once adopted, influence all other levels of logistical control. Regardless of source of origin—internal or external to the logistics sector—the formulation of new or modified policies will require a revision of implementational programs and operational plans. Once adopted, the new operational plan becomes the standard for control at the direction, variation, and decision levels of management.

Summary—Levels of Control and Information Flow

Figure 14-2 will help clarify the four levels of control involved in logistical administration. Adjacent to each level, reference is made to a corresponding organizational rank within a corporation. On the left side of the chart, a data pyramid is developed to reflect the selectivity of information considered at each level of control. As noted earlier, each level is concerned with system monitoring as well as exception reporting. However, as information flows from the direction level to the policy level, the content of subject matter increases in importance to the welfare of the total corporation.

Cost Control

Two important points have been made thus far concerning logistical costs. First, emphasis should always be placed upon total cost in the planning, decision making, and control of logistical operations. Second, the traditional accounting methods of classifying and reporting costs do not adequately serve the needs of logistical controllership. In this section traditional accounting

FIGURE 14-2
Information Flow and Levels of Control

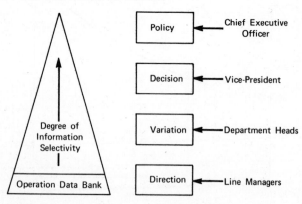

methods are briefly reviewed to illustrate where they are deficient for logistical control purposes. Next, identification of logistical costs and method of reporting are discussed. Finally, the use of budgeting for logistical control and planning is discussed. In total, the section provides the basis for logistical cost controllership.

Traditional Accounting and Logistical Cost Requirements

The main two financial reports in a business enterprise are the balance sheet and the profit-and-loss statement (P&L). The balance sheet reflects the financial position of a firm at a specific point in time. The main purpose of the balance sheet is to summarize assets and liabilities of the firm and to reflect the net worth of ownership. The P&L statement reflects the revenues and costs associated with operations over a period of time. As the name "profit and loss" denotes, the main purpose of this statement is to determine the degree to which operations over the selected period have been financially successful. Logistical operations influence and are an integral part of both statements. However, from the point of logistical control, the primary concern is the method by which costs are identified, classified, and reported in the P&L statement.

Traditionally, the accountant has been concerned with the preparation of P&L statements that are more or less standardized and follow what are considered to be generally accepted accounting principles. It is a financial requirement that all major firms, as well as any firm having investors, be regularly audited to assure that accounting practices are standardized and sound. What has resulted over the years is a standard method of reporting that is designed to meet the requirements of investors and the internal revenue of federal, state, and local governments. Unfortunately, the conventional methods of profit-and-loss accounting do not meet the requirements of logistical controllership.

The first problem results from the fact that the standard accounting practice is to group costs on an aggregate basis as opposed to a functional responsibility basis. For example, the practice of grouping expenses incurred in the conduct of operations into such accounts as salaries, rent, utilities, depreciation, and so on, does not identify with sufficient detail organizational responsibility. To overcome this deficiency, it is common for the over-all P&L statement to be subdivided by internal areas of the enterprise so as to achieve a more adequate measure of each unit's contribution. This process of division helps but does not completely solve the problems of logistical controllership.

The standard practice for generation of internal P&L statements is to group costs along organizational and budgetary lines. Thus, while costs are provided at a more detailed level of refinement than on a total enterprise basis, they become identified by organizational units. The fact that few, if any, logistical operations are totally unified into a single organizational unit illustrates the deficiency of this method of subdividing.

The classification of costs on a natural basis also represents a problem for logistical controllership. In order effectively to control logistical operations, it is necessary to get a handle on costs associated with performing specific tasks. This means that the logistical functions must be identified and costs associated with the performance of each assigned. The data are available in most accounting systems to realize logistical functional groups. Schiff clearly reflects this deficiency in the following paragraph:

What is of primary concern . . . is the suitability of P.D. cost reporting for internal use, and failure to identify these costs and classify them as operating expenses can only suggest that management and accountants do not think these costs are important enough to warrant the attention and concern of the receiver of the report or that they can be influenced by the manager to whom the report is addressed. It is difficult to find a logical basis for this position. The costs are identified and assembled in accounts and in all cases they are of significant dollar value to warrant identification. It would take a minimum of effort and re-education to alter the classification wherein freight and other distribution costs would be identified as operating expenses and thus more closely relate responsibility with reported results.[3]

As an over-all appraisal, a great deal more logistical functional costing is taking place today then ever in the past. However, a great deal more managerial attention and research are needed before standardized practices of logistical cost accounting will be universally practiced.

A third deficiency of traditional accounting concerns methods of handling and reporting transportation expenditures. A standard practice is to deduct freight from gross sales in much the same way as discounts and returns are handled to arrive at a net sales figure. This practice has evolved over the years and is firmly entrenched in accounting practices. In part, the practice seems to be based on the belief that freight is a necessary evil about which management can do very little. Once again, Schiff makes the salient point:

It would appear that the practice of deducting freight costs from sales imputes such characteristics (namely a taxlike quality) to freight costs and suggests the inability of the company to influence the cost. But freight costs *can* be influenced by the shipper in many ways. . . . the fact that rates are basically governed by a public agency or a contract does not restrict a company from influencing the total cost by the decision it makes in how it utilizes the service paid for by a pre-determined rate, or by the alternative it chooses. There is, therefore, no justification for deducting freight costs from sales to arrive at net sales. Apart from its lack of rationality, reporting net sales as a basis for analysis precludes responsibility reporting for this large cost and with it any possibility for control. Despite efforts and successes by Traffic Managers in minimizing freight costs, those responsible for creating demand for freight service are free from any

[3] Michael Schiff, *Accounting and Control in Physical Distribution Management* (Chicago: National Council of Physical Distribution Management, 1972), pp. 1–10.

responsibility for its incurrence since they are measured by net sales and costs related to net sales.[4]

The problem extends beyond where freight is reported. In many purchasing situations, freight is not reported at all. Rather, products are purchased on a delivered basis and transportation costs are buried in the cost of merchandise or material. In order to gain functional control over logistical operations, these practices must be rectified.

A final commentary on traditional accounting practice is the normal failure distinctly to identify the cost of inventory maintenance over an operating period. This deficiency has two aspects. First, costs, such as insurance and taxes, associated with the maintenance of inventory are not clearly identified so as to focus attention upon the importance of this expense. Second, the cost impact of capital invested in inventory is not normally measured and separated from other forms of interest expense occurred by the enterprise. In fact, if internal financing is used by the firm as opposed to borrowing in the money market, no capital cost at all may be reflected in the traditional scheme of profit-and-loss reporting.

In summary, several modifications in traditional accounting are required to realize an effective cost base for logistical controllership. In particular, the two largest individual cost centers of logistical operations, transportation and inventory, are normally handled in a manner that results in obscure identification. Although the situation is improving, the establishment of a commonly accepted practice for isolating total functional costs associated with logistical operations is a long way from realization.

Logistical Costing

How and what costs should be identified for purposes of logistical controllership? One basic problem in logistical cost control is to arrive at agreement concerning the specific accounts to be included in a functional classification. A second aspect of effective control is to identify the time frame for accumulating costs. Finally, a decision must be reached concerning the manner in which cost data will be structured for managerial use.

Each of the above areas is highly judgmental. It should be clear from numerous examples throughout the book that the judgment exercised with respect to cost identification and grouping can substantially influence both logistical system design and operation. Therefore, the judgmental factor should be clearly reviewed at all levels of management in order to develop a realistic set of specifications.

COST IDENTIFICATION. In a general sense, all costs associated with the performance of material management, physical distribution, and logistical coördination should be included in a functional cost classification system. The total costs associated with transportation, warehousing, inventory maintenance,

4 *Ibid.*, pp. 2–3.

communication, and material movement should be isolated and functionally grouped. Total logistical cost involves three types of specific expenditures: (1) direct, (2) indirect, and (3) overhead.

Direct or operational costs are those expenses which are experienced on an out-of-pocket basis during the performance of logistical activities. Such costs are not difficult to identify once an attempt is made to develop a functional cost classification. In particular, the direct cost of transportation, warehousing, material movement, and some aspects of communication and inventory can be accumulated from traditional cost accounts. Likewise, little difficulty is experienced in isolating the administration cost directly consumed by logistical operations.

Indirect costs are more difficult to identify. These costs are experienced by the corporation on a more or less fixed basis as a result of the allocation of resources to logistical operations. For example, the cost of capital invested in real estate, transportation equipment, and inventory, to mention a few areas within the capital structure of logistics, must be reconciled to arrive at a true total cost. The degree to which imputed costs are included in total logistical cost is the main judgmental area in controllership.

All capital allocated to the logistical system represents a scarce commodity within the corporation. Therefore, all expenses paid by the corporation to support this aspect of the over-all logistical operation should be assigned to arrive at a total cost. To the degree that capital investment is internally financed out of the asset base of the corporation, a charge for deployment should be imputed and assessed to the total cost of logistics. When such charges are levied, the practice ranges from the prime interest rate to a figure that takes into consideration alternative uses of capital. The judgment applied in arriving at this standard will greatly influence logistical system design. In turn, system design greatly influences operating costs that will be experienced in logistical processing. Thus procedure and standards used in arriving at imputed logistical costs are at the very heart of controllership.

The final classification of cost important in arriving at total cost is the allocation of fair-share overhead. The enterprise, in total, encounters a great deal of expense on behalf of all functional units and as a result of the need to maintain corporate identity. A question of judgment is involved in how and to what extent this overhead should be allocated to specific cost centers. One method is fully to soak up all corporate overhead by direct assignment on a uniform basis to all functional areas. To the other extreme, some firms follow the policy of withholding all allocations so as not to distort the ability to measure direct and indirect logistical expenditures. Given these extremes, it is impossible to generalize regarding an acceptable practice. From the viewpoint of control, it would appear sound not to allocate any costs that cannot be directly influenced by logistical management practices. This way, costs can be aligned with managerial responsibility on a cause-and-effect basis.

The discussion clearly illustrates that considerable gray areas exist in determining the total cost of logistical operations. What costs are included in total cost is to a large degree a subject of management judgment. As a general practice, a cost should not be assigned unless it is managerially under the control of the logistical organization. Because of the judgmental factor involved, firms in the same industry will report vastly different total cost. It is important to realize that such cost differentials may not have any direct relationship to the actual efficiency of logistical operations.

COSTING TIME FRAME. A basic problem in costing that must be reconciled relates to the period of time over which costs are accumulated for measurement. Generally accepted accounting principles call for accrual methods, wherein an attempt is made to relate revenues and expenditures to the actual performance of sales and services. Significant timing problems are associated with just when to charge for logistical operations. From material management through physical distribution, almost all logistical operating cost is in anticipation of a future transaction.

To overcome the time problem, accountants normally attempt to break costs down into those which can be assigned to a specific product and those which are associated with the passage of time. Using this classification, an attempt is made to match appropriate product and time period costs to specific revenue generation.

From a logistical perspective, a great many of the costs associated with material management and product replenishment operations are absorbed into direct product cost. Thus, because they can be assigned on a specific product basis, the net result is that inventories can be valued on the basis of fully absorbed cost. Such practices can greatly influence the measurement of logistical operations. In situations where a considerable period of time elapses between production and sales, such as in highly seasonal businesses, the costs of logistical operations can be highly disassociated with the time of revenue generation. Unless this potential mismatch is clearly understood and budgeted for, logistical operations can be significantly mismeasured.

COST FORMATTING. Logistical costs can be presented in a number of different ways for managerial purposes. Three common ways are (1) functional groupings, (2) allocated groupings, and (3) activity level groupings. Each method is discussed.

To format costs by functional grouping merely means that for a specified operating period all expenditures for direct and indirect logistical services performed are listed by master and subaccount classifications. Thus a total cost statement is derived that can be compared from one operating period to the next. To the extent that operational planning and budgeting are employed in logistical controllership, comparisons can be made between actual and planned expenditures.

No standard format of functional cost grouping is available to fit the needs of all corporations. Similar to organizational structure, logistical functional cost statements should be designed to facilitate control within the customized situation that each firm confronts. The important points in arriving at such functional groupings are to include as many cost account categories as practical and to maintain a coding system that will facilitate classification of costs into account categories as expenditures are made.

Allocated cost formatting consists of assigning logistical expenditures to a significant measure of physical performance. For example, total logistical cost per ton, per hundredweight, per product, per order, per line item, or some other physical measure provides a basis for comparative analysis between consecutive operating periods. Such classifications formulate a basis for efficiency performance measurement.

Activity level groupings are most often useful in the analysis of costs when different types of logistical system designs or modifications are under consideration. This method of formatting consists of grouping functional costs on the basis of fixed, semifixed, and variable nature as a function of volume throughput. The primary purpose of classifying on the basis of fixed and variable costs is to approximate the magnitude of change in operating expenditure that will accompany different volumes of logistical performance.

For purposes of analysis, all cost elements that do not vary with volume are classified as fixed. In other words, in the short run, these costs would remain given zero volume throughout. All costs that are influenced by volume are classified as variable. This technique of grouping costs on the basis of activity levels was illustrated in Chapter 12 in our discussion of break-even simulation.[5] Although useful in logistical controllership, the basic concept of analyzing fixed and variable costs has inherent limitations, as noted earlier.

Logistical Budgeting

The task of cost control is framed within the period covered by the logistical operating plan. As noted in Chapter 13, the formulation of a budget that covers expenditure expectations is an integral part of the over-all plan.[6] The budget is the key to formulating a logistical cost control-program. Three basic types of budgets are commonly used in logistical controllership: (1) fixed, (2) flexible, and (3) capital. The first two are used to control direct expenditures for logistical performance. The last is used when permanent change involving any component of the logistical system is scheduled during the operating period.

FIXED DOLLAR BUDGETING. As the name implies, the fixed budget is an estimate of functional costs by account associated with an anticipated volume of logistical activity. Given a volume projection, the budgeting process attempts to arrive at the most realistic estimate of costs to be expended for the completion of logistical processing. The budget becomes a base for comparative analysis of desired performance in advance of the operational period with

[5] Page 392.
[6] Page 420.

actual performance during and after the period is completed. To a significant degree, budgeting is a management game wherein top level and operating executives attempt to arrive at joint expectations concerning desired performance. Naturally, top management desires to lower budgets, whereas operating executives desire to build in as much slack as possible. To overcome this fallacy inherent in the budgeting process, many management groups have begun to structure budgets on a line-item basis. On the line-item basis, only minimum variation is permitted in the transfer of expenditures between functional accounts unless plan modification is authorized.

FLEXIBLE BUDGETING. The flexible budget is designed to accommodate variations in volume either up or down during the operating period. Normally, the flexible budget is constructed on the basis of standard costs for performing specific logistical functions. Permissible expenditures float to the level of actual operations. Although it is a desirable method of budgeting, a high degree of cost sophistication is required effectively to use standard cost flexible budgeting.

CAPITAL BUDGETING. Capital budgeting provides a method of controlling the extent and timing of investment in logistical components. As noted earlier, during operational planning a number of different types of logistical system changes may be scheduled to be initiated or completed. The capital budget, for example, provides for the commitment of cash or credit needed to construct a new warehouse, install a new order-processing system, purchase or lease transportation equipment, or institute any other planned expenditure in basic logistical structure.

When major system changes are anticipated, no real difficulty in capital budgeting formulation is normally experienced. Although approval may be difficult to justify on a cost–benefit basis, the actual budgeting technique is straightforward. The difficult aspects of capital commitment involve expenditures for research and development, which at inception are nearly impossible to justify on a cost–benefit basis, and expenditures for creeping capital commitments.

A creeping capital commitment is one wherein the normal process of operation results in a fixed asset investment that is higher than it was previously. All functional areas of the corporation are vulnerable to such elusive capital deployments. However, logistical operations are among the most vulnerable in terms of inventory levels. If inventory plans are not rigorously controlled, a substantial capital investment that was not anticipated may result.

A final note concerns determination of those costs that are applicable to a particular capital investment decision. The accepted practice is to consider in capital budgeting only investments that require new net capital commitment. To the extent that system changes can be implemented that result in operational savings without new net commitment of cash or credit, they are not subjected to the rigid control of capital budgeting.

Summary—Cost Controllership

The development of a sound basis for performing cost controllership is one of the most critical areas of logistical administration. The task is of extreme importance, owing to the large operating and capital dollar expenditures engaged in logistics. The task is complicated by several barriers to effective costing that are well established within generally accepted accounting principles. To develop effective cost control, it is necessary to isolate functional accounts and to reconcile the impact of time upon operational expenditures. The key tool of the logistical cost controller is the combination of operating and capital budgets that regulate cash from within the logistical sector. Of equal importance is the measurement of return on net assets deployed to accomplish the logistical mission.

Service Performance Measurement

The main theme of this book has been that a logistical operating system should be designed to provide a specified level of delivery service at the lowest associated total cost. The last section dealt with controlling costs to planned expectations. This section is concerned with the controllership of delivery service within the material management, physical distribution, and product replenishment performance systems.

The measurement and control of service can be approached from a number of vantage points. The approach suggested here is based upon two specific sets of performance measurement data. The first is built around the total order cycle; the second centers on inventory availability. Each is discussed followed by a brief discussion of performance reporting. To avoid redundancy, the discussion is built around the physical distribution performance cycle. Similar examples could be provided for the product replenishment and material management performance cycles of the total logistical system.

FIGURE 14-3
Illustration Total Order Cycle Physical-Distribution Single-Echelon Example

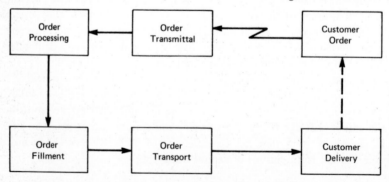

FIGURE 14-4
Time Distribution Four Elements and Total Order Cycle

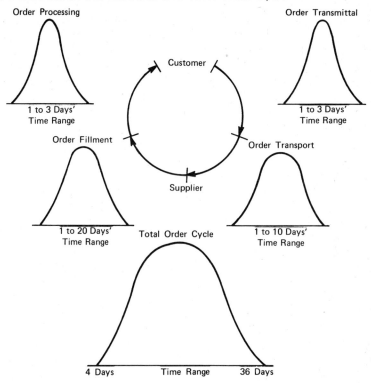

Total Order Cycle Measurement

The total order cycle consists of the time measured in days from order placement to receipt of products. In the case of physical distribution, the cycle is measured from time of order transmittal to delivery of the merchandise at the customer's designated facility. As noted in Chapter 6, the physical distribution order cycle confronts a number of types of potential uncertainties which complicate logistical performance.[7] The task of order cycle measurement is to evaluate the impact of these uncertainties upon operational effectiveness.

At the single-echelon level, the typical total order cycle consists of four time elements. They are (1) order transmittal, (2) order processing, (3) order filling, and (4) order transportation. The basic cycle is illustrated in Figure 14-3. A fifth element of time is the degree of delay experienced in the performance of any one or all four of the order cycle elements. Figure 14-4 provides an illustration of the variable time patterns that normally can be expected in each element as well as the total order cycle. It should be noted that while each form of time distribution in Figure 14-4 is illustrated as a normal statistical distribution, in actual practice other statistical patterns will be experienced.

[7] Page 185.

Using the total order cycle as a measurement framework, statistical analysis is possible concerning each element and the total service time. In Figure 14-4 an individual order can take as few as 4 days and as many as 36 days to reach the customer's delivery destination. The task of total cycle service measurement is to determine the combined impact of all elements and associated delays over time. Table 14-1 provides a review of a number of different measures that can be developed from the total order cycle framework.

The measures illustrated in Table 14-1 are in no way exhaustive of the types of measures that can be generated on a total order cycle basis. They do provide an indication of the usefulness of the order cycle as a measurement framework for service controllership.

Inventory Availability Measurement

The most critical measure of customer service is the availability of inventory to service orders. Variation in inventory, perhaps more than any other element of performance, is the cause of the failure to meet customer service standards.

A typical measure of inventory availability is the percentage of items out of stock to total items carried in stock. The fallacy in the measure is that it does not take into consideration the velocity movement of various items in the product line. For example, 10 slow-moving items may be out of stock and not create serious customer service problems with respect to inventory availability. On the other hand, one fast-moving item being out of stock could cause havoc and result in a flood of customer service complaints.

Therefore, the most desirable measures of inventory availability provide an analysis over a time period of performance. For example, orders with one item out of stock, average cases out of stock per order, average percentage availability of all items requested, back-order delay, and frequency of back orders are representative of the types of indicators that can be developed to

TABLE 14-1
Measurement of Customer Delivery Service

1. Average delivery time	A measure of total elapsed time from transmittal to delivery of a number of different customer orders.
2. Standard deviation of delivery time	A measure of delivery consistency for a number of different customer orders in terms of average expected time.
3. Distribution orders within time intervals	A measure of total orders delivered by time intervals over an operating period.
4. Per cent of orders within time intervals	Percentage of total orders delivered by time intervals over an operating period.
5. Dollar distributions	Similar to measures 3 and 4, with dollar sales being used rather than orders.

provide a comprehensive and factual measure of inventory availability and customer service performance.

Performance Reporting

The essential feature of all control systems is the quality of reports generated from the data bank. Unless available information can be presented rapidly, accurately, and on relevant subjects, little in the way of positive control will transpire. In general there are three types of reports used in a logistical control system: (1) status, (2) trend, and (3) special reports.

STATUS REPORTS. As the name implies, a status report is designed to provide detailed information about some aspect of the logistical operation. One of the most common status reports is the stock status report used in inventory management. The stock status report is normally used to keep track of multiple-item inventories at more than one stocking location. The amount of information contained on an individual report will depend upon the firm, its degree of inventory management sophistication, and the extent to which automated data processing is used. Table 14-2 provides an example of a typical inventory stock status report.

In the example, items of inventory are being controlled from one central management location for distribution warehouses located in Detroit, Chicago, Atlanta, Newark, Tacoma, and Fresno. The unit inventory of the ABC Company is being maintained on a computer using techniques of scientific inventory management. Individual items have been assigned to stock controllers, who are responsible for inventory status at all six distribution warehouses. This particular report is for a controller referred to as A.

The individual item or unit number is printed in column 1. These item numbers do not appear in numerical sequence, because only items requiring controller attention are printed. However, if an item requires action at a specific distribution warehouse, status of that item in all other warehouses is also printed on the report. Thus, when a controller directs specific action concerning an inventory item he is able to view status at all stocking locations. The location is displayed in column 2 and status is reflected in column 3. Of particular interest is the printing of required action in the status column 3. Based upon the rules of the inventory control system, the controller is informed of the reason the particular item appears on the stock status report. The remainder of the columns are for the most part self-explanatory. They provide the necessary information for the controller to direct the inventory procurement program.

Status reports exist for all logistical activity centers. Some relate to individual unit or transaction control; others are financial in nature. The purpose of the status report is to provide line managers with relevant information to fulfill their responsibility in the over-all logistical system.

TABLE 14-2
Example of a Stock Status Report

ABC Company
Distribution Warehouse
Stock Status Report

Date 3-10-74
Controller A

(1)	(2)	(3)	(4)	(5)	(6)	(7)	(8)	(9)	(10)	(11)	(12)	(13)
			Unit Inventory		Forecasted	Back	Suggested	Dollars	Inventory	Open Purchase Order Detail		
Item	Location	Status	on Hand	on Order	Av. Week Use	Order	Order Quantity	on Hand	on Order	Date Placed	Date Due	Quantity
10-326-01	Detroit	Normal	183		25			457.50				
	Chicago	Out of stock		365	40	45		0	912.50	2-15-67	2-26-67	365
	Atlanta	Expedite	29	145	15			72.50	462.50	3-1-67	3-12-67	145
	Newark	Overstock	293		30			732.50				
	Tacoma	Order	55		10		75	137.50				
	Fresno	Normal	103		23			257.50				
Totals			663	510	143	45	75	1,657.50	1,375.00			530
10-327-05	Detroit	Normal										
	Chicago	Normal										
	Atlanta	Overstock										
	Newark	Order										
	Tacoma	Order										
	Fresno	Order										
Totals												
10-365-00	Detroit	Normal										
	Chicago	Expedite										
	Atlanta	Out of stock										
	Newark	Out of stock										
	Tacoma	Expedite										
	Fresno	Expedite										
Totals												

TREND REPORTS.   Trend reports are normally used by administrators at levels of control higher than the line manager. In keeping with the flow of data outlined in Figure 14-3, trend reports are more selective in content than status reports. To illustrate, Tables 14-3 and 14-4 provide examples of trend reports that might be based upon the inventory stock status report.

Table 14-3 provides an inventory recap for all items, controllers, and stock locations. This type of report is used by department heads for review of the over-all inventory situation for the total logistical system. The data contained in the daily inventory summary are developed as a by-product of the stock status report printed for inventory controllers. Thus management is provided a quick recap of the total system and can evaluate over-all performance.

Table 14-3 provides a variety of information. General performance is available on all locations as well as individual controllers. For example, the Newark warehouse is 75 per cent in stock (column 1), 21 per cent of the items have been out of stock longer than 5 days (column 10), and 92 per cent of the orders scheduled for shipment were shipped as planned (column 12). From the viewpoint of a given individual, controller C is having problems. He is in stock on only 82 per cent of his items (column 7), 15 per cent of his items that are in stock currently require expedite efforts in order to prevent future stockouts (column 8), and the items of which he is out of stock fall heavily into the critical area of a classified merchandise (column 9).

Armed with this information, the department head is in a position to review activities and take corrective action. If desired, he can request special reports, which will provide an abundance of detail to help further analyze a possible trend. For example, the department head in this case would probably desire more detailed information concerning the Newark facility and the activities of controller C. There is virtually no end to the selective information that can be generated from a data bank of the type maintained to develop Tables 14-3 and 14-4.

Table 14-4 provides an executive summary of selected critical facts regarding inventory performance. Condensed information of the type presented in Table 14-4 would most often be used by executives at the vice-presidential or decision level of an operation (Figure 14-2). As noted earlier, it is a rare executive who is content to wait for exceptions to appear. Most executives would prefer to see the trend of performance in his areas of responsibility.

Table 14-4 covers a 4-week period. The first 3 weeks are presented in aggregate; however, the fourth week is developed on a daily basis. Reports of this nature provide the basis for evaluation of trends and are useful in selecting areas for diagnostic activity. For example, the data in Table 14-4 point out that inventory performance over the past 3 weeks has deteriorated; however, performance on the most recent days indicates that corrective action has been taken. Of particular interest in Table 14-4 is line 2, weighted performance. The weighted performance is a measure of stock availability in the quantities desired by customers. A system may enjoy a very high level of in-stock items but be out of stock of the items most wanted by customers. Measures of weighted performance will normally run lower than measures of system in-stock.

The data presented in Table 14-4 provide inventory trend information generated from the inventory stock status report (Table 14-2) and the daily inventory summary (Table 14-3). In all probability the executive receiving the performance recap would also be responsible for other logistical system activity centers. The report could be expanded to provide data on transportation, warehouse performance, order processing, material movement, and any

TABLE 14-3
Daily Inventory Summary

	(1)	*(2)*	*(3)*	*(4)*	*(5)*
	Total Items	*Per Cent*	Dollar Values Inventory		
Location	*Stocked*	*in Stock*	*In Stock*	*On Order*	*Forecasted*
Detroit	1,075	92	17,385	3,231	7,115
Chicago	1,093	91	20,265	3,695	5,940
Atlanta	1,041	88	15,197	3,780	8,201
Newark	1,073	75	18,243	9,361	11,116
Tacoma	1,075	89	23,116	5,143	4,307
Fresno	1,026	90	19,450	2,184	1,993
Total System	6,383	87.5%	$113,656	$27,394	$38,672

	(6)	*(7)*	*(8)*	*(9)*		
		Per Cent	*Per Cent*	*Out of Stock by Class*		
Controller	*Total Items*	*in Stock*	*Expedite*	*A*	*B*	*C*
A	1,250	91	10	30	40	50
B	1,300	89	09	36	71	38
C	1,100	82	15	65	47	91
D	1,275	85	09	15	81	95
E	1,458	95	08	20	70	40
Total	6,383	87.5%	10%	166	309	314

	(10)	*(11)*	*(12)*
	Items	*Items*	*Orders Shipped*
	Out of Stock + 5 Days	*Overstocked*	*on Schedule*
Detroit	12	31	96
Chicago	16	11	97
Atlanta	11	38	99
Newark	21	5	92
Tacoma	14	17	87
Fresno	19	0	94
Total	93	102	96%

TABLE 14-4
Logistical Performance Recap

Performance Area	Week C-3	Week C-2	Week C-1	Current Week by Days				
				1	2	3	4	5
1. System in-stock (%)	88.0	86.0	81.0	82.0	85.0	86.2	87.3	87.5
2. Weighted performance (%)	83.8	84.2	90.0	79.8	83.2	84.0	86.3	87.0
3. Dollars inventory	121,614	119,381	111,843	95,417	98,106	96,412	110,807	113,706
4. Shipments on schedule (%)	99	97	98	99	96	97	98	96
5. Back orders	365	691	780	193	217	238	165	101
6. Selected data								
7. Other system								
8. Activity centers								

other areas of concern. In addition, similar reports can be generated in material management and product replenishment operations. Because the information is selective and highly condensed, reports of this type can often be presented on a single page.

SPECIAL REPORTS. Special reports may be created at any level of logistical administration and for a variety of reasons. Most often special reports are developed to provide detail on specific areas of performance. These general types of special reports are commonly utilized in administration.

The first type is a diagnostic report, which provides detail concerning a specific phase of operations. For example, a report might be requested to provide greater detail regarding current back orders and corrective action that has been taken. If the firm in question operates a real-time system, special diagnostic reports may be obtained from either hard or soft copy by direct interrogation.

The second type of special report is a position paper. Given a current or anticipated problem, a report outlining alternative courses of action and expected consequences is often desirable. In terms of control levels (Figure 14-2), position papers are normally developed by line managers and department heads for use by executives at the decision level of the organization. Such position papers will often request additional resources and will, therefore, necessitate that the operational plan be modified if adopted. In accord with the levels of administrative control, position papers and related action may involve a greater allocation of resources to get a job accomplished. However, they will not involve changes in performance objectives.

The final special report is concerned with policy modification. Earlier in this chapter an example of a policy report was provided when the marketing department requested that customer service objectives be substantially improved or upgraded. Policy reports always are directed to or result from the chief executive officer of a given firm. Their content almost always involves areas of corporate activity beyond that normally responsible to the logistics sector of the firm.

In conclusion, the content of control reports is highly customized to the individual firm, its organization, and the degree of automated information handling enjoyed. The content of reports should be geared to levels of administrative control. The higher level of control, the more selective is the nature of information contained on the report.

Status reports for the most part are used by line managers for purposes of directing logistical activities in accord with predetermined operational plans. Trend reports are highly condensed and are used by executives at the variation and decision levels to monitor progress. The higher the control level, the more condensed and selective is the trend report. Trend reports prepared at the decision level should contain information related to all aspects of an integrated logistical system. Special reports consist of selected information concerning certain units of the system. From the control center, interrogation of status and performance of individual units located at any geographic point may be initiated. Performance can be evaluated with respect to the operating plan and so permit fast and efficient management response to any externally or internally generated change.

Summary

The process of control is one of the most complex aspects of logistical management. The problem is not one of informational availability. In today's business enterprise data are abundant. In addition, the continued refinements in management information systems occurring daily will make data more available in the future. The problem confronted in logistical controllership is to get necessary data formatted in a manner that is conducive to performance measurement.

Two main types of data are required for logistical controllership. Cost control data, although most readily available, require a great deal of restructuring to be useful to logistical administration. Service performance data are not normally available within the corporate record base. However, the fact that all elements of the total order cycle are under logistical management control in a unified organization structure renders the data for service measurement attainable. The task of logistical controllership is to isolate cost and performance data to provide management with facts concerning the over-all logistical operations. All levels of management control require timely and accurate data. In final analysis, a logistical operation can be only as efficient and as effective as the control system that guides its destiny.

Questions

1. Discuss the relationship between the operational plan and the logistical control process.
2. Describe the different types of control commonly found in a logistical system.
3. Compare and contrast the concepts of efficiency and effectiveness.
4. Discuss the difference between control at the direction variation decision and policy levels of an organization.
5. Does variation in control necessarily mean that a problem has developed?
6. In the scheme of decision making presented in the chapter and illustrated in Figure 14-2, is it reasonable to conclude that system redesign decisions would reach the policy level while system administration decisions would be concerned with the direction variation and decision levels? Why or why not?
7. What are the deficiencies of the traditional profit-and-loss statement with respect to logistical control?
8. What justification can be found, in arriving at a net sales figure, for treating inbound transportation as part of the cost of goods?

9. Schiff feels that it would not be difficult to develop a set of internal costs that would be highly useful in logistical management. Do you agree or disagree, and why?

10. Describe the differences among direct, indirect, and overhead costs. What is the importance of timing and cost measurement?

11. Why is allocation extremely important to the design and administration of logistical systems?

12. Describe the differences among fixed, flexible, and capital budgeting. Which method do you prefer, and why?

Appendixes

Appendix I

Simchip I:
A Physical Distribution
Game

Simchip I is a physical distribution management decision simulation based upon four firms supplying five market areas with potato chips. Each firm produces potato chips in 1-pound bags and distributes to the five areas in the week following production. The over-all objective of the simulation is to make maximum gross distribution profits for a time period specified by the umpire. Product sales result in revenue generation. Warehouse and inventory costs, production costs, transportation costs, and distribution costs result in expense generation.

The general purpose of Simchip I is to demonstrate to the student the basic interrelationship between several important elements of the physical distribution task. The game has not been designed to present all possible alternatives in a dynamic setting, but to focus on the key elements of the task in such a manner as to provide important background perspective for the student.

In order to focus on the physical distribution task, some simplifying assumptions have been made. These assumptions include a simplified market structure, a limited product line, and the elimination of promotional and advertising decisions.

The explanation of Simchip I is divided into three general parts. The first part, entitled "Information on Key Variables," presents detailed data on all the variables used in the simulation. The second part, entitled "Explanation of Forms and Procedures Used by the Student," explains the forms and procedures used in actually playing the game. The third section illustrates the forms utilized by the players in recording decisions.

The game may be played for as many periods as specified by the umpire. The student should carefully review all materials in the appendix and thoroughly understand the simulation procedure before completing any decision forms.

Information on Key Variables

Market Data

Consumer demand for the product is the key determinant in the firm's sales. Each firm starts the simulation with an equal share of the total market. Consumer demand based on past sales history fluctuates ± 15 per cent. As the simulation develops, each firm's market share will vary depending on the efficiency of production and physical distribution.

Raw Materials

	Cost	Package	Pounds/ Cubic Foot
Potatoes	$ 4.21/cwt	100-lb bags	6.66
Salt	1.735/cwt	100-lb bags	12.50
Oil	16.21/drum	50-gal drum, 400 lb	44.44
1-lb bags	22.00/M	1,000 bags, 260 lb	9.64

Warehouse and Inventory

Each firm has two types of warehouse facilities available for raw materials storage.

Private.   12,500 square feet, 20 feet clear.
80% usable cube = 200,000 cubic feet.
Warehouse overhead charge = $1,443/week.
Warehouse operation = throughput = total receipts + total production
   (from status report) ÷ 2 × $0.16/cwt.

Public.   A public warehouse will be used after 200,000 cubic feet have been placed in a private warehouse.

Cubic Feet	Cost/Cubic Foot
0–100,000	$0.015
100,000–500,000	0.010
500,000 and above	0.005

(*Note:* Cost includes delivery from warehouse to factory.)

Raw Material and Finished Inventory Carrying Cost

Ending raw material inventory (at cost) × 10% ÷ 52.
Finished goods inventory carrying cost = waste × unit wholesale
price × 20% ÷ 52.

Production Capacity

CAPACITY.   Each firm operates a cooking plant located at its home market
location (see Figure E1-1). This plant has a cooking capacity of 20,000 pounds/
day normal, 5,000 pounds/day overtime, and an additional 20,000 pounds
by scheduling Saturday production. Production must be completed in the
week prior to the following week's anticipated sales.

PRODUCTION OVERHEAD.   Fixed overhead charge regardless of production—
$3,750/week. A portion of this overhead is for the reusable cartons utilized in
delivery.

FIGURE E1-1
Simchip I—Market Structure

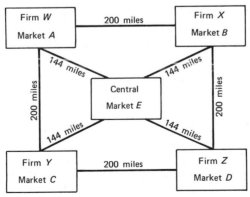

COOKING COSTS. The production of finished potato chips requires raw potatoes, oil, salt, and bags. Costs are incurred as raw materials are converted to chips.

Cooking Conversion—1,000 lb of Finished Chips

Potatoes (lb)	4,370	$183.970
Salt (lb)	50	0.868
Oil (lb)	400	16.210
Bags (lb)	1,000	22.000
		$223.048
	Total cost	Cost/lb
	223.05	$0.223

Cooking Costs—Regular

Basic (lb)	lb/day	Saturday/lb
10,000	$0.220	$0.319
11,000	0.215	0.319
12,000	0.210	0.319
13,000	0.205	0.319
14,000	0.200	0.319
15,000	0.195	0.283
16,000	0.190	0.283
17,000	0.185	0.283
18,000	0.180	0.283
19,000	0.175	0.283
20,000	0.170	0.283

Cooking Costs—Overtime

Basic (lb)	Per lb
0–2,500	$0.284
2,501–5,000	0.246

Transportation Costs (Inbound Raw Materials)

Transportation of raw materials is accomplished by rail, common carrier motor truck, and private truck. All raw materials are received from Central City.

Company Truck (No Lead Time)

	Capacity (lb)	
	Truck A	Truck B
Potatoes	60,000	24,000
Salt	50,000	20,000
Oil	96,000	38,000
Bags	10,000	4,000
	Cost	
	Truck A	Truck B
Basic	$100/week	$65/week
Per mile	$0.15	$0.10
Average mile/hour	40	45
Loading–unloading time	4 hours	4 hours
Driver's wages	$6/hour	$6/hour

Central City—Rail (2 Weeks Lead Time)
(No Maximum)

0–480,000 lb	$0.15/cwt
480,000–960,000 lb	0.13/cwt
960,000–1,440,000 lb	0.125/cwt
1,440,000–any Q lb	0.120/cwt

Central City—Truck (1 Week Lead Time)

	LTL	TL
Potatoes	0–30,000 lb	30,000–50,000 lb*
	$0.50/cwt	$0.35/cwt
Salt	0–25,000 lb	25,000–60,000 lb*
	$0.55/cwt	$0.35/cwt
Oil	0–48,000 lb	48,000–96,000 lb*
	$0.30/cwt	$0.20/cwt
Bags	0–5,000 lb	5,000–10,000 lb*
	$0.85/cwt	$0.65/cwt

* Maximum weight/shipment.

Distribution Costs (*Finished Product*)

Company Truck

	Truck A	*Truck B*
Per mile	$0.15	$0.10
Average mile/hour	40	45
Unloading time	1 hour	1 hour
Driver's wages	$6/hour	$6/hour
Capacity		
Cartons	1,620	600
Pounds	9,720	3,600

Common Carrier

	LTL: *0–9,000 lb*	*TL:* *Over 9,000 lb*
Central (144 miles)	$3.50/cwt	$3.00/cwt
Adjacent (145–200 miles)	$3.90/cwt	$3.40/cwt
Distant (over 200 miles)	$4.20/cwt	$3.80/cwt

Distribution in Market Area—Basic Cost/Market $250.00*

	Cost/cwt
Under 2,000	$0.27
2,001–5,000	0.26
5,001–10,000	0.25
10,001–15,000	0.24
15,001–20,000	0.23
20,001–25,000	0.22
25,001–30,000	0.21
Over 30,000	0.20

* The cost is added once each decision period for each market in which distribution is made. This cost represents storage in transit and distribution in the various market areas.

Explanation of Forms and Procedures Used by the Player

Status Report

The status report provides the basis for planning each period's actions and aids in preparing the operating statement. It is filled out by the umpire. The form contains your company's share of each market and the amount of waste you had last period. You are to assume that you will sell the amount proposed if you produce and distribute that amount to each market. The percentage share may be compared to past percentages to get an idea of your distribution in each market as compared to that of the other companies. Waste is the amount produced and distributed to each market that was not sold.

Remember, this is a physical distribution simulation and your score will be determined by how well you control your logistic system. Coordination among team members is of prime importance!

Decision-Recording Form

PRODUCTION SCHEDULE.   This schedule will be completed showing production for each day and the total for the week.

RAW MATERIAL INVENTORY STATUS.   Beginning inventory and purchase orders due will be provided by the umpire at the start of the simulation. After this, you will be responsible for completing this form in duplicate and returning one copy to the umpire each period. The starting inventory will be the same figure as last period's ending inventory. Usage (obtained from the production worksheet) and receipts (obtained from the warehouse worksheet) are applied to beginning inventory to obtain ending inventory.

All new orders placed and those placed in previous periods and not received during the period are deleted.

DISTRIBUTION SCHEDULE.   This schedule is provided in three parts:

Total Distribution.   This form is to be filled out completely showing the market and the day of distribution. Total q will show the daily distribution; Total p will show the total distribution to each market. These two totals must be equal.

Company Truck Distribution.   This schedule will show your truck schedule for each day of the week and the total pounds distributed. If the truck is used to pick up raw material, the route will be entered in the market column and miles recorded. [*Example:* Your firm is located in market B. You make a raw material pickup in Central (E). Market column would show B–E–B–; miles, 288; pounds and distribution stops, blank. If you loaded your truck with 9,000 pounds of chips and delivered 4,500 to market D and 4,500 pounds to E, and then picked up the raw material, the form would be Market, B–D–E–B, miles 488; pounds, 9,000; distribution stops, 2.]

Common Carrier Distribution.   This schedule will show the daily distribution by market and pounds when using common carrier.

Note: The combined totals of parts 2 and 3 must equal the total distribution in part 1.

Operating Statement

The work sheets provided are cross-referenced to assist you in preparing your operating statement.

General

The decision recording form and the operating statement will be completed and turned in to the umpire on the day announced by your instructor. Fill out these forms completely and accurately, for they are subject to audit at any time during the simulation. File each period's work sheets so that you will be able to support your figures.

STATUS REPORT

Company _____   End of Period _____

Market	Proposed demand in pounds	Per cent share last period	Waste last period in #
A			
B			
C			
D			
E			

Total   _____   _____   _____

Sales Computations:

    Total distribution in $ = distribution last period x .845¢
    Total waste in $ = waste last period x .845¢

Total Distribution Less Total Waste = Total Net Sales

    $ _____ - $ _____ = $ _____

DECISION–RECORDING FORM

Company _____   End of Period _____

Production schedule:

M	T	W	TH	F	S	S
#	#	#	#	#	#	#

Raw materials inventory status:

	Potatoes #	Oil #	Salt #	Bags #
Starting inventory				
Usage (−)				
Receipts (+)				
Ending inventory				
Order due				
# period				
_____ _____				
_____ _____				
_____ _____				
_____ _____				
_____ _____				
Total Committed				

DISTRIBUTION SCHEDULE

1. Total distribution:

	M	T	W	TH	F	S	Total(p)
Local							
Mkt							
Mkt							
Mkt							
Mkt							
Total(q)							

2. Company truck distribution:

	Truck A				Truck B				
	Routing	Miles	Pounds	Stops	Routing	Miles	Pounds	Stops	Total #
M									
T									
W									
TH									
F									
S									

Total   ____ ____ ____   ____ ____ ____ ____

3. Common carrier distribution:

	Market	Pounds	Market	Pounds	Market	Pounds	Total #
M							
T							
W							
TH							
F							
S							

OPERATING STATEMENT

A. Sales (in Dollars) $ _____

B. Warehouse and Inventory Costs

    B-1. Warehouse overhead $ ___1443___

    B-2. Warehouse operations $ _____

    B-3. Extra warehousing (public) $ _____

    B-4. Raw material inventory carrying cost $ _____

    B-5. Finished good inventory carrying cost $ _____

       Subtotal $ _____

C. Production Costs

    C-1. Overhead $ _____

    C-2. Cooking conversion $ _____

    C-3. Cooking costs—regular $ _____

    C-4. Cooking costs—overtime

       Subtotal $ _____

D. Transportation Costs—Inbound Raw Materials

    D-1. Company truck

       Fixed charge $ ___165.00___

       Variable charge $ _____

    D-2. Common carrier—rail $ _____

    D-3. Common carrier—truck $ _____

       Subtotal $ _____

E. Distribution Cost—Outbound (Finished Product)

    E-1. Company truck variable $ _____

    E-2. Common carrier truck $ _____

    E-3. Distribution in market $ _____

       Subtotal $ _____

         Total Cost $ _____

           Profit for Period $ _____

WORKSHEET — WAREHOUSE AND INVENTORY COST

B-1. Warehouse Overhead (Private) $ _____

B-2. Warehouse Operations (Raw Material Handling)

Raw Material Receipts During Period

	#	Order No.
Potatoes	_____	_____
Salt	_____	_____
Oil	_____	_____
1 # Bags	_____	_____
Total Receipts (a)	_____	

Raw materials used
during period (#)
(Production worksheet) (b) _____

Total (a) & (b)_____ ÷ 2 x .16/cwt =_____

B-3. Extra Warehousing (Public)

Cubic ft. used during period _____
x Appropriate rate _____
Extra warehousing cost for period $ _____

B-4. Raw Material Inventory Carrying Cost

Beginning Raw Materials Inventory

Potatoes_____ x 4.21/cwt = _____
Oil _____ x 4.05/cwt = _____
Salt _____ x 1.735/cwt = _____
Bags _____ x 22.00/Bale =_____

Total (a) $ _____

Ending Raw Materials Inventory

Potatoes_____ x 4.21/cwt = _____
Oil _____ x 4.05/cwt = _____
Salt _____ x 1.735/cwt = _____
Bags _____ x 22.00/Bale =_____

Total (b) $ _____

Total (a) and (b) $_____ ÷ 2 = (c) $ _____
(c)_____ x 10% ÷ 52 =
Period raw material inventory carrying cost $ _____

B-5. Finished Goods Inventory Carrying Cost

Period waste (status report)_____
x Unit wholesale price_____ $ .845 ___
$_____ x 20% ÷ 52 =
Period finished goods inventory carrying cost $ _____

C. Production Costs:

C-1. Overhead .... $ _3750_____

C-2. Cooking Conversion

Quantity cooked this period _____ (finished)

Potatoes   _____ x $.0421/lb = _____

Salt   _____ x $.0017/lb = _____

Oil   _____ x $.04/lb   = _____

Bags   _____ x $.022/bag = _____

Total Conversion Cost _____

C-3. Cooking Costs — Regular

Quantity cooked x   rate/lb   =   total cooking cost

M _____ x _____ = _____

T _____ x _____ = _____

W _____ x _____ = _____

TH_____ x _____ = _____

F _____ x _____ = _____

S _____ x _____ = _____

Total _____

C-4. Cooking Cost — Overtime

Daily output in excess of 20,000 lb x rate

_____ x _____ =

_____ x _____ =

_____ x _____ =

Total _____

D. Transportation Costs:

Inbound Raw Materials:

D-1. Company Truck ..... Fixed Charge $_____

    *Total mileage per period x rate

    Truck A_____ x _____$.15_____ = _____

    Truck B_____ x _____$.10_____ = _____

    (Driving time + loading time) x driver's wages

    (_____ + _____) x $6 = _____

                             Total_____

*Serarate truck mileage between raw materials hauling and finished goods delivery.

D-2. Common Carrier — Rail

    Total lbs   x   Rate

    _____ x _____ x

    _____ x _____ x

    _____ x _____ x _____

                Total _____

D-3. Common Carrier — Truck

                Total Lbs/   x Rate
                Shipment   (LTL OR TL)

    Potatoes_____ x _____ = _____

    Salt   _____ x _____ = _____

    Oil   _____ x _____ = _____

    Bags   _____ x _____ = _____

                           Total_____

E.   Distribution Cost:

Outbound Finished Product

E-1. Company Truck

*Total mileage per period x rate

Truck A _____ x _____ $.15 _____ = _____

Truck B _____ x _____ $.10 _____ = _____

Driving time + unloading time   x   drivers' wages   =

(_____ + _____) x $6.00   = _____

                                                    Total _____

*Separate truck mileage between raw materials hauling and finished goods delivery.

E-2. Common Carrier — Truck

Market	Pounds	x	Rate (LTL or TL)	
_____	_____	x	_____	= _____
_____	_____	x	_____	= _____
_____	_____	x	_____	= _____
_____	_____	x	_____	= _____
_____	_____	x	_____	= _____
_____	_____	x	_____	= _____

                                                    Total _____

E-3. Distribution In Market

No. of markets in which distribution is made x fixed distribution charge =

_____ x $250. _____ = _____

Pounds delivered in Market:

A _____ x _____ = _____

B _____ x _____ = _____

C _____ x _____ = _____

D _____ x _____ = _____

E _____ x _____ = _____

                                                    Total _____

Appendix II
Plant Location Factors

Current economic literature contains many contributions aimed at developing a general theory of industrial location. Several such contributions were reviewed throughout the text. These theoretical studies address the problem of explaining geographic distribution of plant capacity. The main criterion permeating the majority of published works is the rational allocation of scarce resources. Thus, most location literature has been devoted to explaining socially acceptable goals generated from classical competitive economics.

However, the principle of free economic action and profit maximization may lead to personal goals inconsistent with social goals. Given imperfections in social and economic organization, individual entrepreneurs may find profit opportunities derived from astute location decisions. It may appear that economic theory and applied business practice are, therefore, incompatible. This view is quite incorrect. The function of location theory is to abstract from practice so that all elemental forces affecting location may be identified. Once these forces are appropriately defined, they implicitly form the foundation of public policy, which is aimed at achieving maximum economic welfare. One result of location theory is, therefore, the formation of adequate public policy to guide the nation's economic welfare. Given this orientation, the complete acceptance of general location forces for the purposes of solving an individual location problem may be inappropriate. However, theory aids in the identification of fundamental forces affecting location and thus assists in the organization of an applied method for locating a specific plant. Applied methodology can be developed within the guideposts so conveniently developed by economic theorists.

Least-Cost Location Factors

The contributions of location theorists point out that all location factors can be grouped and summarized under three broad categories: (1) least-cost factors, (2) profit-maximizing factors, and (3) intangible factors. To select a proper plant location, a complete evaluation of the influence of each category of factors on a particular location problem is necessary. Thus it is important that all location factors be clearly understood. This and the following two sections are devoted to a detailed discussion of each category.

Location cost factors may be divided between transfer costs and production costs.[1] Transfer costs are defined as the costs that result from the movement of raw materials to the proposed plant site and those that are incurred by shipping finished products to market.[2] Production costs include all other costs related to plant operation. To achieve the least-cost location, the sum of all transfer costs and production costs must be minimized.[3] Intangibles may be defined as those elements affecting costs which may not be classified in transfer or production accounts.

Transfer Costs

Transfer costs as a factor in plant location have traditionally been considered by assuming that all other location influences are negligible.[4] Such an assumption tends to minimize important location forces and, therefore, should be employed with considerable caution. On the other hand, this approach allows a detailed and unrestricted treatment of this very important factor. Transfer costs frequently are a dominant element in plant location. Because they are readily quantifiable, transfer cost analysis provides a convenient starting point for solving locational problems. In Chapter 12, an analytical technique is

---

[1] Hoover presented as the core of his thesis two influential cost categories—transfer and process. Although not utilized in a similar manner these cost categories have been adopted for the present treatment. See Edgar M. Hoover, *The Location of Economic Activity* (New York: McGraw-Hill Book Company, 1948).

[2] Transfer costs are defined to include all cost components as developed in the total cost discussion. For a complete discussion of all costs included in transfer costs, see Chapter 4.

[3] Only costs that vary between alternative locations are influential in plant location. For example, the cost of raw materials, per se, is not important unless this basic cost is geographically variable.

[4] For example, see D. Philip Locklin, *Economics of Transportation* (Homewood, Ill.: Richard D. Irwin, Inc., 1947), p. 43.

developed which may be employed to arrive at the geographical point of least transfer costs. However, it is essential to keep in mind that transfer costs are only one of many location influences. The point of least transfer cost will normally have to be amended to accommodate other location elements in selecting the profit-maximizing plant site. Five principal methods of movement are available to transport raw materials and finished products. These are rail, truck, air, water, and pipeline. The particular method capable of solving a given movement problem depends upon the commodity to be moved, distance, weight, size of shipment, speed required, cost, and so on.[5] Given the alternative methods capable of moving a particular commodity, the specific method or combination of methods employed is selected on the basis of cost and type of service required. Cost in all cases should be held to a minimum under the standards of service necessary to satisfy market requirements. Thus, when service requirements are satisfied, the combination of methods that results in the lowest total transfer cost may be determined by utilizing the total cost techniques introduced in Chapter 10. The combination of transfer methods and resultant costs can be materially altered by the geographic point at which the production plant is located. Consequently, in selecting a plant location, it is necessary to isolate the one best geographical point from which service requirements may be satisfied at the lowest total transfer cost.

Intercity transfer costs may be divided into two components: the costs associated with accumulation of raw materials and those related to product distribution. Accumulation costs result from the movement of raw materials or semifinished products to the point of manufacture. Distribution costs are derived from shipment of finished products to the final market through all intermediary steps. A particular plant location may be pulled toward the market or toward the source of raw materials, depending on which location minimizes the sum of accumulation and distribution costs. In some cases, as will be shown, a location between the market and the source of raw materials may yield the lowest total transfer costs.

Materials-Oriented Industries

The plants in a particular industry may be located near the source of raw materials because of the unique location of the raw material or because of a great weight loss in the process of production. Extractive industries as characterized by agriculture, mining, and lumbering must be located at the point where raw materials are available in economic quantities. In agriculture, the supply and quantity of land suited to particular crops plays the dominant role. In mining, it is the location of deposits; in lumber, it is the location of forests.

Industries in which, because of the nature of the product, great weight loss is experienced in production tend to locate plants near the source of raw

[5] The capabilities and limitations of various modes of transport are discussed in greater detail in Chapter 5.

materials.[6] Sugar beet refining and cotton ginning are excellent examples.[7] The net result of such locations is to reduce total transfer costs, because the weight shipped to market is significantly less than the weight of raw materials. A third element causing plants to be located near raw materials is the perishability of the materials. Many agricultural canning and freezing processes are examples. The great canning and freezing complex in central New Jersey, with its vast fresh fruit and vegetable acreages and large processing centers, illustrates this condition. To some unmeasurable extent, this location factor is offset by technological improvement in transportation equipment, for example, refrigerated cars and trucks.

In summary, several major forces influence transfer costs for particular industries, thereby making the point of least transfer cost one in close proximity to the source of raw materials. These forces are (1) great loss of weight in raw materials during processing or production, (2) availability of raw materials for extractive industries, and (3) perishability of the raw material.

Market-Oriented Industries

Industries that add weight during the production of finished products, experience large differentials in rates between raw materials and finished products, or produce a highly perishable finished product tend to locate plants near the market.[8]

A typical weight-gaining process is found in the average industry. Water, a major ingredient in the final product, causes substantial weight gains during production. Because adequate water supplies are found in most potential locations, it is economically desirable to ship concentrates rather than finished products. The weight added to the final product by the addition of water causes transfer costs to be lowest when it is added near the market.[9]

It is interesting to note that in the total marketing effort of the firm, advertising may somewhat modify the impact of transfer cost factors. If advertising can develop a product image that allows a higher price to be commanded, this increased revenue may sufficiently absorb the added transfer expense associated with a location at a point distant from the market. This is of partic-

---

[6] J. Russell Smith and M. Ogden Phillips, *Industrial and Commercial Geography* (New York: Holt, Rinehart and Winston, Inc., 1950), p. 48.

[7] For example, about one sixth of the weight of sugar beets is retained in the extracted sugar. This is also important in cane sugar production; the mature cane is about 10 per cent fiber, 18 per cent sugar, and 72 per cent water. Stanley Vance, *American Industries* (Englewood Cliffs, N.J.: Prentice-Hall, Inc., 1955), p. 557.

[8] There is considerable confusion in current literature regarding whether perishability, service, and so on are location forces requiring a market orientation as a result of transfer expense, or location forces requiring a market orientation owing to consumer preferences. Unquestionably, both forces are important. A clear separation could be obtained only by studying specific industrial location problems.

[9] In some cases where other than "any quantity" rates prevail, for example, if rates in carload lots are lower than rates on less-than-carload lots, it may be possible to increase weight without increasing total costs. Furthermore, within a limited range, increased weights may decrease cost. See Locklin, *op. cit.*, p. 55.

ular importance to firms selling to a national market in which the production process does not allow the use of concentrated syrups. In the beer industry, for example, the accepted meaning of a "premium beer" is that it sells at a price above that of locally brewed products. Although there may indeed be quality difference, it is not the only foundation for classifying a beer as premium for marketing purposes. However, the basic market orientation rule is not greatly influenced by this special case. If concentrates can be employed, the location impact of advertising may be channeled toward more productive sources while lower transfer rates are enjoyed. Primary examples of such physical distribution decisions are the policies followed by the major soft drink producers.

Even when weight differentials between raw materials and finished products are negligible, the plant may be attracted to a market location. A general characteristic of rates is that lower rates are placed upon cruder materials, with the rate increasing as the product reaches final stages of fabrication.[10] Therefore, transfer rates tend to increase with the stage of manufacture. Historically, this condition reflects the value of the service principle in rate making. That is, in some loose way it was assumed that the higher the value a commodity could command, the more easily it could absorb a higher freight rate. The monopoly position enjoyed by the railroads up to the 1930s allowed such discrimination to be practiced. Newer modes of transportation in competition with the railroads have readily impaired the railroad's ability to continue such practices. Value of service in modern rate-making theory refers to the rate that may be charged by a competing form of transport equivalent service.[11] Under this new concept, the spread between raw materials rates and finished product rates is likely to diminish in the future. To the extent that this differential diminishes, such discrimination will become of lesser consequence in plant location.

If the final product is characterized by extreme perishability, there may be additional reasons why a market-oriented location should be selected. Special handling and the requirement for extreme speed may tend to increase the cost of transferring such commodities. Under such conditions, production close to markets minimizes such transfer expense, for example, baked goods, ice cream, and delicatessen foods.

In summary, transfer forces pulling plant locations to a market proximity are (1) weight gains during production, (2) differential freight rates between raw materials and finished products, and (3) perishability of the finished product.

Location at Other Points

A third group of industries has traditionally been labeled "foot-loose." This is because the transfer costs related to their particular manufacturing

---

[10] Locklin, *op. cit.*, p. 47.

[11] For an excellent discussion of competition in rate making, see Joel Dean, *Proceedings Railway Systems and Procedures Association*, 1959, Fall Meeting, Chicago.

process allow selection of a plant location either at markets, at raw materials, or at an intermediate point. If a particular industry is truly foot-loose, transfer costs may play a small role in determining plant location. For example, research and development firms are quite independent of the transfer forces under consideration.

But this is not the situation for all the firms that select plant sites at points separated from raw materials or markets. In some special cases, a plant located at an intermediate point represents the least-cost transfer location. The earlier discussion illustrating why plants are attracted to materials or markets was based upon the assumption that freight expense for a through movement was less than the expense incurred from movements to and from an intermediate point. Although this is normally true, there are some notable exceptions.

Probably the best known exception to the general rule is the granting of in-transit privileges by the transport companies. The most widely utilized in-transit privileges are milling and fabrication. In both cases, the raw material may be shipped to a production point, then to final destination, at a combined cost slightly higher than the through rate. Utilization of this artificial removal of the "diseconomy" of short hauls is particularly influential when the pull of the materials and the pull of the market are otherwise almost equal. Examples of in-transit privileges can readily be found in the grain and steel industries. The impact of in-transit privileges is to allow management considerably more freedom in the selection of plant sites. The net effect of in-transit privileges is to promote the dispersion of industry.[12]

Intermediate location may also stem from the use of transshipment points. Location at transshipment points can be highly beneficial to industries processing raw materials which have low transport costs into final products normally associated with high transport costs. In such cases location at junction points may greatly reduce aggregate transport costs. Water facilities are among the cheapest methods of movement and may economically be used for the transport of bulky raw materials. Processing may then take place during the rehandling operation. This has the net effect of reducing unnecessary rehandling cost. Location at such junction points means that raw materials may move via water transportation, and finished products may be shipped via the cheapest satisfactory means of reaching the market. The importance of Pittsburgh and Youngstown as steel centers may be attributed in part to the availability of water transportation facilities.

Additional factors that pull plants to intermediate locations result from the need to utilize several raw materials or serve several different markets. A firm that utilizes a number of raw materials in processing can usually realize lowest transfer costs by locating at collection points. A collection point is a location that has minimum aggregate accumulation costs for various raw materials. On the other hand, a distribution point is a location that has minimum distribution costs to various markets. When one material or one market

---

[12] Truman C. Bigham and Merrill J. Roberts, *Transportation* (New York: McGraw-Hill Book Company, 1952), p. 25.

cannot be identified as the primary determinant of lowest transport costs, an acceptable compromise location at intermediate least-cost points may be the alternative.

In summary, if an industry can be categorized as truly foot-loose, plants may be located at any point, and transfer costs may not be a dominant location element. Particular industries tend to locate plants at intermediate points depending upon certain economic forces. In these special cases, transfer costs will be minimized at an intermediate location.

Distorting Influences

The transfer factors thus far indicated combine to point out the one best location that results in lowest total transfer costs for each plant. Several factors may act to displace the least-cost location based only on minimum transfer costs. Processing costs, competition, and intangible elements that displace this location will be considered shortly.

At this point, some additional transfer factors of an institutional nature must be considered. One such element is simply the availability of transportation facilities. Extensive industrial development of the northeastern United States may be attributed in part to this condition. At one time, no geographical point within this region was farther than 10 miles from a railroad.[13] The influence of topography and its resultant effect upon transportation facilities cannot be overemphasized. Waterways are restricted to rivers, valleys, lakes, bays, and relatively level areas where canals can be constructed. Other natural barriers influence the character of various modes of transportation. The transportation network is a powerful element that limits the availability of locations to points along the current configuration of transfer routes.

Rate discrimination among commodities and geographic areas will also modify location decisions. Utilization of base-point pricing or uniform blanket rates may completely distort the influences of transportation costs. In addition, rate policies of the various carriers can greatly influence the location of industries. Although rates are subject to regulation, the point must be kept in mind that effective rates are set by the carrier. Close proximity to facilities does not necessarily mean lowest rates. Another important point is that published rates do not necessarily reflect the rate at which freight actually moves. It is necessary to make a detailed study of rates under which relevant commodities actually move rather than to accept published rates.

In conclusion, transfer costs as location factors can attract plants to the point of raw materials, or of markets, or to some intermediate point. Which prevails will depend upon the service necessary to meet individual market requirements and the cost of achieving this service at alternative locations. Because of the general importance of transfer costs in plant location, techniques

[13] Locklin, *op. cit.*, p. 49.

that minimize this factor offer convenient starting points for the solution of location problems.

Production Costs

Production costs consist of all expenses necessary to convert raw materials into finished products. The production costs related to any given manufacturing process are geographically variable. Such geographical differences may be directly traced to forces of immobility. To the extent that any factor necessary for production of a product is mobile, it will tend to move to the geographical area of greatest reward.[14] From the viewpoint of production costs, the most economical location is one that combines the cheapest critical immobile factors with the necessary array of inexpensive mobile factors. Major production costs may be grouped into three categories, each of which is, in varying degrees, an important location factor. These are (1) rent, (2) labor, and (3) power.

RENT. In broad perspective, rent includes the following production costs: land, taxes, and capital.

Land Cost. Land prices may reflect wide regional differences. These cost differences result from the immobile characteristics of land and the wide variation in the natural endowment of individual sites. Variations in costs among specific sites stem primarily from scarcity. The general rule is that the more intensive the demand for land in a given area, the greater will be the cost. Normally, land cost diminishes as distance increases from the city center. Although the cost of land within the central city may be high, it usually offers certain economies that offset this high purchase price. Among these advantages are more adequate transport supply and a more flexible labor market. The price of a parcel of land must, therefore, be considered in light of other location advantages it may provide.

For any manufacturer, there are two classes of plant sites. First, sites with existing structures may be purchased or rented. Although vacant plants are found in abundance, the adaptability to specific location requirements may be limited. Because the average life of a real estate improvement is often in excess of 60 years,[15] this quality of durability results in a standing stock of plant facilities that have limited adaptability to individual tenants. The second alternative is to purchase vacant land. Construction normally requires a substantial capital outlay that tends to bind the firm to a permanent location, thus decreasing mobility. Whether to rent or buy is primarily a financial question to be considered in light of company policy.

Tax Cost. The influence of tax cost on location decisions is elusive, to say

[14] Hoover adequately summarizes the influence of mobility on location in the following quote: "The price of a freely mobile factor would be the same everywhere and would not affect the location of production or other factors at all." See Hoover, *op. cit.*, p. 69.

[15] Ernest M. Fisher and Robert M. Fisher, *Urban Real Estate* (New York: Holt, Rinehart and Winston, Inc., 1954), p. 162.

the least. Common knowledge dictates that a firm will attempt to locate at the point of least aggregate tax cost. It also follows that the 50 bodies of state tax laws, not to mention uncounted community ordinances, will render distinctly different tax assessments in various geographical areas. Yet numerous empirical studies point out that tax costs are, at best, relatively unimportant, secondary influences in location. Greenhut reviews four studies which all agree that the incentives offered by lower taxes were not the determining factors in locating industries.[16] The location influence attributed to taxes was concluded to be of primary concern only in selecting between various sites within a particular area. Additional support is given to this conclusion by a study completed by Stopler concerning the influence of taxes on plants locating in Michigan.[17] He concluded that taxes rank far down the list of factors influential in location decisions.

These observations also agree with the study of taxation effects on industrial location completed by Floyd.[18] In discussing the theory that higher-than-average industrial taxes in a community will restrict its industrial growth, he concluded that tax considerations are influential only in selecting between alternative sites situated under different taxing jurisdictions when a firm finds such sites satisfactory in all other respects. A study completed by Bergin and Eagan supports these findings. Only 32 out of 272 respondents mentioned a favorable tax structure as an important location factor.[19] Normally, few firms will relocate because of high taxes. Taxes may play a minor role in the decision to relocate, but the combined role of these and other costs casts the influence. Tax costs are especially influential when political boundaries, such as state lines, separate the communities under consideration. In addition, taxes are primary cost factors for firms with a high proportion of assets which are taxable under state and local ordinances. For example, if a firm requires a large acreage of land to undertake production, property taxes may become important location elements. In such cases, the firm tends to move toward areas offering comparatively lower property tax levies.

Capital Costs. The cost of capital is an important factor in plant location, but this does not mean that the manufacturer must be geographically near the source of funds. Capital is the most mobile of the elements influencing location. The major significance of capital rests upon availability and cost. For a business to grow, it must have ready access to capital at reasonable cost. Neither of these requirements is directly related to location. Availability is more nearly connected to the financial status of the firm requesting loans and the character of executives employed by the firm than it is to location. The

[16] Melvin L. Greenhut, *Plant Location in Theory and Practice* (Chapel Hill, N.C.: University of North Carolina Press, 1956), p. 126.

[17] Wolfgang Stopler, *Special Study for Michigan Legislature*, Michigan House of Representative State Printing Office, Lansing, Mich.: 1958.

[18] Joe Summers Floyd, Jr., *Effects of Taxation on Industrial Location* (Chapel Hill, N.C.: University of North Carolina Press, 1952).

[19] Thomas P. Bergin and William F. Eagan, "How Effective Are Industrial Development Programs?" *Michigan Business Review*, Vol. XII (January 1960), p. 25.

cost of capital is a direct result of the money market, although this, too, may depend upon the intrinsic character of the firm. Historically, capital has been considered an influential factor in location. Today, financial requirements are rarely, if ever, critical determinants. The decline of the influence of capital upon location is generally attributed to the rise in mobility of capital funds.

LABOR. The location influence of labor affects various manufacturing firms in different ways. These variations tend to pull the location of particular industries toward the geographical point that will best satisfy labor requirements. Although the accumulative influence of labor upon location is difficult to measure, for some companies it is the greatest single influence motivating plant relocation.

Granted that there are great variations in labor requirements among industries, a number of firms are attracted by the presence of low labor rates. Traditionally, wage levels in the United States have been lowest in the southern states. Accordingly, many firms that are labor intensive and operate on low margins locate in the South to take advantage of large numbers of low-wage, unskilled workers. Wages paid are important determinants of location but only one aspect of the labor cost factor. From the viewpoint of the employer, productivity, skill requirements, stability, and labor legislation also must be considered.

Location advantages of an area that offers low wage rates may be offset by low productivity rates. Hoover points out that high wage rates do not necessarily attract job seekers or repel employers.[20] Low production costs may be found in areas with relatively high wage rates. The essential concern for the manufacturer is the productivity of labor and labor's response to maintaining low overhead costs. Hot climates are normally considered to be areas of low productivity. Although this statement has not been substantiated, to the extent that it is true, the low-wage advantages of the South may be offset by decreased productivity.

Firms that require highly skilled labor normally locate in close proximity to the areas that offer such skill. When other critical factors force manufacturers to move from areas of skilled labor, this loss may be offset by bringing skilled operators to train the local unskilled labor force. Such a procedure was followed by shoe manufacturers when they first located their processing facilities in St. Louis.[21] It is possible to offset the lack of skilled workers, but this is a costly and time-consuming process.

Regardless of the planning and analysis taken prior to locating in a particular area, low labor costs will not be realized if the local labor force proves unstable. High labor turnover is expensive. Retraining and loss of productivity are cost factors that cannot easily be recovered.

Labor laws can also cause cost differences between geographical areas. Virtually all industries are subject to state labor laws. Workmen's Compensa-

[20] Hoover, *op. cit.*, p. 103.
[21] Smith and Phillips, *op. cit.*, p. 51.

tion insurance rates normally are applied against payrolls at rates varying substantially among the states. Although not a limiting factor to some firms, compensation charges may represent a substantial cost to the manufacturer when a large work force is employed.

The size of the necessary labor force can also limit location possibilities. Those manufacturers who require large work forces normally are restricted to densely populated areas. In any community, the available supply of labor is basically represented by the workers unemployed. Response of labor to geographical wage differences is often restricted because of movement expense. Although the mobility of labor may be somewhat "sticky," migration can materially affect the local labor supply in times of increased demand.

POWER.   Historically, the location of power resources has been an outstanding factor in the selection of plant sites. But power, like capital and labor, has gained mobility throughout the years. For some early industries, the most attractive sites were located at the fall lines of navigable streams. At this point, water could be harnessed to turn power wheels at minimum cost.

Technological developments have greatly altered the location influence of both power and fuel. Although some plants are still attracted by the availability of cheap and abundant power, in most industries the cost of power as a percentage of total cost is small. Aluminum reduction plants are examples of firms attracted to water-power sites. Natural gas, in the production of glass, and accessibility to coal and coke in steel production are other examples of power-oriented industries. On account of more or less uniform availability, the location of the average plant will not be chosen solely because of power or fuel cost differentials.

In summary, the various location factors of rent, labor, and power can materially influence the cost structure of a plant located at different geographical points. To the degree that production factors are immobile, costs will be geographically variable. Thus, to find the point of least production cost for a given plant, it becomes necessary to evaluate alternative cost structures resulting from different potential locations. To a large extent, these geographical cost differences result from forces of external economies of location. Therefore, prior to concluding the discussion of location cost factors, attention is briefly directed to external economies of location.

External Economies of Location

External economies of location refer to cost reductions which result from the geographical clustering of plants.[22] The forces of concentrations explain

---

[22] External economies of location, as the phrase is used here, are similar to the forces referred to by Weber as agglomerative. He defined an agglomerative force as "An aggregate cost-reducing influence resulting from spatial interdependence." In external economies of location, economies of spatial interdependence are considered from the viewpoint of direct and indirect reductions. The original discussion of agglomerative forces did not develop this distinction in great detail. See Carl J. Friedrich (trans.), *Alfred Weber's Theory of Location of Industries* (Chicago: University of Chicago Press, 1928), p. 134.

to a large extent why the least-cost locations for many plants tend to congregate within a few industrial areas. For particular plants such cost reductions may be direct or indirect. Direct cost reductions evolve from the increased demand for interchangeable factors of production and transportation resulting when a large number of plants locate within a single industrial complex. Indirect cost reductions stem from other benefits realized from location in close proximity to an industrial population.

Examples of direct cost reductions are (1) lower total transfer costs resulting from better transport facilities, (2) reduced production costs due to a ready supply of technically trained labor, and (3) specialization of supplies allowing lower unit costs for materials, supplies, and services. These direct cost reductions explain to a large extent the forces underlying least-cost analysis.

Indirect cost reductions are not as easily qualified. Greenhut refers to this category of influences as a group of generally neglected location forces.[23] He points out that indirect cost-reducing factors may be separated from basic cost factors, because they emphasize the relationship between physical distance and costs in terms other than those of transfer and labor costs. Insurance is an example of a cost factor reduced by locating in an industrial community. A particular type of insurance may be available because of better protective facilities or familiarity of an insurance company with local hazards. Although the cost of insurance is a direct expense, the reduction in cost resulting from excellent protection represents the influence of indirect economies of concentration. Advertising costs can also be reduced by location in highly populated areas. Lower expense may be incurred to achieve equal population coverage.

The combined influence of external economies of location is to attract plants to industrial complexes. Individual firms attempt to locate plants in close proximity to other plants in order to enjoy mutual benefits of spatial concentration. To a large extent these same forces may influence a particular firm to centralize individual plants in order to realize maximum benefits from external economies.[24]

Intangible Location Factors

A final group of location forces influencing site selection is often classified as intangible factors. Intangible factors may be divided into two categories for discussion purposes. The first category contains cost-revenue influencing factors that result from personal contacts of company executives. The second group is personal preferences that influence site selection.

[23] Greenhut, *op. cit.*, p. 168.
[24] Hoover expands this consideration to include individual benefits realized by centralizing all plants owned by an individual firm. See Hoover, *op. cit.*, p. 80.

Cost-Revenue Influencing Factors

Plant locations may be altered to capitalize on the personal contacts and influences of management. Such factors may directly influence the availability of materials, capital, and sales. The availability of capital may be related to personal friendships and confidences that exist between management and creditors. Special requests for rush materials or spare parts in order to eliminate production bottlenecks may be given urgent consideration if friendly relations exist. Last of all, additional sales may be realized by community contacts developed by executives.

All of these intangible factors influence the cost-revenue structure of a particular firm. Without this aspect of personal consideration, location forces are impersonal results of cost and competitive factors. With consideration of personal influence, locations may be altered to increase profitability. Obviously, this influence is most paramount to small manufacturing firms, which in rare cases may find their only economic justification based upon such personal relationships.

Personal Preferences

Personal preferences influence plant location as a result of adjustments made to accommodate human needs and desires. A particular community may be selected because it offers desirable types of recreation, housing, or educational facilities. A particular region may be selected because it offers an enjoyable climate. Although such factors cannot be conveniently analyzed within the framework of economic analysis, the fact remains that purely personal considerations can be important determinants of plant location.

The net effect of intangible considerations is to alter the ideal economic location. The range of freedom available in selecting sites to fit intangible specifications is somewhat narrow if profit-maximization principles are strictly employed. For any particular firm, these factors may be influential only in selecting between communities located within close proximity to each other.

Appendix III

Plant Location—
General Procedure
and Check List

General Procedure

Plant location procedure consists of an organized development of location factors within a working framework. Selection of a plant site is a compromise among various location forces. Because location is conceivably possible at an infinite number of geographical points, the final decision requires an orderly elimination of undesirable locations until the one best plant site is selected. Fortunately, the natural and logical process of plant location provides a satisfactory location procedure, which consists of plant analysis and field analysis.

Plant Analysis

The first step in applying location theory to practice is an appropriate evaluation of the three categories of location factors as they apply to the individual plant location problem. This stage of evaluation is referred to as plant analysis. For plants currently operating, one purpose of plant analysis is to determine if relocation is desirable. With the assumption that a new location is desirable, careful analysis of all location elements will determine what specifications the new location must meet. Similarly for new plants, analysis must be completed to isolate relevant location specifications.

It is during plant analysis that the contributions of location theory can be applied to the specifics of an individual problem. The critical cost factors for the new plant should be identified, and a detailed cost study of current operations should be completed. This will allow comparative cost analysis between the current location and potential new sites. In most cases identification of cost factors requires extensive data collection. The net result is ideally a number of specifications that can be transposed into dollar costs. For example, the amount of labor required, the point of raw material procurement, the power requirements, and the many other factors noted earlier should be quantified in order to guide field research. A detailed study of market areas and competitive forces should be completed in order to determine what general geographic areas appear to contain a profit-maximizing location. Finally, the impact of intangible elements should be given complete analysis.

The final result of extensive plant analysis is a set of location specifications designed to guide the process of site selection. If one or two location factors evolve as critical, they should be identified during plant analysis. Only after the location problem has been analyzed in the magnitude here indicated is field analysis ready to be undertaken.

Field Analysis

Field analysis consists of three steps necessary to reduce the geographic area of concern to a few potential locations. Evaluation of location alternatives should be completed at the regional, community, and site levels of consideration. Field analysis procedure is not viewed as a limiting process. Selection of the one best community need not be made prior to conducting a search for satisfactory factory sites. Several search areas can be considered simultaneously, including their alternative communities and respective factory locations.

Individual states are not considered focal points of attention. Beyond doubt, some states offer advantages for location while others have distinct disadvantages. The potential geographic territory included in a search area is indifferent to political boundaries. Consequently, several different states may simultaneously be considered as location prospects.

Regional Evaluation

The first step in selecting a specific site from a potential geographic area is regional evaluation. The task at this stage of selection is to determine what areas qualify for detailed field examination. The total area under consideration will vary according to the specifications of individual firms. In cases where cheap labor is the primary location influence, regional examination may be limited to only a few regions. If proximity to markets is a primary requirement, regional possibilities will be in the general locale of major market areas. Extreme competitive or intangible influence may limit the regional areas to a few in number. Whatever the specifications, the first step is to identify the geographic areas that meet the broad location requirements.

The second step is to determine which of the alternative regions will be most economical for achieving location objectives. Consideration begins with the assumption that all costs are regionally variable. Each potential region is evaluated by examining the expense of satisfying location requirements. The differential in cost between alternative regions will vary with particular industries. For any particular firm, regional evaluation will identify geographic areas that will satisfy location requirements at least cost. The regions that present possibilities for most economic operation become the search areas for particular communities.

Community Evaluation

Up to this point, the firm considering plant location has, by the process of elimination, selected a few general areas within which communities capable of satisfying location requirements must be identified. Community evaluation should include the availability of necessary facilities. Such factors as availability of utilities, adequate labor force, and transportation must be examined. If a particular community appears to have the necessary characteristics in this respect, a more detailed investigation is undertaken.

Detailed investigation consists of measuring all facilities in terms of potential costs of manufacturing. If all facilities are available at a reasonable cost, investigation is extended to include intangible characteristics of the community. The character of local politics and the community's attitude toward industrial development must be considered. Of primary concern is the question of compatibility between the firm and the community. For example, will the proposed building and manufacturing operations meet with the approval of the community? Not understanding all implications of such intangible factors can result in a serious and expensive mistake on the part of the firm. The firm must also consider if the community fulfills the environmental desires of the personnel to be transferred. Living conditions must be examined in terms of such factors as recreational facilities, cost of living, and adequate housing. If the community offers incentives, complete details should be examined. Analysis of these and all other factors of importance will point out which communities are the best potential locations for conducting manufacturing operations. Evaluation of potential sites still remains.

Site Evaluation

Evaluation of available sites represents the last step in plant location. Only if the community meets all other requirements will the search be necessary.

Selection of a site to construct a new plant can normally be completed in all industrially minded communities. In location problems where a ready-constructed plant is sought, evaluation of sites may be necessary prior to community delineation.

In selecting a site, attention must once again be directed to cost analysis and consideration of intangibles. In addition, physical requirements and topographic features must be considered. Naturally, the direct cost of procurement is one governing factor. Other costs such as obtaining rail sidings, utility hook-ups, and highway access also require evaluation. From the intangible aspect, the firm must determine if the neighborhood is consistent with the desired image of the firm. For some firms, location in close proximity with "linked" industries may be desirable.

Only after satisfactory plant sites have been determined is the location process near completion. At this point, the firm's executives are armed with the necessary facts to make an intelligent location decision. Sufficient information should now be available to determine which area, what community, and the site that offers the best plant location.

Because all location factors have been under consideration throughout plant and field analysis, the forces of cost, market competition, and intangible location factors have guided the selection procedure. To aid in selecting between alternative sites, comparative cost analysis is helpful. The total costs of operation at each potential site should be compared to total costs experienced at the old location. Such cost analysis will clearly point out the benefits gained from relocation.

Plant Location Check List

I. Plant Analysis
  A. Distribution Analysis
    1. 1. Distribution System Analysis
      a. Current Production Points
      b. Current Warehouse Locations
    2. Long-Term Expansion Plans and Policies
    3. Primary Transfer Requirements
    4. Modes of Transportation Capable of Satisfying Transfer Demands
      a. Raw Material Movement
      b. Finished Product Movement
  B. Production Analysis
    1. Raw Material Requirements
      a. Present Point of Purchase
      b. Quantity Purchased
      c. Alternative Purchase Points
    2. General Characteristics of Production Process
      a. Special Factors Dependent upon Location

3. Labor Requirements
   a. Number of Skilled and Unskilled Workers
   b. Degree of Labor Organization Acceptable
   c. Number of People to Be Transferred
4. Power and Utility Requirements

C. Market Analysis
   1. Geographical Location of Major Market Segments
   2. Competition Analysis
      a. Production Locations
      b. Major Markets Serviced and Relative Strength in Each

D. Managerial Location Preferences

E. Location Specifications for New Plant
   1. Distribution Requirements
   2. Production Requirements
   3. Market Requirements
   4. Managerial Preferences

F. Cost Analysis at Present Manufacturing Location
   1. Transportation
   2. Production

II. Field Analysis

A. Regional Analysis
   1. Least-Cost Transfer Location
      a. Arrival at Alternative Points Using Different Raw Material Purchase Points
   2. Selection of Region(s) to Be Given Detailed Analysis
   3. Analysis of Location Factors Variable Between States
      a. Legal Structure
      b. Political Environment
      c. Corporate Laws and Tax Structures
      d. Labor Laws and Labor Conditions
      e. State Financial Status
      f. Industries Currently Located in State
      g. Cost-of-Living Index
   4. Selection of State(s) to be Evaluated in Detail Based upon Regional Analysis and Location Specifications

B. Community Analysis
   1. General Description of Community(ties)
   2. Population and Growth Patterns
   3. Industrial Climate
      a. Existing Industry
      b. Local Laws
      c. Labor Situation
      d. Community Attitude Toward Industry
      e. Amount of Cooperation Available

    4. Supporting Facilities and Services
       a. Transportation Facilities
       b. Utilities
       c. Municipal Services
    5. Living Conditions
       a. Cost of Living
       b. Housing Conditions
       c. Educational Facilities
       d. Recreational Facilities
       e. Character and Quality of Local Government
    6. Selection of Cummunity (ties) on the Basis of Location Specifications to Be Evaluated for a Plant Site
  C. Site Analysis
    1. Geographical Considerations
       a. Size
       b. Soil Content
       c. Drainage
    2. Utility Availability
    3. Availability of Required Transportation Facilities
    4. Costs
       a. Procurement
       b. Landscaping, etc.
    5. Selection of a Site(s) Based upon Location Specifications

III. Final Location Selection
  A. Proposed Costs at Alternative Sites
    1. Continuing Production and Distribution Costs
    2. Initial Establishment Costs
  B. Comparative Analysis of Proposed Costs with Costs Experienced at Current Location
  C. Final Selection of New Location Based upon Least-Cost Comparison

Selected Bibliography

ACKERMANN, KENNETH B., R. W. GARDNER, AND LEE P. THOMAS. *Understanding Today's Distribution Center.* Washington, D.C.: Traffic Service Corporation, 1972.

AMMER, DEAN S. *Materials Management,* rev. ed. Homewood, Ill.: Richard D. Irwin, Inc., 1970.

BALLOU, RONALD H. *Business Logistics Management.* Englewood Cliffs, N.J.: Prentice-Hall, Inc., 1973.

BOWERSOX, DONALD J., BERNARD J. LaLONDE, AND EDWARD W. SMYKAY. *Readings in Physical Distribution Management.* New York: Macmillan, Publishing Co., Inc., 1969.

BROWN, ROBERT G. *Statistical Forecasting for Inventory Control.* New York: McGraw-Hill Book Company, 1959.

BRUCE, HARRY J. *How to Apply Statistics to Physical Distribution.* Philadelphia: Chilton Company, 1967.

BUFFA, E. S. *Production Inventory Systems: Planning and Control.* Homewood, Ill.: Richard D. Irwin, Inc., 1968.

CONSTANTIN, JAMES A. *Principles of Logistics Management.* New York: Appleton-Century-Crofts, 1966.

DANIEL, NORMAN E., AND J. RICHARD JONES. *Business Logistics.* Boston: Allyn and Bacon, Inc., 1969.

ENGLAND, WILBUR B. *Modern Procurement Management: Principles and Cases.* 5th ed. Homewood, Ill.: Richard D. Irwin, Inc., 1970.

FETTER, ROBERT B., AND WINSTON C. DALLECK. *Decision Models for Inventory Management.* Homewood, Ill.: Richard D. Irwin, Inc., 1961.

FORRESTER, JAY W. *Industrial Dynamics.* Cambridge, Mass.: The MIT Press, 1961.

HADLEY, G., AND T. M. WHITIN. *Analysis of Inventory Systems.* Englewood Cliffs, N.J.: Prentice-Hall, Inc., 1963.

HEINRITZ, STUART F., AND PAUL V. FARRELL. *Purchasing,* 5th ed. Englewood Cliffs, N.J.: Prentice-Hall, Inc., 1971.

501

HESKETT, JAMES L., ROBERT M. IVIE, AND NICHOLAS A. GLASKOWSKY. *Business Logistics.* 2nd ed. New York: The Ronald Press Company, 1973.

LEE, LAMAR, JR., AND DONALD W. DOBLER. *Purchasing and Materials Management,* rev. ed. New York: McGraw-Hill Book Company, 1971.

LEWIS, HOWARD T., AND JAMES W. CULLITON. *The Role of Air Freight in Physical Distribution.* Boston: Harvard University, 1956.

MAGEE, JOHN F. *Physical Distribution Systems.* New York: McGraw-Hill Book Company, 1967.

———— *Production Planning and Inventory Control.* New York: McGraw-Hill Book Company, 1958.

McCONAUGHY, DAVID. *Readings in Business Logistics.* Homewood, Ill.: Richard D. Irwin, Inc., 1969.

McGARRAH, ROBERT E. *Production and Logistics Management.* New York: John Wiley & Sons, Inc., 1963.

MOSSMAN, FRANK H., AND NEWTON MORTON. *Logistics of Distribution Systems.* Boston: Allyn and Bacon, Inc., 1965.

PLOWMAN, E. GROSVENOR. *Elements of Business Logistics.* Stanford, Calif.: Stanford University Press, 1964.

SCHIFF, MICHAEL. *Accounting and Control in Physical Distribution Management.* Chicago: National Council of Physical Distribution Management, 1972.

SCHORR, JERRY, MILTON ALEXANDER, AND ROBERT J. FRANCO, eds. *Logistics in Marketing.* New York: Pitman Publishing Corp., 1969.

SMYKAY, EDWARD W. *Physical Distribution Management,* 3rd ed. New York: Macmillan Publshing Co., Inc., 1973.

STARR, M. K., AND D. W. MILLER. *Inventory Control: Theory and Practice.* Englewood Cliffs, N.J.: Prentice-Hall, Inc., 1962.

TAFF, CHARLES A. *Management of Traffic and Physical Distribution,* 5th ed. Homewood, Ill.: Richard D. Irwin, Inc., 1972.

WELCH, W. EVERT. *Scientific Inventory Control.* Greenwich, Conn.: Management Publishing Company, 1962.

Name Index

Subject Index